how to manage your agent

how to manage your agent: a writer's guide to hollywood representation

CHAD GERVICH

Focal Press
Taylor & Francis Group

NEW YORK AND LONDON

First published 2014
by Focal Press
70 Blanchard Road, Suite 402, Burlington, MA 01803

and by Focal Press
2 Park Square, Milton Park, Abingdon, Oxon OX14 4RN

Focal Press is an imprint of the Taylor & Francis Group, an informa business

Library of Congress Cataloging in Publication Data
   Gervich, Chad.
   How to manage your agent: a writer's guide to Hollywood
   representation/Chad Gervich.
   pages cm
   1. Motion picture authorship. 2. Television authorship. I. Title.
   PN1996.G47 2014
   791.4502′32—dc23
   2013024318

ISBN: 978-0-240-82377-5 (pbk)
ISBN: 978-0-240-82404-8 (ebk)

Typeset in Akzidenz Grotesk BE
by Florence Production Ltd, Stoodleigh, Devon, UK

Printed and bound in the United States of America by Sheridan Books, Inc.
(a Sheridan Group Company).

For Max and Miles

Contents

Introduction

Brad Wollack

Producer: Chelsea Lately, After Lately, The Wayne Brady Show

"Remember, Brad . . . agents are nothing more than brokers. They go for the easiest, quickest buck." With those encouraging words from my father upon signing with an agency two weeks before graduating college, I was thrust into the world of Hollywood representation.

Thirteen years and three agencies later, I've come to learn that my dad was mostly right. I've had the privilege of dealing with agents in almost every capacity imaginable, both as a "buyer" (a producer and executive looking to hire a client or acquire a project) and a "seller" (as a writer, performer and producer hocking my wares and half-baked ideas).

Basically, my dad was saying that agents, like any form of "broker," only get paid when their clients are working. To that end, they obviously want their clients to work. While you hope that they're taking the time and care to find just the right project for you—their prized client—truth is they fling as much crap (in this case, their clients) at the wall as they can to see what sticks. That is a very broad categorization of what they do, but it's a basic reality (my current agents excluded, of course).

Full disclosure: at the time of writing this introduction, I haven't read Chad's book. He hasn't finished it . . . even though it was due eight months ago. So, I'm not even sure what I'm supposed to be addressing. However, I've bluffed my way through most of my career, so why stop now?

I suppose this book could be a lot of things. In fact, it could read like a classic romance novel because, to me, the evolution of the client-agent dynamic is very similar to a romantic relationship, or even a marriage. I'll elaborate . . .

After signing with an agency (the first date), the next six months to a year are total bliss because you receive what is commonly known as "new agency love" (the courting process). Both client and agent are still trying to impress one another, and you fantasize and talk incessantly about the life you're going to build together. You have shared dreams and projects you want to nurture together. You have found your knight in shining armor—your one true love. You plan to grow old together and take care of each other when no one else will.

Then reality starts to set in. Phone calls are no longer placed everyday to check in; you're not dining at the hottest restaurants anymore; and your knight's armor suddenly has more chinks than shine. You realize he's buried in work and just doesn't have the time for you anymore. But you tolerate it and, over time, you settle in as most couples do and accept your fate. You have some good times and some bad, but you motor through. You put in the minimum effort to sustain the relationship, but eventually you both know it's over. Sure, you still sleep in the same bed, but the lust is gone.

One day, you're at lunch with your friends or co-workers who start talking about their agents and how fantastic they are. You suddenly realize you're stuck in a loveless marriage. What you have isn't right—it's not a healthy relationship after all. You begin having impure thoughts about other agents and what they could do for you, and, one day, you finally act on your deepest desires and secretly rendezvous with a new agency. It's a thrill. They remind you how beautiful you truly are, and if they were lucky enough to have you as a client, they wouldn't ever take you for granted. You agree to run off with these new agents and a flurry of excitement and nerves you haven't felt in years wells in your stomach. You finally work up the courage to announce to your current agents that it's over. To your surprise, they're fairly understanding. They've wanted to end it, too. The split is surprisingly amicable—they still get to receive a commission from your current employment, but you get the chance to start the romance all over again with someone new.

As in love, each client–agent relationship is different, and managing one isn't without its complications. It typically comes down to the age-old battle between art and commerce. You're the talent, or "the show." They're the brokers, or "the business." In fact, "show business" should really be called "show-versus-business." While you both have the same intention—to make money off of your art—you'll often have differing views on how exactly to achieve that. Like any fruitful bond, it takes a lot of communication, understanding and belief in one another.

I trust this book will help you understand the agency culture and how to navigate it so you know what to anticipate. In case Chad doesn't address every single nuance of the agency world, let me offer you a few of my own tips on negotiating this vortex:

Know Your Team—The first agency that represented me was one of the majors. While I was initially signed by the reality TV/non-scripted department, I assumed that other departments (TV lit, TV talent, etc.) would also gladly represent me. Wrong. It took me two agencies to realize that the team that signs me has to be comprised of agents from multiple departments, who cover various mediums and platforms. For example, if you're a TV writer, make sure someone from the motion picture lit department is on your team. The time will come when you want to write a feature film script, only to find out your folks in the TV lit department don't mix well with those guys, and they can't really help you.

Size Matters—Big agencies will tell you little agencies don't have the scope, resources, clients or services they do. Smaller agencies will tell you that at the major agencies you're just a small fish in a big pond, and only they can offer you the personalized attention you deserve. I've been at major and mid-size agencies, and there are truths to both of these conceits. I actually don't have any guidance for you on which option is better—it's a very personal decision—but I wanted to mention it since it's an issue that comes around time and again. There will be advantages and disadvantages wherever you go. Just control what you can, which is your own work. Everything else will sort itself out.

You Know Best—Agents know a lot and can be great resources, but they don't know everything. That's actually a good rule for anything in life: no one knows everything. Remember, you're the creative mind—the talent. Your job is to generate the new ideas. And the more radical they are, the more resistance you'll be met with. Again, agents often want to go for the easiest sell. The more insane your idea is, the more effort they have to put into helping you sell it. I can't tell you how many times agents have told me ideas of mine weren't "right for the marketplace" or "will never work," only to see someone else sell the same or similar project 6–12 months after I initially proposed my concept. If you believe in something, keep pushing.

Play Nice—Just because your professional relationship with an agent or agency may have run its course, doesn't mean you have to sever all ties. This really is a small industry and you will absolutely see those agents again. I have effectively transacted with many of my former agents throughout the years because I made certain to maintain an amicable relationship. There is not one former representative of mine whom I wouldn't feel comfortable calling upon. Plus, a lot of agents end up agency hopping or leaving the agency game altogether and transition into other facets of the industry— often landing in powerful positions. That's when you will definitely pat yourself on the back for playing nice.

Manage Your Representation—Agents want to get you as much money as possible. However, sometimes the demands they make on your behalf are unrealistic and anger the buyer of your project or services. While many agents already have established reputations, they still are an extension of—and reflection on—you. So the greedier and more aggressive they get, the greedier and more aggressive you appear. On numerous occasions I have witnessed a representative cost their client a job. Life is short—and definitely too short to deal with your prick of an agent. It's up to you to be mindful of your agent's approach and always know—and concur with—what they're asking for.

The irony in all of this, of course, is that Chad asked me, in person, to write the introduction to this book. He circumvented and undermined the entire process established whereby he submits a formal offer to my agents, they contact me to gauge my interest, we weigh the pros and cons and reach a decision. They negotiate a fee on my behalf, both parties agree and the deal is closed. Instead, Chad cut out the middle-man, got my services for free and will exploit me for everything it's worth. I'll never see a dime. So let this example serve as the final lessons for you: 1) Everyone will try to avoid dealing with agents . . . even people writing books about dealing with agents; and 2) if you don't utilize an agent, you will most likely get screwed by the sharks in this business.

Enjoy!

Author's Note

I learned a lot of valuable things writing my first book, *Small Screen, Big Picture*, but nothing more valuable than this:

If there's something you want to understand or know more about, the best way to learn it is to write a book about it.

In fact, much of the reason I wanted to write this book was because I have a great relationship with my own agent, but I'm still frequently at a loss for how to communicate with her. Because we're friends—and because I hate confrontation and conflict with people close to me—it's sometimes hard to express disappointment or anger. (Not that I have a lot of dissappointment or anger with her. I don't.) Also, I hate letting friends see my failures or insecurities, so it's hard to share worries and concerns like "I need to sell something *soon*," or "I think I am failing at this job, and I don't know why," because I don't want my agent, as my friend, to see me as a failure.

I'm not alone in these confusions. I'm constantly hearing writers say things like: "I wrote this great screenplay, but my agent says it's 'not commercial enough.'" Or, "I gave my agent my pilot, and he came back with a bunch of *notes*. I'm like, 'Dude, *just go sell it.*'" Or, "I called my manager three times today to pitch a movie idea and he still hasn't called me back. WTF?!"

Most writers understand these frustrations. It's not easy to keep your sanity in an industry where there seems to be so little rhyme or reason to what sells, you're constantly scrabbling for work, and your livelihood seems dependent on others doing their jobs. So when things aren't going the way you'd like, it's easy to blame the people who are supposed to be making sure things *do* go the way you'd like—your representation.

Sometimes this blame is totally warranted. More often, however, blaming your representation is like yelling at a spouse or partner after a bad day at the office—*it's rarely their fault.* They're an easy and available scapegoat, but it doesn't mean the blame is theirs. Or at least, not entirely theirs.

The truth is—most agent-client relationships are just that: *relationships.* And like any marriage, romance, or family, those relationships require mutual communication, trust, honesty, affection, and support. Likewise, they are fraught with expectations, desires, fears, insecurities, agendas, secrets, power dynamics. And to get the most out of a relationship—whether with a partner, family member, or agent—you have to understand how that person sees the world, what they want and expect from you, and their own personal needs, desires, and goals—all of which may be slightly different from yours.

Unfortunately, marriages, romances, and families often have something agent-client relationships don't: *help.* Go to the nearest library, you'll find hundreds of self-help books guiding you through the intricacies of dating, marriage, children, divorce. Jump on Google, you'll find plenty of marriage and family therapists, counselors, and clergy. Yet there's not a single self-help book or therapist for writers wondering, "If I tell my agent I'm frustrated, will I scare him away?" "What should I say to reignite my agent's passion for me?" "How can I leave my representation without burning a bridge?"

So why not a relationship book for writers and agents? After all, many agent/client relationships are just as intense and co-dependent as any family or romance. Why not a book that helps writers understand their agents and managers, as well as improve their communication and overall relationship? Think *Men Are From Mars, Women Are From Venus* . . . for Hollywood.

In thinking about my own misunderstandings about representation, I knew this book needed to tackle two things:

1. Helping writers understand what agents and managers do . . . and how they do it. Many writers' frustrations stem from a lack of understanding about what exactly representatives do—or are capable of doing—and how they go about doing it, so I wanted the book to explain how agencies and management companies work internally and how this affects writers, clients, and their work. If you understand the specifics of how your agents and managers can or can't help you, it's much easier to use them effectively.
2. Addressing common agent/client frustrations and misunderstandings. Both clients and representatives have certain complaints about one another that seem to pop up over and over, and I felt the book should confront these head-on, not only exploring *why* these issues occur, but offering tools and insights for dealing with them.

I've tried to provide in-depth explanations and answers, as well as perspectives and opinions from various agents, managers, writers, directors, lawyers, producers, executives, assistants. (I have occasionally changed names, or made quotes anonymous, at the request of people discussing sensitive topics or stories.)

Having said this, let's get one thing straight: *reading this book will not solve all your problems.* The heavy-lifting must be done by you. This book will not talk to your representation for you. It will not mediate disagreements. It will not tell you who's right or wrong. You must figure those things out on your own. Every relationship—every individual *within* a relationship—is different. What works for you may not work for me . . . or your agent . . . or another writer.

What this book *will* do is help you see things through your agent or manager's eyes. It will help you understand how they approach opportunities, challenges, and conflicts. It will give you language to employ when communicating thoughts, fears, or frustrations. It will offer tactics, strategies, and advice on how to maximize and synergize your team.

You may need to read this book more than once. You may need to scribble in the margins and mark it up with highlighter. You may need to keep it on your shelf, untouched for months, then pull it down in a moment of crisis. Like a patient therapist, it's here to use whenever—and however—you need it.

Personally, writing this book has given me an enormous amount of understanding and respect for Hollywood's representatives. Good agents and managers work non-stop, remaining on call for their clients 24/7. They give creative notes. Business advice. Personal guidance. And when someone breaks into the exosphere, that ultimate level of stardom, their representation gets a mere ten percent of the fortune—and none of the fame. Most people have heard of *Girls'* breakout star Allison Williams . . . but have they heard of Jason Cunningham, her agent at Paradigm?[1] Louis C.K. and Aziz Ansari keep us in stitches . . . but do we ever give a round of applause to Mike Berkowitz at APA?[2] And while Bruce Willis is a household name . . . what about CAA's Michael Kives?[3]

Also, I like to think that writing this book has made me a better client for my own agent. (She may totally disagree, in which case I'd say this book does a great job of sharpening your levels of self-deception.) I understand better what she needs from me. When she needs it. Why I sometimes drop the ball and how it affects her, and my own career, when I do. I've become less apprehensive about communicating disappointments and frustrations. I've become more proactive about articulating my needs and plans.

So I hope this book helps you in the same way it's helped me. If it does, I'll consider it a success. Just don't ask me for marriage advice. I still have no idea how the hell that works.

An Important P.S.

In filling this book with true examples, I've tried to make it as up-to-date as possible. However, clients fire reps, TV shows get canceled, agents, managers, and executives switch companies every day. So please forgive anything that may be outdated—it was right when I wrote it.

Another Important P.S.

A massive amount of research went into this project, and I would like to give a heartfelt thanks to several places who have no idea just how indispensable they were: Nikki Finke and the team at *Deadline Hollywood*; Andrew Wallenstein, Cynthia Littleton, Claudia Eller, and the folks at *Variety; The Hollywood Reporter; The Los Angeles Times; the New York Times; The Wrap; TV Week; Vulture*; and many others, which I've tried to cite throughout. I don't know how people wrote books (at least not about Hollywood) before them.

Part I
Represent!

1   No Vocation Without Representation

As President of NBC Entertainment for nearly a decade, Warren Littlefield had navigated many sticky situations. He'd managed the notorious Jay-versus-Dave battle for *The Tonight Show*. He'd shocked the industry by paying $13 million an episode to keep *E.R.* on the air.[1] And he'd made cultural history by standing by an odd little show that had received a "weak" score on its pilot report and got pulverized in its first season . . . only to metamorphose into one of the most groundbreaking series of all time: *Seinfeld*.

Yet now, as he stared out the third-story window of his office at the Littlefield Company, his TV production company in partnership with Disney's ABC Studios, Littlefield faced a dilemma unlike anything he'd ever encountered. *He had nothing going on.* In the ten years since departing NBC and launching his company, Littlefield had had some successes—he'd shot several pilots and got five shows on the air (*Keen Eddie, Love Inc., Do Over, Foody Call, Like Family*), but not one that had lasted longer than a season.

"My head was bloody from banging it against the wall," says Littlefield. Not only had any big hits eluded him, but he felt he wasn't even being presented with the writers, directors, and underlying properties needed to develop a big hit. He watched in frustration as writers like *Law & Order: SVU*'s Tara Butters and Michele Fazekas teamed up with other production companies like The Mark Gordon Company to create *Eli Stone*. And *CSI: NY*'s Peter Lenkov partnered with K/O Paper Products (*Cowboys and Aliens*) to reboot *Hawaii Five-0*.

"I needed more choices in order to go into production," Littlefield says. "It was this feeling that 'I don't exist outside the rules of the land.' It was about survival." Littlefield knew what the problem was: he didn't have an agent, a representative to scout the marketplace, bringing him appropriate projects and writers to develop and produce. Throughout Hollywood, most professional artists—writers, producers, directors, actors, designers, composers, hosts—used an agent or manager, some kind of professional representative, to help find work and negotiate deals. But Littlefield, by his own design, didn't have one.

"A number of [agents] had pursued me since I left NBC," he says, but "I thought being Switzerland would make more sense. That way we could do business with everybody."

Unfortunately Littlefield was wrong. Sure—being unrepresented did, in theory, allow him to do business with artists from all agencies, but it had also forced him to accept a grim truth: *no one paid him allegiance.* So while the Littlefield Company could, hypothetically, do a show with a writer from powerhouse agency William Morris Endeavor (WME)—which represents writers such as *Homeland* showrunner Howard Gordon and *South Park* creators Matt Stone and Trey Parker—WME was more incentivized to partner clients with its own production companies, like J.J. Abrams' Bad Robot (*Lost, Alias*) or Queen Latifah's Flavor Unit Entertainment (*Single Ladies, Just Wright*). (Bad Robot has since switched from WME to rival agency Creative Artists Agency, or CAA.) And sure, the Littlefield Company could do a show with a writer repped at United Talent Agency (UTA)—like Rene Balcer of *Law & Order* or *Ted* co-writers Alec Sulkin and Wellesley Wild—but UTA's clients were busy being introduced to UTA's own producers, such as Ice Cube's Cube Vision (*All About the Benjamins*, *Are We There Yet*) or Gavin Palone's Pariah (*Premium Rush*, *My Boys*).

"If you're trying to go through a process that has so many obstacles and barriers ... [you have to] follow the flow of the water," says Littlefield. "It's having a source that's supplying you with talent and content. In the world of television today, most of the development is a format from another country, or based on a book, or there's something presold about it ... so [having an agent that can supply that] gives you a leg up in a very, very, very competitive environment."

Littlefield knew what he had to do. He picked up the phone to dial an old friend. A decade ago, Brian Pike had been one of Littlefield's drama executives at NBC. Today, he was a TV agent at CAA, one of the most powerful agencies in Hollywood (representing actors such as Anna Kendrick and Chris Hemsworth, writers like Jonathan Kellerman and Stephen Gaghan, and reality personalities like Gordon Ramsay and Hoda Kotb).

"I've been waiting for you to be ready for this," said Pike, listening to Littlefield's proposal.

"So with the respect of the muscle of CAA and the personal relationship with Brian," says Littlefield, "that's where I jumped in." With CAA at his back, Littlefield felt the change immediately.

"All of a sudden it was, 'We want you to meet with this writer,' 'We want you to meet with that writer,'" says Littlefield. "Now, make no mistake—you don't just sit back and let your agency shove stuff in front of you. But it's a very important artery going into your heart. [It] gives you content, gives you artists, and when you have that direct line of access, it only helps."

A year later, the Littlefield Company had a new series on the air—ABC's *My Generation*, written by CAA client Noah Hawley. CAA also brokered Littlefield's first book deal (for 2012's *Top of the Rock: Inside the Rise and Fall of Must See TV*). They secured him the TV rights to Brandy Engler and David Rensin's memoir *The Men On My Couch: True Stories Of Sex, Love and Psychotherapy*—also represented by CAA—which Littlefield and *Happy Endings* producer Gail Lerner sold to ABC. They facilitated his partnership with *Veronica Mars* creator Rob Thomas to adapt the British miniseries *Metropolis* for the CW,[2] and with *Watchmen* writer David Hayter to adapt *The Damned*, a supernatural comic book series, for Showtime.[3] And they helped Littlefield team with Academy Award-winning writer/directors Joel and Ethan Coen for FX's TV sequel to the Coen brothers' *Fargo*.

Obviously, any Hollywood wannabe would kill for these kinds of hook-ups. Yet few people get them. Getting an agent is considered one of the major stepping-stones in building a Hollywood career, but there's no real blueprint for making it happen. It's tough to get work with no agent ... yet most agents only want clients who have worked. What's a talented young writer, director, actor, or producer to do?

To make matters worse, agents remain some of the most mysterious, elusive, and misunderstood players in Hollywood. Most avoid the spotlight and shun interviews. Thus, there are few places to get honest, helpful insight into how agents work ... and where to get one. And when fictional agents appear in movies or TV shows like *Jerry Maguire* or *Entourage*, they're usually depicted as slick, shady sharks in Tom Ford suits, screaming into cell phones as they cruise through Beverly Hills in Ferraris and BMWs.

"[Agents] get a bad rap," says Christine Crow, director of development at Millennium Films (*Olympus Has Fallen*, *The Expendables*). "It's the nature of being a representative that you're constantly trying to hustle for your clients ... [but] not all agents are slimy, sharky personality types."

The truth is: most agents are dedicated, caring, passionate people who work hard to get clients fruitful deals and opportunities. Having said that, many agents *do* work in strange and secretive ways ... and they often have their own hidden motivations and agendas. So you want to get the most from your agent? . . . Understand what they want, how they get it, and how you can fit your career goals into their needs and objectives.

To do this, let's look at why most of us need–or think we need–representation in the first place.

WHY DO PEOPLE NEED REPRESENTATION?

While we don't always think about it, we actually use representation in many parts of our lives. Sometimes we need to find work, so we hire an employment agency. Other times, we need to buy or sell something–a house, insurance policies, a car–so we hire a representative who understands that particular market. When we need someone to represent our legal interests we hire a lawyer.

These same situations–and many others–crop up in the entertainment industry. Some matters are the province of agents, some fall to other types of representation, like publicists or managers, but understanding when and why we need representation is often helpful in identifying which type of representation we need–and how to use them. In Hollywood, there are nine basic uses for representation:

One: To Find Employment

Artists working in the entertainment industry are–ninety-nine percent of the time–freelancers. Whether you're a writer, director, actor, costume designer, script supervisor, accountant, or grip, you bounce from job to job, company to company. Even if you manage to land a fairly steady gig on a long-running TV show like *The Big Bang Theory* or *Bones*, or as a producer with a two-year studio deal at Universal, you are a freelancer. Once that job ends, you'll be hurled back into the unemployment lines to fend for yourself and find a new gig. This is true for first-timers like Ashleigh Powell, who sold her first screenplay, *Somacell*, to Warner Brothers in 2012, to veteran producers like Tyler Perry, who produces the Madea movies and TBS's *House of Payne*.

"The first job always seems like the hardest to get," says TV writer Rick Muirragui (*Suits*, *Men of a Certain Age*), but "once you've done it before, you have a little more confidence in going to get another job. So in that regard, yes–it gets easier. But at the same time, it's scary . . . [and] the fear never goes away, because you're a freelancer; you could be on a show that lasts six episodes or six years."

Thus, many people hire representation to help them find employment, just like professionals in other industries might use employment agencies such as AppleOne or Lucas Group. In fact, many states categorize talent agents right alongside regular employment agencies, holding them to the exact same laws and classifications. (More on this in the next chapter.)

"[I am] essentially a headhunter," says one Hollywood agent. "I am responsible for getting my clients–producers, production companies, or freelancers–jobs!" Agents and other representatives do this by gathering information and forming relationships with buyers and executives throughout the industry, making them privy to job opportunies and information other industry professionals may not know about. After all, the industry is vast and complex–it would be impossible for a working writer, director, or composer to work full-time *and* stay on top of upcoming openings. There are generally two ways artists get work in Hollywood:

1. "Work-for-hire" jobs, where you're contracted to work on someone else's project–rewriting a script, animating a movie, playing a character, directing a TV episode.
2. Selling your own original material: a screenplay, pitch, miniseries, etc.

"We're used car salesmen," says manager Jeff Holland, a founding partner of The Cartel, "but our 'vehicles' are our clients' material, our scripts, our directors and their reels. You're selling, just a different type of widget."

Aside from helping clients land specific jobs, representatives also help clients architect their long-term careers. You may need a job to feed your family tomorrow—but if your ultimate goal is to be the next James Cameron, you need to do some planning. What kinds of jobs should you focus on? Which companies should you be in business with? How can you find projects that will build your resume and credibility as an artist? Young writers, producers, and directors won't always have these answers themselves . . . but professional representatives will.

Two: To Negotiate Contracts, Deals, and Other Agreements

As a working freelancer, you sign a new contract for every new job or sale. In fact, you'll often have multiple jobs at the same time—each with its own contract! A TV showrunner, for example, may be producing his current series, developing a new show for a studio, and supervising a young story editor developing her own pilot. He'll likely have different deals for each project.

Thus, at any given time, you could be juggling several potential contracts or deals, each requiring its own negotiation. And you don't want to be doing those negotiations yourself.

"When I was in law school, they said, 'If you are handling a case *pro se*, meaning 'representing yourself,' you have a fool for a lawyer and a fool for a client,'" says expert negotiation consultant Donny Ebenstein. "Representing yourself is hard because you're not objective; you're not neutral. And not just 'not objective' in the sense that you won't see things in a fair and unbiased way, but you're hooked, emotionally—especially when what you're negotiating is your own services, your worth as a writer. 'How important are you to the success of this project?' It's hard not to get hooked by that. Being 'unhooked' is a big part of being effective and successful."

This is one reason we hire other people to be our negotiators. Whether negotiating the sale of a screenplay or the purchase of a condo, they can be calm and rational when we can't. Good negotiators also have specialized skill sets most laypeople lack. For example, when a marriage breaks up, the couple turns to divorce lawyers to help navigate the painful, complicated process of dividing assets. When companies merge, they enlist lawyers who understand the intricacies of corporate law. Likewise, entertainment professionals hire people who understand the unique labyrinth of Hollywood. When should a writer ask for a "strike clause?" What's a good definition of "adjusted modified gross?" Why might an "if-come" be more desirable than a "script commitment?"

"There are *so many* contract deal points," says Heather Lazare, a senior editor at Touchstone Publishing. "I look at [contracts] all the time . . . but I still work closely to make sure all the deal points are correct—and there's a lot of language there that agents understand. So an agent can be an important part of the process, especially for a [first-timer] that doesn't know how to do the negotiation."

Lastly, negotiations can be scary, stressful, and confusing; not everyone has the mental or emotional composition to be a good negotiator. Case in point: *me*. I get nervous, jittery, unsure of myself. What if I push too hard and make someone mad? Or don't push hard enough and wind up getting screwed? How do I know when to back off and when to stand my ground?

"Not only are agents not scared of negotiations, but they truly enjoy it," says screenwriter Diablo Cody (*Juno*, *Young Adult*). "They tend to have more aggressive personalities; they're not conflict avoidant. A lot of artists are introverts and conflict avoidant, and that's why we would not be good at making deals. Agents, by nature, tend to be bolder, more extroverted people that are not [worried about being] pleasers."

Three: To Gain Information and Access

We frequently hire representatives because they have information we wouldn't be able to obtain elsewhere. Travel agents, for instance, know about special deals consumers couldn't find on their own. Even today, when online travel sites like Orbitz, Bing, and Kayak have squeezed many traditional ~~traditional~~ agencies out of business, travel agents book seventy-seven percent of all cruises, seventy-three percent of all packaged travel, and fifty-five percent of all airline tickets.[4] Why? Because they have access to information it would take regular people much longer to cull. The same goes for real estate agents.

"Buying a house is something that takes specialized knowledge and skills," says Ashley Sackerman, a real estate agent with L.A.'s Teles Properties. "Finding the house is the easy part. Everything after that can be much more complicated and challenging. We know what red flags to look for in a home, which systems may require additional inspections, and what to do with all that knowledge once we get it. It takes an experienced professional to understand the liabilities and implications of the issues and advise the client what to do. Buyers rely on our expertise, our relationships within the brokerage community, and our negotiating skills to navigate the escrow period and get those keys in their hands."

Representatives in the entertainment business are no different. They have the inside track on what studios or networks are buying, what's getting greenlighted or cancelled, who's getting cast, fired, or promoted, etc.

"My job is fundamentally two things: sales and research," says Ra Kumar, an alternative TV agent at N.S. Bienstock, the talent agency that reps producers and personalities like Anderson Cooper and Bill O'Reilly. "[My job is to] figure out what people are looking for, what they want, and then sell them what I find that fits. We spend a lot of time with the buyers, both in pitch meetings and outside, doing research, talking to them about what they're looking for, having conversations about clients."

Sometimes this info includes hard-and-fast job openings such as specific casting needs. A talent agent, for instance, may learn that A&E's *Bates Motel* is looking for a "male, African-American, mid-40s to 50s" for a guest starring role. Other times, agents hear of vague opportunities or general areas. Maybe Warner Brothers wants R-rated female-driven adventure comedies. Or NBC wants a reality show set in a rugged outdoor locale. Aside from just knowing *what* opportunities exist, agents are also much more aware of going rates and how much you should be compensated.

"My agent represents other writers, knows other agents, is familiar with the marketplace in a way that I'm not," says Cody. "I'm only aware of my own **quote** and what I'm asking for. [I] don't know what other writers are getting [or] asking for. But my agent can say, 'Look, you want to direct this movie. The studio isn't willing to pay for you to join the **DGA**. However, I know this other first-time director they just paid to join the DGA, so I can use that as a bargaining chip.' And lo and behold—I get to join the DGA! So [agents] just have a wealth of knowledge that extends beyond your individual career."

People also hire representatives because they provide *access* to companies, buyers, and decision-makers clients wouldn't otherwise be able to get to.

"I am in contact with agents, whether on the phone, in a meeting, or at some sort of social situation, on a weekly basis," says producer Doug McKay, former VP of Production at Phoenix Pictures (*Black Swan*, *Shutter Island*). "It's in my best interests as a producer to have a good relationship with as many agents as possible because these guys are the hub of all the activity in the business. If we have a script we're developing internally and need a new writer, we go to an agency. Or once it's time to get a director, we go to an agency. We go to agencies to help put financing together. Through every stage of the process, we find ourselves contacting the agencies to get that next piece of the puzzle."

Talk the Talk

Quote–A writers pricetag for rendering certain services. A writer on a TV staff has a "quote" based on what they made at their last staff job. A writer selling a TV pitch, script, or screenplay has a "quote" based on their last sale. Screenwriters even have specific quotes for rewrites, polishes, or adaptations. We'll discuss TV writers' quotes in Part II and screenwriter quotes in Part III.

Talk the Talk

DGA–Directors Guild of America, the labor union representing directors working in film and television.

This means representatives often act as professional yentas, introducing writers, directors, actors, and creatives to employers with appropriate projects or interests. The best representatives have hundreds of relationships, built up over years of working in the industry. In fact, many are former producers or executives themselves, and vice versa. Jay Cohen spent fifteen years producing movies such as *Bride Wars*, *Two for the Money*, and *A Walk on the Moon* before getting hired as a film agent at The Gersh Agency, the company that reps Heather Graham and Chris Noth. Producer Jeff Kwatinetz was CEO of The Firm—a talent management company that represented Cameron Diaz, Kelly Clarkson, and Leonardo DiCaprio—before founding Prospect Park, the production company behind FX's *Wilfred*, USA's *Royal Pains*, and the online versions of *One Life To Live* and *All My Children*. So good representatives understand many aspects of the business; their relationships run deep and broad, and they use those relationships to gather information and help clients advance their careers.

Four: To be a Creative Guide or Sounding Board

Many writers, artists, actors, and directors use their representation as a creative partner—someone who not only guides their overall career, but also offers creative feedback on projects.

Some managers, in fact, are so hands-on with clients' projects they receive a producer credit on the final product. Fabrik Entertainment manager Mikkel Bondesen represents writer/producer Matt Nix and also serves as an executive producer on Nix's hit USA series, *Burn Notice*.[5] 3 Arts Entertainment manager Dave Becky represents Louis C.K., and works as an executive producer on C.K.'s FX sitcom, *Louie* (one of humanity's top three artistic achievements of all time).

While writers often get notes and feedback from producers or executives on a certain project, execs and producers have their own tastes and agendas, and they're not always the same as the writers'. Thus, many writers like having their own go-to partner, someone they trust and whom shares their creative sensibilities. Good reps are also tuned into the marketplace, and they can help clients protect their visions while still creating something sellable.

"I just turned in some pages to my manager," says screenwriter Tedi Sarafian (*Terminator 3: Rise of the Machines*), "and he said, 'These are awesome, but change this because there's [already] a script out there like this,' or 'They're not looking to buy that kind of thing.' [Managers] have good thoughts about everything that's going on, that's current. I'm not out there—I don't know all that stuff, so its nice to have a guy who has his nose out there and can steer you in the right direction."

Five: To Offer Legal and Contractual Advice or Protection

As we've discussed, representatives can be indispensable when navigating a confusing negotiation. But representatives like lawyers and agents also provide certain legal protections and advice, and in Hollywood—where every project is an intense collaboration between writers, actors, directors, networks, studios, financiers, and hundreds of other participants—lawsuits abound.

Between December, 2011, and January, 2012, for example, writer-director James Cameron was sued by *four different writers* claiming he stole their work to create his blockbuster film *Avatar*.[6] And in October, 2012, author Angela Wilder sued CBS TV Studios and Relatvity, producers of *The Talk*, claiming they stole the concept from her own idea for a show called *The Mothers' Hood*.[7] (Interestingly enough, Wilder admitted she never pitched her idea to CBS or Relativity; she only pitched it to Sony, which has nothing to do with *The Talk*.)

"If you're a writer, you're dealing with property," says entertainment attorney Charles Holland. "That's an important legal concept, and you want somebody looking at that. Once you get to the point that you are creating something, you ought to have somebody protecting that."

Now, I'm not suggesting that by starting a career in Hollywood, you'll suddenly find yourself in a maelstorm of lawsuits. Stories, scripts, and ideas *rarely* get stolen. (At the time I'm writing this, two of the Cameron lawsuits have been totally dismissed.) In fact, I often think being overly worried about your work being stolen is the first sign of a newbie who's not yet ready to work professionally in Hollywood, where success depends on open collaboration and the free trade of ideas.

"In TV, it's very hard to have an idea someone else hasn't already had," says writer/producer Lesley Wake Webster (*We Are Men*, *American Dad*). "If you're writing a family sitcom with feuding siblings, someone can point out eighty different shows just like that. But the specifics of your idea [are what should] be very special and unique to you, and that's what would make it hard to steal. It's [all about] execution, and if you have characters that are specific to your experience, specific to what you've thought up, it's hard for people to steal that. They can try, but inevitably their voice is going to take over," distinguishing their work from yours.

Having said this, Hollywood contracts and deals are complicated, and it helps to have a legal representative on board as you grow your career.

Six: To Be a Therapist

As a writer, I think I speak not only for myself when I say—*we're a bunch of fucking messes.* And by "we," I don't just mean writers; I mean actors, designers, painters, artists—creative folks of all stripes. We're neutoric, insecure, compulsive, volatile, paranoid, obsessive—you name it. I mean, come on —J.D. Salinger spent the last fifty years of his life in total isolation. Vincent Van Gogh cut off his ear (although some say it was sliced off by Van Gogh's frenemy, Paul Gauguin—which does little to quell the notion that artists are all insane). Virginia Woolf survived a lifetime of nervous breakdowns before filling her coat with rocks and drowning herself in the Ouse River.

"[Artists] aren't like everyone else," says Goddard, and "it's important for people to get that. We tend to be more introverted and emotional, and that can require a bit more delicate handling. Certainly my most successful relationships (personal or professional) are with people that understand the artists's mentality."

It's true. Artists sometimes need some hand-holding . . . and we often turn to our representation to provide that. This is partly because our representatives are inextricably entwined with our lives and careers. We depend on our agents, publicists, lawyers, and managers to help us get jobs and feed our families. More importantly, however, artists' emotional lives are what fuel our work. Whether you're a singer, dancer, set designer, poet, or stand-up comic, you draw from your own experiences to make your work genuine, soulful, and alive.

Thus, representatives may be our business partners, but they're also an integral part of our personal lives. They celebrate with us when we land a great job; they pick us up when we fall. And as our *creative* partners, representatives see early drafts of work we'd never show anyone else, lead us through agonizingly personal secrets and stories, and help us dredge up our deepest, darkest thoughts or feelings and splatter them all over screens or pages.

Seven: To Promote Our Work and Material

Artists, by their nature, are rarely great salespeople or promoters. Maybe we've been taught not to brag. Maybe we're not comfortable in the spotlight. Maybe we believe our work should attract an audience by itself, and if we have to hype something, it means it's not strong enough to stand on its own merits. Whatever the reason, most writers and artists suck at sales and promotions —which is why we write instead of doing sales and promotions.

Unfortunately, Hollywood is the land where art and commerce meet. On one hand, the industry thrives on visionaries producing wonderul artworks like *Life of Pi* and *The*

Wire. On the other, giant corporations sell these artworks to audiences for billions of dollars.

"You can talk about your accomplishments, but people are more likely to believe someone else talking about you, rather than you talking about yourself," says Alan Moore, a TV agent at APA (Agency for the Performing Arts). "It brings more weight to it if [a third party] says, 'You need to know this person because they did this, this, and this.'"

So writers, actors, and directors occasionally hire representatives to help sell and promote their work to the public. Some reps actually peddle scripts, films, or concepts to producers or studios. Others simply help clients *promote* their work. They get filmmakers' movies featured in magazine articles. They find public appearance opportunties for comics kicking off a new tour. They set up press junkets for rappers promoting a new album.

Eight: Manage Practical and Financial Matters

Four days before his death, Edgar Allen Poe was found wandering the streets of Baltimore, penniless and delirious. Oscar Wilde died broke and in exile. And while I certainly wouldn't mind being known as "the twenty-first century Oscar Wilde or Edgar Allen Poe," I hope it's not because I've died broke, delirious, and exiled.

This is why many writers hire someone to tend to their business affairs—because most of us suck at it. (I literally have not balanced my checkbook in years. I don't even know how to do it.) Being a freelancer, especially in an industry as labyrinthine as entertainment, comes with a host of confusing business issues. You've just started a new job—did you correctly fill out your short-form? How about your long-form? Or your C.O.A., your W4, and all your payroll documentation? Are you "exempt" or "non-exempt?" When should you form a "loan-out?" Is it time to apply for a Business Tax Certificate? Are you eligible for a performing artists' special exemption, IRC 62 (b)(1) and (2)?

Agents juggle some of these issues for us, managers tackle others, and some fall to business managers. But for business-adverse writers, hiring reps to handle our confusing business affairs and decisions can often be advantageous.

Nine: To Architect and Plan Careers

Doctors don't hire agents to map out their careers. Plumbers don't hire people to map out their career. So why are writers and directors different? If you're a reasonably intelligent artist, why can't you map out your own career?

Well, first of all—maybe you can. But Hollywood is different from other industries. Most artists working in Hollywood are freelancers, so you're not on a fixed path of promotions and raises. You gain cache by continually doing good work, and while "good work" is a requirement of any profession, your writing career can leap ahead with one stellar screenplay . . . or take a nosedive with a crappy one. And unlike, say, a plumber unclogging a drain or a doctor consulting with a patient, writing a screenplay doesn't take a few minutes or hours . . . it takes *months*. So you're usually not earning little paychecks, or even a steady paycheck, as you go . . . you're working for the *hope* of a paycheck somewhere down the line. As a result, it's often helpful to have informed teammates advising you as you pour massive amounts of time and energy into a project.

Also, effective representatives have their fingers on the pulse of the marketplace. They know what's selling and who's buying. They can also evaluate their clients' current place in the industry. If you've just made a splash at a film festival with a low-budget, family comedy, a good representative can advise you what to write next. Should you try your hand at a quirky one-hour television pilot like *Shameless* or *Parenthood* . . . or a large-scale comedy like *The Hangover* or *Identity Thief*?

Architecting a career "depends on what the client's wishes are," says Moore. "Then it's about finding the opportunities that will allow them to get there: figuring out who they should work with, what projects are the best stepping-stones, and giving guidance on how to avoid pitfalls along the way."

IN HOLLYWOOD, WHO USES REPRESENTATION?

Almost everyone. Writers, directors, actors, musicians, designers, and cinematographers all use representatives to find jobs, make connections, and negotiate deals. So do models and athletes. And camera operators, script supervisors, florist designers, sound mixers. Production companies hire representation to gain access to talented writers, directors, and performers. Smoke House, the company behind *Argo* and *The Ides of March*, is repped by CAA, one of the largest talent agencies in the world. ShondaLand, which produces TV shows such as *Grey's Anatomy* and *Scandal*, is repped by ICM Partners. Film financiers like the Bandito Brothers (*Act of Valor*) have representation to give them a pipeline to quality investments.

Politicians like former US Representative Barney Frank and former Pennsyvania governor Ed Rendell use representatives to help land well-paying speaking gigs or book deals. International corporations enlist Hollywood reps to find marketing, product integration, and branded entertainment opportunities—like when WME-repped Hasbro turned its toys Battleship, G.I. Joe and Transformers into blockbuster movies, or when CAA orchestrated Hershey's placement of Icebreakers Sours Gum in a four-minute online episode of "LonelyGirl15."

Even executives and producers employ representatives when they're looking for jobs or promotions. Because Hollywood agents talk to everyone in the industry, they're often aware of opportunities before anyone else. Agencies are "the hotbed of all activity in Hollywood," says McKay.

"Every creative part of production or entertainment has to run through an agency in some way, shape, or form," says Gerry Sadowski, an entertainment research consultant for Fox, Paramount, and Playboy TV. "There are six studios, plus Lionsgate-Summit, Weinstein, and everybody else. All the product they make has to run through agencies. The talent, the scripts, the directors—everybody's either represented or getting funneled through an agency."

Of course, different agencies have different skill sets. The question now is—how many types of Hollywood representatives are there? What do they each do? And which type is right for you?

2   Types of Representation

There are four main types of Hollywood representation: **agents, managers, lawyers, and publicists.** Each specializes in different tasks and responsibilities, and some are more helpful for certain careers—or at certain stages of careers—than others. Agents and managers are the two most recognizable forms of representation—if only thanks to characters like *Entourage's* Ari Gold and Woody Allen's *Broadway Danny Rose.* They're also the two most misunderstood. While their jobs and goals often overlap, there are actually critical differences between agents and managers that affect how they nagivate Hollywood and interact with clients.

AGENTS

"An agent's main responsibility is to find work for the client, to generate business on behalf of the client and the agency," says APA agent Alan Moore. Those clients may be actors, writers, directors, public figures. Usually, an agent specializes in procuring work for one specific type of client. **Talent agents** represent actors auditioning for roles in commercials, TV shows, plays, or movies; ICM Partners, for example, reps Sherri Shepherd, Tim Robbins, and Portia de Rossi. (FYI—the term "talent agent" is often used generically to refer to *all* types of agents that represent artists—musicians, directors, actors, writers, whatever. But to entertainment industry professionals, "talent agent" refers specifically to agents handling actors.) **Literary (or "lit") agents** specialize in writers of literary properties such as books, scripts, or graphic novels. TV agent Scott Schwartz, for example, represents writer/producers Kari Lizer (*The New Adventures of Old Christine*, *Will & Grace)* and Gail Lerner (*Happy Endings*, *Ugly Betty*). Paradigm reps bestselling novelist Stephen King (*Carrie*, *The Shining*),[1] and CAA handles *Unbroken* author Laura Hillenbrand. **Public appearance agencies**, such as The Stephen Barclay Agency, help celebrities, authors, comics, and other experts or performers land speaking gigs, corporate shows, and live engagements. **Music agents** work with bands and musicians to book concerts and tours; WME for example, reps Frank Ocean, LeAnn Rimes, Cee Lo, Ziggy Marley, Natalie Cole, Pitbull, and Kid Cudi.

In exchange for helping clients procure work and jobs, agents charge clients a commission on their income. Agents in some fields take five percent of a clients' income, agents in others take ten or twenty.

What makes an agent an agent?

Can anyone be an agent? I mean, if having an agent is so important, why not just ask your best friend or cousin to help you get a job? I'm sure most of them would be happy to do it for a percentage of your paychecks. "Could your Uncle Harry whip up some letterhead and call himself 'Uncle Harry the Agent?'" asks book agent Scott Hoffman of Folio Literary Management, which represents best-selling authors like Garth Stein (*The Art of Racing in the Rain*) and Buddy Valuator (*Cake Boss*). "He could, but . . . this is a relationship-driven business; editors like to buy books from agents they know and trust."

Wanna Read The Talent Agencies Act in its Entirety?

Check out the California Labor Code, sections 1700–1700.46.

License and Registration

California requires all agents to be bonded and licensed, but at companies with multiple agents, each individual works under the license of the agency.

What Is a Surety Bond?

A surety bond guarantees that if Person A fails to live up to certain contractual obligations agreed to by both Person A and Person B, Person A owes Person B money to cover certain damages.

Hollywood works the same way.

"You get a bazillion scripts/ideas a year," says Scott Seiffert of Dreamworks Animation SKG. "It is impossible for the average exec to read all the scripts they get." If a project comes from a trusted agent, however, "the script has gone through a filter and somebody has concluded the script/idea isn't a heaping pile of shit. It's like getting a contractor for your house. You can blindly pull a name off the Internet, or you can get a recommendation from your neighbor. The smart money is to look at the neighbor's recommendation more closely."

Still, many states have laws requiring agents to meet certain qualifications. Without first meeting these requirements, you can't operate as an agent. In Arizona, all employment agents, including talent agents, must pass a written test and background check, apply for a license, and put up a $5,000 bond. Failure to comply results in a Class 6 Felony. In Maine, agents don't need to put up a bond, but they do need to apply for a license. (Failure to do so results in a fine of at least—are you sitting down?— a whopping $100.)

Agent requirements are strictest in California, the home of Hollywood, where most talent agents are based. California's Talent Agencies Act of 1978 requires all talent agents to pay $225 for a special license and deposit with the Labor Commissioner a surety bond in the penal sum of $50,000.

How to get a California Talent Agency License

Talent agency application packages are available from California's Department of Labor Standards Enforcement (DLSE) via:

- Online: www.dir.ca.gov/dlse/Talent_Agency_License.html
- Email: DLSE.licensing@dir.ca.gov
- Phone: (415) 703–4846 (M–F, 8 a.m.–5 p.m.)
- Regular mail: Department of Industrial Relations
  Division of Labor Standards Enforcement
  Licensing and Registration
  P.O. Box 420603
  San Francisco, CA 94142

Completed applications must be returned along with an affadavit of character, personal record, tax documents, premise certification, articles of incorporation, and artist/agency contracts, fee schedules and a handful of other documents. Applicantss must also include proof of their $50,000 surety bond. There are also some fees:

- Annual license fee–$225
- Annual fee for branch office–$50/office (beyond the headquarters)
- Filing fee–$25

For more information, visit the CA DLSE at www.dir.ca.gov/dlse/Talent_Agency_License.html or the Association of Talent Agents, a non-profit trade association representing talent agencies across the country, at www.agentassociation.com.

As part of their mission to procure employment for clients, agents also negotiate contracts, set up introductions for buyers and clients, offer constructive advice on scripts or other work, and help clients identify long-term career goals and strategies for meeting them.

There's one important thing, however, that agents *cannot* do: *produce their clients' work.* In other words, an agent representing an actor may help that actor land jobs in movies, but he can't produce those same movies. WME, for example, represents director Jason Reitman; WME may help Reitman sell projects, find actors, even secure

No Double-Dipping!

Although California's Talent Agencies Act doesn't specifically keep agents from producing, it *does* prevent agents from "dividing fees with an employer," or making money off clients as well as those clients' employers or projects (often called "double-dipping").

financing–all things a good producer might do–but WME can not be credited or paid as an actual producer. This is to keep agents from funneling clients into movies, TV shows, or other endeavors in which they have a financial stake. This would be a huge conflict of interest, not only because agents would be motivated to steer clients toward their own productions or companies, but because producers have incentive to pay talent as little as possible, so it's not right to let agents–who are tasked with making their clients money–be those same clients' employers.

Ironically, there's no official law forbidding agents from producing. Rather, the "no-producing rule" is a provision of agencies' **franchise agreements** with the Guilds, unions representing Hollywood's professional artists. The Writers Guild of America (WGA) represents TV and screenwriters; the Directors Guild of America (DGA) covers directors and assistant directors; the Screen Actors Guild and the American Federation of Television and Radio Artists (SAG-AFTRA) reps actors, hosts, and voice-over performers.

To Learn More About The Guilds

And to see lists of each union's Guild-signatory agencies or its agency franchise agreement, visit the unions on their websites:

WGA–www.wga.org

DGA–www.dga.org

SAG-AFTRA– www.sagaftra.org

Each union has its own agency franchise agreement, regulating how long clients can be bound, how agent-client disputes must be handled, how much agents can charge, etc. (For example, the California Labor Commission will usually approve agency commisions up to twenty percent, but the Guilds restrict commission to only ten percent.)[2] Most legitimate agencies are "**Guild-signatory**," meaning they've complied with the rules of the Guild's franchise agreements. The unions recommend no one sign with an agency that's not Guild-signatory; Guild contracts have been put in place to protect artists from unscrupulous representatives. Guild-signatory agencies are not necessarily recommended or endorsed by the unions; they've simply agreed to follow a specific set of rules.

While franchise agreements prevent agents from producing, there's one important "caveat" to this rule: agencies can own up to twenty percent of a production entity.[3] So while agents can't technically act as bona fide producers, recent years *have* seen agencies start to invest in various production companies. ICM, for example, invests in interactive producer Rides.TV, while CAA has a stake in Funny or Die and UTA owns part of Awesomeness TV. (More on this in Chapter Three.)

TYPES OF AGENTS

There are two types of Hollywood agents: **above-the-line** and **below-the-line**. "The line" refers to the budget of a film or TV production, where an actual line often separates certain elements from others. "Above-the-line" elements–the writer, director, and main cast members–are considered indispensable and must be in place before production begins. "Below-the-line" elements are hired once the project has been officially green-lit: camera operators, dolly grips, make-up artists, etc.

Most agents represent either above-the-line or below-the-line clients. Montana Artists Agency, for instance, specializes in below-the-line clients, representing stunt coordinators such as Charlie Croughwell (*Flight*, *Dawn of the Planet of the Apes*), costume designers such as Durinda Wood (*A Mighty Wind*, *Brothers*), and editors such as Michelle Tesoro (*Newsroom*, *House of Cards*).

This book focuses on above-the-line agents, which can themselves be divided into two categories: **talent agents** (which represent actors and performers) and **lit agents** (writers, authors, directors, producers). We're here to talk about lit agents, which can be further divided into other categories:

- **Motion picture ("MP") lit** agents rep writers of feature-length screenplays
- **TV lit** agents handle TV writers, showrunners, and producers
- **Alternative** agents rep writers and producers of reality, talk, and game shows
- **Digital media** agents work with writers and creators of video games, web series, and online content

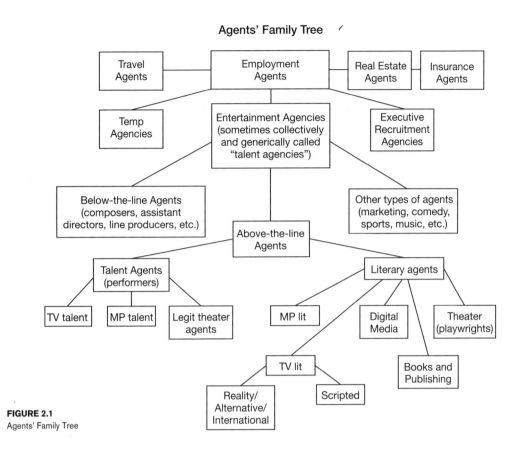

Agents' Family Tree

FIGURE 2.1
Agents' Family Tree

Lit agents come in all shapes and sizes. Some work for tiny one- or two-man shops; others work for international corporations. Some work from their garage or basement; others office in plush penthouse suites. We'll discuss various types and sizes of agencies later—as well as the pros and cons of each—but regardless of size and location, all lit agencies share common goals.

"[We are] the architect for a writer's career," says Tanya Cohen of Verve Talent and Literary Agency, which reps *Star Wars VII* writer Michael Arndt and *Jurassic Park IV* director Colin Trevorrow, "designing a plan for a writer's career that is specific, targeted, and in line with the artist's highest dreams and ambitions. [This means] being ahead of the client at all times, always thinking about what's next, being in front of all opportunities in both the studio and the independent space."

HOW LITERARY AGENTS MAKE MONEY

Literary agents have three primary revenue streams, and they each inform agents' actions and strategies differently. We'll discuss these revenue streams in greater detail in the next chapter, but they are:

1. **Commission**—This is the most common and widely understood form of payment. Most literary agents—whether repping TV writers, screenwriters, playwrights, or authors—charge clients ten percent of their gross earnings.
2. **TV Packaging fees**—TV lit agents often sell shows as "**packages**," providing a buyer not only with a writer and an idea, but with other above-the-line elements such as a director, producer, or actor. When selling packages, agencies become

part owners in the series, taking a portion of each show's weekly budget as well as a piece of its backend profits. Since TV shows can have backends worth billions of dollars (*Seinfeld*'s backend earned $2.7 billion in its first twelve years of syndication),[4] TV packaging can generate serious coin for agents. We'll learn much more about packaging fees in Chapters 3 and 7.

3. **Producer commissions**—MP lit agents not only charge clients ten percent, they also frequently take a ten percent commission from producers to whom they sell. That's right—if an agent sets up a project with a producer, and that producer helps sell the project to a studio, the agent will charge the producer a ten percent fee for providing her with the material.

MANAGERS

"Managers are essentially the artist's partner—whether [that artist is a] writer, actor, director, or producers," says Alex Murray, a manager at Brillstein Partners Entertainment, where he manages clients Jim Gaffigan, Chris Hardwicke, and Michael Waltrip. "We're their right-hand man, their partner in helping them create and execute a blueprint for their business."

Managers often differ from agents because "agents have specific jobs," Murray explains. "There are TV agents, lit agents, talent agents, personal appearance agents, film agents . . . whereas the manager oversees everything. The best analogy is: if there's a football team, I'm the head coach, and agents are the offensive coordinator, defensive coordinator, quarterback's coach, linebacker coach. You need *all* those guys to execute the plan, but it's the head coach that comes up with the X's and O's of what exactly needs to happen."

In other words, while agents focus on on getting clients jobs in the short term, and in specific areas, managers help shape and guide a client's long-term career.

"Your manager is the CEO of your business," says Kara Welker, a partner at Generate, where she helps manage writers and comics such as Al Madrigal, Brian Posehn, and Patton Oswalt, "while an agent or an agency is the sales force."

Managers counsel clients on business choices, introduce them to buyers, and offer creative advice on projects. "You play a lot of different roles—that's what keeps the job fun," says music manager Chris Knight of Career Artist Manager, the firm that reps Maroon 5, Stone Temple Pilots, Barenaked Ladies, and Sara Bareilles. "I like to call it the professional babysitter. Some days you're a therapist, some days you're working out a deal—contract negotaition. Basically, you're overlooking the person's career from top to bottom, helping them make the right decisions."

Of course, agents like to claim much of this is part of their job description as well. So what *is* the difference?

What Makes a Manager a Manager?

It's actually easier to understand what managers do by looking at what they *can't* do. And what managers can't do is fairly simple: *managers can't legally procure work for their clients.*

Managers can guide clients and strategize careers; they can make creative suggestions and notes; they can arrange meetings and send out scripts; but they can't legally get clients paid work.

Why not? Because managers, unlike agents, don't have to be licensed. Remember: in California—and twenty-four other states—talent agents must be licensed in order to procure actual paid work for clients. Of course, the flip side is: because the barrier to entry is much lower, *anyone* can call themselves a manager.

"Not anybody can just become an agent overnight . . . but anybody can do the management path. A dog could probably be a manager," says Jeff Holland, a founding partner of The Cartel, a management company representing writers and producers like

Sheryl Anderson (*Charmed*, *Flash Gordon*) and Pat Charles (*Bones*, *Sons of Anarchy*). "Anybody can decide to [be a manager] any time of day and just start it up, work out of their house, work out of their car, work out of their minivan, whatever they want to do."

Once again, this stems from 1978's Talent Agencies Act, which mandates that anyone getting work for clients must be licensed by the state. Managers don't want to get licensed—and if they did, they'd be agents—so, therefore, they're not allowed to procure work. In fact, if managers *are* caught procuring work, they forfeit any commissions made on that client's employment. Managers, like agents, usually charge clients ten percent commission. But if the state finds a manager actually *getting* work for their clients—*poof!* There goes their commission.

Of course, the meaning of "procuring work" is vague. Let's say a manager introduces a writer to a producer, that producer and writer form a relationship, and the producer later buys a pitch from the writer. Is that "procuring work?" The manager simply made an introduction; the sale of the script happened later.

What if an executive is hiring writers for a TV show and a manager sends over a script, saying, "This is a great writer, someone you should definitely know," and the executive ends up hiring the writer on the TV show. Is that "procuring work?" The manager didn't say, "I'm submitting this writer for a specific job"; he just said, "You should know this talented writer"—and the exec happened to be hiring at the time.

Or what if a manager sends a client's screenplay to a movie studio, the studio says it wants to buy the project, so the manager enlists the client's agent to negotiate and close the deal. Is that "procuring work?" The manager introduced the studio execs to a commercial piece of material, hoping they'd buy it . . . but it was the agent who actually closed the deal and made the sale, the official procurement of work.

Hollywood vs. the Talent Agencies Act

In November, 2012, the National Conference of Personal Managers (NCOPM), a professional trade organization of talent managers, filed a federal suit naming California Governor Jerry Brown, Attorney General Kamala Harris, and Labor Commissioner Julie Su.

The NCOPM's suit claimed the Talent Agencies Act goes against the 13th Amendment of the U.S. Constitution, which outlaws slavery and involuntary servitude. According to the managers, the TAA encourages involuntary servitude because managers are working for clients who can then turn around and refuse to pay managers for doing the very job they were hired to do. This came after various performers—including Arsenio Hall, Rosa Blasi, and Ke$ha—fired their managers and used the TAA to escape paying owed commissions.[5]

The NCOPM also charged that the TAA interferes with due process and equal protection, as well as interstate commerce since it deprives "out-of-state personal managers access to the California talent market on equal terms." The suit claimed that the TAA was established to regulate agents, not managers; an earlier draft of the law even had a clause addressing managers—but it was later omitted—proof, said the NCOPM, that legislators did not intend for the law to apply to managers.

The suit estimated the TAA has cost managers over $500 million in income, and sought a permanent injunction keeping California from enforcing the Talent Agencies Act.[6]

On March 5, 2013, U.S. District Court Judge Dean Pregerson threw the case out. Pregerson ruled that "not being compensated for work performed does not inevitably make that work involuntary servitude. Plaintiff's members have choices. They have the choice to refrain from procuring employment for their clients, to procure employment without a license and risk the voiding of parts of their contracts, or to obtain a license."[7]

As of March, 2013, the NCOPM had vowed to appeal.

These scenarios illuminate the often slippery nature of where managers fit in the context and purview of the Talent Agencies Act.

Another Big Difference Between Managers and Agents

Because managers can't procure work, they're not considered "sellers" in the same way agents are. Thus, managers are allowed to do something agents aren't: *produce their clients' work*. Remember—agents are barred from producing by franchise agreements, but since managers aren't (supposedly) getting clients work, they're allowed to produce!

Thus, when agents and managers try to sell a client's script or pitch, managers often attach themselves as producers. This means that if the project gets made into a movie or TV show, the manager is paid and credited as a producer. You know all those producers, co-producers, executive producers, and co-executive producers you see flashing across the screen at the beginning of a TV show or movie? Some may be managers of the project's writers, producers, or actors! Watch MTV's *The Inbetweeners*—see "Executive Producer Aaron Kaplan" strolling past? Aaron Kaplan manages Damon Beesley and Iain Morris, the creators of the original British version of *The Inbetweeners*.[8] Next time you watch *Crazy, Stupid, Love*, note the credit for co-producer Eryn Brown—she manages writer Dan Fogelman at Management 360.[9]

Does this mean managers are parasites, siphoning money and credit from their client's projects and sales? *Not at all!* Most good managers are hands-on producers, working hard to develop clients' scripts, attach talent, find directors or financing, and sell the project to the right studio or network. Once the show is on the air, or the film is in production, most managers then execute actual producer duties to earn their title and fee.

Some management companies are so heavily involved in production they even have their own production facilities. New Wave Entertainment, for instance, has its own studios, green screens, cameras, lights, and edit bays. This gives clients practical resources for shooting content: shorts, web videos, demos, and **sizzle reels** (short video "teasers" or trailers designed to help sell a reality project).

Good to Know

Managers only get paid as producers *if the project gets made*—and most projects never see the light of day.

It also allows New Wave to "deliver scripted fare to networks that don't have the desire to spend, or the capacity to spend, the money it would normally take to buy scripted fare," says New Wave manager Michael Pelmont, who's a producer on New Wave productions *Stevie TV* or *Munchie the Agent*. "We put together writing staffs. We have internal line producers that budget the show and work with networks in terms of hitting the numbers they want to hit . . . or, if they're beating those numbers, they order extra episodes. We give it to one of our fifty editors to then cut. We're literally making the show soup to nuts."

When managers receive a producing fee, they don't commission their client—just like when agents take a package. "In the perfect world where everything works the way it's supposed to work," says Pelmont, a client sells a show and "will pay no

---

Insider's Tip

If you're hunting for management companies that also produce good shows and movies, *do your research*. "An uninformed writer, a new writer, someone not aware of the situation, will say, 'Oh! This manager's an executive producer! I see their name at the end of the show!'" says one prominent literary manager. But sometimes that "manager just represents the *star* of the show—he doesn't actually have much influence on who's being hired. So while the titles and credits might look the same, it's apples and oranges. That's something you have to look at."

commissions. The studio pays [the client's] manager a fee as a producer, and [the studio] pays their agents a fee as a packaging fee."

So Managers Can't Procure Work . . . But They *Can* Produce. How Else Do Managers Differ from Agents?

One of the biggest differences is that managers have smaller clients lists than agents, allowing them to give clients more personal attention. While an agent may have more than seventy or eighty clients, managers often have fifteen or twenty—sometimes fewer. This also allows managers to be more creatively hands-on than agents.

"Not to say agents aren't creatively involved," says Cohen, but "we're designing the business side of [a client's] career. A manager's role is to be the *creative* partner . . . to read [scripts] page-by-page and act-by-act, and really be a creative soundboard."

Also, because most agencies are ferociously competitive (and rabidly protective of their clients), most won't work with rival agencies when putting together a project or TV package. Managers, however, aren't usually afraid to work with other firms and clients, so a lit manager at Anonymous Content may pair a writing client, like *Terra Nova's* Barbara Marshall with an actor from Industry Entertainment, which reps stars such as *Hawaii Five-0's* Daniel Dae Kim and Beth Behrs of *2 Broke Girls*.

Managers also act as liaisons to clients' other representatives. They coordinate activities and communication between a client's agents, publicists, and lawyers. And because managers have fewer clients than other types of representatives, they're usually more accessible and easier for clients to reach.

"I almost discourage my clients from contacting their agent ten times a week," says manager Geoff Silverman of The Cartel. "That will drive an agent crazy. Managers are there to talk everyday, twice a day, once a week—whatever the client is comfortable doing."

LAWYERS

Fantastic agents and managers know the ins and outs of most Hollywood deals. They know the basic tenets of a standard staffing contract or script deal. But even the world's greatest agent or manager doesn't have legal powers. "Agents tend to focus more on the deal points in broad strokes. What's the fixed compensation? What's the backend?" says entertainment lawyer Greg Snodgrass of Business Affairs, Inc., a law firm representing clients like Fox Searchlight, HBO, and Lucasfilm. "The attorney is able to catch the nuances in the agreement, in terms of legal drafting, protecting rights—like who owns the copyright? Questions that may not be as much of a consideration for an agent are more of a consideration for the lawyer."

Lawyer Up!

"Any writer that's serious about being a creator—get a fucking great entertainment lawyer," says one literary manager. "[Not doing that] is the definition of penny-wise/dollar-stupid. When it comes to those [legal] definitions, in success it leads to a lot of money, and for five percent, it's worth it. Don't skimp. This is your livelihood."

Even if your agent went to law school, he's not spending 24/7 immersed in intricate legal technicalities. "There's almost a 'secret encyclopedia' of what is typical and necessary of people to give, and that changes over time," says entertainment attorney Charles Holland. "Small things: how much expenses someone is going to give, whether these people will give you an advance if you ask for it. A lot of these things are known by agents, but sometimes they're more known by lawyers."

Thus, having a good entertainment lawyer is essential to anyone climbing the Hollywood ladder. "The difference between millions of dollars can be a comma or a period in a contract," says APA lit agent Lindsay Howard. "That's incredibly complicated legal language I can't even pretend to understand, but it can be incredibly lucrative."

Unlike agents, lawyers don't usually get clients work. And unlike managers, lawyers don't usually give clients feedback on scripts or projects. In fact, most law firms discourage their lawyers from doing that. Law firms can get incredibly competitive, so partners discourage any behavior that could potentially backfire and cost the company a client.

Most lawyers focus on perusing contracts, making sure clients are legally protected and keeping them informed about the "legal concepts and effects" of deals. "[Agents and managers] wouldn't necessarily know the legal effect of something," says Holland. "Sometimes a date, even language, the difference between 'shall' and 'must' or 'shall' and 'is' [can make a huge difference]. There is all kinds of . . . magic language we, as lawyers, know is magic. 'Best efforts' is something that gets thrown around by agents like it doesn't mean anything. There will be a provision that writers have to have 'best efforts' to have their script turned in by a certain date. We, as lawyers, know 'best efforts' is something to be avoided. It means you do *anything* to make something happen, even beyond 'reasonable,' even beyond 'prudent,' even if it bankrupts you. 'Best efforts'–you could say, 'Okay, then you don't sleep.' 'You don't go to your daughter's graduation.' 'Reasonable efforts' is what you want."

What Type of Lawyer Do You Need?

There are many different types of entertainment lawyers: intellectual propery lawyers, bankruptcy lawyers, employment law attorneys, immigration attorneys, securities lawyers. What you need, however, is a **transactional attorney**, an attorney who specializes in contracts, deals, and business documents. Transactional lawyers deal with everything from directors' contracts to record deals to film financing to corporate licensing partnerships.

How Are Lawyers Paid?

Many lawyers charge their clients commission, but whereas agents and managers charge ten percent, most entertainment lawyers charge only five percent. Other lawyers charge by the hour. Either way, one thing to beware of–many lawyers also charge an upfront retainer. You or your agent, if you already have one, can sometimes get this waived, and lawyers will often let it go if you already have a job they know will generate income.

PUBLICISTS

Publicists "help create, enhance, and protect the public profile of a celebrity or public figure," says Julie Nathanson, Executive Vice President of Entertainment at Rogers and Cowan, one of Hollywood's top PR firms. "We work with actors, musicians, authors, producers, directors, events–anybody who has a reason to be in the public eye. Or finds themselves in the public eye." This means that rather than finding clients employment, like agents do, or developing and producing material, like managers do, publicists help clients get media exposure. This could include coverage in magazine features and newspaper articles, guest spots on talk shows such as *Jimmy Kimmel Live*, even appearances at live events like the Hollywood Christmas Parade.

"Publicity is a tool like many other tools to help [clients] get more and better opportunities to work," says Nathanson. "If [someone is] an actor on a television series, and they are emerging talent, below the first or second lead, it might behoove them to make sure both the audience and the industry–the people who can hire them for their next job–know them by their real name, not just their character."

Damage Control!

A publicist's job may also be keeping certain clients *out* of the media–like in November, 2012, when Rogers & Cowan pulled Lindsay Lohan out of a planned Barbara Walters interview, afraid Walters would question her on possible criminal charges of lying to police about a car crash earlier that year.

How Do Publicists Make Money?

Unlike agents and managers, who charge clients a percentage of their earnings, publicists charge retainer fees. Some charge $5,000 per month; others charge $200 per hour. This is partly because publicity does not lead directly to employment, so it's tough to say publicists should get paid only if the client gets work. And since clients don't get paid for going on *The Daily Show* or *The View*, or for being interviewed in *Esquire*, it's difficult to link a publicist's compensation to clients' earnings.

Unlike publicists, "agents and managers are committed to clients because they know they could have a really big payday," says Nathanson whose company's client list has boasted Robert Downey Jr., Elton John, and Tom Cruise. "If [a client] makes $10 million per movie, [agents] make $1 million. An agency or manager can work for a client for a long time and never see any money, but when they do it is likely to be a bigger payday. At $5,000 per month, it takes [publicists] a long time to make a million dollars, but our $5,000 a month is guaranteed."

This is also important because there are no assurances in publicity. Publicists can work hard, do a great job, and *still* get the client no helpful publicity. "If you're an actor, you can't hire a publicist and three months later say, 'You didn't get me on Letterman . . . I want my money back.' Or, 'You didn't get me in *People* magazine, so I'm not paying you.' Everyone does the best they can," Nathanson says. Hopefully, you don't take on clients you don't think you can do something for. [And] hopefully, as a client, you are responsible enough to know you have to be watching and making sure your publicist is really working for you. Everybody on an actor's team—agent, manager, and talent—part of their job is to keep a close watch on how the publicity is doing. Sometimes the publicity is great but it's not helping. Sometimes the publicity isn't so good, but the publicist is really pulling out all the stops. And sometimes it's the perfect storm: the publicist is working hard, publicity is coming through, and the additional exposure helps agents and managers build [the client's] career."

Do Writers or Directors Need Publicists?

Talk the Talk

EPK–Electronic Press Kit.

Not usually. Behind-the-camera artists usually get work based on the quality of their work and quantifiable factors like box office receipts, sales, viewer ratings, and awards or nominations—not their public persona or celebrity cache. "The only reason a writer or director would need a publicist would be to keep their name in front of five or six hundred people who can actually get them jobs," explains Nathanson. When publicity needs to done for a new movie—like including the director or writer in the film junket, press kit, or **EPK**—it's typically handled by the studio or distributor's PR department. Some directors even have clauses in their contracts requiring the studio to include them in certain press activities.

Having said that, writers and directors occasionally hire publicists during awards season. Let's say a writer or director's new film is getting a lot of attention; that writer/director may want a publicist to get his name out there in hopes of garnering a nomination for an Emmy or Oscar, or a even a nod from the Directors Guild or Writers Guild Awards.

One Other Type of Representation: Business Managers

Many successful producers, writers, actors, and directors add to their teams the services of a business manager. While business managers are often in regular contact with their clients's agents, managers, and lawyers, they fulfill a slightly different function. To learn more about what business managers do, I decided to ask Ali Iali, veteran business manager at CBIZ MHM, LLC, where "clients range from directors and producers to wealthy individuals."

ME: Ali, what's the nutshell description of a business manager?

IALI: Business management (AKA 'Family Office') deals with all the financial aspects of a client's life. The client can be an individual, a couple or a business. Depending on the level of engagement a client requires, we can do anything and everything. We make sure income is received on a timely basis, bills paid accordingly. We are involved in the wealth management setup, insurance, household employees, business employees (payroll), we purchase and oversee the construction of homes, we engage people to sell homes, get cars and sell them, etc. If we cannot do it ourselves, we know the right people who can.

ME: How is a business manager different from a talent or literary manager?

IALI: Talent and literary managers are involved in promoting the client and making the deals. Our role is managing the money and all aspects of the day-to-day life of any talent so that they can focus on their talent.

ME:	Who has a business manager? Writers? Directors? Production companies? Giant studios?
IALI:	Almost anyone can have a business manager. Definitely, writers, directors, producers and their companies, actors, performers, athletes, wealthy individuals or trust fund babies. I cannot list all of them but you can get the gist of it. Giant studios normally have their own accounting departments that take care of them.
ME:	When might a writer or director turn to a business manager? What problems or situations might a business manager handle that a smart writer/director/client couldn't handle on his or her own?
IALI:	You can be an extremely talented writer, director, or otherwise, but that does not mean you have the time and/or the capability of managing your finances while you are doing the work you do. We make clients' life easier for them. We deal with things that they need not to. We will deal with bankers, investment firms, insurance, real estate brokers … show me any successful director, producer and or writer that does his or her own finances as well as their trade. For example, Steven Spielberg has a team of business managers.
ME:	Are business managers ever involved creatively with their clients? Do they give notes or feedback on scripts, pitches, edits of movies, etc.?
IALI:	Not necessarily. Those that come from that background will. Normally it is the talent manager that will do so.
ME:	At what point in their career might a writer or director want or need a business manager?
IALI:	You will get to that point when you start getting requests for your trade and become pressed for time. In addition, a business manager with a long resume can be costly. So a talent that is just starting does not need a business manager unless an amazing deal falls in their lap with a lot of money. This is when a business manager is needed to protect the talent from themselves. Most tend to spend a lot when that happens. I have seen it with athletes. They are notorious for doing so with few exceptions.
ME:	How are business managers paid?
IALI:	Depending on the client and the engagement, we can go hourly, flat retainer or a percentage of proceeds. Our fees, without naming names, can be as low as $1,000 per month, to $15,000 and $20,000 and sometimes much more.
ME:	When looking for a business manager, what should a writer or director look for?
IALI:	They should look for a history of that manager having writers and directors as clients. A manager that understands the client's trade is much more valuable than one who has no clue. You do not want a baker to build a kitchen cabinet!
ME:	How important is it for a business manager to have experience, in the entertainment industry? Does this industry work much differently than other industries, or could a business manager who mostly has, say, finance clients, also navigate the needs of someone in entertainment?
IALI:	The entertainment industry is a huge monster, and if you do not know about WGA, DGA, and all the other guilds, you will not be able to guarantee the client is getting their fully earned income, may it be fees, residuals, royalties, or participation. Normally, most business management firms will have directors from all aspects of the business world and a good firm will match the client with the correct team leader.
ME:	When a writer or director is looking for a talent or literary agent or manager, it's important to find someone who "gets" you–someone who understands your brand, your creative work, etc. How important is it for a business managers to "get" you–your vision and your brand? Does this even matter?
IALI:	That is very important. It goes along the same lines as [the last two questions]. The ultimate asset that a business manager can have is trustworthiness and integrity.

ME: How and when do business managers interact with clients' other representatives –agents, lawyers, publicists, managers, etc.?

IALI: Whenever there is anything financial on the line, we always get involved since– in most cases–there are tax ramifications for any transactions signed off on by the other representatives. We need to plan ahead based on the deal being presented. We always try to stay in touch with everyone connected to the client through conference calls, meetings and lunch meetings.

Agents vs. Managers vs. Lawyers

Wanna see how different types of reps compare? Here are some general comparisons between agents, managers, lawyers, and publicists.

TABLE 2.1

	Agents	Managers	Lawyers	Publicists
Must be Licensed	Yes (although requirements differ from state to state)	No	Yes	No
Must be Bonded	Yes (although requirements differ from state to state)	No	No (although requirements differ from state to state)	No
Has Legal Powers	No	No	Yes	No
Number of Clients	50–80	15–25	Varies	Varies
Charges Commission	10%	10–15%	5%	No
Charges Retainer	No	No	Sometimes	Yes
Legally Procures Work	Yes	No	No	No
Offers Creative Feedback	Yes	Yes	No	No
Strategizes Long-term Career Goals	Yes	Yes	No	No
Negotiates Contracts	Yes	Occasionally	Yes	No
Arranges Introductions and Meetings	Yes	Yes	Not usually	No
Produces Content (including receiving producer fees and credit)	No	Yes	No	No
Receives Packaging Fees	Yes	No	No	No
Commissions Producers' Fees	Yes	No	No	No
Arranges PR Opportunities (junkets, public appearances, media exposure, etc.)	No	No	No	Yes

THE STATE OF REPRESENTATION TODAY

When I first started working in Hollywood, in 1999, the agency world was dominated by five huge firms: CAA, William Morris, ICM, UTA, and Endeavor. There were also several "mid-level" agencies such as APA, Paradigm, Metropolitan, Writers and Artists, The Gersh Agency, Don Buchwald & Associates, and Innovative Artists. In addition, there were numerous "boutiques," small but effective agencies like Dytman & Associates, Kaplan Stahler, Major Clients, Vision Arts, The Rothman Agency, The

Irv Schechter Company, Abrams Artists, and Broder Kurland Webb Uffner. There were far fewer management companies. The prominent ones were Brillstein-Grey Entertainment and 3 Arts, both large companies representing major players such as Brad Pitt and Nick Lachey. Smaller companies were few and far between.

Over the years, that balance has begun to shift. Small firms lost talented agents to larger companies. In 2002, the Bruce Brown Agency, which repped writers like Cindy Chupack (*Sex and the City*, *Modern Family*),[10] lost agent Dave Brown to the Genesis Agency, which was in turn bought out by Paradigm. Similarly, in 2009, Kaplan Stahler Gumer Braun lost president Bob Gumer to APA[11] and partner Alan Braun to CAA.

Many smaller agencies were bought out. In 2006, ICM gobbled up Broder Webb Chervin Silbermann[12] (formerly Broder Kurland Webb Uffner), a twenty-seven-agent boutique that had become a literary steamroller by repping TV writers like Alex Kurtzman and Roberto Orci (*Alias*) and Chris Gerolmo (*Over There*). That same year, the Gersh Ageny acquired Dytman & Associates,[13] an LA-based boutique that represented top-level writers such as David Amann (*Castle*) and Bob Daily (*Desperate Housewives*), and New York's Joyce Ketay Agency, which specialized in playwrights like Tony Kushner (*Angels in America*) and Neil LaBute (*In the Company of Men*).[14]

The industry's biggest merger came in 2009, when two juggernaut agencies—the 111-year-old William Morris Agency and 14-year-old Endeavor—joined forces. Throughout its history, William Morris had been one of the world's leading agencies, repping legends like Frank Sinatra, Elvis Presley, Frank Capra, Marilyn Monroe, and Clark Gable. It had also built a formidable music business with clients like Kanye West and Willie Nelson;[15] but in recent years its film and TV business had flagged.

Endeavor, meanwhile, had booming TV and film divisions thanks to clients like Tina Fey, Matt Damon, Robert De Niro, Jenna Fischer, Jack Black, Sienna Miller, David Kelley, Ben Stiller, and Amy Poehler. In fact, a year before the merger, Endeavor went head to head with industry leader CAA in a battle to see who would close the most TV deals. The results? CAA: 359. Endeavor: 376. With annual revenue less than half of CAA's, Endeavor was quickly building a reputation as a scrappy, innovative, forward-thinking powerhouse.[16]

While many industry insiders viewed the William Morris–Endeavor merger as more of a takeover (William Morris CEO Jim Wiatt was forced out and 100 William Morris employees were fired; Endeavor's leadership remained intact, and the agency cut a mere six people[17]), the new company, WME, combined the strengths of both former agencies. WME had more than 300 agents—spread across two continents—and boasted clients ranging from Ben Affleck to Tyra Banks to J.J. Abrams.[18] Although a muscular new player had arrived on the scene, the William Morris–Endeavor marriage was also an unmistakable sign of the times: *the agency world was shrinking.*

Another world, however, was expanding. "Every time an agent gets fired," says New Wave manager Michael Pelmont, "you generally have a new manager pop up." It's true. Agent Dave Brown, formerly of Genesis and The Bruce Brown Agency, became a manager at Artist International, which reps writers such as Billy Riback (*Home Improvement*, *The Suite Life on Deck*) and director Jon Amiel (*Entrapment*, *The Borgias*). ICM agent Ron West left the agency in 2002 to help found Thruline Entertainment and its production arm, Tagline Pictures (*Psych*, *Man Up*, *100 Questions*). Former William Morris agent David Lonner launched Oasis Media Group, which represents directors like Alexander Payne (*The Descendants*) and Brad Bird[19] (*Mission Impossible: Ghost Protocol*, *The Incredibles*), while his old agenting colleague Marc Schwartz reps Valerie Bertinelli and Melissa Gilbert at Fusion Management.

"With the consolidation of agencies, and the wash of mid-size boutiques and mom-and-pop shops, there's been a need in the last twelve years for managers," says Brown. "The truth is: this town is so damn tough, you need a whole village to get somebody a job. The volume [agents] work at is more of a plug-and-play business; it's 'Where's the check? When's the payday?' It's not so much, 'How are we going to get this movie made in the next two years?' As a manager, you attach yourself to twenty clients, and your job is to build their long-term careers."

Hollywood's economics were affecting agencies in other ways as well. Studios began making fewer movies. In 2002, Disney put out twenty-two movies and Sony put out thirty-one; in 2012, Disney released thirteen and Sony released eighteen.[20] (That same year, Sony also announced plans to reduce its annual output by two movies a year, starting in 2014.)[21] And while other studios didn't necessarily reduce their output, they began looking to outside financiers to hedge financial risks. In 2005, Fox partnered with hedge fund Dune Capital Management in a multi-million-dollar arrangement that funded films like *Live Free or Die Hard*, *Avatar*, and *The Devil Wears Prada*. Universal partnered with financier Relativity, which made a $2–$3 billion dollar deal to cover nearly seventy-five percent of Universal's films through 2015. In 2007, Merrill Lynch contributed $1 billion to Summit Entertainment, the new studio behind *The Hurt Locker* and the *Twlight* movies, and $500 million to United Artists (*Hotel Rwanda*, *Valkryie*).

Those shifts were due to several factors. One: as films became more expensive, Hollywood has become more desperate for sure-fire hits. This has resulted in a proliferation of two different kinds of movies: 1. big-budget films based on pre-existing properties which execs and producers believe come with a built-in audience, like Disney's $220 million *The Avengers*; and 2. low-budget movies like the $1 million *The Devil Inside*, which was acquired and distributed by Paramount, and grossed over $53 million. What kind of movie is missing? Mid-budget movies ($30 million–$80 million) like *The Proposal* or *The Village*, which cost too much to be risk-free but don't usually generate the hundreds of millions of dollars racked up by something like a *Harry Potter* movie.

Also responsible for this shift is the rise of the global box office, which has become even more important to studios than the domestic box office. Of course, only certain kinds of movies play across cultures and borders—and those tend to be large, action-packed films with some level of pre-existing audience awareness. In 2012, the top ten movies at the international box office were all adaptations or sequels (see for yourself in the margin). This has made Hollywood much less eager to buy or take risks on original material, making it difficult for many agents—especially those who represent writers that don't specialize in large-scale studio movies—to stay in business.

Also contributing to Hollywood's contraction was the the 2007–08 Writer Guild strike, which began in November, 2007. With virtually every scripted writer in Hollywood refusing to work, studios and networks had nothing to buy or air and agents had nothing to sell for 100 days. ICM placed several employees on "strike pay," disallowing them to come to the office or do work. Agents at UTA making more than $100,000 took a twenty percent cut. Assistants' hours were monitored to avoid overtime.[23] Although the strike ended on February 12, 2008, the industry still hadn't recovered that Fall when the global economy imploded, sending Hollywood into yet another tailspin.

As banks' capital dried up, so did much of the industry's spending cash. Some banks, like Merrill Lynch, pulled out of Hollywood altogether. Others grew more exacting about what they wanted in return for their investments; many wanted more control over which movies their dollars supported.[24]

Consumers, meanwhile, curbed their ability, or willingness, to pay for entertainment. Home video sales plummeted by more than $3 billion between 2007 and 2011,[25] and in both 2010 and 2011 the box office slipped (5.2 percent in 2010 and and another 4.7 percent in 2011).[26] Effects from these moves rippled through Hollywood. In June, 2011, Walt Disney studios laid off four percent of its workforce. Five months later, Paramount Pictures axed five percent. The following year, Lionsgate slashed twelve percent of its employees.[27] And in 2013, DreamWorks Animation announced it would eliminate nearly sixteen percent of its workers.[28] With studios shrinking their workforces as well as their budgets, agents found it harder and harder to sell clients' material.

The Ten Highest
Grossing Movies of 2012
(internationally)[22]

1. *The Avengers*:
   $1,511.8 million
2. *Skyfall*–$1,108.6 million
3. *The Dark Knight Rises*:
   $1,081 million
4. *The Hobbit:
   An Unexpected Journey*:
   $1.016.9 million
5. *Ice Age: Continental
   Drift*: $877.2 million
6. *The Twilight Saga:
   Breaking Dawn Part 2*:
   $829.2 million
7. *The Amazing Spiderman*:
   $752.2 million
8. *Madagascar 3: Europe's
   Most Wanted*:
   $742.1 million
9. *The Hunger Games*:
   $691.2 million
10. *Men In Black 3*:
    $624 million

In television, two other factors have decimated much of agents' traditional business. One: as reality TV has blossomed, it has taken hours of prime time programming away from scripted shows, drastically cutting into agencies' packaging fees. Agents *do* take packaging fees for reality shows, but they're much smaller than scripted packages. (We'll discuss this more in Chapter 3.) Two: as cable networks such as USA, MTV, and AMC have grown more successful, audiences have migrated away from traditional broadcast networks (ABC, NBC, CBS, FOX, the CW). With fewer viewers watching broadcast television, it becomes harder for those companies to generate the profits necessary to give agencies big packages. It also makes networks more reticent to program expensive scripted shows that—if they fail—cost millions of dollars. (NBC's *Do No Harm*, a UTA package, premiered January 31, 2013, to 3.1 million viewers— the worst ratings *ever* for a series premiere on one of the four main broadcasters. The show was canceled eight days later.) Instead, broadcast networks program more highly promotable, inexpensive reality shows like *America's Got Talent* or *The Voice*. These shows book recognizable stars like Shakira, Simon Cowell, and Christina Aguilera, generate large audiences, and—because they're cheaper—lose less money if they fail. So while they're great band-aids for networks hemorrhaging viewers and money, they're not great sustenance for agencies dependent on scripted packaging fees.

The upside of the audience's migration to cable is we've started seeing many interesting scripted shows that would never survive on ABC or CBS: FX's *Louie*, AMC's *The Walking Dead*, A&E's *Bates Motel*, Showtime's *Homeland*. The downside: while scripted cable shows are package-able, they have cheaper budgets than broadcast shows, so packages are still smaller than agencies are used to.

All of this leads to one simple analysis: *Hollywood is shrinking*. While there are more companies to do business with, those companies are making fewer, cheaper shows. Less money is being spent. Companies are shrinking both budgets and workforces. As a result, agencies have had to adapt. Some—like WME, APA, and CAA— have found new revenue streams like marketing and advertising. "Everybody is looking for ways to expand their businesses," says APA founder and president Jim Gosnell. "God forbid there's [another] strike, or . . . a proposed slow down. From my point of view, running a business, I'm in other areas that will help me get through those tough times. I have to . . . try to create as many platforms as will help our clients. If you had said to me—five, six years ago—that we'd be in branding and licensing and have a corporate department . . . I would have said, 'You're crazy.' And as we move forward, we may be in *other* businesses. I don't know what they are at the moment, but . . . if we don't, we're gonna be out of business."

Other agencies have survived by slimming their ranks; ten years ago, Metropolitan Talent Agency was a formidable mid-size talent and lit agency with twenty agents; today, it has fewer than five.[29]

"The business is contracting," says manager Jeff Holland, a founding partner of The Cartel. "Agencies are laying people off. But those people have a great client base and great skills. And they're like, 'What do I do with my life?' You can't just say, 'I'm going to work at another agency,' but you can, overnight, become a manager. Or join up with someone who's got an existing firm." Thus, the past few years have seen an explosion of new management companies. Old stalwarts—places like Benderspink, 3 Arts, and Brillstein Entertainment Partners (formerly Brillstein Grey)—are still around, but Hollywood now swarms with start-ups of all sizes, from large companies like New Wave and Anonymous Content to smaller operations such as Rain Management and Omnipop (which used to be an agency before switching to management). In fact, there are now many more management firms than agencies.

For writers, directors, and actors, this can be a huge boon. Since creatives, and actors can be repped by both an agent *and* a manager, artists can double the size of their teams. (On the flipside, your expenditures double as well. But since agents and managers only get paid if you get paid, you pay nothing if you don't work.) (The other flipside: since *anyone* can call themselves a manager, Hollywood is full of unqualified representatives. Some are unscrupulous shysters, others are merely inexperienced wannabes who lack the relationships, skills, and muscle to navigate the industry. You don't want to be with either one.)

3 Anatomy of an Agency— How Agencies Make Money, and How This Affects You

There may be fewer Hollywood agents and agencies than ever, but those that exist are still the most powerful players in the industry. "If you control [most] of the talent in Hollywood, all of Hollywood has to deal with you," says screenwriter/director Drew Goddard (*World War Z*, *The Cabin in the Woods*), "so the big agencies have more power than ever."

The truth is: not *all* agencies are "the most powerful players in Hollywood." The industry has many agencies, yet most of the real power is consolidated in the hands of a very few companies. "It's the world we live in, sadly," says Goddard. "There used to be multiple studios and multiple production houses, and now, at the end of the day, there are four or five. It's the same with agencies."

Agencies in Hollywood can be divided into three categories: the **Big Four**, the **mid-levels**, and **boutiques**. These categories are largely based on agencies' size, but each type of agency also works a bit differently and has its own strengths and weaknesses. No type of agency is inherently better than another; you can find fantastic representation and have a great career at any type, depending on your own personal needs. But understanding how types of agencies work can not only help you find the agency that's right for you, it will give you a better understanding of how agencies interact with and influence Hollywood—and how that affects which movies, TV shows, books, and projects eventually make it to consumers.

THE BIG FOUR

"I would say ninety-five percent of our dealings are with the Big Four agencies," says producer Doug McKay (*What To Expect When You're Expecting*), former VP of production at Phoenix Pictures. Indeed, the agency world is dominated by four gigantic companies: Creative Artists Agency (CAA), William Morris Endeavor (WME), United Talent Agency (UTA), and ICM Partners (formerly International Creative Management, but the agency changed its name to ICM Partners in 2012, when its owner, Rizvi Traverse Management, was bought out by the agents themselves).

These companies are "full-service" agencies. They have tentacles in every nook and cranny of the industry, including offices around the globe and hundreds of agents. CAA has over 300 agents[1] in offices in Los Angeles, New York, Nashville, St. Louis, Chicago, London, Beijing, Mumbai, and Stockholm.

The Big Four represent the lion's share of Hollywood's big-name stars, directors, and writers. UTA handles Johnny Depp, Elmore Leonard, and Sharon Osbourne. CAA has Zooey Deschanel, Jon Favreau, Keira Knightley, and Neil Patrick Harris. WME reps Tom Clancy, Ryan Reynolds, Heidi Klum, Carey Mulligan, Phil McGraw, and Tina Fey.

ICM claims Justin Long, Cuba Gooding Jr., and Eddie Griffin. "The difference [between the Big Four and other agencies] is the elevator," says TV writer Paula Yoo (*Eureka*, *The West Wing*). "Every time I'm at ICM or CAA . . . I'm in the elevator with some A-list Susan Sarandon or Julia Roberts-type person. Whereas when I go to the smaller agencies, it's just me."

But these agencies aren't dubbed the Big Four merely because they represent Hollywood's sexiest and most glamourous clients; they also represent *more* clients than their smaller rivals. One Big Four lit agent told me her department represented approximately 350 clients; the same department at a mid-level agency repped about 250. "That gives [these agencies] a tremendous amount of control," says Debbie Liebling, head of the TV department at Ben Stiller's Red Hour Films. "Those four places have the talent everybody is competing for. And because they control so much talent—actors, writers, directors, everything we're dependent upon—they can drive their agenda."

But the Big Four represent more than household names in film and TV. CAA Sports represents Dwyane Wade and Peyton Manning, while CAA Marketing works with Coca-Cola and Mitchum anti-perspirant. ICM books concert dates for the Beach Boys and Regina Spektor, as well as properties such as *Dreamgirls* and *Jersey Boys*; it also arranges speaking tours for African environmentalist William Kamkwamba and architect Frank Gehry, and does branding partnerships for companies like Joe's Jeans and *Dancing With the Stars*.[2]

With fingers in every corner of media and entertainment, the Big Four synergize clients and broker relationships at stratospheric levels. William Morris (before merging with rival Endeavor to become WME) helped one of its corporate clients, toy manufacturer Hasbro, partner with Discovery Communications to form The Hub, a jointly-owned cable network.[3] CAA paved the way for client Steven Spielberg's DreamWorks Studios to secure a $325 investment from India's Reliance Entertainment.[4, 5] UTA teamed with venture capital firm Kleiner Perkins and the University of South California to create the Viterbi Startup Garage, an accelerator providing grants and other financial resources to tech companies founded by USC students or young alumni.[6]

All these factors conspire to make the Big Four the most powerful forces in Hollywood. It's important to understand, however, that "it's not like mafia power. These are not cigar-chomping, Damon Runyon-esque characters," says former NBC president Warren Littlefield, who has a production company repped by CAA. "They have advanced degrees in literature, history, and business. [They also] have the lion's share of writers, producers, directors, and actors, the critical elements that get product made . . . [so] they have a large voice in where that talent goes."

THE MID-LEVELS

The mid-level agencies are slightly smaller than the Big Four and include: APA, Paradigm, Innovative Artists, Resolution, and The Gersh Agency. Most have offices in New York and Los Angeles, but while a few have branches in cities such as Nashville, Chicago, and Monterey, none has the international presence of the Big Four. Also, they usually have fewer departments. APA, for example, is active in talent, lit, music, publishing, branding, and touring—but has no sports or voice-over departments. Mid-level agencies also have fewer agents. APA and Gersh, for example, each average around 70—compared to CAA and WME's 300.[7, 8] But does this mean those agents are less talented or effective? Not at all.

"Agencies have cultures, and not everyone longs to be part of a giant aggressive culture," says TV writer/producer Lesley Wake Webster (*The New Girl*, *American Dad*). "An agency that's small may have incredibly talented agents who are out busting their ass for you. A lot of times, making it at those giant agencies requires a level of toughness or abrasiveness that may not make an agent a great match with a sensitive writer client."

Mid-level agencies do, however, have less manpower, so they also tend to have fewer clients. One mid-level agent estimated her agency repped less than 1,000 clients across all areas—books, TV, features, talent, etc. Big Four agencies, may often represent close to 1,000 clients in their TV lit department alone! Also, while most mid-levels have many pieces of high-level talent—Gersh reps double Oscar nominee James Woods and four-time Emmy winner Allison Janney; APA reps *24* co-creator Bob Cochran and the world's greatest comic, Louis C.K.—fewer clients means A-listers.

What mid-level agencies are often great at: finding talented up-and-comers and building their careers. In 2011, shortly after landing her first regular TV acting gig, Azita Ghanizada—star of SyFy's *Alpha*'s—signed with APA. Two years later, Innovative Artists signed Broadway actress Becca Tobin (*Rock of Ages*), who had just landed a starring role on FOX's hit series *Glee.*

One of the downsides of this, unfortunately, is that mid-levels often discover talented young artists, only to see them "grow up" and leave for the greener pastures of the Big Four. In 2011, after spending ten years at Innovative Artists, Emmy-winning TV star Jim Parsons (*The Big Bang Theory*) ditched Innovative for CAA.[9] Kyra Sedgeick, star of *The Closer*, chucked Gersh for UTA.[10] Many actors, directors, and writers see the big agencies as having more reach, more muscle, and a better ability to transfer successful people into bona fide superstars. But is this true? Can big agencies really elevate a career in a way smaller agencies can't?

"You want to root for David (the little guy) in that situation," says enterainment research consultant Gerry Sadowski, "but in my opinion, it's true: big agencies have more connections . . . more power . . . and they offer more services. They do branding, they do financing, they do market research. They do other complementary agency things—like CAA is big in sports, so they can leverage [that] in the big picture and expand people's careers. The bottom line is resources. The bigger agencies have resources."

Having said this, many successful professionals don't like the enormity of the Big Four. Because WME, UTA, ICM, and CAA represent so many clients, it's easy to feel lost in the shuffle, and some artists prefer smaller companies where they get more individual attention. Many talented and successful people, for example, turn to the mid-levels to help reignite a career that may have stalled or cooled off—like in 2009, when, after failing to land a starring film role since 2004's *Catch That Kid*), actress Jennifer Beals ditched CAA for Gersh, who immediately helped score her a leading role in Warner Brothers' *The Book of Eli.*[11]

"The big agencies just keep trying to get bigger," says one former Big Four agent. "The big agencies are servicing high-end clients and corporate clients—they have a corporate agenda. WME and CAA have over 1,000 employees, [and] there's really no highly effective agency servicing that next tier, that core business [of traditional writing, directing, and acting clients]."

None of this is to say that mid-levels don't wield enormous power. Most distinguish themselves as industry leaders in at least one or two areas. Paradigm boasts one of the strongest music departments in Hollywood, repping acts like The Gaslight Anthem, Joni Mitchell, and Rachael Yamagata. APA's unparalleled comedy department sets up concerts and tours for headliners such as Aziz Ansari and Anthony Jeselnik. In 2006, Gersh—in a bid to join WME, UTA, and CAA in the cutthroat world of sports representation—purchased sports management firm Steve Feldman & Association, whose clients included NFL players Lorenzo Neal and Corey Dillon.[12] Two years later, after failing to gain the traction they'd hoped, Gersh scaled back its sports operation, focusing instead on an area other agencies hadn't bothered to exploit: Mixed Martial Arts.[13] Today, Gersh has become a front-runner in the world of MMA representation, handling stars like Randy Couture and Gina Carano.[14]

"I've been represented by two [mid-level] agencies," says screenwriter Sean Hood (*Conan the Barbarian, Halloween: Resurrection*). "I had very talented agents who make a lot of deals and get movies and television shows made, but it wasn't so big I ever felt the agenda of the agency was coming before me. The disadvantage of being at a big agency is: do they work for you or do you work for them? Are you suddenly beholden to whatever agenda they have? I never got that feeling [at the mid-level agencies]. I never had an experience where I called my agent and he didn't call back. I never had an experience where I felt my best interests weren't being served. Even when things were going slow—when I suddenly had one of those incredibly lean years— my agent was working just as hard for me. He was getting me tiny jobs that certainly weren't helping his number, but he was still working. I don't believe that would happen at a bigger agency."

BOUTIQUES

While most of Hollywood's power is concentrated in the halls of the Big Four and mid-level agencies, most of Hollywood's agencies are boutiques, the smallest of the agencies. In fact, of the eighty-two WGA-signatory literary agencies, over seventy are boutiques like The Brant Rose Agency or Preferred Artists. Not only do boutiques have smaller client rosters—a boutique lit department may have fewer than 100 clients, compared to several hundred at each of the Big Four—most have only a handful of agents. Some, like Rebel Entertainment Partners, have six or seven. Others, like The Alpern Group, have one or two.

Many boutiques specialize in only one or two specific areas of representation. SMS Talent, for example, is purely a talent agency, repping actors such as *Supernatural's* Misha Collins.[15] The Kaplan Stahler Agency focuses on literary clients like *Teen Wolf* writer Jonathon Roessler and *Nurse Jackie*'s writer Alison McDonald.[16]

Does this mean boutique agents are less powerful than agents at larger agencies? Not necessarily. They may not have huge corporate clients they use to set up movies like *G.I. Joe*, but they make up for it by being incredibly selective in the clients they represent, then plying those clients with personal attention. Many high-level writers and producers prefer this approach. TV producer David Graziano (*Terra Nova*, *Lie To Me*) and *Man Up!* creator Christopher Moynihan are both repped at Rothman Brecher Kim; *Gilmore Girls* producers Stan Zimmerman and Jim Berg are repped at Kaplan Stahler.

"At boutique agencies, the relationship, the marriage, is a little closer," says Disney Channel exec Kristina Speakman, who works with writers and agencies of all sizes. Bigger agencies "have multiple clients who aren't working, [so] they're trying to find more people jobs. By design, if Kaplan Stahler only has a couple people looking for work, they're more likely to help [buyers and employers] find the right fit. They've narrowed it down, just by having a minimal number of clients."

Specialized Agencies

While many agencies specialize in talent or lit, some agencies are even *more* highly specialized. N.S. Bienstock made a name for itself handling TV newscasters, commentators, and hosts like Chris Matthews and Robin Roberts. (It has since expanded into other areas such as reality TV and publishing.) Digital Development Management represents video game developers like Brainz Games (*Vampire Season: Monster Defense*) and Galaxy Pest Control (*Swamp People*). Montana Artists focuses on below-the-line clients like stunt coordinator Mike Smith (*21 & Over*, *Seven Psychopaths*) and costume designer Kelli Jones (*The Following*, *Sons of Anarchy*).

MANAGERS: DOES SIZE MATTER?

Like the big agencies, some management companies house many managers across multiple disciplines. Generate, for example—a management firm owned by Alloy Media, the publishing and production company behind *Gossip Girl*, *Pretty Little Liars*, and *The Vampire Diaries*—has representatives in talent, lit, digital media, and branded entertainment, as well as a research division devoted to gathering data from Alloy's core audience of tweens, teens, and young adults. Its clients include *Broad City* creator/stars Abbi Jacobson and Ilana Glazer,[17] comedian Patton Oswald, and *Filly Brown* producers Amir Delara and Victor Teran.

Other companies are one- or two-person shops. The Radmin Company has only three employees, yet represents successful filmmakers like *Gone* director Heitor Dhalia and *Despicable Me* screenwriter Cinco Paul.

So do big and small *management companies* come with the same pros and cons as big and small agencies? Not usually. "Generally speaking, managers have fewer clients than agents," says Alex Murray of Brillstein Entertainment Partners, which reps clients such as *Book of Mormon* star Josh Gad, Emily Mortimer, Jason Sudeikis, Donny Osmond, Billy Crudup, and Zach Galifianakis. "If an agent has fifty clients, a manager has fifteen . . . so agents don't have the time to have ten phone calls a day with their big clients—they just can't." Thus, managers and clients tend to have much more personal relationships.

When it comes to agencies, however, "the individual agent doesn't matter as much as the [letters] on the script being sent out. Is it CAA? Is it WME? You're being represented by that brand," says indie film producer Charlie Stickney (*The Entertainers*, *Pound of Flesh*), who has been repped at both big management companies like Benderspink and smaller shops like Aaron Kogan Management. "A management company might have a bunch of different managers, but it's the [individual] managers people know by name. It's the managers who build the relationships, so it's [all about] the individual manager and what *their* brand is."

As we'll discuss in Chapters 12 and 13, the manager–client relationship is a much more intimate experience, so writers usually have a much closer relationship with their manager, whether she's at a gigantic company like Brillstein Entertainment Partners (which reps Natalie Portman and Jennifer Aniston), or a one-woman shop like Sekka Scher (who reps Oscar-nominated actor Demian Bichir and award-winning writer/performer Danny Hoch).

What you want from a manager is "a shared philosophy . . . a personal connection . . . [and] someone who knows story," says manager Robyn Meisinger, a partner at Madhouse Entertainment. "We are invested in people's careers, over time. There is a reason why I represent the same people today as I did eighteen years ago. Because the material is better today than it was eighteen years ago. I don't care how accomplished you are as a writer—everybody needs that person. [And] I don't think you need that from an agent. What you want from your agent is aggressive, smart, strategic, and responsive."

Having said this, because *anyone* can become a manager, it's harder to determine if smaller managers are the real thing. Does a tiny one-man shop have the clout and connections necessary to make the introductions you need? Can a decent manager work out of his own garage?

"It depends on who that person is working out of his garage," says Meisinger. "Obviously, you have to be smart and be able to develop, because that distinguishes a manager from an agent. But the other thing is, quite frankly: if that person working out of his garage has no contacts in the community . . . if no one can read the excellent script he developed . . . it's not really helpful."

So how do you know if you're signing with someone who's legit, an inexperienced poser, or a fly-by-night scam artist? How can you be certain someone has the creative chops and business acumen to truly develop your work?

"Do your homework," says manager Michael Pelmont, head of scripted television at New Wave Entertainment, a large bicoastal management and production company. "We have something called Google now. Ideally, you know some people in the business. Any client I've ever taken on has been recommended by somebody. I get tens of submissions a day in queries . . . and I just delete them. I don't even read them. That's not to say a lot of talented people aren't coming in to me—I'm sure there *are* very talented people. [I know] it's tough, especially when you're trying to break in, and you don't know anybody, and you hear something like that, but at the end of the day," recommendations and referrals are the best way to land representation.

Size May Not Matter

But if you're still interested, here are some of the titans of the management world:

- 3 Arts
- Anonymous Content
- Benderspink
- Brillstein Entertainment Partners
- Circle of Confusion
- Generate
- Industry Entertainment
- Levity Entertainment
- Management 360
- Mosaic Media Group
- New Wave Entertainment

AGENTS AND MANAGERS REVENUE STREAMS

In the old days, representation was simple. An agent representing a writer got that writer a job, the writer got paid, the agent took ten percent of the writer's paycheck. Easy, right? "The 10 percent business is dead," says manager Dave Brown of Artist International. Today's agencies have varied and complicated revenue streams, and how those work and balance out bears a huge influence on how agents operate, which projects they champion, and whom they choose to represent. So if you want to get the most out of your representation, it behooves you to know how they intend to make money off you—and how you can help them do it.

Revenue Stream 1: Client Commission

Agents and managers alike still commission clients, and for most firms, commission is their largest, most reliable source of revenue. Most lit agents and managers typically charge ten percent—so if a low-level TV writer grosses $3,700 per week, she pays her agent $370 per week. If a screenwriter sells a feature script for $750,000, she pays her agents $75,000. On extremely rare occasions, a powerful writer may be able to negotiate a lower commission, but California law prohibits agents from ever charging more than ten percent.

Exception to the Rule

Years ago, managers' standard commission was fifteen percent. Today, a handful may still charge that, but ten percent has become the accepted norm.

Agents and managers also commission clients' backend profits. So let's say you sell the screenplay for your new big-budget action/comedy, *Jamie's Crying*, to Warner Brothers for $500,000 and two percent of the net profits. The movie then goes on to gross $140 million—for a net of $80 million—earning you $1.6 million. You pay each rep $50,000 when you sell the script, and $160,000 on the backend, for a total $420,000.

Of course, that's nothing compared to what big agents or managers make from A-list movie stars and directors. Each time Leonardo DiCaprio gets paid $20 million for a movie, he earns his manager, Rick Yorn, a $2 million pay day (DiCaprio chooses not to have an agent, instead using only Yorn, who also reps Martin Scorsese, Jamie Foxx, Cameron Diaz, and Justin Timberlake[18]). Big-name talent can also command large backend fees, sometimes twenty to twenty-five percent of a movie's gross box office take. So let's say Warner Bros casts DiCaprio in *Jamie's Crying*, offering him $20 million and twenty percent of **first-dollar gross**. *Jamie's Crying* then grosses its $140 million, giving DiCaprio twenty percent, or $28 million. This brings his *Jamie's Crying* payday to $48,000,000 and Yorn's payday to $4.8 million. Not bad for a hard-working representative.

Talk the Talk

First-Dollar Gross–Most writers and directors are given backend participation in their movie's *net* profits, getting paid only once the film's studio or financier has paid back all its debts and expenditures. Also, most upfront money paid to these artists' usually counts as an *advance* against their backend payments; in other words, if a writer has been paid $100,000 for his script upfront, he doesn't get any backend profits until the movie has recouped that $100,000 at the box office. A handful of huge stars, writers, directors, and producers, however, get to participate in their movies' *first-dollar gross*. These players' profit participation is calculated from the film's *overall* receipts, not the net, and they don't have to wait for the movie to recoup any money before their participation begins.

Flattening Out

Rather than paying ten percent commission, some giant music acts negotiate a lower rate, while others don't pay commission at all. Instead, they pay their agents a flat rate–say, $10,000 per concert date.

Individual Agents Do Not Keep Their Commissions

Rather, all commissions and revenues go into a department or company pot. Each agent then notes his client's bookings and commissions on a **booking sheet**, which he turns in every month. This is used to track each agent's performance and determine raises, promotions, and end-of-year bonuses. We'll discuss this more in Chapter 4.

But remember, the Big Four agencies represent more than one A-list client. CAA represents Tom Cruise, Al Pacino, and Tom Hanks. WME represents Jim Carrey, Joseph Gordon-Levitt, Mike Myers, M. Night Shyamalan, and Robin Williams. These are all major earners; if each client bags $4.8 million per movie for his agency, that's some nice cash flow.

Music departments are also big revenue streams for their agencies. Music agents, like lit and talent agents, generally charge commission for booking a musical tour. WME, for example, booked Van Halen's *A Different Kind of Truth* tour, which made over $54 million to become 2012's eighth highest-grossing tour. Not bad, but WME also represents two of 2012's other top earners, Lady Gaga ($124.9 million) and Roger Waters ($186.5 million). (FYI–not all that money goes to the band, and agencies only commission the *client's* income–not the tour's entire gross. Unless the band had negotiated a certain guarantee into its contract, the tour promoter usually pays for production costs and other outlays before writing the band their check. So if a tour grosses $54 million, the band may see only $30 million, depending on the deal they negotiated.)

So you want to get a sense of how powerful the WME music department is? They represent over 550 musicians and bands, including Norah Jones, Rihanna, Pearl Jam, Janet Jackson, Lynyrd Skynyrd, Weezer, Slash, Soundgarden, Foo Fighters, Red Hot Chili Peppers, and Snoop Dogg/Snoop Lion. Want some more perspective? When William Morris and Endeavor merged in 2009, the value of the new company was estimated at $300 million[19]–twenty-seven percent of which came entirely from William Morris's $80 million-a-year touring business.[20]

Having said this, not all agency departments charge ten percent. Most sports agents commission less than five percent, as per the sports leagues' rules (NFL players pay three percent, NBA players pay two percent; MLB and the NHL have no specific limits[21]). Marketing departments charge up to twenty percent. WME's marketing arm, for instance, represents Tim Tebow, whose endorsement deals with companies like Nike and Jockey gross an estimated $4 million annually–approximately $800,000 of which could go to WME.[22]

Pay Up, Suckah

When a client gets a job, the agency takes its commission, whether it got you the job or not. So if you're friends with a showrunner who hires you on her series, *your agent will still commission it.* If you meet a producer at a party, pitch him your movie, and he brings you in for a meeting that results in a sale, *your agent will still commission it.*

"Is this fair?" you ask. *Absolutely.* First of all, you may have landed a job through your own hard work, relationships, and networking, but your agent supported and aided along the way. Did your agent arrange the general meeting that led to this particular relationship? Did she give you notes on the script that got you the job? Did your manager talk about you to the executive or producer, helping to keep you at the front of that buyer's mind?

Even if you did score this gig entirely on your own, your agent will—most likely—negotiate the best deal possible. She may get you more money, or better protections, or a higher credit, or guaranteed scripts.

Plus, there are many things agents do once you've closed the deal and started work. They make sure you get paid on time. They peruse and file paperwork. They monitor **option dates** to make sure you keep your job. And if you ever want *out* of the job, they help negotiate a fair and friendly exit strategy.

It's a naive client who thinks his agent only deserves ten percent when she *gets you the actual job*, and if this is all you think agents do, you're probably not getting the most out of your agent.

REVENUE STREAM 2: TV PACKAGES

Who is Package-able?

Studios don't grant packages to agencies who just throw together any random elements, like a writer, a composer, and a cinematographer. Elements must be above-the-line, and they must be sellable. Is your next-door neighbor who guest starred twice on *Hannibal* a sellable element? Probably not. Is Jenna Elfman? Absolutely.

In fact, sometimes agencies don't match together various elements at all. Powerful agencies can command a package simply for providing one fantastic element—usually a super high-profile showrunner.

Hollywood likes to talk a lot about "**packages**", usually when agents put together various elements of a film or TV show to help it sell. In fact, the word "package" may be used as either or a verb or a noun—and it can mean very different things in each case.

We use "package" as a verb when agents (or producers) bundle together different above-the-line elements—say, a screenwriter, a director, and an actor. In television, however, when agents receive a "package" (as a noun) it means something a bit different, and TV packages, or the fees they generate, are one of an agencies' most lucrative forms of revenue. Some agents, in fact, estimate TV packaging fees constitute over half their company's revenue!

In theory, a television package still requires the bundling of various elements. In 2011, for example, WME paired client Rockne O'Bannon, creator of *Farscape*, with WME-repped production company Fake Empire (*The Carrie Diaries*, *Gossip Girl*) to sell *Cult* to the CW.[23] Film packages can be put together the same, but when this happens in television, the agency is compensated in a unique way.

First of all, when a TV agent packages and sells a client's TV show, he does not commission the client. The agent instead receives a **packaging fee** (or, as it's more commonly called, just a "package") from the TV studio. This is obviously a nice perk for both you and your agent. You keep an extra ten percent of your paycheck and your agent has the potential to earn far more dough from that packaging fee than he ever could from your commission.

How Much Dough Are We Talking About?

A lot. When an agency takes a package on a project, it becomes a part owner of the show and participates in that show's profits. William Morris, the agency that packaged ABC's *Who Wants To Be a Millionaire*, has made over $16 million in backend profits

Hands Off My Package!

Agents retain ownership of a package even if the show's primary elements leave the agency. For example, William Morris repped both Regis Philbin and Kathie Lee Gifford when it packaged ABC's *Live! With Regis and Kathie Lee* in 1988. It also repped Gifford's replacement, Kelly Ripa, who took over in 2001. So even though Philbin left William Morris for Paradigm in 2009,[29] and Ripa migrated to CAA two years later,[30] WME retains the show's package. (Coincidentally, Philbin returned to WME in 2011, just as he announced his retirement from *Live! With Regis and Kelly*.)

To Learn More

To learn the ins and outs of packaging, and how agents are paid, take a trip to Chapter 7.

from that show.[24] NBC's hit sitcom *Friends* has reaped over $2 billion in profits, earning its agency, ICM, over $200 million.[25,26]

To put $200 million in perspective: when film financier QED International purchased David Ayers' World War II spec script, *Fury*, for $1 million in February, 2013, it was considered the biggest spec sale of the year.[27] But that sale earned Ayers' agents at CAA only $100,000—a drop in the bucket compared to TV packaging fees. To put that in a bit more perspective, $200 million is approximately ten times the amount WME made from the 2012 Lady Gaga, Roger Waters, and Van Halen concerts *combined!*

Also, the *Friends* gravy train won't stop running any time soon. As of 2011, Warner Brothers had sold reruns of *Friends* through 2017, guaranteeing ICM rakes in plenty of cash for a long time.[28]

The Big Four agencies "are driven by television money, and that's the packaging business," says Pelmont, who began his career as an ICM TV agent. "Our biggest talent agent at the time represented people like Mel Gibson, Michelle Pfeiffer, and Denzel Washington. He still did not come close to doing . . . deals for those people that would generate a billion dollars of revenue."

Ask the Agent

Q: I understand why agencies want packages—they make a ton of money. But what's in it for the studios? Why would a studio even bother *giving* an agency a package?

A: "Agencies could retaliate and say they're not going to give them any more business," says one veteran TV agent. After all, because the Big Four represent the vast majority of television's big-name TV creators and showrunners, these agencies *can* command packaging fees. If a network doesn't want to give WME a packaging fee for a new show by Eric Kripke, creator of *Supernatural* and *Revolution*—fine; Kripke's an A-list showrunner, and there are other networks that will gladly pay the extra bucks to have a Kripke show on their air.

"[A smaller agency] coming in that doesn't have the experience or knowledge might know to ask for a package, but they don't have the clout," says another agent. "A lot of it is saying, 'You're not giving me a package? Okay . . . I've got other stuff and I'm comfortable not coming back to you. Your competitor will get it.'"

Unfortunately, this means packages are usually the province solely of the Big Four agencies, many of which have blanket package agreements with each of the studios. Of the eighty-one new scripted shows picked up to series in 2011 and 2012, only *three* were not packaged by the Big Four. CBS's *Partners* was packaged by Scott Schwartz's Vision Arts, which repped creators Max Mutchnik and David Kohan (*Will & Grace*), and the CW's *Arrow* and *The Carrie Diaries* had no packages at all.

Occasionally, a smaller agency will pair one of its showrunner clients with a production company repped at a different agency, often an agency with a blanket package deal. In these cases, the smaller agency will ask to split the package, which often leads to contentious face-offs between agencies.

"It gets ugly," says Dennis Kim, a partner at boutique agency Rothman Brecher Kim, which reps high-level writers such as Alex Reid (*Up All Night*, *The Middle*) and Alex Herschlag (*Modern Family*, *Hot in Cleveland*). "The studio stays out of it; they're like, 'You guys figure it out.' I was recently in a situation with another agency that wouldn't agree [to split a package]. We wouldn't agree to reduce. It was unfair, basically, so they said, 'Well, the package will go into escrow until it gets settled.' And we did settle it."

How Packages Affect You

Understanding the importance of packages gives us a clue as to how big agents prioritize their clients and projects. "Packaging is far more important to [agencies] than whether or not you go from being a co-producer to an executive producer," says entertainment attorney and former TV producer Charles Holland. "'To hell with you— I want the package! If you can help me get the package, so much the better,' but you're a tool."

Does this mean big agents see no value in mid or lower-level clients? Not necessarily. "[Agents] realize that—particularly in television—that big black box has a voracious appetite, so [they] always have to look to the future," says producer Warren Littlefield. "Maybe last year someone wasn't packageable, but they wrote a script, the script got piloted. Maybe the pilot didn't go to series, but you know what? They established they can take an idea and deliver a piece of material someone will spend five or ten million dollars to make. Now you're a packageable element."

This does, however, illuminate who the Big Four want when considering new TV clients. You may not be package-able now, but for one of the big agencies to sign you, they need to believe you'll be package-able down the road.

Exceptions to the Rule

Feature agents also package. In 2012, for instance, WME sold Universal a package that included *Agent 13*, a sci-fi script by WME screenwriter T.S. Nowlin (based on a 1988 comic book), WME director Rupert Wyatt (*Rise of the Planet of the Apes*), and Oscar-winning actress Charlize Theron, another WME client.[31]

When feature agents sell packages to a movie studio, however, they don't get a package fee; instead, they simply commission any elements repped at their agency. So in the above example, WME commissioned all three elements—Nowlin, Wyatt, and Theron—giving the agency a sizable income. This also gives agents strong motivation to work only with in-house elements. (We'll talk later about how this affects clients and projects.)

Having said that, when agents package and sell an *independent movie*, or find financing for a film outside the traditional studio system, they sometimes receive a small packaging fee—usually two to four percent of the film's production budget. Unlike in TV however, feature agents taking packaging fees on indie films still commission their clients—there's no getting out of your commission in the feature world!

REVENUE STREAM 3: PRODUCER COMMISSIONS

When agents attach a producer to a client's script and sell that project to a studio, they charge their client the expected ten percent commission. Often, however, they will also charge the attached *producer* a ten percent commission. "That's a general rule of thumb," says APA agent Will Lowery. "When you send a producer a script, you're servicing the producer—you're entitled to a commission."

Agents, in fact, often make much more money from producer commissions than from their client commissions. "Mark Gordon, Jerry Bruckheimer, Lorenzo di Bonaventura—these are all $2 million-plus producers," says Lowery. If "I take ten percent of their fee, that [could be] more than a writers fee at $200,000."

How much a producer earns for making a movie depends on that producer's level, clout, track record, and involvement with the project. Carl Levin and Matt Weaver pulled in a $1.25 million producers fee on New Line Cinema's *Rock of Ages*.[32] In his heyday at Universal, producer Joel Silver (*The Matrix*, *Sherlock Holmes*) pulled in a producers fee of approximately $7 million per movie!

One Important Caveat

Producers only get paid *if their movie gets made*. If a producer falls in love with a script and sets it up at Lionsgate, the producer makes no money until Lionsgate greenlights the project into production. As a result, *agents* only receive their producers commission *if the movie gets made*. In other words, if your agent sets up your new script, *The Killing Type*, with *Insidious* producer Jason Blum and the script sells to Lionsgate for $225,000, you make $225,000 and pay your agent his ten percent. Blum, at this point, gets nothing, so he pays nothing to your agent. But if the project is green-lit five weeks from now, or in a year, Blum begins making money, ten percent of which goes to your agent.

REVENUE STREAM 4: REPRESENTING PRODUCTION COMPANIES

Aside from repping individuals like writers, actors, and directors, agents also rep production companies. WME handles BermanBraun, the production banner founded by former FOX president Gail Berman and former ABC president Lloyd Braun, which has produced *Alphas* and *Accidentally on Purpose*.[33] CAA has Rough House–the production company of Danny McBride, Jody Hill, David Gordon Green, and Matt Reilly–and 11th Street Productions, which specializes in reality shows like *Teen Mom*.[34]

Having representation allows production companies exclusive access to writers, producers, actors, and directors from the same agency. Agents, as we know, are incentivized to match together their own in-house clients, which means if WME actor Uma Thurman has a TV show idea and wants to partner with an experienced production company, where will WME send her first? One of their own production companies, such as BermanBraun or Levity Entertainment Group (*Dream Machines*, *The Next Food Network Star*) or Collins Avenue (*Dance Moms*).[35] Likewise, if Rough House needs a suave leading man for its new Jody Hill movie, CAA can easily pave the way for meetings with fellow clients Jon Hamm or Scoot McNairy.

The downside of being a production company with representation: you may miss out on projects being repped by rival agencies. If UTA has a fantastic project, their first priority is to send it to one of their own companies, like Kelsey Grammar's Grammnet (*Boss*, *Medium*)[36] or Barbra Streisand's Barwood Films (*Nuts*, *Yentl*).[37] If your company is repped at ICM or APA, you miss out.

"Every agency has a number of [its own] mouths to feed," says the CAA-repped Littlefield, "so I'm not in another agency's first round, but I get in business with other agencies when I find something and say, 'Hey, we found this article, this book, here's territory we want to play in.' Then I go to other agencies, along with CAA, and say, 'Who do you have? Who's available? Who might be interested in this?' And together we build packages."

When an agency represents a TV production company, they usually take packages on anything the company sells or sets up, even if it's in partnership with another producer or showrunner. In the event that the agency *can't* get a package, they commission any fees the company, or producer, is paid on the project.

REVENUE STREAM 5: CORPORATE RETAINERS: ADVERTISING, MARKETING, LICENSING, AND BRANDED ENTERTAINMENT

Today's agencies work hand-in-hand with some of the world's biggest brands and corporations. Many agencies have full-fledged marketing, licensing, branded entertainment and advertising departments, going head-to-head with heavy-hitting ad firms like McCann Erickson, which has offices in more than 120 countries and works with clients such as Weight Watchers, American Airlines, and the US Postal Service.[38] CAA, for example, represents Best Buy, Chipotle, and Southwest Airlines. UTA's marketing arm, United Entertainment Group, handles Frito-Lay, Hugo Boss, and Quaker Oats.[39] APA works with Lamborghini, J.W. Marriott, and Bombardier.[40]

Brands like working with talent agencies because they provide access to sexy Hollywood stars, properties, and producers. Sometimes this means doing a simple **product integration** deal, in which a specific brand or product is woven into the storytelling of a TV show or movie (like Dustin Mufflin's Staples rivalry on *The Office*).[41] More and more, however, agencies are marrying brands to entertainment properties at even higher, more significant levels. CAA reps toymaker Mattel, and has set up several films based on Mattel products: Hot Wheels at Legendary Pictures, He-Man at Sony, Magic 8 Ball and Max Steel[42] at Paramount, Monster High and Major Matt Mason at Universal.[43] CAA also helped Southwest set up *On the Fly*, a TLC reality show that went behind the scenes of the airline. Similarly, WME is working to transform The Knot's three brands—The Knot (serving engaged couples), the Nest (newlyweds), and the Bump (expectant couples)—into various TV and film properties, much like Lionsgate did with best-selling pregnancy guide *What To Expect When You're Expecting*.[44]

For agencies, corporate clients provide two important things:

1. **Huge retainer fees**. Instead of paying agencies commission, corporations shell out enormous retainers; Coca-Cola was at one time paying CAA $400,00 per month! (They no longer do.) Still, agencies often charge corporate clients $200,000–250,000 per month for their marketing and/or consulting services.[45]
2. **Unique opportunities for clients**. When Cirque du Soleil, for instance, wanted to expand its brand with a feature film, CAA hooked the company up with CAA-repped producer James Cameron. The resulting partnership yielded *Cirque du Soleil: Worlds Away*, a $25 million 3D film (that unfortunately grossed just over $32 million at the global box office).

REVENUE STREAM 6: INVESTMENTS

Ask the Agent

Q: Do I really need to hire my own lawyer? I mean, aren't most of my agency's business affairs execs lawyers? Can't I just use them?

A: Yes—most business affairs execs are lawyers. And no—I wouldn't recommend using them as your own . . . and neither would most agents. First of all, most business affairs execs are so swamped dealing with the agency's high-end deals, they won't even look at a contract worth less than $50,000. Second, business affairs lawyers are charged with protecting the agency's concerns, not the client's, and while there's often overlap, there's also an occasional conflict of interest. Perhaps most importantly, business affairs execs "*are* attorneys," says one agent, "but they won't mark up a contract as diligently as outside attorney—they're so overwhelmed and not paid to do this. I encourage every client to have outside attorneys."

As agencies grow and evolve, they're not only representing production companies and brands, they're seeding and investing in them as well. In 2010 CAA invested a reported $80 million in J Brand Jeans.[46] It also helped find funding for FunnyOrDie,[47] established a film fund for National Geographic, and co-founded Evolution Media, an investment bank and sports consultancy that has greased the wheels for mega-deals like the sale of the Memphis Grizzles and the Pac-12's twelve-year, $3 billion deal with ESPN and Fox Sports.[48]

These types of investments not only contribute to the overall health and strenth of the agencies, they also provide opportunities for writing and producing clients. "Being a writer in today's world has changed," says Richard Weitz at WME, which has invested in video game producer Grab Games and Jingle Punks, a music licensing service. "The staffs on TV shows have dwindled from ten or twelve people to four or six. EP-level writers are now cutting their quotes or being called 'consultants' to make a living . . . so it's knocking out younger writers. People need to make an income, people need to find opportunity. Grab Games—if they need a writer and we have a young up-and-coming writer who has great material, or whose ideas are specific to what they're looking to do—it [provides] jobs."

On the other hand, some investments seem to blur the line between representation and production, raising eyebrows across Hollywood. In 2012 CAA became an equity investor in AXS, a new cable network jointly owned by Mark Cuban, AEG, and CAA client Ryan Seacrest. This came on the heels of WME's 2009 agreement to fund a large chunk of The Raine Group, an investment bank specializing in media and entertainment. Four years later, Raine itself invested $60 million in Important Studios, WME clients Trey Parker and Matt Stone's new production venture, giving the *South Park* creators' company an estimated value of $300 million.[49]

"There are so many things that . . . seem to be conflicts of interests," says entertainment attorney Greg Snodgrass of Business Affairs, Inc. "Agents, managers and lawyers have fiduciary duties to their clients. They have to put their clients' interests ahead of their own . . . and any time [they] don't do that, it starts turning into a conflict of interest. The same thing happens for lawyers and certainly for managers. When [a] client gets hired to write a show . . . it seems almost inevitable the manager is an Executive Producer. Maybe that's fine . . . but if he's doing that, he's got some aspirations of his own. Would he give up something for his client so he could get his own Executive Producer credit?"

While some agency investments indeed tiptoe into gray areas of representation versus production, it's important to remember there's actually nothing illegal about agencies investing in, or even co-owning production entities (up to twenty percent). Also, many of these deals are carefully structured to protect both the agency (the investor) and the producer (the investment). WME didn't actually invest in Important Studios; it merely backs the bank that did. Similarly, in 2007, investor group Broadcast Media Partners Holdings acquired Univision Communications, which includes America's largest Spanish-speaking networks and Univision Studios.[50] Who's one of the key investors in Broadcast Media? TPG Capital, which—three years later—purchased a thirty-five percent stake in CAA, one of the world's largest talent agencies.[51] Interesting? Absolutely. Conflict of interest? A gray area. After all, CAA itself doesn't own Univision, and Univision doesn't own CAA; they just share an important investor.

Land Ownings

Another little-known source of agency revenue is real estate holdings. Not every company owns their building or invests in property, but those that do can be rewarded handsomely. In 2012, Paradigm paid $24.2 million for its Beverly Hills offices.[52] CAA's monolithic steel and glass Century City headquarters, affectionately nicknamed "The Death Star," cost $35 million.[53] And when William Morris merged with Endeavor, it sold it's long-time Beverly Hills home for $143 million—approximately $783 per foot![54]

"Real estate is a great investment strategy for businesses," says real estate agent Ashley Sackerman of LA's Teles Properties. "While the market is cyclical with high peaks (like in 2005) and low troughs (2009), the general trend line of real estate values increases over time. According to the Case Shiller Index for Los Angeles, for example, home prices rose about fourteen percent from February, 2012 to February, 2013. Where else can a business get that kind of return on its money?"

Is Bigger Always Better?

The upside of agencies having all these departments and revenue streams is that they create opportunities for both clients and agents alike. Cirque du Soleil gets to work with James Cameron. Southwest and TLC get to ride each other's promotional coat tails. Agents get to package projects, then profit from the clients they helped develop.

"[Big] agencies want as much synergy as possible," says former CAA agent Roy Ashton, now a partner at Gersh. "Half of all television shows are based on books or formats or underlying material . . . so in order to make your television department a success, you need help from the book department. If you're a TV writer and don't have an idea for a TV show . . . ask your agent to give you the book list, [or] to put you in contact with the book agent directly. Look at [your agency's] talent roster and see who you like. Ask your agent to get you a meeting with somebody. No one knew who Dmitri Lipkin was when he put The Riches on the air. He had never done anything in television, he had never sold anything, he had never staffed . . . and he asked to meet with a pretty high end actor, Eddie Izzard."

The downside of being at a big agency is that certain kinds of clients tend to be more important and attractive than others. A "baby writer" is probably never going to earn his agency a package, no matter how talented he is. Likewise, a first-time screen-writer stands little chance of being paired with Mattel to write the next Hot Wheels movie.

"You go to [any corporate clients] and say 'Hey, do you want to do a campaign with the guys from Homeland?' What are they going to say? 'Of course we would!' When you are Seth MacFarlane, or Tina Fey, or Steve Levitan, you become a brand name. That's where you access that," says one veteran agent. "Unfortunately, ninety-five percent of people are not going to be in that position."

Thus, lower- and mid-level clients often complain about getting overlooked and "lost" at big agencies. "The big agencies are interested in representing Hasbro," says another top-level agent. "They want to represent the company . . . the big deal, the big entity, the property. The writer? Whatever."

Does this mean big agencies won't sign newer, younger writers? Not necessarily; after all, agencies know that today's newbie could be tomorrow's Tina Fey or Ben Affleck. Signing a baby writer is like investing in a start-up company; it's risky, but the rewards can be great. It does mean, however, that young writers repped at these big firms must fight to get the same attention or support as more established breadwinners. This is why many writers, directors, and producers turn to boutique agencies. A smaller company, they believe, can service them in ways bigger companies can't.

"'Synergy' is something that sounds great, but in practice, it doesn't happen all that often," says one long-time agent. "It's an elite client that gets that true attention across the board. Often times, you're one of hundreds of people, and if you're the fiftieth person on the list, you're not getting a good crack at it. Also, is a big agency really going to take the time to nurture and develop [someone] over the course of a writing career? People fall off the radar, they get cold, and nobody wants to put the effort in. [At a] boutique it's a much more hands-on experience. You're developing material along the way, making it the best it can be, putting in the time. You're banking on the fact that this person is going to have a long, successful career."

The question now is: when an agency *does* have all these different areas, relationships, and revenue streams, how do they work internally to create opportunties for agencies' employees and clients? How do agencies structure themselves and operate, on both a macro-level and a day-to-day basis, to try to capitalize on the money and possiblities flowing into its halls?

Other Agency Departments You Should Know

Agencies are often huge corporations, and while high-rolling agents often steal the spotlight, there are several essential departments that make the agency tick and—if you want to have the most productive agency relationship possible—you should know.

Business Affairs—The business affairs department manages all the agency's legal concerns when it comes to contracts and negotiations. This includes fighting for packaging fees or negotiating package splits with other agencies. One of the department's most important duties is recording the many definitions, or precedents, used in the agency's contracts and deals. Say the agency uses a particularly advantageous definition of "net profits" in a writer's contract with Disney; business affairs remembers this definition, so it can cite it as "precedent" in future negotiations.

Public Relations—An agency's PR department manages the agency's public image. They authorize agents to do interviews, deal with any fallout when a big client or agent leaves the firm, and do damage control when the agency finds itself in an uncomfortable public position.

Accounting—These are the people who process your checks. Most clients have paychecks sent directly to their agency, where accountants process the check, deduct any commissions (including to your managers or lawyers), and send the remainder to you. (We'll get up close and personal with agency accountants on page 105.)

Human Resources—Human resources oversees all the company's hirings, firings, and management of personnel—whether it's an agent, assistant, or lowly intern. You probably won't have much interaction with HR unless you're applying for an agency job, which can be one of the best ways to break into Hollywood (more on this in Chapter 16).

4   The Life of an Agent

On the corner of APA lit agent Lindsay Howard's desk sits a marble and brass nameplate. It reads:

LINDSAY HOWARD
Vice Fucking President, Bitches

It was given to her by a client the day she was promoted to Vice President, Television—the youngest VP in the history of the agency. The nameplate always gets a laugh from visitors, but for Howard, it's more than just a funny gag.

"Being an agent can be emotionally challenging," says Howard, "because you work behind the scenes, busting your ass for your clients, working and giving—sometimes believing in people even more than they believe in themselves—and there's not always a ton of recognition. So for me, the best part of getting promoted wasn't the promotion itself, it was just knowing all my hard work—all the time and energy I've poured into clients, all the projects I've cared about—had been acknowledged. I'm not someone who needs a ton of validation . . . but sometimes you go home, flop on the couch, and wonder: 'Is this all worth it?' That's why I love this nameplate. Every time I look it, I am reminded that it absolutely is."

The life of an agent isn't always easy. Agents often work painfully long hours and make themselves available to clients on weekends, over vacations, and at all hours of the night. "When you sign up for this job," says Howard, "you have to go in knowing you don't have personal time anymore."

Of course, agents and managers don't do their jobs *only* to support their clients. They also have their own goals and ambitions, their own lives and families to support. In other words, just like the writers, directors, or actors they represent, they're trying to climb their own professional ladders. So if you want to motivate, maximize, and communicate with your representation, it helps to know how *they* make money and rise through the ranks. Understand what they're up against—and how you can help them navigate it—and you stand a much better chance of being supported, appreciated, and serviced.

Of course, to best understand this, it helps to know a bit about how agencies work from the inside out and the top down.

Agencies' Business Models and Internal Structures

Most of today's talent agencies are privately owned companies with one of three management structures. Many are wholly owned by one individual or a small group of people—like the Alpern Group, which is owned by Jeff Alpern, or the Gersh Agency, which is owned by the family of legendary talent agent Phil Gersh, who repped Humphrey Bogart and Richard Burton.[1] Some agencies are owned, or partly owned, by private investors. In 2010, CAA sold thirty-five percent of itself to TPG Capital for an estimated $165 million.[2] Two years later, WME sold a thirty-one percent stake to private equity firm Silver Lake. Still other companies are owned by their employees. In 2012 ICM president Chris Silbermann and twenty-eight other agents pooled their money to buy the agency back from Rizvi Traverse Management, the investment firm that had paid $75 million for a controlling stake in 2005.[3] While employee-owned businesses may lack the large flushes of capital enjoyed by investor-backed companies like WME and CAA, they offer agents a stake in the firm's success, (hopefully) motivating them to work harder, earn more money, and stay at the firm much longer.

Why Have None of the Agencies Gone Public?

It would be hard. Even in today's market, when big agencies seem hungry for capital to acquire, found, and invest in new businesses, it's tough to take an agency—which is essentially a service provider—public.

An agency "doesn't have any product [or] assets," says Rothman Brecher Kim partner Dennis Kim. "The valuation is the agents. The manpower. It's not like a multinational corporation where you can lay off, and re-hire, ten percent of the workforce and it doesn't matter. The rank and file are important. If five agents [leave] with all their people, it [becomes] a wholly different place."

Also, public investors tend to gravitate toward businesses with consistent annual growth, and agencies rarely have this. Good agencies, in fact, are scalable. As service providers whose strength lies primarily in their human capital, agencies can expand or shrink as necessary, which is great for a company navigating the ever-changing seas of Hollywood, but not great for investors looking for guaranteed profits.

Having said that, some agencies *have* gone public, such as Wilhelmina International (OTCQX: WHLM), the modeling agency that reps Chris Brown, Fergie, and Natasha Bedingfield. And a few decades ago, ICM was part of Josephson International, a publicly traded media and financial organization, but the agency spun off and went private in 1988.

Agenting . . . Gangnam Style!

South Korea's YG Entertainment, which reps hip hop acts like Big Bang and Psy ("Gangnam Style"),[4] is one of the world's only publicly traded talent agencies.[5]

What's the Point of Being a Non-equity Partner?

Not much. "When you're a partner, you're sharing in the fortunes—both good and bad—of the company," says Verve partner Amy Retzinger. "If you're not, if there's no equity—that's not a real partnership. You get to sit in the room and have partner meetings and express your opinion, [but] your opinion means less. Your impact is less. [You just get a] fancy title [and] people outside the company don't always know."

Regardless of how they're owned, many agencies and management companies utilize some type of partnership mode. Some agents become partners by helping to found the company, joining in its infancy, or buying into the firm. Others get hired, or "poached," from rival companies, negotiating partnership as part of their deal. And many, like UTA agents Dan Erlij and Brett Hanson, work their way up internally, starting in the mailroom, or as an assistant, and working their way to the top of the corporate ladder.[6]

"As a partner, you're making decisions that effect your department and the company as a whole," says Gersh partner Roy Ashton. "What's affecting the marketplace as a whole? How are we competing against other agencies? What do we need to do better? [You're discussing] whether we hire more agents, what kind of an assistant training program we're putting together, if we need to hire a publicist."

Agencies generally have two types of partners. **Equity partners** buy into ownership of the company, share in any debt, manage the company's long-term strategy and execution, and participate in profits and losses. This also means equity partners don't receive a regular salary, and if they're booted, or the company is sold, their shares must be bought out.

Non-equity partners, or "guaranteed payment partners," have no ownership in the company; they receive a regular salary and help make decisions, but they share no debt responsibility and don't participate in profits or losses. (Non-equity partners may receive an annual bonus based on the company's success, but regular compensation doesn't depend on the agency's productivity.)

How Agencies Work With Investors

Because agencies are difficult-to-value service providers, they're typically considered risky investments. But in recent years, private equity firms such as Silver Lake, Rizvi Traverse, and TPG Capital have started buying shares of big agencies. So what's in it for these investors? Why place such a notoriously risky bet? And how does the injection of capital benefit agencies, and their clients?

The first thing to understand: agencies *do* have quantifiable assets. Television packages generate an incredible amount of income and agencies retain ownership of these even if a show gets canceled or the packaged clients leave the agency. Agencies also keep commissioning clients on projects they did while represented at the agency. In other words, if CAA books an actor, Robert, into a new movie called *Hang 'Em High*, and Robert then ditches CAA for UTA, CAA keeps taking ten percent of Robert's *Hang 'Em High* income. If the movie goes on to make $350 million and Robert takes home $60 million of that, CAA gets $6 million—even though Robert himself is now repped at UTA. (Robert's new agency, UTA, does *not* get to commission *Hang 'Em High*; they only commission Robert's new business.)

First-dollar gross participants are also quantifiable assets. This is what often interests investors in agencies: reaping the rewards of mega-successful movies, TV shows, and stars without shouldering the risks inherent to being a network or studio. (And by the way, it *is* possible to value an agency; after TPG's 2010 investment in CAA—and a $200 million loan[7]—the agency was valued at $700 million.[8])

Agencies, meanwhile, use investors' cash to hire agents and expand into new business territories. Only weeks after receiving its initial investment from Silver Lake, WME helped fund theAudience, a company dedicated to managing celebrities' online personas.[9] Likewise, shortly after banking $165 million from TPG, CAA invested in celebrity social media site WhoSay and Encore Career Institute, an online continuing education school for baby boomers.[10]

Not every agent agrees, however, that this is the best way to help clients. "Anything that affects agents affects clients," says one agency partner. "If the partners, the people who run the agency, are being leaned on by investors . . . who want their money, they lean on the agents. Agents are then going to be motivated to make money—as opposed to making [client's] careers."

As we discussed earlier, younger writers can get easily overlooked and satisfying investors gives an agency just one more reason to focus on bigger earners. "The burden to the investor is . . . the driving force behind how the agencies do business," the partner continues. "Agents are then thinking about the bottom line . . . instead of about their clients. That's becoming more and more prevalent—and that is not good for all the clients."

The Corporate Ladder

Agencies, like many businesses, are arranged internally as hierarchies that look something like this:

Board of Directors—Bigger agencies are topped by a board of directors consisting of the company's president, or CEO, and a handful of high-level partners. Most boards have fewer than ten people, although some have a couple of rotating seats. The board is responsible for all high-level decisions: evaluating investment opportunities, when to take on outside investors, whom to hire and fire, internal bonuses and compensation, etc. Salary: $3.5 million–$15 million.[11]

Non-Board Partners and Department Heads—While department heads (most of whom are partners) have traditional agenting responsibilities, they also have managerial duties as well: running meetings, approving travel and expenses,

Some companies, like
Brillstein Entertainment
Partners and APA, give
employees corporate titles:
president, vice president, etc.
Others, like WME and Verve,
have no titles—so don't judge
an agent or manager based
on his title.

Talk the Talk

Script coverage—Unlike
when agents "cover" certain
territories, this coverage
refers to analyses readers
and assistants write after
reading a script. A bit like a
book report, most coverage
consists of a summary of the
work, a critical review, and an
evaluation of the piece's
commercial potential.

Words of Wisdom

"Being an assistant is crucial
for making the connections
you'll need to move forward
and be successful in your
career. You'll commiserate
with your fellow assistants
over the long hours, little pay,
and (from what I've heard!)
grouchy bosses, and when
you come out on the other
end, these are the people
you'll turn to for favors. This is
the next batch of executives,
producers, and writers, and
they're already your friends—
not just people who
networked with you out of
common industry courtesy."—
Jillian Profetta, lit agent's
assistant, Janklow & Nesbit
Associates

communicating with upper management, helping allocate salaries and bonuses. They also make strategic decisions for the department. The head of a reality department, for example, may see a trend in cooking shows and decide to bulk up his team's roster of chefs. The head of a talent department may charge his agents with signing more diverse clients. Salary: $600,000–$3 million.

Rank and File–Senior Agents, or **packaging agents**, work with high-end clients (showrunners, executive producers, A-list writers) packaging movies and TV shows. A senior agent's salary is typically based on how much commission, or how many packaging fees, that agent earns. Salary: $500,000–$1 million.

Junior Agents, also known as **servicing agents** or **covering agents**, are usually responsible for staffing lower-level clients. Servicing agents are rarely allowed to package or sell new projects, duties usually left to senior agents; juniors spend most of their time staffing clients already on the agency roster. They also do **coverage**, "covering" the town and gathering information on what's being bought, sold, developed, and produced. Salary: $45,000–$500,000.

Coordinators are like "assistants to the entire department," says Verve coordinator Melissa Solomon. "You usually don't have a single boss, you have many bosses, and your job is to help that department run as efficiently as possible—whether helping people prepare for meetings, keeping lists, or updating grids." Coordinators keep records of feature writing and directing assisgnments, TV shows in development, and pilots in production. Sometimes the coordinator collects this info on her own; other times, she's organizing information gathered by agents above her. She also preps agents for meetings, updates clients rosters, and oversees certain department-wide communications. "Basically," says Solomon, a coordinator handles "all the logistics within the department." Salary: $35,000–$50,000.

Assistants manage the office of one or two particular agents: answering phones, updating the phone sheet, and maintaining not only the agent's schedule, but the schedules of all that agent's clients! Assistants also read a tremendous amount of scripts and write feedback in the form of **script coverage**. Salary: $25,000–$35,000.

Mailroom employees—The nerve center of the agency, the mailroom is the port for all incoming and outgoing scripts, packages, mail, etc. Many agency employees (such as Jim Toth, CAA's co-head of Motion Picture Talent, and WME partner Adriana Alberghetti)[12] begin in the mailroom, learning the ropes of the company and the industry at large, then go on to assistant, coordinator, and agent jobs. Salary: minimum wage.

How Agents Become Agents

Agents have two ways of getting hired or becoming agents:

1. Junior agents are typically hired from within by promoting assistants or coodinators. Because these covering agents mostly service other agents' clients or do recon on networks and studios' needs, most agencies want junior agents who are already familiar with the inner workings of the agency, which is why asistants and coordinators are primed for these positions. They've spent years learning the agency's client list, building a rapport with writers and directors, reading scripts and giving notes, forming relationships with assistants or execs at other companies. Being an assistant is, in many ways, the audition to become an agent.

"You have to work your way up," says APA founder and president Jim Gosnell. "I find that in this generation, [people] want to jump to being president before they ever learn how to be an agent . . . but you have to learn how to get people jobs before you can actually sign people. Why are you signing somebody if you don't know how to get them a job? Master your craft, just like a musician learning how to play an instrument. Learn the fundamentals, get a good foundation, then build from there."

Help Wanted!

Many agencies have sophisticated, rigorous training programs designed to transform promising young assistants into crackerjack agents. To learn more about how these programs work, and how to apply, check out Chapter 16!

2. Senior or mid-level agents are often hired from from other companies. Some come from outside the world of representation altogether, like when Gersh hired movie producers Jay Cohen (*Mad Money*, *Boys and Girls*) and Jennifer Dana (*The Brass Teapot*, *The Art of Getting By*) to run its indie film packaging and financing department. Many agents are "poached" from rival agencies, like in 2011, when Paradigm hired away almost all of Abrams Artists' youth talent department[13] (and when, only a few days later, Abrams in turn poached the youth department of Don Buchwald and Associates/Fortitude[14]).

Most agencies poach an agent from a competitor because they want that agent's client list. In 2012, WME stole talent agent Warren Zavala from CAA, knowing he'd bring with him a client list that included Anna Faris, Joseph Gordon-Levitt, Adam Scott, Paul Dano, Amber Heard, and Elizabeth Winstead.[15] A few months later, fledgling agency Resolution nabbed CAA agent Adam Kanter, whose client list included *There's Something About Mary* directors Peter and Bobby Farrelly and *G.I. Joe* director Stephen Sommers.

Of course, there are other important factors, too. Smaller agencies often steal bigger agents to help bulk up or lead a particular department, like when Gersh wooed away CAA agent Roy Ashton to head their struggling TV lit department, or UTA lit agent Hayden Meyer was stolen to launch APA's Alternative and International TV department.[16]

"Besides a handsome guy that drives a foreign car," says agent-turned-manager Jeff Holland, "we look for someone who has a similar style to us; someone who we want to be in a room or a working environment with for fifty plus hours a week. Someone we can trust. Someone we believe has good taste in material."

Because agencies are fiercely competitive, plans to poach a rival agent are hatched and orchestrated at the highest level of the company, then carried out discreetly through mutual friends or outside lawyers. "A lot of the time this stuff is done in complete secrecy," says literary agent Tanya Cohen, who left Paradigm for Verve in 2012. "Sometimes even the agent doesn't know it's going to happen until it really does, and if it does . . . it happens overnight. A quick rush. [Other] agents might be talking to somebody at another company for six months, going back and forth on deal points,

To Learn More

In Chapter 14, we'll talk more about what happens when agents switch agencies and how this affects you.

What's in an Agent's Contract?

When agents get promoted or take a new job at an agency, they sign contracts outlining the agency's expectations. There are three main deal points agents negotiate and agree to:

1. **Base salary**—Every contract is a new negotiation, but you can get an idea of various agents' salary ranges on pp 44–45.
2. **Length of time**—Most agency contracts last two to three years, with a one-year option to extend.
3. **Break-even number**—Most agents are given a "break-even number" to try to hit. When an agent's income exceeds this number, he has covered his own overhead and expenses. In theory, break-even numbers are a quantifiable way to evaluate an agent's worth and determine compensation, bonuses, etc. A break-even number is, however, an extremely limited valuation. "There are certain people that bring value to an agency, but they don't show you a tremendous commission report," says APA president Jim Gosnell. Instead, "it's the four or five things they do throughout the year that help you retain or sign a client . . . [or] push it over the goal line for the client." Thus, many agencies ignore the break-even number, instead giving discretionary bonuses evaluating performance subjectively.

trying to figure out if they can make a deal or get out of their old contract. Hopefully, their current agency doesn't find out, because they'll probably get thrown out of that office very quickly."

Sadly, agent defections often result in bitter lawsuits between former friends and colleagues. When CAA plundered IMG Worldwide's sports department in 2010, poaching both clients and agents, IMG sued former agent Matthew Baldwin for violating a non-compete agreement and taking with him confidential files. When former CAA agent Dan Aloni joined WME in 2012, taking with him clients like Jay Roach and Mike Myers, he sued his old colleagues for more than $5 million, claiming they had refused to pay out his guaranteed vacation time and bonuses.[17]

How Agents Get Paid and Promoted

First of all, know this: agents do *not* usually keep their commissions or packaging fees. They receive a salary. Their commissions and fees go into a company kitty. Does this mean an agents' commissions are unimportant? Absolutely not. Each time an agent lands a client a gig, he fills out a **booking sheet** containing all the information about the job: what it is, the company, duration, how much it pays, etc. This sheet is then used to determine an agent's value to the company, as well as his annual bonus. (For an example of a booking sheet see p. 50.)

An effective agent should, in theory, be generating commissions worth at least three times his salary. A third covers the agent's overhead, a third goes to the company, a third goes to the agent himself. As an agent grows and begins bringing in millions of dollars, that ratio changes. No agent's overhead is $3 million a year, so an agent generating that kind of income gets to keep more of his income.

This presents a challenge for first or second-year agents, whose overhead alone— once you account for your office rent, parking, utilities, assistant, benefits and health care, their assistant's benefits and health care—probably costs more than their $60,000 salary! But remember, junior agents mostly service other agents' clients. So if a lowly covering agent helps land a $400,000 job for a senior agent's high-level client, earning the company a ten percent commission of $40,000, both agents may be listed on the booking sheet. The client's main agent, or **point agent**, gets $20,000, and the junior agent gets $20,000. Do that for three clients a year, most junior agents have already covered their salary. (Not all commission splits are 50:50; some are 33:66 or any other negotiated ratio.)

How (Some) Management Companies Are Different

Unlike agents, not all managers are paid a salary. At some management firms, the company simply covers the manager's overhead in exchange for a 50:50 commission split. In other words, the firm pays for the manager's office space, an assistant, IT, supplies, etc., and the manager gives the firm half of all his revenue.

How All This Affects You as a Client

While it may seem like you want to be repped by the biggest, baddest agent at the agency, younger agents get promoted by proving they can successfully service other clients and close deals, which means they're often hungrier than higher-ups.

"You have big name [agents] that will open doors and get you into rooms," says Verve coordinator Melissa Solomon, "and then you have people who are going to be just as persistent and won't take no for an answer. They may not be the big name or level, but they're doing their damndest to get you in anywhere. That goes a long way."

The Team Approach: How Agents Work Together

One of the advantages of being repped at the mid-level or Big Four agencies is that departments cover the town and represent clients as a team. This gives these agencies a leg up, especially when gathering information on what studios, networks, and production companies are buying, selling, and developing. "There are just too many shows out there, too many executives to know," says Verve partner Amy Retzinger.

If you were a solo operator, "you certainly couldn't be in a conversation with every show and every executive on a regular basis, at least not frequently enough to be aware of the jobs that might be coming and going."

When it comes to collecting info and doing recon, agencies divide the industry into "**territories**," with each territory referring to a different studio and its subsets. One territory might be Sony Pictures, which would include Sony's **specialty arm**, Sony Pictures Classics, plus production companies such as Adam Sandler's Happy Madison (*Rules of Engagement*), Simon Cowell's Syco (*The X Factor*), Ashton Kutcher's Katalyst (*No Strings Attached*), Jimmy Miller's Mosaic (*Rapturepalooza*), and approximately thirty more organizations that have deals or partnerships with Sony.

Most agency departments assign one agent to "**cover**" each territory. This "**covering agent**" is responsible for knowing what execs at those territories are buying, selling, looking for, developing, and producing. If Rachel, an MP lit agent at CAA, covers Universal Pictures, her job is to check in at least once a week to find out what everyone in the Universal family is looking for. Does Focus Features need writers for upcoming assignments? Does Vince Vaughn's Wild West Picture Show Productions have specific kinds of movies they're looking for? Is Judd Apatow's production company, Apatow Production Companies, working on any movies that may need a director? Rachel reviews all this info with other agents in her department, then reports back to her Universal contacts with appropriate pitches, projects, or clients.

Sounds easy, right? Think again. Connecting with all the companies and divisions at even *one* territory each week takes a lot of time, but agents usually cover *multiple* territories, so Rachel may cover Universal, Dreamworks, New Regency, and all feature animation!

"As a covering agent, if something happens at a studio and [industry journalist/blogger] Nikki Finke breaks it before you sent it out, that's bad," says former ICM agent B.J. Ford. "If something major happens, you send that out to the department. If so-and-

---

Ask the Agent

Q: I'm about to sign with a boutique talent agency—basically, a one-man shop. If the team approach allows bigger agencies to cover the entire town, is a smaller agency even capable of getting the same amount of information? Should I be worried that my agent won't know about certain opportunities?

A: "The reality is: information is pretty free-flowing these days. The Internet has helped that a lot—the ease with which you can get information from other agencies. The electronic age has made information very easy to swap. Do we see everything? Of course not. That's true whether you're at X big agency or Y big agency. [But] we see a very high percentage of information that's out there."—Boutique literary agent.

Tracking Boards

One way agents, coordinators, and assistants gather and swap information is with tracking boards, online groups of people who share inside information, rumors, scripts, job openings, and resources. It's like an Internet chat room, but members trade scripts, early leaks bout sales or job openings, spec script strategies, etc. Tracking boards are usually run by assistants, agents, managers, or execs—like Trackula, which is run by Station 3 manager Kailey Marsh. Most are password-protected and invite-only. There *are* a handful of "public" tracking boards or services, such as rackingB.com, TVTracker.com, inHollywood.com, but most require a subscription fee.

so fell out of a movie, a director fell out, other agents must know so they can call and get their director client in line."

The team approach not only makes it easier for an agency to cover the entire industry, it keeps studios and networks from being bombarded with multiple calls from the same agency, which can get overwhelming, redunant, and annoying.

Bigger agencies also use teams to interface with clients. A low-level writer, just starting a career, may have only one or two agents on his team. A more successful writer/producer—someone who has sold projects, run a TV show, written and directed feature movies—may have four or five agents in both the film and TV departments. He may also have a digital agent working to land online gigs, and a commercial agent trying to score him work producing or directing TV spots. A big movie star—or a "multi-hyphenate" who acts, writes, sings, and directs—may have an MP talent agent, a TV talent agent, a commercial agent, a couple of lit agents, and personal appearances or licensing agent. (And these are just their *agents*; they also have managers, lawyers, publicists, and business managers!) Each client is then assigned a **point agent** who is responsible for organizing and communicating all the various agents on the team. At any given time, one particular agent may be " running point" for ten clients, and on teams for ten other clients.

Advantages to the Team Approach

- Allows agencies to submit clients for more opportunities faster.
- Gives clients more relationships within the agency. If a client doesn't like one agent, he can work with someone else. This also protects the agency if an agent gets fired or poached; if a valuable client feels close to multiple agents, there's a better chance he'll stay at the firm rather than following the departed agent.
- Incentivizes agents to work for co-workers' clients. As we mentioned earlier, when an agent lands a gig for another agent's client, some agencies give a percentage of the commission to the agent who did the booking, and a percentage of the commission to the point agent. Other agencies give the entire booking to the agent who covers the territory. Either way is especially important for junior agents, since most junior agents *only* service other colleagues' clients.

Ask the Agents

Q: I understand how a team approach helps agents internally, but how is it better for clients? I mean, if my agent covers Paramount, but I want to be put up for a job at Universal, aren't I being repped by someone who A) doesn't know me as well, and B) would rather push her own clients harder?

A: "For me, the appropriateness of the client trumps all else," says Verve partner Amy Retzinger. "I'd rather get the job for my colleague's client than not get it for mine . . . which means I better make sure I know my colleagues' clients."

But not all agents agree. "In a perfect agency scenario," says another agent, "you're incentivized to book your own clients *and* other people's clients—and have a share in whatever comes in. [But] people tend to always want to book their own clients. Younger agents will book the shit out of anything, [but] if they're older agents, who have their own people that are priorities to them, [those clients] are always going to be priorities. It's a flawed system. It's different everywhere . . . [and] I suspect it's fucked up everywhere."

FIGURE 4.1
Booking Sheet

DATE 11/1/13   LITERARY BOOKING REPORT   NO. _____

1. CLIENT/LOADOUT CORP. __Mark Stone / Top Jimmy Productions__

2. PROJECT TITLE __We Die Young__   3. AGENT __Mitch Cherone__

4. START DATE __11/15/13__

5. BUYER __NBC / Warner Bros__

6. BUYER CONTACT __Sammy Smyth__   7. PHONE NO. __818-555-2110__

8. ENGAGEMENT IS (CHECK ALL THAT APPLY: MOTION PICTURE ____ T.V. _X_ OPTION ___

       SERIES ___ PILOT _X_ OTHER _____

9. CONTRACT PRICE __$125,000__

    A. TOTAL POTENTIAL FEE __$130,000__ COMMISSION _X_ 10% OR _____

    B. PAYMENT STRUCTURE _____

DESCRIPTION	TOTAL AMOUNT	$ DUE – START DATE	DUE DATE: START	$ DUE – DELIVERY	DUE DATE: DELIVERY
Commencement	10% or $12,500				
Outline	20%				
1st Draft	40%				
1st Revisions	10%				
2nd Revisions	10%				
Polish	10%				
Opt. Polish	$5,000				

10. BONUS AMOUNT __$25,000 for sole credit, red. to $12,500 shared__

11. PROFIT PARTICIPATION __10% MAG red. to 5% (vesting in 1/4 s)__

12. TV ROYALTY/RESIDUALS __$5,000 red. to $2500 / ep__

13. BILLING/CREDIT __CO-EP yr 1 – EP. yr 2 + 3__

14. SEND CHECKS TO: __X__ CLIENT _____ MANAGER _____ OTHER

15. ADDITIONAL REMARKS __Pilot & EP fee – $25 K yr 1 Co EP – $22,500__

Year 2 EP @ $25K , Yr 3 EP – $27,500

Lock 1-1, opt to consult @ 10K / ep

A Year in the Life of an Agent

Departments of an agency are like organs in a body—each has its own unique function and processes, but they all work together for the health of the entire body. Thus, they do their best to find opportunities to maximize corporate synergy. Let's say WME signs a celebrity chef —we'll call her Kiley; the alternative TV department may help Kiley get her own cooking show on the Food Network, which serves as a platform for the branded lifestyle department to license her name and likeness for a line of cookware, which can be promoted through a speaking tour arranged by the personal appearances department and used to help the book department land her a book deal, which increases Kiley's brand awareness enough to score her a spot hosting a non-cooking show, thus breaking her out of the cooking world and onto a much larger stage. This is how agencies like WME, which took Guy Fieri from everyman cook to *Minute To Win It* show host, coordinate their many disparate resouces and "tentacles" to capitalize on their clients.

In order to continue understanding how agencies work internally and holistically—and how this affects agents and clients' day-to-day lives—it's helpful to look first at the factors that shape an agency's annual calendar. Agencies and management companies, like most businesses, view each year according to their fiscal calendar, which usually ends in December and begins in January. "I'm never more bummed than my first day back at work (in January)," says manager Michael Pelmont, New Wave Entertainment's head of television, "and it's not because vacation is over. It's because I'm staring at a year's worth of empty booking sheets."

The year's first few months are always tough for agencies. Many clients aren't yet working, but agencies must keep paying employees, rent, utilities, insurance policies. As the year stretches on, clients begin getting work, money starts coming in. Eventually, summer arrives; summer is not only the busiest time for touring comics and musicians, it's television's annual development season, when new show ideas are bought and sold (more on this in Chapter 7). This can make summer one of an agency's most hectic times, as well as the most profitable. Activity slows down as the year draws to a close; agents usually spend the fourth quarter chasing clients' money and unfulfilled contracts. Many agencies also dole out end-of year bonuses, based on each agent's bookings and how he or she contributes to the agency.

Throughout the year, big agencies' calendars are also shaped in special ways by the annual cycles of some of their most important departments. These are:

- **Television's Annual Seasons**—Most television departments, which are one of agencies' most important divisions (thanks to those lucrative packaging fees!), follow the three regular seasons of broadcast television: **development season**, when many of TV's show ideas are bought and sold (July–October); **pilot season**, when selected scripts are piloted as prototypes (January–May); and **staffing season**, when TV writers have their best shot of getting hired onto shows (March–May). (We'll learn more about these in Part II.)
- **Music's Summer Booking Season and the Summer Concert Season**—While summer is the busiest touring season for giant acts like Bruce Springsteen and Coldplay, music agents' real rat race lasts from November through April, when they book the next summer's concerts and tours.
- **Big Film Festivals and Markets**—Although film departments have no annual cycles like TV or music, buying and selling opportunities often heat up around important festivals and markets (such as the Sundance Film Festival and the American Film Market). See the box on page 152 for a short list of the industry's more important events.

There are a handful of other events which also shape or mark an agency's year:

- **Company Retreats**—Many agencies have an annual two- or three-day getaway with every agent from every department—including those from other cities or countries. Some retreats focus on important business goals, changes, or strategies, with each department preparing a special presentation for the rest of the company. Others are more like TED or Milken Institute Conferences, exploring fresh ways of thinking, communicating, and problem-solving. WME's 2012 retreat featured panels with Al Gore and Sean Parker, plus a 75-minute debate between former Deputy Chief of Staff Karl Rove and Chicago mayor Rahm Emanuel (brother of WME co-CEO Ari Emanuel). CAA's retreats have also had special visits from sports stars such as Andre Agassi and Chris Paul, actors like Tom Cruise[18] and Selena Gomez, and business titans like eBay CEO John Donohoe.[19]
- **Quarterly Company Meetings**—The biggest agencies, especially those with offices in multiple countries, may also have quarterly meetings. WME, for example, brings together the entire company via video conference so each department can give its own status update.
- **Departmental Retreats**—Many departments have their own annual retreats, where they talk about big projects and departmental goals, and review their client list, cutting anyone they no longer want to be in business with.

Occasionally, departmental retreats may include other divisions as well. At the TV development retreat, for example, just before the kickoff of development season, TV agents meet with each of the agency's *other* departments: MP talent, MP lit, video games, personal appearances, books, branded lifestyle, etc. Does a hot pop star have a desire to host a game show? Do any feature writers have ideas for sitcoms? Is there a branding opportunity for a rising reality star? What books or video games can be adapted into a TV series?

Year at a Glance

Many agency departments, such as branding, marketing, and licensing, have year-round business. Others, like music and TV lit, have specific windows when doing business is critical, and these times are big commerce drivers for those departments. Here's a quick look at some important agency departments and how their busy periods fit into the agency's year. (FYI—we'll discuss film and TV departments' annual calendars in much more detail in Parts II and III, so if not all of this calendar makes complete sense, it will soon.)

	JAN	FEB	MAR	APR	MAY	JUN	JUL	AUG	SEP	OCT	NOV	DEC
TV LIT.	Production on current shows continues and wraps			Staffing season			Production begins on new and current TV shows					
	Pilot season through May upfronts						Development season			End of year: business slows down, agents track unpaid monies and unfinished contracts or paperwork, annual bonuses, holiday parties		
TV TALENT	Pilot season					Pilot re-castings	Guest star casting for current TV shows					
	Guest star casting for current TV shows											
MP LIT.	Sundance Film Festival	Berlin Film Festival		Tribeca Film Festival	Cannes Film Festival				Toronto Film Festival		American Film Market	
MUSIC AND COMEDY				Summer concert season (bands, musicians, comics)							Holiday concert season	
	Summer concert booking season										Summer concert booking season	

A Day in the Life of a Lit Agent

"At five o'clock in the morning, the alarm goes off, my fiancé starts getting ready for work, I grumble, roll over, and go, 'What the fuck? Is it still dark out?'" says Lindsay Howard, APA's VP of television lit.

People in entertainment—writers, producers, execs, actors, directors, designers—work hard. But few people work harder than agents. We give them a lot of grief—"When the hell is he gonna call me back?!"–but "being an agent's not necessarily glamorous," says UTA Chief Administrative Officer Michael Conway. "Most people think it's Ari Gold and *Entourage*. The reality is: it's not. You're on call 24/7. The client doesn't care if you're sick or don't feel well or your car won't start and you had a bad day. It's about them; whether or not they're going to have a career, or have anything going on, is dependent upon you as an agent going out and getting them a job."

Thus, most agents begin their business day long before they enter the office, sometimes with breakfast meetings or pitch prep sessions, and their work continues long after they leave, often with dinners or comedy showcases. "The first thing I do each morning," Howard continues, "[is] check the iPhone while I pee, because that's the only thirty seconds I have to myself. I read scripts while I'm getting ready. I dry my hair circling and annotating page notes. Then I bring my iPad downstairs, finish reading a script while making a fruit/vegetable smoothie, continue to answer emails while I'm doing that. Then I start my drive to work while **rolling calls** and answering emails (illegally while I'm driving) and then I get to work and start making [more] phone calls."

Once agents arrive at the office–usually at 10 a.m., the start of a typical Hollywood workday–their schedule is packed with meetings and conference calls (see the calendar on page 54). Of course, many unexpected emergencies can derail an agent's day. Sometimes agents need to chase down a client's missing contract or paycheck. Other times, they have to read a time-sensitive script.

"Today, a client emailed me at 8:30 a.m.–he knows that's when I start checking–about his script," says feature agent Will Lowery. "I haven't read it, [but] I say, 'Let's talk.' He says, 'I'm out of town tomorrow through the end of the week, so I'd like to talk today.' I look at my calendar–I can find an hour to do this–and set the call for 5 p.m. I read the script from 11:30 to 12:30, and talk to the client at 5:00. If it needs to be done, it needs to be done, it's part of the job . . . but I can't just sit around reading [during the day]. It hurts the rest of my business."

Agents also need to be ready to help "clients having an emotional struggle getting something done on time, or having an issue with their producer, and I have to play therapist," says one long-time agent. "Being able to help somebody through that moment is part of my job, and [it] enables them to be more successful, but it takes time away from things that could be more financially lucrative in the short term . . . [like] getting people jobs."

A normal Hollywood workday lasts till 7:30 or 8:00, but most agents have dinner or drinks meetings with clients or execs. These wrap up around 9:30 or 10:00, when agents head home to–go to bed? Nope, they've still got scripts to read! These could be new scripts from clients, pilots looking for writers to hire, screenplays in need of a director, or submissions from aspirants hoping for representation.

"I currently have three scripts I need to read immediately," says Howard, showing me the list of scripts on her iPad. "Then I have ten scripts I have to read immediately. Then I have all these scripts I have to deal with. And then I have ten scripts that I have to read at some point in the imminent future." The list is approximately forty scripts long. And with new pieces of work always coming in, *it never gets shorter.*

"You prioritize as much as humanly possible, but the reality is: I'm probably reading a script while trying to watch *The Bachelor* or something," says Howard. "I cannot read at work; reading at work is impossible. The phone doesn't stop. The questions don't stop. It's not a place you want your agent reading something they have to focus on. [This is why] I do most of my reading first thing in the morning–that's the only time I'm not consistently distracted."

But in between a 5 a.m. wake-up call and falling asleep reading scripts, what's an agent or manager's schedule look like? When we're frustrated they're not calling us back right away, what are they actually *doing*?

Talk the Talk

Rolling calls–Making a series of phone calls remotely using an assistant in the office to patch through consecutive calls. Usually, the assistant then dials everyone his boss needs to call, patching through each call individually. When rolling calls, the assistant never hangs up; he stays on the line, listening, taking notes, and preparing to call the next person. Thus, the agent is "rolling" through calls.

Ripped From the Headlines! (or at least someone's calendar)

The following is a fictional schedule for an agent's day, adapted from calendars of several actual lit agents at various agencies.

Tuesday, March 16

6 a.m.	– Spinning @ 24 Hour Fitness (Read: *In Your Room*/Elise Condon, *I'm Not an Angel*/Wynn Boyd, *American Boys*/Hallie Cornell)
8:30	– Breakfast w/ Tevin Baloche–TNT Entertainment @ Toast
9:30–10 a.m.	– Roll calls
10 a.m.	– Coverage meeting
10:30 a.m.	– Kiersten Wyland & Travis Roth call–*18 and Life* pitch prep
11 a.m.	– Capricornia Productions meeting (in town from NYC–do not reschedule)
12 p.m.	– Jahan Palmer call–review *Flashbacks* contract for HBO
1 p.m.	– Lunch w/ Alyssa Rioux–Coney Island Productions @ Lemonade (FYI–lunch in Hollywood always happens at 1:00. Don't ask me why, it just does. Not 12:00, not 12:30–*1:00.*)
2 p.m.	– Travel to Warner Bros. / Jillette Calise call–*Torpedo* notes (draft #2)
3 p.m.	– TV staffing meeting @ Warner Bros.
4:00 p.m.	– Return from Warner Bros. / Roll calls
5:30 p.m.	– Big Eater Productions–weekly development call (*Euphoria Lane* update?)
7 p.m.	– Dinner w/ Harvey Jane–Omnibus Films @ Bella Roma
8:45 p.m.	– Vince Gellar stand-up showcase @ Laugh Factory (confirm guest list)
10:00 p.m.	– Tonight's read: *Searchlights*/Susan Fisher, *Ocean to Ocean*/Rebecca Cadigan, *Bright Again*/Mark Hobson

Just Another Manic Monday

Every Monday, agents follow up with networks and studios about clients' pitch meetings from the previous week. "If it's a flat-out 'no' and I understand why this network is passing," says one agent, "I won't argue. But if they're wavering, I'll be after them like a gnat," checking in repeatedly until there's an answer. "I [also] check in with clients I haven't talked to in a week to see how they're doing, [and] I start calling my production companies to say, 'What ideas do you have? A&E is looking for [a specific type of show], do you have anything in your stable?'"

Important Weekly Meetings

Agents also have several weekly meetings they attend. Here's a quick glimpse at one TV lit department's quasi-fictional schedule of regular weekly meetings:

Monday

10 a.m.	– Staff meeting (whole agency)
11 a.m.	– Literary department meeting (feature lit, TV lit, alternative/reality TV)
2:30 p.m.	– Casting meeting (TV and MP talent departments review all important casting opportunities in pilots and features)

Tuesday

10 a.m.	– Coverage meeting (Agents in the same department share updates on needs and news from their territories.)
1 p.m.	– TV Lit staff lunch (Usually geared toward a certain topic, like director clients, book adaptations, etc.)

Wednesday

3 p.m.	– Branded Lifestyle meeting (bi-weekly) (The branded lifestyle department shares any licensing opportunities or product integration possibilities for clients.)

Thursday

3:30 p.m.	– Coverage meeting (some agencies have two coverage meetings per week)

4:00   – Weekend read meeting (Agents divvy up scripts to read over the weekend. Some, such as new screenplays from valuable clients, may be read by the entire department; others are read by only one person just to get a sense of the project's quality.)

What Tools and Resources Do Agents and Managers Most Rely On?

Assistant–Assistants are representatives' right-hand men and women. They "know what's going to keep you on track, but they're also 'you' when you're not there," says one agent. Assistants interact with clients and buyers, read scripts, give feedback, and gather valuable (often secret) information from their own contacts. "They're partners in crime . . . tied at the hip to you. They're the biggest thing to help drive the truck smoothly."

Phone sheet–A list of incoming and outgoing phone calls: who the agent wants to call who's called the agent, where the agent has called and "left word," and to-do notes for each conversation. "I return every phone call every day," says ICM agent Melissa Orton. "I return the bottom-of-the-barrel Joe-Schmo-producer-who's-never-done-anything, and I return every client's phone call – that's just the way it works."

(You can see a sample phone sheet in Table 4.1 this is excerpted from an actual agent's phone sheet; only the details have been changed):

Company-wide database–Most agencies maintain a massive database that cross-references every script and project in Hollywood. Each entry contains the project's budget, history, any attachments, and which executives at the studio or network oversee it. It also lists clients who have been submitted for the project. Agents can access this entire system from their phones or tablets, putting massive amounts of up-to-the-minute info at their fingertips no matter where they are. (Many agencies use Database Oasis–www.databaseoasis.com.)

Smartphones–"I could work from a port-o-potty if I had my iPhone," says one agent. Many agents, however, don't have an iPhone, they have *two* phones: an iPhone and a Blackberry, as each excels at different tasks or connects more easily to various internal systems. This keeps agents connected at all times to their phone sheets, calendars, address books, company databases and intranets, and **development grids**.

TABLE 4.1 Phone Sheet Example

Status	Last Updated	Contact	Communications	Subject
TD-CM	May 13, 2013	Lisa Moyers, Paramount	323–555–4235	MTG: Fuller (next time in town) MTG: Sebastian Crow (Jeff Cobain too) 4/30 Sent ABSINTHE 4/1
TD-CM	May 13, 2013	Dmitri Murdock, Showtime	323–555–3598	MTG: Diamond & DeLonge
CU	May 13, 2013	Glenice Krieger, Found It Productions	310–555–4574	Sent McCauley's link, SET MTG IN JUNE
CU	May 12, 2013	Daniel Spitzer, Spitzer Films	310–555–0834	Irving Snow referred him to you. He's in casting. Wants to speak about a project. Robby Howe is a friend.
RET	May 12, 2013	Moti Short, Rawk-n-Roll Prod.	323–555–2892	MTG: Thomas Peacock
RET	May 11, 2013	Morgan Thompson, Dreamworks	818–555–9241	He's a manager. Met you a year ago. Wants to introduce you to a client Dorsey Jackson. She wrote WIDOWER'S HEART stars 3 BAA clients
TRD	May 10, 2013	Tevin Fleder, Horrible Ent.	310–555–1624	Sent VOODOO QUEEN 4/21, BIG TROUBLE, LITTLE DREAMER, Pitchford credits 4/14
TC-M	May 10, 2013	Meghan Franklin, Fortune Films	818–555–7345 DRIFTWOOD	re: DLR interview for NBC story notes–
TC-SM	May 8, 2013	Carly Plotnik	213–555–8435	Re: representation
TC-SB	May 7, 2013	Daria Levin, Spoken Song	310–555–4453	Sent CATHEDRAL 4/18
TC-SB	May 5, 2013	Samantha Kolby, Fantastic Prod.	818–555–3457	Sent HAND COVERS BRUISE 4/9
LM	May 4, 2013	Jonah Cole, MGM	323–555–7402	OOT Sent: for Let Me Lie: Tim Banks, Steven Batali, Dean Chalk, Dale Feaster, Prestwood & Rochell, Melamed, Berg 4/8

KEY

TD-CM – To-Do Client Meeting
CU – Called Us
RET – Returned
TRD – Trading
TC-M – To Call/Follow-up on meeting
TC-SM – To Call/Set Meeting
TC-SB – To Call Submissions
LM – Left Message

Part II
Television Agents

5 A Quick Overview of the TV Business

Heads Up!

This section, "Part II: Television Agents," focuses mostly on writers and agents for prime time scripted comedies and dramas, as these are the genres where writers are most active. However, I've also included some helpful info about reality shows (watch for the "Reality Check" text boxes), and much of the scripted info applies to the non-scripted world.

"I can't tell you how out of my depth I was," says screenwriter Diablo Cody. It was 2008–Cody's first produced script, *Juno*, had just nabbed the Academy Award for Best Original Screenplay, and she was taking on a new challenge: running her own TV series, Showtime's *United States of Tara*. "I had only ever been on a feature, where the director is God and the writer, if they're lucky, gets to visit the set and say, 'Wow, this is cool!'".

Unlike in film, on a TV show, it's the writer, not the director, who gets to be "God." In fact, TV's head writers, or **showrunners**, don't just oversee a show's storytelling, they literally run *every aspect of the show*, from set design and casting to music and wardrobe. A showrunner is essentially the CEO of a $50 million per year, 150-person operation, and Cody–who had gone from being a total unknown to Hollywood's hottest screenwriter in just over a year–was ill-equipped to be a CEO. "The director (Craig Gillespie) kept looking for guidance from me," she says, "and I just wound up rolling over and telling [him], 'Do whatever you want.' He did everything–from production design to casting–without a lot of input from me. I had never done any of those things! I had only done one thing, a single feature film, and I wasn't even a producer on *Juno*, all I did was write the script! So to go from that to 'All right, now you're going to be the Executive Producer of a television show' . . . it was a joke."

Fortunately, Cody was a quick study; the series ran for three seasons, picking up two Emmys and a Golden Globe. Still, "I wish I had gone and started TV the way everybody else does," says Cody, "working as an assistant [or] script coordinator, maybe being a PA, spending time on set, learning how it works, working your way up to Staff Writer, then working your way to creator. Then, by the time you get to creator, you have this incredible knowledge of how everything fits together."

Indeed television, unlike film, has specific paths many writers follow to build a career. In fact, most of Hollywood's professional writers work in television, not movies. In 2011, the Writers Guild of America (the labor union representing writers in TV, radio, and film) reported 3,320 working TV writers, and only 1,562 working screenwriters.[1]

Television also drives the majority of profits for most of the big Hollywood studios. In its first fiscal quarter of 2013, the Walt Disney Company's television networks generated $1.21 billion, a two percent increase from a year earlier. The film studio, meanwhile, *dipped* forty-three percent, racking up only $234 million.[2] To give this even more perspective, Disney's theme parks pulled in $577 million during the same period, and its interactive department, which handles games and online content, made a measly $9 million. In other words, Disney's TV business pulled in more than its film, theme parks, and interactive divisions *combined*!

Also, unlike movies—which get bought, sold, produced, and distributed in a myriad of ways (we'll learn more in Part III)—the world of television follows a specific set of rules. While there are occasional exceptions to these rules, most shows follow a predetermined path from conception to production.

So we begin with television. In the world of TV, there are three basic types of companies:

- **Networks** which are responsible for acquiring and distributing television content (ABC, Bravo, MTV, etc.).
- **Studios** which finance, own, develop, and produce television content (20th Century Fox, CBS Studios, etc.).
- **Production companies** which create, develop, and produce television content (Doozer, The Tannenbaum Company, etc.).

There are hundreds of these companies throughout Hollywood, but the truth is *only five control the majority of what viewers watch on TV.* That's right: five. Those five companies are the **media conglomerates**: Comcast, NewsCorp, the Walt Disney Company, CBS Corp., and Time-Warner.

Each of these five companies is a massive corporation holding numerous companies in media and entertainment. Comcast, for example, controls networks like NBC, USA, and SyFy, studios such as Universal TV and Universal Cable Productions, and production companies like Deedle-Dee Productions (*Parks and Recreation*), Broadway Video (*30 Rock*), and Shine America (*The Biggest Loser*). It also owns the Philadelphia Flyers, Plaxo, and a significant stake of In Demand. CBS Corp. meanwhile owns CBS, Showtime, and half of the CW (in a 50:50 partnership with Time Warner); it also owns Simon & Schuster publishing, CBS Films,[3] GameSpot, BNET, Last.fm,[4] approximately 130 local radio stations, and TVGN and TVGuide.com.

Most importantly, each of the five media conglomerates has one thing almost no other company in America has: **a broadcast network**, the most powerful distribution method in the country.

Other Conglomerates

While the five broadcast networks are each owned by a major media conglomerate, there are other important conglomerates as well. Viacom owns Nickelodeon, VH1, Spike, and Comedy Central. Scripps Networks Interactive owns Food Network, Travel Channel, and HGTV. Broadcast Media Partners owns the Univision networks.

Which Conglomerates Own which Broadcast Networks?					
Conglomerate	Comcast	*Disney*	NewsCorp.	CBS Corp.	Time-Warner
Network	NBC	ABC	FOX	CBS & CW (jointly with Time Warner)	CW (jointly with CBS Corp.)

What's a Network?

Networks have one main function: to distribute television programming (TV shows, newscasts, sports events, etc.). NBC distributes *Ironside* and *America's Got Talent.* Lifetime distributes *Army Wives*, A&E distributes *Bates Motel*, CBS distributes *Person of Interest.*

For most of its existence, the U.S. TV market has been dominated by broadcast networks, companies that use radio waves to distribute content to consumers' television sets. Because radio waves can be received by anyone with an antenna-equipped TV set, broadcasters typically distribute their programming for free, making money by selling advertising time within those programs.

In the last forty years, however, new technologies have created other ways for viewers to watch TV. Cable providers such as Cox Communications and Mediacom deliver content to consumers' televisions via wires. Many distributors—Logo, ESPN, TLC, SyFy, etc.—now avoid radio waves altogether, instead operating only as **cable networks**. Other service providers, such as Dish Network and DirecTV, provide content via satellite signals—some have even started their own satellite-only networks, such as the Audience Network, which airs original series like *The Artie Lange Show* and *Rogue*. Netflix, meanwhile, distributes content over the Internet, streaming content directly to viewers' screens; originally begun simply as a movie rental service, Netflix has since blossomed into a fully-fledged distributor of original content like *House of Cards* and *Arrested Development*.

It's important to note: while cable, satellite, and online distributors are growing and multiplying (as of 2013, ninety percent of U.S. households received cable television[7]), they still rarely garner as many viewers as broadcasters. During the week of February 24, 2012, for example, AMC's *The Walking Dead* wowed the industry by garnering an audience of 11.1 million viewers—over a million more than that week's episode of ABC's *Modern Family*—but it still fell short of beating broadcast hits like CBS's *The Big Bang Theory* (17.9 million) and FOX's *American Idol* (13.5 million). This will undoubtedly change in the future, but for now broadcasters still have the most reach.

Talk the Talk

Sweeps–A quarterly period in which the Nielsen Company, America's primary calculator and analyst of media viewership, takes uber-accurate audience measurements. As a result, sweeps months (February, May, July, and November) are incredibly competitive periods during which networks schedule their most sensational programs in hopes of attracting larger audiences.

Talk the Talk

While broadcast distributors, like ABC and the CW, and cable distributors, like GSN and E!, are all technically networks, when industry professionals refer to "networks," we're generally referring to *broadcast* networks. When talking about E!, GSN, Disney XD, or CNN we usually specify them as "cable networks."

How Networks Make Money

Since it costs almost nothing for consumers to receive radio waves, broadcast networks distribute content for free, then charge advertisers to place commercials within broadcasts. The more viewers that watch a particular program, the more a network charges advertisers. In 2010–11, for example, CBS's *The Good Wife* averaged nearly 13 million total viewers per episode,[8] allowing CBS to charge an average $137,457 for a thirty-second spot within the show.[9] FOX's tenth season of *American Idol* pulled in between 23 million and 26 million viewers per episode, generating between $468,100 and $502,900 per spot.[10]

Networks also charge more for attracting large audiences within specific target demographics. In 2012 CBS's *The Amazing Race* averaged 9.31 total million weekly viewers,[11] compared to *The Family Guy's* 5.98 million viewers on FOX.[12] Yet because *The Family Guy* attracts a larger share of broadcast networks' desired audience (adults 18–49), FOX was able to charge $264,912 for each thirty-second spot within the show, while *The Amazing Race* charged only $124,091.[13]

Cable networks such as Discovery Channel and A&E also charge for commercial time, but because they reach smaller audiences, they charge less per spot. In 2010, ESPN commanded some of the priciest commercial fees in cable at approximately $31,551.[14] That same year, TNT charged only $16,474.[15]

Double Dollars

Aside from ad dollars, cable networks make money another way, too: by collecting subscriber fees from cable providers, like Charter Communications and Cablevision, carrying the channel. The amount of money each network collects depends on viewership in the network's target demographic. In 2012, MSNBC commanded approximately 16 cents per subscriber per month,[16] while Discovery Channel generated 36 cents per subscriber,[17] and Nickelodeon received 50 cents.[18] HBO, which has no commercials and operates mostly on subscriber fees, collected a hefty *seven dollars per subscriber per month*![19]

Despite the double revenue streams, most cable networks still don't generate as much income as broadcast networks. In one three-month period of 2011, CBS generated $1.99 billion;[20] compare that with the $2.1 billion generated during the same time by *all* of NBC Universal's cable networks combined: USA, SyFy, Oxygen, Bravo, and MSNBC.[21]

What is a studio?

Networks distribute TV programming, but they don't usually produce that same programming . . . which is where studios come in.

A studio's job is to develop, produce, finance, and own scripted television content. This means the studio pays every cent going into a show's production: writers', actors', and designers' salaries; costume rentals, paint and lumber, insurance, catering, pencils, *everything*. For a one-hour drama such as *Chicago Fire* or *Nikita*, this usually comes to about $3 million per episode. Half-hour comedies, such as *2 Broke Girls* or *Mom*, cost a bit less—usually between $1.5 and $2 million per episode. The studio then "sells," or **licenses**, each show to a network, which distribute it to viewers.

Here is where media conglomerates once again flex their muscles. The conglomerates not only own the networks that reach most of America's viewers, they own the production studios providing them with content! So NewsCorp.'s TV studio, 20th Century Fox, finances and produces *Raising Hope* . . . then turns around and licenses it to FOX, which is also owned by NewsCorp.! Likewise, *Revenge* is produced by Disney's ABC Studios and airs on Disney's broadcast network, ABC.

Which Conglomerates Own which Studios?

	Comcast	Disney	NewsCorp.	CBS Corp.	Time-Warner
Network	NBC	ABC	FOX	CBS & CW	CW
Cable Nets (Partial list)	USA, E!, Bravo, SyFy	ABC Family, ESPN	Fox Sports, FX, Fox News	Showtime TBS	HBO, TNT, TBS
Studio:	Universal TV	ABC Studios	20th Century Fox TV	CBS Studios	Warner Bros.

Each studio, in fact, is charged with making as much content as possible for their parent networks. ABC Studios' mission? Make shows that fit on ABC. 20th Century Fox's mission? Make shows that fit on FOX. *However ...*

While studios aim to make shows for their own distributors, *they can actually sell shows to any network.* Warner Bros. makes *Revolution*, which airs on Comcast's NBC. Comcast's Universal TV makes *The Mindy Project*, which it licenses to NewsCorp's FOX. Still, each conglomerate's goal is to keep as much content and money as possible in-house. Of the fifteen new and returning scripted shows announced for NBC's 2012–13 schedule, only *two* were produced by outside studios: Warner Bros.' *Revolution* and 20th Century Fox's *The New Normal.*

Even Studios Can Be Homeless

There's one studio (and conglomerate) we have not yet mentioned. Sony—the massive corporation that makes everything from cameras to televisions to movies—owns Sony Pictures Television, which makes shows such as *The Dr. Oz Show, Jeopardy, Drop Dead Diva,* and *Community.* Yet Sony has no network, no "home" waiting to snatch up its content! (It does, however, own pieces of GSN and FEARnet.) Thus, Sony shops its shows to every network, giving it a wide marketplace. *Justified* airs on FX, *The Goldbergs* airs on ABC, and *Breaking Bad* airs on AMC.

How Studios Make Money

A network, as we know, makes money by acquiring television programs from studios, then charging advertisers to plant commercials within broadcasts of those shows. So obviously, a studio makes money by covering a show's expenses, then selling it to the network for a markup ... right? If one episode of *Revolution* costs the standard $3 million, Warner Bros. TV (the show's studio) probably charges NBC (the show's network) $4 million. Or $5 million. Enough to make a profit, right? *You would think.*

The truth is, studios usually sell their shows to networks for *less* than it costs to make them. If *Revolution* costs Warner Bros. $3 million per episode, NBC acquires the show for $1.8 or $2 million per episode, meaning every hour of *Revolution* leaves Warner Bros. $1 million in the hole. That also means a standard twenty-two-episode season puts Warner Bros. out $22 million. Which, in turn, means if Warner Brothers has twenty-six shows on the air (twenty one-hour dramas and six half-hour comedies), they're potentially losing over $500 million a year! This is called **deficit financing** but how can it work?!

Here's how ... As I mentioned, studios don't really *sell* their scripted shows to networks. (We say "sell" in the industry, but that's inaccurate.) Studios **license** their shows to networks. The $2 million per episode NBC pays to Warner Bros. is a **license fee**; it doesn't give NBC ownership of the show, it just gives NBC license to broadcast the show's episodes a certain number of times, usually once or twice. The studio itself retains ownership, which means it's able to resell the show's episodes to other distributors for reairing. In other words: *reruns.*

Traditionally, selling a show's reruns has involved selling, or **syndicating**, the show to hundreds of local television stations across America. Studios approach each local station, or a **station group** consisting of several stations, and peddle their available shows. The goal is to syndicate a show in every **market area** in the country. This can be incredibly lucrative; the U.S. has just over 200 markets, and second-run episodes of hit shows can sell for hundreds of thousands of dollars—even millions. In 1986, Viacom syndicated *The Cosby Show* to 172 local stations for a record-shattering $4 million per episode.[22] In 2006, Warner Bros. syndicated *Two and a Half Men* for approximately $2 million per episode.[23] And after *Seinfeld's* first round of syndication sold for $3 million per episode;[24] it has gone on to make almost $3 *billion*.[25] Thus,

Most networks have a right of first refusal on their studio's shows. So if CBS Studios has a new show they hope to sell, they must first pitch it to CBS, their sister studio. Once CBS "passes," the studio can shop the project to other buyers.

Talk the Talk

Deficit financing—When a studio pays more to make a show than it receives as payment, hoping to make up the difference by reselling the show later.

while studios usually lose millions on a show's front end, they aim to make it up on the backend.

Because local broadcast stations often **strip** syndicated shows, airing them daily instead of weekly, the rule of thumb has typically been that studios need one hundred episodes—or about four seasons—before selling a show into reruns. Since the growth of cable, however, cable networks have been hungry for content to fill airtime, and they've been started buying second-run shows much earlier in the show's lifecycle. In 2010, after a single season on ABC, *Modern Family*'s cable, or **off-network**, syndication rights, were sold to USA for $1.5 million. That same year, TNT nabbed *The Mentalist* for over $2 million per episode, while Oxygen picked up FOX's hot newcomer, *Glee*.[26]

One huge syndication sale not only turns a profit for that particular show, it recoups a studio's losses for all the shows that never make it to syndication—which is most of them. The 2012–13 TV season saw the passing of *666 Park Avenue*, *Last Resort*, *Do No Harm*, *Emily Owens M.D.*, *Made in Jersey*, *Partners*, *Animal Practice*, *The Mob Doctor*, *Ben and Kate*, and *Guys With Kids*. These new shows never even made it to season two, and they'll remain permanent losses for their studios.

But syndication isn't important only to studios. Syndication is also where producers, creators, and stars make their big money. Remember when we learned about agency packages back in Chapter 3? Syndication is also where agents with a package earn most of their profits. (Most agencies with a package get ten percent of a show's backend. We'll discuss this more in Chapter 7.) So when *The Cosby Show* first sold into syndication, Bill Cosby took home approximately $166 million,[28] and William Morris, his agency at the time, pocketed $50 million (back then, a jaw-dropping sum).[29] *Two and a Half Men*'s first foray into syndication earned its studio, Warner Bros., an estimated $250 million (although some analysts estimate that by the time it completes its run in 2021, the show could generate $2 billion).[30]

Reality Check

Because reality shows are much cheaper and easier to produce than scripted shows (one half-hour reality show could often cost between $100,000 and $500,000, compared to almost $2 million for a scripted half-hour), there's usually no need for a studio to deficit finance a reality series. As a result, few studios participate in reality TV. Many networks purchase their reality shows directly from production companies, then finance and own the projects themselves.

What Are Production Companies?

We know what networks do—they acquire and distribute television content. We know what studios do—they develop, finance, and produce television content, then license it to networks. But what about the third type of company, production companies? What do they do?

First, let's discuss what they *don't* do. In the world of prime time scripted programming, most production companies *do not* physically produce the show. Production companies do not have their own cameras, their own lights, their own edit bays. People always think they do, but they don't. In truth, production companies develop and produce television content just like studios, except studios have one thing production companies don't: *money*. Most TV production companies do not have their own money. Rather, they fund themselves through special arrangements with studios—which, in turn, don't have something production companies have: *talent*.

This special arrangement between studios and production companies is called an **overall deal**, and it works like this: a studio comes to a writer, producer, or director

First-Look Deals

Some TV production companies, rather than having an overall deal, sign a **first-look**. With a first-look deal, a company isn't totally exclusive; rather, it gives the company's studio the right of first refusal on any projects the producer develops or acquires. If the studio passes, the company is free to take the project to other studios or buyers. First-look deals are less lucrative than overalls, and less common in television. In film, on the other hand, most producers have first-looks rather than exclusive overalls. (We'll talk about first-looks more in Part III.)

Do Agencies Commission Their Clients' Overall Deals?

Absolutely! However, if the writer sells a show while under an overall, and her agent receives a package on that show, the agency reimburses the client for any commissions she has paid. In other words, they won't double-dip, keeping both the writer's commission *and* their packaging fee.

(we'll call him Eddie) and says, "Eddie, we are such fans of your work—you've written and produced so many fantastic hours of television—we'd like to give you an overall deal." The studio then pays Eddie, the writer, a specific amount of money (usually about $1 million per year) to "own" Eddie exclusively, and any television work Eddie writes or develops, for a specific amount of time (usually one to four years). The studio pays Eddie's salary and producing fees, his staff, and any overhead. This means if Eddie comes up with a hilarious sitcom or outrageous reality show, it belongs to the studio. It also means if the studio has needs on any of its current projects, it can assign Eddie to work on them. In simplest terms, an "overall" is the exchange of money for talent and vision.

Good to Know

Overall deals usually only cover a producer's *television* work. J.J. Abrams' Bad Robot, for example, has an overall deal at Warner Bros., which covers only television. The company has a separate deal for film at Paramount. Chuck Lorre's Life's Too Short (*Mike & Molly*, *The Big Bang Theory*) and Greg Berlanoti's Berlanti Production (*Brothers & Sister*, *No Ordinary Family*), meanwhile, both have eight-figure, four-year Warner Bros. deals that cover both television *and* film.[31]

Each studio usually keeps a stable of about thirty to fifty overall deals, giving it a go-to well for new ideas or high-level staffing opportunities. Universal TV has overalls with executive producers such as *30 Rock's* Jack Burditt, *Parenthood's* Jason Katims, and *Up All Night's* D.J. Nash. Warner Bros. has *Cougar Town's* Bill Lawrence, *Will & Grace's* John Riggi, and *Celeste and Jesse Forever* writers Rashida Jones & Will McCormack.

So the Network/Studio/Pod Relationship Looks Something Like This . . .

	Comcast	Disney	NewsCorp.	CBS Corp.	Time-Warner
Network	NBC	ABC	FOX	CBS & CW (50%)	CW (50%)
Studio	Universal TV	ABC Studios	20th Century Fox TV	CBS Studios	Warner Bros.
Pods	Liz Brixius	Mark Gordon	Jason Winer	Craig Turk	Dan Lin
	Matt Hubbard	Evan Katz	Matt Reeves	Gary Fleder	Damon Lindelof
	Mike Schur	Jack Estrin	Gregg Mettler	Kevin Wade	Kevin Williamson
	Will Packer	Laurie Zaks	Dana Klein	Greg Garcia	Conan O'Brien

A couple of important things to know:

1. When we talk about television "production companies," or pods (**P.O.D.**'s) most consist of only one to three people—usually, the writer, an assistant, and maybe an executive. There's rarely a huge infrastructure.
2. Because studios have these in-house writers and pods, where is the first place they turn when they need a new idea? To winners of high-profile screenwriting contests? No. To talented staff writers writing on their shows? Doubtful. They may eventually entertain ideas from these people, but the place studios turn *first*? Their

Talk the Talk

P.O.D.–Production Overall Deal; another name for an overall deal. We often refer to overalls, or producers and companies with overalls, as "pods."

stable of overalls. Likewise, where do studios go when they need a seasoned producer to shepherd someone else's idea? To highly trained valedictorians right out of film school? Definitely not. To brilliant professors teaching structure and character at top-rated grad schools? Nope. When studios need someone to shepherd a project, they turn to the people they already trust and have invested in—their stable of overalls!

Thus, when other writers, and their agents, are out pitching or selling projects, they often go first to a successful producer or pod. After all, if you hope to sell Sony TV your great procedural idea, you're much stronger walking in with a Sony-based producer like Carla Kettner (*Bones*, *The Mob Doctor*), whom you know Sony already likes and is eager to buy from.[32] If you want to sell your single-camera comedy, you might first pitch *Up All Night* creator Emily Spivey, who has a two-year deal at 20th Century Fox.[33]

Most television projects are sold by traveling up the ladder from writer/creator to pod to studio to network. Now, let's explore how that happens.

Reality Check

Unlike scripted production companies, reality companies often *do* physically produce their own shows. Since reality programming can cost as little as five percent of a scripted show's budget, many reality companies have their own equipment: edit bays, cameras, lights, etc. This also allows them to produce shorts and web material, or selling tools like **sizzle reels** and **demo reels** (a video of clips highlighting the work of a particular actor, producer, or company).

TELEVISION'S ANNUAL SCHEDULE

For years, the broadcast networks and studios have bought, sold, developed, and produced TV shows on a rigid annual cycle. This cycle has three "seasons," each with a different purpose:

Development Season (June/July–October/November)—When shows are pitched, bought, sold, and developed.

Pilot Season (January–May)—When networks "pick up," or select, a handful of projects to shoot as pilots, or prototypes.

Staffing Season (April–June)—When broadcast networks decide which pilots will become actual series, and each show hires a staff of writers.

The television industry has been stuck in this cycle since the 1970s.[34] Every year, various networks crow about how they're breaking the mold and doing "year-round development," but I'm here to tell you . . . *it's not true*. Sure, networks occasionally order an off-cycle pilot—like in October, 2012, when NBC ordered pilots for Sascha Penn's *The Secret Lives of Husbands and Wives* and a new medical drama from *90210* executive producers Gabe Sachs and Jeff Judah[35]—but the bulk of broadcast development still follows the traditional schedule.

Cable networks *don't* follow this same annual cycle. Many have their own annual cycles, some have quarterly cycles, others buy and develop projects as they want to, willy-nilly. Most shows, however, whether on broadcast or cable channels, still undergo the same basic process—development, pilot, staffing—so it helps to understand how this process works.

Development Season (June/July–October/November)

Unlike in movies, most TV projects are sold as pitches, not pre-written scripts or **spec pilots**. TV show ideas can also spring from anywhere. Some are completely original,

Talk the Talk

Spec Pilot—A pilot script written independently of any network, studio, production company, or financier; it's simply written by a writer wanting to write a great script.

right from a writer's imagination. NBC's *Hannibal* and the CW's *The Vampire Diaries* are based on books. Showtime's *Homeland* is based on an Israeli series, *Hatufim* (*Prisoners of War*), and ABC's *Red Widow* is an adaptation of the Dutch *Penoza*. Even music can serve as the inspiration for TV shows—like in 2010, when HBO and the BBC teamed up to develop a series based on Nine Inch Nails' *Year Zero* album.[36]

Projects can also come together in a myriad of ways. Many travel the traditional writer-producer-studio-network path. Other times, a network hears a pitch first, buys it, and "lays it off" on its studio to finance and produce. An actor may have an idea and pitch it to a writer. A studio may come up with its own idea, then call agents to try and find a writer to execute it. A TV director may team up with a feature writer, then "attach" a big-name actor to star.

Also, most projects are partnerships between a writer and producer, or pod. Together, these two "entities" develop the project and take it to studios. If a studio likes the concept, they purchase it. Remember, studios, not networks, own television shows, so studios usually buy a project *before* taking it to networks. This involves making a **script commitment**, a deal in which the studio commits to paying the writer to develop and write one pilot script. Once the deal is in place, the writer, studio, and production company pitch the project to networks.

Depending on its needs, a network may allocate up to $125–$150 million a year for new development.[37] When a network's development fund runs out, usually in October or November, it's "closed" and stops taking pitches. Most networks hear about 1000 pitches per year, buying between 100 and 150 projects (both comedy and drama).

When a network buys a project, it works with the writer, studio, and production company to shape the idea into something appropriate for their audience. This may involve tweaking characters or relationships, outlining a pilot story, or brainstorming episode ideas. At every stage, the writer receives feedback from executives at the pod, the studio, and the network—all of whom may have slightly different perspectives and agendas. Finally, usually some time in early November, the producers, the studio, and the network approve the pilot outline, and they send the writer to script.

Writers usually deliver final drafts of their pilots just before the winter holidays, sending network executives home with stacks of scripts to read. Comedy execs take comedy pilots, drama execs take dramas, and higher-ups or department heads take the most important, high-profile scripts in both. When execs return in January, they sit down to discuss what scripts they liked, disliked, and what deserves to be picked up as a pilot. And thus begins Pilot Season.

Pilot Season (January–May)

Each broadcast network selects about fifteen to thirty pilot scripts, both comedies and dramas, to be produced as pilots, sample episodes the network will use to evaluate which shows should be picked up to series.

When a pilot is green-lit for production, usually in January, its writer and producers race to get to work. Most pilots must be turned in to their networks in early May, about four months down the road, and actors must be cast, designers hired, sets built, locations scouted. Because the point of a pilot is to convince the network to pick up the show to series, studios often pour more money into pilot production than they would into subsequent episodes. Many pilots cost $4–6 million, twice the cost of a regular broadcast episode.

Producers deliver their finished pilots in early May. Network executives then review all the projects, announcing which pilots will become series at May's New York **upfront presentations**, massive gala events where networks unveil their new fall schedules to advertisers, the press, and local stations from across the country.

Each network picks up about four to eight pilots to become fully-fledged series. Some shows premiere on the network's fall schedule and others are held till **mid-season** (winter or spring of the following year). At its 2012 upfronts, CBS announced four new fall shows—*Partners*, *Elementary*, *Vegas*, and *Made in Jersey*—and two new shows for mid-season, *Golden Boy* and *Friend Me*.[38] NBC announced seven for fall—*Revolution*, *The New Normal*, *Go On*, *Guys With Kids*, *Chicago Fire*, and *Animal Practice*—and one, *Do No Harm*, for mid-season.

Most new shows have a low survival rate. *Made In Jersey* and *Do No Harm* had such low ratings they were canned after two airings (CBS's *Jersey* premiered to less than 8 million viewers, then fell thirty percent in its second week;[39] NBC's *Do No Harm* opened to less than half that[40]), and, *Golden Boy*, *Vegas*, and *Men With Kids* soon joined them on the chopping block. If a network is lucky, two to four shows survive to get second seasons . . . and if a network is *really* lucky, one of those becomes a bona fide hit.

TV Development: Playing the Numbers

Pitches heard by each network:	1000
Projects bought/developed by each network:	100–150
Pilots ordered per network:	15–20
Pilots ordered to series at each network:	4–8
Shows surviving to second season per network:	2–4
Shows that become hits (hopefully) per network:	1

Staffing Season (April–June)

Almost every scripted show on television is written by a staff, or **writers room,** a team of eight to fifteen writers who—led by their showrunner—map out the show's season, outline individual episodes, and write scripts. When I worked on Disney Channel's *Dog With a Blog*, our showrunner liked using the entire staff to brainstorm story ideas and

TABLE 5.1 A Year in the Life of a TV Writer

JAN	FEB	MAR	APR	MAY	JUN	JUL	AUG	SEPT	OCT	NOV	DEC
Pilot season						Development season				Writers write and turn in pilots	
TV shows shoot, begin wrapping production			Staffing season			TV shows begin pre-production	TV shows shooting, in full production				

Talk the Talk

Punch Up: To focus on and improve specific lines, jokes, or moments within a script.

Talk the Talk

Beat Out: To outline a story in stark, simple, logical bullet points, or "beats." Each beat contains one specific piece of story information.

.

write detailed outlines for each episode, but he'd then assign a different writer to write each script. At E!'s *After Lately*, we'd come up with story ideas as a staff, then split into pairs to outline and write each episode. Other showrunners divide their staff into groups; one "**punches up**" this week's script while the other "**beats out**" episodes for next month. Some showrunners even write every episode themselves, just using their staff as researchers!

Talk The Talk

Writers room—The "room" can refer to one of two things: 1. the physical place where a writing staff meets and works, or 2. the staff itself. We often say, "Our room works this way," or "Here's how our head writer runs the room," using the words "staff" and "room" interchangeably. Physical writers rooms are often small conference rooms, with a large table in the middle and white boards tacked to the walls. Writers use these white boards to scribble story ideas, jokes, and characters arcs.

Regardless of how a staff works, most network shows hire staffs during staffing season, which means April and May are writers' best chance of getting a job each year. Sure, there are occasional cable gigs, but these are sporadic and unpredictable; staffing season is the only period when writers *know* jobs will be available. Also, many new shows don't hire until mid-May, when networks announce their upcoming schedules, creating a huge feeding frenzy, as every broadcast show scrambles to hire its writers at the same time. As a result, staffing season is an incredibly hectic, stressful time.

Good to Know

While development execs tend to specialize in comedy or drama, current execs often cover both

---

The Hierarchy of a Writers Room

Most writing staffs work as a hierarchy, so when you watch a TV show tonight, watch the names that flash by at the beginning of the episode. See all those producers, co-producers and executive producers? Those are most of the writers on the writing staff! Many writers are given producer titles, and while they may be helping with some "producing duties," the truth is, most of them are actually writers. Here's how a writers room organizes itself:

Upper Level Writers

- **Executive Producer**—Showrunners, creators, and other high-level writers. Although a show usually has only one showrunner (or a writing team serving as showrunners together), some have multiple writers with executive producer (EP) titles.
- **Co-Executive Producer**—A showrunner often selects a co-EP to be her "Number Two." Because running a show is so time and energy-consuming, most showrunners want help filling in the gaps. If the showrunner needs to go to a casting session or promo shoot, the Number Two takes over the room.
- **Supervising Producer**.

Mid-Level Writers

- **Producer**
- **Co-Producer**
- **Executive Story Editor**

Low-Level Writers

- **Story Editor**
- **Staff Writer**—A show's entry level-writing position.

For writers, staffing season begins in April, as network, studio, and production company executives begin taking meetings with writers. **Current executives** cover shows already on the air. **Development executives** cover new shows hoping to get picked up. They then make suggestions to their showrunners, who read hundreds of samples, meet with writers, and assemble their staff in May. Most writers rooms begin work in June, giving staff seven or eight weeks of writing time before production begins in late July or early August.

Reality Check

Unlike scripted television, reality TV does not follow a rigid annual calendar. While reality shows often go through the same development process—development, pilot, series pick-up—they're pitched and bought year-round. This is for three main reasons:

1. **Reality shows are cheaper and faster to produce**—so they don't often need months and months of development or pilot production time. A network can buy a reality idea, develop it, produce the pilot, and determine its fate in a matter of weeks.

2. **Broadcast networks often use reality shows to plug holes when more expensive scripted shows fail**. When NBC canceled expensive period drama *The Playboy Club* in October, 2011, it replaced it with two months of *Prime Suspect* reruns, then gave the time slot to reality series *Celebrity Wife Swap*. While *Celebrity Wife Swap* may have taken longer than two months to develop, it would have taken more time to develop another scripted series.

3. **Reality TV is the bread and butter of most cable networks**. Unlike broadcast networks, cable networks have twenty-four daily hours to fill. (Broadcast networks program about half that, as several hours of their days are programmed independently by local stations.) Thus, cable networks are constantly hunting for new content, so they like shows they can develop, and air quickly and cheaply.

---

6   Staffing Season—How Agents Help Clients Get Hired

"You always hear stories that things can abruptly end," says Jessica Kaminsky, "but you never really understand it until it happens to you." Kaminsky was unemployed. Which, to be fair, is not unusual, especially for TV writers. Every year, numerous TV shows get canceled midway through their runs, casting all of their writers, producers, actors, designers, editors, accountants, crew members, and assistants into the unemployment line. Kaminsky knew this, of course, but it didn't lessen the pain.

She had always dreamed of being a writer—first a playwright, then a TV writer—and after spending years as a writers assistant, clawing her way up the ladder, Kaminsky had finally—in spring, 1999—landed a job as a staff writer on the second season of CBS's *Ladies Man*. Five months later, only days before Thanksgiving, the network pulled the plug on the entire production, obliterating everything for which Kaminsky had worked.

That was six months ago, and Kaminsky hadn't written professionally since—not that she'd had any opportunities to do so. Writers who don't land a job during staffing season, or lose their job later, are out of luck until the following year. So Kaminsky took jobs as a substitute teacher for a swanky West Hollywood private school, a gig that kept her afternoons free so she could go to meetings or interviews. So when her agents at UTA called to tell her she had a meeting to be a writer on the sixth season of NBC's *Just Shoot Me*, she was ecstatic: "I'm like the hugest *Just Shoot Me* fan, so just the idea that I could even be meeting on that show was—I was swooning I was so happy!" says Kaminsky.

There was just one problem: Kaminsky sucked at showrunner meetings. "I would get the meetings and prepare like crazy—read the script, watch the show, and figure out exactly why they needed to have *me* (adorable, funny me) on staff. Then, when I didn't get the job, I'd be crushed. So I turned to my friend, Amanda, who at the time was doing *way* better than I was. Every time she met on a show, she got an offer. What the hell?! So I asked her—What was her secret? And more to the point, what was I doing wrong?! That's when she laid it out for me. *I wanted it too badly.* And they (showrunners) could tell. She explained that meeting with showrunners was a lot like dating. You can't be over eager. It comes off as desperate. You need to funny, relaxed, confident. Whether you really are or not. You need to be someone they would want to spend countless hours in a room with. Mainly, you have to find that balance between complimenting the show but also seeming a little detached. As if you were interviewing them too."

Kaminsky went in for her meeting, "over-prepared" as usual, but doing her best to relax. "It was a wonderful meeting," she recalls. "I was relaxed . . . we all got along super well . . . and [when] I walked out of there, I didn't know if I had it or not, but I was very pleased with how I had presented myself—which, trust me, was not always the case."

Often, when writers meet with showrunners about joining a staff, they get an answer fairly quickly. But Kaminsky heard nothing that week. Or the next week. Or the next. "I was going absolutely crazy," she says. "Experience teaches you not to assume you'll get the job—so then you assume you *won't* get the job—and then, for thinking you won't the job, you think you should be rewarded by *getting* the job."

Kaminsky began thinking up excuses to call her agents and check in, but they hadn't heard anything. "Clearly, I was freaking out," she says. "I became superstitious like a baseball player. I'd do tons of weird things—like walking to the gym the same way every single day. Then, I went through this weird period where I would set up things for myself that made absolutely no sense. 'I have to drive downtown and hit five green lights in a row.' One time, I ran a red light and got pulled over by a cop who was like, 'You just went through a red light.' And I said, 'I know, sorry. It was not because I was drunk, it was because I set a goal for myself: I had to go through five streets in a row,' So I mean, you go crazy."

By the time Memorial Day rolled around, Kaminsky had accepted the fact that she wasn't getting the job. So she did what every writer does when they hit rock bottom. "I went to a movie and I turned my phone off, which [normally] I would never do," Kaminsky says. "I came out, turned my phone on, and it immediately rang. It was my agent, and he said, 'Where were you?' 'In a movie, why?' And he says, 'You got the job!'"

Six months later, Kaminsky and her agents were standing on stage, watching David Spade and Wendie Malick spin Kaminsky's words into comedy gold. "After that," Kaminsky smiles, "I realized what a desperate nerd I'd been acting like in meetings, and I'm happy to report I've changed my ways. And yes, I've gotten the jobs."

Indeed, Kaminsky has worked steadily ever since, rising to supervising producer via shows such as *Jonas*, *So Random*, and *Men At Work*. Nevertheless, Kaminsky—like every other TV writer in Hollywood—still endures the annual agony and uncertainty of staffing season. "In a way, it gets easier, because you have the experience to know you can do the job," she says. "But noooo, it never gets easier. We chose a career where literally every six to ten months we are out of work, hustling for a new gig. We don't have a 401k. There's no security. It's a nightmare. That said, I would shoot myself if I ever had to have a regular job. So obviously, it's a very specific type of person (crazy) who seeks out this type of employment."

Of course, writers aren't the only ones stressed out by staffing season. Agents and managers, the representatives who get one window a year to find their clients' work, are equally anxious. And while for most writers, staffing begins with casual meetings in March or April, then builds to a tumult as networks announce their new and returning TV series in May, agents begin their process much sooner.

Staffing—from an agent's perspective—can be broken into five stages:

1. Preparation (January–February)
2. Network/studio meetings and script submissions (March–April)
3. Writer meetings (March–May)
4. Getting the offer (late April–late May)
5. Negotiations.

JANUARY–FEBRUARY: PREPARATIONS FOR STAFFING

As agents return from the holidays in January, they immediately begin preparing for the upcoming staffing frenzy. Their first mission: assess which clients have the best shot at getting hired. Several components factor into these decisions:

- **Which writers will be available?** In order to accept a job on a staff, a writer must be available to take a job. For some, this isn't a problem; they don't have a

On the Bubble–A term for
shows whose future is
uncertain: they have iffy
enough ratings that they may
get canceled, they may get
renewed.

current job and are eager to find one. Others are employed on returning shows,
making them unavailable. But many may be working on shows that are **on the
bubble**. In these cases, the writer may not know his or her availability until well
into staffing season, which puts agents in a sticky situation.

"Often, the client who's not available is a little hotter," says Jennifer Good, a
TV lit agent at the Alpern Group, "What's difficult is when . . . I think a show has
a thirty percent chance of coming back, and executives think, 'No, it's [definitely]
going to come back.' [Because] executives don't want to spend time on someone
who might not be available, you have to fight that perception" in order to get the
client any meetings.

These situations are also sticky because good agents don't want clients
competing with each other for jobs–especially if one client may ultimately be
unavailable. Thus, most agents take fewer chances with clients on bubble shows,
putting them up only for jobs on highly appropriate, specific shows.

- **Which current shows are returning?** Tracking which current shows may return
  and which won't helps agents prepare game plans for working and non-working
  clients alike. It obviously helps them know which clients may have jobs to return
  to, but it also helps them identify which returning shows may have *new* needs.
  After all, first-season shows aren't the only ones hiring writers. Perhaps *The Big
  Bang Theory* needs a new story editor or *Grimm* has mid-level openings. These
  are opportunities agents need to know about.

Get a Report Card

Many agents check in
periodically with their clients'
showrunners to see how
clients are performing. If it's
not going well, this helps the
agent prepare their clients for
the eventual next step. The
agent can also get
constructive criticism the
showrunner may not feel
comfortable giving directly to
the writer.

- **Which working writers may not be returning to their current show?**
  Working writers don't always return to the series they're writing on. Some get
  fired midway through the season because they're not the right creative fit. Many
  complete the current season, but aren't invited back. Others ask to be released
  from their contract for personal reasons. Occasionally, the studio fires a series'
  showrunner, and the replacement clears out the staff and hires his own writers.
  Other times, writers aren't brought back because their contract requires them to
  receive a raise and promotion, and the showrunner feels they're not worth a higher
  pay grade.
- **Which writers have the necessary samples?** To land a job, writers need
  writing samples to show executives, producers, and showrunners. There are
  generally two types of samples writers use to get TV jobs: **spec scripts** and
  original material.

Spec scripts are sample episodes of shows currently on the air. In other words,
if you hope to staff on quirky character-driven dramas, you might write your own episode
of *Parenthood* or *Suits*. If you like single-camera comedies, you might spec *The Mindy
Project* or *The New Girl*.

Original material is a piece of writing–usually something in script form: a
screenplay, pilot, or stage play–that springs wholly from the writer's imagination; it's
not based on a pre-existing property or idea. Recently, there's been a trend toward
"**spec pilots**," pilots that are written without being pitched or sold first, mainly because–
thanks to the sale of *Desperate Housewives* in 2003–networks and studios have
actually started reading them. (More on this in the next chapter.) But this doesn't mean
sample specs of current shows aren't valuable and necessary.

Exception to the Rule

Although most agents and
producers want to read
something in script form–a
pilot, screenplay, or play–I've
seen people get work using
beautifully written short
stories, essays, or articles.

"Looking at pilots is okay; it can show the the breadth of a writers work," says
executive producer Richard Gurman (*Still Standing*, *Married With Children*). "But you
still want to see a spec of a show, because it's a different art. I'm often just as–if not
more–impressed with an *Office* or *Community* [that makes me say,] 'Wow, I haven't
seen that on the show, yet this feels like one that was on the show.'"

Thus, many agents kick off their Januaries by ensuring clients are on track to deliver
new material before staffing season. Your job, as a writer, is to be constantly refreshing
your portfolio, which is why many representatives insist clients deliver at least two or
three new pieces of stellar material a year.

Plan Ahead!

Knowing that your agent or manager will want new material in January, plan accordingly to give yourself time to write and polish it. While every writer's process is different, it's safe to assume it takes three to four months to write a spec pilot. So working backwards, you want to start working on new material in August or September. This should allow you to deliver a draft to your representation in December, so you can incorporate their feedback and give them the final version at the start of the year.

What Makes a Good Writing Sample?

Most agents want writers to have a portfolio of at least three or four scripts, both sample specs and original material. Besides, the writer must not only have *enough* well-written scripts, she must have the *right* samples: scripts that are current, appropriate for jobs, and reflective of the writer's unique talents and sensibility. If your goal is to staff on a romantic comedy like *Mike and Molly*, your agent won't want to submit your gritty *Homeland* spec, no matter how brilliant it may be.

Having said this, you should try to write specs that show off different strengths. If you're a comedy writer, write a spec that illuminates your skills at hard jokes, like *The Big Bang Theory* or *Men At Work*, and another highlighting your understanding of characters and emotion, like *Raising Hope* or *Modern Family*.

Lastly, every year, certain specs become "hot." A few years ago, every aspiring TV writer in town pumped out his or her own spec episode of *The Office*. A year or two later, agents and execs were so sick of *The Office* specs, they refused to read more. The spec was cold. The best way to learn what specs are hot is to ask friends working at agencies, networks, or studios. If you don't have friends in those positions, here are a few tips you can use to figure out what shows are "specable":

- **Never spec a show in its first season**. There's no guarantee a new show will last, and a spec becomes useless once the show is off the air. Also, new shows go through growing pains as the writers learn what jokes work, which actors can deliver, which characters have chemistry, etc.
- **No shows older than four years**. Even if they're still hits, shows tend to lose their freshness for execs and producers. Maybe readers have already waded through 6000 specs of that show, or maybe they're just sick of talking about it, but most shows start to age round season four.
- **Check into the zeitgeist**. What shows are selling well on iTunes? Which get a lot of high-caliber guest stars? (You knew FX's *Louie* was taking off when it started having guest appearances by people such as Chris Rock, Jerry Seinfeld, and David Lynch.) What are critics raving about at important cultural publications like *The New York Times*, or perhaps more importantly, at hipper places like *L.A. Weekly*, *Salon*, and *The Onion*? This will give you a fair idea of which shows people are buzzing about.

Your agent won't want to send out your five-year-old stage play, either. Sure, it may be a small-town comedy perfect for *Parks and Recreation*, but if it's no longer indicative of your current writing ability or worldview, it's not a great sample. Besides, execs and showrunners hate reading pieces they've read before, so if your agent already submitted your play last year, it's no longer an effective calling card.

Joke Packets and Sketch Packs

Talk shows (*The Tonight Show*, *Conan*), clip shows (*The Soup*, *The Daily Show*), and sketch shows (*Saturday Night Live*) also hire based on writing samples, but since these shows aren't story-based, writers usually use **joke** or **sketch packets**. These usually include ten to twenty monologue-style jokes, and a handful of comedy sketches. Sometimes writers submit material they've already written or produced; other times, shows request new material based on certain themes or suggestions. A talk show, for example, may want jokes about current events or ideas for man-on-the-street bits and pranks.

Tweet This!

Many joke writers (and stand-up comics) work out new material on Twitter, which favors funny and forces brevity. Some writers even submit their Tweets as part of their joke packs, and many talk shows and showrunners monitor Twitter for new voices!

As agents make sure clients have new material to go out with, they also collect and read all the greenlighted pilots, thinking about each project's tone and which clients may be appropriate to write on it. Agents then start checking with execs about various shows' needs. Development executives cover new show or pilots; current executives cover shows already on the air.

In late January and February, development execs are juggling all the pilots entering production, so they're not yet focused on staffing. Current execs, meanwhile, are busy helping shows finish their seasons—writing, producing, and posting their final episodes. They're also looking ahead to next season, thinking about each show's upcoming creative needs. Will the show be looking for fresh blood in the writers room? Firing or hiring directors? Replacing a showrunner? Agents also use late January and early February to begin sending current execs samples of potential writers for returning series. After all, new shows may not hire till they receive an official pick-up in May, but current shows often know their fate earlier. In March, 2013, two months before it announced its new shows, CBS renewed four comedies and nine dramas, including *The Big Bang Theory*, *Mike and Molly*, *NCIS*, and *Person of Interest*. This allows current shows to hire new writers as early as March or April.

Aim for the Bottom

Because execs are so busy in January and February, it's not always easy for managers and agents to get the attention they want. Thus, many reach out to junior execs, coordinators, or assistants, knowing if they can get a low-level exec to fall in love with a writer early on, he'll champion the writer to upper-level execs down the road.

Here's the hierarchy of current and development executives at most networks, studios, and production companies:

- Sr. Vice President
- Vice President
- Director
- Manager
- Coordinator
- Assistant

Agent Communication 101

Starting in February, read all the pilots and tell your representative which are your favorites. This helps them concentrate their efforts. (Any good agent should be able to provide you with all the pilots being produced. If your agent can't, you need a new agent.)

"I try to limit [submissions] to two or three writers per exec," says TV agent Jen Good. "If you send two or three good samples, the door is open for me to make another call later, [but] if you send five things that are terrible [the exec isn't] going to take your call again."

Exactly what samples the agent chooses to send depends on the level of the writer. "TV writing jobs are two-fold," Good explains. "There's the writing part, and the producing part, the ability to come up with story and also cast and run your own episode. [With] a higher-level writer, you have more leeway in what you can send, because they've been working on a show for the past five years. If there's a show looking for a strong Number Two, someone who can run their own episodes, maybe even the room, it's important to have a great sample, but it may not be as important for the sample to be perfect for that show. If I'm submitting someone more junior, it's more about writing than producing, so I better have a sample that's going to speak to the tone of their show."

As agents are monitoring pilot progress and contacting execs, TV lit coordinators are busy putting together one of the agencies' most useful staffing tools: **staffing books**, a giant volume containing resumes or credits for almost every TV writing client—even if they're already working and not technically available to staff. The book is divided into comedy and drama sections, which are in turn divided according to upper-level writers, mid-level writers, and low-level writers. Writers within each level are arranged alphabetically. (To see what a writer's credits look like, take a peek at the sample credits on page 76.)

Once coordinators complete the first draft of the staffing book, the TV lit department convenes to scrutinize each page and make sure every client's credits are up-to-date and accurate. The only writers not included are uncredited baby writers who have never staffed or sold anything. "When an agent's representing somebody with no credits, it's their responsibility to make sure that person gets the job," says ICM lit agent Melissa Orton.

In other words, while the entire agency may band together to help a credited writer land a gig, this doesn't happen with newbies, or **baby writers**. "**Breaking a baby**," or landing someone his first gig, is such a Herculean task, "it's your individual agent's job to sell you," says Orton. As a result, most agencies don't include babies in their staffing books.

Exception to the Rule

There is one type of baby writer that *does* get included in agency staffing books: **diversity writers**, writers who qualify as ethnically "diverse" (black, Latina, Native American, etc.). Many studios have "diversity programs" that encourage shows to hire minority staff writers. Each studio defines "diversity" a bit differently, but for years, Hollywood has been anxious to get more diversity onto traditionally writing staffs dominated by white males. Diversity writers aren't paid from a show's production budget; they're paid through a special fund established by the studio, essentially making them "free" to any show that hires them. As a result, diversity writers are much easier to staff than white male writers.

Most coordinators finalize their staffing books by late February, when the next stage of staffing season kicks into gear.

MARCH–APRIL: NETWORK/STUDIO MEETINGS AND SCRIPT SUBMISSIONS

March usually kicks off with agents setting **staffing meetings**, which are a chance for each agency's entire TV lit department to sit with each network or studio's current and development departments to present their staffing books and discuss the network or studio's staffing needs. Most agencies take separate meetings with the comedy development, drama development, and current departments at each network and studio—meaning agents spend most of March going on approximately twenty staffing meetings.

"We start [each meeting] by asking, 'Is there anything specific you have needs for right now?' 'Do you need a showrunner on anything?' 'Is there a returning show you're going to have needs on?'" says Orton. Once the network or studio's needs have been

BUFFY WINTERS
Writer/Producer

TELEVISION

Unchained	Supervising Prod.	ABC
Feel Your Love Tonight	Producer	ABC
Take Me Back	Co-Producer	USA
Blind Script Deal (half-hour comedy)	Writer	20th Century Fox
Bullethead	Co-Producer	NBC
The Trouble With Never	Exec Story Editor	NBC
Atomic Punk	Staff Writer-Story Ed.	CW

FILM

Sorry For It All (in development)	Writer	Paramount
Dirty Work (optioned)	Writer	Relativity
Empty House (w/ Xander Willow)	Writer	Happy Madison/Sony

THEATER

Adelaide	Playwright/Director	Final Stage Theater
The Welding Game*	Producer	Piebenga Players
Welcome To Splitsville	Director	Final Stage Theater

* Winner of the 2009 Sophocles Drama Award

2533 Glen Drive • Los Angeles, CA 90034 • P: 323-555-5150 • F: 323-555-1984 • www.bigassagency.com

discussed, everyone opens their staffing book. Each executive has their own copy, which has been sent to them ahead of time by the agent's coordinator. The agents guide the execs through the book, giving a "sales pitch" on each writer, beginning with upper-levels.

"You know Curt Tindell," the agent might say. "He's no longer working on *Once Upon a Time*, so he's available. He just did a mini-series for Starz, and he's got a novel coming out this October. He's also got a killer *White Collar* spec, which you have to read—it kind of turns the whole show on its head in a really wonderful way."

Many execs know or have read most working mid- or upper-level writers. Occasionally, there's a writer an exec doesn't know and wants to familiarize himself with. Other times, agents encourage execs to read a new piece by an older writer. All this is captured by the agency's coordinator, who jots down which scripts to send where.

The only writers who don't get the full treatment are the low-levels. "[Staff writers] don't play a huge role in shaping the voice of the show," says co-producer Anupam Nigam (*Psych*, *Defiance*). "That's the showrunners and upper-level writers; staff writers are there to just carry the ball. They're not expected to break stories on their own; they're there to replicate what's already been done in the pilot. That's a big thing when execs read people's samples: does it seem like they can replicate the showrunner's voice?"

As a result, execs often ask agents to spotlight just one or two low-level stand-outs, usually those with unique backgrounds that could be nice matches with a specific show. "If you just say, 'Hey, this guy's a great writer,' an executive's ears are not going to perk up," says Verve agent Amy Retzinger. "Nobody wants a 'good writer.' There are a million 'good writers.' They need: 'This person used to be a former CSI tech themselves.' Or, 'This person was a lawyer in a former life.' Whatever meshes with what they might need."

After the staffing meeting, agents compile and send over execs' requested scripts. Big agencies may send over 50–100 scripts, boutiques may only send five or six. The hope is execs will enjoy the scripts enough to meet with the writers for staffing.

Covering agents send their scripts and writers to production companies as well. If sending the same scripts and writers to networks, studios, and production companies seems like overkill, think again. All this redundancy is essential, because in order to get staffed on a series, *writers must be approved by the show's network, studio, production company, and showrunner.*

Ask An Agent

Q: If my agent's going to be pitching me at all these network and studio staffing meetings, should I have a conversation with her first so I can fill her in on my plans and goals for next season?

A: If you're an upper-level writer—sure. "If someone says, 'I don't want to staff this year, I just want to sell a pilot,' you should prep your agent so they don't do a bunch of legwork if you're not planning on taking the job," says Melissa Orton of ICM.

But for younger writers, "sadly, it doesn't matter much," counters Verve agent Amy Retzinger. "If you tell your agent, 'I really want to go on *Breaking Bad*,' your agent is going to roll their eyes. Everybody wants to be on *Breaking Bad*. [Staffing] is much more about what positions are open at the time [and] 'does this person fit?' It's rare that the show someone's most passionate about also happens to need someone—at that moment—with their specific skill set, and they find a match. As an agent, you have to consider all opportunities, and pursue all opportunities, within reason. We're going to pitch you for everything you're right for."

Talking to your agent before these meetings *can* be helpful if you have some useful info to offer. For instance: "You know, [*Breaking Bad* creator] Vince Gilligan and I go to the same yoga class," or, "I used to cook crystal meth in my younger days." "Something that can give me a talking point to pitch you," says Retzinger, "that's helpful!"

Exception to the Rule

Some "races" have more "horses" than others. Sometimes, says TV agent Jen Good, "you're covering the creator and the showrunner, the non-writing producer and the other non-writing producer, the studio executive, the junior, the high-level, and the network executives. You'll be covering seven different people for one show that may not even get picked up!"

A Quick Break for a Helpful Metaphor

I like to think of staffing as a horse race. There are four horses: Network Approval, Studio Approval, Production Company Approval, and Showrunner Approval. But instead of competing *against* each other, these horses only win if they *all* cross the finish line. Your agent is the jockey, riding and managing all four horses at the same time, and your competition is all the other teams of horses out there—racing to get *their* horses across the line. If your agent manages to get all four of your horses across the finish line before anyone else, *you get a job.*

Sound tough? A little. But remember: you're not just in one race, you're in a different race for *every writing job out there.* If your agent has put you up for jobs on ABC's *Once Upon a Time*, NBC's *Revolution*, and the CW's *Arrow*, you need separate sets of approvals for each one.

TELEVISION AGENTS

Now, imagine you're a drama writer. It's staffing season, and each of the five broadcast networks currently has eight eight dramas on the air. Let's also estimate each network has ten drama pilots contending for one of next season's timeslots. That's eighteen potential dramas per network, or ninety potential dramas across all five networks.

Of course, most shows won't get picked up, and those that do won't hire at every level, and those that do often hire friends or colleagues the showrunner has already worked with—so no writer actually has ninety chances to land a job. But since agents don't know which shows will go—or which will hire at certain levels—they must pursue every possible opportunity for each client.

Estimating the average TV lit agent has twenty-five drama clients, this means each agent spends staffing season managing *2,250 different "horse races,"* or staffing opportunities—just for drama (ninety possible shows x twenty-five clients = 2,250 different drama "races"). Add in an agent's comedy writers, and you're talking about almost 4,500 different "races" the agent has to manage! (2,250 drama possibilities + 2,250 comedy possibilities = 4,500 total staffing possibilities.)

"What's really stressful," Good says, "is you have to track it all, be on top of it all, and you know it may all be for nothing. But you have to do it. You have to act like every single show is going to happen."

So when writers complain their agents aren't calling them back during staffing season—"*What the hell are they doing all day?!*"—this is what they're doing all day. I'm not excusing your agent for not calling you back. You deserve the courtesy of a call, and two-way communication is the foundation of any good business relationship. But juggling all of this can be crazy-making, even for the most efficient representative. So understanding and empathizing with your agents' situation may, hopefully, help you consider how to better approach or communicate during staffing season.

You Can't Handle the Truth!

There's an unhappy fact every writer must eventually accept: *not all clients are created equal.* And when it comes to the feeding frenzy of staffing season, agents focus their energies on clients who have the best chances of bringing in revenue. As we discussed earlier, these chances are based on several factors, including availability, diversity status, and having the right writing samples. But other factors also affect where agents pour their energy:

- **Level of the writer**–"Higher level people with more fans and a proven track record are going to be your priority," says Good, "especially early on, because they get staffed first." Upper-level writers also bring in more money, allowing agents to keep their lights on. If an agent staffs two mid- or upper-level writers, each making $300,000 a year, the agent brings in $60,000 in commission ($30,000 x 2). A low-level writer earning **WGA minimum**, or "scale," may make $130,000—but for an agent commissioning ten percent, that's only $13,000—not enough to sustain a business.
- **New material**–"A big priority are people who have a new piece of material that I am excited about," says Good. "They get a little more attention; they just do." A new piece of writing not only helps an agent introduce a client to new execs and showrunners, it allows her to re-excite producers and executives who already know the writer. (It also lets an agent re-introduce the writer to people who may not be fans. A new piece of writing can change their minds!)
- **Studio writing programs**–Many studios also have writing programs designed to find talented young writers and groom them for staffing. Because these programs are a direct pipeline to the studios' shows, acceptance is extremely competitive. In fact, agents often swarm these programs looking for new clients, knowing they have a huge leg up when staffing rolls around. (We'll learn more about studio writing programs on page 261.)

- **The writer's current job**–Young writers working as a writers assistant, script coordinator, or showrunner's assistant also have a distinct advantage during staffing. Hopefully, an aspiring writer works for a showrunner who likes to promote his assistants, giving her a direct pathway to an actual writing job, but even without a promotion, these assistants and coordinators often have a cadre of professional friends and colleagues who can either hire them or make referral calls. They also have a much stronger sense of what it takes to survive and succeed in a writers room. "One of the the first times I was in a writers room," says Kelly Galuska (*Emily Owens, M.D.*), "I realized that the writing is really a small part–not a *very* small part– but it is only part of the skill set you need to be a writer in the room. Learning the dynamics of being in the room, pitching ideas, is a whole other ballgame . . . so it helped to spend time in that environment and get used to it."

So considering all these factors, who is an agent's top priority? "Being brutally honest," says Good, "the priority will be a higher-level client with a fresh piece of material." Thus, if an agent were to rank her client list according to each client's priority level, it might look something like this:

1. Upper-level clients with a new piece of writing.
2. Mid- or upper-level clients coming off shows.
3. Diversity staff writers or writers currently in a studio writing program.
4. Baby writers with a good professional job (writers assistant, etc.) and new material.
5. True baby writers–those with no professional job, experience, or inroads.

For baby writers "who aren't a writers assistant, script coordinator, or diversity writer," says Good, "it's going to be tough to even get on the radar."

MARCH–MAY: WRITER MEETINGS

This begins the period most writers view as staffing season, when they actually start getting involved and taking meetings. There are three types of meetings writers take during this time: **generals, staffing meetings,** and **showrunner meetings**.

General meetings are casual meet-and-greets, opportunities for executives or non-writing producers to sit with a writer, gauge his personality, see how he might fit with one of their writing staffs. Most execs take generals throughout the year, even beyond staffing season, simply to maintain relationships and meet new writers.

Staffing meetings, like generals, take place with executives or non-writing producers, but they're for specific shows. If *Modern Family* is hiring, you may have a staffing meeting with a current executive at ABC, the network that airs the show, and another meeting with a current executive at 20th Century Fox, the studio that makes the show. Neither of these execs has the authority to hire you, but they can recommend you to the show's creators and showrunners, Steve Levitan and Christopher Lloyd. (You'll also need the network and studio's approvals if Levitan and Lloyd want to hire you.)

Showrunner meetings are the most coveted kind of meeting, as they're with a show's ultimate decision-maker, the creator or showrunner. Showrunner meetings are the last taken, as A) many showrunners don't know if their show will be picked up until the final moments of staffing season, and B) showrunners are so busy, producing pilots or running shows, they rarely think about staffing until the last possible moment. As a result, most showrunners don't take a meeting unless they've read and truly appreciated a writer's work. If you get a showrunner meeting, it's the final job interview; the showrunner likes your writing, she just wants to judge whether you'll be a good fit for her staff.

Unfortunately, showrunner meetings aren't easy to come by. You usually need to have a personal connection with a showrunner, or know someone who has a connection. This is where agents come in and why their weeks of preparation and communication with executives and producers is so important.

How Agents Get You Meetings

Remember all those scripts agents sent to execs in February? About two weeks after sending them, agents begin following up to see what scripts the execs liked and which writers to schedule for generals. Even getting generals is harder than you might think. One studio exec estimated that during staffing season, she receives over 150 scripts per week. As if that's not enough, development execs are busy overseeing pilots, and current execs are still embroiled in production on airing shows. Thus, execs must prioritize which scripts they actually read.

"Most agents send you material that has nothing to do with what you've asked for," says Kristina Speakman, Disney Channel's Director of Current Series, who also spent several years at Spelling Television (*Beverly Hills 90210*, *Melrose Place*). So "based on a writer's experience and credits, we have a preconceived notion of whether that client is right for the project. We know when agents are pushing their A clients, their B clients, and their C clients. A-clients are 'Oh my god, here's who I called to request— we know this person would be right for this show!' B-clients are: 'I'm familiar with this person, but they're not right for my project, so I can't spend my time looking at the material.' C-clients are unknowns. 'This is a brand new person [who] doesn't have the experience I'm looking for, but I'll give the writer the courtesy of becoming familiar with them.' That's when the pile grows—the pile of priority reads, and the pile of 'I'll get to this [later] so I can be familiar with the writer, but its not for here and now.'"

Unfortunately, sometimes an exec "doesn't respond" to a script. In these cases, the execs tell the agent it's a "pass," and the agent tries to get feedback. Did the story not track logically? Were the characters poorly drawn? Was it not funny or suspenseful? "One opinion is not necessarily going to change my [mind] on something," says Good. However, "there are certain notes worth hearing, and I give feedback to clients, good or bad. I might say, 'They have a point,' or '[This note] is not worth doing; that was just their feedback.' But if I hear the same comment from four or five people, I might say, 'Before we get [the script] out to more people, maybe this is worth addressing.'"

TABLE 6.1

Name	Level	Credits	Rep	Comments	Status
Freeman, Amy	EP/Co-EP	*Outta Space*, *Spanked*, *Bad Women*	Tony Menken, Excellent Artists	*Photo Booth* (spec pilot)—Divorced mom realizes she's a lesbian, begins dating women–feels a bit schticky, some funny jokes; *The New Girl*: "Generals"–Good spec, feels like show, hilarious drunk scene, love	Good for *Capricornia*? Possible dev.? SET MTG
Martin, Jacques	Prod.	*Heaven Help Us*, *Don't Need Love*	Gina Stoker, GBA	*Be Mine Tonight* (pilot)—Family adopts problem child–UGH – how does this guy work? Lame story, not funny, feels totally unbelievable. NO.	PASS
Greene, Eloise	SE	*Jar of Fireflies*	Ava Negry, Eclectic	*Scandal* (spec)—Ok, voices=good, story a bit dull, read something else; *Natural Tendency* (play)—Woman's stalker traps her in apartment–cool! Premise feels a bit cliche, but great execution.	General mtg: 3/14–fun in room, talked re: UCLA, hilarious story re: mom's shirt

The agent must also determine whether the exec is going to "**block**" the client, or keep him from getting a job. "I cover [a particular studio]," says Orton, "and one of the execs there, a VP, is picky; he knows what he likes and what he doesn't. So when I cover shows with him, I literally say, 'Are you going to block this person? Are you gonna tell your exec producer not to hire him?' And he'll say, 'No, but I'm not going out of my way to get this person a job.'"

If the executive does like the script, the agent schedules a general meeting for the writer, usually for a week or two later. This is also when agents begin "**agenting**," leveraging positive feedback from one place to generate heat at another. For example, let's say an agent has submitted her client, Bob, to a network, studio, and production company. The studio and production company haven't yet read Bob's material, but a network executive just read Bob's script, loved it, and wants to set a meeting. "If I've gotten a little bit of traction on Bob from the network," says Orton, "I will email the studio, and CC the network, saying, 'So-and-so read Bob's script and we're setting a meeting. Just wanted to let you know, if you want to check him out soon.' Any tiny inkling of interest you can turn into heat is the name of the game."

What Happens in a General or Staffing Meeting

Some writers grumble and complain about generals because they don't lead directly to getting hired or making a sale; they're more like "first dates" to let two people get to know each other. Personally, I love generals. I've had generals that have led to jobs down the road, but also to double dates, parties, and lifelong relationships. And because generals are specifically *not* about an immediate sale or hire, there's no pressure. You can go in relaxed, comfortable, ready to chat and enjoy yourself.

Most general meetings are held in the executive's office at network or studio headquarters, which means you'll often be driving onto a studio lot. Your agent will

Getting Agented—"'Agented' is just another word for being sold or manipulated, which happens in every business every day," says Andy Bourne, Sr. Vice President of Television at Closed on Mondays Entertainment. "It comes down to someone else imposing their will on you in a way that makes you feel like you were sold. I recently read the Steve Jobs biography, and you could apply that term to him. He made everyone else around him see his vision and buy in. Some people assign that term a negative connotation—I think it's just part of selling and part of the business."

What's it sound like to "get agented?" And how do execs respond? Probably something like this. This is the transcription of a semi-imaginary conversation between Cooper, a (fictional) literary agent, and Ellen, a current executive at a prominent cable network:

COOPER: So what'd you think of Nolan's script? Pretty great, huh?
ELLEN: To be honest, I didn't really respond to it.
COOPER: Really? Everyone else loves it. The guy's on fire right now.
ELLEN: Who else read it?
COOPER: They just read him at 20th for *Modern Family*, and they're reading him at Nickelodeon for the new Victoria show.
ELLEN: Okay, well, send me something else. I just didn't get into this one.
COOPER: You want to go ahead and set a meeting and I'll shoot something over tonight?
ELLEN: Let me read him first.
COOPER: All right . . . I just don't want you to miss out.
ELLEN: I'll take my chances.
COOPER: (Calling to his assistant, but so Ellen can hear) Hey, Lily—can you email Nolan's *Chicken Switch* pilot to Ellen at Disney? Then follow up tomorrow about setting a meeting. (Back to Ellen) Awesome—we'll get it to you tonight.

Luckily, Ellen didn't get *too* agented, although she did get roped into reading a second script. "That's the agent doing they're job," says Disney Channel executive Christina Speakman. "I'll never fault the writer. If your agent is strong-arming people and getting you in the door, kick it wide open! Sometimes [as an executive,] you get into a room with a writer and their personality might fit the bill. [So] come in and impress me!"

have called to ensure the executive's assistant gets you a "drive-on," a pass to enter and park on the lot. I'm not gonna lie: even after almost fifteen years in the industry, there's something thrilling about driving onto a lot. This is where movies are made, TV shows are shot! You'll see cameramen carrying equipment, producers strolling to lunch, writers and actors discussing scripts. It is, if nothing else, a reminder of why you love this business.

When you arrive at a general meeting, an assistant will greet you in the lobby, offer you a water, and ask you to relax in the lobby. Eventually, the execs will be ready, and the assistant guides you into the office or conference room to begin the meeting.

"It always opens with a bit of small talk," says writer Paula Yoo (*Eureka*, *The West Wing*), "You talk about the weather, or if you're both fans of *American Idol*: 'Oh my God, did you see last night's episode?' Eventually, the executive will steer the conversation: 'I really enjoyed reading your sample. How'd you come up with that idea?' [Or], "I see your last credit was (whatever TV show). What was that like?' You say, 'It was such a great experience working with so-and-so,' or, 'I grew up watching my favorite TV shows on this network,' or, 'I never thought in a million years I'd ever be able to work on a science fiction show. I was such a geek in high school!' You have to talk

How Many General Meetings Should I Expect During Staffing Season?

Writers always get anxious during staffing season, fearing they're not having enough meetings, or they're having fewer than other writers. The truth is that the number of generals you have is not an accurate gauge of your chances at success. In fact, your number of generals depends on several things:

- **Mid- and upper-level writers often have fewer meetings.** The purpose of a general is to introduce you to execs at networks, studios, and production companies. Veteran writers who have been around tend to know more people, so they require fewer generals.

  On the other hand, "if you haven't worked in a while, it's important to get out there and do some generals," says manager Jeff Holland of The Cartel. "Executives and producers change; they move into different positions at different companies, whether it's studios, producers, pods . . . so it depends how active you've been in the business lately. And, frankly, how hot you are, because you're only as good as your last credit."

- **How many generals did you have outside of staffing season?** Good agents get generals for their clients year-round. In fact, most generals happen *outside* of staffing season, when execs have more time to read and meet new talent. This way, by the time staffing starts, "the client should have met everybody in town, all the networks and studios," says Roy Ashton of The Gersh Agency.

  "[Last fall], we signed a guy from *Californication*," says Holland. "He started as a staff writer and moved up to co-producer, but he had never met anybody in the business because it was his first job and he signed [right away] with CAA. He's not working now because *Californication* is wrapping up. So we probably had, in two months, about six generals . . . and we expect to have another six in the next two months. And I suspect during staffing season, since he hasn't been exposed, [he'll have] twenty-some odd generals."

- **Do you have new material?** Writers with a great new piece of material get more generals, as agents can use it to put a writer back on an exec's radar. Other times, agents use pitches as reasons to introduce writers to new execs. A writer with a well-delivered pitch can impress—even if the pitch isn't exactly right for a particular exec or company.

  "The executive can think, 'That idea didn't quite work, but it was well thought-out, and I really like that writer,'" says Jen Good of the Alpern Group. Often, this leaves an even stronger impact on an executive than just having a good meeting.

  Thus, the question writers should be asking is *not* "How many generals should I have?" It's "Where do I not have contacts or relationships? At what companies do I *need* a general?" These are the places you and your agent want to target for meet-and-greets, and ideally, *before* staffing season.

about yourself, but don't come off as [bragging]. Talk about your passion for storytelling; everyone—whether an executive or agent or writer or producer—we're all passionate about storytelling."

Hopefully, you've also done your research on the executive: their background, their career trajectory. I have a friend who peruses people's Facebook pages. If she sees a particular exec is a ski buff, she'll do some quick reading on current ski trends and conditions, so she can talk like a ski buff herself!

"You want to make *them* feel good, too," says Yoo. "Once you've talked about each other, the executive will say, 'Well, these are the types of shows we're looking at for the fall season. Some of the shows that may return are classic nuggets like this procedural show, or this character drama.' That's your turn to say, 'I love that show!'

What Should I Wear to a General Meeting?

"Don't dress up, but don't look homeless. Jeans, a nice shirt, not a tie. Casual, but so they know you're not going to stink up a room when you walk into it."–Francisco Castro (*Without a Trace*, *Urban Games*)

"This is a bit of a double standard for women, but you have to be a bit more fashionable, without trying to hard. You want to be yourself, just a bit more enhanced. If you're going to interview for something at the CW, or a young hip channel, dress [like] what the show would be [or] the brand of the network. If you're a Gen X woman like me, I'm not going to wear blue jeans and a nice shirt; I'm going to wear a cute outfit that doesn't look too young but still shows I'm fashion forward and hip."–Paula Yoo, co-producer (*Eureka*, *The West Wing*)

Or, if it's not your type of show: 'I'm not a procedural fan, but I love the actor on that show. I love what you do with his character.' Play off your strengths, but come across as sincere."

The exec may also ask which pilots you've been reading. Your agent or manager should have supplied you with all the picked-up pilots. Read them all–especially ones from the company where you're meeting. Let the exec know which pilots you enjoyed; try to find a personal connection that proves why you'd be a valuable contributor to the series. If the show is about a professional gambler, mention that you used to work in a casino. If the show's about twentysomethings working at their old high school, talk about your experiences teaching, or how you're still haunted by your own traumatic high school experiences.

I usually end a general saying something like: "Well, this has been really fun. I'd love to find something to do together, so if there's anything you need, or anything I can help you with, please let me know." This is a gentle way of saying "I hope you hire me for something" without seeming desperate.

Ask the Executive

Q: I was recently fired from a show I was working on. I got along with the showrunner and staff–it just wasn't the right show for me. What do I say when I'm meeting with other executives and producers? Do I say, "I had a great time, but it was a hard procedural, and to be honest, I'm not a hard procedural guy"? If I say that, will it cut off opportunities for me?

A: "No, because then you're going to tell me what you *are* good at: '[*Grey's Anatomy*]– I can knock it out of the ballpark. I can pitch you three or four story ideas right now.' And you start selling yourself. Demonstrate to me what you are good at– you know yourself better than I do. You're a writer, it's all in your head, so if you don't tell me I don't know it."–Kristina Speakman, director of current series, Disney Channel

I call my agent immediately after the meeting to brief her, especially if there was anything particularly positive (like the executive saying "I'm sending your script to the showrunner tonight!") or negative (like me accidentally insulting one of the network's shows). This helps my agent prepare for her follow-up call to the executive, which she usually puts in the next day.

The goal of a general is to get the writer on one of the execs' show lists. Each staffing season, execs keep lists of writers for each show they cover, divided into the

The Top Eight Ways to Ace a General Meeting

1. Get some background info from your agent. Learn "how long [the exec] has been at the company, if they are married, single, kids, whatever. I try to give a little personal information so people can connect on that level. I'll say, 'She's got a daughter who's four and your son is four, so mention that.'"–Jen Good, agent The Alpern Group

2. "Find out from your agent all the shows this executive covers. Watch as many of those shows as you can. You want to act like you're an authority on these shows."–Anupam Nigam, producer (*Defiance, Psych*)

3. "Be prepared to listen with genuine interest as a producer or exec talks about their children for more than half the meeting. That's not a dig; it's just a realization that even though you may consider this a big opportunity, the person sitting across from you just thinks of this as another day at work. What these meetings are really about is demonstrating you're a genial, intelligent human being, the kind of person other people like to be around. It also helps to be super attractive."–Gabe Uhr, writer (*People's Choice Awards, Spike TV VGA Video Game Awards*)

4. "Re-read your own script, whatever script your agent sent to the exec, and be ready to talk in-depth about it: why you made certain creative decisions, what inspired you to write it, etc."–William M. Akers, screenwriter/author (*Lois & Clark, Deserter, Your Screenplay Sucks!*)

5. "Be able to verbalize what your strengths are . . . I'm not saying your strength is only writing for legal shows, but if you stand out in that area, brand that so executives . . . can sell you to shows that are going to hire you." Karen Horne, Vice President of Programming, Talent Development, and Inclusion, NBC Entertainment/Universal Television

6. "Get up to speed on current pop culture topics and trends. Watch the hot shows on TV. See whatever movie is winning the box office. Listen to the top songs on iTunes. Tune in to NPR or Rush Limbaugh to find something interesting or provocative to chat about. Present yourself as someone who loves staying current and absorbing pop culture." Gil Cunha, Supervising Producer (*Hello Ross, Love You, Mean it with Whitney Cummings*)

7. "Paint a vivid picture of your background. You never know, an interesting experience you've had might trigger an idea for a show."–Melissa Sadoff Oren, writer (*State of Georgia, First Day*)

8. "Never underestimate the power of a hand-written thank-you card. If you get a meeting or interview, a proper old-school thank-you card is golden. (Your mom was right on this one.)"–Scott Seiffert, executive, DreamWorks Animation SKG

various levels of a writing staff. Thus, when it comes time for showrunners to begin hiring, execs pass along their lists of pre-approved writer recommendations. Show-runners are so busy, says Orton, they "tend to need guidance from the network, studio, and producer of whom to read. If you're not on those lists and approved by those three areas, it's that much harder to get the creator to read you and take you as a serious submission."

Unfortunately, not all generals go as well as Nolan's (see the textbox at top of p. 87). "I have an upper-level client who has worked for so long he's never really done generals," says one Big Four agent. "He went in (for a general) and was really quiet, passive. So when I called this specific executive, I said, 'This man has a tie to the creators of [a hit sitcom]; do you think we can put him in the room? And the exec said, 'I've just met people I like more. I'll bring him up, but I'm not going to go out of my way to get a meeting.'"

How Do Agents Follow Up After a Meeting?

Here's what a conversation might sound like when Cooper, our agent from a few pages ago, follows up with Ellen about his client, Nolan:

COOPER: So, Nolan thought you were awesome yesterday.
ELLEN: Yeah, he was great. Talk about an interesting background!
COOPER: Did he tell you the Alaska story?
ELLEN: Incredible! He'll dine out on that story for years!
COOPER: So, can you put him on your lists?
ELLEN: Of course! He'd be perfect for *Light Up the Sky*.
COOPER: Oh, he loves that show. Is Debbie (the showrunner) reading yet?
ELLEN: No, but I'll send his stuff over as soon she is. Hit me back in a couple weeks.
COOPER: Terrific—thanks.
ELLEN: Also, if you haven't called Marta in development, give her a shout. Nolan would be good for her demon-hunting thing.
COOPER: The Merz and Martin project?
ELLEN: Yeah.
COOPER: Nolan adores those guys. He's seen every episode of *Drop Dead Legs*. You cool if I say you told me to call?
ELLEN: Tell you what—I'll call Marta today and give her a heads-up, tell her how much I like this guy.

Once Cooper gets off the phone, he immediately does four things:

1. Emails Marta in development.

2. Makes a note to check in with Ellen in a couple weeks to see if she's submitted Nolan to *Light Up the Sky*.

3. Calls execs at other networks and studios, using the success of Nolan's meeting with Ellen to try to get another. Cooper may say, "Nolan just had a great meeting at NBCU. Ellen's sending him to Debbie for *Light Up the Sky*. You wanna schedule a time to sit down with him?" Or, "Warners is pushing him for *Light Up the Sky*. You wanna sit down with him for *Born at Zero*? I'd hate for you guys to miss out."

4. Records his notes in his own staffing charts. (See the box on page 88.)

In It for the Long Haul

The point of the general is not just to meet someone for thirty minutes, it's to *start a relationship*. So your job, once you leave, is to nurture your relationship with that executive or producer. Send a casual thank-you email the next day to thank them for sitting down with you. Mention something specific you talked about, to personalize the experience and plant something memorable in the exec's head. Also, friend that person on Facebook. "You might not see them for another three or four years, and it's easy to forget a face," says Jeff Holland, a lit manager at The Cartel, "but if you're on their Facebook page, you can help keep up and network."

Does this mean the client has no chance of landing a job on that sitcom—or any other of the execs' shows? Not necessarily, but it does mean the agent must work a bit harder. "It's going to be up to your agent to get the [show] creator on the phone and say, 'You have to hire this person,'" says Orton. Of course—as we'll see in a moment—that's easier said than done.

As agents are busy getting their clients generals at networks, studios, and production companies, they're also following up and tracking every exec's response.

Which doesn't sound hard, except remember: they're doing that with over fifty clients in contention for over 150 opportunities. How do agents keep all their info straight?! It's not easy, but most use two kinds of highly detailed charts:

Show Charts–Agents make charts and lists for each and every potential show, both new and returning, containing:

- The name of the show
- A quick synopsis
- The showrunners
- Executives covering the show at the network, studio, and production company
- Which writers and materials the agent has submitted (and when they were submitted)
- Any responses to each submission

This not only allows agents to monitor shows' status and track their own clients' progress, it lets them access info quickly when talking to execs or showrunners about specific projects.

What a Show Chart May Look Like

Title:	Hacienda Motel
Format:	1-hr drama
Stats:	NBC / 20th Century Fox / Baxley Productions
Synopsis:	The staff of a haunted roadside motel must deal with ghosts and poltergeists as well as the strange guests who show up every week.
Showrunners:	Tom Howe and George Simon (EP), Mel Hardy (creator/Co-EP)
Network Executives:	Lisa Pendleton, Tori Graves
Studio Executives:	Sunny Schwartz, Jake Fulton
Pod Executives:	Darren Baxley, Bridget Chaplin

TABLE 6.2 Show Chart

Name	Credits	Notes	Net. Submission	Studio Sub.	Pod Sub.	Showrunner	Status
EXECUTIVE PRODUCER							
Melville, Alfred	Brothers in Arms, Black Roses	Parents owned hotel in Georgia	Diver Down–3/31 (L.P.); LP: PASS	Diver Down–2/17 (JF)– JF: PASS	The Unknown–3/1 (DB, BC)		PASS
Pickwick, Bella	The Dark Age, Act of Truth	Worked w/ Baxley on Turnpiked	Unbalanced–4/2 (LP)	Genetically F*cked–3/12 (LP)– LP: LOVE	Unbalanced–3/18 (DB)– DB: LOVE	Unbalanced–4/16 (MH)	Pod/Stud: LOVE, FU w/ MH 4/25
CO-EXEC PROD.							
Waters, Sid	Harvest, Never Run Away	Friends w/ S. Schwartz, T. Graves	Ugly Baby Chronicles–3/15 (TG)	Heaven In My Hand–3/15 (SS)	Heaven In My Hand–3/15 (BC)	Ugly Baby Chronicles–4/16 (MH)– MH: PASS	PASS
PRODUCER							
Sharpe, Ivan	Ship of Fools, Cadillac Desert	Worked as carnival psychic in college	Pear-Shaped Heart–3/15 (TG)	Pear-Shaped Heart–2/23 (JF, SS)	Cell Phone Mercy–2/23 (BC)	Cell Phone Mercy–4/16 (MH)	Only hiring teams at this level

Network, Studio, and Production Company Charts–Agents also keep separate charts for current and development departments at each network and studio. With five broadcast networks and six main studios, this means each agent keeps approximately thirty separate network/studio charts, plus charts for all the important production companies! Each chart lists:

- All executives in that department
- What shows each exec covers
- Which writers and materials the agent has submitted (and when)
- Responses to each submission

TABLE 6.3 What a Network or Studio Chart May Look Like

UNIVERSAL TV					
Drama Development					
Name	*Level*	*Covers*	*Notes*	*Submissions*	*Status*
Horton, Sal	Sr. VP	*Rogue State, Nibblers, Family Grind*	Univ. of Chicago, wife: Shelley	Cal Spitz–*Sexy Eyes* (3/19); Staci Port–*Special Needs* (3/19	FU re: Port; PASSED on Spitz
Ruhde, Vince	VP	*Rogue State, Stake in the Heart, 1777*	Used to be at Sony, divorced	NA	Set lunch
Torres, Kami	Director	*Stake in the Heart, 1777, Blood Rites*	Son goes to Pennybrook Middle School, knows Ben	NA	
Elzinga, Kirk	Manager	*Speed Demons, Nibblers, Blood Rites*	Lunch set for 6/23	Stormy Parkes–*Blowing Smoke* (3/24)	Liked *Smoke*, send *Paper Fools*

Agent Communication 101

Don't be afraid to nudge your agent, but do it with empathy and compliments: "Hey, Adam, I know you're pounding the pavement, but I just wanted to put a bee in your bonnet and remind you I really love these four drama pilots: *Intruder, Mean Street, House of Pain,* and *D.O.A.*" Or: "Hey, Jess–Just a reminder: I'm friends with Eric Miller over at *Ice Cream Man,* and he'll put in a call to Wilkerson and Gray, the showrunners, if I need it. Lemme know!"

Agent Communication 101

While communication during staffing is important, you don't need long, in-depth conversations with your agent. "The only communication that's really necessary is: 'What's the update on where I've been submitted," which the agent should give the client and the client's reps. The other update, from the client, is: 'I ran into so-and-so, my friend who works on this show, and this is the information I have.'"–Roy Ashton, partner, The Gersh Agency

Ask the Agents

Q: How much should I talk to my agent during staffing season? I know they're super-busy, and super-stressed, so I don't want to bug them, but I also want to know what's going on. Should I call once a day? Once an hour? Once a week? What?!

A: "It's not about how frequently you call," says Verve agent Amy Retzinger, "although please do not call every single day, and do not call once in the morning and then again in the afternoon . . . and don't *never* call, because there are certainly clients you don't hear from for weeks and that's dangerous, too. In a perfect world, you might be talking to your agent a couple times a week, [but] it's more about the *content* of the conversation. Do not call your agent and just say, 'What's up? What's going on?' It puts your agent on the defensive. I like if a client can say, 'Hey, what's going on with [*Blue Bloods*]? A friend told me [a showrunner] is looking to meet people.' Most agents welcome information, and even the best agent isn't going to have every piece. So be specific, bring something to the tabl–even if you're ultimately hoping to have a wider staffing season conversation."

Eventually, execs and producers start to get a sense of which shows will get picked up and which won't. They also learn one may need a mid-level writer with medical expertise. Another needs a female staff writer. Another wants a team. Another needs an African-American. Another wants someone with a stand-up comedy background. "A lot of shows know–before they get a renewal–what their needs will be," says Karen Horne, NBC Entertainment/Universal TV's VP of Programming. "They let the network's current executives know what their needs are, so we know if the show comes back *Grimm* is looking for something, or *Chicago Fire,* or *SVU* needs this."

As the landscape takes shape, writers' general meetings give way to "staffing meetings" with execs and producers. Unlike generals, staffing meetings are targeted for specific shows. You may go to 20th Century Fox to meet with a development exec

If you're going in for a
meeting with a producer or
exec on a current show,
"know the show. Come in
with a few pitches–stories,
characters–and impress me,"
says Disney Channel current
executive Kristina Speakman.
Story ideas shouldn't be long,
just one or two sentences,
but make them "visual . . . and
[if] you're a comedy writer,
always try to get a joke in
there."

covering two new comedies, or you may meet with a current exec covering *Modern Family*, *How I Met Your Mother*, and *The New Girl*–all of which may need writers.

Based on these general and staffing meetings, execs revise their writer lists, which they pass on to showrunners in mid-April. Showrunners have their own lists of writers for staffing, but they know that writers recommended by the network or studio are already "pre-approved," making their hiring process much easier.

Agent Communication 101

"Always be positive with your agent. And be prepared. Read the trades. Keep up with *Deadline Hollywood*. Find out what shows seem to be getting good buzz. During staffing season, I always send my agents and manager emails saying, 'Here's a link to an article about a show that just got green-lit. If it goes to series, I'd love to be considered; it takes place in my hometown and has something to do with what I have a passion for!' Keep your agent and manager updated. Other than that, leave them alone. Let them do their job."–Paula Yoo, co-producer (*Eureka*, *Side Order of Life*)

Showrunner Meetings

Because showrunners have the final word in who's hired, showrunner meetings are the most important. Yet in order to get a showrunner meeting, you must first get to the showrunner. This often requires a personal connection, or an agent or friend with a personal connection.

"There are generally three places writers come from" during staffing season, says executive producer Richard Gurman (*I'm In the Band*, *Still Standing*). "One: your own personal contacts, people you've worked with, people you know and can depend on. Two: the studio and the network–people they've been looking to staff, or people that have been on other shows. That's the path of least resistance because [those writers] are already approved–although that doesn't mean anything unless you like them. [Three:] agents you've developed relationships with. If you've staffed on dozens of shows as I have, you have a group of go-to agents you trust."

While agents need to be
aggressive, they also need to
understand that showrunners
are being bombarded 24/7
with calls from anxious agents
and managers. "You'll get
called by every agent and
manager in town. At first it's
flattering, then it's annoying,"
says executive producer
Richard Gurman (*Married
With Children*, *Still
Standing*). But "if I get a cold
call and [an agent] intrigues
me with someone, if the
agent or manager takes the
time to say, 'I know your
show, I've seen your show,
I've read your script–this
person would be perfect for
it,' I'll take a look."

This "is why it's important for
agents to read their pilots,"
adds ICM TV agent Melissa
Orton. "If you're covering a
show, you should know what
the show's about, what the
tone is. Not every agent does
that."

It's not unusual, in fact, for showrunners to hire entire staffs of friends or former co-workers. This is partly because showrunners receive hundreds of submissions–more than they could ever read–and it's easy for familiar names to rise to the top. But showrunners also want to hire people they know they can spend fifteen hours a day with, trapped in a tiny room. And while there are undoubtedly great unknown writers out there, unknown writers are wild cards, and many showrunners, swamped with the pressures of running a $60 million/year TV show, don't have time to deal with wild cards. Thus, even aggressive, persistent agents find the barriers to entry high when it comes to contacting showrunners.

"We have a really limited window to submit writers to the actual showrunner," says Good. "If you call too early (in February or March), they say, 'You're calling too soon, we're in production.' If you call too late, [the assistant] tells you, 'We've got two hundred submissions. You're S.O.L.–see you next year!' A lot of anxiety comes from people saying, 'Get your scripts in this week. If you don't get them in, you're going to miss the boat and you can't get people in later. We're going to read right now.'"

This is also where showrunners' assistants prove invaluable. Many assistants read submissions before their bosses, so agents reach out to assistants in February, as pilots begin production. Some assistants tell the agent to call back in a few weeks, others are already reading. At the very least, assistants provide agents with information about when the showrunner may start reading and what kinds of writers he'll be looking for.

Most agents get showrunners on the phone in April, as showrunners shift from principal photography to post-production and begin contemplating their writing staff. When a covering agent calls a show creator, they ask four important questions:

1. **What are you looking for?** Does the showrunner want writers with specific specialties or skill sets, such as former doctors or police officers? Are they looking for strong female writers? Hard joke writers? Hard procedural writers? Writers familiar with certain subcultures or communities, like the circus or local politics? "In some ways, it's like a sports team filling roll players," says Gurman. "You've got a good center and a couple of forwards, [and] you know you need a guard. In another sense, it's like a dinner party, figuring out who's going to get along with whom, and who you want to spend an evening with—because there are so many evenings."

2. **How big is your staff?** The size of a staff is determined by two primary factors, the show's writer budget and the showrunner's personal preference. Most broadcast network comedies have a writer budget of about $100,000 per episode, but budgets can vary slightly between comedies and dramas, network shows and cable shows. Also, some showrunners like large staffs with writers at all levels; others like smaller, intimate staffs of experienced upper-level writers.

Double Header

Many showrunners like to hire writing teams, pairs of writers that work as a single unit. This is often advantageous because even though there are two people, teams are paid as as a single unit, so showrunners literally get two heads for the price of one.

3. **What levels will you be reading?** Some showrunners already know they have a friend they're hiring as Co-EP, or an assistant they're promoting to staff writer, so there's no need to read submissions at those levels. Others know they only want mid-level writers, or a few upper-levels and two low-levels, so they don't bother reading other positions.

4. **What kinds of material would you like to read?** Many showrunners want to read original material—pilots, plays, screenplays—to feel out the writer's unique voice. Some want sample specs to ensure the writer can mimic another writer's tone. Others simply want the strongest sample, whether it's a spec, pilot, essay, or sketch packet.

Based on this info, agents pitch the showrunner clients they feel are most appropriate. "If you've got a family show, you want some people to be family people," says Gurman. "If it's a workplace show, [you want some] people who came from business or law. There's usually some pressure to have a mix, gender-wise. If you have no female voice and there are women characters, it's A) the right thing to do, and B) it usually benefits you. There's [also] pressure to have minorities. Black can write white, white can write black, old can write young, young can write old—I believe in that—but if you're writing a show where there's a 'hip factor,' it's helpful to have some hip voices in the room."

Insider's Perspective

When submitting scripts to showrunners, good agents are much more discerning than when they send massive packages to network or studio executives. Showrunners only want submissions an agent believes could be 100 percent perfect for their show. "If I say, 'I only want three [scripts], and I want them to be lower-level teams,' I want that agent to send me what I've asked for," says executive producer Stacy Traub (*Notes From the Underbelly, Glee*). "If that agent then sends me twenty scripts, I'm pissed; and I will remember that. Or I'll just say, 'Now I'm not reading any of your scripts.' I understand their job is to get people hired, [but] the agent really has to listen to what the showrunner is asking for. I want to help, but I can't hire every one of their clients."

Thus, agents often send writers they know are liked or "pre-approved" by the network, studio, and production company—another reason generals and staffing meetings are so important.

Even when showrunners have requested or agreed to read certain scripts from an agent, not every script gets read. "There are so many scripts and so few hours," says Gurman. As a result, showrunners must prioritize what they read, and scripts that move to the top of the stacks tend to be those from friends or close colleagues.

"I'm always going to read someone from my own agent," Gurman continues. "I'm not going to hire them just because it's my agency, but my agent will get a leg up because I will read almost anything my agent sends me."

This is where big agencies have a distinct advantage. Over *ninety-two percent* of new scripted series announced by broadcasters for the 2012–13 season were packaged by one of the Big Four agencies.[1] So do the math: if showrunners are more inclined to read their own agents' submissions first, and over ninety-two percent of shows come from the same four places, it becomes clear whose clients have a direct pipeline to showrunners and staffing opportunities.

Does this mean smaller agencies stand no chance of getting clients read? Not necessarily—many mid-level and boutique agents have terrific relationships with showrunners they don't represent. But those numbers do speak to the muscle of the Big Four, not only in getting shows on the air, but in funneling clients into job openings.

How Many Showrunner Meetings Should I Expect During Staffing Season?

According to most agents and managers, three to five seems to be a happy number, a number at which "they better be locking down one of those jobs," says one manager. Having said that, "a lot of high-level writers at a big agency will get fifteen showrunner meetings just because [their agents] make them happen," says one agent. "But some of those meetings aren't even real meetings, they're just favors."

Also, many showrunner meetings end up being for shows that never make it to air. "I've had a writer take six showrunner meetings and not a single one of those shows gets picked up," says Jen Good of The Alpern Group.

This is the important thing to remember: while it's nice to have a lot of meetings, "it only takes one to get a job," says Jeff Holland of The Cartel. However, "if you're getting zero meetings throughout a complete staffing season, and if you're getting zero within *two* full staffing seasons, there's a problem. You probably need to start looking for new representation, or you need some new material."

About a week after submitting scripts, agents follow up with showrunners. If the showrunner hasn't read everything, the agent may steer him toward two or three scripts he thinks are the strongest contenders. Other times, the showrunner may have changed his mind about what he needs. Perhaps he's already hired writers at upper levels, so he's now reading only for co-producers and story editors. Or perhaps he's hunting for African-American or Asian writers, nullifying all the agent's submissions! Unfortunately, it's hard for agents to now make new submissions, since they've presumably already said, "These are my best writers."

Hopefully the showrunner *has* read the agent's submissions. If he "didn't respond" to a specific writer's work, it's probably the end of the road for that writer on this show. If the showrunner *did* like a writer's work, however, the agent schedules a **showrunner meeting**.

Showrunner meetings are often scheduled fairly quickly—sometimes only two or three days away, other times, that very afternoon! This is partly because as we near mid-May, when networks announce season's schedules, showrunners are more focused on staffing. Plus, each writer they hire affects their other options. If a showrunner hires one writer whose strength is story, he starts looking for another writer who's strength is jokes; if he hires a co-executive producer and supervising producer, he may start looking for co-producers and exec story editors. Showrunners also must move quickly because *every other show* is trying to hire, which means talented writers get snatched up fast. This makes staffing season as stressful for showrunners as it is for writers.

Do Your Homework

Although pilots are supposed to be top-secret, most of them seem to get leaked every single year. Starting in April, agents and managers get their hands on cuts of various pilots. A good agent should be able to slip you DVD copies of whatever you want. If you can, watch this *before* you go into your meeting. The showrunner may screen a more recent, polished version, but at least you'll be able to start thinking about the project before you go in.

When you first arrive at a showrunner meeting, an assistant usually takes you to a private room to screen the pilot. Throughout pilot season, producers and executives work hard to keep their pilots-in-progress under wraps, but they allow writers to watch them in the office so they can have an informed discussion.

Once you've finished the pilot, spend a few moments contemplating the project. I usually carry a journal with me so I can jot down thoughts on characters, possible stories, interesting thematic territory. You're about to have a critical conversation with the writer who created the show, so go in with some organized insights. "The first thing I think of when watching a new pilot is: can I come up with more ideas for this show?" says producer Anupam Nigam (*Defiance*, *Psych*). "Is there an organic way to get into new stories? Am I excited about the stories my brain is coming up with? If I watch a pilot and don't know what the second or third episode [might be], or if I was tasked with writing the second or third episode and don't know if I can do it, I'm probably not a great fit for the show. But if I watch and think, 'Oh, from there I can write this story,' and I learn something about this character and can tell five different stories, then I feel like I'm a good fit."

With a comedy, says Gurman, think about "the style of humor: whether it's hard jokes or character driven, whether there's a lot of physical humor. If you are in sync with that style, if you're comfortable with it, you should be able to talk about that style of show in the meeting. Compare it to other shows like it. Talk about the characters and why you liked them. That would be reflective for the showrunner of the type of humor you're going to add to the mix. 'I loved it when she walked through the door and said that!' 'I loved it when these two characters talked around each other!' Pick out little runs you like, or you'd like to see more of, and work that into the conversation."

Ask the Producer

Q: I have a showrunner meeting next week, and while I want (and need!) the job, I'm not that crazy about the show. Should I lie and say I love it? I don't want to jeopardize my chance to get the job, but I don't want to be disingenuous either. What do I say?!

A: "It's hard to fake it. If you don't like the show you're meeting on, it usually shows. I try to find lines, or character moments, I legitimately like. If I can somehow link that to some quality in myself—if I can point out how I'm like a character, or have the same background as a character—the more that showrunner looks at me and thinks, "She's going be a good resource for the show.""—Lesley Wake Webster, co-executive producer (*The New Girl, We Are Men*)

Once you've watched the pilot, the assistant ushers you into the showrunner's office and the meeting begins. "Usually, the writer starts off flattering [the showrunner], telling you how much they like the show," says Gurman. "If the feeling is mutual, a showrunner will talk about your script. Everyone is feeling each other out. I kind of believe in [Malcolm] Gladwell's *Blink* theory: you can tell within the first few minutes if you're going to click."

You can also use this opportunity to talk a bit about your own life and background. Showrunners want writers with rich life experiences, especially if those life experiences relate to the show. If you're single and meeting on *The New Girl*, tell some dating or break-up stories. If you're meeting on *Parks and Recreation*, and you used to manage a department of quirky workers, bring them to life. Also, be prepared to talk about your own work. The showrunner most likely read and enjoyed something you wrote, so be ready to talk about what inspired you, your process, etc.

Showrunner meetings can be nerve-racking experiences. As much as you want to relax, it's hard to "just be you" when your dream, a professional writing job, is within your grasp! Of course, good showrunner meetings can also be exhilarating. Meeting with a writer is different than meeting with an exec, a suit. Even if you don't get the job, you're now sitting across from someone who speaks your language, shares your passions, is programmed with identical chips. At the very least, you'll hopefully have a fun, interesting conversation!

When the meeting ends, the writer calls his reps to tell them how it went, and the agent or manager calls the showrunner to follow up. If a showrunner has no intention of hiring a writer, he usually tells the agent up front. At this stage, however, most showrunners have no idea—even if they liked the writer a lot. Assembling a staff is fraught with constantly changing variables. Let's say a showrunner has six slots to fill. He may know who he wants as his "Number Two," but if that writer's deal doesn't close, the showrunner has to take his second choice. And swapping in that second choice affects other decisions. Maybe the second choice is more expensive, forcing the showrunner to give up another co-executive producer. Or maybe that second choice is *less* expensive, freeing up more money to hire a story editor. Thus, showrunners usually tell an agent their client is "**in the mix**," but there are no solid answers till everything starts to coalesce. Other times, the showrunner says something like, "I'd love to hire Jessie, but it's all going to come down to money. I'm waiting to hear how two upper-levels play out, so I'm hoping to have enough left to bring on your client."

The Top Seven Ways to Ace a Showrunner Meeting

1. If you have a relationship with execs at the show's network or studio, pick their brains. "I'll prepare you on how to win him over . . . how to try to break the ice, see through his stoic face. 'He's kind of an introvert, so don't take it personally. Get in a joke. Here are the kinds of things he responds to: what he likes, what he doesn't.' If I know anything personal, I'll tell you that–'On weekends he plays with a band.' I would arm you with enough information to win him over–that's the goal."–Kristina Speakman, director of current series, Disney Channel

2. "The biggest mistake people make, time and again, is not knowing the show. I can't tell you how many times people would come in and not know the characters' names, or not know episodes of the show, or not know the spirit of the show. It was shocking to me, because the easiest thing to do is to watch old episodes of the show, but people wouldn't do it! And it usually got them nixed immediately, because when you're talking to a showrunner, somebody who has devoted the last five years of his life to this show, the least you could do is research the show in the two days before your meeting."–Drew Goddard, co-executive producer (*Lost*, *Alias*, *Buffy the Vampire Slayer*)

3. "Follow the lead of the person you're hoping to impress. Sometimes they want to talk about your credits, sometimes they want to hear where you're from. My goal in those situations is to steer the conversation toward my strengths as a writer and my good stories, because everyone who's coming into that meeting is super qualified and super funny–at least in the comedy world–so you're trying to show you're different, you're special."–Lesley Wake Webster, co-executive producer (*We Are Men*, *American Dad*)

4. "You can ruin yourself by coming into a room and being shticky to the point where I don't want to spend my whole day with [you]. [You don't] have to fill every second with a joke. If I read someone I thought was brilliant and they came in and were socially awkward, I'd think, 'Well, writers aren't always the most complete people; that's why they write.' So air on the side of less shticky."–Richard Gurman, executive producer (*The Facts of Life*, *Uncle Buck*)

5. "Find something in the show that you liked. Last year, I did a Mandy Moore show about family . . . I loved the people who came in and said, 'Oh my God–the brother reminds me of my brother!' I'm not saying you should lie, but if there's a character you relate to, tell me, because when I'm sitting there, I'm trying to figure out: *do you have stories to give to the show?*"–Stacy Traub, executive producer (*Notes From the Underbelly*, *Glee*)

6. "It's important to know what the climate of the room is going to be, how it's going to be run. Are we going to be splitting into groups? Are we going to be pitching all the time? What's the make-up? How many people will be there? That's a huge deal to me–feeling comfortable in a room and being able to do my best, knowing what to expect."–Alison Brown, story editor (*Dog With a Blog*, *Worst Week*)

7. Research the showrunner online. "Facebook is the most genius thing for figuring out who these people are. If you went on [the showrunner's] Facebook page and saw he's a big motorcycle guy, and so are you, start talking about it. Nine times out of ten, you'll get the job."–Melissa Orton, agent, ICM

Sometimes these statements are completely true; other times, they're early negotiating tactics.

Once they know their client is "in the mix" on a particular show, agents work the phones to gin up excitement and momentum at the network, pod, and studio. "I don't know if you've heard from David (the showrunner) yet," the agent says, "but the meeting went great. I'd love to make this happen, so let me know what I can do to help."

GETTING THE OFFER AND NEGOTIATING THE DEAL

Agents and clients live for the moment when the phone rings and a studio executive is on the other line. It's usually a current or development exec who calls first, telling the agent to expect an offer. This is the moment you and your agents been working towards—and for most baby writers and their representation, it's been months and years in the making.

Getting that call "is a gigantic euphoric feeling," says Gersh literary agent Roy Ashton. "When you begin an agent-writer relationship, you tell them you're going to help further their career and develop the skills to become a show creator or showrunner. Now you have a client who's in the game, legitimizing themselves in the marketplace … someone who networks, studios, and other talent—producers, actors, directors—are going to pay attention to and get to know as a potential creator. Every promise you've made is fulfilled. It's a tremendous feeling. Plus, getting paid doesn't hurt."

The official offer comes later, from Business Affairs, the studio department responsible for analyzing, formulating, offering, negotiating, and closing deals, whether hiring a writer or acquiring a piece of intellectual property (IP).

When making an official offer, the Business Affairs exec first calls the agent to check the writer's quote (how much he or she gets paid for similar jobs, usually based on the writer's last comparable writing job) and lays out the initial terms. There are five main deal points that are usually negotiated:

1 Compensation
2 Script fees
3 Title/credit
4 Guaranteed scripts
5 Exclusivity

Negotiating 101

"There are three essential things [to being a good negotiator. First,] the ability to analyze a position dispassionately and tell how much it's worth. Second, being able to communicate forcefully your position. A lot of writers tend to be passive-aggressive personalities that don't want to communicate verbally in an assertive way. The last part: emotionally detach yourself. People vary in their ability to compartmentalize," and writers tend to remain very attached to their work.—Charles Holland, entertainment attorney

---

Standard Deal Points in a Staffing Contract

Talk the Talk

WGA-covered—Shows or companies that have agreed to the terms and rules laid out by the Writers Guild of America, the labor union representing professional TV, film, digital media and radio writers.

The WGA MBA

Every three years, the WGA and the **Alliance of Motion Picture and Television Producers (AMPTP)**, the trade organization representing Hollywood's main studios, networks, and production companies, re-negotiate the WGA's **Minimum Basic Agreement (MBA)** and **Schedule of Minimums**, agreements regulating compensation for TV and film writers.

Compensation—When it comes to compensation, writers on WGA-covered TV shows fall into two categories: **Article 13** or **Article 14**.

Article 13 pertains only to staff writers, the lowest-level of writer in a staff's hierarchy. Staff writers are considered "pure writers." Their job is simply to *write*; they don't have additional responsibilities such as editing, casting, meeting with designers, etc. Article 13 writers are paid a weekly salary, usually the minimum weekly payment required by the WGA (aka "**Guild minimum**" or "**scale**"). Article 13 writers are also "**term writers**"; they're hired for a specific term (say, twenty weeks), and they receive a set weekly salary for this amount of time. The longer the guaranteed term, the less the show must pay them per week. This incentivizes productions to hire staff writers for longer terms.

Article 13 Writer: Week-to-week Term Employment Minimums			
Weekly Compensation	*Effective 5/2/11–5/1/12*	*Effective 5/2/12–5/1/13*	*Effective 5/2/13–5/1/14*
Week-to-Week	$4,171	$4,244	$4,3239
6 out of 6 weeks	$4,171	$4,244	$4,3239
14 out of 14 weeks	$3,877	$3,945	$4,024
20 out of 26 weeks	$3,576	$3,639	$3,712
40 out of 52 weeks	$3,268	$3,325	$3,392

Learning On the Job

Although staff writers aren't technically, or contractually, obligated to shoulder producer responsibilities, many showrunners want–and expect–staff writers who will participate in these processes. It's not only how staff writers make themselves invaluable to the show, it's also how they grow into capable, competent producers.

Article 14 refers to all TV writers *above* staff writer: story editor on up to executive producer. These writers are considered to have certain producer responsibilities beyond basic writing: editing, casting, set and costume design meetings, etc. Article 14 writers also have WGA minimums, but instead of being paid per week, most Article 14 writers are paid per episode, and their agents negotiate an "**episodic fee.**" Why are Article 14 writers paid this way? Because the episodic fee is not meant as compensation for any writing work; it's meant as compensation for writers' additional writing/producing work–the casting, editing, costume meetings, etc.

So let's say Greg, a supervising producer on a new half-hour comedy, *Addicted To Love*, receives an episodic fee of $14,000 per episode. And let's say *Addicted To Love* has been picked up for thirteen episodes. Greg is guaranteed a gross of $182,000 (thirteen episodes x $14,000/episode). He still receives a weekly paycheck, but it's based on his episodic fee, pro-rated per week. So if Greg has been hired for thirty weeks of work, he will receive a weekly paycheck of $6,067 ($182,000 ÷ 30 weeks). (Actually, the reality of how Article 14 writers get paid is a bit messier and "mathier." For the full scoop, check out the text book below. But read on at your own risk!)

Script Fees–If episodic fees earned by Article 14 writers working on a TV show are considered compensation for writers' "additional producing work," how do writers get paid for their actual writing?–Script fees.

Script fees

Article 14 writers are paid a fee, based again on WGA minimums, for each script they write. Half-hours and hours have different minimums, as do broadcast prime-time shows and cable shows.

Script Fee Minimums (Broadcast and Cable, Traditional Half-Hour and Hour Programs)

Weekly Script Fees	Effective 5/2/11–5/1/12	Effective 5/2/12–5/1/13	Effective 5/2/13–5/1/14
30 minutes (broadcast, prime time)	$23,358	$23,767	$24,242
30 minutes (cable)	$13,144	$13,343	$13,610
60 minutes (broadcast, prime time)	$34,355	$34,956	$35,655
60 minutes (cable)	$23,837	$24,254	$24,739

So, looking at the above text box, if Greg, our fictional supervising producer on *Addicted To Love*, writes three scripts this season, he receives $72,000 in script fees ($24,000 × 3). These script fees aren't usually negotiable; a handful of powerful upper-level writers may be able to negotiate higher fees, but most receive the same amount: WGA minimum.

How Article 13 Writers Are Different

Unlike Article 14 writers, staff writers are *not* paid script fees atop their weekly salaries. Rather, Article 13 writers' script fees are counted *against* their weekly salaries. In other words, let's say A.J., a staff writer on a new drama called *Fire Walker*, grosses $100,000. During his season on the show, A.J. writes two scripts. If WGA minimum for a half-hour script is $24,000, those two scripts *should* earn A.J. an additional $48,000 in script fees. But since A.J. has already been paid $100,000—well over the $48,000 in script fees—he is not paid any more money. However, if A.J. were to write *five* scripts in the season, earning him script fees totalling $120,000; $20,000 over the $100,000 he's already been paid—the show would owe him an additional $20,000. (Sounds great, right? Don't get excited; I've *never* heard of an Article 13 writer writing enough scripts to make anything beyond his or her weekly salary.)

Cable vs. Broadcast

Cable shows have lower minimums than broadcast shows because, traditionally, they've had smaller budgets—a "fact" that doesn't always hold true anymore. The first season of HBO's acclaimed drama *Game of Thrones*, for example, cost an estimated $50–$60 million, about the same as a single season of a broadcast drama. But one season of a broadcast drama typically has twenty-two episodes; *Game of Thrones'* first season had only ten, bringing its average episodic budget to over $5 million per hour—almost twice as much as a typical broadcast episode![2]

Title/Credit—When an agent negotiates a writer's TV deal, "title" is one of the first things discussed. Will the writer be a staff writer (Article 13) or story editor (Article 14)? Co-producer or producer? Producer or supervising producer? Except for Article 13, staff writers, titles are not tied to a specific pay scale; the only rule is that writers must make WGA minimum or above. Having said that, as writers move up the hierarchy, they demand more money, and there are basic pay ranges for each level. (FYI–there's no rule saying a staff writer or story editor can't make *above* Guild minimum, and an exec producer could, in theory, get paid the same as a story editor, although it would take a pretty terrible agent or lawyer to let that happen.)

Pay Ranges for Various Staff Levels

Staff Writer–WGA Article 13 scale (see chart on page 97)
Story Editor–WGA Article 14 scale (see chart on page 98)
Exec. Story Editor–WGA Article scale + five to ten percent (or, if you negotiate an episodic flat fee, it's probably about $11,000/episode)
Co-Producer–$12,000–$15,000/episode
Producer–$12,000–$16,000/episode
Supervising Producer–$15,000–$18,000/episode
Co-Executive Producer–$16,000–$25,000
Executive Producer–$25,000–$50,000/episode

Some shows also have **consulting producers**, writers who have a special arrangement with the show. Perhaps they're working on another show, so they only come in part-time. Maybe they're semi-retired and want limited responsibilities. Depending on their experience and contract, most consulting producers make approximately $15,000–$25,000 per episode.

Most agents try to get their clients the highest title possible, including a bump from their last job. If a writer was "co-producer" on her last show, her agent tries to land her "producer" on this show. This isn't always easy when many writers are competing for only a handful of slots. It's not unusual, in fact–especially in lean times–for writers to take a *drop* in credit, settling for a lower title, and sometimes a lower fee, just to have a job.

Agents also try building automatic promotions into clients' contracts. Since most contracts bind a writer to a show for two to three years, agents want guaranteed annual raises and title bumps. So a writer hired as an executive story editor is often guaranteed a co-producer title in her second year and a producer title her third year.

The biggest–and most difficult–leap is from staff writer to story editor, or Article 13 to Article 14. This is because this is the only title bump that comes with a mandated and significant pay hike. Plus, Article 14 writers receive script payments atop their weekly salaries or episodic fees. Together, this amounts to several thousand dollars a year in extra payments, so some studios insist staff writers serve at least two years as Article 13 before bumping them up. Other times, shows simply fire staff writers rather than promoting them to story editor and paying extra money.

Guaranteed scripts–Because agents rarely negotiate higher script fees for clients, they often convince studios to guarantee a writer a certain number of scripts per season. While most shows won't guarantee *any* scripts to Article 13 writers (some staff writers never get to write their own script the entire season!), higher-level writers are often promised one or two scripts, ensuring they'll make at least those script fees atop their episodic paychecks.

Exclusivity–When a studio hires a writer, they want to know all the writer's creative energies are focused 100 percent on that particular project. Thus, they often try to make the writer "exclusive," contractually forbidding him to work on any other projects. They may do this in several ways:

1.   Declare the writer exclusive to the studio "in all media." This means the writer is not allowed to write, work on, produce, or publish any material, in any medium, for any company besides the studio. The writer cannot publish a book. He cannot

sell a movie. He cannot write a video game. If this seems draconian, it is–and most agents negotiate out of it.

2. While studios may back off exclusivity "in all media," they often insist the writer– especially a low-level writer–be exclusive in television. In other words, the writer can publish his novel or write a film, but he can't work on other TV projects. Sometimes, if the writer is already working on other TV projects, the agent can carve those out of the deal, or excerpt them.

3. It's harder for studios to bind upper-level writers to 100 percent exclusivity, even just in television. Most upper-level writers have reached a point in their careers where they want to have their own show, and they won't accept deals that restrict their abilities to take that step. Thus, studios insist on a "first-look" clause in writers' contracts, giving them first crack at any ideas those writers develop while on staff. Unlike a paid first-look deal given to a successful producer or production company, these deals don't pay the writer extra money; they're simply stipulations included in the writer's for-hire contract.

Regardless of whatever exclusivity a writer's representative negotiates, most studios require staffed writers to be in "**first position**." This means the current show takes precedence over all other projects or opportunities. So if Greg is writing for *Addicted To Love* on NBC and suddenly sells his sitcom, *Personality Crisis*, to CBS, he must sell it in "**second position**." This means Greg can only render his writing and producing services to *Personality Crisis* if they don't interfere with his duties on *Addicted To Love*. Thus, many studios won't buy projects from or hire writers in second position.

Going Breach

Sometimes, when writers are exclusive to a particular show and need to get out of their contract, they simply "go breach," or quit the project in breach of their contract. While this isn't something I'd recommend, it rarely results in legal action; it can, however, damage your reputation with the producers and executives working on that show.

Once the agent receives all the deal points from the business affairs exec, he imme- diately calls his client's other reps–managers or lawyers–to bring them up to speed. Then he calls the client. Together, they decide whether or not they want to counter, or try to improve the terms of the deal. If the writer has heat on other shows, the agent may try to see if he can use this offer to quickly elicit other job offers. This is often tough to do with low-level writers; jobs are scarce, and thousands of young writers want them.

As the agent and business affairs exec haggle over the main deal points, they also negotiate other contractual issues such as travel, workman's comp, and whether or not the writer gets his own office. Throughout negotiations, how much leverage your agent has depends primarily on two things:

1. **Your level as a writer**. Mid- and upper-level clients often have fair amounts of leverage, but staff writers and story editors are usually offered "take-it-or-leave-it" deals. "It's supply and demand," says agent-cum-manager Jeff Holland. Because so many young writers are clamoring for staff writer positions, "studios and producers know they can get away it. But if you survive that initial staff writer position, your salary almost doubles when you become story editor (this is the jump from Article 13 to 14), and you start getting script fees. All you have to do is survive that first season, and you can get out of the staff writer mold."

2. **Competitive situations**. If you're being offered a job, and it's your only offer, your agent has little leverage. But if you've got two or more offers, you're suddenly free to take the best deal–and your agent can play studios off one another. "I had a situation recently," says one TV agent, "where I had an offer from Lionsgate, then eOne put in an offer at the eleventh hour. We were literally a day away from closing the (Lionsgate) deal and eOne said they wanted to make an offer. The deal was a joke, but I was able to use that eOne deal to get [my client] the best deal at Lionsgate, to make it seem competitive–even though it was not competitive in our eyes at all."

Unfortunately, competitive situations are uncommon, especially for low-level writers, so good agents, managers, and lawyers must create the *illusion* of leverage and competition.

"Sometimes [leverage] is psychological and sometimes it's real," says entertainment lawyer Charles Holland. "Sometimes the leverage is real because I'm at a firm that has a bunch of people [the studio] wants to work with. Sometimes the leverage is because even though this [project] didn't work out, they want to work with the client again. Sometimes the leverage is psychological; there are plenty of people in Hollywood who have reputations of being cool who aren't cool. They don't want people to know they're not cool. Sometimes there's a gentle blackmail–'People are going to find out you're a monster.' Sometimes that kind of psychological leverage works."

Most staffing deals are fairly standard, so negotiations rarely last long. Negotiating an upper-level writer's contract can be more complex, with backend and development discussions (perhaps the agent wants the studio to give his client points in the show or an overall deal), but a low-level contract should take only one or two days–sometimes a single phone exchange! (Agents always consult their clients before asking or agreeing to anything, but staff writers have such little wiggle room that negotiations are fast and easy.)

Important and Helpful Questions to Ask Your Agent About Your Contract

- What's my payment schedule?
- When must I be told if I'm going to be brought back for the next season?
- What are my obligations on the show? What duties are required of me?
- When is the end of season one–or how many episodes is it? (Some studios, once a show is up and running, will continue to add episodes to the season– "Congratulations! We're picking up an extra eight episodes!" "Guess what?! We're giving you three more episodes!" "The show's doing great–five more episodes please!" What they may be doing, however, is squeezing more episodes out of the show without having to pay people the higher salaries they've negotiated for next season.)

It's important to note, however, that deals can fall through. Maybe the studio and the writer don't come to terms on compensation. Maybe the studio refuses to carve the writer's prior development out of the deal. "It's difficult to blow a deal in this day and age," says manager Jeff Holland, "unless the client is being very difficult. Most business affairs execs come back to you multiple times, and you really know when you're going to blow the deal. Eventually, they tell you, 'It's take it or leave it.' [The writer] might not be satisfied or love the deal, but it's difficult to blow a deal."

If I'm a First-time Staff Writer, with Little or No Leverage, What Can I Negotiate?

Not much. As a low-level staff writer, you or your agent probably can't negotiate a higher salary. There are, however, some deal points a good agent can move on–mostly option deadlines within the contract.

Every TV contract specifies **option dates** by when a studio must notify a writer of whether or not he is being brought back to the show. An option date may be a specific date–"September 30, 2014" –or it may be tied to certain events or benchmarks, such as "within fifteen days of the show being picked up." A good agent can move these dates up–say, from September 30 to September 1. This doesn't mean the studio will or won't "pick up your option," or bring you back to the show, it just means that if they don't move quickly, you're free to begin searching for a different job.

Eventually, the agent and studio usually come to terms and the deal is "**closed**." Which means . . . CONGRATULATIONS!! You've just staffed on a TV show! You're on your way to becoming the next Greg Daniels or Aaron Sorkin! "It's never old-hat to get staffed," says David Weinstein (*The Closer, Death Vally*). "When you do the [showrunner] meeting with the Executive Producer and it goes well, it's very buzzy. Then, immediately after the meeting, you start second-guessing yourself about every stupid thing you might have said. You start bugging your agent or your manager–whoever set up the meeting–for answers. Then you wait to see if they liked you as much as you liked them . . . and when the offer finally comes in, it's intoxicating. It means so many things–money, professional validation–the promise that things will go great, and the insane fear you'll fuck up and never work again."

While done verbally, "closing the deal" still constitutes a legally binding agreement. Business affairs then rushes over a **deal memo**, a simple document outlining the basic points of the deal, which the client signs and returns. The studio will also have you sign a **certificate of authorship (C.O.A.)**, saying they've negotiated your services, pursuant to a deal being signed, and own any work you do for them. *You can not show up to your first day of work without signing a C.O.A.!* The studio won't let it happen, so be sure you sign this before starting! (Signing the C.O.A. doesn't mean a deal has been made; it simply confirms the studio owns any work you do for them and a negotiation is underway.)

Ask the Lawyer

Q: I just received my first offer for a staff writer job, so I know don't have much negotiating room in my contract. I also know that most staff writer contracts are pretty standard. Do I need a lawyer to look over my deal, or can my agent handle it himself?

A: "Depends on the agent. Some agents and managers are good at this–I've seen comment letters that were as good as from a lawyer. Managers are usually more thorough than agents. A lot of managers are lawyers [or] ex-agents, but they only have twelve to fifteen clients, as opposed to fifty, so they have time to really look at the thing, read it carefully. The agent doesn't have that kind of time, they have to get on it and start selling the next person. [But] the truth is, there could be something wrong in there. It's always in how something is worded, and companies have incentive to update their form contracts to try and get a little bit more."–Charles Holland, entertainment attorney

---

The Longform

Once your deal has closed verbally, the studio's legal department puts together your actual **longform contract**. While a deal memo covers sixty-five to seventy percent of the main deal points, the longform is comprehensive and detailed. "The part you need to get people to work–that part is the deal memo. It's the meat," says entertainment lawyer Charles Holland, but "there are many things that have to be in the longform to protect the studio, to deal with all kinds of eventualities. What happens if this doesn't work out? What happens if there is an emergency? What happens if there's an act of God? What happens if there's a strike? Studio lawyers want to protect the studio; the client's lawyers want to protect the client."

Agents, lawyers, and the studio's legal affairs department often spend *months* quibbling over language in the longform. In fact, many writers spend months or years working on a show without ever signing a final, official longform contract!

How Do Agents or Managers Stay Involved Once You Begin Work?

Once a writer starts work, things settle down, but that doesn't mean the agent's job is finished. Good agents stay in touch with clients, and good clients communicate with their agents—even when there aren't immediate issues to address. There are, however, several important ways in which agents service working clients:

1. **Staying on top of options**—Most writers have various "**option dates**" built into their contracts, deadlines by which the show or studio must exercise their option to "pick up" (re-hire or retain) the writer on staff. Many low-level writers have a twenty-week option, so after their first twenty weeks on staff, the show must decide whether to keep or fire them. Writers also have option dates at the end of a season; if the show or studio wants the writer back next year, they must notify the writer by a particular deadline. Agents and managers make sure these options don't lapse in order to keep their clients working in good stead.

2. **Checking in**—A good representative follows up periodically to make sure his client is happy in her job. Does she like her boss and co-workers? Did she get the office she was promised? Is the show running smoothly? Many managers and agents also call the showrunner. Is their client listening and participating appropriately in the room? Pitching too little? Pitching too much? Monitoring clients' progress helps agents advise and instruct their writers. It also prepares them for upcoming staffing seasons; if they're aware a client is struggling, they can better prepare to find that client a new job if she's not asked back.

3. **Scheduling generals**—No job lasts forever, especially in Hollywood, where TV writers get fired, shows get cancelled, and staffs downsize almost daily. Thus, agents always keep one eye on the future, watching for opportunities and helping clients pave the way to their next gig. One important way to do this is by constantly introducing clients to execs and producers, usually through general meetings. Just like during staffing season, writers take generals throughout the year. In fact, many agents *prefer* their clients take generals outside of staffing. It eases the chaos of staffing, and allows the writer more time to nurture a relationship. Plus, writers often seem "hotter" when they're working on a show rather than looking for a job.

Save Away!

It's important for writers to be good financial savers; TV writing paychecks may look cushy, but that money has to get you through inevitable periods of unemployment—sometimes weeks, months, or even years.

How Checks Are Processed at an Agency

Unlike in most jobs, where a paycheck travels straight from an employer's accountant to the hands of the employee, writers' paychecks travel an interesting journey. First of all, when writers take a job, they sign a **check authorization**, allowing the employer to send their paychecks directly to their agents. At the agency mailroom, the check is sorted into a pile with other incoming paychecks, which are delivered to the accounting department. Accountants sort each check according to client and deal (some clients have more than one active deal), verifying the information on each check is complete and accurate. They then make a copy of the check, depositing the original into the agency's client trust account. (Agencies, management companies, and law firms all have client trust accounts at various banks, and writers sign **bank authorizations** permitting their agencies to deposit checks on their behalf.)

Using the copy of the check, accountants deduct the client's ten percent commission. They also deduct commissions owed to other representatives, such as the client's lawyer or manager. The accountants then cut new checks for each of these payees, including the agency itself! So one check goes to the client's point agent, another to the client's manager, and another to the lawyer. Finally, the accounting department prints one last check—the writer's—which it mails to the client.

Ask the Agent

Q: I'm a writers assistant on [a popular drama] and was just offered my first freelance script. Should I pay my agents commission on this?

A: This is always a touchy subject among young writers and agents. After all, freelance scripts don't pay much, and most go to young aspirants who could use the money. On the other hand, writers with representation have certain contractual obligations—and one of those obligations is to pay their agents for any writing income, no matter how big or small. Besides, most young writers have young agents, and young agents also have careers to grow—which they do by commissioning clients and building up bookings.

"The question I ask," says Verve agent Zach Carlisle, is "did I help him get the freelance? If I was lobbying shows and showrunners once a week, pushing, pushing, pushing to get the writers assistant a freelance, and it was based on my relationship with the showrunner, in concert with their writers assistant position, there's definitely an argument to commission. This situation just came up. I had a [writers assistant]—who I certainly helped—but he worked very hard to get that [freelance] job himself, and I didn't feel right commissioning it. He asked me to, but I didn't feel it was right. It's not a ton of money, I believe in him long term, and I didn't feel I had done enough to deserve the commission. For the most part, with these guys, if you believe in them, you hope they get staffed and continue to advance their career."

Talk the Talk

Freelance Script–
According to the WGA, every scripted TV show picked up for more than thirteen episodes must assign at least two episodes to **freelance writers,** writers who aren't part of the regular staff.[3] The idea is to give unemployed writers, especially aspirants, a chance to break in. Thus, most showrunners give freelances to writers assistants or low-level friends they weren't able to officially hire.

4. **Getting clients paid**—An important part of an agent's job (and, often, a huge time-suck) is simply making sure clients get paid appropriately. This usually requires teamwork with the agency's accounting department, which is responsible for monitoring each clients' pay dates to make sure checks come in at the scheduled time. When a writer is working on a staff, she usually gets paid weekly, so checks show up regularly. But sometimes there's a glitch in getting payments started, or a check goes missing, and accountants or agents must contact the employer to investigate. Did the writer fail to sign her contract? Has she completed all her payroll paperwork? Once the employer has everything they need, they send the agent the check, but prodding networks, studios, and production companies to pay can be a pain-staking, time-intensive process.

What if a Show Gets Canceled Mid-season?

Reality Check

Fortunately, reality shows—which are cheaper to produce and air–rarely get cancelled midway through their run, and new reality shows start up and staff all year long, so reality writers and producers have many more job opportunities than their brethren in scripted television.

On October 19, 2012, ABC announced it would not renew *Private Practice* after the series' current thirteen-episode season. Less than two months later, on December 7, the show wrapped its final episode, leaving most of its cast, crew, and writing staff unemployed.

When a show gets canceled mid-season, it's usually because ratings have been too soft to warrant further production. Unfortunately, this leaves writers in an uncomfortable situation. "If a show gets cancelled, there isn't much that can be done as a representative," says one agent. "You can try and get [your clients] back out there for gigs, but on the scripted side, there's nothing to do. You have one staffing season, that's it."

In the case of *Private Practice*, knowing of its demise ahead of time helped agents prepare to get clients new jobs. In these cases, says Good, "I'll say, 'Get your spec ready, or your new pilot, or rewrite that script you've been meaning to rewrite for six months.'" In other words, write something new, either a new sample for the upcoming staffing season, or something you can sell. Which brings us to our next chapter: **Development Season**.

A Staffing Season Calendar

How do the activities of staffing season fit into the context of a regular year? Use this calendar to help you understand and plan your own staffing season strategy.

TABLE 6.4

	JAN	FEB	MAR	APR	MAY	JUN	JUL	AUG	SEP	OCT	NOV	DEC
Writers	Deliver new material to agents	TV shows shooting, begin wrapping production		STAFF-ING: Generals and staffing meetings	STAFF-ING: Show-runner meetings	TV shows begin pre-production		TV shows shooting, in full production				
								Works on new staffing material to deliver to reps in January				
Agents	Agents touch base with network and studio execs re: possible staffing needs, submit scripts and writers to execs		Agency hold staffing meetings with networks and studios	Agents schedule generals for clients, submit material to show-runners	Agents schedule show-runner meetings for clients, negotiate and close staffing deals		Agents check in with clients working on shows, make sure working clients get paid, and schedule general meetings to introduce clients to new executives					
What else is going on through-out the year	Pilot season						Development season				Writers with development deals write and turn in pilots	

Staffing Prep Schedule/Checklist

Whether staffing season is eight months or eight weeks away, it's not too late to start planning—especially since writing new material takes time and energy. Here's a checklist and schedule of important to-do's and benchmarks to help you be 100 percent ready for next year's staffing onslaught.

- ☐ **June/July**—Reach out to execs, producers, and other professional contacts—set lunches, coffees, etc. (to maintain and nurture relationships)
- ☐ **August**—Discuss ideas for new material with representation
- ☐ **September**—Begin writing new material
- ☐ **Early December**—Deliver draft of new material to your agent or manager for notes and feedback
- ☐ **December**—Make list of helpful professional contacts and relationships
- ☐ **Early January**—Deliver final draft of new material to agent or manager for staffing submissions
- ☐ **January**—Meet with agent to discuss helpful contacts and relationships
- ☐ **January/February**—Start reading all pilots, inform agent of favorites

7 Development Season— Selling Your Own TV Show ... and Beyond

Stacy Traub was sitting on her couch, exhausted. She had just finished shooting and editing her first pilot, and she was now on the phone with her executives at Warner Brothers, who wanted to talk about staffing possibilities. *Why?* she wondered. The show hadn't yet been picked up . . . it may *never* get picked up . . . and all she wanted was to relax.

In fact, Traub hadn't wanted to develop in the first place. She had been happily working as a supervising producer on *Kitchen Confidential*, FOX's Bradley Cooper-starring adaptation of Anthony Bourdain's acerbic memoir, when producers Eric and Kim Tannenbaum (*Two and a Half Men*, *Sit Down Shut Up*) had called to see if Traub would be interested in writing a TV version of *Notes From the Underbelly*, Risa Green's comic novel about a reluctant mother, for ABC. Traub had met the Tannenbaums a year earlier, after her agents–Larry Salz and Dan Erlij at UTA–had sent her in to pitch on another development project. Unfortunately, Traub hadn't gotten the job, but the Tannenbaums had remembered her, and she seemed like a perfect fit for this new project. After all, she was a rising star in the TV comedy world and had just given birth to her first daughter. Who could be better for a comedy about new parents? Yet Traub wasn't interested.

"It felt very overwhelming to be on a show and develop," Traub recalls, "so I thought, 'I don't think I should do this.' It didn't feel right." But the Tannenbaums didn't give up. They came back and asked Traub to take a look at the novel. If she didn't love it, fine, they'd go away. So Traub agreed to read it and despite herself, wound up liking Green's tale of a Bel Air guidance counselor whose husband convinces her to have a baby.

After that, things happened quickly. Traub wrote the pilot in a matter of weeks. It was green-lit to series. Barry Sonnenfeld (*Men in Black*) came on board to direct; indie film darling Jennifer Westfeldt (*Kissing Jessica Stein*, *Friends With Kids*) was cast as the lead. From there, the four-month pilot process swept Traub into a production whirlwind–rewrites, casting sessions, early morning shoots, late-night edits–an overwhelming experience for anyone, especially a first-time developer.

Through all this, Traub had leaned on her agents, Salz and Erlij, for professional, moral, and emotional support. "When I'm in the middle of something like that, going through shit, I probably call Larry Salz every day," says Traub. "Your family, your spouse–they can help you, but no one understands it the way an agent understands it. They're like your therapist."

It was now early May, 2006, and Traub–like all the other writers with pilots in contention at various networks–was waiting to hear the fate of her show. ABC would either pick it up to series, or flush it–along with half-a-year's worth of blood, sweat, and tears. But at this moment, collapsed on her couch, all Traub wanted was to sleep, or to hang out out with her new daughter, yet Warner Bros. wanted to talk about writers for a TV series that didn't even exist. And probably never would!

That's when "someone runs into the office at Warner Bros., screaming, 'You're picked up! It's picked up! We're picked up!'" says Traub. "And I'm on the other phone, and everyone starts screaming, and I'm like, 'Wha?! Oh my God—Wha?! Wow!' We're screaming and excited, and then I hung up and – I. Started. Bawling."

This is how her husband found her when he walked in a moment later.

"What happened?" he asked.

"The show got picked up."

"Why aren't you happy?"

"And I say, 'I have to run a show!' I literally did not have one moment . . . not one second of joy. I just went to complete terror and panic. *'How the fuck am I going to run a show? I have no idea what I'm doing!'*"

Fortunately, years of experience on shows such as *Spin City*, *Suddenly Susan*, and *What I Like About You* had given Traub all the knowledge she needed. She guided *Notes From the Underbelly* through two seasons on ABC, and while the show didn't come back for a third, ABC hired her to write and produce an adaptation of the BBC's hit sitcom, *Pulling*. "I was very fortunate," Traub says. "The fact that I was allowed to run my own show, having never run a show before, was the hugest, most amazing—as much as I was sobbing, it was incredible that they let me do it—that they trusted me—and for something I was so completely terrified to do . . . I loved it."

Today, Traub has become one of Hollywood's premiere showrunners. She has written, produced, or developed pilots for networks including ABC and HBO; she has co-executive produced FOX's hit musical *Glee*; and she has a lucrative two-year overall deal at ABC Studios. She has also become a seasoned veteran of TV's labyrinthine development system. The twists, turns, and obstacles that once had her sobbing on her agents' shoulders have become old hat.

Yet Traub's favorite takeaway from that first experience? A gorgeous, professionally hardbound copy of her script, given to her by her agents. In fact, her agents now give Traub a hardbound copy of the script every time she produces a pilot—which, since saying goodbye to *Underbelly*, has been every single year.

This isn't to say, of course, that Traub relies on her agents any less. In fact, now that she's a go-to producer, she depends on her agents even more to guide her through development season's Rube Goldberg-esque obstacle course. Fraught with pitfalls, development season is the slim window when TV's creators and showrunners take their shots at selling the next *Elementary* or *Trophy Wife*, backed, hopefully, by an agency powerful enough to make it happen.

But how *do* agencies make it happen? What goes into selling a project? And perhaps more importantly, how do agents and managers give certain project the edge they need to get picked up to pilot, and eventually to series? Understanding how representatives navigate—and, in some cases, control—development season not only gives us valuable insight into how shows get sold and produced, it also helps us build and strategize our own projects and careers.

APRIL–JUNE: PRE-DEVELOPMENT SEASON

As we've discussed, development season—for producers and execs—kicks off in late June or early July. As new and returning series ramp up production for the upcoming season, networks, studios, and production companies begin hearing pitches for the *following* year, which means agents who set those pitches must begin preparing a bit earlier. "I first start thinking about [development] in March," says UTA agent Joel Begleiter. "You start to realize what shows are definitely not going to come back, which clients are available, which clients don't want to staff."

"As an agent, it is my job to call the different studios and networks and get ideas of what they think will come back and what won't," explains APA lit agent Lindsay Howard. "But we also keep track of the ratings throughout the year. [We watch] when something looks like it's trending downward and not likely to come back, and [when] something is stable."

Hurry Up and Wait

While studios and upper-level writers may put their blind script deals in place in April or May, they still won't begin developing ideas together until development season, two or three months down the road.

This early in the game, most development action centers around upper-level writers. Agents get a sense of which Executive Producer or Co-Executive Producer clients have their own show ideas, which don't want to return to a staff, which are working on shows that won't be renewed. Agents then begin calling studio execs, trying to land their upper level clients a **blind script deal**, a financial commitment to write an as-yet-unspecified project. A "blind" allows the studio to secure a writer's services before the writer takes

---

To D or Not To D?

Young writers are often bursting with ideas for TV shows, but developing for a low-level writer isn't always the best idea. "I don't *discourage* low-level writers from developing," says UTA lit agent Joel Begleiter, "but it's a hard road for them to go down. The system is set up for [execs and buyers] to say no to everything; if you just bring in a low-level writer naked (without attachments or a shepherding producer), unless that idea is spectacular or they have a specific fan at a network or studio, it's really hard to get something going."

Still not dissuaded? Fine—here are some other reasons to reconsider developing as a low-level writer:

1. **Development is time-consuming**. Most low-level writers are (hopefully) busy writing on an actual staff, which takes massive amounts of time and energy. You're often in the writers room, or on stage, for fifteen hours a day or more, leaving little time for anything else, especially trying to develop and write a whole new series. Many studios, in fact, contractually ban low-level writers on their shows from developing.

   "It's just not fair to the show," says Dana Honor, senior VP of comedy development at 20th Century Fox TV, "[when] we're putting forth all of our energy to make the show as big of a hit as we can, and you're physically out of the room, out of the story-breaking process."

2. **Developing too early can damage your "quote."** "Let's say you're a story editor," says Begleiter, "and you sell a piece of development. You're going to get paid close to WGA minimum (about $50,000) to write that pilot script, so now it's your 'quote.' So you write the pilot, it doesn't go forward and then you go on staff. Three years later, you're a supervising producer, you're going out with development again, and a business affairs executive says, 'Do they have quotes?' You *do* have a quote, and your quote's near WGA minimum," when it *should* be much higher—perhaps two hundred thousand dollars higher. "You might be better off having never developed before than having development and having a bad quote."

3. **You're missing out on valuable experiences**. As Honor points out, if you're trying to juggle both a staff job and development, one or both of them will suffer. And the truth is: staff writers are helpful to a staff, but if they're not delivering, they're inexpensive and easily replaceable. So during the early stages of your career, you should have one goal: *impress the showrunner, execs, and producers you work with*. You can't do that if you're preoccupied with other projects.

   Having said that, writers with great ideas *can* use the spring to prepare their pitches. Often, for instance, writers like to partner with successful producers or studio-based pods, as this gives them a leg up going in to studios and networks.

   March or April is often a good "time to go to big producers who can be an eight-hundred-pound gorilla in the process," says Begleiter. "Producers aren't jammed the way studio and network executives are at that time. If they've had a pilot go, they're busy, but they have enough time to sit with somebody and work on an idea. [Also] . . . if we're trying to add a big element, that's a perfect time to start that conversation."

his project to the marketplace, thus avoiding a competitive situation that could drive up the project's price. It also allows the writer to know he has income, should he not land a job (or want to land a job) on an actual staff.

For lower- and mid-level writers, March, April, and May are consumed with the demands of staffing season: non-stop meetings, script reading, pilot watching. And while younger writers may have their own show ideas, agents don't usually focus on younger clients' development until after 'upfronts', as it becomes clear which writers won't staff.

Deciding What to Develop and Pitch

As staffing season winds down, some agencies host TV development retreats for the entire agency, usually at a posh Southern California hotel or resort. The retreat begins with the TV lit department combing through its entire list of clients, from the uppermost showrunner to the lowliest baby, discussing who's working, who's not, who wants to develop. TV agents then meet with every other department in the agency, exploring where there may be television crossover. Does a feature screenwriter have an idea for a TV show? Is there an author who has a book that could be spun off as a TV series, like *The Carrie Diaries* or *Bones*? A successful blog or web series that could become a sitcom, like when Comedy Central adapted Jordan Pope Roush's blog, "Bad Advice From My Brother?"[1] A high-profile musician who wants to break into television, like Ricky Martin, who landed a 2012 NBC development deal?[2]

Just as agencies commence staffing season with network and studio "staffing meetings," they also begin development season with network and studio meetings. Most agencies' TV lit department goes around town, meeting with each network and studio and gathering information about what they hope to find and develop. Sometimes, a network or studio's wants are specific: "We want serialized male dramas like *24* and

TABLE 7.1

NBC–Comedy Title	Writer	Auspices	Studio	Commit-ment	Logline	Comments	Status
F*ck I'm In My Twenties	Emma Koenig, Jeff Lowell	EP: Gail Berman, Lloyd Braun, Gene Stein/ BermanBraun	Universal	Script	20-something girl faces realities of post-college city life.	Based on blog and book	Dead
Untitled Ron Weiner Project	Ron Weiner	EP: Peter Chernin, Katherine Pope/ Chernin Company	20th	Script	Two co-workers who hate each other learn to get along and manage a team together.		Dead
Joe & Joe & Jane	Joe Port and Joe Wiseman		20th	Put pilot + penalty	Autobiographical multi-cam about author who must navigate relationship b/w wife and his friend/co-author, who hate each other.	Cast: Larry Wilmore, Sally Pressman	Pilot
Undateable	Adam Sztykiel	EP: Jeff Ingold, Bill Lawrence/ Doozer Prod.	Warner Bros.	Script + penalty	Two buddies who can't attract women navigate the dating world.	Based on book *Undateable: 311 Things Guys Do That Guarantee They Won't Be Dating Or Having Sex*, by Ellen Rakieten and Anne Coyle	Pilot
Untitled Ricky Martin Project			Thru Universal TV			Talent holding deal; Martin repped at CAA	

Prison Break." Other times, they're more general: "We want a medical show," or "We don't want anything with a supernatural element."

This is why most TV projects are bought as pitches, concepts, instead of fully written scripts. Because networks have only broad ideas of what they want, they look for good ideas they can mold to fit their own unique brand. It's harder to do that with a fully written script. Also, "as an agent or manager, you don't want your writer to take five months to bang out a script, to come to find [the network] already bought their cop show," says one lit agent.

While early meetings are great recon missions, covering agents track each network and studio's development slate as it evolves throughout the season. Many agents use comprehensive grids such as Table 7.1 (this is information culled from the 2012–13 development season):

Covering agents also gather info on properties a studio owns and may wish to develop into TV shows. In 2012, for instance, Sony Television wanted to develop TV versions of its movies *Bad Teacher* and *A Knight's Tale*, so agents try to find clients to fill these needs. In this case, Sony hired UTA-repped Hilary Winston, a *Community* writer, to adapt *Bad Teacher* (which it then sold to CBS[3]) and *Battlestar Galactica* executive producer Ron Moore, repped by CAA, to write *A Knight's Tale* (which it sold to ABC[4]). *Bad Teacher* was eventually picked up to series for the 2013–2014 season; *A Knight's Tale* was not.

In addition, agents track other helpful information, such as which producers and pods have deals at a particular studio. A partial 2012 list for NBC may have looked something like this:

Universal TV Overalls

- Liz Brixius (Exec. Prod: *Nurse Jackie*)[5]
- Tucker Cawley (Exec. Prod: *Up All Night*)[6]
- Gina Fattore (Exec. Prod: *Californication*)[7]
- Jason Katims/True Jack (Michelle Lee: head of dev.)[8]
- D.J. Nash (Exec. Prod: *Up All Night*)[9]
- Sarah Watson (Co-EP: *Parenthood*)[10]
- Harris Wittels (Sup. Prod: *Parks & Recreation*)[11]

Insider's Tip: Keep Your Own Development Reports

You can maintain your own development reports and overall lists by tracking projects or deals reported online or in the trades. You'll not only stay current on what's happening in the TV world, you'll start to spot trends in projects being bought and writers or producers landing deals. Are writers from certain series all scoring valuable development overalls or selling pitches? Are there many shows with similar themes—such as shows about the supernatural, or serial killers, or political scandals—that may be tapping into cultural currents? Here are some great sites and publications for monitoring TV sales and deals:

Daily Variety—www.variety.com
The Hollywood Reporter—www.hollywoodreporter.com
Deadline Hollywood—www.deadlinehollywood.daily
TV Week—www.tvweek.com
Broadcasting and Cable—www.broadcastingcable.com
Cynopsis—www.cynopsis.com
Futon Critic—www.thefutoncritic.com
TV Tracker—www.tvtracker.com

As writers consider TV ideas, they often bounce pitches off their representation. Some do this over email, others prefer a phone call, and many like to sit face-to-face. Also, some agents want to read a one-pager, others like hearing slightly fleshed-out ideas, and still others want the simplest presentation possible. "I prefer one-liners," says Begleiter, "to be able to say, 'I've never heard that before' or 'I've heard that forty times.' It allows me to get into the creative process a little bit, so they're not working in a vacuum, [then] coming in with something fully conceived before you say, 'That'll never sell.' If you identify an area that's great, you can be involved in working it up with them. That can be valuable."

How, then, do agents evaluate whether a show is "sellable?" Actually "That is not the most important question," says Ra Kumar, an alternative agent at N.S. Bienstock. The important question is: "Is this the kind of show a network wants to see *from this client*? If a producer known for doing game shows walks through with a docu-soap, the network will question whether or not they can pull this off. You always want to know how hard it's going to be to sell something based on the **auspices**. Sometimes a network will buy a show they've heard many times before, but they buy it from the sixth person they hear it from because they really want to be in business with [this particular producer]."

Thus, it's not unusual for writers to bounce fifteen or twenty ideas off their agents. Most get axed in a quick fifteen-minute conversation, but hopefully your agent finds one or two that excite him. In a way, this part of the process is as much about quantity as quality. Sure, you want to find that one brilliant idea you're passionate about, but being a television writer is often about generating quantity as well as quality (after all, when you have a show on the air, you need to be pumping out hundreds of stories a year). So this stage is about generating several ideas that excite you, then letting your agent help weed out the **MOPs** (**Most Often Pitched**).

"'It's a cop who can read the memories of the deceased.' I've heard that idea literally a hundred times in my career," says Begleiter. "Everybody thinks they've cracked it ... [but] there's nothing that sets it apart from the hundreds of versions that have [already] been pitched. It's not their fault, but it's my job to say, 'Don't pitch that. It's been pitched a thousand times.'"

Talk the Talk

Auspices—A project's attachments or partners; auspices could include a producer, an actor, a director, a host, or even a corporate sponsor.

JULY–OCTOBER: DEVELOPMENT SEASON

Winding Up for the Pitch

Once you and your agent land on one or two ideas, it's time to go off and flesh out the pitch. This should happen quickly. "If it takes you more than a week," says Begleiter, "it's probably not a very good idea and you're not completely invested in it."

Also, it's the writer's job to do the heavy-lifting of development. Most agents do not want to be bombarded with creative questions and issues. Sometimes "we've spitballed something in the room and come to a point where we've [agreed] about the right way to do something," says Begleiter, "and a writer will send me an email two days later saying, 'I thought of something else, I want to go this way, does that make sense?' 'Yes, that makes sense, go do it.' But I don't want them peppering me with questions every twelve hours."

This is where managers can be much more effective. "We take on fewer clients, whereas at agencies there could be twenty TV lit agents and hundreds, if not a thousand, of clients," says manager Geoff Silverman, a partner at The Cartel, which represents writers and creators of shows such as *Alphas*, *Charmed*, *Judging Amy*, and *White Collar*.

When a writer first approaches his manager with an idea, "I explain, first and foremost, what we need to go in there and *sell*," says New Wave manager Michael Pelmont. "The main difference between selling a TV show versus a feature is: in a feature, you're selling concept over character; in a TV show, you're selling character over concept. When you pitch a feature, you're pitching something beat by beat. When you sell a TV series, you're selling great original characters.

"[In fact], I never have people pitch pilots. I don't like to get bogged down going through Act One, Scene One, Scene Two . . . You're not selling that pilot, you're selling the ability to make a hundred of these things with characters that are great. [So] we'll say, 'We don't have a pilot, we have some episode ideas, we could probably use this first one for the pilot, or we could pick any of them for the pilot.'

"If you go in there and set up these characters, by the time you deliver these one-liners (story ideas), that executive should know these characters so well they literally laugh at the idea of seeing them in that scenario. You could have put the characters from *The Office* at the DMV or as flight school instructors—it wouldn't matter. But you don't get to that point unless these characters are so real and distinct they're immediately going to be pictured in these scenarios, and you get that laugh. If you're getting laughs out of your two-line episode ideas, you're on the way to a sale."

Once the pitch is fully baked, the writer presents the idea to his agent. A writer should know the basic premise of his show, the central characters and relationships, how a typical episode works, and several episodic story ideas or areas. You should "be able to sit in the room and pitch me, in the most compelling way imaginable, why this show is great and why you're the right person to write it," says Begleiter. "If you want to have visuals, great. If you want to have music, great. If you just want to pitch

---

Should I Pitch My Show or Write It as a Spec Pilot?

This is a question that plagues many writers, "In my opinion, there is never a situation where a great idea is better being taken out as a spec pilot," says UTA agent Joel Begleiter. "If it's actually a great idea, and if the client can pitch, take it out as a pitch. If it doesn't sell, and you still believe in it, *then* write the spec."

Why is this? For better or worse, studios and networks rarely buy spec pilots. Sure, you'll occasionally hear of a spec pilot getting bought or even made, but look at examples from recent years. CBS's *Two Broke Girls* hails from *Sex and the City* showrunner Michael Patrick King and long-time comedy producer/performer Whitney Cummings, Fox's *Touch* came from *Heroes* creator Tim Kring, and *Don't Trust the B*[12] came from *American Dad* executive producer Nahnatchka Khan. In other words, *they're all from veteran writers and producers.*

Having said that, even most spec pilots from seasoned showrunners wind up in the circular file. In 2012, Josh Schwartz (*The O.C.*) and Chris Carter (*The X-Files*) both wrote spec pilots that failed to get picked up. The point is: it's rare for *any* spec pilot to get picked up, *but even rarer from a novice writer.*

"[Writing] things on spec to try to sell them, with the intention of marketing them, is a one-way ticket to not getting paid to write your spec," says UTA agent Joel Begleiter. "It's something we should all be disincentivizing our clients to do."

Does this mean you should *never* write a spec pilot? Not necessarily. There are certain times it may be beneficial to write something on spec:

1. **If a writer is switching genres**—If an established comedy wants to write a drama (or vice versa), and there's nothing to convince networks this particular person can write outside her wheelhouse, the idea may be worth speccing.
2. **If the idea is provocative or potentially uncommercial**—Networks, for the most part, like to develop shows that are safe, conventional, and not going to upset audiences. Not many networks would develop a series about a morally ambiguous policeman who kills, tortures, and lies . . . which is why Shawn Ryan chose to write the pilot for *The Shield* on spec.
3. **You want a killer sample**—This may be the most common reason to write a spec pilot: the story is burning inside you and you want a fantastic sample to help land a staff job. Execs and showrunners love reading "original material," and a spec pilot is an excellent way to display your voice. "Write the thing you're passionate about," says Begleiter, "but the goal can't be 'I have to sell this.' If it's that, you're fucked from the beginning."

it verbally, great. If you want to come in and read off a document, great. It just has to be compelling."

Now your agent begins to strategize. If the writer is an upper-level producer, he may immediately call studios to drum up excitement. (In fact, if the agent loved the idea from the outset, he may have begun calling last week, before the writer even had his prepared pitch!) "If [the writer] already has a blind somewhere," says Begleiter, "I like to call the studio and say, "They just pitched me this idea. It's fucking great. You're gonna love it. Get him in there. Call him today and get him in there to you to pitch it to you in the next week."

Taking Out the Pitch

Every year, the agencies, collectively, take out thousands of pitches. One Big Four agent estimated that his agency alone takes out between 500 and 750 pitches a year, selling approximately seventy-five percent. Smaller agencies have fewer agents and fewer clients, but one boutique agent estimated his firm took out between seventy and eighty pitches a year.

The first step in the pitching process is usually to meet with producers or production companies. When it comes to picking a production company with a studio deal, you generally have two options or strategies. Most writers and agents find one particular pod, or producer they gel with, then partner with this "entity" exclusively. As a writer, for instance, you may partner with *The Walking Dead* writer/producer Glen Mazzara, who has an overall deal at Fox TV Studios (20th Century Fox's sister studio, which focuses on low-budget, cable, and alternative programming).[13] Together, you and Mazzara would take the project to Fox TV Studios; if they pass, Mazzara can ask permission to go elsewhere—a request that may or may not be granted.

Occasionally agents let multiple companies take it to their home studios simultaneously. In other words, the writer might pitch the idea to various producers—Mazzara at Fox TV Studios, Andre and Maria Jacquemetton at Warner Brothers,[14] Baz Luhrmann's Bazmark Films at Sony[15]—but instead of choosing one person he likes best, he'd choose one entity *at each studio*, then let those people compete by taking the project to their execs at the same time. Mazzara would take it to Sony, the Jacquemettons would take it to Warners, and Bazmark would take it to Sony. This can not only create a more competitive marketplace, it forces production companies to be more aggressive in applying pressure to their studios. (This strategy, as we'll learn in Chapter 9, is much closer to the process used by feature agents.)

How an agent approaches potential producers depends on the writer who created the project. "In the case of a talented but relatively unknown entity to these pods," says Begleiter, "I'd [call and] say, 'I've got a young writer. It's something I really believe in. Here's the basic area. Can we set a time for him to come in a pitch?' Ninety-five percent of the time they will, for all the reasons involved: I'm calling from UTA, I have good taste, and I have a track record of being right about things."

If the production company has never met or heard of the writer, execs might want to read samples before hearing the pitch. A good agent may convince them to go ahead and schedule the meeting, then send over samples to be read beforehand. If the writer is a mid- or upper-level writer, someone who's already well-known, the exec is probably already aware of their work. Likewise, if there's already a substantial star or director attached, the exec probably won't ask to read samples; they'll simply take the pitch. (Usually, however, the producer helps attach a star or director; we'll examine this more in a moment.)

An agent generally tries to set producer pitches as close together as possible. This not only creates competition, it gives pitchers energy and momentum. Like any performance, the spiel gets better each time you do it, and there's a fun excitement in driving from pitch to pitch.

Agenting 101

"Sometimes it's good to set the [meetings] that aren't as important (smaller, less powerful pods) first. Treat them like practice pitches. The first one or two are not going to be smooth . . . [so] it's a little scary to have your biggest meeting up first. Writers that have pitched the idea to four or five pods—when they go in on the seventh or eighth, they've really got it down. They're not looking at notes, they know all the talking points, they know where people are going to laugh."–Geoff Silverman, manager/partner, The Cartel

TELEVISION AGENTS

All In the Timing

Some writers and agents think certain times of day are better for pitches than others. Is this superstition or smart strategic planning to connect with someone when they're most eager to listen? I have no idea, but here are some (supposedly) good pitching tips I've hard writers swear by:

- I always try to be an exec's *first* meeting of the day or her *last* meeting of the day. People tend to be better at remembering things at the beginning or end of their days; all the stuff in the middle becomes white noise.
- I know other writers who *never* pitch at the end of the day, as they fear execs just want to pack up and go home.
- Some writers like to go in right after lunch, when the exec feels refreshed. But if you can help it, *never* go in right *before* lunch, when people tend to be hungry and unfocused.

Most production company pitches are held at the company's main offices or, if they have a project in production, the show's production office, so you'll often be driving onto a studio lot. Your agent will call ahead to ensure the company gets you a "drive-on," a pass to enter and park on the lot.

"If you are a young writer, you are going to be pitching to the bottom of the food chain," says showrunner John Peaslee (*Liv and Maddie, According To Jim*). "For beginner writers, the likelihood that you get a decision maker in the room is low. If you are a well-known writer and have had success with that network before, you'll get a higher-level development person. Sometimes you get the highest, depending on who you are, and what commitment they have to you."

Two is Company, Your Agent's a Crowd

Most agents don't attend pitch meetings, especially if the writer and execs already know each other. A pitch should be about creative minds meeting and connecting over a particular idea; having an agent, a salesman, present often gives the meeting a weird, "business-y" feel that can undermine the connection and creativity that need to happen. Agents, however, sometimes attend if the writer and execs don't know each other, or if the agent fears their personalities may need help connecting.

"There are execs who are very stone-faced; they don't give a lot of emotional feedback," says Kumar. "It's hard to pitch someone who's not giving you a lot of reaction. My role is to guide the conversation and fill in the gaps. [Also,] if it looks like there's no further reason to be there, I cut the meeting. I've had to kick clients under the table to tell them to stop talking."

The pitch usually begins with small talk. I usually have a funny anecdote in my back pocket—something I know will be an ice breaker if the meeting doesn't kick off with an energy of its own. After a few minutes, the small talk may segue naturally into your pitch (if you're pitching a family show, and you're chatting about your kids, you can use a crafty, "Speaking of kids . . ."). Or the execs may shift the spotlight themselves—"So, tell us what you have"—at which point, the floor is yours.

"You're under a little less pressure [when pitching] the pods," says Peaslee, "because they need to come up with product. They want you to succeed, so striking out with them doesn't necessarily mean you've struck out. They [may] go, 'I didn't like anything about your pitch except that one character. You think we can take that character, and put him in another world, another arena?' Your calling card is your idea, [so] you want to come in, not be too nervous if you can help it, look them in the eye, tell a story. They're waiting for you to entertain them."

Most writers begin their pitch with a quick description of what the show is about and why it's personal to them. "Most things should be—in some way—personal to you," says Traub. "Even if it's a cop show, it might be underlying a father-son relationship based on you and your dad. Then pitch the lead characters, and a quick synopsis of the pilot story—basically when we're going to drop in to meet these people, and why. Some people don't include a pilot story at all, they just do characters and sample stories."

The writer or creator of the show should aways be the "point person" in the pitch, but if you're pitching with an actor or director, you may want to find some places for them to jump in as well. "[Buyers] want to know there's synergy, that you're not just two people who were '**paper teamed**' and have nothing to do with each other," says Gurman. "They're buying that synergy between you."

Some producers or execs wait till you finish to ask questions; others ask as you go. I always take it as a great sign when they're asking questions along the way—it means they're engaged! "[A pitch] should be more of a conversation than just a sales piece," says Verve agent Amy Retzinger. "Whether [pitching] a pod, a supervising showrunner, a director . . . this person is going to be your partner, so you want to have a bit of a back-and-forth. Be open to input; they're there to be creative, to roll up their sleeves. You want their knowledge and expertise. Otherwise, why would they want to get in business with you?"

As the pitch winds down, execs usually give some indication of where their heads are. This may be something polite but dismissive, like, "It's a fun world—it's just not right for us," or, "I don't think we're the right home for this, but thanks for thinking of us." They may "buy it in the room," saying, "Great job, we'd love to be a part of this!" Most likely, however, they'll ask for time to think and tell you they'll be in touch.

Talk the Talk

Paper Team—When a studio or agency pairs together two writers to make them cheaper to hire. Since writing teams get paid as a single unit, it's often more cost-efficient to hire duos. Thus, some studios will offer a job to two solo writers—as long as they agree to be paper teamed, essentially allowing the studio to pay them each half their normal quote. *("That sounds sleazy," you say? Yeah—it is.)*

Should I Leave Behind a Treatment or One-page After a Pitch?

"I generally encourage [clients] *not* to leave a paper treatment," says N.S. Bienstock agent Ra Kumar. Contrary to popular belief, this isn't because producers may steal your idea. In fact, if you've developed your idea properly, it should be so personal and distinctive that it can't done without you. Rather, there are two reasons not to leave behind a treatment.

Reason One: "A lot of times you'll get input from [executives] about the pitch: 'we're looking for this, not that,'" says Kumar. Maybe they think the show should be set in a beach town instead of a ski resort, or should have a female lead instead of a male lead. USA's *Suits*, for instance, was originally set in an investment firm, until USA suggested creator Aaron Korsh transfer it to a law office. By not giving execs a "leave behind," you can integrate their notes into your concept and send them a perfectly tailored treatment a day or two later. This not only allows you to give execs precisely what they want, it allows you to snag their email addresses and open a channel of communication. Even if they don't buy this idea, you can keep in touch, take them to drinks, and nurture a relationship that will lead to them buying your *next* idea.

Reason Two: When you leave the meeting, execs have to go pitch your idea to their boss, and you want them to be the most passionate, enthusiastic pitchers possible. They have to transfer your fire and excitement to the head of the company! Leaving a treatment gives them a crutch; they'll be constantly glancing at the treatment, making sure they have details and words right. Or worse yet, they'll just say, "Here, read this." But details, words, and pages are much less effective than passion and excitement—so don't give them anything that could sap that energy!

Reality Check

Unlike in scripted television, producers pitching reality shows often put together sophisticated **sizzle reels** and beautiful, comprehensive **treatments**, which they *do* leave behind with buyers. While much of the process and theory of selling a reality program is the same as selling a scripted program—you're still trying to bring the show to life for buyers—most reality programs don't use traditional scripts or actors, making it hard for networks to evaluate a show's potential based on writing samples, or box office cache. Reality shows, rather, are often based around real people or events. If it's a docusoap like *Duck Dynasty* or *Dance Moms*, it mines stories from the lives of actual people like the Robertson family or Abby Miller. If it's a personality-driven idea, like *Nathan For You*, or even a talk show like *The Late Late Show with Craig Ferguson*, it's based on the charm and personality of the show's host. It doesn't really matter what Craig Ferguson or Nathan Fielder do each week; audiences simply want to spend time with them. Thus, producers pitching reality shows need some way to prove to buyers their real-life characters "pop" on screen.

"A **sizzle reel** is the only real way of showing it," says alternative agent Ra Kumar. Sizzle reels, or "tape," are short videos highlighting the characters, their personalities and relationships, and how they conflict with each other to create story. Most "sizzles" look like commercials or trailers for a movie or TV show; they show the characters interacting in their natural habitats (fighting at home, joking around at work, being friends at school, whatever their dynamic), talking in confessional (one-on-one with the camera), and embarking on the kinds of adventures audiences can expect to see on the show. Most sizzle reels are about two to five minutes long, and can take a few weeks to produce.

A good sizzle "shouldn't cost more than $5,000," says APA alternative/international agent Alan Moore, "but people spend more. If you can do it while shooting another show, that helps bring costs down, because you can share resources. But I'd never advise anyone to spend more than five grand on tape. You should be calling in favors. It's like a student film. It should be as cheap as possible."

A **treatment**, meanwhile, "could be as little as a one-sheet with some graphics and a quick description of the show," adds Kumar, or it could be "as detailed as a show bible [illustrating] what episodes are like. If it's a **format-based** show like a game show or *Survivor*, what are the episodes going to be? If you're selling a show like *Snapped* on Oxygen, [buyers] want to know those stories exist."

Indeed, treatments work well for format-based shows that aren't based on actual people, but instead have specific challenges, events, or structures. The point, of course, isn't just to give dry information about the show, it's to make the show "sexy. You want to sell it," adds Moore. "If it's *Ice Road Truckers*, you would talk about the world it's set within. You would identify some great characters in that world. You would have pictures, bios—not just background info, but what makes them a great character, what their stories are like, so you can see what the show might capture. And if there's a business, [you might include] what their next step of growth might be so you can see the [bigger] storyline—not just for the people involved, but for the business as a whole."

One reason reality producers often use leave-behinds—and scripted producers don't—is that in scripted television, buyers are investing less in the fictional details of the pitch than in the unique vision and talent of the writer. In other words, TV is full of scripted ideas which, on paper, seem frighteningly similar: *Fringe* and *The X-Files*, *Psych* and *The Mentalist*, *Grimm* and *Once Upon a Time*. But these shows are actually wonderfully different, because the visions and worldviews of their creators are so wonderfully unique and distinct. And before these shows were developed, buyers *knew* these creators' worldviews were different because they had read writing samples, looked at past work, etc.

In reality TV, buyers also want unique and distinct ideas, but because reality characters are springing from writers' imaginations, instead of real life, reality buyers look at sizzle reels and treatments rather than sample scripts. Thus, reality producers often leave behind treatments or sizzles that illuminate a show's (and producer's) tone, sensibility, stories, and characters.

After each pitch, the writer's agent or manager calls the execs to push them toward buying or partnering on the project. "I'll say something like, 'We have strong interest at one or two places,'" says Silverman, "which hopefully is not a lie. There's nothing wrong in saying, 'They just had a great meeting. J.J. Abrams was actually in the pitch', if that actually happened—'you should think about taking this out . . . it's getting some definite heat.'"

As you finish all your production company pitches, you and your agent discuss each company: how the meetings went, who responded and who didn't, who would be an appropriate and enthusiastic partner, and who actually has the muscle to navigate Hollywood and get a show on the air. "I definitely want the strongest producers," says Silverman, "[but] passion speaks volumes, so I [also] want them to be passionate."

The agent or manager then calls the lucky company to give them the good news. Now the writer, with the help of his new partners, begins tweaking the pitch, a process which could take a few days—or a few weeks. This may involve redeveloping the concept creatively, or even attaching elements, like stars or directors, that could help get the project sold.

Attaching Elements

If the writer isn't a veteran developer, or the pitch is a trickier concept, it often helps to attach other elements, or auspices, like an A-list "piece of talent" or a director with a unique visual style. When you're pitching a TV show, "you're selling a pig in a poke," says Gurman, "and if [buyers] can have an element they're familiar with, like a director or an actor, it helps them visualize something."

Attaching talent also helps persuade execs that audiences will watch a show. After all, stars come with a built-in audience, right? Cast a big name in the lead, and audiences will come running. That's the thinking that drives many network and studio decisions—but is it true? In 2008, FOX canceled comedy *Breaking In*, starring Christian Slater, after seven episodes. (Weirdly, they "un-canceled" the show three months later, revamping it for a second season. It re-premiered on March 6, 2012 and lasted five poorly-rated episodes.) Similarly, ABC was happy to announce Christina Ricci in its 2011 drama *Pan Am*, only to unhappily announce its cancelation fourteen episodes later. The truth is: execs think audiences care about big-name stars, but the only people who actually seem to care about big-name stars are executives!

Agents may also try to attach high-profile producers or showrunners. Sometimes this is the whole purpose of having the pod itself aboard; other times, the showrunner and the pod are different. When I worked at the Littlefield Company, we developed a romantic comedy with Andrew Secunda, a *Saturday Night Live* and *Late Night with Conan O'Brien* writer just dipping his toe into the sitcom world. We paired Andy with *Friends* executive producer Adam Chase. The show, *Love, Inc.*, made it on the air at UPN, where Secunda was the creator, we were the pod, and Chase was the showrunner. Attaching a showrunner is, in many ways, more valuable than attaching an actor or director, because while a showrunner may not guarantee the show will be a hit, he gives buyers confidence that there's an experienced leader at the helm.

Attaching auspices up front is also helpful because if your project goes to pilot or series, you're going to need to hire these elements anyway. Yet as development and pilot season progress, actors, showrunners, and directors get hired onto other shows,

The Bigger They Are . . . Doesn't Mean Much

Like their friends in TV, movie producers and execs also fool themselves into thinking big-name stars are all audiences care about. Unfortunately, this has been proven painfully *wrong* on more than one occasion. Check out the box on page 179 to learn more!

TELEVISION AGENTS

giving you a smaller pool from which to hire and less control over your own project. So attach the right elements now, and it may make for a better product.

When thinking about attachments, agents confer with colleagues in other departments to figure out which clients may be right for the project. What actors or hosts in the agency's talent department are desirable enough to get this project sold an on next year's schedule? Agents also look at the studios' list of overalls, development deals, and **talent holding deals**. Has a hot up-and-coming actor just signed with the TV talent department? Do the MP agents represent an aging movie star who may consider doing a series?

There are several factors to consider when attaching actors, directors, and showrunners:

1. **Are they creatively appropriate for the project?** J.J. Abrams is a brilliant writer/director who has developed amazing shows—*Alias, Lost, Felicity, Person of Interest*. But is he right for your multi-camera sitcom about a blended family? Probably not, since Abrams seems to excel with intense and mysterious dramas. Similarly, *Two and a Half Men* creator Chuck Lorre is a highly respected and coveted showrunner; but is he right for your dark, serialized drama about a juvenile correctional facility?

2. **Are they someone valuable to networks and studios?** Each network has a "wish list" of actors, showrunners, and directors they'd like to work with; the goal is to find attachments attractive to as many networks as possible, or at least to networks you're targeting with your pitch. Unfortunately, networks and studios have different tastes and needs, and an actor or director who's great for one place may not be great for another. Agents keep tabs on who networks and studios want to be in business with by covering their territories and watching the trades.

3. **Are they someone "get-able?"** Does the possible attachment seem like someone who might be interested in this particular project? (Tom Cruise may be perfect for your action-adventure series, but there's little likelihood Tom Cruise will attach himself to a TV show, so why waste time pursuing him?) Even if a particular star is interested in TV, most genuinely valuable stars won't attach themselves to just "any" project. Their representation is going to reserve them only for the biggest writers or producers.

   "I heard Demi Moore's going to want to do TV this year," says Silverman. "I just don't think she's going to walk in with anyone below Chuck Lorre. I don't know if she wants to do drama or comedy, but when her representative at CAA says to the town, 'Demi Moore's going to do TV,' they're going to contact [only about] five producers. If I was to call and say, 'I have the greatest project for her,' they'll say, 'Great, who's the writer?' Or, 'Is Imagine involved?'"

   It's true; A-list talent wants to know a respected producer is steering the ship—another reason it can be helpful to go first to big producers or those with overall deals. They have access and influence even many agents don't actually have. (Also, as we'll discuss in a moment, it's not always easy for agents from one agency to attach an artist repped at another.)

   "Cameron Diaz is never going to do TV," muses one manager, "unless she's walking in with Steven Spielberg and Dreamworks, saying, 'I'll do six episodes on a TV show this year, and I'll be the executive producer.' And then we just let Dreamworks go get her."

4. **Is there enough time?** In-demand actors and directors have busy schedules, and most studios and networks exhaust their development coffers in early October, so get in early. "You don't want to run out of time while you're busily trying to attach elements," says Begleiter, "and then you look up and its September 15th and you still haven't gone to a studio."

5. **Does the attachment have a studio deal, a first-look, overall, or talent-holding deal?** We know big writers, producers, and even directors sign deals

with studios, but so do top-shelf actors. In some cases, the actor simply wants to produce projects; in others, the actor intends to perform as well. In 2012, *30 Rock* star Alec Baldwin signed a two-year overall with Universal Television. Ryan Reynolds launched DarkFire, a TV company with a first-look deal at 20th Century Fox TV. And MMA and UFC champion Randy Couture signed a two-year overall, starting in 2013, with Spike.

Better Late Than Never

It's also possible to attach an element *after* pitching a studio. Maybe the studio has an overall with a sci-fi producer who would be perfect for your futuristic drama. Or perhaps the studio has a holding deal with a hilarious young actress looking for a smart romantic comedy. Of course, in order for this to happen, the studio first has to want your project; this can sometimes put younger, inexperienced writers at a disadvantage, as it's harder for them to sell a show in the first place, and studios may not want to pair valuable talent with an unproven writer.

Finding an attachment with a deal can be advantageous because you know their studio or network is hungry to find projects for them. But there's also a downside. "Often times, people who have a deal just at NBC might not be able to go somewhere else," says Silverman, so if you fail to sell your project to that person's home studio, you can't take them with you to pitch other studios. "A lot of times there are good outside producers that just don't want a deal, like [*Sideways* producer] Michael London. Sony pods, and Warner Brothers or Warner Horizon, are usually good because [their] pods can go anywhere." (Remember: Sony and Warner Brothers have no network of their own; they're just studios.)

How Can I Find Out Which Actors, Directors, or Showrunners Have Deals?

There isn't necessarily one source that maintains this information. Most agents and managers keep their own lists of overalls and holding deals, updating them regularly by reading trades or talking directly to friends at networks or studios. You can sometimes find assembled lists on **tracking boards** or services like TVTracker.com, but most representatives still maintain their own. This means you can, too, simply by monitoring industry trades, publications, and websites!

When attaching elements to a project, agencies obviously like to go first to their own clients. In-house talent is not only easier to approach, it guarantees the agency won't have to split its packaging fees, which most agencies abhor doing. Occasionally, however, the perfect attachment is someone repped at another company—in which case, the agent has some challenges to tackle.

"I'm happy to go outside" the agency, says N.S. Bienstock agent Ra Kumar. "It's just a question of: is the agency of the [other element] open to ideas brought to them by another agency? Will they be willing to split the package, make my client a good deal, et cetera? Ultimately, it's about is this [element] the right [match] for the idea? Will my client make money?"

Unfortunately, many agents, especially at the Big Four and mid-level agencies, aren't receptive to calls from other agents. Not only do they hate splitting packages, but in a competitive industry where client-poaching is all too common, agents get uneasy about rivals sniffing around their talent. Thus, agents trying to attach an actor or director would rather reach out to that person's manager.

"I don't want an agent at another company telling me to fuck off because they'll have to split a package," says one Big Four agent. "If I know the [agent's] a normal human being I can have a conversation with, I'll call the agent. If I can call [the client's] manager, I call the manager."

Whether it comes through a manager or an agent, a representative's first task is to vet the project. If it's an official offer, with actual money attached, he's obligated to inform the client. If it's just a submission looking for an attachment, the representative evaluates the pros and cons. Is this project from a worthy production company? Does it involve valuable auspices, such as a well-regarded writer, actor, or director? If it feels appropriate for the client, the representative forwards it on.

For an actor or director to be interested enough to hear the pitch, "it usually has to be a genre I'm intrigued about," says Emmy-winning director/producer Todd Holland (*Go On*, *Shameless*, *Malcolm in the Middle*). "Of course, I hear a lot of comedy pitches. That's my business. But the genres I'm most *excited* to hear are usually not comedy; it's usually sci-fi or suspense or something that's a break from comedy."

The manager or agent then schedules a meeting for the writer to pitch the project to his client. Because artists tend to be more creatively involved than networks and studios, "at any point during the pitch, I stop, ask questions, interrupt," says Holland. "I'm trying to glue together the universe in my head. Is there conflict? Do I understand it? Do I like the characters? Is the character listing complete? Every pitch has a unique thumbprint; you're not trying to compare it to anything else—you're just trying to figure out if it feels like a living thing. 'Does this feel like a living story, a living world? Do I want to watch this?'" This meeting could end one of several ways:

1. It could be a love-fest, with the actor/director immediately hopping on board. This is great when it happens. It almost never does.
2. The actor/director could already know they're not interested and pass in the room.
3. The actor/director could be intrigued, but they'd like the project developed more. Maybe they want characters fleshed out or the story revised. Maybe they feel there's a flaw in the series concept.
4. Most likely, the actor/director will ask for time to consider the project and weigh other options and obligations.

"Usually, I talk to my agent and make sure he supports this union on a business level," says Holland. "Agents have a much keener sense of the political environment with writers and their odds of getting something made." During this time, feel free to pitch your idea to other people; until someone agrees to attach themselves, or offers you money, no one has any claim on the project.

"You should be pitching six places at a time," Holland advises. "Five of them will likely not like it. You're trying to find a passionate creative partner, not just a businessperson. It's like finding your soul mate—the odds of finding that person are low, so you have to play the field."

Ask the Executive Producer

Q: How much should I change my idea to accommodate a big piece of talent?
A: "Limit how deeply you're going to redevelop something for someone that's attached, because it's easy for that executive or director or actor to just keep asking for more until they 'fall in love with it.' If someone is box office gold, you'll do backflips for [them]. I've seen writers work their asses off for years to try to have that perfect attachment and it never happens. This can [also] happen where a development executive says, 'Email me,' 'Just give me a one liner,' and people do it because it's the easiest thing to do. [But] a lot of writers get trapped. It's free work and people do it because there is so much competition. I wouldn't discourage people from doing a certain amount of free work but you really have to decide if someone is just jerking you around."–Richard Gurman, executive producer (*Still Standing*, *The Facts of Life*)

If the actor/director ultimately passes, you and your agent move to the next person on your list. But if they accept, the project progresses to the next step—taking the pitch to studios! In most cases, attachments have no formal contract, just a gentleman's agreement. When the project eventually sells to a network and studio, each party then makes his or her own independent deal with the buyer. Sometimes, however, you or the attachment may want to put in place a "**shopping agreement**," a short document stating something like:

> JANE WRITER and JOE ATTACHMENT agree that as of March 14, 2014, "BLOOD AND FIRE" will become the mutual property of both parties for 18 months. At the end of 18 months, ownership of the Project will revert solely to Jane Writer. If, at the end of 18 months, we are in negotiations with a meaningful studio or network, we will extend this option for as long as it takes to negotiate the deal.

A shopping agreement guarantees that both parties must be satisfied with their deal with a buyer before the project can move forward; neither the writer nor the attachment can move on without the other.

Once you've solidified the working arrangement with your new attachment, it's time to prep the pitch to take to pods, studios, and networks. Much of the prep is already done, but your attachment may want some changes. Perhaps a comic actor wants to make her character nerdier, funnier. Or give her a sidekick. Other times, prepping a pitch may involve finding places for the actor or director to jump in and participate, talking about their passion for the project, or telling a funny joke or personal anecdote that complements the show.

Out of Sight, Out of Mind

One important note: if you've attached an actor to the project, *the actor must actually go to the pitches*. "If they're not going to the pitches, it doesn't mean anything," says Begleiter. "If you have Idris Elba, who's busily acting in the next season of *Luther*, you tell the networks you have Idris Elba attached, and Idris makes some phone calls to the network people. That's fine, that works. But they have to engage in some way, they have to stand forward and say, 'Yes, my name is Idris Elba. I am attached to this project.'"

The Studio Pitch

When the pitch is ready, the production company execs call their home studio to schedule a pitch. This is not done by the agent, because the pod usually has a closer relationship with the studio. Your producer or production company partners then accompany you to the pitch.

"[A studio pitch] is more of a sales presentation," says Retzinger. "You have to be more polished, know everything you're going to talk about. Be much more confident about your choices, less open to suggestion. With your producer, you want some back-and-forth, let them help mold it, guide you. With a producer, you might say, 'I think this feels single-camera, but it could be multi-camera.' You don't say that at the [studio or] network. You want to tell them what your show is. Come in and say, 'This is a single-camera half-hour comedy about a guy who blah blah . . .' Don't leave any question as to what it is."

Because you want your studio execs to quickly grasp the basic idea of your show, it's often best to "sell your idea with a great one-liner," says Dana Honor, Senior Vice President of comedy development at 20th Century Fox Television "Think about how the network's going to be viewing things. What does that poster look like? With five hundred channels, the Internet, YouTube—how are you going to get viewers into network television? Make sure you can summarize quickly what the show is, what your hook is, what sets it apart from everything else.

"Then get into characters, which is what ultimately sets things apart. It's less important to know your pilot story and more important to get across characters and the world you're creating. We usually like to hear an example of a pilot story, and a few quick examples of episodes. You're selling a series. A pilot is a sales tool to get that show on the air. If you're selling characters that are rich and specific, in a world we haven't seen before, and you're selling how they interact with one another, it's going to be obvious how you get a hundred episodes out of that. And just do—literally—three sentences on episode examples."

Ask the Agent

Q: I understand that when I'm pitching the studio, I need to be crystal clear on what my show is. But what if they suggest a change? What if they want it to be a female lead instead of male? Or single-cam instead of multi? How do I respond?

A: "You say, 'That's giving me a lot to think about. Let's have a further conversation.' That [way,] you're not so wishy-washy that you've bent with their suggestion, yet you are leaving the door open to a further conversation."—Amy Retzinger, agent, Verve Talent and Literary Agency

---

After the studio pitch, it's the producer's responsibility to follow up and gauge the execs' response. If the writer's agent or manager has her own relationship with the studio, she may also put in a good word, but most of the communication stays between the producer and studio. Just like with pod pitches, the studio may buy the pitch in the room, pass immediately, or need time to mull the project over. They may want changes of their own. Maybe they're not crazy about this particular pitch, but they love the writer/producer/actor team, and they want to discuss some other ideas.

If the studio passes altogether, a production company with an overall can ask to take the project to other studios. If the studio grants permission, the producer will schedule pitches at other studios. If the studio declines, the project is dead with this particular company. Agents now may set another round of pod meetings, or you may return to pods you'd already rejected at other studios. Hopefully, they're still willing to take the pitch, but if they've moved on, or found their own project in similar territory, you may be out of luck.

But—fingers crossed—you won't find yourself in this situation and the studio "buys your pitch in the room," putting you one step closer to the promised land: *having a TV show on the air!*

NEGOTIATING THE DEAL

The next step: pitch the show to networks. But before this happens, one important thing has to get done: your agent must negotiate your deal. Remember, TV shows are financed and owned by studios, not networks, so the studio must officially acquire the project before trying to sell it as its own.

If-Come vs. Script Commitment: Which Is Right for You?

When a writer sells a project to a studio, there are generally two types of deals agents try to negotiate: a **script commitment** or an **if-come**. With both types of deals, agents negotiate all current and future terms: how much the writer gets paid for writing the pilot, how much the writer gets paid per episode, how many backend points the writer receives, etc. There's just one major difference between a script commitment and an if-come:

With a script commitment, the studio agrees to pay the writer a specific fee (say, $60,000) to write a pilot script—*even if that pilot never gets set up at a network.* (Remember: the writer and studio pitch the idea to networks *before* writing the script. So with a script commitment, the studio must pay the writer even if a network never buys the idea.)

With an if-come, the studio only pays the writer *if the idea gets sold to a network.* In other words, the studio and the writer will develop the idea together, with both sides working for free, then pitch the show to various networks; if the show never sells, the studio owes the writer nothing. If the show *does* sell, the studio must then pay the writer the agreed-upon price (the $60,000). (The studio doesn't actually pay the $60,000 in one lump sum; it's dribbled out over the course of writing the pilot. More on this in a sec.)

Script commitments have an obvious upside: they put money into a writer's pocket. But certain script commitments can also have a hidden downside: some, like blind script commitments, obligate a writer to pitch at least three ideas to networks. Not to studios, to *networks*. Which means that before the studio is required to pay you, you must develop and pitch *three separate ideas* to various networks. If a network buys one of those ideas: great, you get paid. If *none* of those idea sells, you don't get paid until you've pitched all three. (FYI—developing and pitching an idea can take several weeks or months; many writers pitch only one idea a year!)

"What usually happens in the case of a young or mid-level writer with a blind script," says Begleiter, "is that the first idea doesn't sell, allowing the studio to say, 'Well, you didn't sell it. We're rolling [your deal] to next year. Come back next year and we'll pitch another thing. Oh, that didn't sell? Let's pitch another thing.'"

So that single script commitment, which was supposed to pay you a nice $60,000, gets stretched over two or three years, and you, the writer, don't get your paycheck till the end.

More importantly, "those networks have now passed on you three times in a row," says Begleiter. "They [now] have no interest in buying from you until you are on a hot television show and a hot writer again. [The studio] has to pay you, but you've ruined your career."

If-comes, on the other hand, put no money in the writer's pocket unless the project sells, but they commit the writer to *nothing* beyond the development of a single idea. "If it doesn't work, everybody walks away," explains Begleiter. "You can still do whatever you want to do next, with whomever you want to do it with. You're not locked into having to do something with [one particular studio] who's now disincentivized to put you with their producers because you failed to sell the first thing. All of that gets washed away if you do the if-come."

Because if-comes are risk-free propositions for studios, they also allow agents to negotiate higher potential fees for clients. In other words, instead of negotiating a guaranteed script fee of $60,000, the agent may negotiate a script fee of, say, $80,000. This $80,000 fee is contingent on the writer and studio selling the project to a network, but if the project *doesn't* sell, the writer isn't forced to continue developing and pitching ideas, unpaid.

Reality Check

Remember, in reality TV, studios don't usually develop or deficit finance shows; most studios don't even participate in reality television. Networks fund and own the programming themselves. Thus, reality writers and producers partner for free with a production company (or make an informal if-come), then negotiate their deal directly with the network that buys the show. Having said that, much of what we're about to discuss in terms of negotiating the deal still applies to reality—it simply takes place at the network level rather than the studio.

The Negotiation

Negotiations begin with the studio's business affairs executive calling the writer's agent to check the writer's quotes. An agent usually gives one of three answers:

1. "No, she doesn't have any quotes."
2. "Yes, she has quotes. Here they are."
3. "No, she doesn't have any quotes" . . . *which is a total bald-faced lie.* The writer *does* have quotes, but they're far below what the agent thinks the writer deserves, so the agent, hoping to get his client a better deal, lies.

Let's take a look at each of these answers and what they mean:

"No, she doesn't have any quotes"–THE TRUTH. If it's your first time developing, you probably don't have any quotes. You're an untested newbie, which also means you'll probably get scale, the minimum payment required by the Writers Guild for writing a pilot.

"Yes, she has quotes. Here they are."–THE TRUTH. When the writer has developed before, and has good quotes, the agent offers the quotes as a starting point for the negotiation, then urges the studio to beat them. "When I give quotes, I tell them up front: 'If you come in at the quote, it's not going to be acceptable,'" says one TV agent. "I also try to have a fair amount of market intelligence–like what other people are getting paid, perhaps on the same show, or on similar shows at that studio or network. If you have that intel, you can use that as leverage against that business affairs person."

If the writer's quotes are fairly reasonable, the business affairs exec probably won't question them. But if the quotes seem egregious, the exec may doubt their veracity. "I like to be honest in those moments–'He's a fucking great writer, there were no circumstances, he's that good,'" says Begleiter. "Or, if it's some egregiously aggressive deal, [I say], 'Here was the situation, I know it's a little egregious, but this is how it happened.'"

Sometimes, execs even call rival studios to verify a writer's quotes, and studios gladly hand out this information. "There are definitely agents who lie about [quotes]," says Begleiter, "but I find honesty gets me favors down the road. Once I have a history of being honest with a business affairs executive–giving up on stuff I know is fair to give up on, and being aggressive on stuff I know is fair to be aggressive on–I'm able to call that executive back down the line, on this deal or another, and say 'Listen, I need you to foot another $5,000.' Or, 'I need the definition on the backend to be better.' If you have that history with an executive, where you've been honest and straightforward and they trust your business relationship, they become your advocate internally, and you have a much better chance of getting the thing you're asking for."

"No, she doesn't have any quotes"–TOTAL BALD-FACED LIE. If an agent deems a writer's previous development quotes are too far beneath what the writer is worth, he may just deny their existence. In these cases, the writer is usually a mid- or upper-level writer who, for whatever reason, has quotes more appropriate for a lower-level writer. (Perhaps, as we discussed earlier, the writer developed something as a baby writer, the project wasn't picked up, but the writer continued to ascend the staff hierarchy. She's now a much more experienced writer saddled with inappropriate quotes.)

By refusing to acknowledge previous quotes, the agent can marshall an argument as to why the writer deserves more money. Perhaps the agent touts the writer's relationship with a valuable producer or executive. Maybe she's about to land a movie deal or another writing opportunity. "If they're true," says Begleiter, "those are things that can help you get a little more money out of the studio."

Once the agent and the business affairs exec establish a starting quote, the business affairs exec presents the agent with an official offer. The negotiation has

This negotiation doesn't
define just the terms of this
pilot deal; it usually defines
the terms of your employment
for the next three years—what
you'll receive if the show
goes to pilot, to series, and to
second and third seasons!

begun. Some points are more negotiable than others, but the main issues to be hammered out include:

Title/Credit—One of the first things your agent negotiates is the title, or credit, you'll receive when the show goes to series. While your agent fights to get you an appropriate title, "you don't want to give somebody falsely inflated credits," says one TV agent. "Obviously, the holy grail is for everybody to be an Executive Producer, [but] if you're not equipped to do an Executive Producer job then you shouldn't have an Executive Producer credit. Newbie writers generally fight for anything from Producer to Supervising Producer."

Having said this, agents usually build in guaranteed title bumps for your first three seasons. So if you're a producer in season one, you get bumped to supervising producer in season two, and co-executive producer in season three.

Fee—The total amount of money the writer shall be paid for writing the pilot, whether the project goes to pilot or not. The money is dribbled out in installments as the writer hits various benchmarks throughout the development process:

- Commencement (beginning work)—ten percent
- Outline—twenty percent
- First Draft—forty percent
- First Revisions—ten percent
- Second Revisions—ten percent
- Polish—ten percent

Backend Points—Backend points are percentage points referring to the amount of ownership each party has in the show and, therefore, how much of the show's profits each party receives on the "back end" of the the show's lifecycle. Remember, TV shows don't usually make money until they're sold into syndication or home video, so while you may see *Seinfeld*-esque billions when your agent tells you that you have ten points on the backend, don't get your hopes up. Most shows never make it that far.

Every show begins with 100 percentage points. These are divided between the studio, the creator or showrunner, the production company or pod, and any big-ticket attachments such as a high-profile director or star. The studio keeps the vast majority of the backend points; after all, the studio is the entity taking the biggest financial risk, and it sees no return on its investment until the show earns a backend by selling into syndication. As a result, studios hate giving up backend points, even to the show's creator. It may seem like this would be an easy place to get the studio to budge—after all, chances are no one will ever see that money; why not give some of it up?—but since this is the studio's only chance to make any real income, it keeps as much backend money as it can for itself.

Also, while studios may give up some of their backend points, they also try to protect themselves by negotiating various definitions of backend participation. There are three basic types of backend participation—**net profits, adjusted gross profits** (or **modified adjusted gross profits**), and **first-dollar gross**—and all three are defined differently by different studios.

Let's say you create a series
that goes into syndication,
racking up millions of dollars,
and you own ten points. You
don't actually get your full ten
points just for creating the
show; your participation has
to vest. So you may vest one
quarter, or one third, for
producing the pilot, another
quarter, or third, for sticking
with the show through its first
year, etc.

- **Net Profits**—This is the most common type of backend, "which usually doesn't result in profits because of all the deductions," says entertainment lawyer Michael Plonsker. This includes gross receipts (based on a certain definition), less distribution fees (which vary depending on how the content is distributed: syndication, home video, online, etc.), less distribution expenses (marketing, advertising, etc.), less the **negative cost** (the cost of production), less interest (a percentage of the negative cost) and overhead (also a percentage of the negative cost). "Each of those categories is defined in different ways by different studios," says Plonsker, "and they are long, complicated definitions."

How much money can be
hidden under a "bad"
definition of net profits?
According to a jury in
Riverside, California, almost
$320 million. That's how
much they awarded Celador
International, the production
company behind *Who Wants
To Be a Millionaire*, when
Celador sued Disney in
connection with a profit
participation case. To learn
more, check out the box on
page 133.

- **Adjusted Gross Profits or Modified Adjusted Gross Profits**—These usually involve the reduction of the distribution fee, interest, and/or overhead fee. In rare cases, the studio may even eliminate the distribution fee altogether. These definitions are more appealing than "net profits," because there are fewer deductions taken off the top before calculating the artist's share.
- **First-Dollar Gross**—This is the best definition, as it includes (almost) the entire gross of the product, minus certain expenses different studios like to include. Few people ever see first-dollar gross in television *or* movies; in fact, only a select handful of movie stars are ever considered "**first-dollar gross participants**."

Because there are multiple kinds of backend, and even these have very different definitions, be sure to ask your agent and lawyer not only how many backend points you got, but how those backend points are defined.

Series fees—Your project may not go to series, but agents and studios still pre-determine your script and episodic fees. In fact, *this* is where agents can often get clients the most money. This is because studios try to pay as little as possible in upfront writing fees, expenditures they *know* they'll have to pay just for buying the project. They also hope to give away as few backend points as possible, since this is usually their best chance of making any profit.

But let's say your agent negotiates an extra few thousand dollars in episodic series fees. First of all, the show probably won't go to series, so the studio most likely won't have to pay it. But if the show *does* go to series, all the studio cares about is making a good show and getting its potential backend; and compared to that backend, what's a few thousand extra dollars per episode? As a result, agents often have the most wiggle room when negotiating these fees.

Exclusivity—When you sign a development deal, even for only one script or project, studios often want you to be exclusive to them in "all media." In other words, you're not allowed to write or work on any other projects for any other companies—even projects in other mediums such as film, books, theater, or the Internet. The good news: this is a fairly easy point to negotiate out of.

One thing you probably can't negotiate out of is your "**position**," or the priority level of this particular project. If this is the first project you've sold this season, the studio will demand that it's in "**first position**," meaning it takes priority over all other projects and jobs you may work on. If you sell another show or receive an offer to write on a series, that project must be in "second position."

So, let's say you've just sold a drama pitch, *Loss of Control*, to ABC Studios. This project is in first position. You later accept a job on NBC's *Revolution*, where you're in second position. If *Loss of Control* gets picked up to pilot or series, you're contractually obligated to leave *Revolution* to work on *Loss of Contol*, because it's your first priority, claiming importance over all other projects.

Studios obviously don't want their projects or writers in second or third position. If they're spending thousands of dollars on something, they want to ensure it's the writer's top priority and won't get shortchanged by something else. In fact, studios often refuse to buy a project, or a hire a writer, if it puts their project in second position. Other times, agents arrange for the writer to render "non-exclusive services" in exchange for slightly lower script fees.

Bonuses—Agents may also negotiate bonuses for you if your pitch sells to a network, or if a network chooses to green-light the pilot or pick up your series. For example, you may get an additional $10,000 if your pitch sells to a network, and another $25,000 if your project goes to series.

Locking—Being "locked" to a project means the studio or network can't fire you at will. Agents often negotiate a "two-year lock," guaranteeing the creator stays with the show for the first two years. You can also be "locked to consult," which means that after the two-year lock, you can render part-time consulting services instead of full-time services.

Leverage and How To Use It

With the deal points spelled out, having room to negotiate requires one thing: leverage. And what's the best kind of leverage? "A competitive situation," says Begleiter. After all, if you have have only one buyer interested, it's difficult to convince them to improve the terms of their offer. But if you have two or more interested buyers, you can pit them against each other, forcing each to boost their offer until you get the best possible deal.

"If I have three job offers, what's a factor that would lead me to pick one over another?" asks Donny Ebenstein, a conflict resolution expert who has taught negotiation on five continents. "Ask a roomful of people that question and—invariably—the first factor everyone shouts out is 'money.' It's natural; we're in a capitalist society. And it's not that that's wrong, but money is only one of many things. So what else would attract you to one job or another? What's the most interesting work? Which firm has a better reputation? Which job has a better chance of advancement? Is there travel involved? There are many different factors, interests, drivers, motivators, things people want satisfied. There's a tendency to fixate on money, and that tendency is made worse when you're emotional, nervous, afraid of being a sucker or being too aggressive."

Show Me the Money!

There's no pre-determined amount of money all writers receive for selling or writing a television pilot, no standard price tag. The only rule: every writer must receive "WGA minimum," or "scale." Beyond that, each sale is a new negotiation, and the writer's fee depends on his or her level, track record, and the project itself. However, here are some benchmarks to inform your expectations.

Low-Level and First-Time Developers:

- **Script Fee**: $45,000–$50,000 (WGA minimum + ten percent; most agents persuade business affairs execs to add ten percent so the writer doesn't lose much money paying commission)
- **Title**: Producer, Supervising Producer, or Co-Executive Producer credit on the pilot and first two seasons of the series
- **Backend**: three to five percent
- **Pilot producing fee**: $12,000–$15,000
- **Series Fee**–$14,500–$22,000 per episode
- **Royalty**: $2,000–$2,500 per episode

Mid-Level Developers:

- **Script Fee**: $50,000–$150,000
- **Title**: Co-Executive Producer or Executive Producer
- **Backend**: five to ten percent
- **Pilot producing fee**–$20,000–$25,000
- **Series Fee**–$17,500–$22,500 per episode
- **Royalty**: $3,000–$5,000

Upper-Level Developers:

- **Script Fee**: $150,000–$500,000
- **Title**: Executive Producer
- **Backend**: fifteen percent
- **Pilot producing fee**–$25,000–$40,000
- **Series Fee**–$25,000–$50,000 per episode
- **Royalty**: $4,000–$6,000

Talk the Talk

Royalty–A bonus paid to a show's creator each time a new episode of that show airs. If you have a $2,000 bonus, and your show runs 100 episodes, you'll make $200,000, in addition to your regular fees, salary, and backend.

So when you and your agent are weighing multiple offers, think about other things you'd like from each job. Do you want to make sure you're free to develop your own projects? Would you like a shorter contract so you can leave if you're not happy? Are there certain decision-makers you want to have face-time or access to?

Of course, not every situation is competitive, which means agents, doing their best to service clients, must often create the *illusion* of competition. One way to do this, quite simply, is to lie. Tell a studio, "I'm holding another offer on this." Studios inevitably ask who the offer is, but unless the offer's real, agents rarely tell. Does this smell of B.S.? Sometimes. And sometimes studios will investigate. But not always, and many agents are willing to take the risk. (Agents caught in a lie, however, run the risk of damaging their reputations.)

More often, agents use vague interest from one possible buyer to spark or fuel others. "I recently took out a spec pilot," says one agent. "Sony wanted to make a deal, but they wanted to make an if-come. ABC Studios and 20th were both interested, but neither had said whether they were going to make an if-come or a guarantee. The minute Sony threw their hat in the ring on the if-come, I called those other places and said, 'I am holding a competitive offer from Sony. You need to check it out? Check it out.'"

The agent knew that if ABC or 20th called Sony, Sony would never admit they'd only offered an if-come—it would leave them too vulnerable to getting beaten out. "I was able to force ABC Studios to offer a guaranteed deal," she says. Then, "I was able to go back to 20th and say, 'I am now holding two competitive offers. Check 'em out. Call ABC and see what they're up to.' I was able to take them from sniffing around to a moment where they were suddenly like, 'Oh, God, we're going to lose it!' It was some of the best agenting I've done, and the only white lie was, 'I'm holding a competitive offer.' I didn't say the competitive offer was virtually worthless."

In some competitive cases, especially with mid- or upper-level writers, agents are even able to get competing studios to commit to giving the writer a **blind script deal**, a development deal to write an as-yet-undecided pilot.

Eventually, the deal "closes," meaning everyone agrees upon terms. A mutual commitment has been reached and it's time to for the final phase of setting up a new television show: shopping the project to networks!

AND NOW A NOT-SO-BRIEF WORD ABOUT PACKAGES

When a client sells a project, the agent commissions ten percent of that client's income, unless, of course, the agent gets to take a "package."

What Exactly *Is* a Package? How Much Is It Worth?

At most studios, a "full package," the most the studio ever grants an agency, is "3:3:10." In other words: three percent of the show's license fee or budget; another three percent of the show's license fee or budget, *deferred*; ten percent of the show's modified adjusted gross profits.

If these numbers and definition sound confusing—they are. Not only are many agents often unclear about what exactly these numbers and definitions mean, but the rules and definitions of a "package" vary a bit from studio to studio and network to network. But let's look at the most common definitions and explanations for each of these numbers.

Three percent of the show's license fee or budget—When an agency gets a package, they take three percent of the project's license fee (sometimes, the license fee is equal to the show's budget; most of the time, it's slightly less). So let's say *Downward Spiral*, a (fictional) drama series, has a license fee of $2 million per episode; the agency receives $60,000 per episode (three percent of $2 million). For every

Reality Check

Since reality shows aren't produced on a deficit like scripted shows, agencies usually receive three percent of the budget itself, which is often the same as the license fee.

episode the show produces, this $60,000 is a line item in the show's budget, just like wardrobe supplies or the visual effects artist's salary. If that TV show produces twenty-two episodes a season, the agency makes $1.32 million. If the license fee goes up the next year to, say, $2.5 million per episode, the agency brings home $1.65 million.

The Incredible Shrinking Package

Think those three percent budget commissions sound like a nice chunk of change? They are. But until the 1970s, agencies took *five* percent of shows' budgets! Then ICM instituted a new policy: they'd take three percent of the budget until a show became a hit, then they'd bump their take up to the full five. In a competitive move, CAA—at the time, a hungry upstart—decided it would forego the three percent altogether, reducing its budget commission to three percent across the board. ICM and UTA soon followed suit. The only holdout was William Morris, until, in 2001, Disney's TV studio, Touchstone Television (which eventually became ABC Studios), announced it would no longer pay *any* agency, including William Morris, the traditional five percent. Disney would pay three percent, not a penny more, on all shows, and that has been industry standard ever since.[16]

Three percent of the show's license fee or budget, deferred—You know how I explained the agency takes three percent of the show's license fee or budget? Well, I lied—kind of. Technically, the agency takes *six percent* of the show's license fee or budget, but it takes half that upfront, while the show is in production, and the other half later, once the show earns a backend. So if *Downward Spiral* has a $2 million per episode license fee, the agency actually receives $120,000 per episode. But rather than paying the agency its full $120,000 from the show's episodic budget, the studio gives the agency half ($60,000) from each episode's budget, and half when the show turns a net profit. "Net profits" is usually defined as the money existing once a show is completely in profit; in other words, whatever profit is left once the show and the studio have paid back all outstanding people and expenditures.

Ten percent of the show's modified adjusted gross profits—In this case, "modified adjusted gross profits" refers to the entire backend of the show, or the profits *before* they've been "modified" to account for repaying expenditures. In other words, this ten percent comes out of the show's *gross* profits rather than its *net* profits, so it's paid from a considerably larger pot of money. Except for one thing: The definition of "modified adjusted gross" is not always set in stone. In fact, agencies sometimes negotiate themselves a different definition of backend than they negotiate for their clients! Some agencies are able to define their gross profits, or modified adjusted gross profits, as the pool of backend profits that exists even before their client, or other gross participants, have been paid. This means those agencies take their ten percent from a much larger amount of money than their clients do! As a result, agencies not only stand to make far more money than their clients, but, because they're taking money from the show's profits before their clients are paid, those clients are essentially paying their agents' packaging fees (thus undermining the client, who's not supposed to pay any kind of fees or commissions when the agent takes a package).[17]

Most of the time, in the best cases, the agency's definition of gross, or adjusted gross, is identical to the client's. Thus, agents are incentivized to negotiate as powerful a definition as possible for their clients.

As we saw, taking three percent of a show's episodic budget can earn an agency some impressive cash—$1.32 million per season is nothing to sneeze at. (In *Friends'* eighteen-episode final season, from 2003–04, NBC paid Warner Brothers a license

Back of the Class

In 2011, writers Michael Elias and Richard Eustis–creators of Warner Bros.' sitcom *Head of the Class*, which ran on ABC from 1986–91–sued their former CAA agents for allegedly negotiating a better backend for themselves than their clients. According to the suit, the show has racked up over $200 million in backend revenue,[18] yet while Elias and Eustis have never received a dime, CAA has received millions thanks to a backend definition that allowed Warners to pay CAA before Elias and Eustis.[19] As of spring, 2013, there's been no official settlement or verdict.

Similarly, in 2010, Celador Productions sued Disney for refusing to pay owed profits on Celador's hit game show, *Who Wants To Be a Millionaire.* During the lawsuit, Disney lawyer Marty Katz suggested that if Celador was unhappy about its profits, the cheat wasn't Disney, it was Celador's former agency, William Morris. According to Katz's proposal, Celador's reps at William Morris structured a package agreement so large they essentially siphoned profits away from their client, Celador. While Celador had made $21 million from *Millionaire*, William Morris had made $16 million–eight times what they would've made from a straight commission.[20] Celador never pressed charges against William Morris, but the judge ordered Disney to pay $269.4 million in damages, plus $50 million in interest.[21] Two years later, Disney appealed the decision to the 9th Circuit Court of Appeal; they were denied.[22]

fee of approximately $10 million per episode, earning the show's packaging agency, ICM, a tidy sum of $5.4 million for the season.[23]) But taking ten percent of a show's backend is where agencies make their *real* money–like the $200 million-plus ICM has earned from *Friends*.

A show's backend can stretch far into the future. Reruns of *I Love Lucy* and *The Cosby Show* are still being sold and aired, which means an agency with a package on a successful series can plan on counting its cash for years, or even decades. Packages also extend to spinoffs or format sales of a particular show. So because CAA landed a package on *The Bachelor*, they also own pieces of *The Bachelorette*, *The Bachelor Pad*, and all *The Bachelor's* international versions, like those in Chile,

The Incredible Shrinking Package: Part II

"When packages first started–and that model was invented by William Morris in the 1940s and '50s–[agencies] would deliver a project that already had a director, the main talent, the writer," says New Wave agent-turned-manager Michael Pelmont. "They were true R&D for the networks."

Sometimes, however, packages don't spring wholly from one agency. In 2011 UTA and Gersh split a package when ABC Studios purchased *Red Widow*, a pairing of UTA-repped writer/showrunner Melissa Rosenberg (*Twilight*) and Gersh-repped executive producer Alon Aranya (who acquired the rights to the Dutch series, *Penoza*, on which *Red Widow* is based).[25] When this happens, agencies often split a package; each agency takes a half-package (instead of 3: 3: 10, it's 1.5: 1.5: 5), but other splits can be negotiated.

Agents hate doing this, and this is another reason why declining packaging revenues have helped fuel a contraction of the agency world. "Not only are packages getting smaller," says Pelmont, but "as they become split more and more, less money is coming to these agencies, and that's why you saw a lot of these agencies collapsing into each other and merging."

Wait a sec–so if my agents get a package, I never pay them *anything*?!

Not exactly. Packages don't kick in until a show gets picked up to series and begins production. So a client must first sell the pitch or script in development season. That script must then be one of the network's fifteen to thirty scripts picked up to pilot. And that pilot must then be one of the four to eight projects picked up to series.

Up until this point, the client has been paying the agency the regular ten percent commission. Once the client's new series actually begins production, however, and the agency receives three percent of the budget, the agency then rebates the client all the commission she's paid.

Israel, Ukraine, Norway, and Finland.[24] (Backend can even include merchandise–toys, clothing, games, etc.)

How Do Agencies Negotiate Packages?

An agency obviously can't take a package unless a client closes a deal. So package discussions often go hand-in-hand with writer negotiations, and whether or not an agency takes a package depends on how much leverage they have. An agency with a lot of leverage can command a full package simply for providing the studio with the show and a desirable showrunner. But what's in it for studios to even give an agency a package?

"Agencies have become so powerful and control so much of the talent, I'm not sure the studios are in a position to say no," says Andy Bourne, Sr. Vice President of Television at Universal-based Closed On Monday Productions. This may be true, but while a Big Four agency may get a package for selling a show with certain auspices–a writer and director, a producer and star, even just a high-profile showrunner–a smaller agency may get nothing for selling a project with the exact same attachments. Studios dole out packages at their discretion, and not always fairly. In his book *Desperate Networks* (a must-read for anyone interested in the behind-the-scenes machinations and politics of television), Bill Carter tells the story of how, in 2003, Paradigm brought Warner Brothers a spec pilot written by Marc Cherry, a veteran yet unemployed TV writer. Tony Krantz, a producer with a Warners overall, was eager to develop the project, but Warner Bros. refused to give Paradigm a package. When Krantz and Paradigm pointed out that Warners would unquestionably give a package to a Big Four agency delivering the same project, Warner Bros. agreed–but they weren't about to establish a precedent of giving packages to any mid-level or boutique agencies. So Paradigm took Cherry's project to Disney.[26] A year later, *Desperate Housewives* debuted as ABC's highest rated premiere in eight years (since 1996's *Spin City*).[27] *USA Today* credited the show with reviving audience's interest in scripted TV, which had been losing ground to sensational reality shows like *American Idol* and *Survivor*.[28] And by the time *Desperate Housewives* reached it's eighth and final season, it not only continued to be a huge hit on ABC (and internationally), generating over $5.2 million per hour in ad revenue,[29] it had been syndicated to Lifetime for approximately $500,000 per episode.[30]

Nonetheless, studios still rarely give packages to smaller agencies. "Agencies like WME or CAA, which control about eighty percent of the A-list talent in town, have so many pieces they can put into a show in the future that it warrants it," says one executive. "Smaller agencies just don't have those [carrots] to dangle and say 'Here's how we can support it.'"

Ironically, supporting a show isn't always in an agency's best interests–even when it might help their clients. "What really happens is: agencies get packages, then don't want to put any clients on those shows because they can't commission them," says one high-level agent. "When you have a good client on a show you're making no money on, it's annoying. So when you have a package on something, you want everybody else to put their elements on it."

Most agents ask for "confirmation of a package" during their first phone conversation with a studio's Business Affairs department. If an agent is feeling especially aggressive, he may not even discuss the client's contract or respond to deal points until he's sure he's receiving a package. If the studio refuses to grant the package, or hedges, the agent may spin the deal points to the client in a less flattering light, hoping to dissuade her from accepting the deal–especially if there's a competing offer from another studio.

Agent-to-English Dictionary

When a studio refuses to grant an agency the package the agency wants, the agent may subtly try to steer the client away from the offer. Here are some things your agent may say if he's trying to talk you out of a deal:

- **"They're not paying you enough"**
- **"They're refusing to lock you"**—The studio or production company is refusing to "lock" you to the project, or guarantee you a job on the show.
- **"The network's no good"** or **"They're not a top five network"**—No writer or producer wants their project at a poor, unwatched, disrespected network; your goal is to have a hit show somewhere popular and powerful. So implying a network is too small or insignifiant is an easy way to suggest the offer is a terrible career move.
- **"The network's too big; you'll be lost in the shuffle"**—An agent may also spin the negatives of a *big* network, claiming it's too big, corporate, and busy: your project will simply be one on a large list, you'll receive no personal attention, and the show will get lost or trampled amidst all the studios' other projects.
- **"The backend definition sucks"**—Obviously, writers want the best possible backend definition. However, especially for a first-time creator, backend definition may not be that important; after all, most shows—especially reality shows—never have a backend, so it's not always worth worrying about.
- **"They're not giving you a good credit"**—Everyone wants to improve their credit, moving up the hierarchy of writers and producers. But if the production company or studio won't give you a better title, perhaps you can negotiate something better elsewhere, like better episodic fees, a better backend definition, or a guaranteed lock to the show.

How Studios Negotiate Against Packages

While packages have become an accepted part of doing business, especially with big agencies, studios occasionally try to negotiate out of them. A studio may tell a writer's agent: "Listen, we'd love to give you a package, but then we can't afford to pay your client $20,000 per episode. If you can reduce your client's fee, we'll be glad to give you your package." Other times, especially with reality shows, buyers tell agents, "We'll give your producers a budget of $300,000 per episode. We don't care if you take a package or not, but that's what your clients get to produce the show."

Most clients in this situation opt to give the agency its package: 1. it allows both the client and agency to make more money, and 2. most clients recognize that packages are essential to an agengy's survival. Besides, an agency that can't package certain clients is not going to concentrate on those clients for long, so clients who refuse their agency's package may soon find themselves hunting for new representation!

Not surprisingly, this kind of studio behavior enrages agents, as it pits them against the very clients they're working hard to support and protect. One agent told me that when studios pull this, the agency vows to "hurt" them in return. Maybe next time the network wants one of the agency's shows, the agency ensures it goes to a different buyer. Or when one of the network executives needs a job recommendation, or a job contract negotiated, the agency refuses to help. Execs, after all, need agents as much as—if not more than—agents need buyers, so most execs don't want agents as enemies.

Do Packages Harm Clients?

"There are all kinds of reasons we explain to clients why they don't get fucked," says one high-level TV agent, "but they get fucked all the time." As we discussed earlier, a package that dampens a client's profits is clearly not in the best interests of the client. Other people have alleged that package-hungry agencies sometimes pair people who don't work well together, or convince clients to join packages against their better interests, simply to secure the package.

On the other hand, packages keep clients from paying commission, which is nice for the client. And clients "forced" into packages probably aren't high-level clients who would've sold something (or commanded a valuable **penalty**—which we'll discuss in a moment) on their own anyway, so if a package helps them make a sale they wouldn't have otherwise made, maybe it's not the worst thing.

Having said that, the truth is: for certain agencies, packaging is a huge source of revenues, and as commercial enterprises those agencies will do whatever they can to protect their revenue opportunities. "I won't *not* sell a show because of the package," says N.S. Bienstock agent Ra Kumar, "but I *will* not sell a show to one network over another."

As another agent says, "it's an imperfect system. But [clients] also get lots of great benefits. Just like our government, just like our healthcare system. It benefits a lot of people, and occasionally there are a few casualties along the way."

PITCHING TO NETWORKS

Once the writer's deal has closed, the studio, pod, and writer begin preparing the network pitch. Perhaps the studio wants to add or delete a character. Maybe they want to tweak the pilot story or brainstorm new sample episode ideas.

Finally, the studio execs call the network to schedule the pitch. When they do, they usually tell the network a bit about the project. If the network immediately knows it's not the right fir for them, they may say, "Thanks for letting us know about this, but we're never going to do a show about an alien invasion—you're free to take this to other outlets." The studio can then go about setting pitches with more appropriate networks. (The studio, in fact, may actually call the network before even buying the project, just to test the waters. If the network is uninterested or reticent from the beginning, it may help determine whether the studio offers the writer a script commitment or an if-come, or buys the project at all.)

"Obviously, it's a win-win when one of our projects goes to FOX," says Dana Honor, an executive at 20th century Fox TV. "But we pride ourselves on tailoring the project for the appropriate network, and there are plenty of projects that go straight to CBS or ABC if they're not right for FOX. Everything is very above-board."

Most of the times, the network agrees to hear the pitch. Network pitches can be large meetings—they're usually attended by the writer, the producer or production company executives, studio execs, and any attached director or actors. Most agents and managers don't attend these pitches; there are enough bodies in the room, and with this much firepower, there's little for a representative to add.

After the pitch, parent networks usually take a day or two to respond to any pitches from their in-house studio. If the network passes, the studio is free to present the project to rival networks. Just like with an agent shopping a pitch to various studios, studios hope to generate a competitive situation between networks. A studio, with the help of the project's agents, can then negotiate a higher license fee or, more importantly, a special **penalty**. In fact, when pitching a project to a network, the ultimate goal isn't just to "sell" it—it's to sell it with a penalty. There are three basic kinds of penalties:

1. **A "put pilot"**—A guarantee that the network will produce a pilot episode. Come January, when the network execs debate which scripts to actually shoot, this project will already have a green light.

2. **Penalties**–The network must pay the studio a specific amount of money, anywhere from $50,000 into the millions, if they don't green-light a pilot. Usually, this money is intended only for the studio, but a top-level showrunner may be able to take a slice as well. (Penalties for writers are usually negotiated as part of a writer's overall deal, not just part of a script commitment or sale.)

3. **Series commitments**–Some projects are so special a network guarantees to air the show even before developing a script. This was the case with a package UTA pitched in August, 2012. The show followed a father struggling to navigate his job, his family, and a chronic, progressive disease. Although it was being written by Sam Laybourne, a young *Cougar Town* writer, UTA attached Will Gluck (*Easy A*, *Friends With Benefits*), a producer/director with a Sony deal, and beloved TV star Michael J. Fox. With just "Gluck and [Laybourne] taking that project out, it would have sold [with] a heavy penalty," says Begleiter. "Attaching Michael J. Fox made it a twenty-two-episode production commitment."

Thus, when networks select which scripts to shoot as pilots at the top of pilot season, many decisions are preordained, thanks to networks weighting certain projects more heavily than others. In 2013 over forty-seven percent of ABC's twenty-three pilots came with penalties or put pilot commitments. This makes it exponentially harder for a first-time developer, a younger writer, or a script without big-name attachments to actually get selected as a pilot; not only is it simply a bigger risk, but networks have already placed extremely large bets on the projects they most think will–and want to–go.

"If a network buys your pitch," says Begleiter, "it will be one of sixty things on a development report competing against Greg Berlanti or J.J. Abrams or Chuck Lorre or Steve Levitan. So the dream scenario of a little baby [writer] going out and [pitching an idea that] becomes a big giant television show? It happens, [but] the odds against it are beyond calculation."

This also further solidifies the big agencies' control over Hollywood. Because they represent most of the blue chip showrunners and producers who would even qualify for a penalty, and because they're also the gatekeepers for eighty percent of Hollywood's talent, it's easier for them to fight for penalties for projects they believe in. These agencies' shows then have a better chance of getting on air, cementing their ruling-party status.

While much of these negotiations are between the studio and the network, agents often get involved to help their clients' projects. "The networks start calling the agents to get a sense of what the studio's saying," says Begleiter. "'Where do you want it to land? Where does the client want it to land? Here's why you should do it with us.' [They'll look for] any way to be able to have that conversation with the client and have that information relayed."

Agents, of course, have their own agendas, their own hopes for where the project will end up. Maybe they think one network is a better creative fit for the show than another. Maybe they like certain execs better than others. Perhaps one network screwed them on a recent deal, so they *don't* want to sell something to them. "I usually have a good sense of where I want [a project] to land," says Begleiter, "so I tend to be stand-off-ish with networks I don't want it to go to. And I tend to be honest with the network I do want it to go to. I say, 'Listen, I am not in total control of this process. I want to deliver this to you. You are not being used as a stalking horse. Tell your business affairs to step up here. This is real; you're in consideration, So if you're talking about throwing the extra fifty grand at the penalty on this project: *do it.*'"

Agents also rely on information from their research departments. They pull up demographic information and viewership on each network's shows, allowing them to form compelling arguments about why a network should buy a particular pitch. Agents can see where networks are losing viewers, where schedules have holes, which current shows need a stronger lead-in.

Eventually, the studio accepts one network's offer, which means: CONGRATULA-TIONS–YOUR PILOT IS SET UP AT A NETWORK!

Does this mean your show will be on the air? Nope. It still has a long way to go. *Does this mean your script will be shot as a pilot?* Not even close. *Does this mean you'll make more money?* Probably not–although if you have a sale bonus structured into your deal, you may get a few thousand extra dollars. But you are now much, much closer to having your show on the air, and you've made it over a hurdle many writers never leap! The next step: working with the network to develop the show further and write a great pilot script.

How Agents Stay Involved Once a Project Has Been Sold

Once a writer is off and working, agents become less involved in their daily lives. Agents may check in occasionally, just to see how things are going, but they don't usually peruse drafts, give notes, or offer feedback. This is the department of managers, who may also be attached to the project as producers. Agents tend to get involved only if there's a problem–if, for example, their client is not being paid on schedule.

Most writers deliver pilot scripts to networks just before Christmas. Execs then read over the holidays, returning in January to select which scripts to produce as pilot episodes. While networks obviously want the best possible shows on their air, they consider many factors when greenlighting pilots. First and foremost, has the network already committed to a put pilot or penalty? Is the project from an important showrunner with whom the network wants to maintain a relationship? Is it a high-profile project from the network's sister studio, giving it greater synergistic potential (like in 2013, when ABC greenlighted ABC Studios' *Agents of S.H.I.E.L.D.* based on Disney's *The Avengers* movies)?[31] This is when agents sometimes get re-involved, calling networks and trying to use their muscle to get client's scripts picked up.

"Agents all pretend that we can be incredibly persuasive in that moment," says one agent, but "there are [only three] agents, traditional TV lit agents, in the city of Los Angeles capable of doing that: Joe Cohen at CAA, and Ari Greenberg and Richard Weitz [at WME]. The volume of business those people have is so vast that they can be punishing to a network that crosses them. But the general answer is no–the networks don't really give a fuck what agents want or think."

Well, okay–so let's ask WME TV agent and partner Richard Weitz. Weitz reps clients such as director/producer Jamie Widdoes (*Two and a Half Men*), writer/producer/performer Tina Fey (*30 Rock*), and actor/musician/producer L.L. Cool J (*NCIS: Los Angeles*). So, Richard, tell us–when it comes time for networks to decide which pilots to pick up, how influential can agents be?

"The influence of an agent in today's marketplace [goes] back to August, September, October, when you're selling projects and everybody–if it's competitive–wants them," Weitz says. "When you have a *real* project, and we had several this year, we *expect* [them to get made]. I *expect* Sean Hayes's pilot to get made. I *expect* David Kelley or Howard Gordon's pilot to get made. [Those networks] took it off the market and they put it in penalty. We don't get the money directly, the studio does–we're interested in the opportunity. So that's where you have muscle. And muscle really is: if it's good product and people like it, they just need a push."

As if to prove Weitz's point, Sean Hayes' half-hour NBC comedy with producer Victor Fresco, *Sean Saves the World*, was indeed picked up to pilot and eventually to series. So was David Kelley's CBS pilot, *Crazy Ones*, starring Robin Williams and Sarah Michelle Gellar. And Howard Gordon's TNT pilot, an adaptation of Robert Littell's novel *Legends*, starring Sean Bean and Ali Larter.

If a client's script does *not* get picked up–and most of them don't–agents may work to find the show a new home. This happened with 2012's *The Mindy Project*, which Universal originally developed for NBC. When NBC stiff-armed the pilot, Universal sold the project to Fox. Unfortunately, reselling a "**busted**" pilot isn't always easy. The show's studio must first ask the original network's permission to take the project elsewhere, and while the network may not want the show itself, it may not want other networks to have it either. This isn't always pettiness; perhaps ABC developed two pilots about firefighters–*Ablaze* and *Hot Times*–and it opts for *Hot Times*. ABC may have passed on *Ablaze*, but it also doesn't want *Ablaze* on a rival company's air, competing with *Hot Times*.

Also, broadcasters rarely want projects that have been killed by other networks. Most networks are already committed to their own development, and "sloppy seconds" tend to carry the stink of rejection. Thus, if a pilot is going to find a new home, it's usually on cable, like in 2012 when Lifetime snatched up ABC's rejected Marc Cherry pilot, *Devious Maids*. When these deals happen, they usually begin with the show's agents and studio execs having a conversation about other networks that might make a good home. Agents, not execs, then put in a call to the new networks. Although the show's studio stays with the project, political reasons often keep execs from calling other networks to try and resell the show. So agents step in.

When trying to find a busted pilot a new home, "I call the other networks and say, 'I don't make this call very often,'" says Begleiter, but "'this got developed [and] it's extraordinary and special. You know I don't call you like this more than once every two or three years, [so] this is real . . . you should pay attention to it. Read it. I'm going to take it to all the other networks [and] someone's going to buy it.'"

When a pilot gets picked up, whether by its own network or someone else, agents rush to support their clients. They introduce the showrunner to the agency's talent agents, directors agents, below-the-line agents. Having a client get a pilot or series picked up, after all, is a direct pipeline for getting jobs for other directors, designers, or actors.

As we learned in Chapter 6, a showrunner's agents are especially helpful during staffing season, providing their showrunner clients with other writers for staffing. "Because I've had a relationship with my agent for thirteen years, anyone he sends me I'm going to read before [submissions from] an agent I don't know," says executive producer Stacy Traub.

Showrunners and producers deliver their finished pilots to networks in early May, when network execs decide which current shows to renew and which new shows to green-light to series. Just like when greenlighting pilots, networks must consider more than just the quality of a pilot. What holes do they have in their schedule? Which shows could be paired together for a solid one-two punch?

During this time, agents and managers are in constant contact with networks, learning which pilots are looking hot, which are "dead," and which have specific challenges blocking their paths. If a show has an expensive license fee, for example, the agency can work with the producers and studio to lower the fee. (This often happens with "bubble shows," like in 2012, when CBS and Sony TV negotiated an eleventh-hour license-fee deal to pick up a seventh season of *Rules of Engagement*.[32]) Or if a new show has a big star commanding a large paycheck, and that's keeping the network from giving the green light, the agency may convince the star to reduce her salary. Often, the biggest leverage agencies have is their ability to provide–or not provide–networks and studios with talent and product, which is why big agencies wield an enormous stick. Networks and studios "rely on a handful of major guys, at CAA and UTA and WME and ICM, who control the clients," says one Big Four agent, "and if they fuck us, we're going to fuck them down the road. We can push and get [things] over the top. We use our muscle to do that. That's why you're represented by us rather than the other agencies."

Finally, in mid-May, at upfront presentations, the networks announce their new season's schedules. Every writer longs to have their series picked up. But hearing your show announced at the upfront presentations isn't just a dream come true for writers– it's also a triumphant moment for agents and managers who have supported, believed in, and championed those writers along the way. "It feels pretty awesome," says Lindsay

Howard, APA's VP of television. "In this job, you have to let people down so much that when you get to call and give anybody good news, your adrenaline shoots through the roof. You're ready to run up and down the halls, high-fiving! You feel a massive sense of accomplishment and you're pumped for your client. You've gone through a ton with them, and you are just so happy and proud for them. [And] for me, personally, because I get so creatively involved in the process, I feel like 'Hell yeah! I did that!'"

TABLE 7.2 Staffing, Development, and Pilot Season: How a Year Looks For Writers and Agents

	JAN	FEB	MAR	APR	MAY	JUN	JUL	AUG	SEPT	OCT	NOV	DEC
Writers	TV shows shooting, begin wrapping production			STAFF-ING: Generals and staffing meetings	STAFFING: Showrunner meetings		TV shows begin pre-production	TV shows shooting, in full production				
	Deliver new staffing material to agents								Work on new staffing material to deliver to reps in January			
	Networks pick up pilots	Pilot production			Show-runners finish pilots; deliver to net-works	Show-runners com-plete staffing	Writers conceive, pitch and develop ideas with pods, studios and networks				Writers with pilot deals write scripts, deliver to networks	
Agents	Agents touch base with network and studio execs re: possible staffing needs, submit scripts and writers to execs		Agency hold staffing meet-ings with net-works and studios	Agency schedule generals for clients, submit material to show-runners	Agency schedule showrunner meetings for clients, negotiate and close staffing deals		Agents check in with clients working on shows, make sure working clients get paid, and schedule general meetings to introduce clients to new executives					
	Networks pick up pilots; agents lobby on behalf of clients' projects	Pilot production begins; agents provide show-runner clients with other resources		Agents shop for develop-ment deals for upper-level clients	Networks pick up new series; agents lobby on behalf of client's pilots		Development season: agents setting meetings and pitches for clients to pitch pods, studios, networks					

140   TELEVISION AGENTS

Part III
Feature Agents

8 A Quick Overview of the Feature Business

It's Friday night. All over America, thousands of people are getting off work and going to the movies. Many are paying $8.00 to see a quirky romantic comedy. Some are paying $16.00 to see an action flick in IMAX and 3D. Others are paying $3.50 for an arthouse film in a second-run theater. But how did each movie get there? Why do some make it to theaters and others don't? How does an indie film travel a different path than a studio film? And how are agents and managers involved in this process?

Let's first look at the four main types of companies involved in a film's lifecycle—**exhibitors, distributors, production companies,** and **financiers**—going backwards from the moment most audiences first meet movies.

Exhibitors are most consumers' first, and only, point of contact with Hollywood. They're the companies that show movies to audiences, the theaters where all those Friday-night viewers go to see their movies (e.g., AMC, Landmark, Regal, or your own local theater). But most exhibitors don't make those movies themselves, they acquire them from other companies—distributors.

Distributors provide exhibitors with movies to show. They are, in essence, middlemen who obtain movies from producers (companies that actually *make* movies), and get them to exhibitors. So when you see a movie this weekend at the CineMark North Grand 5 in Ames, Iowa, or the Harkins Park West 14 in Peoria, Arizona, those theaters didn't acquire the movies from producers themselves; they received them from a distributor such as Sony Pictures Classics, which distributed *Blue Jasmine* and *Austenland*, or FilmDistrict, which did *Insidious* and *Olympus Has Fallen*. Some distributors specialize in **theatrical distribution** (showing a movie in a theater), others focus on direct-to-video or television releases, and still others distribute movies strictly online or in foreign countries.

Production companies and producers are the organizations or individuals responsible for actually *making* the movies distributed by distributors. Like TV production companies, they're usually based around the visions and talents of one creative person or team. Overbrook Entertainment, for example, is the company of movie star Will Smith and his long-time business partner, James Lassiter; Stars Road is director Sam Raimi's company; Elton John has Rocket Pictures. Good producers oversee every aspect of a film's production, from developing the script to hiring the director to editing and delivering the final version of the movie. Producing a movie, of course, often costs millions of dollars, and most producers and production companies don't have their own money. So they bankroll movies with the help of another type of company—financiers.

Financiers supply production companies with capital needed to fund a film's production. Some fund entire movies, some fund portions of a film's budget, others invest in production companies themselves, treating companies like hedge funds that decide how to spend their investors' money.

So, in its simplest iteration, Hollywood works likes this: Production companies receive money from a financier. Using this funding, the production company makes a movie, which it sells or licenses to a distributor. The distributor then delivers prints of this finished movie to exhibitors, who screen the film for audiences.

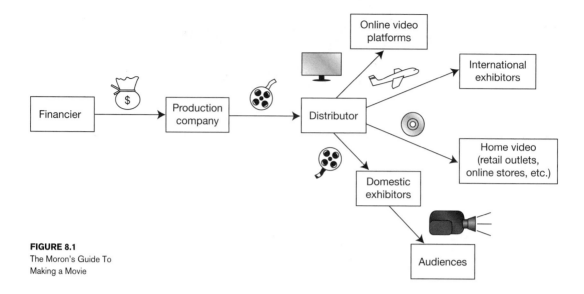

FIGURE 8.1
The Moron's Guide To
Making a Movie

There is, however, a fifth type of company, and this type of company dominates almost every aspect of the American film industry: *studios*.

Studios are massive corporations with enough resources to provide the services of all the other types of companies. They have their own money to finance films, their own creative or practical production capabilities, and their own distribution arms to supply movies to exhibitors. (The one thing studios don't usually do is exhibit films themselves, although their distribution executives have relationships with exhibitors around the world.) Today, Hollywood has six "**major**" studios: 20th Century Fox, Paramount Pictures, Warner Brothers, Columbia Pictures/Sony, Walt Disney Pictures, and Universal Pictures.

Because studios fund, produce, and distribute their own work, they're one-stop shopping for filmmakers, and agents representing filmmakers. Studios also have much deeper pockets than most independent companies, allowing them to make more—and bigger—movies. Look at the top twenty movies each year between 2008 and 2012; of those hundred films, *ninety* are produced and distributed by major studios. This makes studios some of the most powerful players in the industry.

Ironically, most of the movies released each year are *not* studio films. In 2011, the six major studios (20th Century Fox, Paramount Pictures, Warner Brothers, Columbia Pictures/Sony, Walt Disney Pictures, Universal Pictures) released 141 movies domestically, compared to 469 independent films, or movies made outside the studio system.[1] Yet while studios released less than twenty-four percent of 2011's movies, they dominated almost *82 percent* of the U.S. box office.[2]

This doesn't necessarily mean studios make *better* movies; it simply means they have such powerful distribution mechanisms, as well as well-funded promotional and marketing machines, that they can corner and control a vast majority of the market. Many studios spend $100–$350 millon on one film's marketing costs alone!

Occasionally, an independent film can capture and grow an audience without the backing of a studio. Dinesh D'Souza and Gerald Robert Molen's indie documentary, *2016: Obama's America*, for example, premiered at Edwards Cinema in Houston, TX on July 13, 2012, then spread to over 2,000 screens over the next two months, pulling in $33.5 million and becoming history's second-highest grossing doc of all time. Similarly, Alex Kendrick produced his Christian football movie, *Facing the Giants*, for $100,000; it opened September 20, 2006, on 441 screens, and over the the next seventeen weeks racked up $10 million—a 10,000 percent return!

FEATURE AGENTS

These feats are exceptions, however, not rules, and most commercial filmmakers still want to work with one of the six major studios (or one of a handful of "**mini-majors**," slightly smaller studios we'll discuss in a moment). So let's look at how Hollywood makes movies and delivers them to audiences, through the lens of the companies that rule the roost: the studios.

Studios

There are hundreds of elements, resources, and processes needed to make and release a movie. Many are practical: cameras, lights, make up, costumes, microphones. Some are human: actors, designers, editors, writers, gaffers. Others are financial: location fees, travel expenses, print fees, etc. Thus, a movie studio is usually defined as a company possessing the financial and creative resources (or immediate access to those resources) to develop, produce, and distribute films. They have stables of creative talent (usually in the form of producer deals, which we'll discuss in a moment), billion-dollar development and production budgets, and, often, their own soundstages, costume departments, office spaces, etc. They also have their own resources for marketing and distributing films, getting them to exhibitors that screen them for audiences.

Remember back in Chapter 5 when we talked about the six media conglomerates, the massive corporations that own both TV networks *and* TV studios? Well, guess what else most of them own? That's right—the six major movie studios. NewsCorp. owns 20th Century Fox, Time-Warner owns Warner Brothers, Comcast owns Universal Pictures, the Walt Disney Company owns Walt Disney Pictures, Sony owns Columbia Pictures, and Viacom owns Paramount. (I didn't list Viacom as one of the major TV conglomerates because it doesn't own a broadcast network. It does, however, own several cablers, such as MTV, Logo, CMT, Comedy Central, etc.)

The "majors" not only produce and distribute most of Hollywood's big hits, they also have a hand in the success of many of the independent films that make it to theaters. Director Ramin Bahrani's *At Any Price* (2012), for example, was independently produced by producers like Teddy Schwarzman's Black Bear Pictures,[3] then acquired for distribution by Sony Pictures Classics, a branch of Sony specializing in indie and arthouse pictures.[4] Lorene Scafaria's *Seeking a Friend For the End of the World* (2012) was co-financed by manufacturer-cum-producer Steven Rales's Indian Paintbrush, then distributed by Focus Features, Universal's arthouse division.[5]

Thus, there are two types of movies released by studios: **studio films**, projects developed and produced in-house, and **acquisitions**, independently produced films a studio purchases, or licenses, and distributes. Studios tend to focus on their own films, which are often big-budget movies like Universal's *Fast and Furious 6* or Paramount's *World War Z.* "If a smaller or moderately priced film is successful, the

What the Conglomerates Own

	Viacom	Disney	NewsCorp.	Sony	Time-Warner	Comcast
Broadcast Nets	–	ABC	FOX	–	CW (50%)	NBC
Cable Networks (partial list)	MTV, VH1 Logo, CMT	ESPN, Disney Channel	FX, Fox News Fox Sports	GSN (50%)	TNT, TBS, HBO	E!, USA, Bravo
TV Studio	–	ABC Studios	20th Century Fox TV	Sony TV	Warner Bros.	Universal TV
Film Studio	Paramount Pictures	Walt Disney Pictures	20th Century Fox Pictures	Sony Pictures	Warner Bros. Pictures	Universal Studios

studios have the potential to make a few million dollars," says Scott Seiffert, an executive at DreamWorks Animation SKG (*The Croods*, *Rise of the Guardians*). "When a big-budget movie is successful, the studios have the potential to make a billion dollars. One billion-dollar hit makes up for seventeen misses. It's playing the odds."

Indeed, of 2012's ten highest grossing movies, only *two* cost less than $100 million: Universal's *Ted* and Lionsgate's *The Hunger Games*. This also means the quest for high-concept, big-budget tentpoles (and low-budget acquistions) has all but pushed out mid-budget movies within the $30–$50 million range. (Even *The Hunger Games*, which cost Lionsgate $78 million, is considered high-budget.) Univeral's *Ted*, which–at $50 million–came in on the high end of "mid-budget," shocked the industry by grossing over $330 million worldwide to become one of the year's most profitable films.

When it comes to producing or acquiring lower-budget product, most of the major studios have **speciality arms**, branches that produce and distribute films that aim for more "niche" audiences. Columbia Pictures, for instance, has Screen Gems, which focuses on genre movies: thrillers, comedies, urban, and horror films. Fox Searchlight, a specialty arm of 20th Century Fox, does low-budget films–usually around $8 million[6]–like *Ruby Sparks* and *The Best Exotic Marigold Hotel*. Movies from Paramount's Insurge Pictures, which was founded after 2007's $15,000 *Paranormal Activity* grossed $194 million worldwide, are even smaller; it aims for "micro-budget" projects costing less than $100,000 each.[7]

"A studio movie is more likely to be very high concept, very plot-driven," says manager Aaron Kogan, who founded Aaron Kogan Management after working for *The Dark Knight* and *Man of Steel* producer Charles Roven's Atlas Entertainment. "A specialty arm-type of project may be more character-based, more filmmaker driven." Thus, managers and agents stay in constant contact with producers and studio execs to know what they're looking for, what they're developing, and what they're avoiding.

In addition to the six majors and their speciality arms, Hollywood also has six "**mini-majors**," smaller studios not owned by one of the main media conglomerates. These produce fewer movies than their gargantuan counterparts, but they still have their own development, production, and distribution resources. The mini-majors are Lionsgate (*The Hunger Games*, *Tyler Perry's Madea's Witness Protection*), Relativity (*Act of Valor*, *Mirror Mirror*), CBS Films (*The Woman in Black*, *Salmon Fishing in the Yemen*), FilmDistrict (*Lockout*, *Drive*), MGM (*21 Jumpstreet*, *Skyfall*), and The Weinstein Company (*The Artist*, *Bully*). Some people also consider Dreamworks a mini-major, although Dreamworks distributes its films through Disney.

In the first half of 2012 alone, the six majors and and six mini-majors accounted for over ninety-seven percent of the domestic box office,[8] which gives us an idea of where agencies and managers like to focus most of their selling energies. "Financially speaking, at least ninety percent of all [our] business . . . is at the studio level," says manager Adam Kolbrenner, a partner at Madhouse Entertainment, which reps writers such as Aaron Guzikowski (*Contraband*) and Dan O'Keefe (*Seinfeld*, *The Tonight Show*, *The League*). "Independent production companies usually will not compete with studios in terms of fees."

Producers and Production Companies

Production companies in film–like in television–create, develop and produce content. This content can originate from virtually anywhere. Some ideas are sold as pitches–like in March, 2013, when Universal Pictures and Jason Bateman's Aggregate Films acquired playwright Jay Reiss's pitch for *Family Therapy*.[9] Others are fully written spec scripts, like Olatunde Osunsanmi's *Eden*, which was reportedly purchased by Gold Circle Films (*Pitch Perfect*) for a low six figures in March, 2013.[10] Other times, production companies purchase a valuable piece of IP; this could be a novel–like when Leonardo DiCaprio's Appian Way purchased the film rights to Dennis Lehane's

What Makes the Majors Major

Hollywood's six major studios are also members of the Motion Picture Association of America (MPAA), a trade organization founded in 1922 to represent studios' political and business interests. You kow the film ratings you see on movies, like PG-13 or NC-17? Administered by the MPAA. They also spearhead massive efforts against piracy and copyright violations. Only the six majors belong; even the mini-majors are not part of the MPAA.

Agencies: Power by the Numbers

On page 28, one producer claimed ninety-five percent of all his business came through the Big Four agencies. Assuming this is true for most mainstream movie producers, and knowing the majors and mini-majors control ninety-seven percent of the market, this suggests over *ninety-two percent* of mainstream movies are being put together, in some way, by the Big Four agencies.

unpublished *Live By Night*[11]–or a memoir, like when Reese Witherspoon's Pacific Standard nabbed Cheryl Stayed's bestselling *Wild*[12]–or a video game, like when Lionsgate scooped up Deep Silver's zombie adventure, *Dead Island*.[13] IP could even be somebody's life, like when Paramount and Atlas Entertainment bought the life rights to U.S. Postal Service biker and Lance Amstrong teammate Tyler Hamilton.

The production company is then responsible for working with writers, directors, or other producers to develop the material into a shootable script. Once the script has been green-lit by all the producers, director, and financiers (which could be a major studio, a mini-major, or an independent investor), the production company then guides the film through preproduction, principal photography, and post-production until, finally, it's delivered to a distributor.

Like in TV, film production companies don't usually have their own money or practical filmmaking resources, so many successful companies stay afloat by making **studio deals**, also known as **production deals**, or **producer deals**. Again, these deals involve a studio paying a producer a specific amount of money in exchange for that producer's work over a specified amount of time. In 2011, for instance, Paramount closed a three-year deal with Sacha Baron Cohen's company, Four By Two Films, which produced *Bruno* and *The Dictator*.[14] In 2013, Dreamworks inked a first-look with Paper Pictures, the production company of former ICM agent and New Regency president of production Carla Hacken, who worked on *Unfaithful*, *Walk the Line*, and *Diary of a Wimpy Kid*.[15]

In features, most studio deals are **first-look deals**, which are usually less exclusive than the overall deals found in television. In a first-look deal, a producer gives a studio the right of first refusal on any of his projects. If that studio "**passes**," or has no interest in the project, the producer can take it to other studios or produce it independently. When producer Scott Rudin had a first-look at Paramount, for example, and they passed on *The Life Aquatic With Steve Zissou* and *The Royal Tenenbaums*, he took both projects over to Disney.[16] (Rudin subsequently terminated his Paramount first-look and signed a five-year deal with Disney. When the Disney deal expired, he signed a three-year deal with Sony, taking him through 2014.[17])

Even mini-majors and specialty arms occasionally make producer deals. Relativity has a two-year deal with actor/producer Channing Tatum's Iron Horse Entertainment;[18] The Weinstein Company has a first-look with producer Cary Woods (*Scream*, *Godzilla*).[19]

An Exception to a Rule

On rare occasions, movie studios do offer production companies and producers exclusive deals rather than first-looks. Ron Howard and Brian Grazer's Imagine, for example, used to have an exclusive deal with Universal Pictures, as did Working Title, which produced *Rush*, *Closed*, and *Anna Karenina*. But in 2012, Universal amended both deals to be first-looks, extending Working Title through 2015[20] and Imagine through 2016.[21]

How many producers a studio has under contract at a particular time varies depending on its needs and financial situation. In 2000, studios boasted a combined total of almost 300 deals. Ten years later, as the U.S. economy struggled to recover from the 2008 financial crisis, studios had only 133. As of 2012, there were approximately 160 deals.

If a production company proves successful over the course of its deal, providing its studio with quality projects, the studio will renew the company's deal. In 2005, for example, Warner Bros. inked a deal with director Todd Phillips' Green Hat Films (*The Hangover*,) after Phillips' big-screen reboot of *Starsky and Hutch* grossed $170 million worldwide. In 2012, after Green Hat's first three movies earned Universal $1.2 billion, Universal extended the deal through 2013.[22] If a company is not successful, or has a poor relationship with the studio, the deal will be terminated. In 2012, Warner Brothers declined to renew its long-time deal with producer Joel Silver. Although Silver had produced some of the studio's biggest movies, including *The Matrix* trilogy, he was also responsible for some of its biggest flops (like 2008's *Speed Racer*), which left him owing Warner Brothers almost $30 millon. His pricey deal covered a $7 million-per-film producer fee, as well as overhead for twenty employees, a personal driver, and a projectionist for his home screening room![23] Ultimately, Warner Bros. figured, the money Silver's movies brought in wasn't worth the outlays they were putting out.

An Exception to a Rule

While studios usually want to buy projects for—and provide material to—their own producers, they also want the most appropriate shepherd for every project. In 2012, Universal paid $5 million[24] for the adaptation rights to author E.L. James's *Fifty Shades* trilogy *before* finding a producer. They then sat down with some of Hollywood's most successful production companies, including Ron Howard and Brian Grazer's Imagine Entertainment[25] (*Angels and Demons*) and Scott Stuber's Stuber Pictures (*Ted*), both of which have Universal deals.[26] Ultimately, however, the studio chose to lay the project off with Mike De Luca,[27] a Sony-based producer who'd had recent success with two other red-hot book adaptations, *Moneyball* and *The Social Network*.

Talk the Talk

Vanity Deal—A production deal offered simply to stroke somebody's ego. When a studio fires a top executive, for example, it may give her a first-look deal as part of her severance. Or it may offer "vanity deals" to actors it wants to lock down for casting purposes. Studio execs may or may not view a particular actor as a bona fide "producer," they simply hope by offering the actor a producer credit on films he stars in, they can keep him in their movies. Actors, however, often turn out to have impressive producing chops. Leonardo DiCaprio, for example, has had a first-look with Warner Bros. since 2005. Although DiCaprio was once considered just a pretty heartthrob from movies like *Titanic* and *The Beach*, he has established himself as a powerful and talented producer, producing and developing projects such as *The Wolf of Wall Street* and adaptations of Michael Armour's novel, *The Road Home*, and anime classic *Akira*.

Of course, studios don't just hand production deals to anyone who wants one; they give them to people they have firm reason to believe will generate quality commercial material: established entities, producers and companies who have long, successful histories, or those who have produced a recent significant hit. Companies that don't have deals must find other forms of funding. Some are started by wealthy wannabe producers using their own cash. Thomas Tull, for example, was part-owner of the Pittsburgh Steelers when he decided to use $500 million to start Legendary Entertainment (*Wrath of the Titans*, *Man of Steel*), a production company specializing in sci-fi and comic-book movies.[28] Cross Creek Pictures (*Black Swan*) was founded with a $40 million investment from the Thompson brothers, five children of a wealthy Louisiana oil family.

Other producers solicit money from friends or relatives, or find backing from outside investors and venture capitalists. In 2012, Union Bank and UBS together invested $225 million in the Weinstein Company.[29] British producer Graham King (*Traffic*, *Dr. T and the Women*, *Gangs of New York*) launched GK films with private equity from oil and real estate tycoon Tim Headington, then went on to produce Oscar winners such as *Hugo*, *The Departed*, and *Rango*.[30] And when veteran theater producer Scott Sanders (*The Color Purple*) launched his film and theater production company in 2007, he scored investments from Robert Kraft, owner of the New England Patriots, and investment bankers Jim Fantaci and Roy Furman. (In an interesting arrangement, the investments from Kraft, Fantaci, and Furman fueled Sanders' theater division, while Sanders' film division was funded through a first-look deal with Walt Disney Pictures.[31]) Two years later, Sanders' theatrical division inked a five-year overall deal to produce stage versions of Sony Pictures' films, with Sony also buying twenty percent of the company. This brings us to the next type of company critical to the filmmaking process:

Financiers

Independent financiers (a financier who's not a studio) come in all shapes and sizes. Some fund entire companies. Others invest in a company's **slate**, a group of projects in development. Many provide financing for one or two specific films.

Traditionally, independent financing has been reserved for movies being created and produced outside the major studios, such as 2003's terrifying *Open Water*, which writer/director Chris Kentis paid for with $130,000 from his own pocket.[32] But today, as films have grown more expensive, even the majors are turning to outside financiers to help fund films and hedge bets. Paramount, Fox, Universal, Sony, and Warner Brothers have all partnered with financiers in various ways; only Disney still funds all its own movies (although it had a $500 million Credit Suisse deal that ended in 2009).[33]

Other financiers like to handpick the movies in which they invest, like when Michael Benaroya, son of wealthy Seattle real estate magnate Larry Benaroya,[35] personally ponied up $3.4 million to produce 2011's Oscar-nominated *Margin Call*.[36] Some fund portions of a film's budget. For example, energy magnate William O. Perkins' venture capitalist firm, Small Ventures, put $10 million toward Crystal Sky Pictures' $30 million adaptation of the video game *Tekken*.[37] Still others are foreign companies, such as Europe's StudioCanal, which made a name for itself funding movies budgeted under $30 million (*The Last Exorcism*).[38]

Also, some financiers begin as pure moneymen, then grow into a more hands-on role. Relativity Media founder Ryan Kavanaugh, for example, gained entry into Hollywood after his venture capitalist company tanked in 2001, leaving him with nothing but a Rolodex full of East Coast multimillionaires. Supporting himself writing business proposals for Hollywood studio execs, Kavanaugh started to learn a bit about the world of film finance, and realized he could be a matchmaker for his venture capitalist friends and Hollywood producers needing cash.[39] Relativity Media began making a name for itself by helping studios like Sony and Warner Brothers structure lucrative financing deals, and Kavanaugh quickly established himself as a bona fide producer. He has since worked on over 200 movies, including *The Fighter* and *Les Miserables*, which have collectively more than $17 billion at the box office.[40]

As films find funding in more and more unconventional ways, agents have begun to adapt to the evolving world. Some, like ICM and Gersh, now have departments devoted entirely to helping independent films, producers, and production companies find financing and/or distribution. Just as traditional feature agents sell films to studios by "packaging" scripts with directors or actors, these divisions package scripts with directors, actors, and monetary attachments. Sometimes, they put together a project and sell it to an indie production company or financier; other times, they package a project with partial funding and sell it to an actual studio. In fact, in addition to repping writers, directors, and projects, these agents also rep financiers *looking* for writers, directors, and projects.

Creative Cash: Part I

Recent years have seen indie artists invent some incredibly unique ways of funding their work. In April, 2013, TV writer Rob Thomas used Kickstarter to raise over $5.5 million for a big-screen adaptation of his cult TV hit, *Veronica Mars*.[41] A few days later, Friends Media released its first feature, *Not Today*, starring John Schneider and Cody Longo, which it produced with $1.6 million in donations from the congregation of Friends Church in Yorba Linda, California.[42]

Distributors

Distributors are middlemen who get movies from producers who make them to exhibitors who screen them. Studio films don't usually need to find distribution; they simply use their studio's in-house distribution arms. Independent producers, however, need to find distribution companies to acquire their movies and license them as rentals to exhibitors such as Regal Cinemas, North America's largest theater chain, or Flagship Theatres, an independent exhibitor specializing in foreign, independent, and arthouse films. Other distributors, like iTunes and Netflix, acquire films and distribute them to audiences via DVD, television, or the Internet.

There are many different avenues through which to distribute films, and many different companies working to do so. When it comes to theatrical distribution, however, *almost all major distributors are owned by or affiliated with one of the main Hollywood studios.* This is one of the reasons studios dominate the industry. Sure, there is a handful of indie distributors, like Freestyle Releasing (*Me and Orson Welles*, *The Illusionist*) and Magnolia Films (*Universal Soldier: Day of Reckoning*, *John Dies at the End*), but most of these specialize in finding "alternative" strategies for releasing small independent films. "It's so expensive and hard to open a movie," says former agent and manager B.J. Ford, "that it's a big barrier to entry into the distribution world. That's why the studios thrive."

First of all, the major studios have more money to produce and acquire movies. And while this doesn't necessarily guarantee studios release *better* movies, it does guarantee studios release *more* movies. In 2011, Paramount and Warner Brothers, the year's top-grossing majors, released fifteen and twenty-six movies, respectively, generating $5.17 billion and $4.67 billion.[45] Mini-majors, on the other hand, released fewer and brought in less money. Lionsgate released only nine pictures and generated $1.58 billion.[46] Relativity released seven, Summit released eight, the Weinstein Company released eleven. Compare that to even smaller, more independent distributors like Open Road Films or Freestyle Releasing, which each released one–*Killer Elite* and *Dylan Dog: Dead of Night*. (*Killer Elite* grossed $25 million, barely a third of its $70 million production budget, and *Dylan Dog* brought in just over $1 million.)

Second, studios have millions of dollars to promote, advertise, and market their movies, often spending as much on marketing or **P&A** as a movie's production budget itself. For example, 20th Century Fox spent about $300 million making James Cameron's *Avatar* in 2009, and another $350 distributing and marketing it.[47] While this may sound like excess, it's a reality of the film world; whether you're a big-budget producer like James Cameron or an indie producer like Sidney Kimmel (*Gone*, *Parker*), if you want your film to be financially successful, you need to have major marketing money. Which means a filmmaker who wants his films to succeed will probably, at some point, cross paths with one of the majors, mini-majors, or a specialty arm.

Indie films looking for distribution tend to find it in one two ways, and agents can be instrumental in both:

Way To Find Distribution 1: Finding distribution for a completed film. Many independent filmmakers make a movie with no distribution in place, then attempt to find it once the project is finished. This usually involves submitting the completed movie to film festivals frequented by buyers and distributors. Producer Travis Stevens, for example, submitted his low-budget comedy *Cheap Thrills* to the 2013 South By Southwest (SXSW) Film Festival, where he sold its North American theatrical and VOD distribution rights to Drafthouse Films and Snoot Entertainment. And at the 2013 Sundance Film Festival, UTA's Rena Ronson sold Stephanie Meyers and Jerusha Hess's *Austenland* to Sony for over $4 million.[48]

Other producers peddle their wares at film markets like Cannes' Marche du Film or the American Film Market (AFM). Unlike festivals, where there's usually an evaluative acceptance process and a competition component, film markets are open to any buyer or seller willing to pay the entry fee. Film markets are like giant farmers markets, but instead of going booth to booth buying carrots and peppers, buyers go booth to booth, or room to room, buying movies and distribution rights. The annual eight-day AFM, for instance, takes place at Santa Monica, California's Loews Santa Monica Beach Hotel. More than 8,000 attendees from over seventy countries bounce from room to room, watching films, trailers, clips, and promotional packages, and–hopefully–buying and selling films. At 2012's AFM, Paradigm agents Nick LoPiccolo and Ben Weiss helped clients Sarah Siegel-Magness and Gary Magness (who also produced the Oscar-winning *Precious*) sell their adaptation of April Stevens' novel, *Long Time Gone*, starring Virginia Madsen, to Canada's Phase 4 Films (*Milkshake*, *The Last Gladiators*).[49] And at 2013's European Film Market, Chilean film director Sebastian Lelio's *Gloria* sparked a feeding frenzy from distributors around the world, selling U.S. rights to Roadside Attractions, German rights to Alamode, and French rights to Ad Vitam, as well as rights to many other territories like Switzerland, Greece, and Spain.

What Are the Relevant Film Festivals and Markets?

There are hundreds of film festivals and markets around the world. Some are prestigious, some are hip and underground, some are small and regional. But only a few attract the powerful buyers distributing films on a national and international playing field. Want your film to have the best shot at wide-scale distribution? Pray it gets into one of these:

- **Sundance Film Festival** (www.sundance.org)—January
- **Berlin International Film Festival** (www.berlinale.de) and **European Film Market** (www.efm-berlinale.de)—February
- **SXSW** (www.sxsw.com)—March
- **Tribeca Film Festival** (http://tribecafilm.com/festival)—April
- **Cannes Film Festival** (www.festival-cannes.fr) and **Marche du Film** (www.marchedufilm.com)—May
- **Toronto International Film Festival** (http://tiff.net)—September
- **American Film Market** (www.americanfilmmarket.com)—November

---

Way To Find Distribution 2: Pre-sell a movie's distribution rights. "Pre-selling projects is a large component of the independent financing space," says Alexis Garcia—an agent at WME Global, WME's department specializing in indie film—who helped pre-sell *Drive*, starring Ryan Gosling, to FilmDistrict. "Pre-selling is basically licensing a film to distributors around the world, and even in the U.S., prior to finishing the movie."

Convincing a distributor to commit to distributing a movie before the movie has been made is never easy, and it usually involves a well-connected agent who can put together a commercially attractive package. "[If] you're trying to convince a distributor in France to commit a specific amount of money on delivery of this project, they're going to want to know who's in it, who's directing it, [and] they're going to want to read the script," Garcia explains. "In special instances, they may not even care about the script if they know it's a certain size movie with this filmmaker and these actors. In very, very special instances, they might love the script so much they say, 'As long as the actors [are of] a certain caliber . . . we'll make a commitment.' In any of those instances, you're aiming for them to give you a contractual commitment saying, 'Upon delivery of this movie, we're paying you X amount of money, irrespective of how good it is. As long as it's this script, this filmmaker, a few other parameters [like] running time, then we're committed to paying you.'"

Foreign Sales Agents

Most traditional agencies, including the Big Four, don't take on foreign distribution sales themselves. Most use **foreign sales agents,** based in the various foreign territories, whose whole job is selling foreign distribution rights of American films. While you'd think this might be big business for Hollywood agencies, big enough to warrant them having their own foreign sales departments, "there's not a lot of money in it," says APA feature agent Ryan Saul. "You have movies selling in territories for $30,000."

Foreign distribution rights are usually sold by geographic region, or **territory**. Wild Bunch International, for example, distributes films in Italy, France, Germany, and Spain (where they've handled hits such as *The Artist*, *The Wrestler*, *Spirited Away*, *Fahrenheit 9/11*, and *Vicki Cristina Barcelona*). United International Pictures, which is owned jointly by Universal and Paramount, distributes movies in eighteen countries including Hungary, India, Norway, Poland, Chile, Taiwan, and Colombia (where it has distributed *G.I. Joe: Retaliation*, *This is 40*, *The Guilt Trip*, and *Mama*).

Also, when a distributor pre-buys a movie's distribution rights, it doesn't pay upfront cash. Rather, it gives the producer a contractual agreement stating the terms of the commitment and the specific dollar amount. The producer can then take this agreement to a bank, or an equity financier, and use it to get funding for the film.

Thus, raising money by pre-selling distribution rights often means patching together a mish-mash of sales in hopes of making enough money. Let's say you're trying to raise funding for a movie budgeted at $10 million. You may sell your French and Portuguese rights to one company for $1 million, your Turkish and Japanese rights to another company for $2 million, and your Chinese and Danish rights for $1.5 million—giving you a total of $4.5 million in pre-sales. A bank may then loan you $3 million, leaving you another $7 million to raise, usually through private equity. (Banks rarely match the amount of pre-sales—especially pre-sales from foreign companies, which they often view as less reliable and harder to monitor than American companies.)

"The ultimate goal," says Garcia, "is to license a movie for more money than it costs [to make]. You have zero performance risk. If you can license the movie for more money than it costs, even prior to making the movie . . . you don't need equity financiers at all. You can go to a bank and, hopefully, cover the whole thing. That's pie in the sky—but it happens." A successful example of this process? Writer/director Rian Johnson's *Looper*, which raised its $30 million independently and presold its distribution rights to FilmDistrict.

Agents' Sales Fees

So far, we've talked about independent film agents making money three different ways: 1. They commission their writers and directors, just like feature agents selling scripts to studios; 2. They collect retainer fees from financier clients; 3. They take packaging fees—usually two percent of the budget—when they package an indie project. But agents have a fourth way of making money as well: *sales fees*. These are fees an agent collects for finding distribution for a film, and they're usually taken off the top of whatever money the distributor pays to the financier. (Sales fees often range anywhere from ten percent to thirty percent, depending on how much international pavement-pounding the sales agent is doing.[50,51])

Talk the Talk

Output Deal–An arrangement in which a distributor pre-pays for the rights to distribute a certain number of films produced by a particular company. In 2012, for example, Wild Bunch, a European sales and distribution company, forged an output deal with Mark Burg's Twisted Pictures, the company behind the *Saw* franchise. Under the deal's terms, Twisted produces two movies a year, with Wild Bunch claiming worldwide distribution rights in all media through 2015.[52] Thus, Wild Bunch has agreed to distribute these Twisted movies—even before seeing them—and Burg and Twisted know they have distribution (as well as some possible upfront cash). Wild Bunch, meanwhile, must distribute those films—as long as they meet the agreed-upon criteria (running time, stars, etc.)—no matter how wonderful or terrible they may be. If the movies are unwatchably bad, Wild Bunch still distributes them. Sounds like a great deal for Twisted, right? It is. On the other hand, if the movies are fantastic masterworks, Wild Bunch gets a bargain, because Twisted may have undersold pictures it could've gotten a higher price for elsewhere.

Sometimes pre-sales don't even involve an actual price tag. In other words, a distributor may say, "We're not willing to commit to an advance on the budget, but we'll guarantee you two thousand screens domestic and twenty million dollars in **P&A**."

Now you've "presold domestic not for money, but for something that could be more valuable," says Garcia. "That's going to help you drive up your international numbers, drive interest if you still need equity. There are a lot of times when you see these movies that aren't very good still going out on over two thousand screens—they had that commitment before the film was ever finished, and the film never would've gotten made without that!"

Of course, a big part of a distributor's job—whether a studio or an independent—isn't just getting films to exhibitors, it's advertising and marketing that film. As we've discussed, a film's marketing and distribution costs can often exceed the film's production budget itself. But not every movie is, or should be, marketed and distributed the same way.

One of the biggest factors in shaping a movie's marketing campaign is its opening weekend. Flashy, expensive tentpoles like *Pacific Rim* or *Iron Man 3* open simultaneously on thousands of screens across the country. "You have the rollout of the large, nationwide release in the theaters . . . a lotta buzz . . . Hollywood premieres—it's a time-tested and proven launching platform," says Richard Hare, Senior VP and CFO of Carmike Cinemas, America's fourth largest exhibitor with nearly 250 theaters and 2,500 screens.

The Avengers, for example, opened domestically on May 4, 2012, in 4,349 theaters, averaging $47,698 per screen for an opening haul of nearly $207.5 million.[53] Films opening at this level need to generate massive amounts of business, so marketers bombard consumers with trailers, billboards, online ads, and TV spots—as well as partnerships with toy companies, fast-food restaurants, convenience stores, etc. Whenever you see a movie-based toy in a Happy Meal, or a character on the side of a 7–11 cup, thank the studio or distributor's marketing department. Many times, they've begun planning these campaigns close to a year in advance of the movie's release!

On the other hand, smaller indepedent movies usually appeal to much smaller audiences, so distributors open them on fewer screens, testing the waters to see how they fare. As a result, these films need much smaller marketing blitzes. If a movie succeeds in its opening weekend, the distributor rolls it out slowly to other theaters. On January 11, 2013, for example, the Weinstein Company opened first-time director Dustin Hoffman's *Quartet* in two theaters—one in L.A., one in New York. When the movie averaged an impressive $23,561 per screen, Weinstein expanded it to thirty more locations. That second week, it averaged a still repectable $10,000 per screen, giving the Weinstein Company a 579 percent boost in profits.[54] The next week, Weinstein added another 131 screens and averaged $7,111 per screen the next week. Week four: almost fifty new theaters at $5,900 per screen.[55]

Aside from strategizing movies' releases, distributors have one other very important duty—getting the movies themselves to the actual theaters! This involves making prints to be projected, delivering those prints to theaters, and negotiating deals and relationships with theater owners and managers. Which brings us to the final step in a film's theatrical life cycle: *the exhibitor.*

Exhibitors

In the U.S. alone, there are over 100 theater owners and chains, or exhibitors, boasting over 30,000 screens. The largest chain, Regal, has nearly 7,000 screens, AMC has over 5,000, and Cinemark USA has almost 4,000.[56] These exhibitors not only receive prints from distributors (whether those are digital prints either beamed by satellite or stored on a hard drive, or actual canisters of film), which they then project for audiences, they also negotiate schedules, set ticket pricing, sell concessions, and do small-scale advertising, such as publishing ads or showtimes in local newspapers.

For exhibitors, each week begins with a phone conversation with distributors to discuss each film on each screen in each of the ehxibitor's theaters. "It's a very involved . . . labor-intensive process," says Hare. "When you agree to a film, you're not just negotiating the price, you're also negotiating how many screens you're going to put it on and how long you're going to hold it on those screens. [For example,] you may hold a film on three screens in a certain theater, and if the movie does better, you will agree to add a screen. If it doesn't do well, you work with the studio. In some cases, we'll be required to keep holding it—but in [other] cases, the studio will say 'Hey, you can take it off, we understand. Help us out with the next movie.' It's a very fluid dialogue and discussion, almost on a daily basis."

Hostage Crisis

Because movie studios control distribution of the biggest, most commercial movies—*James Bond*, *The Hobbit*, *Spider-Man*, *Ice Age*, etc.–they can occasionally hold exhibitors hostage, demanding theater owners show one of the studio's less attractive films if the theater also wants to show next weekend's hot opening tentpole. Often times, studios must do this to keep big stars or directors happy. When negotiating deals for big-name talent, agents sometimes push for special guarantees, like convincing a studio to commit to opening a client's movie on at least 3,500 screens. When the movie turns out horribly, or gets bad reviews, or tanks in ticket pre-sales, exhibitors are anxious to yank it, but studios must honor their contracts.

Exhibitors and distributors also negotiate the price the distributor pays for each movie. Although exhibitors and distributors split the box office gross, the amount of the split is determined by the success of the movie; this is called a **scale deal**, and the better the movie does, the more money the distributor gets to keep. So if a movie

FEATURE AGENTS

Agents and Exhibitors

I understand how agents interact with production companies, studios, financiers, and distributors. But do they ever interact with exhibitors?

Not usually, although agents occasionally pitch "alternative content" ideas to exhibitors. New York's Metropolitan Opera, for instance, has its "Live in HD" series, in which operas are beamed live from Lincoln Center to over 1,500 movie theaters in more than fifty countries.[57] Theaters have also shown live rock concerts and sporting events like marathons and UFC fights.[58] This is still a relatively new and experimental revenue stream for exhibitors, but this is the one area where they're occasionally pitched by agents.

makes $100 million domestically, an exhibitor may pay the distributor 45 cents of every dollar; if the movie makes $150 million, the exhibitor pays 50 cents. Scale deals are always negotiated *before* a movie screens, but the exhibitor doesn't pay the distributor till after the screening period.

Once negotiations are complete, the distributor must deliver the actual movie to exhibitors. For most of Hollywood's existence, exhibitors projected physical films; each movie would contain three to five reels of celluloid, which would be delivered to the theater and projected with an actual projector. When the industry started using digital prints and projectors, prints started coming on hard drives that simply slid into the digital projector. Today, many films have left the physical world altogether and are beamed straight to theater projectors via satellite.

This is where, on all those Friday nights, the business of Hollywood meets the consumers of America. Movie-goers sit in a dark theater, munching popcorn amdist their stadium seating, while behind them, a projector whirs away—the final step in an often years-long journey.

The Feature World's Annual Calendar

Unlike the broadcast television industry, which works on a rigid schedule, film studios buy projects year-round . . . or at least until they run out of development money. Thus, many agents monitor each studio's fiscal year, trying to gauge when each studio may be low on cash or flush with new funds. Here's a quick look at each major's fiscal year:

- **20th Century Fox**: July–June
- **Disney**: October–September
- **Paramount**: January–December
- **Sony Pictures**: April–May
- **Universal**: January–December
- **Warner Bros.**: January–December

Certain times of the year, however, are also better for selling scripts than others. Many agents and managers go out with scripts in spring or fall to avoid some of Hollywood's slower times, such as:

- **Winter**—Hollywood slows down between Thanksgiving and Christmas. Then, a month after New Year comes Utah's Sundance Film Festival, which feels like an extension of the holidays, so most buyers and sellers don't start thinking about new projects till February.
- **Summer**—Summer begins with the Cannes Film Festival, which attracts many of Hollywood's power-players, so there's no point in trying to sell a script during Cannes. As days heat up, people are more interested in going on vacation or hitting the beach, and no agent or writer wants their script read by some exec lounging on the shore with his kids.
- **Holidays**—Hollywood will find any excuse to take a day off—it embraces holidays unlike any other industry. (I can't prove this statistically, but I swear it's true.) We not only take off the Mondays of Labor Day and Memorial Day, but many companies also take off the preceding Friday (or they take a half-day)! Also, if a holiday like Independence Day falls in the middle of the week—forget it; many companies take off *at least* the day before, if not the entire week. Many agencies close the day before, and sometimes the day after as well, so the entire week is shot. Also, for an industry that takes a lot of heat for having no religious grounding, we *love* religious holidays. We'll take off Christmas, Easter, Good Friday, Passover, Yom Kippur, and Rosh Hashanah!

So when *are* the best times for going out with scripts? Summer or fall.

Ask the Exhibitor

Q: I'm an indie filmmaker about to finish a new movie. Why can't I act as my own distributor, skipping festivals and markets and going straight to exhibitors myself?

A: "You can!" says Richard Hare, Senior VP and CFO of Carmike Cinemas. "The challenge with that is scale. With the advent of digital, you can give us a digital print, and we can put it on our projector, but distributors pay for advertising costs, and has anyone ever heard of this movie? We have to look at the economics of our screens and say, 'If we're going to put something on this screen, we have to take something off of this screen.' Can we take something off of this screen? How much money do we think we're going to make by doing that? What I've learned is the enormous importance of advertising and marketing for these movies. You'll see where people will buy movies from Sundance or other sources–the movies are already made, already in the can–and how much money distributors have to [spend]. Sometimes the distributors spend more on advertising and marketing than they do on making the movie! And that's *crucial*.

   "The other thing, economically, you have are virtual print fees, which are fees studios typically pay facilitators of digital projectors. The way it works: you have a company that buys digital projectors and [leases them to exhibitors]. In our case it's Cinedigm, a public company. We put projectors they own into our circuits, and they collect virtual print fees from studios. Virtual print fees are what studios pay to subsidize digital projection in the industry; in lieu of studios having to pay the money they normally pay to produce a 35 mm print, they pay an amount of money, or part of it, to subsidize digital projection. A lot of smaller independent [distributors] have a hard time coughing up the virtual print fee. So it can be very difficult [for exhibitors] to make money off of those."

9 Original Material— Specs and Pitches

No matter how hard he fought, Jeremy Garelick's eyes were closing. He'd been on set for more than fourteen hours, and the weights within his head kept pulling down his eyelids. All Garelick wanted was a bed, but as he glanced at the Irish countryside, where he was shooting second unit for Joel Schumacher's upcoming movie *Veronica Guerin*, he knew he still had a couple of hours to go. Garelick pried his eyes open— he could not mess this up. He'd spent the last several months working as an assistant to the award-winning director, and Schumacher had finally agreed to let him shoot second-unit. It was a huge break, but "I still wasn't making any money," says Garelick. More importantly, "I wasn't really seen as a writer and a director, which was my ultimate goal."

And then his phone rang. "Is Jeremy Garelick there?" asked the unfamiliar voice on the other line.

"This is he."

"It's Mike Sheresky from William Morris." Suddenly, Garelick was awake. "We just read your script, *The Golden Tux*—we absolutely love it! We want to meet with you tomorrow. We want to sign . . ."

"And then I got cut off," Garelick remembers. "I tried calling back the William Morris main line, but I couldn't remember his name. The name I remembered was Mike Krzyzewski, the basketball coach at Duke, so I just asked for Mike Krzyzewski." Finally, Garelick was put through to Sheresky. The young feature lit agent had gotten the script from Allen Fischer—a manager who repped Garelick's writing partner, Jay Lavender— and felt he could sell it.

A few days later, Garelick—who had spent time as a CAA assistant before leaving to work for Schumacher—was being led through the halls of William Morris. "When you're an assistant, most people walk by and don't notice you—you're there to serve them," says Garelick. "Then, suddenly, *I* was the one walking past the assistants. I kept saying hi [like] they were my peers, but I was getting looked at by the agents in a very different way—which felt weird, but cool at the same time."

Sheresky was waiting for Garelick and Lavender in his office. They sat down, chatted casually for a few moments, and then Sheresky laid his cards on the table. "If you sign with us," he said, "we can sell this script tomorrow."

Of course, agents make these promises all the time and they *never happen*. The next day, Garelick was driving through L.A. with his father, a construction worker from New York, when the phone rang. Garelick hit the speaker button. Sheresky's voice crackled into the car: "We have an offer."

That afternoon, *The Golden Tux*—the story of "a professional best man for grooms with no friends"—sold to Dimension Films, a division of Miramax (then owned by Disney) specializing in horror and comedy. Sheresky had sent it only hours earlier to a young director/producer named Todd Phillips, who had a first look with Dimension and was in the middle of directing his second comedy, *Old School*.

Although Phillips and Dimension never made *The Golden Tux*, the sale launched Garelick's career. In fact, Garelick was the guy Phillips called a few years later when he needed extensive rewrites on a new script he was prepping—a relatively low-budget comedy called *The Hangover*. Garelick also got to know Vince Vaughn, who was briefly interested in *The Golden Tux* but instead pitched Garelick and Lavender an idea for a romantic comedy called *The Break-Up*. Garelick, Lavender, and Vaughn broke the story together and sold it to Universal for $2.25 million;[1] it was eventually produced, starring Vaughn and Jennifer Aniston, for $52 million, and grossed over $200 million worldwide. Garelick is now one of Hollywood's most sought-after screenwriters, often getting called to pen high-profile projects such as New Line's *Police Academy* reboot and Paramount's *Baywatch* feature. And in a weird twist of fate, *The Golden Tux* finally entered pre-production in 2013—thirteen years after its original sale—with a new director at the helm: Garelick.

As extraordinary as Garelick's (literal) overnight success story is, it actually illuminates a fairly standard path traveled by scripts aiming to get sold: agent–producer–studio. But how does this path work? What detours and pitfalls might a script and its agents encounter? And how can you, as a writer, be prepared to navigate this process alongside your representation?

There are five basic stages to selling a script:

1. Deciding what to write.
2. Script development.
3. Going out with the script.
4. Getting an offer and creating a competitive situation.
5. Negotiation.

DECIDING WHAT TO WRITE

As writers, we like to think a well-written and compelling story should be enough to sell a script. Unfortunately, this isn't always true. In fact, it's *rarely* true. Sure, selling a script requires a well-told story, but there are other, equally important factors that make a script attractive to buyers. Perhaps the five most important factors are:

1. **Is your script based on intellectual property?** Are you adapting a true story? A well-known play? A best-selling game or graphic novel? Studios are much more willing to bet money on properties that have already proven their worth in the marketplace, so a writer or producer who can secure the rights to a recognizable property increases their odds of a sale.

2 **Does your script fall squarely within the boundaries of a particular genre?** Is it a horror movie? A teen sex comedy? A found footage film? Genre movies are easier to sell because they're easier to market. Look at the marketing campaigns for genre movies; whether it's a horror movie like *Mother*, a sci-fi movie like *Star Trek Into Darkness*, or a romance like *Safe Haven*, it's crystal clear what those movies are. But take something like *Warm Bodies*, which mixes elements of horror and romantic comedy, and it's less clear. It may not appeal entirely to horror fans, or entirely to romantic comedy fans. Second, producers and studios believe, rightly or wrongly, that attaching a big star makes movies more attractive to audiences (see the textbox on page 179). But if a movie lands firmly in a specific genre, it helps mitigate some of that need. Horror fans tend to like horror regardless of who's starring; fantasy fans love fantasy movies even without a big star.

    "When you have an opportunity to do a [genre] movie, you're not cast dependent anymore," says manager Lenny Beckerman of Hello and Company. Those movies "have a better chance of getting made because you don't need A-list stars in it. [Plus,] the budget's going to be smaller, so they have a better chance of selling."

3. **Does the concept have strong foreign value?** Today's studios rely on a film's international box office almost more than domestic box office. Fox's $112-million *Gulliver's Travels*, starring Jack Black, bombed in America when it took in less than $43 million. But overseas, it chalked up almost $200 million. Many studio

executives consult their international distribution departments even before buying a script or greenlighting a project, letting international execs weigh in on creative decisions such as casting and location.[2] Perhaps most importantly, certain types of movies—like comedies, which rely on language and culture-specific jokes and humor—simply don't play well overseas, making them a much tougher sell to American execs. Thrillers and action flicks, meanwhile, transcend national and cultural borders much easier than other films, making them more sellable as scripts or pitches.

4. **Who is the audience for your movie?** Today, tween and teens make up a massive movie-consuming audience. Many kids spend their entire weekend at the mall, where they may watch two or three movies in a weekend. This makes the PG-13 rating incredibly valuable; it means movies like *Twilight* and *The Hunger Games* are mature enough to attract older audiences, but kids aren't exempt from seeing them.

5. **What is your movie's budget?** Today, most movies tend to be either big-budget blockbusters based on familiar IP (*Star Trek*, *The Avengers*), or smaller "**contained**" movies like *Moon* or *Buried*. Contained movies can usually be done for a specific price point— *Phone Booth's* budget was made for $13 million, *Moon's* budget was $5 million, and *Buried* reportedly cost less than $3 million—making them attractive to studios and indie producers alike.

Talk the Talk

Contained movies take place almost entirely in a specific, isolated location—it could be a single room (*12 Angry Men*), an apartment (*Rear Window*), a boat (*Dead Calm*), a cabin (*Misery*), a new house (*Paranormal Activity*), a convenience store (*Clerks*), or a school library (*The Breakfast Club*).

Ask the Manager

Q: I just had a general meeting with an executive at a production company with a studio deal—a friend of mine, an assistant, set it up. The exec told me they're looking for supernatural thrillers with female protagonists. What's the best way for me to use this information and try to sell them something?

A: Don't bother. "Don't try to satisfy a whim of a studio. There might be a situation where Paramount says, 'We're looking for a micro-budget horror movie.' They think that way, [but] we wouldn't necessarily recommend clients [write] things to satisfy one studio. It doesn't make strategic sense. What we advise our clients is: write commercial movies. You know what they are, because they're in the movie theater. And hopefully, it's what you like, too."—Robyn Meisinger, manager, Madhouse Entertainment

---

Thus, you shouldn't start thinking about how to sell your script after you've finished writing. You should begin those strategizing conversations with your agent *before you even sit down to write "Fade In."*

"It's annoying if someone just drops a script in your lap that you don't know anything about," says APA feature lit agent Will Lowery. "Ideally, you know it's coming. If you're a good agent or manager, you've already discussed the idea [with your client] and whether it's good or not. You know your client is writing a comedy about dogs that talk. You know your client is writing an action-thriller. It's our job to sell, but it's also our job to tell you what can or can't sell."

Agents and managers spend most of their days on the phone, chatting with producers, studios, and executives, learning what buyers want and what they don't. For example, says Mike Sablone, director of development at John Krasinski's Sunday Night Productions (*Promised Land*), "John has a specific vision of what he'd like to be developing and producing. It's not 'I only want to produce movies about small town America,' it's more 'I want to work on movies about bigger issues.' With *Promised Land* we were looking to write something Capra-esque, whether it's 'I just read an amazing book about coal mining,' or 'Oh my God, I just read a book about early unions,' or 'I just read an amazing story about two brothers that has nothing to do with anything political or charged.' It changes with his interests, and what stories we've told in the past. With *Promised Land*, we learned what was great about that story, and now it's like, 'We've told that story, let's find something different we can put our spin on.'"

If a political scandal captures the country's attention, producers and execs may suddenly want politically themed stories. If a new teen horror flick becomes a box office smash, every exec in town will want his own version of a teen horror film. And if, the next day, there's a national tragedy like the Newtown massacre, everyone will just as quickly drop it. "Good scripts don't sell," says Lowery. "*Marketable* scripts sell."

Ask the Agent

Q: I'm an aspiring screenwriter living in the middle of Wisconsin. I don't have an agent or any industry friends. Is there any way I can learn what producers are looking for and buying?

A: "The Internet is an amazing tool, and it's probably where you will get all your information if you are not in L.A., working in the industry. Blogs like *Deadline Hollywood* (www.deadline.com/hollywood)–Nikki Finke has amazing amounts of information, constantly updated. *The Hollywood Reporter* (www.hollywoodreporter. com) and *Variety* (www.variety.com)–they've got websites, as well. There's also *ScriptShadow* (scriptshadow.net), reading and passing judgments on scripts, and Agent Trainee (twitter.com/AgentTrainee)."–Melissa Solomon, coordinator, Verve Talent and Literary Agency

---

So how do you know what's marketable? Ask your representation! "Artists are often so close to their work that they want to pursue it for art's sake," says Scott Hoffman of Folio Literary Management, an agency representing both literary and film rights. "The role of the agent is to filter the goals of the artist through the lens of commerce, let the artist know whether what they're doing is going to be commercial, and allow the artist to make the correct decision for him or herself in an informed manner. If I have a client who wants to write a three-hundred-thousand word novel about his great-grandmother's bunions, that's fantastic, and that might be exactly the right project for him to do artistically, but it's probably not the right project to do commercially at this point in his career. The role of the agent is to explain that to the client, then let them make their own decision. And because I work with that client on a commission basis, whether I want to be involved in that project, or whether I want to be involved with a client whose commercial goals might differ from my own."

Ask the Agent

Q: What does an agent do if a client is passionate about writing something the agent feels is un-commercial?

A: "It depends on the client, and it depends on the project. There are projects you think are entirely wrong projects, career killers, and there are projects that are just not the right *next* project for a client, in which case you have a dialogue about each of your respective roles, and what the benefits and drawbacks are to each specific party. [Likewise], if a client turns in work that happens to be not their best work, or not up to the kind of quality you as an agent feel you would like to represent, it's up to you to have an open and frank discussion and say, 'I don't feel comfortable sharing this [with buyers]. When I send something [out], there's an implicit endorsement of it. I don't think this work is your best work, and I don't think it's the kind of thing I would like to be professionally associated with.' But, in general, if the dialogue is working between the agent and the client, what needs to happen for both parties will happen for both parties."–Scott Hoffman, founding partner, Folio Literary Management

---

FEATURE AGENTS

Consulting your representation also gets them personally invested in the process and helps them begin strategizing. "If it's [an idea] I'm excited about and I know I'll have it in a month," Lowery says, "if I'm at lunch [with a studio executive or producer], I'll say, 'You're going to have this great thing from me in a month.' I do that a lot."

Some writers pitch their agents a small handful of fleshed-out ideas. Others present a list of **one-liners**. Either way, consulting your representation lets your agents help pick the most seaworthy ideas and tweak them to be as sellable as possible. They may suggest changing the backdrop, switching characters' genders or ethnicities, or adding or removing certain storylines or set pieces.

One thing to consider: when bouncing ideas off your agent, make sure ideas are as well-developed as possible. It's fine to pitch your agent one-liners, but anything beyond this should be fairly fleshed out. Agents "are not producers," says Lowery. "We're your reps. So it's annoying when a writer says 'What about this?' and you come back with 'What happens in the second act?' and they don't have an answer. *You're the writer!* I don't have time to sit down and do development sessions. That's where managers come in. It's their job to sit down and flesh out the idea and make sure it's agent-ready."

Because managers often have smaller client rosters, they often have more time to work with writers on development. Plus, as potential producers on projects, their job is to shape those projects both creatively and commercially. "'Manager-ready' is way more ready than 'agent-ready,'" says literary manager Robyn Meisinger, a partner at Madhouse Entertainment. "'Agent-ready' doesn't mean 'good'; 'agent-ready' means 'I barely have to do anything to sell this script.' [Managers] are involved in every aspect from the conception to completion of a script, and every writer's process is different. They might come to us with an idea; we then do a two-page or three-page on characters, which then evolves into a beat sheet, which becomes an outline, which then becomes a script. And there could be multiple drafts of a beat sheet, multiple drafts of an outline, multiple drafts of a screenplay. Agents have four hundred clients and don't have time to read sixteen drafts of scripts, so for us to have a script that's ready, [the script is] far more complete than a lot of . . . scripts that go out from agencies and haven't been worked on with managers."

Ask the Agent

Q: I worry that if I ask my manager for too much help developing a project, they'll get annoyed and lose interest. How much help is too much to ask for?

A: "When it's too much is really simple: *when the work is not good.* I could do a first act with the writer, and we could do three or four sessions trying to get that first act, but if the writer can't get there, then the writer is not talented enough to get there. That's when you start to figure whether to cut your losses or not. I mean, the only thing [managers] have is time, but you have to use your time correctly. So if the writer is taking too much of your time, but not getting there, then you bet on the wrong horse."—Lenny Beckerman, manager, Hello and Company

---

Script Development

Once a client and his reps agree on which idea to pursue, the client goes off to write. Most agents expect to see a script within two or three months of sending a client to script. "It's always impressive, but also kind of scary when writers write really fast," says Lowery, and "it's annoying when they're really slow. [I want to see a script] as soon as it's ready, but [not till] it's good. Treat it like a full-time job. I treat my job like a full-time job! It's so bizarre and frustrating how many writers don't take the time to write."

When the writer feels he finally has a worthy draft, he emails it to the agent, who puts it into his nightly or weekend reading stack. Client material goes to the top of the stack, "and the most important clients go to the [very] top. And by "most important," says Lowery, "I mean the ones who make the most money."

When reading a client's new script, agents are obviously gauging their emotional response to the script. Are they laughing? Crying? Falling asleep? Is the story firing on all cylinders? Do the characters seem believable and relatable? "The notes I give are broader: tone, character, structure," says Lowery, who claims the biggest issue he sees in first drafts is a lack of character development. "A lot of writers get caught up in cool plots, set pieces, or gimmicks and ignore character. Characters have to have an arc. I always refer to *Family Man* or Ebenezer Scrooge. They go from one place to another . . . so when we meet our main character in the beginning of a script, he really needs to change."

Agents are also starting to think about the script strategically. "As an agent, I'm thinking of everything," says former ICM agent and ROAR manager B.J. Ford. "What studio is this right for? What producer is this right for? Is there a big A-list actor or actress that would be perfect for this material that we could attach? Is there a director we could bring on? You're looking at your agency roster, thinking 'I want to make my agency money, so I want to put our clients in it . . . and it's beneficial for our clients; it's adding value to what they're paying for.' Is it an established writer or brand new writer? Is it good enough and strong enough to attach someone before we go out with it? Or is it just a piece of material I want to sell to get into development?"

Forget the Face Time

Don't expect an in-person notes meeting with your agent. Agents are busy; finding time for an in-person meeting could take days or weeks; phone calls are faster and more efficient.

After hearing the agent's notes, it's the writer's job to go away and rewrite. How long the rewrite takes depends on the extensiveness of the notes. "No one wants to see their draft turned around too quickly," says Lowery, "because you feel like they didn't digest and absorb the notes. But it depends on how deep and broad they are. If they're small: a week. If they're big: a month. In an ideal world, the manager's done their draft, [the agent] gets a draft and gives some notes, [the writer] comes back within two weeks so you can go sell it."

Sometimes the agent has more notes on the revised script. If, however, after that, the script *still* isn't ready, he may start to get anxious. "I don't want to give more than two [rounds of notes]," says Lowery. "If the the third time you hand me the script, it's not ready, I'll complain to the manager. It's like, 'Why are we sending the writer down this road that he can't achieve? If he can't do it, he can't pull it off. Maybe he's not a good writer, or maybe this isn't the right idea for him.'"

Of course, writers occasionally disagree with their representatives' notes. Sometimes they feel the agent is trying to make the script too commercial. Other times, they disagree on how a plot or character should evolve. Just the other day, a friend of mine who had recently gotten script notes from his agent told me, "I want to say to my agent, 'Dude, are you a writer? No. So stop giving me notes and just go *sell* this!'" Now, I'm the first to admit: it's easy and enticing to want to dismiss your agent's notes. It's important to remember, however, *your agent is on your team.* He's not giving you notes to make your script *less* sell-able; he's trying to make your script as strong and commercial as possible!

"If you like and trust your agent," says Hoffman, "think about why the agent may have made a particular suggestion. It's okay to ask. Unless the agent specifies otherwise, suggestions are just that—suggestions. I don't require all my clients to make editorial changes, but if there's a point of contention, it's a good dialogue starter. In a lot of cases, the author will say, 'Here's why I made this creative decision: later I wanted to do X, Y, and Z.' And [I] will say, 'That makes perfect sense. Disregard the note entirely.' In other cases, the client will say, 'You're right, that definitely clarifies the story or enhances this character. Let's do it.' It should be a good constructive working dialogue."

Sometimes, if a writer and agent disagree about the readiness of a script, the agent may say, "Look, I don't want to send this out wide and burn it, but let's see if we can get some feedback from a handful of people. Let me send this to four or five execs who know this type of movie better than I do. Maybe they'll see something different than I do." But hopefully, this doesn't have to happen. Hopefully, the writer hands his draft to his agent and the agent says, "Great—let's go slam-dunk this thing!" And that's when things start to get exciting.

GOING OUT WITH THE SCRIPT

As the writer rewrites, the agent and manager devise the best strategy to go out with the script, or present it to buyers. Because the film industry is structured a bit differently than the TV industry, there are four general plans of attack:

1. **The Shotgun Approach** exposes a script to multiple producers or studios simultaneously. In other words, the agent or manager sends the script to twenty, thirty, even fifty producers, hopefully generating a competitive situation in which various buyers are bidding against each other.

2. **The Targeted Producer Approach** exposes a script to a select number of producers, often one at a time, in hopes of making each feel special about receiving an exclusive script.

3. **Attaching elements** involves attaching a high-profile actor or director to a project in order to raise its marketability. The thinking goes that a project with a big-name star or director, like Tom Cruise or Judd Apatow, is more attractive to studios (and audiences) than an unencumbered project.

4. **Finding independent financing** is usually reserved for A) quirky scripts that don't fit the mold of mainstream Hollywood studios, or B) projects that have failed to get set up via more conventional routes.

Every script, every strategy, is a bit different, and agents select their approach based on several factors, including the nature of the script, the level of the writer, and the project's production requirements.

Plan of Attack 1: The Shotgun Approach

This **Shotgun Approach**, or "**going wide**," is designed to expose the script simultaneously to as many parties as possible. This is also called a "**Spec Day**," because agents send the spec to all the companies on the same day. It's not unusual for agents to send scripts to thirty, forty, or fifty companies—all at the exact same time! At Disney, for instance, an agent may send a script to Jon Turtletaub's Junction Entertainment (*National Treasure*), Scott Rudin Productions (*Moonrise Kingdom*), Andrew Panay's Panay Films (*Hit and Run*), Andy Fickman's Oops Doughnuts (*You Again*), and Sean Bailey's Ideology (*Gone Baby Gone*). All have Disney deals. The agent then sends the script to multiple companies at Sony: Chuck Roven's Atlas Entertainment (*Man of Steel*), Laura Ziskin Productions (*The Amazing Spider-Man*), Graham King's GK Films (*Hugo*), and Neil Moritz's Original Film (*The Fast and the Furious 6*). The script also goes to various companies at Fox, Paramount, Warner Bros., Universal, and the mini-majors.

Ideally, the script generates interest from multiple companies at each studio. The agent and client then select one company per studio—say, Ideology at Disney, Original at Sony, etc.—and these companies present the script to their respective studio at the same time. Hopefully, this creates a competitive situation in which studios are bidding against each other to acquire the property.

Planning a Spec Day takes the coordination and cooperation of every member of the screenwriter's team. But first, there are five important areas of attack agents and managers discuss:

1.   Which studios or specialty arms are most appropriate for this script?
2.   Which producers or production companies to target.
3.   Which studio executives to approach.
4.   Which reps should contact which execs or producers.
5.   When to go out with the script.

Which Studios or Specialty Arms are Most Appropriate?

"For the most part," says Ford, "big studio movies will work at any of the studios. They all like the same kinds of material. Disney's the one place [that's a bit different]; they're kind of family-oriented." Thus, if your script is clearly a big-budget studio blockbuster, your representatives will probably want to send it to all the big studios. This doesn't mean, however, that your script has an equal chance at each studio. "It's based not just on what they like," Ford adds, "but on what they need. Say your script is about something Fox just did. You may bring it there, but they're not going to want it."

Does this mean it's not worth submitting to Fox? Definitely not! Any bit of interest helps agents and managers create competition—or the illusion of competition. Plus, if Fox likes the script, they'll meet with the writer, which could begin a productive new relationship. "I'm always searching for [great] writing," says Sablone, "so even if a script is not right for Sunday Night Productions, I want to read anything agents think is exciting work by new writers, just so I can be aware of them for future situations."

Of course, some movies aren't big blockbusters, making them more appropriate for studios' specialty arms. A biopic about folk singer-songwriter Jeff Buckley and his relationship with his father (*Greetings From Tim Buckley*), for example, would probably be more suitable for Universal's Focus Features than Universal Pictures proper. This would mean it may also be more right for Fox Searchlight and Sony Classics than those divisions' parent studios.

Determining which Producers or Production Companies to Target

Occasionally, reps skip this step, not even bothering with sending scripts to producers first, instead submitting straight to studios. But this usually happens only if A) the writer already has a fantastic working relationship with a particular studio, or B) the writer's managers are attached as producers and are strong enough to not need another company. There are only a few managers that fit this bill. Jimmy Miller's Sony-based Mosaic, which has a Sony deal, manages clients like comedian Will Farrell and directors Judd Apatow and Jay Roach and has produced films such as *Bad Teacher* and *The Other Guys*. BenderSpink, based at New Line, reps writers Evan Daugherty (*Snow White and the Huntsman*) and Karl Gadjusek (*Oblivion*) and has produced *Arthur* and *Leap Year*.

Most of the time, however, partnering with a production company housed at a studio is the smartest way in. The thinking goes that a company like Shawn Levy's 21 Laps (*Date Night*, *The Internship*), which has a deal at 20th Century Fox, has a better chance at setting up a movie than an independent company like Polsky Films (*The Bad Lieutenant: Port of Call–New Orleans*). The question is: which production companies to target? Sometimes it's best to go to long-standing giants, like Imagine at Universal, or Jerry Bruckheimer at Disney, which both have lots of power and muscle. Other times, it's smarter to go to new companies, the studio's "flavor of the week."

One of the main criteria in selecting production companies is finding those who share the sensibilities of the writer and the script. If you're sending Sony a high-octane action movie, you probably don't want Adam Sandler's Happy Madison, since Sandler tends to focus on broad comedies. You might, however, choose Neal Moritz's Original Film, since Moritz produced the *Fast and Furious* and the *xXx* movies. Likewise, if you're going out with a raunchy male-driven sex comedy, you may want to go after Jimmy Miller's Mosaic Media Group, which produced *Bad Teacher*, *What Happens in Vegas*, and *She's Out Of My League*. All of these companies–Happy Madison, Original, and Mosaic–have Sony deals, but they all have profoundly different tastes and sensibilities.

Ultimately, of course, what's most important is finding "somebody who can get a movie made," says Meisinger. "Somebody who has tight relationships with directors, actors. Who you know that . . . can call Reese Witherspoon . . . and the next day, we're in a room with her, and the movie gets made. That's what you want. People who can get into places, into things, that you can't otherwise get to."

Which Execs to Target

Good agents "know who at each studio is right to call for [a specific] writer," says Debbie Liebling, Vice President of Ben Stiller's Fox-based Red Hour Films. "If there's [an agent] whose taste you like, and you like his clients, and you like things he's sent you in the past, you'll probably say, 'Yeah, I want to read what you have. Send it to me.' If an agent sends you five [pieces of junk] in a row, you go, 'Ugh–I'm not rushing to read what you send me.'"

However, there are other things to consider besides executives' individual taste. Has the writer had a studio movie made recently? Are there key execs he already has a relationship with, making one studio a more welcoming home? Does this also mean other studios will be competitive and eager to steal him away? Also, in order to officially attach a production company, you (or your agents) must get the president of the

Yes, You Read That Right

In case you were just thinking "Wait, did I just read that *management companies* have first-look deals?" the answer is: *yes, you did.* Because managers also function as producers, some form first-look deals with studios. The Gotham Group, a management/production company that reps screenwriters Robert Harling (*Steel Magnolias*) and writer/director Boaz Yakin (*Remember the Titans*), has a first-look feature deal at Sony Animation and a first-look TV deal at ABC Studios.[3] Similarly, BenderSpink–which reps digital agency Jetset Studios[4] and *90210* writer Allison Schroeder–has a first-look in television at CBS Studios and a first-look in film at New Line.[5]

Talk the Talk

Put Deal–It's especially helpful if you can get to a producer with a "put deal," which requires the company's home studio to buy and make a certain number of their films. Chernin Entertainment's deal with 20th Century Fox requires the studio to fund at least two Chernin movies per year; if they don't, the studio owes Chernin $9 million per movie.[6] Getting the support and partnership of a company with a put deal can give your project a huge edge.

FEATURE AGENTS

company to sign off. "Presidents hire underlings to do their work," says Lowery, "so sometimes it's more valuable to go to a junior and empower that person." An excited, passionate junior executive can be an incredibly persuasive voice in a boss's ear. Besides, busy presidents don't usually read scripts by younger, less established writers; they rely on their support staff to field those.

Agents and managers also submit to execs with whom they have the best relationship. An executive receiving a call from a stranger is never going to prioritize that agent's script; likewise, an agent will never be particularly influential with an exec he or she has never met. As a result, newer, lower-level agents tend to have more relationships with newer, lower-level executives; higher-level, experienced agents have more relationships with older, veteran executives.

Once agents and managers have specified which companies and execs to approach, they figure out how to split up the phone calls and submissions. If there are two agents and a manager, and they're submitting to twenty-six companies, they may split it up eight, eight, and ten, depending on where each person has the strongest relationships.

When to Go Out with the Script

Many scripts go out on a Monday; this way, if execs don't read right away that night, they have four more days. You don't want execs taking the script home on the weekend when it can get lost amidst social plans and family obligations. Monday keeps it far enough from the weekend, but still gives people ample time to read. Agents also make sure no one else at their agency is going out with a script on the same day. "We'd shoot ourselves in the foot if we all took out a spec on the same day," says Lowery. "I'd want to stagger it. That's why we have staff meetings, to talk about that kind of stuff."

And We're Off!

Finally, Spec Day itself arrives—the day your script meets the world for the first time. The day producers and execs lay their eyes on this virgin story. There's a brilliant new piece of writing in the world—perhaps the next *Hamlet* or *Gone With the Wind*—and until this day, no other living person has seen it. Or have they?

Sometimes, agents and managers like to leak a script *before* Spec Day. If the plan is to go wide on a Monday, they'll sneak it on the preceding Friday to a select number of producers or execs—often high-level people the writer has already worked with—to create momentum. Going wide "is not always the best [approach]," says Meisinger. "If you don't get the heat you want, the bidding war you want, you might be diluting [your chances of a sale]. So slipping it out, having people start hearing about it, getting some good feedback, having that drive things . . . sometimes that makes more sense."

Leaking a script also gives agents the chance to find a **preemptive deal**, a producer/studio willing to pay a premium for the script before it goes to everyone else. In June, 2010, Relativity Media paid six figures to preemptively buy Melissa Wallack's *The Brothers Grimm: Snow White*, the script that eventually became Disney's *Mirror Mirror*. Occasionally, even independent producers find the money to buy something preemptively—like in January, 2012, when indie producers Steve and Paula Mae Schwartz and Nick Wechsler used their own money to preemptively purchase *The Counselor*, a spec from ICM-repped novelist Cormac McCarthy (*No Country For Old Men*, *The Road*).

When a studio or production company's development execs decide to buy something preemptively, they notify their business affairs execs, who calculate how much money to offer. "Business affairs looks at the [writer] involved: what kind of money have they made before?" says entertainment lawyer and former business affairs exec

Charles Holland. "If somebody has gotten a million dollars a script, $750,000 is not going to get it done. [Business affairs] then makes a recommendation to the ultimate decision-maker (usually the president of production or president of the entire studio) of how much this ought to cost. [The president tells] you 'yes,' 'no,' 'not a bit more than that,' or 'are you sure?' Then business affairs makes a determination of whether they want to shoot their whole wad right away, which you almost never do, or if they offer a bit less than they could, so they have somewhere to go" in negotiations.

Preemptive deals usually cost buyers a bit extra, but they can often be a win-win for both the buyer and the seller; A) they lock down a sale for the agent and writer, and B) they keep the script from becoming a competitive situation that drives up the price even more.

However, preemptive offers can be risky propositions. In order to convince a studio to make a preemptive offer, an interested producer must convince the studio to purchase the script. Sometimes, that takes a few hours; other times, it can take one or two days. Hopefully, the studio responds quickly. The agent and writer can then decide whether the studio's offer is worth accepting. "It's up to my client and me to determine what our selling price is," says Lowery. "A bird in the hand is awesome . . . [but] do you try to shop it and get more? If a studio makes a [preemptive] offer, then I begin shopping it to other people and those people pass, that will get back to the first studio and they'll pull the offer. So you have to be careful. I try to negotiate the highest selling price possible based on it being preemptive."

If the studio and producer do pass on making a preemptive offer, the agent and manager repping the script must make sure the info doesn't become public knowledge. "You don't say [the script has] a pass," Beckerman explains. "You say, 'This producer took it to Universal yesterday; he had a preexisting relationship with the writer, the writer gave him one day, he loved it enough to take it to the studio. Now we're going out wider. The studio hasn't made an offer yet.' You're not lying—the studio has not made an offer, the writer did have a preexisting relationship, he did take it to the studio. They only thing you're *not* saying is they passed."

Other times when agents leak a script, they simply *don't* get a quick response. A day passes. Another day passes. Now the plan to possibly score a pre-emptive deal has failed and the script has been exposed, risking a pass and compromising the potency of going wide to everyone else. "If I don't get an offer by the end of the second day," says Beckerman, "I have to benefit my client by going out wider." The agent immediately blasts the script out to as many producers as possible, telling them it's already gone to Warner Brothers—so the clock is ticking.

Most scripts, unfortunately, don't generate preemptive offers. They go to market, as planned, on Spec Day.

Spec Day begins with every member of the writer's team—each agent and manager—placing calls or emails to the producers or executives he's been assigned to contact. "I always say something like, 'Listen, I don't want to waste your time,'" says Lowery, "'[so] don't read this as a favor to me. If I'm sending you a comedy about talking monkeys and you already have a comedy about talking monkeys, just tell me. But if you're interested in the idea, I'll send it to you.'"

The agent then emails over the script with a short cover letter introducing the writer and giving a one or two-sentence logline of the project. Remember: the goal is to get the script to everyone on the same day, which, in an age where phone tag can last days, isn't always easy. If this happens, the agent may just email late in the afternoon—assuming he's got a good relationship with the producer or exec—saying, "I'm sorry we keep trading calls, but I'm calling about a spec I'm super-excited about, and you really need to read this tonight."

The Spec Grid

When going out to forty or fifty different producers, agents and managers' assistants and coordinators track who's submitting to which companies, as well as each company's response. They do this with a **"spec grid,"** which organizes submissions by studio and production company, like this:

TABLE 9.1

Contact/Submitter	Prod. Co.	Prod./Exec.	Comments	Status
WARNER BROTHERS				
Melanie F., BAA (Agent)	Galactic Productions	Kyla Cornell, 310–555–3567	Have similar project in development	PASS; submitted 4/22
Melanie F., BAA	5150 Films	Otis Wilkerson, 310–555–2978	Liked script, not right for them, would meet with writer–interested in true adventure stories	PASS–but set general mtg; submitted 4/19
J. Lytle, Lytle Management (Manager)	Ansara Productions	Ansara Dawe, 818–555–4965	Didn't respond to script–felt overly familiar, didn't find funny	PASS; submitted 4/22
UNIVERSAL				
Melanie F., BAA	Lemonhead Entertainment	Miles Riley, 323–555–5813	Enjoyed, passing on to Lucy Cooper (head of dev.)–could be right for Chloe Moretz? Directing vehicle for W. Miller?	Follow up 5/1; submitted 4/22
J. Lytle, Lytle Management	Cade Carter Productions	Owen M., 424–555–3280	Shooting on location in AK–will return next week	Follow up 5/6; submitted 4/22
J. Lytle, Lytle Management	Diver Down	Lincoln Noble, 818–555–8371	Enjoyed, but not what they're doing right now–only looking for family-friendly films, esp. something with animals	PASS; submitted 4/23

What Agents *Don't* Put in the Cover Letter

When sending out a spec, agents don't usually suggest possible actors or directors. After all, if they love the idea of a certain actor or writer so much, why didn't they just attach that person? "Or," an exec might wonder, "did they *try* to attach that person and fail?"–a thought that then colors the script in the exec's mind. Either way, suggesting a writer or director simply highlights the agent's own inability to attach that person.

Working for Free

When a writer chooses to develop the script with a particular producer, he's usually working for free. Occasionally, a producer may option the script with money from a discretionary fund, but these times are rare. It's a good agent's job, therefore, to make sure the writer doesn't get stuck in development hell, doing endless rewrites for free.

Hopefully, responses start pouring in immediately–sometimes that same day. In a perfect world, they're all saying, "We love it!" But this isn't always the case. Some producers call back to say, "I *like* this script, but I don't love it. I'd want to do some development before taking it to the studio." Obviously, this response isn't ideal if you're trying to whip up a competitive frenzy. So you need to weigh your options. Is this producer strong and valuable enough to do some extra work? Or are you getting so many positive responses elsewhere that you don't need to entertain notes?

Sometimes, of course, a script may strike out completely, finding no interested producers at a particular studio. This stings; no writer likes getting all passes–and neither do agents or managers. "I work closely with my writers in developing material," says Beckerman, "so when you finally go out with it, and people poke holes in it, or pass–or even worse: when everyone *likes* it and it still doesn't sell because the studio has a competing project–it hurts. And what hurts more is when a client blames you for them passing. You work hard on it for six months to a year, and in three weeks everyone passes, and the client says, 'Well, you didn't do your job.'"

Can't Agents Submit Straight to Studios?

Absolutely, but, with no producer attached, this has several possible disadvantages:

- Producers are often persuasive salesmen and champions, especially with their own studio execs.
- A hot producer with vision can earn a greenlight for a project that may otherwise never have caught a studio's attention.
- With no producer attached, studios often wonder: *why is there no studio attached?*–shading their read of the script.

Passing the Bad News Buck

When you inevitably decide to go with one production company over another, good agents know how to take the heat from jilted producers so clients don't look bad. Besides, says Lowery, "I get passed on most of the time, so every once in a while, I don't mind passing on other people. [Producers] can get mad all they want, but no one's doing [agents] any favors; we're the ones providing them with material."

"No Deal" Can Be a Great Deal

In a traditional "shotgun" scenario, producers do not meet with the writer before taking a script to their studio. They don't even put together a contractual deal or agreement. Because the goal is to move quickly, everything is done in good faith, with a casual, verbal understanding. The writer himself is rarely involved.

Reps usually accept a producer's rejection with a disappointed "No worries, man–thanks for reading it. I'll send you the next one." Sometimes, however, they like to take a little shot. "If I'm feeling pissy," says one agent, "I'll say, 'Oh, no, it's cool–I've already got like ten people who want to read it.' Then I usually get this, 'No, no–wait! Who wants it?' And I say, 'Don't worry about it, you passed.' It makes me feel good and it prevents that person from saying anything bad [about the script] around town because they're afraid to look foolish."

When agents don't find an interested producer at a specific studio, they can A) send the script to a new batch of companies at that studio; B) call producers at other studios and, without sounding desperate, say, "Hey, Universal's still open if you want to take it in there." If one of those producers is already excited to take it to their home studio, they'll probably grab the Universal opportunity as well; and C) submit directly to the studio with no producer attached.

Hopefully, however, each producer calls the agent gushing about how much he loves the script, and why he's the perfect shepherd to take it to his studio. The producer may even say, "Listen, I'd love to take this to Universal (the studio where I have a first-look) immediately." This is the kind of enthusiasm agents love–but agents' goal, just like when going to producers, is to have the script go into all the studios simultaneously. So if an excited producer wants to take the script in immediately, an agent must think carefully about how to play it–and that depends on who the producer is.

If it's a prominent producer studios are anxious to buy from, the agent may say, "Great! Let the studio know they have it exclusively for one day, but after that we're going into other places." This lets the studio (and the producer) feel special; they're getting an exclusive first shot at the script. If the producer isn't someone with a ton of muscle, however, the agent may hold them off till he hears from other producers. Either way, as soon as the agent hangs up the phone, he calls every other buyer he has sent the script to. "Listen," he says, "take your time reading. If it's not for you, it's not for you. But just so you know–someone else wants this. So if you think might be interested, you need to read it now. I'm not trying to be a jerk, I'm just letting you where we are." The agent may even tell other producers who has expressed interest–if name-dropping will push people to read faster.

How Your <u>Agents</u> Make Money

Remember back in Chapter 3, when we talked about agents commissioning producers? This is where that happens. Before letting a producer take a script to a studio, an agent will often make sure he can commission that producer's fee. In other words, the agent not only takes ten percent of whatever his client, the writer, makes–he also takes ten percent of whatever the *producer* makes. So if the studio pays the producer $500,000 to produce a movie, the agent repping the script gets $50,000. "Here's why agents get away with [that]," says Madhouse manager Robyn Meisinger. "If they have a hot spec, [but] a producer says, 'I want it,' and there are four [other] producers on the lot who want it, the agent says, 'I'll give you the territory . . . but I'm commissioning you.' And the producer says okay, because she wants the script."

One important catch: producers only get paid by their studio *if the movie gets made.* They don't make money simply for being attached to a script that sells; the movie has to receive an official green-light and enter production. As a result, agents only collect their ten percent producers' commission *if the movie gets shot*; they don't commission producers on a movie that sells but never goes into production. (Also, producers rarely pay agents these commissions themselves; rather, they send the bill to their studio, which doesn't make studios happy, but has become a fairly accepted practice.)

How Your __Managers__ Make Money

As we discussed in Chapter 3, if your managers are attached as producers to your script, they earn producer fees. And when they do, they *do not charge you commission.* As producers, however, managers only collect their fees if the movie gets made. So let's say your movie, *Blank Spaces*, sells to Universal for $200,000. Your managers, Crackerjack Management, commission you ten percent. You begin rewriting the script with Universal. Several months later—congratulations—Universal gives *Blank Spaces* a greenlight! At this point, the studio begins paying your managers their producers fee, and Crackerjack Management reimburses your $20,000. (Producers aren't paid in one lump sum. Their fee is amortized over the course of production. So if their fee is $300,000, and there are thirty weeks of production, they get a weekly paycheck of $10,000.)

Ask the Producer

Agents vs. Managers

If your managers are attached as producers to your script, your agents may try to commission ten percent of *their* producer fees as well, a practice managers abhor and often refuse to let happen. "It's bullshit," says Meisinger. "If someone hands us a piece of material and they want to commission us, okay. But if we've worked a year and a half to develop a script, then give it to the agent, who didn't do anything, and he wants to commission us? *No.*"

Q: If my agent can commission producers' fees, isn't she incentivized to steer me towards a producer who will give her a larger commission, rather than a producer who may be more appropriate for my script?

A: "Ideally, an agent is going to look for someone who's both [commissionable and appropriate for the script]. They're running a business—they're trying to make money like anyone else. If they have producers they can commission, it would logically follow they would be effective producers that get things done. So [what] makes sense to an agent . . . is a marrying of these things. The producer who ran the company I worked for for many years, Mike Medavoy, was not a producer who was typically commissioned. [But] this didn't stop agents from going to him, because he can get things done. Were they also submitting those scripts to people that *did* get commissioned—or who were clients of the agency? Absolutely—it's an additional revenue stream! [But] ultimately, they want these projects to be executed. Getting that project done is good for their client, and also good for them."–Doug McKay, producer (*What To Expect When You're Expecting*)

"No one makes decisions on their own anymore," says Lowery. "No one wants anything unless they know someone else wants it, and once they know someone else wants it, that's all the validation they need."

Ideally, the agent starts hearing from other interested producers, which means he and his client need to make decisions. Which producers do they feel are best for the project? Who seems to connect most with the script? Are some producers "hotter" than others, giving them more cache at their studio? Some producers may be so excited they want to take the script to the whole town, submitting it to other studios even beyond their own. This is another a big decision for writers and their reps. Do they want one passionate producer going to multiple studios? Or are they stronger going in with different producers to each studio? Also, you don't want to alienate producers at other studios who are excited about your work; you may need to re-approach them later or work with them on future projects.

When an agent "gives a producer a territory," allowing a producer to take the script to a certain studio, the agent may quickly call or email to the studio execs to voice enthusiasm, but the producer makes the submission herself. "As a producer, you have to call and say, 'This is the one! I love this! I really want you to buy this for me!'" says Liebling, who ran production at Universal before joining Red Hour Films.

"When I was a studio executive, if a producer called me with that kind of passion, I read it right away."

If the situation is incredibly competitive, studios read that day. Other times, however, they take their time, responding in a few days or a week.

"The great thing about spec [screenplays]," says Jonathan Eirich, Dreamworks' Senior VP of Production, "is you can read and assess: is this something we can get into production in eight months, nine months, a year? . . . as opposed to hearing pitches [or] looking at books [and] articles which are inherently deeper development—with those, it's a more long-term strategy."

Execs also consider the financial and production realities of making this film. "If we love the script, we'll certainly buy a spec if it's a big adventure movie with a $100 million-plus budget, but the bar is raised that much more," says Eirich. "Whereas if someone has written their version of *Chronicle*, you start thinking, 'This is fun . . . this is fresh . . . we can do this for $15 million. This is not star-dependant. This could be a way to get in business with one of those hip young filmmakers we love.' There's a lot of appeal to those pieces of material, and realistically, they are often much more make-able."

Development executives even consult other departments before shelling out big bucks for a script. Does the marketing department think this project has wide enough commercial appeal? Do the international execs feel they can sell this movie overseas? You start thinking about the screenplay's "bigger hook," says Eirich. "What do you think this trailer will be? What's going to be the sell of the movie? What's your two-line pitch—how do you frame this movie in a way that feels fresh, original, and different? If it's a *Cloverfield* or a *Chronicle* or a *District 9*—one of those movies that feels like, 'Wow! This is unique!', I know how this can distinguish itself in the marketplace—then [the budget] becomes the next thing you have to consider.

Eventually, the studio responds to the producer, usually with one of three replies:

1. **"Sorry, we pass."**—In which case, the project is dead at that particular buyer. Studios "pass for a number of reasons," says Liebling. "'We have something like it.' 'We can't wrap our head around that concept.' 'We already have a movie in that arena.' 'We're doing fewer movies of this type.' 'I didn't like the writing.' 'I don't think it's our brand.' 'I don't think it's right for what we're talking about right now.'"

"Development mandates change constantly. You look at what you have, you look at what you need, you look at what's doing well in the marketplace. Something will do well and surprise everybody, and then everyone goes, 'We need one of those!' Suddenly, that other [project] that seemed so good, it's not 'of the moment.'"

Sometimes, when a studio passes, a production company may decide to use its own money to acquire the project. Unfortunately, only a small handful of companies have the ability to do this; most are highly successful companies that have **discretionary funds,** pools of money used to buy, option, or develop properties on their own. While it's wonderful to find a well-heeled organization willing to plunk down its own coin, discretionary fund money usually can't compete with actual studio money. In other words, says Liebling, "if you're working out of your discretionary fund, and somebody at Sony is spending Sony money, [the project] is probably going to Sony."

On rare occasions, when a studio passes, the producer who took in the project may be so enamored he wants to keep trying. Maybe he wants to take the project to other studios (assuming the project hasn't already been submitted to those studios via other producers). Or maybe the producer is game to travel the long, hard road of finding independent financing. "It's always a breath of fresh air when a producer says, 'You know what? Big Shit Studio didn't buy it, but I'd love to figure out a way to make this for half the budget, or rework it or something," says Lowery. But "most producers are lazy, and if they get a pass, they say, 'Hey, man, that was awesome, thank you.

Couldn't sell it, let's move on.' Most people don't have the time or patience to seek out independent film. Ironically, that's how most movies get made, which is the whole joke of it—most producers don't know how to produce a movie outside the studio system."

2. **"We like it, but we have some issues."**—Maybe execs feel the script's third act doesn't work or a main character isn't likable. Or it's too commercially risky without a big star or director. This may mean the writer works with the producer to further develop the script (writing for free; no money is exchanged), or the agent and producer must try to attach an actor or director. Or, if you have offers from other studios, you may just thank the studio for their interest and move on.

3. **"We love it—we'd like to make an offer!"** Mazel tov—someone wants to buy your script! Does this mean you hurriedly accept and sign on the dotted line? Nope—this is when your agent does what he does best: agenting. We'll discuss in a moment how agents work to get you more money and a better deal, but first, let's explore some strategies agents use to get scripts to studios.

Hold On—Not So Fast!

Before we talk about agents' other strategies, there's something important you need to know about this Shotgun Approach. All the stuff we just talked about? The whole "Spec Day" strategy? "Specs don't really sell that way anymore," says Lowery. "Competition doesn't mean as much as it used to. Attachments are really important, and people, studios, don't react based on their gut anymore. They send it through their financial model. 'Who do we cast?' 'How do we market it?' What do we put on the poster to put X number of people in seats?'"

Does this mean there's no value in the Shotgun Approach? Not necessarily. It's actually a very effective way of introducing a fresh young writer—or re-introducing an older writer who hasn't worked in a while—to the industry. "When I went out [wide] with specs of brand new writers," says former agent and manager B.J. Ford, "I wanted to sell it, but it was also a good way to introduce the writer to a ton of executives. Ultimately, it's an executive who will give the first read, so there always came thirty or forty meetings out of these specs. Even if it didn't sell, if it was good, it got the writer in the door and helped him build relationships."

How Many Scripts and Projects Do Studios Develop Each Year?

"It ranges from studio to studio," says Jonathan Eirich, Dreamworks' SVP of Production. Mini-majors like Dreamworks and Lionsgate, which release about six to ten movies a year, usually have slates of thirty-five to sixty projects at any one time. Major studios, like Warner Bros. or Paramount, have hundreds. Some are spec purchases, others are based on IP, like books or video games, and still others are based on executives or producers' internal ideas. Also, about 200 of these are "active" projects, and another 500 or so are "inactive" projects still hanging on for various reasons. "You go through them all the time and say, 'Let's put this one in a storage bin for now," says Red Hour Films' Debbie Liebling. "Then you have executives [who] create their own slate, [so] when an executive leaves, things they bought go into 'purgatory.'"

Also, adds Eirich, most studios have twenty or thirty projects they're really focusing on, and "those twenty-or-so projects are always changing. You get a great actor attached to one, suddenly it's a priority project. A bad draft comes in, or the actor or director loses interest—they take another movie—suddenly that project moves back down the ladder."

Plan of Attack 2: The Targeted Producer Approach

Like with the Shotgun Approach, the "Targeted Producer Approach" involves submitting scripts first to specific producers or production companies, usually those with studio deals. *Unlike* with the Shotgun Approach, however, agents and managers don't send scripts to hordes of companies at the same time. "Ten or twelve years ago," says Beckerman, "I would make fifteen calls to fifteen producers on a lot, and I'd easily have another twenty-five incoming calls. 'Hey, I heard you're going out with a spec—can I read it?' It becomes a competition: who can get into the studio first? Then studios become competitive, and the price starts going up, and you've got a bidding war."

But after years of buying expensive scripts that never got made, studios are now more wary, which means agents and managers have had to change their approach. Today, most representatives target a small handful of producers they feel are best suited for any given project and approach them one by one. It's less about generating competition than creating a perfect marriage. "If I go to Mike DeLuca, if I go to Kevin McCormick, those guys say to me, 'Thank you so much for giving me this first. How are we going to do this together?'" says Beckerman. "It's [about] feeling included in the process. Blasting it out wide, odds are people will read thirty pages and pass, without even notes."

Agents and managers begin the process of finding a producing partner by creating a shortlist of producers they feel will gel with the script. The truth is, there's usually *not* a vast array of producers worth submitting to. "[Years ago,] there were about 350 producers who had deals at studios," Beckerman says. "Now, there's maybe 110, 120. Of those, sixty to seventy percent are talent-driven: a writer, director, or actor. The studios want to keep that talent working, so that leaves only a handful of [actual] producers. And those are mostly vanity deals, studio executives who need to get paid out somewhere. So it leaves you with a small number of people—do you want to go into the studio with them or not?"

It's also important to partner with a producer who has some heat, some of-the-moment cache. This could be someone who opened a smash movie two weeks ago, has recently been nominated for awards, or just landed a studio deal—making them the studio's sweetheart du jour.

Building a Foundation

When the trades print news of a new company signing a studio deal, agents rush to set a lunch or drinks to meet the new executives. Similarly, the new executives rush to set meetings with agents or managers. Both sides are aware this is a fresh opportunity to do business, so it's a natural time to sow the seeds of new relationships. In other words, it's more organic for an agent to call now—when change is in the air—and say, "Hey, this is Cindy Seller, I'm a feature agent at Big Powerful Agency. I read about your new deal on Deadline—congratulations! I'd love to take you to lunch or drinks and see if there's something we can do together." This is how relationships begin, as casual meetings over beers, and they hopefully result in sale or producing partnerships—even months or years down the road.

When deciding which producers to approach, it's important to choose only one or two at each studio. Agents aren't trying to create competition or a bidding war; they're trying to make each producer feel special, coveted. Also, agents or managers don't send all the producers the project at the same time. An agent may send it to one producer on a Friday, making her feel special and exclusive, but telling her she has the weekend to read and respond. On Monday, the agent sends it to another producer; on Tuesday, another. If an agent sends the script to too many producers and they all want it, people wind up feeling angry and betrayed, which is not a great way to convince someone to become your business and creative partner. (The downside of the Targeted Approach is that with little sense of competition, or urgency, it's sometimes tougher to get producers on board.)

If, by the end of the week, all the producers have passed, it may be time to reassess the project. Perhaps all the feedback has made you realize the story is flawed, needs more jokes, or your main character is unlikeable. Or perhaps you and your representatives are all still confident and passionate about the script you have, and you decide to simply start anew with another round of producers.

There are still times when producers say they like the concept, but the script needs work. In these cases, the writer may choose to work with a particular producer on the rewrite. It's important, however, for a good agent to make sure his writer doesn't get stuck in development hell—doing endless rewrites (for a producer) for free. Or worse, working on different versions of the script for different producers at different studios.

But my prediction is: you won't be in this situation, because your script is gonna get snatched up by the first producer who reads it! And when it does, your relationship may transpire in one of two ways: 1. the producer could offer to option your script with his own discretionary fund; or more likely, 2. you'll agree to partner up for free, each of you working for free as you go into studios or develop the script further.

Ask the Agent

Q: I had a general meeting with a producer yesterday, and I mentioned the screenplay I was developing. The producer loved it and suggested developing it together. On one hand, I'm thrilled to have someone excited about my project! On the other, it's my idea. Is working with this producer a valuable partnership? Is it worth attaching a producer before the script is written?

A: "It's a case-by-case situation. If a writer came up with an idea [on his own], I don't see the value in developing it on spec with a producer—unless that producer adds a substantial amount of creative value in terms of breaking the story. "If you have a writer who is a great executor, but has a hard time coming up with the next great thing, and a *producer* gives *him* an idea—something he loves—then I would encourage it. In some situations, it's [even] easier to just go and pitch it, to try and get a studio or financier to put up money for development. If you're a brand new writer, and there's a great producer who has a track record, fantastic actor and director relationships, and is invested in the project . . . it can open doors where there are paying opportunities that the producer is working on."—Tanya Cohen, literary agent, Verve

---

Plan of Attack 3: Attaching Elements

This is the strategy most people think of when agents talk about packaging a particular project, or adding filmmaking components that will be attractive so studios. Those components may include—along with the script—producers, actors, a director, or any combination thereof. So instead of going out with just the brilliant script you wrote, you go out with your brilliant script as well as Russell Crowe committed to play the lead and Christopher Nolan committed to direct. In 2012, for example, Paramount purchased *Draft Day*, a football-themed script by Gersh-repped Rajiv Joseph and CAA-repped Scott Rothman that had CAA director Ivan Reitman attached to direct.[7]

"As a producer, you know the people who are valuable to studios," says Todd Lieberman, founding producer of Mandeville Films (*The Muppets*, *The Fighter*). "Tom Cruise is obviously a big movie star. Anyone would want to make a Tom Cruise movie, so if Tom Cruise has already read the project and shown interest, that's one step closer to getting that movie made. If a big director has shown interest in directing, that's one step closer to getting that movie made."

Attaching valuable elements is also a helpful approach if the project isn't a typical studio picture. "Studios only want to make studio movies," says Lowery. "You drive down the street, you see what the posters are. *Sherlock Holmes*, *Snow White*, *Fast and the Furious 8*, *Step Up 4*. It's source material, nonfiction, sequels, games like *Battleship*. So if that's not [our project], we have to find another way to do it," like by attaching a big movie star.

When preparing to attach elements, your representatives' first step is to make a list of potential attachments. Which directors would best understand the script and execute it artfully? Who would make the perfect leading man–Don Cheadle? Jeremy Renner? Could Halle Berry or Jennifer Lawrence play the amazing female lead? "You try and think of talent that will add value," says Lowery–which, I know, seems like a no brainer, but what you *don't* want to do is add talent that *won't* add value. There are plenty of talented actors and directors, even those with extensive credits, that aren't box office draws or don't get studios excited. You may know a fantastic character actor, a tremendous artist who would do a great job in your movie, but if he doesn't bring audiences to theaters, attaching him will only harm your project.

Film Packages vs. TV packages

As we discussed in Chapter 8, feature agents–unlike TV agents–do *not* get giant packaging fees and backend participation for selling a film package. They get to commission all the clients and, hopefully, any producers' fees. If it's an indie film, agents occasionally receive a packaging fee of about two percent of the film's budget, but they have no participation in the film's backend.

Agents, of course, first think about actors or directors represented at their agency. But most will also consider talent repped outside as well. In February, 2013, for example, Lionsgate/Summit picked up *Spinback*, a spec script from Paradigm writer John Swetnam, with WME's Scott Speer (*Step Up Revolution*) attached to direct.[8]

Once agents and managers have completed their list of possible attachments, the next question is: *how do we get to them?* If they're actors or directors repped in-house, contact is easy. If they're repped elsewhere, the task becomes more challenging. There are three basic ways of getting to talent:

1. **Through the talent's production company.** Not every actor or director has a production company, but when they do, it's "one-stop shopping." You not only get the talent as a performer or director, but you can also attach them as a producer. And if their company has a studio deal–like Tobey Maguire's Sony-based Maguire Films or Robert Downey Jr.'s Warners-based Team Downey–you know you're getting someone with whom the studio wants to do business. When submitting to an actor or director's production company, agents usually have relationships with the company's top executives. For example, Jason Bateman's Universal-based Aggregate Films is run by Jim Garavente, a former lit agent and manager who previously had a producing deal at Mandate Pictures (*Mr. Magorium's Wonder Emporium*). So while Bateman is busy acting in Aggregate projects, Garavente–who comes loaded with relationships–takes care of the company's executive duties: forming relationships with sellers, meeting writers and directors, searching for projects, etc.

The Downside of Going to Elements with First-Looks

While attaching an actor with a studio deal can make a project more valuable, it can also mean a smaller paycheck. "If an actor has a studio deal, that studio has a first look at things that actor brings in," says manager/producer Aaron Kaplan of Kaplan/Perrone Entertainment. "When you have a first look, you are viewing it without competition, which would make it a smaller deal. If you take [the project] to every studio at the same time and let the market bear whatever the market can bear, it generates competition, which drives up the price."

2. **By attaching a producer first.** This puts the job of "selling" the project to actors and directors more on the producer than the agent, which can be more effective for several reasons. First, producers often have stronger relationships with talent than agents or managers. Second, producers work with reps from every agency and management company, so their relationships are less insular than agents at specific company. And lastly, an actor or director who's approached by a producer—rather than an agent—knows the project already has the validation of someone who's not just a salesman, someone with a vested interest.

"A big misconception [is] that agents sell," says Lowery. "Of course we sell, but producers are really the best salesmen. Let them put the right cast on it, let them put the right director on it, let them convince the studio they're the right producer for the movie."

"When searching for a producer, the most important thing," says Beckerman, "is to know which producer is able to get the script into an element's hands that could go slam dunk it somewhere."

In 2005, Beckerman and his client, screenwriter Jeff Rake (*Bones, Beauty and the Beast*), shopped around an adaptation of Jennifer Cox's whimsical memoir *Around the World in 80 Dates*. Part travelogue, part dating guide, the book chronicles Cox's romantic adventures around the world. Perfect for a globe-trotting romantic comedy, right? That's what Beckerman and Rake thought. Unfortunately, it didn't sell. "So I got Mike De Luca's company (Michael De Luca) interested," says Beckman. De Luca, one of the producers behind *Moneyball* and *The Social Network*, is widely known as one of Hollywood's most competent, creative, and well-connected filmmakers. Thanks to the muscle and relationships of De Luca, "we went and got Reese Witherspoon. And then we were easily able to sell it to Universal!" (Unfortunately, it never got made.)

Managers Come in Peace

Unlike agents, managers don't poach or steal each other's clients. "Because we help our clients produce," says New Wave manager Michael Pelmont, "we want access to the best talent out there, so we have to be friendly with other managers. We never want them to worry about giving us access to their great talent because they're worried we're going to try and poach them."

3. **By calling the actor's representation.** This is usually the least desirable approach. While it's not unusual for artists at one agency to work with artists at another, agents themselves are wary of calls from other agencies, as their first instinct is that the other agency is trying to poach their clients. As a result, many agents call an actor's manager rather than his or her agent, since managers are more welcoming of outside calls.

When a talent agent or manager gets a call inquiring about a client, regardless of who that call comes from, he acts as his client's first line of defense. "When you represent actors, you don't want them attached to a bunch of things that aren't set up," says Ford. "You don't want to attach a client to something that then gets passed on by the town. It has to be special." Thus, a talent handler assesses several things even before discussing the project with his client.

First: basic info. "You have to know the producer, know he's credible, know he's someone you want your client working with," says one high-level talent agent. Most talent agencies handling A-list talent "don't take unsolicited submissions. So you're wasting your time if you're a producer with a piece of material and no financing, no real relationships to get it going, and you're looking to lock in a piece of talent to be a catalyst."

"Part Two: what state is the project in? Is it in book form? Pitch form? Script form? You make an assessment about whether that's something your client would be open to. "Thirdly, once they've told you what the project is about, you read it. If, at that point, you feel it's of the quality your client deserves attaching to, [of] lending his or her brand equity to, you talk to [the producer] about the strategy: where they're going, how they'd want to set it up, to what buyers, in what fashion." An agent will also ask if the submission is exclusive to his client. If it's not, most agents simply pass. But if the submission is *exclusive*, and everything else checks out, the agent sends the script to his client.

In order for a high-level piece of talent to be interested, his reaction must be "more than 'I like it,' it must be exceptional—a part [the actor] is wildly passionate about playing," says one agent. It could also "be a part [the actor] hasn't been allowed to do. If she's a dramatic actor, and there's a comedic role . . . or he's a character actor,

Exception to the Rule

The only time a talent agent or manager takes a non-exclusive submission to a piece of A-list talent is if it's a project based on a well-known property, like a bestselling book or play. When Baz Luhrmann was casting *The Great Gatsby*'s role of Daisy, for example, he supposedly auditioned Scarlett Johansson, Blake Lively, Natalie Portman, Michelle Williams, and Keira Knightly—all A-list actors who are typically "offer only," meaning they don't audition, they simply receive—and accept or deny—offers.[9] The role eventually went to Carey Mulligan.

and he gets a chance to play the leading man. Is it something he can't get through the normal channels of casting?"

If it's not an unusual role, "if it's a part the actor just 'likes,' many factors other than the script come into play. Who's directing? Who's financing it? When does it go? What's the 'opportunity cost' of doing it? What are they going to comp you? Since they're lending something additive . . . [being] a catalyst for the movie to get set up . . . the client may want to be a producer on the project as well. If, as an actor, you're going to attach yourself to something, it has to be something you value to the point where you want to control it."

Assuming all systems are go, the agent arranges a meeting for the actor and producer. They'll talk creatively about the project: the producer's strategy for selling it, possible directors, the film's size and scope. The actor may also have certain creative requests like script changes or director pre-approval (if a director isn't already attached). Finally, after a process that usually takes two weeks to a month, the actor attaches himself! He and the producer may "memorialize" the attachment with some official paperwork, but usually—with well-known producers—a verbal agreement is enough.

Case Study: *Next*

It was 2003, and Anonymous Content manager Lenny Beckerman (now at Hello and Company) had been approached for representation by Gary Goldman, screenwriter of *Total Recall* and *Big Trouble in Little China*. Unfortunately, Goldman was "cold"; he hadn't had a successful movie in years, and while he'd written the first draft of Steven Spielberg's *Minority Report*, he was fired from the project, given no writer credit, and relegated to "executive producer."

"Nobody wanted to do business with him," says Beckerman. "They felt he was old hat." So Beckerman started racking his brain. How could he revive Goldman's career? The guy was a fantastic writer—it wasn't his fault his last movie, 1990's *Navy Seals*, had been a flop. But *Total Recall* was a sci-fi classic. And while Goldman wasn't credited on the final version of *Minority Report*, the movie still got made. "I said, 'Let's go back to the well. You have a good relationship with the Philip K. Dick estate . . . lets get a short story and see what we can do.'" So Goldman optioned the rights to a Dick story called "The Golden Man," about a man who can see the future. He and Beckerman developed the concept over the holidays, and Goldman wrote the project on spec. The final script? Fantastic.

"We said, 'All right, we have a great piece of material. What should we do with it?'" Beckerman knew the script was strong enough to sell on its own. But he also knew agencies were eager to package their actors with interesting projects, and the right piece of talent would drive up the script's price. So Beckerman approached CAA lit agent Jon Levin, who had a reputation for being savvy with genre material and was a Philip K. Dick fan. Levin loved the script and presented it at his next CAA staff meeting. "All of a sudden," says Beckerman, "Nicolas Cage (a CAA client) was interested in the script!" Cage had just finished shooting Disney's *National Treasure*—which, with a box office of $173 million, was 2004's ninth highest grossing feature—and attached himself to star and produce (along with his producing partner, Norm Golightly).[10]

"You get an actor that means something—and Nic Cage meant something—you double, triple the price," says Beckerman. "Then, when the studio spends so much money in development, the odds of it getting made become higher and higher and higher. We went from *potentially* selling the script to getting a preemptive offer for $1 million versus $2.5 million. The movie got made, Gary got paid $2.5 million, the Philip K. Dick estate made [money], and everybody was happy."

Then, with a sad smile, Beckerman adds, "Except the movie just didn't *work*." Released in April, 2007, the film—retitled *Next*—barely grossed $18 million.[11]

FEATURE AGENTS

Plan of Attack 4: Finding Independent Financing

For studios, movies are a financial investment. They plunge millions of dollars into developing, producing, and marketing each movie; if one succeeds, the studio stands to profit handsomely. In 2009, for example, *The Hangover* cost Warner Bros. $36 million, but it generated a 1,297 percent return when it hauled in $467 million worldwide.[16] If a movie fails, however, the studio takes a multi-million dollar hit—like in 2013, when Universal bet $130 million on the success of *R.I.P.D* . . . and earned a pitiful forty-three percent return of only $56 million.[17]

Part of a good agent or producer's job when setting up a movie is minimizing the studio's financial risk, or at least proving the risk is minimal. One way of doing this is to attach a commercially attractive movie star or director—someone studios believe will draw in audiences. Another way is to provide some of the funding. If a movie costs $70 million, like Millennium Films' *Olympus Has Fallen*, and you can reduce the studio's financial exposure by providing $35 million, the studio will see the venture as much less of a risk. (E.g., *Olympus Has Fallen* was co-financed by West Coast Film Productions, which entered a three-year, $100 million co-financing agreement with Millennium in 2012.)[18]

Thus, agents hoping to sell studios on an unconventional movie may try to secure partial financing before approaching studios (or *re-approaching* studios; sometimes, if a studio likes a script but has reservations, agents will try to find financing, or attach talent, then re-present the project). Other times, agents may help secure *full* financing for a film, bypassing studios altogether and making the film independently. This is also a viable route for a movie that has been passed on by the major studios. "I'll take a script out [to studios], get all passes, and then the real work starts," says Beckerman, "because then it's me putting the movie together, getting the director, getting the pieces. There are enough foreign sales companies, enough equity, and enough people to re-ignite the script if you get it to the right place."

Finding full or partial financing can be a long, challenging road, fraught with obstacles and false starts. Funding often comes from fairly unconventional places—venture capitalists, foreign investors, wealthy friends and uncles—places where many traditional lit agents don't necessarily have relationships. Which is why, as we discussed

Like a studio . . .

Millennium Films funds and produces its own movies. It doesn't, however, have its own distribution, so it doesn't qualify as a full-fledged major or mini-major. (Millenium's *Olympus Has Fallen* was distributed by FilmDistrict, while *The Expendables* movies were handled by Lionsgate.)

in Chapter 8, many big agencies now have special divisions devoted exclusively to finding funding or distribution for independent projects. There are several ways an agency may find independent financing:

1. Production companies with their own financing. Some production companies are fortunate to have their own well-lined pockets. Richard Branson used profits from his Virgin Airlines to fund Virgin Produced, an independent production company run by Jason Felts and Justin Berfeld (best known for playing Reese in FOX's *Malcolm in the Middle*). The company produced its first film, 2011's *Limitless*, starring Bradley Cooper, for a mere $27 million, then watched it haul in over $160 million worldwide. Similarly, in 2010, David Ellison's Skydance Productions–which has a first-look deal with Paramount Pictures–landed $150 million in equity and a four-year revolving credit facility from JPMorgan Chase to the tune of $200 million. Skydance has used this money to co-produce Paramount movies like *Mission Impossible: Ghost Protocol* and *World War Z*. It's also allowed the company to acquire and develop projects other companies could not afford on their own, like in January, 2013, when Skydance plunked down over $1 million to preemptively buy a disaster movie script from *Leverage* producers Dean Devlin and Paul Guyot.

Of course, Skydance and Virgin Produced are well-backed heavy hitters. Not all films require–or attract–this level of financing. Companies like Super Crispy Entertainment, which produced the award-winning *Like Crazy* for $250,000,[19] specialize in smaller, quirkier films. Agents often turn to these types of companies when trying to finance films that don't fit a typical studio business model. Director Nicolas Refn's $15 million *Drive*, for example, had originally been acquired by Universal, but when Universal couldn't make the film work and it went into **turnaround**, WME's indie film branch, WME Global, hit the streets to find independent financing. It was eventually released by FilmDistrict and made over $35 million.

Talk the Talk

Turnaround–Sometimes a studio works on a project for a while, before losing steam, so they offer the producer, or her agents, a chance to take the project to a new studio. When a script is in this state of homeless limbo, it's said to be in **turnaround.** If a new studio or producer wants the project, they must then reimburse the original buyer any costs incurred: the script's original purchase price, any money paid to rewriters, etc. In 2004, Focus Features decided to throw in the towel on developing an offbeat family comedy it had spent $150,000 on acquiring for producer Marc Turtletaub. The project went into turnaround, but Turtletaub paid $400,000 to reimburse Universal and acquire the rights for himself–and went on to produce the Oscar-winning *Little Miss Sunshine.*[20]

---

2. Investors and financiers. Sometimes, representatives and filmmakers venture outside Hollywood altogether, finding investors or financiers who don't normally play in Tinseltown at all. When filmmaker Nate Taylor needed financing for a new film, his wife introduced him to a girlfriend's husband, Dennis Wallestad, who happened to be the CFO of JPMorgan Chase's Treasury services department. Wallestad had long backed promising artists and agreed to put up $300,000 for Taylor's new project, *Forgetting the Girl*, which went on to win the audience award at the 2012 SoHo International Film Festival.[21] Taylor and Wallestad found each other without the help of an agent, but Wallestad is the type of unorthodox investor many indie film agents have on their radar.

Other times, filmmakers or agents target investors who have unique personal passions. Chat Reynders, CEO of Boston-based Reynders, McVeigh Capital Management, has been a proponent of socially conscious initiatives; he's worked with organizations such as The Whale Conservation Institute and the One World One Ocean Foundation.[22] So when he founded Reynders, McVeigh Capital Management, he began funneling finances to environmentally-themed IMAX movies such as *Grand Canyon Adventure: River at Risk* and *Into the Arctic*. Reynders typically invests in films in the $8–$12 million range, organizing his deals so clients always make their money back. Over the course of eight years, investors in his first film, *Whales*, recouped their investment . . . plus an additional thirty-five percent.[23]

Unfortunately, these types of non-Hollywood investors can be difficult to find, which is why independent film agents work hard to pinpoint and nurture these relationships. This is also a place where lawyers can come in handy; investors often enlist the services of an entertainment attorney, so a good lawyer specializing in independent film usually has many relationships with unconventional film investors.

3. **Pre-selling a project's distribution rights.** As we discussed in Chapter 8, many indie films find financing by pre-selling distribution rights. In the case of *Drive*, for example, WME presold its domestic distribution rights to FilmDistrict. Its foreign distribution rights—as is often the case—were sold to a plethora of random distributors; Blue Sky Media handled Eastern European countries such as Poland and Bulgaria, Svensk Filmindustri covered Scandinavia, Nu Metro Cinemas handled South Africa, etc.

Similarly, producer Carl Mazzocone financed 2013's $15 million *Texas Chainsaw Massacre 3D* by first getting a domestic distributor, Lionsgate, to agree to $25 million worth of prints and advertising. Mazzocone then partnered with Millennium, who presold the film's foreign rights.[24] The film opened on January 4, 2013, racking up over $21 million and snagging the number one spot of the weekend.

Agents decide to independently finance projects for several reasons. Sometimes they've tried selling the project to studios and failed. Other times, they successfully sold the project to a studio, but it went into turnaround—like *Drive* and *Little Miss Sunshine*—so agents scramble to find a new buyer or independent financier. Occasionally, agents take a project to studios and indie companies simutaneously, hoping the two approaches will help each other, either coming together in a mutually beneficial arrangement, or creating a bidding war.

Agents generally begin looking for financing by either taking an unencumbered script straight to financiers, or attaching talent. Many first attach talent, since financiers love investing in movies with known stars and directors. In the indie world, however, it's often easier to attach actors to *less* commercial projects, even films that don't yet have financing. This is because most actors want to do indie films with some kind of "artistic" appeal—adaptations of literary novels, projects from artsy directors, etc. "You can appeal to the filmmaker, or the actors, on the [basis] of doing something more . . . 'elevated,' more indie feeling, not something purely for commerce," says WME feature agent Alexis Garcia. "If it's purely for commerce, they want to know if it's real, [and] how much they're going to make before they dive into it. If something is clearly a genre movie, you're going to have a hard time attaching elements before getting financing."

Sometimes, of course, attaching talent first isn't possible, so agents go directly to financiers. This is usually the case with indie projects that are more traditionally commercial. This also puts much of the creative control in the hands of the money men; they now control the project, or a portion of it, and can take the reins on casting, finding a new writer or director, or hiring designers.

Getting the Offer

"Way back around 2000," says screenwriter Sean Hood (*Conan the Barbarian*, *Halloween: Resurrection*), "I wrote a spec script [in film school] called *The Dorm*, a supernatural thriller set in a freshman dorm. I knew it was good, but I knew how hard it was to sell specs, so I wasn't confident it would sell." Hood's agents sent the script to several producers, and over the next few days, responses trickled in. "So-and-so

Independent Thinking

Sometimes agents and managers sell a project to a studio through a **progress-to-production** deal, in which they contractually require certain conditions be met for the studio to retain the project. These conditions often include certain time thresholds or production benchmarks; for example, a progress-to-production deal may give the studio specific deadlines by which it must attach a director or star, green-light production, or release money to begin casting. "We did [something like] this with *Babel*," says Hello and Company manager Lenny Beckerman, who previously worked with *Babel* producer Steve Golin at Anonymous Content. "We had a relationship with [director] Alejandro Gonzalez Iñárritu, he had an idea for a movie, so we hired Guillermo Arriega to write the screenplay internally. Steve had a relationship with Brad Pitt through *Sleepers* and *California* (both produced by Golin). He got it to Brad. Then we made Brad's deal, we made the screenwriter's deal, we made every deal inside, [and] we got a budget made for less than $30 million."

Thus, Golin and Beckerman presented studios with a ready-to-be-shot project; they had all the main above-the-line elements in place—writer, director, and star—as well as a concrete, comprehensive budget. They also had Brad Pitt—for a limited window. All a studio had to do was hand over the money and green-light the movie *for the specific window when Pitt was available*—and the producers could deliver an on-budget, on-schedule Brad Pitt movie.

If this sounds like a smart way to package a project . . . it is. There are only two main downsides. One: unlike Anonymous, few production entities have the financial resources to fund development on a project of this magnitude. Most A-list writers, actors, producers, and directors won't work for union scale, so the management or production company needs to have deep enough development or discretionary funds to pay everyone.

Two: when presenting a studio with this kind of deal, the production entity is on the hook for the proposed budget, so you need skilled and reliable directors and line producers to put together an accurate budget. "We took that package out to studios—a Brad Pitt movie for less than $30 million, with Alejandro Gonzalez Iñárritu directing—[and said,] 'Who wants it?' We had four studios bidding on it," says Beckerman. "In the end, Paramount bought it, because Brad Grey and Brad had a relationship through Brillstein-Grey (Paramount CEO Grey's old management company, which represented Pitt). They bought it for more than the budget—so we hadn't even made the movie and we were ahead of the game."

Babel went on to garner seven Oscar nominations and make over $135 million at the worldwide box office. Since then, many films have been sold with progress-to-production deals, including *The Change-Up* and *All You Need Is Kill*.

---

passed," "So-and-so's still reading," "So-and-so's interested and wants to take a meeting."

"You ride this roller coaster," says Hood. "Then one person says, 'We're going to take it into Sony Studios,' 'We're going to take it into Paramount,' and you're really excited." Amidst all this hope and promise, Hood's agent received a call from MTV. They had read the script and loved it—but they also knew they didn't have the money to compete with the majors. So they said, "Listen . . . if all the majors pass, come back and talk to us."

"And that's what happened," Hood says. "All the major studios passed, so we went back to MTV. They said, 'We're not paying $500,000 for a screenplay,' but they wanted to make an offer!"

When a studio or financier wants to buy the script, the agent gets a call from either the exec or the producer, happily telling him to expect an offer. As soon as the agent hangs up, he calls the client to tell him the great news. (If the writer has both an agent *and* a manager, they'll usually phone him together.)

"It's exciting," says screenwriter and producer Charlie Stickney, who sold his first script, *Exorcism For Dummies*, to Revolution Studios, "but I don't think it's as exciting as you dream it's going to be, because you've already put in a lot of hours to make that happen. We had been working on that script for three years before it got set up. So when it finally happens, it's more like, '*It's about fucking time.*'"

A few hours later, after the studio exec or producer, the studio's business affairs department calls to begin the actual deal-making. "That first call is the nice call," says Beckerman. "They do this fact-finding mission about who the writer is, what his role is in the industry, his credits, all that stuff." (Sometimes studios already have this info, or they get it from other studios. It's not unusual for business affairs execs at rival studios to call each other to find out what a writer was paid.) After business affairs' fact-finding call, the studio begins putting together their official offer, which is a critical period for the agent. This short time between receiving notification of the offer and receiving the offer itself is when serious agenting starts to go down.

"The first thing I do," says Lowery, "is call every [other] potential buyer I can, even ones I haven't gotten to, and say, 'I've got an offer on the table, what do you think?' If I send a script to Warner Brothers right now and say, 'Read this,' [it may take] two to three weeks," says Lowery. "But if I say, 'Your biggest competitor is making an offer,' they'll read it tonight." The agent works as hard as he can getting competitive bids *before* he receives the first studio's official offer.

Things "get a little sticky," says one agent, "when the offer actually comes in and you've got a number, because then you're '**shopping the offer**.'" Studios would rather you not shop their offer, but we do it anyway in hopes of getting a better offer." Studios *hate* it when agents shop their offers—they view it as a betrayal of their enthusiasm and support—"but we do it anyway," says the agent.

Eventually, the first studio calls back with their terms. This is when "they [begin] the process of negotiation," says Hood, "and *that's* what's gut-wrenching."

If this is the writer's first sale, and there are no other offers on the table, the studio will offer the smallest amount of money they can—usually WGA minimum. "They'll say, 'Hey, we're giving this kid an *opportunity*,'" scoffs Beckerman. "All of a sudden, he's a 'kid' and it's an 'opportunity.'"

If this is not the writer's first sale, if he has established quotes, the studio hopefully offers to increase those quotes, paying the writer more than he made for his last sale. Often, however, studios try to lowball writers. (This is, after all, a negotiation.) If the writer's last movie was an independent movie which sold for $80,000, the studio will try to use that as a quote. The agent argues, saying, "That was a contained thriller and an independent movie. This is a sci-fi epic, and you're a *studio!*"

Once the agent has the terms of the offer, he and his client discuss their next move. If it's a great deal, they may just accept. Most likely, however, they want to improve the terms of the offer. Maybe the agent has already received a competitive bid from a rival studio, and he can use this to counter. Perhaps he has no other bid, but he wants to shop the offer, or try to leverage a competing bid from a rival studio. The downside of shopping an offer: it takes time. If other studio execs haven't read the script, they need to read, mull it over, run it up the flagpole, get approvals to buy. This usually takes longer than the original studio is willing to wait—and the offer will be pulled. Plus, if it gets back to the original studio that their offer is being shopped, they'll likely pull the offer altogether. Many business affairs execs even give agents a time limit or an exclusive negotiating period—perhaps twenty-four or forty-eight hours to counter. If the clock expires, the studio pulls the offer.

"If I shop the offer without [the first studio] knowing, and I get a better offer, I win," says Beckerman. "If I shop the offer and don't get a better offer, and they find out, it puts me in a bad spot." Most agents try to avoid this situation, especially if the difference in offers is likely to be a small amount of money—say, $50,000. (Granted,

Quote Me!

Writers have quotes for everything they do. They have purchase-price quotes, rewrite quotes, polish quotes, option quotes. Writers who have worked in independent film even have indie or low-budget quotes.

$50,000 is not "small" to most of us, but as Beckerman says, "it's not worth alienating a studio for that amount of money for yourself, the writer, or the project. Deals come and go, but studios are here forever.")

Negotiating 101

When shopping an offer, agents don't always tell one studio what another has offered. This way, if Universal has offered Agent Joe $500,000, and Agent Joe–trying to generate competition–gives this info to Warner Bros., Warners can't come back and offer $500,001. So instead, Joe calls Warner Brothers and says, "This is really competitive; other studios want it. I'm looking for $750,000." Or, "I'm looking for mid-six figures." This gives Joe the best chance of earning the most money possible for himself and his client.

Having said that, it sometimes benefits agents to be more specific. If the offer is terrible, or far below the writer's quote, an agent may call rival studios and say, "Just give me his quote." In these cases, it helps to have hard data, specific numbers, so studio execs can say to their bosses, "Here's what it will take; here's what we're getting into." The studio head then decides whether the price is worth it or not.

Good to Know

When a studio purchases a script that comes with attachments, the entire purchase price goes to the writer; the attached actor or director does not share in the money. Attachments obviously bring value to the script, and they may even help develop it creatively, but they earn no money until the project actually enters production.

An agent's goal, of course, is to create a bidding war that jacks up the price of the project. In September 2010, UTA and CAA orchestrated a bidding war between Sony, Paramount, Fox, New Regency and Summit for *Snow White and the Huntsman*, a package that included UTA screenwriter Evan Daughtery and CAA director Rupert Sanders. Universal won, acquiring the project for more than $3 million.[25]

Sometimes, however, it takes studios more than just big money to win a bidding war. As CAA and UTA were out peddling *Snow White and the Huntsman*, WME was shopping *Abraham Lincoln: Vampire Hunter*, a package including WME screenwriter/novelist Seth Grahame-Smith, WME director Timur Bekmambetov, and WME producer Tim Burton (who had used his own cash to option the rights to Grahame-Smith's original novel). Nearly every studio in town was clamoring for the project, but Fox pulled out all the stops. When WME and its clients arrived at the Fox lot on Friday, October 1, 2010, they found reserved parking spots labeled, "Parking for Vampire Hunters only–park at your own risk!" They were escorted down a pathway of bloody footprints, past a Confederate bugler playing "Taps," to the door of their meeting. The co-chairs of the studio and president of production then won them over with an in-depth presentation about their production plans for the movie, which included a $69 million budget, as well as marketing and release strategies.[26] Less than one week later, after losing *Snow White and the Huntsman* to Universal, Fox won *Abraham Lincoln: Vampire Hunter*. When the movie was released two years later, it grossed less than $40 million domestically. (*Snow White*, meanwhile, grossed over $155 million.)

Eventually, whether you have a bidding war or not, buyers make their final offers, and agents and writers must decide which to accept. Sometimes this decision is based solely on an offer's financial terms; other times agents talk to studio execs to learn other information. How fast can the studio get this movie into production? Do they have high-profile directors or stars they could put on the project? How many competing projects are on the studio's slate–and what are this script's odds of rotting in development? "A movie getting made is so much more important than extra money," says Beckerman, "because then the writer has a credit–he accomplished something–as opposed to being a writer with a bunch of development deals."

Finally, the agent calls the lucky studio to tell them they they've won–and it's time to negotiate the nuts and bolts of the actual deal.

Negotiating the Deal

When negotiating a feature script deal, the first thing to determine is whether the studio is buying the script outright or optioning the script. If a studio or producer purchases the script, they own the material into perpetuity. If they **option** it, they own it temporarily; the contract usually stipulates a deadline on which the rights revert back to the creator or original owner (usually in eighteen months). During this time, the producer or studio can develop the material further, attach a director or cast, rustle up funding, or try to find other creative and financial partners. If the producer or studio wishes to extend the option past the deadline, they must cough up more money.

What's the yin and yang of purchasing versus optioning? A purchase usually nets the writer more money up front, but the movie runs the risk of languishing on a studio shelf, never getting made. Another danger: the writer could—and probably will—be fired from the project and replaced with another writer. An option, on the other hand, costs less, and because the rights eventually revert back to the writer, he and his agent can try reselling the script if the first buyer chooses not to make it. "As an agent, and as a client, you want the big splashy sale," says Carlisle. "But there are certain types of material you are not going to sell for $500,000 or $1 million, and trying to do that is a disservice to the material. If there is an interesting compelling, high-school-set, character story, that we love, and the client loves, we would rather someone option it ... under certain guidelines, so they're not hoarding a piece of material for a long period of time, and put it in a position where it can get made. That's what any writer wants—they want their material to get made—and that's what we want in order to advance their career."

To Learn More

To learn more about options, flip to page 190!

When negotiating a script sale, the main deal points are:

• **Purchase price**—The purchase price of the script is determined by a writer's "quote," which could be "scale," or WGA minimum, if he's never sold anything; or—in the case of heavy-hitters like James Vanderbilt (*The Amazing Spider-Man*)—it could be $3 million (which is what Vanderbilt got for selling his spec, *White House Down*, to Sony in March, 2012.) Hopefully, a good agent increases her client's quote each time the client makes a sale.

Minimum Screenplay Purchase Prices

While every script sale is a negotiation, the WGA mandates minimum purchase prices based on the film's budget. Low-budget movies are anything under $5 million; high-budget movies include anything over $5 million. The WGA renegotiates these minimums every three years with the AMPTP. Here are current minimums through 2014:

Minimum Compensation	Effective 5/2/11–5/1/12	Effective 5/2/12–5/1/13	Effective 5/2/13–5/1/14
Original script, including treatment:	LOW/HIGH $63,895/ $119,954	LOW/HIGH $65,013/ $122,054	LOW/HIGH $66,313/ $124,496
Original script, excluding treatment **or** sale/purchase of original script:	LOW / HIGH $42,930/ $87,897	LOW / HIGH $43,681/ $89,417	LOW / HIGH $44,555/ $91,205

Negotiating 101

"Research shows the higher your aspiration at the outset of the negotiation, the better your outcome at the end of the negotiation. One mistake [people make] is not having an ambitious or specific enough goal. Saying 'I want to do well' is not as specific as 'I want to get at least $50,000 for this piece of work.' And not ambitious enough: maybe $50,000 is too low! You want specific goals that are sufficiently ambitious. In general, the higher your aspiration, the better you're going to do. You may not reach your goal, but you'll get closer to it."–Donny Ebenstein, expert negotiation consultant and author of *I Hear You: Repair Communication Breakdowns, Negotiate Successfully, and Build Consensus . . . In Three Simple Steps*

The writer's quote helps establish his "**guaranteed compensation,**" the purchase price of the script. Most negotiations, however, are a "teetering seesaw" between "guaranteed competition" versus "**contingent compensation,**" the amount the writer gets paid *only* if the movie gets made (often called a "production bonus"–more on this in a moment). Studios try to pay less guaranteed compensation and more contingent compensation–since they may never actually pay it. Thus, strong agents do their best to get as much up-front guaranteed compensation as possible. "If you're going to buy my script for a dollar," says Lowery, "but you promise you're gonna make the thing, I'll say, 'Fine, I'll sell you my script for a dollar, but when you make it, I want ten million dollars.' Now, that's not guaranteed, but you have a little more leverage to negotiate some contingent compensation."

It's also important to note that the writer's quote doesn't usually cover the mere acquisition of the script; it's the price for a pre-determined amount of work. So a writer's quote of $200,000 may actually include the purchase of the script, plus two "**sets**," or two sets of notes and revisions. Or a quote may include two revisions and a polish. Or one revision and one polish. These extra drafts are called "guaranteed steps," because they're steps in the process that the writer must contractually deliver.

The studio can also request "**optional steps**," additional rewrites it may or may not need. These cost money, of course; if the studio's already paying $350,000–that's for the script and, say, two sets of notes and rewrites–it may build in two more *optional* steps for $150,000. The writer only gets this $150,000 if the studio asks for the extra work. Most studios try to contract *fewer* guaranteed steps, and *more* optional steps– allowing them flexibility to use the writer if necessary, or let him go if they feel he's not delivering.

Having said that, "I think there is a misconception that studios love to buy something, then replace the writer right away," says Eirich. "I don't think that happens as much as people think, and generally [executives] are very good about giving a writer a shot. Quite honestly, if you do a step or two with a writer and it's not getting there, you replace the writer and it's usually not that dramatic. Ninety-nine percent of the time, writers are very respectful and very thankful to say, 'Listen, I understand your job is to do whatever you can to get this movie made. This is my baby–I want to see this get made. So if you think the best thing is to hire so-and-so A-level writer who can revamp the dialogue before we send it to actors–great. Do whatever you can to get the movie made.'"

You Have the Right to Sell these Rights

Purchasing an original screenplay, entirely dreamed up and executed by the writer herself, is usually a fairly straightforward negotiation. But if the script is based on underlying material, or another person's life rights, things get a bit more complicated. First of all, the studio will want to ensure the writer has the necessary sign-offs and permissions to write and sell the project. Most likely, the studio's deal with the writer will be contingent on the writer having secured these rights; if it turns out she hasn't, her deal with the studio cancels out. Sometimes the writer does not own the rights to the original property herself, but she's shopping the project in partnership with the rights owner. (Perhaps a screenwriter has partnered with a novelist to adapt the novelist's book, or perhaps the screenwriter and a living person are shopping a project based on this person's life.) In these cases, the studio first makes a deal with the original rights owner . . . or at least makes their deal with the screenwriter contingent on their ability to close a deal with that original owner.

• **Production bonus**–Writers often receive bonuses if their script gets produced. A successful screenwriter, for example, may make $850,000 in guaranteed compensation for selling his script, then an additional $650,000 in contingent compensation if the studio greenlights it into production. Like everything else, this bonus is negotiated up front, and we say the script sold "for $850,000 against $1.5 million" (the purchase price versus the ultimate price, including the production bonus). In May, 2011, CAA reportedly sold Matthew Aldrich's spec script, *Father Daughter Time: A Tale of Armed Robbery and Eskimo Kisses*, to Warner Brothers for $500,000 against $800,000. So that's a purchase price of $500,000 and a $300,000 production bonus–for a grand total of $800,000.[27]

Talk the Talk

Sole/shared production bonus–When a writer receives his entire production bonus, it's considered a "**sole production bonus**"; when he shares it, it's a "**shared production bonus**." The amounts a writer earns for both his sole and shared production bonuses are, like everything else, part of his quotes.

If the studio later hires another writer to do a rewrite or polish–as often happens–the original writer's production bonus is reducible, usually by half. In other words, you might sell a script for $700,000 against $1.2 million–a $700,000 purchase price with a $500,000 production bonus–but if another writer comes on for a rewrite, your production bonus is reducible to $250,000. If a third writer comes aboard, the original writer's bonus is not further reducible (although the *second* writer's might be).

• **Backend compensation**–Standard backend compensation for a screenwriter is often about five percent of the film's net profits. So if the movie nets $100 million, the writer receives $5 million. Most writers, however, receive no "net profits" until all other expenditures have been paid and the studio breaks even, which means many writers never see any backend at all. Studios are notorious for redefining and recalculating a film's profits and expenditures to keep a movie from ever "officially" breaking even. This is why it's incumbent on a watchful agent to negotiate a fair definition of the writer's "net profits" or backend compensation.

Occasionally, an A-list writer like Aaron Sorkin (*The Social Network*) or Diablo Cody (*Juno*) may be able to negotiate a piece of their film's gross compensation, but this only happens in the case of special writers so powerful the studio can use their name in marketing efforts (e.g., "From the Oscar-winning writer of *The Social Network* . . ."). Many agents and managers try instead to build **box office bonuses** or bumps into clients' contracts. Box office bonuses usually kick in once a film has recouped some of its costs, say, one-and-a-half times its negative cost. So if a film cost $50 million, it must make $75 million ($50 million plus another $25 million) before the writer begins receiving bumps. But once the movie hits this benchmark, a writer may begin seeing $5,000 or $10,000 bonuses for every additional $5 million or $10 million the movie makes. (Most contracts also require the studio use box office numbers reported by a public source such as *Variety* or *The Hollywood Reporter*. The studio is *not* allowed to use its own figures or say, "Our research says the movie has only sold $20 in tickets, so we're not paying you.")

"Box office bonuses are not a guaranteed thing even on an original piece of material," says literary manager Jeffrey Thal, a partner at Ensemble Entertainment. "They arose because [writers] never see profits, and because a lot of times [studios] wouldn't give you what you wanted on your guaranteed compensation. So this is a way to give you a sop; in success you'll see something better than just net profits."

How Do Studios Keep Movies from Breaking Even?

Sometimes they factor in expenditures unrelated to the movie, like producer deals or production fees from other movies. Other times, they charge themselves exorbitant distribution fees–like the $212 million Warner Bros. charged itself for *Harry Potter and the Order of the Phoenix*[28]–or marketing fees, like spending ridiculous amounts of advertising money with in-house TV networks or magazines. In one historic case, writer Art Buchwald sued Paramount, claiming they used his idea as the basis for 1988's *Coming To America*, starring Eddie Murphy, and didn't properly compensate him. One of the arguments Paramount used in its defense was that the movie, which was made for less than $40 million, never actually turned a profit–despite grossing almost $300 million worldwide. The California Supreme Court called Paramount's accounting methods "unconscionable," and Buchwald and the studio settled.

• **Set-up bonus**–This bonus applies only to situations where a producer has optioned or purchased the rights to a script *without* the partnership of a studio. If the producer then succeeds in selling the project to a studio, the writer receives a bonus, which could be anywhere from $25,000 to $1 million.

- **DVD bonuses**–DVD bonuses, when you can get them, are triggered by a certain number of domestic DVD sales. The writer gets paid each time DVD sales pass certain thresholds–say, for example, 100,000 units, 250,000 units, and 500,000 units. Agents aren't always able to negotiate DVD bonuses on theatrical films–and when they are, they're rarely that lucrative–but they become more important with direct-to-video releases.

"I had a writer, a young kid out of USC, who wrote a screenplay called *Band Camp* as a senior paper," says Beckerman. "He got it to me, and I knew somebody at Universal Home Video. [They bought] his script and adjusted it to make it *American Pie: Band Camp*. He got paid, there were a million steps, but then–because it was a direct to DVD movie–you could negotiate DVD bonuses."

- **Strike price**–Screenwriters with a tremendous amount of leverage occasionally negotiate a "strike price," or penalty the studio pays if it decides *not* to make the movie.

- **Perks**–Agents and lawyers also negotiate special perks for their clients. These may include extra tickets to the premiere, special travel arrangements if the writer is flown to set (a certain class of flight or hotel, per diem), etc.

As negotiations stretch on, most writers are wringing their hands back in their offices or apartments. "First," says Hood, the studio "comes in with an offer that's very low, then [your agent] comes back with an offer that's impossibly high. It goes back and forth, and everyone's threatening to walk away from the table. 'The deal's going to fall apart!' It's nerve-racking. Then, eventually, you get the call. 'The deal is done. We're closed.' And you feel a great sense of relief . . . [this] strange sense of–'the world is

---

Directors Contracts

Directors' contracts often have a few more provisions than writers' deals. In features, after all, unlike in TV, directors are afforded much more responsibility than writers; they're not only in charge of the project's creative execution, they're responsible for delivering the film on time and on budget. Thus, a studio may stipulate that if a project goes over budget, the director loses backend points. Studios also try to control the movie's final running time. The shorter the movie, the more screenings an exhibitor can show, the more tickets that exhibitor can sell, and the most dollars the studio collects. Directors' contracts used to keep movies under two hours; now they're often kept under 100 minutes.

Two Other Important Deals

As the agent closes your deal, two other possible deals are being negotiated: the manager's producing deal and the agent's commissioning of the producer. Just like writers have quotes for writing, managers and producers have quotes for producing– and they usually use lawyers to negotiate their studio contracts. Writers don't usually know what their managers' quotes are and, as one manager put it, "they don't need to." But remember–managers only get paid *if the project gets made*. So if you sell a screenplay to Universal tomorrow, you still pay your manager his commission. If the movie gets green-lit, and your manager collects his producing fees, he'll reimburse you whatever commission you've paid.

Like managers, other producers attached to the script (including move stars receiving a producer credit) don't get paid unless the project enters production–so your agents don't collect their ten percent producers' commission until then. (Also, FYI–when agents commission a producer, they still commission their client.)

How Options Are Different

If the buyer options the script, instead of purchasing it outright, they still negotiate all the relevant deal points up front. Options also have a few other points to be negotiated:

1. **Time period.** How long does the buyer's option last? Twelve months? Eighteen? The WGA mandates that no option last longer than eighteen months. Or rather, they must pay additional fees for each eighteen-month period.
2. **Extensions.** Many agents will cap the number of times a producer can extend his option, allowing ownership of the material to return to the writer after a specified amount of time.
3. **Option payments.** On the open market, a buyer can purchase or option a script for however much or little they negotiate. However, if the buyer is a WGA-signatory company—as most legitimate Hollywood studios and production companies are—they must purchase your script for no less than WGA minimum, as laid out on page 186. If they're optioning the script, the WGA mandates they "pay not less than ten percent of the applicable minimum due upon the sale of such material, for each option period of up to eighteen months."[29] So if the agent negotiates a purchase price of $45,000, the option may cost a mere $4,500. Or, for a high-level writer getting $500,000 or $1 million per script, the option could be $50,000 or $100,000—or more (there's no rule saying an agent can't negotiate an option price *more* than ten percent). Having said this, many companies—even Guild-signatory companies—skirt this ten percent rule, paying much less for options. Director Deepa Mehta, for example, paid author Salman Rushdie only $1.00 for the film rights to Rushdie's award-winning 1981 novel *Midnight's Children*, which Rushdie then adapted himself.[30]
4. **Option price vs. purchase price**—Studios and producers often want their option payments to count against the script's final purchase price. Let's say the negotiated purchase price is $500,000, and the studio pays the writer $50,000 for the option. Later, the studio decides to purchase the script entirely—they now owe the writer only $450,000. Agents (and writers), however, always want the option and the purchase to be two separate, unrelated payments—so if the buyer pays $50,000 for the option, they still owe the full $500,000 to acquire the full script later. This is often a big part of option negotiations.

Dollar Options

Sadly, "dollar options"— literally paying $1.00 to option a property's film rights—aren't uncommon in Hollywood. Sometimes, this is just a way to formalize a gentleman's agreement. Other times, it's a way to take advantage of young writers desperate for an opportunity.

opening up . . . I'm alive . . . from here on in, I'm on easy street!' Even if you don't sell it for very much, even if it's not splashed across the trades, it's a great moment. It's that first validation.

"[Of course,] as months and years wear on, you realize that was just the first step of another long process. There's going to be more spec scripts and more writing assignments, but that first one—there's something pure about it. *You're a professional writer!*"

What Now?

Once the deal is closed, the agent stays involved by monitoring the project's progress. He helps ensure his client turns in drafts and rewrites on time (and protects the client if she needs *more* time) and makes sure his client gets paid in a timely and appropriate fashion. They're less involved creatively; they're no longer reading drafts, giving notes, or going to meetings. Managers may be a bit more involved, especially if they're attached as producers. Once the project gets green-lit into production, however, says Lowery, "you want to be first in line to potentially cast it with your talent or your director."

If it's an independent film, some agents may also get involved once the project is in the can, helping it to find distribution at film festivals or markets. For both indies and studio films, an agent may also enlist a publicist "to renew client interest," says Original Artists agent Matt Leipzig, who reps clients like Ryan Engle (*Ben 10*, *The Rampage*)[31] and writer/producer Alessandro Camon (*The Messenger*, *Wall Street:Money Never Sleeps*).[32] This is especially important during awards season, when an agent may "lobby the studio to promote your client. The best way to get the most things for a client is the fact that there's going to be a huge publicity push behind the making of the movie. How do we have some of that accrue to the benefit of the writer? You want to start getting a bunch of visibility for your client."

Turnaround

Agents also get much more re-involved with a project if it it goes into turnaround. In these cases, a studio decides to cease development on a property, making it available for another studio to grab and re-develop. It's the job of the project's agent and producer to find a new buyer—which isn't always easy. In order to get a project out of turnaround, the new buyer must reimburse the original studio the price of the script and any development costs. The film rights to Stephanie Meyer's *Twilight*, for example, were originally purchased in 2004 by Paramount's MTV Films, but after three years of failed development, Paramount called it quits. Summit Entertainment, a nascent studio that had released only five movies—four of which bombed—picked it up. Less than two years and $37 million dollars later, Summit had a $393 million global hit on their hands.

Unfortunately, not all turnaround stories end this successfully, and many studios don't want to pick up another studio's "sloppy seconds." "If there's $2.5 million against it, there's a big stink on it," says Beckerman. And "because [the first studio] couldn't get it made, nobody's going to make that movie and give the other studio two and a half million." Sometimes, a project that felt ripe and relevant when it was purchased now, months or years later, feels dated and stale. Other times, a script may have initially sold thanks to the attachment of a hot director or A-list movie star . . . but by time the film goes into turnaround, the attachment has lost interest, devaluing the entire project.

Occasionally, however, producers and agents *are* able to re-sell a project in turnaround, often using creative deal-making. One producer told me a story of getting a project out of turnaround by saying to the studio, "Tell you what—if I get this movie made for less than $5 million, I reimburse you only $100,000. If I get it made for *more* than $5 million, I'll pay you the full freight." The studio agreed. (Most studios consider $5 million the threshold between indie films and low-budget studio films.) The producer financed the movie independently—for less than $5 million—and is currently seeking distribution.

So How Did the Sean Hood Story End? Did MTV Ever Make *The Dorm*?

Unfortunately, they did not. The script withered away on the shelves of MTV, until almost thirteen years later—when MTV re-approached Hood about doing it as a four-hour miniseries. By then, some of the rights had reverted *back* to Hood, which means MTV had to re-purchase the same script they'd already bought over a decade earlier!

"[The project had] changed over the years," says Hood, "but there are still some scenes and sequences that are just as I wrote them thirteen or fourteen years ago. And it's finally going into production."

10   Writers-for-Hire—Open Assignments and Rewrites

While every screenwriter dreams of having his script arrive on the screen unchanged, exactly as he wrote it, this doesn't always happen. Actually, scratch that: it *never* happens. In fact, not only will your script get rewritten–probably countless times–it probably won't even get rewritten by *you*. "Rarely does a writer who sells [a script or a pitch] take it all the way home . . . from the start of the script to actual production of the movie," says David Boxerbaum, Senior Literary Agent at Paradigm. "I would say ninety percent [of scripts] become [**open writing**] **assignments** at some point, [meaning] they'll be open for other writers to come in . . . to lend their expertise in a certain area: a dialogue polish, production polish, character polish, structure." There are generally two kinds of open writing assignments:

1. **A writer is hired by a studio or production company to write a script based on an idea or property already owned or generated internally.** This could be a novel, magazine article, video game, TV show, old movie, even the life of a real person.

2. **A writer is hired to rewrite or polish another writer's script.** Sometimes, this is a script the studio has been developing for a while. Other times, studios buy a spec with the sole intention of firing the original writer and hiring someone more experienced to re-conceive or rewrite it. One agent told me he sold a client's script (a horror-movie version of a classic novel) for approximately $150,000, only to have the studio turn around, boot the writer, and bring in a bigger screenwriter for about $500,000 to redo the whole thing as a family movie.

First Rewrite

The Writers Guild mandates that a script's original writer must always get the first rewrite, but it's easy enough for studios to give the writer his rewrite, then axe him and bring in someone new.[1]

Up until the late 2000s, Hollywood was lush with open writing assignments. In fact, many screenwriters made the bulk of their living simply rewriting other people's work. Unfortunately, "the world of open writing assignments has changed quite a bit since the 2007 WGA strike and the collapse of the economy," says lit manager Adam Kolbrenner, a partner at Madhouse Entertainment, the management arm of Alcon Entertainment (*Beautiful Creatures*). Because studios are now making fewer movies, there are fewer scripts needing rewriting. As a result, "there are only a small amount of available job opportunities. [Now,] most feature writers earn from selling original material."

Where Do Open Writing Assignments Come From?

Assignments can come from studios, producers based at studios, or independent companies. Agents usually learn of assignments when covering their territories each week. Perhaps Universal wants someone to do a four- to six-week rewrite of their new vampire comedy. Maybe Scott Free, Ridley Scott's company at Fox, needs a **closer** for a two-week polish on their latest political action thriller, which begins shooting in a few weeks. Whatever the parameters of the job, the covering agent then takes this information back to his co-workers to help find the perfect writer.

Talk the Talk

Closer—A writer brought in to give a script one final polish before it goes into production. Most closers are highly paid for excelling in a particular area—dialogue, characters, set pieces, etc.

"There are writers who have probably written [only] one or two original things, but they're closers because they know how to bring a script home," says APA feature agent Ryan Saul. In the final stretch of development, he continues, studios often find "there's a problem with the script. 'We need one of six writers who does this . . . to finish the movie!'"

Closers are usually extremely high-level writers who command extraordinary fees for polishing a screenplay in need—often $250,000–$300,000 per week. *Angels and Demons* writer David Koepp was reportedly paid over a million dollars to rewrite Adam Cozad's script for Paramount's Jack Ryan reboot.[2]

Other writers are in the "**incoming call business**," and they—and their agents—learn about assignments when producers or execs call specifically to work with them. Especially at the rewrite stage, or as a script gets closer to production and time is short, execs compile "wish lists" of three or four A-list writers they hope to hire for a rewrite or dialogue polish. An exec needing a rewrite on a post-apocalyptic horror movie may call WME to ask about Alex Garland (*28 Days Later*). A producer needing someone to adapt a chick-lit novel may call CAA to hire Abby Kohn and Marc Silverstein (*The Vow*, *He's Just Not That Into You*).

Occasionally, a particular incoming-call writer will be too busy to accept an assignment, but execs want him so badly, they put the entire project on hold! "It's more important [to have the] marketing hook of: 'From the Academy Award-winning writer of X,' than to give a young kid an opportunity," says manager Lenny Beckerman of Hello and Company. When Beckerman was a lit manager at Anonymous Content (*Winter's Bone*, *Fun Size*), Anonymous client William Monahan, writer of *The Departed*, "was backed up close to eight assignments. [This is why] the assignment game is fool's gold in a lot of ways."

Indeed, it's tough for younger writers to nab assignments as many are reserved for a handful of writers. "I'll call and say, 'I hear this [assignment] is open,'" says Boxerbaum, "and they'll say, 'Yeah, we have our list of two or three [writers] we're going to first, our wish list, and if that doesn't pan out, we'll come to you. Even if one on the wish list responds, [execs] may wait to see what the other two think as well. Wish-list writers have to compete, too, sometimes."

Of course, not all assignments have wish lists, and execs and producers often call agents to solicit writer suggestions or submissions. "You go to the agency and say, 'Send me your number one guy for sci-fi adaptation,'" says Brendan Deneen, who worked in development for producers Scott Rudin and Harvey Weinstein before founding MacMillan Films, the film production branch of Macmillan Publishing. The key, for execs, is to contact agents who they know will send terrific material. "You don't want billions of scripts and samples, so you pick and choose [which agents to call]. The longer you're in the business, the more agents you know. You start to see: this guy always sends good stuff, this guy always sends bad stuff. You have your A-list choices, you have secondary choices. I don't think anybody only goes to agencies with only three letters; that's a silly way to go. A lot of boutique agencies have great clients."

Relationships are Everything

"I've spent the last fifteen years working in the theater, so if we have a piece of work we want adapted, I'll listen to agents, but I'm also going to have a list of playwrights. I think, 'I can finally get so-and-so! This is exactly the kind of play they are writing—I would love to have them take a crack at this!"—Mike Sablone, director of development, Sunday Night Productions (*Promised Land*), and former dramaturg at Center Theater Group

When an agent learns of an open assignment, he immediately enters it into a company-wide database that records pertinent info abut every project in town: the title, what it's about, its history, who the executives and producers are, etc. It also notes which of the agency's writers or directors have been submitted (e.g., "Submitted Ryan Johnson's *Gross Intentions* script—Sheila hated—do not resend."). This entire database connects directly to the agency's database of contacts, so when an agent pulls up a particular exec, he can immediately see every project that exec has ever worked on, going back years, as well as everything the agency has ever sent her. The covering agent then emails his co-workers, detailing the project and asking for writer suggestions. With his co-workers' input, he compiles a list of writers. (FYI—this means the agent may be pushing clients not on his personal roster. If one of them books the gig, the covering agent and point agent split the commission, incentivizing agents to work for each other's clients.)

How Long Are Writers Given to Write an Assignment?

While every assignment's different, here's a basic range for different types of jobs:

Full script: 12 weeks
Rewrite: 8–10 weeks
Polish: 4–8 weeks

"You try to narrow it down to the fewest people possible," says Boxerbaum. "You don't want to send a laundry list, or a vast amount of people for one job. You want one, sometimes two or three people that make the most sense for that job." When agents submit writers for a job, they consider not only the writers' skill sets and samples, but also their personalities. Like with TV staffing, an assignment writer must be approved by the studio, any involved producers, possibly an attached director or actor. Thus, will these writers click with the other people on board? Can they write on deadline? After all, when a writer's off on his own, writing a spec, he can take as much time as needs to perfect that script. An assignment, however, usually has to be delivered in a matter of weeks.

Once the agent has a short list of writers he thinks could actually get the job, "you call the executives in charge of the assignment, you call the producers in charge of that assignment, you call everybody that needs to be called to make sure your clients have the best possible chance," says Boxerbaum. "In a perfect world, I'm trying to get the job offer on the phone, but that rarely happens . . . [and only with] major established writers. Sometimes you get, 'That's a great idea! Let me see if [the studio] would be interested—I'll call you right back.' They talk to their boss and if they're interested, they

FEATURE AGENTS

call back to say, 'We'd go exclusively to them and make this their job.' Unfortunately, that's a rarity these days."

Most of the times, these phone calls end in one of two ways:

1. **"Sure–let's schedule a meeting!"** Maybe the exec met the writer earlier, during a general meeting, when his agents were out with a spec screenplay. Feature writers, like TV writers, often go on general meetings, meet-and-greets that allow them to form relationships with producers and execs. (Remember in the last chapter, when we discussed going wide with a script? The Shotgun Approach may no longer be the most common or effective way of selling a project, but it's a great way to introduce a writer to the industry and generate thirty or forty meetings. And when do those meetings pay off? *Now.*)

"I'm always searching for [great] writing," says Sablone, "so even if a script is not right for Sunday Night Productions, I want to read anything agents think is exciting work by new writers, just so I can be aware of them for future situations."

This way, when open writing assignments pop up, "you've already established a relationship between the writer and the producers or executives," says Boxerbaum. It's much easier to get a job for a client already known to execs than a complete stranger–however talented he or she may be.

2. **If the exec or producer has *not* met the writer, he asks the agent to send writing samples.** He then reads and decides if this writer is someone who may be appropriate for the job.

Preparing the Pitch

As the exec reviews the writing samples, the agent fills in his clients about the project. Since many assignments are adaptations or rewrites, writers need to read the source material or the original draft and come up with their own unique "take."

"If it's a novel or a graphic novel, the first thing I ask myself is: 'how is this a movie?'" says screenwriter Sean Hood, who's been hired to write installments for franchises like *Halloween* and *The Crow*. "Novels take a particular form—they often contain a lot of characters' thoughts and feelings, things that don't show up on screen—and that presents problems. I try to imagine whatever imagery or premise is contained in the underlying material, [and] how that story could be told visually and cinematically."

It's also important to find some sort of personal connection to the material, an emotional attachment. "That's the secret to making a great movie, and quite honestly, there's no other real way to do it," says *The Cabin in the Woods* writer/director Drew Goddard. "You have to make it personal. Anybody can format the book into a screenplay in final draft. The best adaptations are ones that find the spirit of the piece and make it into something else, into cinema. Otherwise, why are you there?"

Perhaps a studio's looking for someone to adapt a book about pregnancy and childbirth—something like *What To Expect When You're Expecting*—and you recently had your first baby. Maybe a producer wants to make a film version of a video game set in a war-torn future, and you served three tours in Iraq. Other times, the connection could just be a profound love for the material. "As a little kid, I happened to have read a lot of *Conan the Barbarian* comic books," says Hood, who penned the 2011 reboot of Robert E. Howard's classic character, "so when that particular assignment came up, that was my connection. I hadn't thought about Conan in years, but I pulled out the old comic books and looked at them again. When I [went in to pitch], I was thinking of my own chest of ideas and thoughts about a character I hadn't uncovered since I was a little kid, [so] it was very personal."

Writers then put together a short presentation—no more than fifteen to twenty minutes—to enchant execs with their vision of the project. Often this is a simple verbal pitch, detailing their approach to the story, the characters, the world. "I pretend I'm telling a bedtime story to kids," says screenwriter Tedi Sarafian (*Terminator 3*, *The Road Killers*). "When I pitched *Sinbad* over at Sony, I remember saying, 'He looks down at the water and sees this spec of light. This giant wave crashes over us—and then there's this ship. This ship's on fire . . . houses are burning . . .' and I literally narrated the story."

Other times, writers create visual aids or props to help bring the pitch to life. "One of our jobs as writers is to make a pitch entertaining and memorable. Nothing is off limits," says writer/director James Seale (*Black Sash, Juncture*). "I've brought in music, created sizzle reels, projected graphics, even used actors—anything that helps the room see the vision of what I'm presenting. In this day and age of viral videos and ten-second attention spans, we must evolve as writers and do whatever is necessary to hook whoever we're pitching in unexpected ways."

When I was an executive at the Littlefield Company, we bought several pitches from Seale. In one of the best pitches I've ever seen, he came in and pitched a time travel series, but his entire pitch was "choreographed" to an actual soundtrack. The music swelled during the exciting parts, softened during the quiet parts, and exploded at the climax! "I generally write to film scores," Seale explains, and "I remember hearing a certain piece of music and how closely it mirrored the beats of my pitch. I had never used a music cue in a pitch before, but the development process at The Littlefield Company was so open and warm, it felt like a good place to try it out. Once I got over the fear of messing up the pitch and falling out of sync with the music, I presented to the room and to my relief, the execs seemed to appreciate 'hearing' a pitch in a new way." Not only did we "appreciate" it—we bought the show in the room.

How Pitching a Movie is Different than Pitching a TV Show

"TV pitches always focus more on the 'who.' Movies are more and more concept-based. Characters matter, but if you come up with a great premise and can expand on that premise in the pitch, it tends to be enough since most films are one-shot deals. For me, TV shows pitches are more about establishing a unique lead character, or characters, and pitching the journey they will go on throughout the life of the series. A great premise never hurts, but I tend to explore more character-related issues in a TV series pitch. Their arcs, back stories, interactions, goals. The best series live and die on their characters and the better pitches I've had in TV have been designed to do that. My movie pitches tend to be more plot-driven, focusing on the 'what.'"—writer/director James Seale (*Momentum, Throttle*)

FEATURE AGENTS

Ask the Executive

Q: I have my first pitch next week for an open writing assignment! It's with a producer who needs a screenwriter to adapt a novel he's optioned. I'm nervous; the producer obviously loves this book, and I want to have a unique take, but how much should I deviate from the original story to make it into a fabulous movie?

A: "A book and a movie are two different things—everybody who understands multimedia understands that. [So] it depends on the book. [If it's] *Harry Potter*, you want to stay pretty close to the source material. If it's a book no one has heard of, you can make deviations . . . as long as you're true to the core of the character, the core of the plot, the core of the intent. I write the *Flash Gordon* comic book, and I've stayed true to the core of the character, and the original concepts of Alex Raymond, but I update it for the twenty-first century. That's proven very successful for us. You can't be so constrained that you're not bringing your own original concepts or sense of adaptation. Otherwise, they don't need you. You don't bring anything to the table."–Brendan Deneen, Macmillan Films

This is another place agents and managers can be extremely helpful to their clients. As a writer prepares his pitch, his reps can be terrific sounding boards or advisors. "A lot of times we'll read the material with [our clients]," says New Wave manager Michael Goldberg. Managers and agents then have "them send us treatments, pitch us on the phone, pitch us in person. We talk with the producers involved, execs at the financier's company—getting the landscape. Just last night, I was talking to an exec at a mini-major, saying 'Who are they up against? What directions should they go in? What directions should they stay away from?' [Then you] quickly download to your writers so that they can be prepared with as much information as possible."

Writers don't always have much time to read the project's source material and prepare their own take. An agent may call and say the meeting is in a week, or it could be tomorrow. Or it could be two weeks down the road—then get pushed a month. "If I'm the executive trying to fill an assignment right away, I want to get that person in as soon as my schedule allows it," says Boxerbaum, "so as an agent, you try to get the meeting as soon as possible. You try to continue to bring in opportunities for your client, to have them continue to be working. So you want to get those meetings on the books right away, especially if there is strong interest in your client on that assignment."

Pitching the Producer

In Chapter 6, we talked about how television writers need the approval of at least three or four different entities to land a staff job: the network, the studio, the production company, and the showrunner. Scoring an open writing assignment works the same way. Writers need the approval of every party involved. Occasionally, this is only the studio and a producer.[3] Sometimes, this could be the studio, producer, and director. Or it might mean the studio, the producer, a director, and an attached star.

Having said that, producers are usually the project's first line of defense, charged with meeting all potential writers, hearing their fifteen-minute pitches, and deciding which to introduce to the studio.

When you meet with a producer to pitch your vision for an open assignment, "have a real pitch," says Deneen. "Read the source material closely and come up with specific ideas that are your own, so you're not just regurgitating the plot of the book or article you're going to adapt. Come in and say 'I read the book, I loved it, but here's what I would do with it.' [Tell] a story. 'You open with this, you go here, this is this character's arc, my third act is different than the book because I'm adding this.'"

Ten Ways to (Help) Land an Open Writing Assignment

1. "**Practice your pitch before you go in.** We, as managers, like to sit down before our clients go in and help them hone their pitch. Some people practice in a mirror, some people record themselves, some people just say it out loud a few times. Whether you have a manager or not, have it as clear and concise as possible."– Aaron Kaplan, Kaplan/Perrone Entertainment

2. "**Do not try to pull it out of your ass.** The last writing assignment I got was for the remake of a Bollywood film–I had twenty-five pages of notes. You're basically writing a beat outline of the whole film; you know your jokes, you know everything inside-out, so if they ask you a question, you can 'pretend' you're pulling it out of your ass, collaborating with them, but you already know all the questions someone might ask."–Charlie Stickney, writer/producer (*The Entertainers*, *Pound of Flesh*)

3. **Try to pitch to low-level execs and producers.** "If you're pitching producers, you always want to work with the lower levels–those are the [people] that you can riff off of, that you can engage quickly. Once you go into the studio, the producers [will be] on your side and they'll help you workshop further."–Producer

4. "**Do *not* go soft, do *not* go expected.** If you're doing a page-one rewrite, or adapting IP–an article, a book, a fucking napkin with a sentence on it–go crazy. Most of the time, [when] my clients book something or lose out to someone else, it's because the wheel has been reinvented. Go balls to the wall–one of two things is going to happen: you either book it, or you're going so far away that the conversation's over–but the exec will respect you no less."–Michael Goldberg, manager, New Wave Entertainment

5. **Make your characters seem real.** "The best pitch is when it feels like you're gossiping about people you know. You know the joy you have when you're gossiping about somebody? 'You have to meet my friend so-and-so, he's such-and-such . . .' You can tell when you're doing it at a dinner party, you're doing that to capture some-body's interest. It's the same thing with [pitches]. The more it feels like you observed it, rather than created it, the better it is."–John Peaslee, writer (*Crazy On the Outside*)

6. **Do *not* act.** "I have been to pitches where people act scenes out. It's always a bad idea. Execs want to be entertained, but they don't want to think you're trying to get a part in the movie."–Brendan Deneen, Macmillan Films

7. "**Use phrases execs like to hear.** 'This will make it more cinematic.' 'This will make it a four-quadrant movie.' 'This will make it a big movie star role.' Think like a movie exec. How is this movie going to open and make lots of money for everybody involved?–Brendan Deneen, Macmillan Films

8. **Collaboration is key.** "Do not argue. Do not be combative. Do not get frustrated. Do not look disinterested. You see a different ending? The exec is right; the exec is the one writing the paycheck. Find a way to match up to what the exec is looking for."–Feature lit manager

9. "**Be one of the last ones on the project to pitch.** It's better to be the last person to pitch than the first person to pitch. It's better not to pitch right before lunch. The best time to pitch is late morning . . . but not before lunch, because they're thinking about getting out to lunch. [And] not at the end of the day, because they're tired and want to get out for the end of the day. A 10:00 or 11:00 or a 3:00/3:30 timeslot–that's awesome."–Manager/Producer

10. **Don't** "**go on too long.** A good pitch should be no more than fifteen to seventeen minutes. Longer than that, you're on the edge of losing your audience. Now, if it's an amazing story, you can open it up for questions, [let it be] a dialogue, a conversation–that's the best way to get somebody involved."–David Boxerbaum, senior literary agent, Paradigm

Most pitches "start with telling [the execs or producers] what you love about [the project]," says Goddard. "Chances are, they love it, too, which is why they bought it. When people go in there: 'Well, this doesn't work, but maybe you could do something else,' the executive's face falls."

From there, simply tell your version of the story, casually and conversationally, as if you're telling a story to friends over drinks. Don't "have too much stuff written down in front of you," says Sarafian. "If you're worried about 'I have to do this part, this part, this part,' and you want to say it exactly the way it's written, you're looking at a page and reading. It's boring hearing somebody read—that's not going to get your idea sold."

This is not to say, of course, that you shouldn't be prepared. "Just about every single time I've had a bad meeting, where I wound up with egg in my face, it was an open assignment," says screenwriter Diablo Cody (*Juno*, *Young Adult*). "People will sit there, ask you what you're going to do, you'll do your whole spiel . . . and then they'll go, 'Okay, and?' They want you to recite the entire fucking rewrite! So you have to be triple prepared, have as much information as possible to fill that silence—because they're not going to provide you with anything. They're waiting to hear what you have to offer, so even if you're talking out of your ass, have a lot of options and be prepared for a sudden left turn. They'll say, 'Wait a minute—we didn't want to make it more romantic. We don't like that idea!' And you go, 'Did I say romantic? I meant more action-packed for the eighteen to twenty-four males!' Give them whatever they want and give them a lot."

After the pitch meeting, your agent steps in to work some agenting magic. "You know this guy's perfect for the project," the agent tells the exec. "You've seen his other movies—he had the number one teen romantic comedy last year. And you read the spec he sold to Sony, right? Tell me he's not the guy. And, for what it's worth, I haven't seen him this fired up about an assignment since *Ice Cream Man*, which just got a green-light at Universal with Melissa McCarthy attached. I'm telling you—this guy will knock it out of the park for you."

What happens next depends on several different variables. If you pitched to a high-level executive, a decision-maker, the exec could immediately say, "We love this writer's take; let's take it to the studio!" If you pitched to a lower-level exec, he may need to run your thoughts up the flagpole. His boss may then want to meet with you himself—in which case you return for another meeting—or he may simply empower his exec to pull the trigger.

Ask the Manager

Q: I had a pitch this meeting at an indie production company for a job I *really* wanted. I thought it went well, but my manager followed up with the production company, and the producer said he didn't respond! Can a good manager change his mind?

A: Probably not. "Assuming [the project] is set up with a financier [and] not just a producer, you can call the financier and try to back it in. You need everyone on board to make this work. Not to mention, you don't want to make enemies of yourself as a rep, because you're going to need that relationship in the future. More importantly, you don't want to make enemies with the client and the producer. There's no open writing assignment that's worth burning bridges for."—Michael Goldberg, manager, New Wave Entertainment

---

Working with a Producer

Congratulations! The producer loved your pitch! He has some notes, of course—"small" things he wants tweaked: he'd like to lose the sidekick, add a love interest, and revamp the entire second act—but he'd like to develop the pitch with you to take to the studio. One important thing to understand: *you are not the only writer on this project.* In fact, as you and the producer work on your version of the story, the producer is likely working on totally different versions with two or three other writers (maybe more). This is often a studio mandate; studio execs instruct the producer to bring in a certain number of writers—say, the best three or four—to present different takes on the material. "I weed it down to the ones I absolutely love," says *The Muppets* producer Todd Lieberman. "If I love them and they happen to be different, that's great. If I love them and they happen to be similar, that's fine, too. I'm not steering one in any different direction—it's the writer coming in and giving their particular take. [I'm just] supplementing and helping what they've already come in with."

It's also important for producers to develop more than one pitch, says Boxerbaum, "because if one goes south, where are you at? Half the time, you get a take ready, spend months getting this pitch perfect . . . it's the big day . . . you go in, the studio hears it, and they go, 'Ehhh, I don't like that version of the movie.' Then where are you at?! You say, 'We can fine tune it with this writer, then give it back!' 'Nah, I'd rather you bring me more ideas.' Back to square one! After all that, months of work. So to protect their own asses, [producers] have multiple options to bring their executive."

Sometimes the studio has an idea of what they want in these pitches—perhaps they're looking for someone to give the project a dark, creepy edge; maybe they want a writer to infuse the script with some raunchy comedy set pieces. Other times, the studio is open to hearing various versions, but they let the producer pick his favorites. "It's difficult to determine what [a studio] has in mind for a project," says producer Doug McKay (*Shutter Island*), former VP of production at Phoenix Pictures, "so it's helpful to try and get some of that information from a friendly studio executive or an agent close to the process. Bearing that in mind when designing a pitch is a smart idea, but usually, when I'm developing a pitch with a writer, we just work on making sure the writer's vision and delivery is clear."

Throughout this process—which, by the way, could take several weeks or months—you, the writer, are working for free. That's right—the producer shepherding the pitch is not paying you. The studio, which hasn't yet heard the pitch, is not paying you. You are simply preparing for your chance to audition for the assignment. "Sometimes you do treatment after treatment after treatment, and you finally go into the studio and they go, "Nah, we [don't like it],'" says Boxerbaum. "Sometimes you do all that work, the studio hears the pitch and goes, 'You know what? It's great. I just don't think we want to make this movie anymore.' It's a real crap shoot."

Thus, good agents track how many writers a producer is working with and make sure they're not "bringing in twenty different writers to their studio executive," says Boxerbaum. Agents "try to minimize that, as much as possible, to their own clients . . . to make sure [you] have the best opportunity to get that [job], to go pitch the executive." If it looks like a producer is taking too many writers to the studio, just "throwing spaghetti against a wall to see what sticks," an agent may advise his client to back out of the running. "You sure you want to do this?" the agent tells his client. "They're casting a pretty wide net—ten or twelve people. To be honest, I don't think the producer has any idea what the hell he wants—or what kind of movie this is. Which means even if you get this, there's a good chance you're going to end up going around in circles, working on this forever. That's my gut. But if you really want to go in on this, do it—just do it with your eyes open."

Agents also want to avoid situations where clients spend weeks working with a particular producer, only to find—upon pitching the studio—that the studio execs aren't fans of that writer's work. To avoid this, agents "take the studio's temperature" on the writer *before* sending the client into the producer. In other words, let's say an agent learns of a particular assignment from a producer, not a studio. In addition to suggesting a handful of writers to the producer, the agent will call his contacts at the producer's home studio to make sure those writers are "approvable." If execs don't know one of the writers, the agent sends them writing samples even before the writer meets the producer. The last thing an agent wants is to waste hours of his client's time, or the producer's time, by discovering too late that the studio won't approve the writer.

Should Writers Work for Free?

When I was just out of grad school, I was invited by a struggling indie producer I knew (she'd been an exec at a company where I'd interned) to write a haunted house script . . . for free. This is not unusual. Movie producers sometimes come up with an idea on their own, then "hire" young writers to write the script for free, on spec. If the script sells, the producer and the writer both get paid; if the script doesn't sell, no one gets anything. In a business that often feels impossible to break into, many aspiring writers view this as a great way to form relationships and have a shot at selling a script with a producer attached. But is this really a fair arrangement, a good opportunity? Should writers be working for free?

That depends on the situation. If the producer has a bona fide studio deal, these situations "are good for younger writers to at least get the development experience working with a producer," says APA feature agent Ryan Saul. And as Adam Kolbrenner, a manager at Madhouse Entertainment, adds: "If you trust the producer to sell the material, it's a good strategy. When it's a producer who has no real relationships and is not quite established, it becomes a much more difficult proposition."

The question, then, is how does a young writer know whether a producer is legit—or at least powerful and connected enough to make this collaboration worth the writer's time? "Do your research," says Verve literary agent Tanya Cohen. "There are definitely individuals out there who claim they're producers, and a writer who has never done this before can fall into those traps. [Most] agents and managers have a great working knowledge of producers around town. And if there is one that an agent or manager hasn't heard of, [they] vet them. Sit down with them, see what they have going on. Make sure the people you are dealing with are reputable and have a track record."

You can also research most genuine producers online, via IMDB.com, Studio System, or Variety's "Facts on Pacts," which keeps a fairly updated list of producers with studio deals. If the producer doesn't have a studio deal, or a track record of producing legitimate films, be wary. Protect yourself. Put together a working agreement—*on paper*—to which both you and the producer agree and adhere. "After a certain period of time," says Cohen, "the rights of the project should revert back to the writer. Whether it is an original idea that the writer came up with or an idea the producer gave to the writer, if the writer is writing completely on spec there should be an agreement stating the producer has eighteen months, or nine months, to set this up. If they are unsuccessful, [the rights] revert back to the writer, and he owns that piece of material." Don't be afraid to ask for this if you're asked to write a script for free. I'm never a fan of writers not getting paid, but at least with this arrangement, both writer and producer have skin in the game. If the producer refuses—*no deal*! You don't want to be in "business" with someone who values your work so little they refuse to take any risk themselves. (As for me—I initially told the producer, my former internship boss, that I'd write the haunted house script. But as we got into the process, and I realized how much work it would entail and that I was essentially writing for free with no real path to getting a movie made—I bailed. She wasn't happy, but it was the right decision. To this day, that woman has never produced a movie on her own, and writing the script would've been a wasted six months to a year of my life.)

Pitching the Studio or Financier

You and the producer finally feel your pitch is ready to take to the studio! It's now the producer's job to call the execs at the studio and schedule the meeting. Now remember, the producer is probably working with a handful of other writers on *their* pitches for the same material. Some producers like to take each pitch to the studio whenever it's ready, pitching one idea tomorrow and another in three weeks or a month. Others try scheduling meetings all within the same week. Still others schedule with a bit of Machiavellian strategy; one producer told me he schedules his favorite pitch right after his weakest pitch—making the better pitch look even stronger.

When pitch day finally arrives, the writer and producer, and any other important parties—a director, actor, or executive from the production company—head to the studio. As the pitch begins, "I set up the room a bit," says Lieberman. "It's always good to break the ice, make the environment a little more comfortable. Then we set up why this [project] is a passion of ours, I pass it off to the writer, and he or she goes into the presentation we've rehearsed. It's kind of a rehearsed job interview. The executive will ask some questions, and hopefully, by that point, we have poked as many holes into the story and presentation as possible, so we're prepared to answer those questions."

After the writer has talked through the creative part of the pitch, the producer may talk about practical and logistical factors. If this particular take would allow the movie to be done for a relatively low price tag—he brings this up. (Conversely, if it's a big-budget pitch, he dances around it.) If the pitch allows for special tie-ins or merchandising opportunities—toys, books, games, product integration—he brings this up. Anything that could whet the studio's appetite and help make a sale—the producer spells out.

When the pitch is over, the studio execs put their heads together to evaluate the pitch. Obviously, they need to have liked it. But there are other factors to weigh as well. How expensive is this particular writer? How much development money does the studio have left in it's annual coffers? Ultimately, however, the decision comes down to the studio's "gut instinct" about a particular writer and his or her take. "You never want to take a meeting with a writer you don't think you might hire for this project," says Eirich, "so going in, they're already at a certain level of qualification where you believe, with the right take, they can get this job. That said, there are writers at different levels. There's going to be a writer who's had his last three movies produced and has a $1.5 million quote, and there's going to be a writer you believe in whose spec was on the Black List but didn't sell—who has a $200,000 quote. There's a version of both of these writers writing your assignment. You'll occasionally have meetings with the $1.5 million writer who comes in and says, 'Yeah, I really want to do it; let me know if you want me.' And you're [thinking], 'Well, there aren't a lot of ideas there … we don't necessarily know what he's going to do with it, but he's incredibly talented and he's proven he knows how to solve problems and can write great characters.' Then there might be a less-expensive writer who gives you the beat-by-beat take: That's where it gets challenging, because on the one hand, there's a writer who's a little safer, who's had a lot of success, but then there's a writer you believe in but doesn't have the track record to back it up. There's no science to it, no formula; it just becomes about a gut instinct and an internal conversation with your President of Production to decide who gives us the best chance to get us a script we can go make."

At this point, agents and managers jump back in, calling to get feedback from the studio and trying to convince execs to hire their client. "Half our job is selling and positioning," says one veteran lit manager. "We never lie, but we'll say, 'Just so you know, this writer just sold X, Y, and Z. And this writer has this other A, B, and C cooking. But he's very passionate [about the project] and we might have a finite window here. We'd love for you to strongly consider the writer … [but] we'd love an answer sooner rather than later.' But you never want to go overboard. In the current climate, financiers have the power."

He's right; studios not only have power and money on their side, they have time. Some pull the trigger on a writer only hours after the pitch. Others take a couple days. On rare occasions, execs are so excited they buy the pitch in the room, hiring the writer on the spot. Unfortunately, on many occasions, studio execs make no decision at all.

　　　　　　　　　　　　　　　　　　　　　　　　　　　FEATURE AGENTS

In fact, one of the dangers of open writing assignments is that many never get filled. "In some cases, studios have been looking for years," says feature agent Jim Ehrich of Rothman Brecher Kim. "You send someone in, and they say, 'Okay, we're waiting to hear more takes,'" and that could go on ad nauseum, because they don't know what they want. It's one of those things they know when they hear it, [but] it could stay 'open writing' forever. Some never get filled—it's incredible." Knowing this, most agents try to be judicious about which assignments they pursue, not wanting clients to prepare pitches that have little chance of getting accepted.

The Economics of Open Assignments

A few years ago, many writers made their livings primarily on open writing assignments. Today, however, much of that has changed. "The open writing world has shrunk," says Paradigm senior lit agent David Boxerbaum. "Now it's much more original material: specs, pitches, articles, IP. Studios are making fewer movies; because of that, fewer assignments are being filled." Indeed, in 2002, Disney released twenty-two movies and Sony released thirty-one; ten years later, in 2012, those outputs had dropped nearly twenty-four percent—Disney released only thirteen movies; Sony released eighteen.[5] Movies have also gotten more expensive. In 1995, the average cost of a Hollywood movie was $42 million.[6] A decade later, the average movie cost $60 million.[7] Six years after that, the average movie price tag had hit $78 million.

This is partly because Hollywood blockbusters have been incorporating more expensive high-tech visual effects and computer wizardry. It's also because, as ticket sales dropped more than twenty percent between 2002 and 2012[8]—Hollywood, desperate to find viewers, has started making fewer original movies and more sequels, spinoffs, and adaptations. (Of 2012's ten highest grossing movies, only two—*Ted* and *Brave*—were not sequels or adaptations.) Believing these movies have a built-in audiences, making them less risky investments, studios pony up big bucks for stars, effects, sets, costumes, and marketing campaigns.

What this means for writers, however, is that because there are fewer movies, there are fewer assignments. "You have so much competition to get these jobs," says Boxerbaum, "a lot of writers don't want to put their names in the hat."

Complicating things further, when an assignment comes along, the stakes are high; a studio with $200 million riding on a film isn't going to throw a rewrite or adaptation to the first writer who comes along. "Studio executives are scared of putting forth something to their bosses if they don't think it's 100 percent right," says Boxerbaum. "They're going to their boss saying, 'Give me $200,000,' 'Give me $400,000 or $500,000,' 'Give me a million dollars to hire this writer. That's a lot of pressure on your shoulders if that doesn't work."

Sometimes, however, a savvy young agent or writer can use these financials to his advantage. APA agent Ryan Saul tells of learning about a rewrite job at one of the studios' specialty arms. They were looking for a five-star writer in the $2 million range. Saul had a talented client who had recently had some heat from selling a spec, but "he wasn't getting this assignment." Saul arranged for the writer to have a general meeting at the studio—not a pitch, just a meet-and-greet. Based on the success of that general, he convinced the execs to give this writer a chance to pitch on the assignment. So the writer went in, pitched a great take on the source material, and said, "Look, I know you want to hire this expensive writer, but you can hire me at fifteen percent of his quote and I'll deliver a terrific first draft. If you don't like it, go get the other guy. Even if you end up replacing me, at least you won't have to pay him to do an expensive page-one rewrite, so you pay him $1 million instead of $2 million. What do you have to lose?" The studio hired him. He did a great job, and "off of that sample," says Saul, "he is now on a couple other major studios' lists of writers to go to."

Fortunately, not every open writing assignment is a fool's errand. Many get filled by top-shelf writers that pull down $60,000 per day. Oscar-winner Alexander Payne (*Sideways*, *The Descendants*), for example, did rewrites on *Jurassic Park III* and *I Now Pronounce You Chuck and Larry*.[4] Other assignments go to younger, more untested writers, who earn closer to $1,500 per day. Regardless of what level you're at, when the offer comes in, it's time for your agent to negotiate the deal, and assignment negotiations can be slightly different than spec negotiations.

Negotiations

To Learn More

Read about the details of a traditional script purchase negotiation, see page 185.

Negotiations begin, as usual, with the studio's business affairs execs calling to check the writer's quotes. Although assignment negotiations play out similarly to a script purchase, there are some differences worth knowing about:

- **Guaranteed steps vs. optional steps**—A strong agent tries to get his client as many *guaranteed* steps as possible, since this translates to more money and a better chance of receiving credit on the movie. A studio wants to give the writer more *optional* steps; this way, if studio execs want to fire the writer after a single draft, they can. If they feel the writer's doing a great job and they want to keep her on they can exercise more optional steps, paying her more money, but they're under no obligation.

Back in the Day

Years ago, rewriters were normally hired for a guaranteed rewrite, set of revisions, and a polish; now they typically get just one guaranteed rewrite.

- **Compensation**—Just like with original specs, the WGA has established pay minimums for non-original screenplays, as well as rewrites and polishes, and all WGA-signatory studios and production companies must abide by these rules. Having said that, good agents, lawyers, and managers always try to get clients bumps in their quotes, so every new assignment, every new deal, is a new negotiation.

- **Increase in backend compensation**—Most screenwriters hired to write a film adaptation get a share of the film's backend. If the writer gets sole credit, he'll receive the traditional five percent; if he shares credit with another screenwriter, that percentage becomes reducible by half—or sometimes more, if credit is shared with additional writers. Even rewriters usually get to participate in a film's backend. However, if a screenplay goes through multiple drafts by multiple writers—which

TABLE 10.1A Minimum Prices for Screenplay Adaptations*

Minimum	Effective	Effective	Effective
Compensation	5/2/11–5/1/12	5/2/12–5/1/13	5/2/13–5/1/14
Non-original script, including treatment:	LOW/HIGH $55,910/$103,975	LOW/HIGH $56,888/$105,795	LOW/HIGH $58,026/$107,911
Non-original script,* excluding treatment *or* sale/purchase of non-original script:	LOW/HIGH $34,936/$71,899	LOW/HIGH $35,547/$73,157	LOW/HIGH $36,258/$74,620

TABLE 10.1B Minimum Rewrite or Polish Prices*

Minimum	Effective	Effective	Effective
Compensation	5/2/11–5/1/12 LOW/HIGH	5/2/12–5/1/13 LOW/HIGH	5/2/13–5/1/14 LOW/HIGH
Rewrite	$20,965/$31,961 LOW/HIGH	$21,332/$32,520 LOW/HIGH	$21,759/$33,170 LOW/HIGH
Polish	$10,489/$15,980	$10,673/$16,260	$10,886/$16,585

*Films budgeted under $5 million are considered "low budget"; films over $5 million are "high budget."

FEATURE AGENTS

Many rewriters receive *no* on-screen credit. This is because the WGA–*not* the studio–determines which writers get credit. And since the WGA often favors the original writer, a rewriter must do a significant amount of work–usually an entire page-one rewrite–to qualify for any screen credit at all.

Inside Info

"At the end of every project you get the final credit determination. I had writers on *Curious George*, and at the end . . . I got a list of the writers that had worked on *Curious George*. It was five pages long with probably ten names on each page! Some were drama writers, some were big animation writers. How do you determine who wrote that script?! And how much money do you think they spent on development?"–Ryan Saul, lit agent, APA

is not unusual–there may be a situation in which the studio feels they've already given out too much backend to earlier screenwriters, or creators of the source material, like a novelist or playwright, and they refuse to give away more.

- **Production bonus**–Writers of non-original scripts negotiate guaranteed compensation and contingent compensation much like a writer who sells a wholly original script. They get their guaranteed compensation just for writing the script and then, hopefully, a bonus if it goes into production.

  Writers hired for a rewrite, however, negotiate a bit differently. "When you're coming in to rewrite somebody else, it's assumed you're not going to get sole credit," says manager Jeff Thal of Ensemble Entertainment. After all, you're already not the script's "sole writer"–you're coming in behind someone else, so many rewriters get a "shared credit" bonus, usually about half the writer's regular production bonus. Often, a smart agent argues that because it's almost virtually impossible for someone hired to do a rewrite to get "sole credit," the rewriter should get his full bonus as long as he shares credit with *no one other than the original writer*. In other words, the writer will most likely have to share credit with the script's original writer . . . but as long as no one comes on after the rewriter, he still gets his full bonus. If other writers come on later, the rewriter is reduced to his "shared credit" bonus.

- **Last writer bonus**–Since rewriters seldom get screen credit, especially if there's been a long list of writers before them, agents sometimes negotiate a "last writer bonus." This is a bonus given if the writer is the *last* writer on a project, the writer who takes the ball into the end zone. That writer may not get screen credit, but at least they get some extra cash for delivering the draft that gets the project green-lit.

- **Box office and DVD bonuses**–If you can get them at all, box office and DVD bonuses for work-for-hire assignments are negotiated similarly to those for original script purchases.

- **Perks**–Assignment writers, especially rewriters, get fewer perks than writers who sell specs. If the project has cycled through many rewriters or polishers, for instance, the studio probably won't invite them all to the premiere unless they also have a screen credit. And unless you're being hired specifically to be an on-set writer, the studio probably won't foot the bill for any travel arrangements.

Unattached and Unpackaged

When a writer gets hired for an open writing assignment, whether a page-one rewrite or a quick polish, his managers don't usually get to attach themselves as producers. Managers only get to produce when they have generated or developed the bulk of the IP (which also means you're paying them commission on all your open writing assignments). Similarly, when a client gets hired for assignment work, agents don't commission ten percent of the producer's fee or take a two percent packaging fee from the budget.

The Deal Closes

Finally, the deal closes and the writer begins working. While much of the agent's job is done, he still needs to remain in the process. "You need to make sure your writer is not taken advantage of," says Verve agent Zach Carlisle. "[Writers] don't want to rock the boat and screw things up . . . that's our job. We're the ones who rock the boat. If your [client] turns in a draft you need to make sure the producer doesn't immediately come around and say, 'Here's a whole series of notes and you have to go do a whole other [draft].' [That's when we say,] 'If you want them to do more work . . . trigger the polish!' Pay more money!"

Ask the Managers

Q: I recently got hired for my first open writing assignment job—rewriting a low-budget thriller for a small indie production company. The draft is due next week but to be honest, I don't think I'm going to have it done. What happens if an assignment writer misses his deadline?

A: "The vast majority of the time: nothing," says manager/producer Aaron Kaplan of Kaplan/Perrone Entertainment. "You might have an angry studio exec or an angry producer, but very rarely does anything happen financially or contractually."

This doesn't mean, of course, that writers should simply ignore deadlines. "If you've got a problem, communicate it," says New Wave manager Michael Goldberg. "You might have eight weeks, but it might take ten weeks to crack a couple of problems. People are understanding. Theoretically, as you're doing open writing assignments, you should be talking to the producers, showing them half drafts. Don't go into a dark hole, because if you accidentally go in the wrong direction creatively, you're off the project and you might not get hired again in the future."

Part IV
Digital Media

11   Navigating a New World

Shilpi Roy needed to *make* something. She had spent over $100,000 to get through USC's graduate film program, and what did she have to show for it? *Nothing*–except a handful of three-year-old student films and some videos she'd edited for Playboy TV and Brave New Films. "The whole point of being a filmmaker is to make things," Roy says, and "I hadn't made anything in a long time."

Unfortunately, making films requires money, and Roy's online editing jobs weren't leaving her flush with cash. She wanted to make something of quality, but she needed to do it quickly and cheaply, which pretty much ruled out TV or features. "With a TV show, you have to get an agent or manager, you have to pitch it, somebody has to buy it, somebody has to put money behind it, and then *maybe* it'll get made and *maybe* it'll get on the air," Roy explains. So she settled on another idea. "With a web series, you can literally do all those things yourself, and it's guaranteed to have people see it, because you're the one putting it up."

Roy had recently moved to Silverlake, L.A.'s idiosyncratic hipster haven, and she hit on an idea for a serialized romantic comedy about two hipsters continually failing to make an emotional connection. This was something she figured she could do with very little time or energy. After all, her husband was a cinematographer who had much of his own equipment, and Roy could edit the series herself. For everything else, she'd call in favors and beg local businesses to let her shoot on location. How difficult could it be?

As it turned out, "it was as hard as doing a short film," says Roy, "and people say doing a short film is as hard to produce as a feature; features are just longer.

"[First of all], I was literally doing it all myself. I had to deal with all [the same] problems you do on any size film set. Just because it's a web series doesn't mean those things go away."

One big challenge was Roy's lack of budget. She was paying for the project entirely out of her own pocket, so she could only spend a few hundred dollars. She quickly realized, however, that she could make her work stronger by embracing her weaknesses and turning them into strengths. For instance, shooting on location meant she had to contend with ambient sound, and getting a good sound mixer, as well as an acceptable sound package, was going to cost at least a grand. So, she thought, *what if she eliminated all the dialogue*? Roy designed the show as a series of run-ins between "Cereal Guy" and "Faux Fur Girl," but neither was confident enough to confront the other. Instead, we'd hear only their inner monologues. "I saved myself at least $1,000 right there," says Roy, and it "meant I could shoot while locations were open and serving their customers."

But the challenges kept coming. "I had written myself eight locations, so I had to find eight different locations willing to let me shoot for free, or really cheap, and I had to work around their schedule. Then, I had to work [around] the actors' schedules– and my own, and my crew's–so it became this juggling thing. For episode one (which runs less than two minutes), I shot eight half-days; I couldn't ever get a full day of shooting because nobody was ever available!"

Roy persevered, and nearly ten months and $2,000 later, she began posting weekly episodes on YouTube and Blip. Her first episode pulled in 30,000 views, and after nine months, she had 200,000 views and 4,200 subscribers. Sure, these numbers were a fraction of the subscribers amassed by Internet celebrities like Shit Girls Say (175,00 subscribers) or MysteryGuitarMan (2.6 million subscribers). But Roy had made something people had *seen*. It would have been nearly impossible for her to amass 200,000 viewers in the traditional mediums of film or TV. More importantly, *Hipsterhood* was spotted by executives at Blip, who offered to finance a second season.

This, of course, is the power of digital media: giving new producers and content creators a stage to showcase work that would otherwise never be seen. While it's rare that something rises above the clutter of the Internet (aspiring actor Jonathan Nail pulled the plug on his nine-episode web series, *Solo*, after it pulled in only about 4,000 views per episode—and cost him $20,000[1]), some projects and creators *are* getting spotted—and not just online. Comedy Centrals *Broad City* is based on Abbi Jacobson and Ilana Glazer's web series of the same name.[2] In 2012, Disney XD developed a series for YouTube comedian Zach Fox, and ABC cast the singing Stella sisters, Lennon (thirteen) and Maisy (six), on *Nashville* after their videos went viral online.[3]

"Digital media is the future," says Roy. "The line between TV and the Internet is going to disappear. You'll still have your TV, and it'll be big and beautiful with surround sound, but you'll be able to watch whatever you want on it, whether it's *Hipsterhood* or *The Sopranos* or *True Blood*. You [will] find all those shows in the same space within three seconds of each other." Thus, as Hollywood finds more and more inspiration in "new media," agents have taken notice. Many agencies now have digital media departments, and there are even a few that specialize solely in the digital space. In some ways, these agents work just like traditional agents; in other ways, they work totally differently.

Digital media departments usually cover four distinct areas. Some agencies play in all four, some in just one or two, but the four main "sandboxes" where agents play are:

1. **Online entertainment** includes everything from web series like Felicia Day's *The Guild* to online channels and distribution outlets like the Cheezburger Network and Smosh. Agents working in this space mostly represent two kinds of clients.

   They help *individual content creators*—bloggers, comics, sketch artists, filmmakers, performers, etc.—make the leap from the digital world to film and television. In June, 2013, WME, for example, signed writer/comic Ray Williams Johnson, host of his own YouTube show, =3, which (as of May, 2013) had nearly 5 million subscribers and nearly 2 billion views. They then enlisted *Search Party*-writers Mike Gagerman and Andrew Waller, also WME clients, to develop a TV series based on Johnson's life and sold the project to FX.[4] But agents also help artists and creators working in traditional media make their way into the digital world, like in 2008, when WME helped Lisa Kudrow set up her web series, *Web Therapy*, at LStudio.com, an online portal owned by Lexus. (In an interesting twist, two years after the show's web debut, Showtime acquired the rights to adapt *Web Therapy* as an actual TV series, which premiered in 2011.[5])

   They represent *companies* needing guidance as they strategize how to create, distribute, market, promote, and monetize original online programming.

2. **Social media advisory services** help actors, writers, producers, directors, musicians, and even major companies and organizations like NPR[6] use social media to expand audiences, market projects, and generate income. In a way, this is similar to what publicists do—managing a specific area of a celebrity or company's public profile. Agents, however, don't accompany clients to PR events or pull press clippings. Instead, agents "sit with a client and talk strategically about how they can use platforms like Twitter or Foursquare or Reddit or Pintrist to grow and capitalize on a fan base," explains Brent Weinstein, head of UTA's digital

In 2006, UTA became the
first Hollywood agency to
launch a digital media
department. Four years later,
it became the first to start a
specialized social media
practice. Today, UTA remains
an industry leader in the
world of digital and online
representation.

media department. "Sometimes we'll do that in partnership with media companies in business with our client. If the client has a TV show coming out, we might be asked to contribute to the conversation with the network or the studio about how to market the show through social media. If they have a film coming out, sometimes the client will say 'Hey, UTA—can you sit at the table when we're having marketing conversations so I know people that have my back are part of the conversation about leveraging social media to get the word out about this film?'"

3. **Video games**—In 2012, according to market research firm DFC Intelligence, the burgeoning video game industry was worth $67 billion (this includes both software and hardware)—over $19 billion of which came from online games. Hollywood sold only $10.8 billion worth of movie tickets that same year. By 2017, DFC predicted, the entire gaming industry would be worth an estimated $82 billion![7] And all those games, whether online or purchased in boxes, must be developed and written by artists, engineers, developers, and writers—many of whom have agents. Thus, gaming has become one of the fastest-growing areas of business for talent and literary agencies across the country.

As of 2012, *World of
Warcraft*, the world's highest-
grossing video game, had
earned over $10 billion[8]—
more than the world's top six
highest-grossing movies
combined.[9] (Those movies
were *Avatar*, *Titanic*, *The
Avengers*, *Harry Potter and
the Deathly Hallows Part II*,
*Transformers: Dark of the
Moon*, and *The Lord of the
Rings: The Return of the
King*.)

4. **Corporate consulting**—Many agencies provide digital consulting services for large corporations and Fortune 500 companies. This could include anything from advising executives on the marketability of a Web site or mobile app to actually incubating a start-up. UTA, for example, reps video game maker Electronic Arts[10] and social media analysts Crimson Hexagon,[11] while CAA helped launch—and owns a stake in—comedy site Funny Or Die and mobile entertainment producer Creative Mobile Labs.[12]

In this chapter, we'll focus on the two areas where digital content creators and writers typically work: *online entertainment* and *video games*.

ONLINE ENTERTAINMENT

When people think of "online entertainment," many think of web series like Issa Rae's *The Misadventures of Awkward Black Girl* or Maple Blood Productions' *Divine*. Yet while there are some wonderful projects out there, selling shortform web series is not a big focus for agents—mainly because it generates so little money. In fact, online entertainment is mostly important to an agency not as a legitimate revenue stream (one Big Four agent even suggested digital media was the *least profitable department* of the entire agency), but for two other reasons:

1. **As a mechanism to identify and grow new talent.** The Internet can be a fantastic stage to showcase your work and transition to more lucrative platforms, as WME did with Ray Williams Johnson. The monetization of most online entertainment, however, is not about representing or selling "shows"; it's about building brands and communities around unique personalities like YouTube stars comic/impressionist Shane Dawson or comedian/blogger Jenna Marbles. For digital media agents and managers, this could mean anything from helping personalities promote content to actually matching them with paying sponsors or brand integration deals—like when rapper DeStorm shot the music video for "Tools" in Home Depot (a partnership arranged by his representatives at Big Frame).[13]

2. **As a value add for corporate clients and big-name stars.** While there may be little money in selling a web series, especially from an undiscovered or rising talent, celebrities occasionally have online passion projects. Ben Stiller's hilarious *Burning Love*, for instance, began as a Yahoo series before being picked up by E![14] For agencies, therefore, what these projects don't generate in dollars they make up for in good will for servicing high-end clients.

Agencies *do* stand to make a lot of money, fortunately, in other types of online deals, but these deals are often at much higher levels than simply selling content or arranging an artist's product integration deal. In 2012, for example, UTA helped writer/producer client Brian Robbins (*Smallville*, *So Random!*) launch Awesomeness TV, a YouTube channel aimed at teens and tweens.[15] Less than a year later, after becoming one of the fastest-growing channels in history, Awesomeness was purchased by Dreamworks Animation for a tidy $33 million (and by 2015, the channel's success could boost the deal's final price to $117 million).[16]

Let's look, then, at how the digital industry, still an untamed frontier with few rules or standards, operates . . . and how agents navigate their way through the wild.

The Structure of the Industry

Unlike the film and TV industries, which have been around for decades, the embryonic digital world doesn't yet have an established power structure. Or rather, its power structure changes and evolves on an almost daily basis. While a few years ago, there were no real buyers or distributors in the digital space, "there's now a wide range of places to shop different types of projects," says Kara Welker, a partner at Generate, a management/production company owned by Alloy Digital (Smosh, *Chocolate News*).

As untamed and amorphous as the digital landscape is, the marketplace can be divided into four tiers of buyers or distributors: **premium digital content platforms, general content platforms,** and **channels** and **vertical brands** or **multichannel networks**.

Premium digital content platforms, like Netflix, Amazon, Hulu, and XBox, have well-lined pockets that allow them to develop and acquire high-quality, full-length original content like Netflix's *Hemlock Grove* or Amazon's *Alpha House* and *Betas*. Hulu, for example, spent $50 million developing original web series for a summer 2012 launch. Out of that sizable investment came ten series, including *Spoilers* and *Up To Speed*, from feature directors Kevin Smith (*Clerks*) and Richard Linklater (*The School of Rock*), respectively.[17] As these buyers grow, agents and managers have even started including them when taking shows out to traditional buyers like CBS and MTV.

General content platforms like Funny Or Die, AOL, Blip, and Yahoo not only distribute user-generated videos, they've also begun investing in their own development and acquisitions. These companies usually "don't have the same types of budgets (as premium platforms), but they have great audience reach, followers, or subscribers," says Welker. Like television networks, general content platforms often make exclusive deals to distribute content funded by outside financiers. In July, 2012, for instance, Yahoo premiered *Electric City*, Tom Hanks's $2.5 million[18] animated series, funded by Yahoo and Reliance Big Entertainment, the feature company behind *Dinner For Schmucks* and *Fright Night*. Two months later, Yahoo debuted *CSI* creator Anthony Zuiker's $6 million[19] cybercrime series *Cybergeddon*, which was part of Dolphin Digital Media's $25-million development slate. Whereas many professional web series cost about $500,000, Dolphin—the production company that also bankrolled Facebook and Cambio's *Aim High* in 2011[20]— often spends $2 million to $5 million per series.[21]

While digital production companies and general content platforms may be increasing their development slates as well as their budgets, "one big difference between the television business and the digital landscape is the seasonality and consistency of the buying cycles," says Brent Weinstein. Broadcast and cable networks, after all, must keep acquiring and producing content in order to survive. In the digital world—not so much. "Whereas NBC's business will cease to exist if they don't buy shows, Yahoo's business won't. They still have a fantastic ad-supported business around a lot of their products and services, from mail to stocks to everything else. [So] if they do original programming—great. If they don't—you're not going to see the stock go to zero. That eliminates the sense of urgency that normally propels the traditional film and television business."

As a result, online distributors only acquire or produce content when it's exactly right. There's no need—like in television—to develop 100 projects in hopes of having ten air-able shows. General content platforms can develop whatever they want, whenever they want, ensuring they only focus on projects that fit specific and immediate needs or goals. Plus, those goals can change instantaneously, based on what a particular advertiser wants or an executive's sudden whim. (This doesn't mean online studios and distributors don't make or try things that don't move forward. In April, 2013, Amazon Originals placed its first batch of fourteen original pilots online for viewers to watch and vote on. One of the first to get axed was *Zombieland*, a series version of Rhett Reese's 2009 movie of the same name.[22])

Also unlike in television and film, different sites can develop totally different types of content. In TV, for example, various networks have different brands, but the *formats* remain the same. An hour-long drama is an hour-long drama, whether it's a light action series like USA's *Burn Notice* or a dark mystery like FOX's *The Following*. A news commentary show is a news commentary show, whether it's Fox News's *The O'Reilly Factor* or MSNBC's *Hardball with Chris Matthews*. Online, however, one general content platform might experiment with feature-length ideas, like YouTube's *Girl Walks Into a Bar*,[23] while another might try its hand at choose-your-own-adventure style film-making, like Land Rover's *Being Henry*.[24] A single company may even try many multiple approaches, offering audiences interactive games, feature-length movies, shortform series, and user-generated content. This constant free-for-all not only makes it hard for producers to sell content to online distributors, it makes it hard for agents and managers to track what various platforms want or are developing.

Welcome to the NewFronts

In April, 2012, six major online outlets—Yahoo, YouTube, AOL, Microsoft, Digitas, and Hulu—launched the "NewFronts," their answer to May's television Upfronts. Like TV's gala presentations, these companies wooed advertisers by presenting their new shows and content, like Yahoo's *Electric City* and *Cybergeddon*,[25] amidst performances by superstars like Jay-Z and and car giveaways by AOL CEO Tim Armstrong.[26] Advertisers responded, pouring hundreds of millions of dollars into these companies. The following year, the NewFronts expanded to include non-video content creators such as game company Zynga and online magazine publisher SpinMedia.

Channels, most of which live on YouTube, are content creators' home-pages, the central destination for viewers to access that producer's work. A channel can be customized aesthetically (you can change the background, the fonts, the colors, etc.) and features all videos uploaded by the user. The creator can also embed other users' videos, comments, etc., making it a social networking hub. Go to YouTube right now, you'll see a column recommending various channels based on your viewing habits. Right now, YouTube is suggesting I check out The Ricky Gervais Channel, BuzzFeed, and Sub Pop Records. If I click on Sub Pop, I see all the Sub Pop-created content, which is mostly music videos from Sub Pop bands.

Vertical brands (or "**verticals**"), sometimes called **multichannel networks** (or "**MCN**'s") are organizations that aggregate related channels at a single destination. Think of a vertical brand as a media conglomerate, just like Comcast or Viacom. Comcast owns NBC, USA, E!, Bravo, SyFy, etc.; Viacom owns MTV, VH1, Logo, CMT, Comedy Central, etc. A vertical's channels, however, are all user-generated; a single vertical could contain YouTube channels from a fifteen-year-old comedian in Bluewater, Arizona, a professional singer in Kuna, Idaho, and an armchair political pundit in Mississauga, Ontario. Most verticals have some kind of thematic or tonal unity. Revision3, for instance, is a MCN specializing in video game and tech-related content; its YouTube channels include Tekzilla (technology reviews and tips), GeekBeat.TV (teaching viewers to "upgrade your life"), and The Ben Heck Show (gadgetry how-to and inventions).

By being part of a multichannel network, content creators join similarly branded producers and channels, making their work easier to find. Producers aiming for geeks and fangirls, for example, may want to be part of Wonderly, which includes content from producers like Nerd In Translation, Squaresville, and Books And Quills. Producers trying to reach urban audiences may want to join Forefront, which features content from rapper DeStorm Power and hip-hop publicist Karen Civil.

Most multichannel networks also offer "infrastructure to allow or enable content creators to produce more, produce bigger, produce better, market better, [and] monetize better," says Dan Weinstein (no relation to UTA's Brent Weinstein), a founding partner of Collective Digital Studios. In other words, companies running MCN's often act a bit like a TV or film studio. Big Frame and Maker, for instance, supply their content creators with cameras, edit bays, even financing. Some even offer more traditional management services, guiding clients' careers and helping them book roles or jobs in television and other mediums.

The main difference, however, between typical managers and multichannel networks, is that a "manager represents a piece of talent and acts as the CEO of that talent," says Dan Weinstein, whose Collective Digital Studios formed as an offshoot of The Collective, a traditional Hollywood management firm. A manager "manages all the different aspects of that talent's business . . . from an advisory, 'bird's-eye' position. He works with the publicist [and] the agents, [liaising] everything, whereas a multichannel network has infrastructure to actually *execute* everything: a marketing team, a sales team, technology infrastructure, all that stuff." Thus, many homegrown content creators are eager to join MCN's in order to have creative and practical support and resources. In a moment, we'll discuss how multichannel networks market, sell, and monetize producers' content.

One important difference between premium digital content platforms, general content platforms, and multichannel networks: premium platforms charge for their content, usually through subscription fees. Thanks to the strength of its original series *House of Cards*, for instance, Netflix boasted more than 29 million subscribers, and revenue of more than $1 billion, in the first quarter of 2013 alone.[27] In 2012, on the other hand, Funny Or Die, which allows users to watch videos for free but makes money via branded content and corporate sponsorships, was projected to pull in less than $50 million for *the entire year*. Thus, many distributors are still working hard to figure out exactly how to monetize digital content.

Also, while these three tiers seem to organize the industry nicely—much like television's organization of networks, studios, and production companies—it's important to note that these categories, and the organizations within them, are constantly shifting and redefining themselves.

Are Multichannel Networks Worth Joining?

"If you are going to join a MCN," says Blip.com's Kent Nichols, "think hard and long about what values they are actually providing you. What are the perceived advantages, the things they're telling you the advantages are, and what's actually in the contract? A lot of times those things do not match up. When I was a creator looking at these contracts (Nichols also created 2005's seminal web series *Ask a Ninja*), the only thing I really cared about was promotion, and most of the time, promotion was not written into those contracts, although they paid lip service to it. To me, it's much more about: are they delivering what they are [promising]? Are they giving you more money than you would be making [without them]? It's the same sort of analysis about any representation in Hollywood. Is this person [earning] their fee, plus? Sometimes the answer is yes, sometimes the answer is no, [but] you need to start thinking about that in a deeper way."

What Makes Great Web Content?

The Internet is not only a different distribution method than film or television, it's an entirely different artistic medium. Just as TV stories work differently than stories in novels or plays, and films, online material works differently than TV and movies. So if you're going to make something for the web, it should be something made specifically for the web's special canvas. "We've seen a lot of examples of 'this didn't work on TV, throw it on the web,'" says Sarah Penna, who founded Big Frame, a MCN/management firm. "Well, guess what? That doesn't work all the time. There are outliers and exceptions, of course, but . . . most of the time it doesn't [work]."

What, then, makes a digital idea unique? What makes successful online entertainment different than entertainment on TV or in a movie theater? According to Penna, it's "the interaction with the audience, and I'm not talking about an interactive series where the audience votes on things—I think that's kind of a gimmick, a layer on top of what makes great digital content. We have this content creator, Tyler Oakley, who's constantly talking to his fans. He's on Instagram, he has a big Tumblr, he's providing them with entertaining content multiple times a day, he does meet-ups—he does Skype calls with his fans. It makes total sense for someone like that to be online because that's where their audience spends their time."

Dan Weinstein illustrates it this way: "When a normal, everyday person runs into a celebrity on the street, there are three scenarios: if they run into George Clooney or Brad Pitt, they whisper to themselves, 'Oh my god, that's George Clooney!' and they let him be because he's almost unattainable. When [people] run into their favorite TV star, it's more like, 'Hey that's the person from [some TV show]—maybe I should go say hi! Should I ask her for a picture?' because that person is in their home every week, on television, in more of an intimate setting. She seems more accessible than a George Clooney. [But] when one of these web stars—and I've been around many of them—walks down the street and one of their fans picks them out, they walk up and say, 'Hey, remember me?!' like they know the person! 'You responded to my comment on your video, you know who I am!' It's because they're watching that content on their laptop, proactively, in their bedroom, in the privacy of their own home. The person is often talking directly to camera; they're engaging, asking for feedback, responding. It's a much more intimate relationship. Bottling that, or producing with that in mind, is what makes great web content. It's got to engage, be a two-way conversation, and there needs to be a reason to use the platform, because everybody who has tried to repurpose television content for the web has mediocre to poor results."

This is why many of the biggest Internet stars aren't people who were already celebrities—rapper/impressionist Alphacat, comic vlogger Daily Grace, comedian/host Kassem G, *My Drunk Kitchen*'s Hannah Hart. The very notion of "celebrity" suggests or encourages a certain aloofness, and while aloofness may work in the less intimate mediums of film and television, it's suicide in the digital world. "You have to really talk to the audience," says Penna, "and they have to *believe*. We throw this word around a lot: authenticity. That's really at the core of it. Things that get bubbled up on Reddit or Mashable or Huffington Post have this homegrown authentic feel. If the audience feels like your duping them, or there's a big company behind [a piece of content], it's less appealing then some kids doing this on their own. It doesn't get more authentic than [a] cell phone video [of] a corgi playing with a spoon. Even the very high quality content—*The Lizzie Bennet Diaries*, *Squaresville*, Freddie Wong, Mystery Guitar Man, DeStorm—some of our content creators shoot on the Red. They have editors. They have a team. Writers. [But] it still feels authentic . . . it's still a personality kids can idolize and mimic."

How Agents Find and Sign New Clients

Big agencies don't necessarily hunt aggressively for digital writers, performers, or artists working solely in the digital space. First of all, the bread-and-butter of big agencies' digital departments is *not* selling original content; it's working with corporate clients who have specific digital agendas. Second, because there's so little money in creating original web content, agents need to believe a digital content creator has significant crossover ability to traditional media. When UTA signed Justine "iJustine" Ezarik in 2013,[28] for example, her five YouTube channels not only had more than 430 million views, she had acted in *Criminal Minds*, *Law and Order: SVU*, and *The Vampire Diaries*. She also had on-camera hosting experience and voiced "Passion Fruit" in the Cartoon Network's *The High Fructose Adventures of Annoying Orange*. In fact, digital agents often consult their film and TV departments before signing a new client. Signing iJustine wasn't just about capitalizing on her enormous online success, it was about expanding her brand and presence into other more lucrative mediums.

"There are lots of things we see online that are interesting," says UTA's Brent Weinstein, "but maybe we don't think the person has what they would need to have a long career. Even though something has millions of views or fans, [it may not have] the right voice or foundation for us to build a career on the back of it. [Signing a client] is not about any particular metric, it's just about that gut feeling of 'Wow, this person's unbelievably talented.'"

Most digital agents find new clients by referrals, just like film, TV, and music agents. Some clients come via managers or lawyers; others come via platforms or publishers who call to say, "Hey, we've been working with this fantastic writer—we think she could probably benefit from having an agent."

In fact, "if they're not coming to us through those channels," Brent Weinstein says, "we're not sure how seriously we should take it. Now, sometimes we'll find someone before they have a chance to come to us, but if we're receiving a lot of unsolicited

---

How Do Digital Media Agents Get Paid for Selling Online Entertainment?

Just as there are few rules to creating digital content, there are few rules determining how digital agents get paid. Digital agents usually take a ten percent commission, just like with regular film or TV agents. Agents take this commission off anything the artist or performer makes—AdSense income, hosting fees, sponsorships, product integration partnerships, development deals. Digital managers, also commission, but since some managers, like Big Frame, also double as MCN's, commissions can range, depending on what services the manager's providing, from ten to fifty percent. Corporate clients, meanwhile, often pay flat fees or retainers, sometimes even paying in stock shares or options.

The Collective, a management firm which was founded in 2005 and quickly joined UTA as a pioneer in the world of digital representation, doesn't commission some clients at all. Rather, the Collective produces or co-produces clients' work, in exchange for retaining ownership if the property sells to a larger distributor. For example, when the Collective signed online creator Dane Boedigheimer in the spring of 2010, Boedigheimer's self-produced web series *Annoying Orange* had been viewed approximately 100 million times in its first six months of existence.[29] The Collective took the series to Cartoon Network, offering to deficit finance a TV version in exchange for owning the property (just the TV version, not the original web series).[30] Cartoon Network agreed, and the Collective paired Boedigheimer with Emmy-winning client Tom Sheppard (*Pinky and the Brain*), who wrote the six-episode series. The show premiered in June, 2012, as Cartoon Network's number-one Monday night show among boys, prompting an order for additional episodes.[31] While *Annoying Orange* was already earning Boedigheimer a comfortable living online, the real value—for the Collective—was participating in ownership of *Annoying Orange's* TV show and any ancillary products, such as toys from The Bridge Direct and clothes or accessories from Hybrid Apparel and Accessory Innovations.[32]

emails from people who have clearly been trolling for agents and managers for the past five years, those are the things we tend to put in the discard pile."

Many digital representatives are also accessible online, much more so than their traditional media counterparts. Companies such as Big Frame and Collective Digital Studios, which are multichannel networks as well as management companies, can be emailed directly over their websites. "Somebody will look at your content, evaluate it, and make a determination," says Collective Digital Studios' Dan Weinstein. "We tend not to turn people away. It's not a game like the agencies play. We want more creators. They may not be at a place today where we are 'all hands on deck,' turning it into the next *Annoying Orange*, but they may be tomorrow. Conversely, we have a team of seven to ten people combing the Internet for creators and content, reaching out proactively."

Ask the Producer

Q: I spent four years in Los Angeles trying to get an agent so I could start a career as a TV and film producer. It never happened. I signed with a couple managers, but it was a terrible experience. Now, I've moved back to Oklahoma, and while I'm obviously far from Hollywood, I'd still like to create stuff, put it online, and hopefully have a career. As an online producer, do I still need an agent or manager?

A: "Absolutely not," says *Hipsterhood* producer Shilpi Roy. "For TV and film, you have to have an agent or manager to get anywhere. In the world of digital media, you can totally do it by yourself, it just takes a little more work and effort. [The truth is,] a lot of agents and managers don't understand the space very well yet; they don't know how to move in it."

The one place an agent or manager *can* come in handy, however, is in arranging for brand deals and sponsorship. "If brand sponsorship is vital to your show," says Roy, "then yes—you're going to need help with that." It doesn't necessarily need to be an agent or manager, however. Many online distributors and MCN's, like Big Frame or Blip, shop their producers' work in hopes of finding advertiser partners. "Blip is doing that for me," Roy says.

MONETIZING ORIGINAL CONTENT ONLINE

While smart creators and representatives alike are always experimenting and inventing new ways of capitalizing on content, agents and managers typically have two basic ways of selling clients' product: selling an idea to one of the premium digital or general content platforms, which often follows a more "traditional" TV-like path, or monetizing homegrown content, which involves utilizing the benefits and resources of a MCN.

Monetizing Content Method 1: The TV-ish Path: Selling to Premium or General Content Platforms

As in both film and TV, the first step when developing an online project is to bounce the idea off your representation. This is especially important for writers or producers who work regularly in other mediums; since producing a web series often requires a huge amount of time and energy—usually on a shoestring budget—it helps to have agents weigh in on a project's commercial viability. "There are lots of reasons why a successful television writer may want to experiment in digital," says Brent Weinstein, "but it shouldn't be driven by the expectation they're going to make a lot of money, because even in success—they likely won't, at least not today, and relative to their earning power in traditional media. [Maybe] there's an idea they just want to see made, a passion project they want to get out of their system, someone they've always wanted to collaborate with and they don't feel it's possible in the traditional system. [Maybe] they [are afraid] this idea they have will die in development if they take it through the typical TV process. If Lisa Kudrow had pitched *Web Therapy* directly to Showtime—maybe it gets made, maybe it doesn't–[but] doing it digitally and seeing it moved to Showtime was probably incredibly rewarding for her and the people who surround her. But again, the economics are changing and it won't be long before the earning potential in digital is similar to that of traditional media."

Once you and your agents agree on a seaworthy project, your agents may ask you to write a short proposal or put together a formal presentation. This may include a treatment, video, animation—whatever they can send to prospective buyers. "In digital media, as opposed to traditional media, buyers often like to get material to review," Brent Weinstein explains. "It's not a 'meeting culture,' so having materials you can send on is smart. Now, I prefer to have the client in the room to pitch—especially if we're talking about film or television—but I also don't want to waste the client's time, so if I can send the synopsis of a web series to a potential buyer and get that buyer's gut-check as to whether or not they're interested, I can potentially save my client a lot of time."

Online buyers and producers also look for projects with "star power," says Rich Hull, film producer and CEO of Latin Anywhere, America's top digital distributor of Spanish language film. "If you can come in with a James Franco, who will come in for free because he's your roommate, that's going to move you to the top of the stack. Beyond that, they look for anything that might have an existing following or brand." Indeed, in April, 2013, AOL unveiled a slate of fifteen original shows, twelve of which had some kind of major celebrity involvement. Celebs starring in and producing shows included Gwyneth Paltrow, Rocco DiSpirito, Sarah Jessica Parker, Jonathan Adler, Nicole Richie, Hank Azaria, Anthony Anderson, and NASCAR driver Dylan Kwasniewsk.[33] Similarly, Yahoo announced six new shows, boasting talent such as Cheryl Hines, John Stamos, Ed Helms, Rachael Harris, and brands like Conde Nast, WWE, CNBC, and ABC News.[34]

Some buyers, unfortunately, don't accept new proposals at all, choosing instead to back projects that are already up and running. Blip, for instance, funds and supports shows on its platform (like Roy's *Hipsterhood*), but only once the projects have attracted a certain level of attention. "We're very selective about what projects we allow onto our platform," says Kent Nichols, Blip's Director of Creator and Talent Relations. "We track those new shows and try to promote them. If they respond to promotion, we try to promote them even more. Then if we fall in love, as we did with *Hipsterhood*, we see if there are additional steps we can take to [help] more production happen. *Hipsterhood* is a delightful little series, but just looking at the specs on paper, even watching a video or two, we would not have been like, 'Oh, of course we have to pick this up.' It was only after we saw how the first season performed, [and] were impressed with Shilpi's organization and attitude, [that we said], 'This is a special filmmaker with a project that's resonating with promotion. There has to be a way for us to make sure we can see season two.'"

Different buyers have different processes for developing or producing projects. Some, when they find a project they like, have a fairly TV or film-like process with various developmental steps: treatment, script, pilot, etc. Other buyers can't afford to develop, so they only acquire projects they intend to make. All those differences make it hard for agents to track who wants what, and this is compounded by the fact that "the buyers change," says Hull. "In movies and TV, the buyers are fairly established, whereas in digital media, the buyers change every day. There's a new company here, they go out of business. There's a new company there, they go out of business. It's constant revolution."

Similarly, there are no industry-standard contracts or deals in the chaotic, unregulated, non-unionized world of digital media. Some contracts work like traditional TV or film deals, with writers receiving an agreed-upon paycheck, plus a share of the project's backend or ad revenue. Other times, buyers simply negotiate a purchase price or budget for the overall show. The writer/producer then has this lump sum with which to produce the project. If the project goes over budget, the writer/producer is responsible. If the project comes in under budget, the writer/producer can pocket the leftovers.

No Packages

Because the needs and interests of online buyers change so frequently, it's often tough to package projects in the online world. Usually, if any kind of "package" is going to happen, it begins with an agent submitting a packaged project to a general content platform like Yahoo or AOL; that buyer then says, "We like it—let's talk about casting possibilities." The buyer can then contribute it's two cents worth—as opposed to having to accept or reject a pre-packaged project.

Negotiating a Deal in Digital Media

While there are no standard contracts in digital media, and crafty artists, representatives, and platforms are constantly devising news ways of partnering, buying, or selling material, here are some of the most common issues hammered out in digital media contracts:

- **Ownership**—Who will ultimately own this piece of IP, the creator or the buyer? This is an important question, as the hope of many digital creators and distributors is to help the project make the leap to film or television. This is where there are much bigger paydays, so both the creator and the distributor want to own or control the property.
- **Compensation**—Payment often works differently in the digital world, where instead of negotiating fees *within* a budget, buyers often give producers one lump sum and let him decide how to budget the money. If the producer spends the entire chunk of change on production values, he takes home nothing. If he keeps the money and puts *none* of it into the production, he'll have a lackluster show and never get hired again. (And remember, budgets could range from less than $3,000 into the hundreds of thousands or even millions.) Also, buyers sometimes agree to pay the creator a higher fee or bigger budget in exchange for ownership of the property. Other times, they pay less money but let the artist retain ownership. You either get high "money and sell the IP, or low to no money, and you get control of your IP," says Nichols. "Too often, [artists and agents] want high money *and* complete control of the IP, and [they] can't have everything. You have to make it attractive to the buyers in some way or another . . . either through a lower upfront fee in exchange for keeping more control, or throwing off total control and [getting] a higher dollar amount."
- **Number of episodes**—How much content is the buyer getting? Enough to release an episode each week? Is the project a one-off sketch that needs enough star power to capture millions of eyeballs? How many episodes the producer makes, or expects to make, determines what the platform is willing to pay, as well as any promotional or marketing strategies.
- **Length of episodes**—Many buyers want to make sure they're getting webisodes with Internet-friendly running times, although different audiences have different attention spans. "I made *Hipsterhood* specifically to be two minutes long," says Roy. "If you asked me, 'why didn't you just make a TV show?' two-minute voice-over sections—that's just not going to work in a TV show. But on the web it works well—a little vignette, you watch in between reading emails. Just think about somebody sitting at their computer, watching your content. What do you want them to be going as they're watching? Have that in the back of your mind."
- **Deadlines**—When is the project due? This is obviously important so the platform can sufficiently promote the work and generate an audience.
- **Where will the content live?**—Will the content ultimately live on the distributor's home platform? On YouTube? On the creator's website? On all of these? Everyone wants to know this, as audiences will often be driven back to this particular site.
- **Distribution Windows**—Online content creators frequently want to distribute their material to as many sites and platforms as possible, allowing them to reach the widest audience. Platforms, on the other hand, want to be a projects' *exclusive* distributor, so all traffic is driven to their own site. Thus, agents negotiate distribution *windows*, or time frames. Each episode, for example, could premiere on Vimeo, then move to YouTube after a week.
- **Promotion**—Promoting a project is essential to helping something transcend the clutter of the Internet and actually find an audience. Thus, agents and buyers may try to negotiate various promotional commitments, like how much money the platform must spend on promotion, or assigning the artist himself special promotional responsibilities, like certain social media duties.

How Much Commission do Reps Deserve?

"A lot of time [agents or managers] feel they're owed compensation for the [project's] entire budget," says one producer, "because they feel that's what they negotiated. But shouldn't they really be getting paid on a slice of the talent's fee itself? [Plus,] there's so little money, giving ten percent to an agency, ten percent to a manager, and a lawyer's fee—all that really starts cutting into the ability to get anyone paid. It's a conundrum . . . because [agents] help get fees raised and help raise our budgets. But since we're starting at such a low budget level, having all the machinery really starts to bog down the process."

Web budgets vary wildly. Depending on the buyer and producer, one six-episode series of five-minute episodes could cost $100,000, another could cost $1 million.[35] One executive told me of paying creators $3,000 to make a single one-off sketch, whereas nine episodes of Rocket Jump Studios' *Video Game High School* cost $636,010.71, and Bryan Singer's 48-episode *H* cost over $1 million.[36, 37]

Back to the . . . Past?

While some say "branded entertainment" is the future of advertising, "it's actually going backwards," says TV and digital media writer Jordana Arkin. "That's how they did *The Milton Berle Show* and *Caesar's Hour*—all those things were sponsored by advertisers. That's the past!"

Staffing in the Online World

Unlike in traditional media, there are very few staffing or assignment opportunities in the digital world. First of all, cyberspace doesn't have a staffing season like the broadcast networks, so there's not a singular window of time when employers look to hire. And since companies can produce whatever they want, whenever they want, with no pressure to generate content, there's no ongoing stream of possibilities for agents to track and monitor. Plus, with online content so hard to monetize, producers rarely have the cash to pay entire staffs. Many content creators are one-man teams, writing, filming, and editing all their material themselves. In the infrequent cases where someone *does* sell a project or get funding, the money is usually so small the buyer or financier expects the seller, the producer, to be a solo operator. Thus, if you *are* going to make money writing or producing digital content, it's probably going to be by selling original material, not staffing on an existing project. *Having said that . . .*

The one time writers and producers *are* sometimes able to get hired onto a project is in the case of **branded entertainment**, advertiser-funded content designed to engage audiences while promoting a product or service. Perrier's interactive movie "*The Secret Place*," for example, allows users to become one of several characters invited to a mysterious Parisian party where they must find "The Golden Woman" and the "Secret Bottle."[38] Google's complex mobile game "Ingress" invites players to unravel a *Matrix*-like conspiracy via their Android phones.

When creating these campaigns and projects, advertisers often partner with traditional media producers, like movie studios or production companies, who understand how to write and produce stories. And how do companies often find these writers and producers? Through agencies. Some companies, like Mattel (repped at CAA[39]), have agency representation for exactly this purpose—agencies can connect them with Hollywood producers and filmmakers. Other advertisers partner first with a studio or production company, then use that organization's contacts to find writers.

A few years ago, my agent got me a job with Fox TV Studios, developing an online series for Jose Cuervo about young people throwing parties in their New York apartment. Although no Jose Cuervo products were mentioned in any of the stories, the goal was simply to create a cool atmosphere in which Cuervo drinks could organically exist. That same year, I was hired by Warner Bros. to write on the staff of "Wig Out," an online sitcom sponsored by Unilever and set in a beauty salon. Unfortunately, neither "Wig Out" nor the Cuervo project ever saw the light of day. (We actually shot a full twenty episodes of "Wig Out" before Unilever switched gears and canceled the whole campaign.) Instances like these are the rare occasions when you may be able to "staff," or get hired onto a project. Since many of these projects spring not from production companies but from corporate advertisers, however, finding them often takes connections not to Hollywood, but to Madison Avenue—or at least an agency that has a strong corporate division.

How Do I Pitch an Online Spinoff

Q: I'm a huge fan of *Revolution* on NBC and have a fantastic idea for a web series spinoff. How could I find an agent to help me pitch this?

A: Unfortunately, you probably can't. Most online spinoffs are written by the original show's writing staff or other people in the production office. *Psych*'s Emmy-nominated "Hashtag Killer" series, for example, was written by writers assistant Brittany Hilgers Hollenbrau.[40] *The Office*'s "Girl Next Door" was written by assistants Kelly Hannon, Mary Wall, and Jonathan Hughes. If you're interested in writing online spinoffs of current shows—which, by the way, can be a great opportunity to collaborate with working writers and get your work seen—the best avenue is to join the staff or crew of a show and ask for the opportunity.

Monetizing Content Method 2: Representing and Selling Homegrown Content

In terms of programming and monetizing online content, the Internet is still very much the "Wild West." Producers and distributors alike are experimenting not only with the web as an artistic medium, but with the web's business models as well. Revenue from online advertising is quickly growing—in 2012, advertisers spent $36.6 billion on online and mobile ads,[41] (a healthy eighteen percent increase from 2011's $31 billion,[42] if still only half of the $72.1 billion spent on television)—but little of that money has trickled down to artists and content creators. In *Hipsterhood*'s first nine months online, for example, Roy turned a profit of only $600.

"There's money flowing into production," says Hull, "but ad rates are still so low compared to television it's difficult to break even on that production spend. It's still pennies compared to the dollars of traditional distribution, and it's spread out over so many eyeballs that it's tough for content creators to make any money. Even YouTube takes almost half of every ad that runs on YouTube. It's hard for content owners to make any money when their ads are only generating pennies per click, if that, and YouTube's taking half right off the top."

Speed vs. Quality?

While it's tough for any producer to make big money online, some content creators have a tougher time than others, depending on what kind of work they produce. "There's low quality content that has really high volume [and can be made] fast and cheap," says *Hipsterhood* creator Shilpi Roy. "Those people can crank out content like there's no tomorrow. When you're cranking out content, it's just not going to be as good . . . [but] those people do see some of that [advertiser] money because that's what companies are looking for: engagement, view count, how long is somebody watching your video on your website, interacting with you or whatever brand is there? For people going for quality . . . those people, at least in the beginning, are not getting as much money, because there's going to be a limited number of episodes, you're going to take your time [creating] it. You can't create the [same] kind of engagement you can when you're cranking out content."

For years, digital distributors have tried various methods of monetizing product. Many use advertising models. Some try subscription models. Yet even when one of these seems successful, it unleashes a host of other challenges. Do ads work best when integrated directly into the content? Do they work best as pre-roll ads, appearing on-screen before the video begins playing? Should they be post-roll? Text-based ads layered over the content itself? "We're still experimenting," says Hull, "and that's what the 'Wild West' part of it is. We know what works in television; it's tried and true, we've [been doing] it the same way for the last fifty years. But we're constantly evolving the business model in the digital universe."

The television analogy is apt, especially because "people compare this time to the cable revolution," says Penna. "The monetization wasn't there at the beginning either."

Part of the reason the Internet has grown up as such a lawless frontier is that it created "an era of disintermediation where an artist, or a piece of content, did not have to go through a traditional third-party gatekeeper like a movie studio, record label, or network to reach an audience," says Dan Weinstein. Digital agents, managers, and distributors then realized that if they could "enable [a] creator to build their audience, aggregate a big enough community, there was a tremendous amount of value to be extracted from that one-to-one relationship. We didn't know how it was going to manifest itself at the time, but that was the theory."

Verticals have become one of the most popular and effective ways for content creators to maximize their earning potential. In exchange for offering promotional, financial or practical support to channels, MCN's "represent distribution rights of the content creators that are in our 'system,' or network," says Dan Weinstein. "We represent the rights to monetize that content, we represent the rights to distribute that content."

Thus, the job of a MCN—or a manager representing a creator or artist that may work with a MCN—is to figure out how to successfully monetize content or brands living in a space that doesn't offer traditional monetization. In fact, many MCN's also act as de facto managers, and many managers operate MCN's with their own practical, production, and financial resources. The Collective, for example, has both a management division and its own MCN, Collective Digital Studio, which has a sales force of twenty-five people in New York, Chicago, Detroit, Los Angeles, and San Francisco. Similarly, places like Big Frame and Generate have relationships with new media distributors like Hulu, Amazon, and Yahoo—buyers most agents and managers don't even bother to know. A traditional "manager or agent . . . is a servicer, but does not have that infrastructure [or] those relationships," says Dan Weinstein.

A multichannel network's job is also to figure out what "success" means—and the definition is often different for each creator, artist, or channel. As of May, 2013, for example, filmmaker and YouTube personality Freddie Wong had over 5.5 million YouTube subscribers. Wong's material was also garnering about 30 million views per month, a number rivaling viewership of TV shows like History Channel's *Vikings* and USA's *WWE Monday Night Raw*.[43] So Wong and his managers at the Collective found themselves asking, "How do we leverage that one-on-one relationship (between creator and audience) to create value?" says Dan Weinstein. "There are a lot of ways to do that: create bigger content, merchandise, ad sales, sponsorships, all that sort of stuff."

With Boedigheimer's *Annoying Orange*, the Collective had recognized they had a property that was scoring with boys ages six to fourteen, so they took the show to another platform that was aiming for the same audience: Cartoon Network. The move paid off. But Wong was not an animated fruit; he was a living, breathing filmmaker who not only produced content, he made himself accessible to fans and followers. Because Wong had an especially strong and "personal" relationship with his audience, the kind of relationship that can't be transferred to television, the Collective decided to take an even bigger gamble. They decided to help raise the cash to produce *Video Game High School*, a longform web series. Wong and the Collective knew they were wading into murky waters; scripted web series don't have a strong tradition of success. But they raised $273,276 via Kickstarter, plus more than $350,000 through other avenues, like sponsorships with Monster energy drink and Evike.[44] Two months after the series premiered, in May, 2012, it had been viewed over 30 million times, and it was soon licensed to Netflix and iTunes and sold internationally.[45]

One of the most important things good digital managers seem to understand is that what sells online is totally different than what sells in film or television. Unlike traditional lit agents and managers, "we mostly deal with personalities who make content on a consistent basis," says Penna. "Our model with the personalities is creating weekly, if not daily, content. Frankly, I do not know how you monetize an eight-episode web series unless you get a brand attached to it."

When a content creator signs with a multichannel network, the first thing he does is terminate his partnership with YouTube or Google; he is now a partner of the MCN, which signs him into the company's **Content Management System** (**CMS**). This allows the network's execs or managers to publish the creator's content via YouTube or Blip, attach ads, etc. A digital manager or MCN may also begin introducing the client to other content-creators in the network, allowing them to collaborate on projects, cross over into each other's work, or otherwise promote one another. "If I have 100,000 subscribers and you have 10,000, but I really like your content, I'll say, 'Come on my channel and I'll promote you,'" says Penna. "Maybe we go to lunch and I vlog our lunch. [Maybe] I'm a singer, you're a singer–why don't we do a song together? There are a million different ways to do it."

That's "the best kind of cross promotion there is," agrees Roy, "so different audiences can be introduced to each other. Having said that, it's not like you put it on the network and you're done. You still have to be constantly promoting it yourself."

Beyond basic promotion, managers evaluate each content creator or digital channel on a case-by-case basis, strategizing how best to grow and monetize it. The evaluation "is some version of cost, scale of audience, and quality of content," says Dan Weinstein. "If the cost is low, the content quality is great, and the audience is there–it's a no-brainer. If the cost is high, the audience is high, and the quality is low–maybe less so. It's some version of that algorithm that makes sense–but ultimately it's a gut [feeling]. It's like traditional A&R: do we like it? Do we think it has potential as IP in and of itself? [Other] things we look at are: scale of audience; is the content really resonating and engaging, or is it sort of passive? Are people actually responding to it and interacting with it, or is it just blanket views? Is it growing? Month to month are we getting more viewers, are we getting less viewers, or has it plateaued? What is the cost? What is the audience? Is it meant for very specific males who have had their left-arm amputated, are thirty-six years old, and live in Washington? [If so,] the marketplace is probably not that big. But if it's right down the middle: boys and girls, eighteen to twenty-four, Millennials, comedy–[there's a] bigger opportunity. There are a lot of determining factors, but it's certainly not a science."

Once managers or MCN execs have evaluated and analyzed a content creator's marketability, the question they ask themselves is: *what do we do with this?* There are few well-paved paths through the untamed digital wilderness; each content-creator is a new riddle to be solved in a creative way. A few, like *Annoying Orange* and *The Young Turks*, hop to television. Some, like Rebecca Borucki, whose inspirational fitness videos have racked up more than 13 million views and 72,000 YouTube subscribers, sign spokesperson or product integration deals (Borucki is a "brand ambassador" for Delta Labs).[46] Others, like hip-hop musician Macklemore–who rocketed up *Billboard's* Hot 100 Chart as his music video for "Thrift Shop" received more than 310 million YouTube views–use the Web as a stage to attract the attention of more traditional buyers. Many use a combination of strategies; Rocket Jump and Collective Digital Studios, for instance, did brand integration deals to help pay for *Video Game High School*, then re-edited the web series into a two-hour feature film to sell to Netflix and iTunes. The beauty, and the challenge, of the Internet is its relative lack of order, making things that would be impossible in traditional media totally do-able–as long as you have the right clever approach.

The Collective used a clever approach after signing Lucas Cruikshank, creator of YouTube character "Fred Figglehorn," whose YouTube channel became the first to amass more than one million subscribers.[47] "A traditional manager would have walked [Cruikshank] in as an actor to Nickelodeon and said, 'I've got this really talented kid. He's created this rabid following online; he's got this character. Let's develop something together!'" says Dan Weinstein. "Nickelodeon would have had seven meetings over the course of four months … and three years later, maybe something would have happened. But the one thing, for sure, would have been that Lucas, the performer, would have gotten treated as just that: a performer, a work-for-hire actor, even if they developed this character he created. He might have gotten a better deal than someone fresh off the boat, but Nickelodeon would own the whole thing. [So] we decided, 'Look, we know the guy has an audience. We know there's value there. What's the bigger thing to do?' So we financed and produced a movie! We didn't know what we were going to do with it. We didn't know if we were going to take it theatrically or TV or if we were going to sell a DVD. Ultimately, we ended up licensing it to Nickelodeon.

We own 100 percent of it with Lucas, the creator, and it blew up. We've got three movies and thirty episodes of television, all of which Lucas owns and controls with us, and [he] has made a tremendous amount of money on. So those are the things we're more interested in. If you're a performer and you have an audience, you have more leverage than you've ever had before. There are better ways to exploit [your work] than going to be a host on an MTV show or something like that. Not to say those aren't viable options for some people, but we're less focused on that and more focused on how we can create bigger, better, more—and exploit and leverage the audience that's been created."

Because there are few established paths to success, cyberspace is a world many traditional agents and managers don't like playing in. They don't understand it, they can't make enough money in it, and they lack the resources, knowledge, and experiences to properly service clients. "These massive agencies—they get $30,000 from a commission, [and it] doesn't mean anything—that's a drop in the bucket for them," says Big Frame's Penna, "which is why they've struggled, frankly, to try to figure out what their digital strategy is."

While the Internet's entrepreneurialism and uncertainty can be exciting for content producers, it's also what makes it a tough world for traditional agents and managers. Even representatives working solely in the digital space are trying to figure out what everything means, what has value, how the landscape is best navigated. "There's a lot more gray area in this space in terms of what value a manager is really adding," says Penna, who sometimes shares clients with traditional agents. As Big Frame works on building a client's business online, the agent peddles them for jobs and opportunities in old-school media. "A combination of a Big Frame and a WME can be really powerful. We share a client and we're working on growing their audience, bringing in brand deals, setting up collaborations. Those are not scalable things an agency would want to do, but we do enter into a typical management/agency relationship with them, and that combination can be powerful. This particular client just got sent on a commercial shoot and we just hooked them up with a brand deal for their YouTube channel. So we're generating multiple revenue streams, and . . . the agency sees a check, albeit a small one, come in every month for that client, [and] they can say, 'Okay, this fits into the grid of our understanding of what a client is.' If you can't capture a monthly revenue I think its hard for them to wrap their heads around it."

The good news is: representation is rarely a necessity in the digital realm. Regardless of your goals or focus, online entertainment is opening up business and storytelling possibilities that never before existed. Sure, much of the industry is still in its salad days, with writers struggling to figure out where and how they fit in, but it's a time of enormous promise and opportunity. Whether your passion is writing serialized web series or first-person shooters, "don't focus on the economics," says Brent Weinstein. "Focus on the creative opportunity. There are no limitations, no gatekeepers, no one telling you what to create when, what, where, or how—just make it. Make something you're proud of. Let it be a banner you can wave high above your head, where people can take notice and say, 'I get it. I can see exactly who this person is and what they stand for.' And it's a fantastic calling card."

VIDEO GAMES

One of the best things about my grandfather was—when I was ten years old and my parents wouldn't let me play video games—he'd give me quarters every time we went to Michael's Hot Dogs in Highland Park, IL. They had all the usual arcade games there —Frogger, Galaga, Donkey Kong, Tapper—but the one that most intrigued me was Dragon's Lair. Even when I ran out of change, which happened quickly, because it cost fifty cents instead of twenty-five, I'd stare at the screen, watching snippets of Dirk the Daring stumbling and slicing his way through Mordroc's castle. What captured my imagination most, however, wasn't the game's groundbreaking animation—it was that this game told an actual *story*! You weren't just sliding mugs of root beer to thirsty customers, or guiding a lonely frog across the street—this game had characters and plot! It was a full-on interactive movie!

Now, thirty years later, I may not be a massive gamer, but I still love strolling through Best Buy, looking at *Dungeon Siege* boxes, reading the back of the latest *Red Dead* release. Video games are no longer simple kids' diversions; we see their influence not only at the box office in the form of big-budget adaptations like *Resident Evil* and *Prince of Persia*, but in interactive web series like Chad, Matt and Rob's low-budget *Time Machine*. Perhaps more than any other medium, video games are having a profound effect on the economics of entertainment, as well as the age-old techniques and traditions of storytelling itself.

Yet while writers and storytellers now have a much larger place on the playing field of game development—Activation's *Singularity* was written by *Eli Stone* writers Marc Guggenheim, Lindsey Allen, and Emily Silver,[48] and *Call of Duty: Black Ops* and *Black Ops II* were written by *The Dark Knight* screenwriter David S. Goyer—story is still not the driving force behind most games (and, as we'll discuss in a moment, probably never will be).

Thus, in order to understand how writers are utilized in the video game realm, and how they work with agents, you must first understand a bit about how video games are made and what makes them tick.

Structure of the Industry

Video games, unlike the world of online and mobile entertainment, has a much more clearly defined power structure and organization, a bit like TV and film. The video game industry can be divided into two types of companies: **publishers** and **development studios**.

Publishers, like the networks and studios of traditional Hollywood, are the big dogs of the gaming world. Their job is to distribute, market, and oversee development and production of video games. Today's video game world is dominated by a handful of major publishers, including Microsoft, Nintendo, Sony, Square Enix, Sega, Ubisoft, Activation Blizzard, and Electronic Arts.

Development studios are smaller companies that act like TV or movie producers, directors, and production companies—all rolled into one. Their job is to create, develop, design, and actually produce the video games publishers distribute and market. Like TV and film production companies, development studios have strengths and specialties; some are great with role-playing games, others excel at first-person shooters. Also like production companies, development studios usually lack the money and resources necessary to mass-produce, distribute, and market their games. What they do have is the vision, creativity, and design skills not always found at a gargantuan publishers (similar to the TV studio/pod dynamic). As a result, game development studios sometimes work on projects handed them by publishers; other times, they pitch publishers their own original ideas.

Warning: Confusion Ahead!

In film and television, "studios" are the multi-billion-dollar entities funding projects, acquiring indie films, releasing blockbusters, etc. In video games, "studios" are smaller entities creating and developing projects—like TV pods or film production companies. It's a strange dichotomy in definitions—so be prepared as we move forward!

"The difference is: in [the film] world, the studio has all the power, and they pretty much tell the production companies what they can or cannot do," says one video game publishing executive. "In video games, the developer—because we feel they are the creative people—should be allowed to pretty much do whatever they want. We figure they make successful games, so they must know what they're doing. The publisher is there to give them money and provide structure for getting marketing, PR, legal and all those other things they don't need to deal with. They should just be focused on creating the game. We give them a lot of license, a lot of freedom to do what they want to do, whereas in [film and television] it's reversed ... it's a different power structure."

There are two kinds of developers: "**first party**" and "**third party**." **First party** developers are those that make video game consoles, as well as video games made exclusively for those consoles. Sony, for instance, is a publisher but it's also considered a "first party developer" because it makes consoles like the PlayStation 4 and PSP E1000, plus games like *Little Big Planet 2* and *God of War: Ascension*–both of which can be played only on Sony machines. **Third party developers** make games that can be played on *any* console. Double Helix's *Silent Hill Homecoming*, for example, can be played on Sony's PS3, Microsoft's XBox 360, or Microsoft Windows. Grasshopper's *No More Heroes* can be played on PS3, XBox, or Nintendo Wii.

It's also helpful to note there are both internal development studios, owned by the publishers, and external development studios, which are free-standing entities that contract with publishers on specific projects. Raven Software, which developed games like *Call of Duty: Modern Warfare 3* and *X-Men Legends*, began as an external development studio, but was purchased by Activation in 1997; it now operates as an internal development team within Activation–kind of like production companies that have exclusive pod deals with television studios.

Who Agents Want

Most video game agents represent third party development studios, *not* writers. As we'll see, studios are the primary creative forces behind most games; writers are often, for better or worse, incidental.

Game development studio Platinum Games, on the other hand, makes games like *MadWorld*, which Sega publishes for Nintendo. But Platinum Games is neither owned by nor contracted solely to Sega. It also makes *Metal Gear Rising: Revengeance*, which Konami publishes for PlayStation and XBox, and *The Wonderful 101*, which Nintendo publishes for Wii U.

How Video Games Are Developed

In film and television, studios and production companies have many irons in the fire. Big production companies may be developing ten or twenty TV shows at any one time, while film studios often have hundreds of projects in various states of development. Not so in the world of video game production, where publishers often release only two or three titles a year and developers usually work on only one game at a time. This is because games take much longer to develop–a single game usually takes two or three years–and cost much more money. On the low end, a game could cost $20 million; *Star Wars: The Old Republic*, one of the most expensive video games ever invented, came in at an estimated $150 million.[49] While these price tags don't sound far off from film budgets, remember: motion pictures only get expensive once they go into actual production. A movie studio can buy and develop a screenplay for less than $100,000, but developing a video game requires an entire staff of designers, engineers, and artists, plus computers, machines, and infrastructure. In other words, a movie or TV studio can tinker around with an idea for very little money, but with video game development, it's either all or nothing. (Developing a screenplay just takes paper, pencils, a computer, and Final Draft). Thus, publishers are incredibly picky and analytical when it comes time to selecting which projects they want to commit to.

Video games tend to originate in one of two ways. Sometimes, publishers own or license a valuable piece of IP. Activision, for example, owns licenses to make video game versions of Spiderman and James Bond; Warner Bros. Interactive owns rights to Batman, Superman, and Harry Potter. In these cases, the publisher may assign development of the game to one of its internal teams, or it may hire an external development studio. Ubisoft owns the license to create video games based on Sony's *Smurfs* properties, but it handed development of 2011's *The Smurfs Dance Party* to Land Ho and 2013's *The Smurfs 2*, based on the film, to WayForward Technologies.[50,51]

Other times, development studios come up with their own original ideas, which they then pitch to publishers. *Fuse*, for instance, was an original idea created by Insomniac, the development studio, then pitched and sold to Electronic Arts. Electronics Arts also purchased the *Crysis* series, an original idea from Crytek.

Original Ideas vs. Adaptations

In film and TV, it's often a huge advantage to develop a project based on pre-existing properties—comic books, novels, plays, toys, etc. And while there are certain benefits to making video games based on IP as well (EA's *Harry Potter and the Order of the Phoenix*, Bethesda Softworks' *Pirates of the Caribbean: The Legend of Jack Sparrow*), many properties come with such expensive license fees that it can be tough for publishers or developers to make much money. Original ideas often prove much more profitable. Also, game producers usually agree to make video games based on studio projections; the studio says it's committed to making at least three movies, or five movies, etc. But often, the studio's first movie is a hit, and maybe the second movie is a hit, but then the franchise starts to flounder. As the movies lose steam, so does the audience's interest in ancillary products—like video games. Unfortunately, the publisher, the licensee, has already agreed to produce a certain number of expensive games, so they're now locked into spending massive amounts of time and money making games no one wants.

Now let me guess: you're sitting there thinking, "Okay, I get it! Just like in film and television, once the publisher or developer has an idea, they bring in a writer to help them flesh it out. Makes total sense!" *Nope*. Writers have nothing to do with any of this.

In fact, pitching a video game often has *nothing* to do with story—which is why writers accustomed to film and television seldom make great game creators. After all, what's most important in video games—to the chagrin of most writers—is not the story, but the *playing experience*. "It's about what the player is going to *feel*," says one publisher, "what the player is going to *do*. Ideas are not like, 'Spider-Man breaks up with Mary Jane.' Ideas are more like, 'We're going to make it feel like the player is really swinging all around New York City. The player is really going to feel the web.' It's about the technology . . . the gameplay. The story comes later."

A few years ago, a development studio came to its publisher with a new technology they believed could reinvigorate a kids property that had been sitting, untouched, on the publisher's shelf for years. The studio had invented a small figurine, in the shape of a character, which could be placed on any video game console, sending its character into the game. The figurine then retained the character's stats when it was transferred to another console. In other words, a player could place her figurine/character on an XBox in her bedroom, play the game, and the figurine would log her character's stats and data. She could then take her figurine to a friend's house, place it atop her friend's PS3, and her character—complete with its updated stats—would jump into the world of the PS3 game! "*That*," says the publisher, "is the kind of concept that [makes] a publisher like us say, 'We want to put our money behind this. We want to see if this could work, because this will change the whole industry.' It's the concept of the game—not the story."

When execs at a publisher hear an idea they like, they immediately send it through an intense gauntlet of analysis. Every department from marketing to licensing to legal weighs in, looking at various factors. If it's a hardware or technology-based idea, like *Dance Dance Revolution* or *Guitar Hero*, it could require special manufacturing. How much will it cost to manufacture the game's dance pad or guitar? How will the pieces be boxed and shipped? Also, does the property have the ability to be franchised, launching sequels and entire series? Because games cost so much time, money, and manpower to produce, a franchise-able game—something that can recycle the original's gameplay or technology—allows the publisher to churn out other games and spinoffs quickly and easily. In fact, "one-offs" stand little chance of making back their money; publishers rely on franchises so they can amortize costs over multiple games.

Once the publisher's initial analysis is complete, which takes (hopefully) about a week, the idea is presented to the company's CEO, who must sign off. That's when the real development begins. "And now," you're thinking, "the writer is finally brought in?" *Nope.* The writer is still out of the picture.

Negotiating a Development Studio's Video Game Deal

When it comes to video games, the big deal to be negotiated—and where agents come in handy—is not the writer's deal, but the deal between the studio and the publisher. "For a larger project, we have about fifty deal points we like to settle in advance," says agent Joe Minton, President of Digital Development Management (DDM), which represents studios like Ninja Theory (*DmC: Devil May Cry*) and Slant Six Games (*Resident Evil: Operation Raccoon City*). Smaller games have far fewer deal points. Regardless of a game's size, there are usually five main deal points agents negotiate for every game.

- **IP Ownership**—One of the first things to be agreed upon, as it affects many other deal points, is whether the publisher is simply *licensing* the game rights from the development studio, or *purchasing* the intellectual property outright. (The publisher may also license or buy not just the creative content of the game, but any unique technology behind it.) This determines who controls the game itself, as well as—most importantly—the rights to spinoffs or ancillary products like toys, movies, books, TV shows, etc. With Hollywood eager to churn out movie adaptations of games like Freestyle Releasing's *In the Name of the King* and SyFy's *Red Faction: Origins*, IP ownership can be worth millions of dollars.

- **Advance/Guaranteed Compensation**—Just like in features, video games agents negotiate their client's advance, or the guaranteed upfront compensation. There are several factors that help determine this. First, has the game already been made? Some games are created on spec, like screenplays, and taken to publishers fully baked. Others are pitched, then developed only once they've been purchased or licensed. In these cases, the advance being negotiated is based on the studio's **man month rate**, or how much it needs to pay per month to hire the game's designers, programmers, etc.

  "A studio in central Europe might charge $600 per person per month," says Minton, while a "studio on the west coast [in] California might charge $13,000 per person per month." This cost is then multiplied by the number of people needed monthly and added to cost projections for other development expenses: motion-capture, music, writers, etc. Final price tags vary wildly; a smartphone puzzle game like tap tap tap's *The Heist* or Namco Bandai's *Bird Zapper!* might cost as little as $100,000, whereas a console game like *L.A. Noire* may cost $50 million.[52]

  In addition to negotiating the total amount of the advance, video game agents also negotiate the **milestones** by which the advance will be paid. Milestones are delivery dates for various stages of the game. Usually, every "month or so [the developers] have a set of deliverables they have to match up against," Minton explains, and "at the end of that month the publisher checks it and . . . if it's approved . . . pays [the studio]."

  Often, in addition to negotiating when and what those milestones are, agents will try to limit the time publishers have to review the deliverables, clarify what's "passable," and give publishers time limits by which they have to pay. This protects studios from publishers not looking at material quickly enough or sending studios back time and again to redo acceptable work. If the game has already been made, payment negotiations revolve less around milestones and more around distribution

Talk the Talk

Open Beta Testing–When a game is available for the public to play, but it's not yet charging the players; this period is used by publishers and developers to make sure the game is working correctly.

Go up live–When a game is officially up and running online, charging players to play.

Talk the Talk

Revenue Share vs. **Royalties**–"In the game business," says video game agent Joe Minton, 'royalties' and 'revenue share' are "the same thing. Different publishers use different terminology. Depending on what territory a publisher's in, there may be certain internal financial implications . . . for their own books . . . [depending on] whether or not they label something a 'royalty' or a 'revenue share,' but to the client there is really no difference."

agreements. "It's more like 'what's the advance fee for getting the rights to put the game out in, say, the Russian territories?'" says Minton. "That advance fee might be paid upon execution, or there could be milestones for that, such as when the game goes into open beta testing or when it goes up live."

- **Length of Term**–If the game hasn't yet been made, this is the amount of time the development studio has to finish it (which obviously affects the studio's man month rate and overall budget or advance).

- **Backend**–One of the most important deal points to negotiate is the **royalties** or **revenue share**. What percentage of the game's profits will go to the development studio–and what's the definition of "profits?" Just like in movies, "many folks get hung up on what a percentage is," says Minton, "and not so much the definition [of that percentage]. The definition, of course, is critical. It's essentially: off the sales of the product, at what point do you begin to get a piece of it, and how much? When the publisher has broken even, [paying off] their expenses–is that when the revenue share kicks in? Or does the publisher need to earn a huge amount *more* before it kicks in? And what are the deductions that are made before the payment of that percentage? The calculation of backend revenue share is one of the most important things that you're negotiating."

- **Non-compete clause**–Many publishers also want studios to sign a non-compete clause, often one of the contract's most controversial clauses, preventing the developer from making any similar games or clones. "It doesn't happen much in the console world," says Minton, "but it's a big issue in the mobile world, when you can sometimes put out another version of a game in days."

Video Game Development

Once the contract is finalized, the development studio begins working on various pieces of the game, making sure the gameplay and technology work the way they're intended. Each part is tested by **Quality Assurance (QA)** testers, low-level employees whose job is to play every section of the game over and over, testing for flaws, glitches, mistakes–anything that could affect the experience.

"When I first moved to Los Angeles in 1996, I met a guy who was video game testing for Dreamworks Interactive," says WGA Award-nominated game writer Duppy Demetrius (*Wet, 24*). "I went and met him [at work] one night–he was there all night doing the *Jurassic Park II* game. He was playing a dinosaur, running into walls to see if he could walk through. He was bug testing these games to see if he could walk through certain things. Could he walk through a tree? If he did, he made a little notation–'The programming's bad here . . . I shouldn't be able to do that.' That is the [entry-level] job, but from there you can get bumped up."

The programmers then take the QA testers' notes and fix any bugs or glitches. As the game evolves, designers sit down at every milestone to present their work to the publisher's top executives. If the work's not approved, the developer must go back and revise. Unlike in film and television, projects are rarely killed when development goes off track. So much time, money, and human resources have already been invested, it's more cost effective to simply redo the work until it's approved than to actually pull the plug.

All this time, the story is evolving along with the game. A basic story may be worked out at the beginning, but developers continue shaping it as the game evolves–writing dialogue, molding characters, etc. Which means somewhere–and it could be different for every game–designers realize they need help. Video game producers "tend to work in triage mode," says one exec. "They'll be like, 'This story sucks. These characters are bland. We need to fix this.' And they bring in a writer."

Who Are Video Game Writers?

First of all, it's important to understand that most video games have no literary or storytelling needs. Puzzle games, racing games, strategy games, card games, massive multiplayer games, board games, simulations—these types of games have almost no use for writers. If a game *does* need a handful of lines written, it's usually done quickly by somebody in-house.

As video games have advanced, however, a small subset has evolved. Games such as Quantic Dream's *Heavy Rain* and Naughty Dog's *Uncharted* series take their players through sophisticated narratives that clearly require expert storytellers. For years, as games like these came of age, video game writers were simply developers or designers pulling double shifts as writers. A few, however, like *Red Dead Redemption's* Christian Cantamessa and *Assassin's Creed's* Corey May, emerged as great storytellers.

In most games, the dialogue was "written by people who were there at midnight just trying to get the game out," says one high-level publishing exec. "That's where you got a lot of the really stupid writing, stupid dialogue you hear in games. They just piecemeal the writing out ... and that's why it [feels] jumbled and not consistent, just really bad. It's not writers who are writing that; it's developers. They don't [always] understand the idea of one voice, one tone—somebody overseeing and making sure everything is consistent."

Today, the video game world has started turning to Hollywood for help. Developers hire different kinds of writers depending on the game's needs. Story-driven games often use writers to help break story; in these cases, developers bring on blue-chip writers who not only have a deep understanding of narrative, but whose names can help market the final product—like when Activision hired *X-Men: The Last Stand* screenwriter Zak Penn to write *X-Men: The Official Game*. Other times, the majority of the story is broken, or beaten out, and developers simply need a writer to fill in holes and smooth out bumps. Some games—say, sports games with sideline commentators—just need someone to write jokes, banter, or 300 different ways to say "Score!" In these cases, developers rarely go to expensive A-listers such as David Goyer or Zak Penn, instead hiring talented joke-writers or people who specialize in dialogue.

Unfortunately, it's not always easy for screenwriters to adapt to the gaming world. First of all, most developers want writers to be on site, and not all companies are located in Los Angeles. So accepting a game assignment may mean packing up and temporarily relocating to Montreal or Silicone Valley or Vancouver or Cambridge, England, for the length of the job. Which brings us to problem #2: video game jobs can last a few weeks, several months, or the full two-year term of development—and not all screenwriters are eager, or able, to sign on for that long. Many have families they can't leave for great lengths of time; others don't want to put their regular careers on hold while dabbling in a new medium.

Traditional screenwriters also face creative challenges when writing games. Most film and TV writers are trained to think linearly: Scene A is followed by Scene B, which is followed by Scene C. Video games, however, are non-linear. Depending on players' choices, any given scene could lead to countless different scenes or situations. A video game script must encompass all of these—and every path must make logical sense. Some video game scripts are over 2000 pages long! Thus, many traditional writers *think* they're interested in writing video games—until they learn about the job requirements, and then run screaming in the opposite direction.

How Video Game Writers Are Hired

When in need of a writer, most developers turn to the small community of game writers who started as designers, or have worked at studios and understand the processes, the language, of game making. Others call contacts in agencies' digital media or interactive departments. If they're looking for writers who already have game experience, digital/interactive agents may already have the perfect person—or be able to find them. If developers want an actual screenwriter, the digital agent may need to consult his colleagues in TV or feature lit. "Ironically, [traditional lit] agents don't understand video games and don't really want to send their clients in," says one video game exec. "You spend a lot of time educating them on our process," and it usually takes a digital media agent to "explain why their client should do this."

The digital agent, just like lit agents, returns to the developer with a list of writers. Often, the developer begins by asking about the writers' levels and pay scales. "Well," the agent may say, "they're all on **AAA**-level budgets exceeding some thirty-odd million dollars." If the game developer is interested in a big-name writer, a Marc Guggenheim or Zak Penn, the agent will cut right to the chase: "Here's his quote. How much time do you need? Here's his availability. Are you interested or not?"

Because video game execs, unlike film and TV execs, don't spend their days reading and working with writers, most are unfamiliar with many screenwriters' work. In these cases, agents—just like in film and TV—send over writing samples, usually screenplays or television scripts. Some developers also ask writers to write a sample for free, a practice that rankles writers and agents alike (not to mention the Writers Guild). "This is not wise," says one exec. "[Developers] should be able to take a script someone has written, read it, and understand what kind of writer that person is. But they don't have that skill, [which is] why the industries are very separate."

Game developers usually peruse samples from about ten writers, then meet with their three favorites. Unlike in the movie world, writers don't go into these meetings pitching their take on the game. In fact, the *last* thing a game developer wants to hear is an original take! "We're pitching them *our* take," says one publishing exec, "but what we are really looking for is someone who is enthusiastic. A lot of times, writers come in very skeptical, thinking, 'This is a frivolous industry'—kind of like how the outside world views entertainment. [Or] they know it will be cool for their kids if they say, 'I'm writing a video game,' but they don't really 'get' video games. So that meeting is important to figure out how passionate this person is. Ideally, they have some connection to the property. [Maybe] they're gamers or understand something about games. [Or] if you are doing a *Call of Duty*, the guy comes in and says, 'I wrote a script [like this] . . . and I did [a ton of] research.'"

Unlike in film or television, however, it's rare for game developers or execs to share too much about the project they're working on. Because studios and publishers develop so few projects at a time, they're extremely protective, letting out no information until they're ready for a public announcement, and usually making writers sign a Non-Disclosure Agreement (NDA). "When I went in for the meeting [on *Wet*]," says Demetrius (*Major Crimes*, *24*), "they already had their characters. [They said] 'we have a female bounty hunter.' They knew they wanted her to be named Rubi Malone, they knew they wanted her to be a Pabst Blue Ribbon-drinking, lives-in-a-desert-trailer-type, as opposed to Lara Croft, who lived in a mansion and had all the toys. This woman had a gun and a sword. They knew they wanted to have it set in San Francisco and Hong Kong, and they knew they wanted these three or four villains: one named Tarantula, one called the Collector—the guy who can do the sword, this woman who can climb the wall. They would ask my opinion on certain things . . . but, for the most part, they had what they wanted."

Often, these introductory meetings are less about writers auditioning for the job and more about developers convincing the writer to come aboard. As Demetrius says, "The guy basically said, 'We like your sensibilities. We saw what you did with [*24: The Game*], we know what you can do writing-wise. We know, based on the other video games you did, [you can do] twists and the turns,' which is exactly why they wanted me for this. I was going into that meeting thinking, 'I have to make them want to hire me.' And, it turns out, they wanted to hire me before I even arrived."

Talk the Talk

AAA–A gaming term referring to the processes involved in developing, publishing, and marketing most big-budget games being released by major publishers like Square Enix, Nintendo, or Sega.

After the meeting, the writer's representation kicks into agenting gear to get the writer the job. If it's a screenwriter, the agent usually calls the developer and applies some pressure—"You guys want him or not? If you want him, we need to get on this right away because he's about to get busy with a film project at Universal. So get me the paperwork and we'll kickstart this thing." The developer then sends over a contact, and negotiations begin!

Do Video Game Writers Need to Be "Good in a Room?"

While developers or publishers sometimes want writers on site, working closely with designers, video game writers often work from home. "There may be times when the development studio has an in-person [meeting] with the writer," says video game agent Joe Minton, President of Digital Development Management, but "often the writer goes off on their own and tap, tap, taps on their keyboard. It's much more solitary, similar to working on a short story, then checking in, getting feedback, working on it some more." This doesn't mean, however, that video game writers can be antisocial hermits; writing video games still requires a high degree of teamwork. Designers and developers "need to be in contact with [the writer] a lot," says one publishing executive. "You need to tell them, 'This mission just went away,' or 'We can't afford to do this,' or 'We're thinking of changing this.' It's very collaborative, so it has to be somebody you feel you can work with, connect with, you're on the same level with."

Negotiating a Writer's Video Game Deal

Video game deals, for writers, are usually very straightforward. They lack most of the complexity and nuance that gum up movie or TV show negotiations, or even publisher/developer negotiations. There's little back-and-forth on fees or quotes, and no haggling over vague backend negotiations. Video game writers retain no rights to the material they create; they are employees of the game, all material owned by the studio. Game producers also have very specific budgets and tasks—"We need him three days a week to help shape these particular missions," "We need jokes and quips for these characters and situations"—making negotiations quick and painless. There are typically four main deal points video game writers and their agents can negotiate on:

- **Compensation**—Video games, in many ways, are still in their infancy, and the notion of hiring bona fide writers is relatively new. Only recently have some video games been covered by the WGA, and most games still aren't. As a result, there are few standards or templates regulating writers' compensation, and writers are compensated in many different ways. Some developers say, "We need you two or three days a week for X number of months," and they pay the writer a daily or weekly rate. Others pay a negotiated salary for the entire project, usually between $20,000 and $75,000 (which sounds like acceptable money, but remember—you could be giving two to three years of your life to this game). Lucky writers may see $100,000 to $150,000, and a few A-listers, in rare situations, have earned close to $1 million.

- **Milestones**—Like game development studios, most writers are compensated according to certain milestones, or benchmarks, such as rewriting the game's first four missions or levels. Milestones also allow the developer to terminate the relationship if the writer is not meeting expectations. Thus, writers can negotiate their milestones a bit; a writer may negotiate, for example, getting paid after every three missions instead of every four.

What's *Not* in a Video Game Writer's Contract

Backend. Video game writers, unfortunately, almost never, *ever* participate in the video game's backend, or profits. You could write a video game that goes on to gross, like *Grand Theft Auto IV*, $1.35 billion—you won't see a dime.[53]

- **Term/length of time**—Since many games can take two or three years to finish—and often pay less than TV or feature gigs—it's important for an agent to determine how long a client may be tied up. Sometimes, especially with higher-level writers who can't agree to long terms, developers may opt to bring them in only in at strategic points. Other times, agents may negotiate a certain amount of time for a writer, or a limited number of revisions (like "sets" in a screenwriter's contract), and if the studio needs to keep them on longer, they must pay more money or a higher rate.

- **Location**—Some developers want their writers on site, so agents may negotiate how long the writer needs to be away from home. This negotiation could also include travel arrangements such as airfare, hotel, and per diem (which is usually just rolled into the writer's daily rate).

How Video Games Are Written

Most writers begin the game-writing process by meeting with developers to discuss story. The creative team usually has some general ideas about the game's narrative, characters, and missions, but they often look to the writer to do the heavy-lifting. In this first meeting, developers also fill the writer in on any special technologies or unique game-play that must be incorporated into the story. Maybe the game is based on players' ability to shoot a special gun or feel like they're flying a certain airplane. The story must be based around, or heavily incorporate, that technology.

While writers are often allowed to offer changes or revisions to story ideas, what they *can't* do is alter the game in ways that would require different technologies or types of gameplay. In other words, if the entire game centers on the experience of wearing a special glove or helmet, the writer can't suggest story changes that eliminate the glove or helmet. The story is there to serve the gameplay, not the other way around.

Many games are written in stages. The first stage may involve writing a treatment; after that, stages often correspond to different levels, or missions, within the game. Throughout the process, the writer and developers are in constant contact, with the developers often calling to say, "We can no longer afford to do this particular part of the game," or "We have to do this level differently." It's the writer's job to adapt quickly and easily. "When I came into [*Kung Fu Panda*] they already had it sort of plotted out," says video game writer Jordana Arkin, so "[the designer] would send Level Seven and I would have to write a **cutscene** at the beginning, almost like putting your own scene in a movie that doesn't exist, then a bunch of incidental dialogue between the characters in that level. You write it out of order, which was confusing to me because I kept going 'I don't know what scene's before [or] after this!'"

Other games don't need heavy plotting, they just need tight, entertaining dialogue. When Arkin was hired to rewrite Activision's *Madagascar: Escape 2 Africa*, for example, "it was joke writing. It was taking every line somebody wanted to be a joke and turning it into a joke—*for 300 pages!* You have to be really creative because you have to find sixty different ways to say the same thing, like 'Shoot him in the head!' I'd end up beating my head against the wall trying to do that."

When the writer turns in a particular stage of the script, he usually needs approval before getting paid and moving to the next stage. Getting approval is not always a quick, easy process. The work must be reviewed by the developer, the publisher, and—if it's based on pre-existing IP, like a movie, TV show, or celebrity—the original licensor. Unfortunately, video game makers have a tendency to get hung up on technical or design problems and often neglect reviewing writers' work as quickly as they should, leading to long delays in writers' paychecks. (Yet another reason many writers quit or refuse to get involved with video game writing.)

Talk the Talk

Cutscene—A narrative scene in a video game, usually at the beginning or end of a level, over which players have no control. Cutscenes usually feature characters chatting, planning the next level, or taking actions that propel the story.

How Video Game Agents Find Clients

Remember: most video game agents don't rep writers; they rep development studios, and "we're approached every week by studios" looking for representation, says Minton. "We've frequently had publishers call us up and say, 'Hey, we just had this studio come in and pitch us. They have most of their stuff together, they're just not quite in sync. [But] if they had an agency like you who would help them, they could be rock stars."

On infrequent occasions, video game agents may represent a particularly high-profile writer, but this is rare—although not for writers' lack of trying. Many agents are approached by writers with ideas for story-based games, and agents have to discourage them from pitching. First of all, most writers fail to understand that video games aren't about story, they're about gameplay. And unless the writer has invented a new technology—or has the technological know-how to engineer a groundbreaking technique—a simple story-based idea isn't usually sellable. If you're Christopher Nolan or J.J. Abrams, you can get some meetings, but unless you have a name that's a marketable brand, you're probably not getting through the door.

Second, just like TV studios want to buy ideas from showrunners who can produce and deliver an entire series, publishers want to buy games from organizations or companies capable of designing and making an entire game—and most writers, unless they have a solid background in designing or programming, can't do that.

Lastly, even when a passionate writer convinces an agent he wants to pitch an idea, the writer often ends up bailing. Here's how this usually plays out: a writer, often someone who's had enough success in film or television to believe he has some street cred in the game world, tells his agent—or his agency's video game department—he wants to pitch a game. The agent tries to talk the writer out of it. The writer insists. The agent offers to set the writer up on some general meetings with publishers or development studios. The writer goes to the meetings, upon which he learns how much time game-writing takes, and how little it pays, and he opts out. When a video game writer *does* find representation, he's usually been working successfully in video games for several years and has proven he can write other kinds of material. Christian Cantamessa, for example, had been writing and designing games since 1996 before signing with CAA and selling his screenplay *Wake Cycle* to Boss Media in 2011.[54] Other times, a screenwriter may be able to find video game representation if he's reached a stratospheric level of success—like WME-repped David Goyer, who wrote *Call of Duty: Black Ops* and *Call of Duty: Black Ops II*.[55]

In addition to having professional game-producing experience or a marquee-value name, video game writers must think differently than traditional writers. Screenwriters and TV writers tell linear stories, but video game writers must think *non-linearly*. This doesn't necessarily mean "non-chronologically"; it means you must be able to tell a story that can diverge and branch into a myriad of permutations and storylines. Each storyline must track perfectly, even as it intersects with and affects other storylines, creating whole new interactions and permutations.

How Video Game Agents Get Paid

Just like traditional lit agents—they commission ten percent of their clients' income.

So if I Dream of Becoming a Video Game Writer, How *Do* I Break in?

Whether you want to write for other people's games or happen to get invited to pitch your own ideas, "what you need to do is become an expert in the style of writing" you aspire to, says DDM agent Joe Minton. "Study how games are written so you're not handing someone a short story, pretending it would be a good example of a game script. Look at how dialogue is broken down; begin learning the cadence and how it's done, which you can do from simply playing games and paying attention. [Write] your own game storylines [then post them] online. [Start] your own blog about writing and video games. Review different writers and games from a writer's perspective."

Another great way to break in is to get a job with a development studio. This could mean getting an entry-level Quality Assurance job or an unpaid internship, or even offering to write some games or lines for free! "If you can write and speak, you can get a QA job," says one veteran game maker. "The way you move up the ranks in QA is by playing the game and looking for problems. If you're able to articulate [problems you find], especially on paper, you will move up the ranks until you jump into the production realm, which is the AP (Associate Producer). [From there,] you just move up the ranks, but it's a long haul, and a lot of it comes from understanding how video games are made."

Fortunately, video game studios, unlike most movie studios, aren't confined to Hollywood. Zombie Studios (*Special Forces Team X*) is based in Seattle, WA; Armature Studio (*Batman: Arkham Origins*) is headquartered in Austin, TX; Disruptor Beam (*Game of Thrones Ascent*) is in Boston, MA. You can even find studios in foreign countries, like Finland's Bugbear Entertainment (*FlatOut*), Iceland's Gogogic (*Godsrule: War of Mortals*), and Spain's Tequila Works (*Deadlight*). Also, unlike many movie and TV companies, game studios tend to post available job opportunities on their websites, which are much easier to find and navigate than those of networks and studios. "Going to work for a developer is like being crew on a movie—you have to have some kind of specialty," says one video game executive. "Either you're a programmer, an artist, or a designer. So unless you have some kind of specific production skill, you're not going to get a job at a developer. You're going to have to go to a publisher where there are marketing, PR, and finance [departments]."

The good news: numerous colleges and universities now have programs offering degrees in video game design. So in a medium where the interactive experience is more important than story, it behooves writers to train themselves in something other than storytelling—whether it's game mechanics or writing code.

Another great way to begin your entry into the world of video games is to attend industry conventions where you can rub shoulders with designers, publishers, writers, and artists. "One great thing about the video game space is that somewhere between ninety and ninety-five percent of the people who work in it are really terrific," says Minton. "They're happy to talk and give their time. They're not arrogant; they're not surrounded by handlers and protectors, and there's none of the star thing that happens in Hollywood. In fact, I know a guy right now whose been trying to break in as a writer. He spent his time networking, and he's now up for a very key writing job in the industry—all through simply talking to people at shows, going up to the booths, finding out where the writers are. It's not easy doing that, but that's the only way."

You can also network or job-hunt through professional industry organizations which host special events, celebrations, and opportunities. Some of the biggest are the **Academy of Interactive Arts & Sciences** (www.interactive.org), the **International Game** Developers Association (www.igda.org), and the **Entertainment Software Association** (www.theesa.com).

The Best Gaming Conventions for Networking

- **AOC App Developers Conference & GDC Next**—www.gdcnext.com
- **Electronic Entertainment Expo (E3)**—www.e3expo.com
- **Game Developers Conference**—www.gdconf.com
- **Games Summit**—www.game-summit.com
- **Penny Arcade Expo (Multiple conventions in Seattle, Boston, and Australia)**—www.paxsite.com

Video Game Trades

Just as Hollywood turns to Deadline and *Variety* for industry news, video game professionals also have trades and news sources. You can use these to keep abreast of industry developments or familiarize yourself with the names of significant players:

- Gamasutra.com
- Gamesindustry.biz
- Joystiq.com
- Kotaku.com
- Polygon.com

Entertainment of the Future?

As video games continue to meld cinema and storytelling in new ways, where will they end up? As games become more immersive and interactive, will they someday replace TV and film as America's dominant form of entertainment? Why *watch* a story unfold, when you could *live* the story? "Now you have these games [where] there are cameras on the consoles," says Demetrius. "If I turn my head to the left, the camera moves to the left. If I turn my head to the right, the camera turns to the right. If I raise my arm, my sword or gun arm raises. That's where technology is able to [take us]. [Video games] will never replace movies and TV, but, as far as video games have come, I don't think we've seen *anything* yet."

Part V
You and Your Agent

12 Finding Representation

So you're ready for representation. You've got four great scripts under your belt, a desk full of brilliant ideas, and—most importantly—*you've read this book*, so you understand how agents and managers function: when they staff, how they find assignments, where they sell pitches and projects. *You could not be more ready . . . or could you?*

Before spending time, energy, and possibly money hunting for representation, it may be helpful to ask yourself: "*am I really ready for an agent or manager?*" This is different than asking: "do I *want* an agent or manager?" Lots of people *want* an agent or manager, but that doesn't mean they're ready, career-wise, to attract or have an agent or manager. And if you're not ready to actually *have* representation, to participate fully in an agent-client relationship, your time is better spent gathering or building the tools, resources, and credits necessary to eventually attract and use representation, rather than pursuing it prematurely.

The question to ask, then, is: "*what do representatives look for and need in new clients . . . and how can I fit the bill?*" Because television and film are such different industries, TV and film agents often look for slightly different things in potential clients. Sure, they all want fabulous scripts, but fabulous scripts are rarely enough. So in order to make yourself as attractive as possible to managers and agents, it helps to know what different kinds of reps look for in new clients.

WHAT TELEVISION AGENTS AND MANAGERS LOOK FOR IN NEW CLIENTS

While TV lit agents and managers are almost always open to signing new clients, they're not always open to signing any *type* of new client. Namely, "baby writers."

In fact, many TV lit agents and managers won't sign baby writers at all. Not because they don't like finding and nurturing new talent, but because "breaking a baby," or getting a first-time writer his first TV job, is a near-impossible task, with very little payoff.

"It's very, very tough to represent someone who has never worked in this business before," says agent-cum-manager Michael Pelmont. "To get them that first break, to put in all that work, to trust they're going to appreciate that and not walk away—there's a huge risk you take on as a manager or an agent."

Let's break down what, exactly, makes a baby TV writer so risky:

1. **They don't have tons of relationships.** As we've discussed, having a large network of professional relationships is essential—especially in television—for young writers hoping to work. Showrunners tend to hire or promote friends and colleagues they already know; execs and producers recommend writers they've met and enjoyed. Unfortunately, baby writers may come brimming with talent, but they rarely come with a deep Rolodex of contacts. Even those who have been working as assistants or P.A.s come with only limited connections—and while these connections are helpful, it takes as many relationships as possible, with almost every network and studio, to really "break" a baby writer. This means agents must begin introducing writers to all the relevant producers and executives around Hollywood. This not only takes time, but one

quick meeting with an exec or producer isn't usually enough to lock down a staff job. So while agents and managers can make introductions, or plant the seeds of relationships, it's up to writers to nurture those seeds, turning them into bona fide relationships, which takes even longer.

2. **The focus is staffing, not selling.** In television, most writers' work comes from staffing, but the biggest paydays, especially for agents, come from selling or packaging original ideas that make it to air. Unfortunately, most baby writers, even those that are extremely talented, don't have the experience or skills necessary to sell a show. So while a good agent or manager may believe a baby writer has the talent to *eventually* pitch and sell a series, it often takes years of work before a client can actually sell her own show. "If I have a kid [with a show idea] right out of college, I can't go to a network because he's never produced," says N.S. Bienstock agent Ra Kumar. "That's like going to an architectural firm with a drawing of a house and saying, 'Okay, now we can start construction!' You have to have people that know what they're doing and have done it before."

Also, baby writers are not package-able. As we've learned, TV packages are big agencies' largest source of revenue. But not every sale garners its agency a package–and even if a young writer manages to sell a pitch, or a spec pilot, most studios won't allow the agency to take a package. A low-level writer may grow to be a package-able showrunner, but that could take years–if it ever happens at all. Thus, agents have little hope of getting any kind of impressive payday from a young writer, even a young writer with her own terrific show ideas, for many years.

3. **Competition is high.** There are thousands upon thousands of baby television writers clattering on keyboards across America, and only a handful of entry-level jobs. In 2012, for example, broadcast networks aired only ninety-six scripted shows, and not all of them offered staff writer positions. While cable shows also offer other opportunities, there are fewer scripted opportunities on cable than on broadcast. And because cable shows have smaller budgets, many staffs don't staff writers at all. So these thousands of writers are competing for–in all of television–less than 200 openings a year! Not to mention, most shows get canceled early or don't last past their first season. So staffing a baby writer doesn't mean an agent's job is done. The odds are that writer will be unemployed again in a few months, chucked back into Hollywood's unwashed masses of wannabe TV writers, and the agent will have to start all over again.

4. **Baby writers take a lot of time and earn little money.** "I've heard of [writers] taking seven years to get their first job," says one entertainment lawyer, and all that time, "you don't know if you'll ever get paid as a representative. Ever!" Plus, when a baby writer *does* get his first job, it's fairly low-paying. Let's say a lucky staff writer makes $100,000 during his first year on a TV staff. $100,000 may not be spare change, but that writer's agent or manager only pockets $10,000–which certainly isn't enough to sustain business or put food on an agent's family's table. Even if that agent or manager staffed four baby writers, that's only $40,000 in commission; but let's say that agent staffs four upper-level writers, each making close to $500,000 per year. Now that agent's bringing home $200,000 in annual commission–and seasoned upper-level writers are much easier to staff than inexperienced babies.

5. **Baby writers don't earn agents or managers a promotion.** While agents and managers love and promote their clients, they also have their own careers to manage; they want to get their own promotions and raises. "The more invaluable [to the company] you become, the higher you go up," says Pelmont, "whether it's by raising more money, increasing the company's profile in the marketplace, [or] running things internally." Yet while breaking a baby may be personally gratifying, it usually generates little money–or press–for an agent or manager's company, which means it does little to further an agent or manager's career.

For all of these reasons, agents and managers think carefully before signing a baby writer. "We'll take on someone that's really special," says WME TV agent Richard Weitz, "but we're not going to take on a ton of people who will collide against each other. Maybe one or two or three. Not more than that."

Thus, most writers need to have more going for them than just phenomenal writing samples. In fact, "they actually don't have to be great [writers]," says manager Jeff Holland of The Cartel. "[I won't sign] a bad writer, but I will sign someone who is solid [if they're] working for an individual, a showrunner, who is known to promote from within. If they're on a show like *Justified*, which is going to go a couple more seasons, or a comedy like *How I Met Your Mother*, and you know they're going to get promoted from within . . . sometimes you're willing to work with somebody who you don't feel has material as good as somebody you already represent, but they have connections and networking."

What, then, are the most important elements for a TV writer to have in place in order to attract representation?

• **Great writing samples**—A writer needs to prove he can write, and most agents and managers will want to see between two and four writing samples. This could be two sample specs and one piece of original material, two pilots and a *Girls* spec, or a *Homeland* spec and a one-act play, or a spec pilot and a sketch packet. Different representatives want to see different things, but if you don't have at least two to four scripts—and, preferably, a mix of specs and originals—don't bother searching for representation.

• **Professional connections**—"Let's be honest, this is a business where you hire your friends, and that's why it's tough to break in," says one lit representative. "You have to get into those circles." It's true; for better or worse, writers who come with their own network of relationships are imminently more staff-able. This could be someone working as a writers assistant, or a grip who has spent years working with and impressing showrunners throughout the industry, or even someone who's the daughter/ husband/partner/sister-in-law of a prominent director/executive/agent/producer.

Having said this, the *quality* of your relationships is just as important as the quantity. One "person came recommended to me by two substantial people," says Dennis Kim, a partner at Rothman Brecher Kim, one of Hollywood's top boutique literary agencies. Kim read the writer's samples and was impressed enough to meet him. After the meeting, came "an avalanche of calls from everybody—known entities—it was insane, and I was thinking, 'Wow, this person knows a ton of people!' Then, one of the calls ended up being a close friend of mine [so] I said, 'What is the deal [with this writer]?' 'Oh, he knows everyone.' [So] I go, 'Are you falling on your sword for this? Are you saying—if you have a show—you are going to put them on, no questions asked?' 'Uh . . . no.' It was one of those things: they knew this writer, they were asked to make a call, [but] it wasn't sincere."

• **Living in Los Angeles**—"Anyone who says they want to work in this industry—if they're not living in Los Angeles, then they're really not serious about writing for television," says Karen Horne, NBC's VP of Programming, Talent Development and Inclusion. Writers outside of L.A. hate hearing this, but it's true. You may be the world's most talented TV writer, but when an agent or manager receives a script from an out-of-towner, they immediately know certain things before reading even the first page. They know this writer probably has no professional connections to help them staff, and has no real means of making them. They know this writer probably has little first-hand knowledge of how TV shows are written or produced. They know they can't begin setting up meetings for this writer because the writer isn't here to take them. (Writers love saying, "But I'll jump on a plane at a moment's notice." No, you won't. Jumping on a plane "at a moment's notice" isn't cheap or easy, and meetings get spontaneously scheduled and rescheduled all the time.

Lastly, the agent knows that if—by some miracle—you're up for an actual job, you're probably not in a position to start immediately. In other industries, people accept jobs and are given start dates several weeks or months down the road. (When my wife lived in Chicago and took a job at Goldman-Sachs in Los Angeles, the application/interview process lasted months. When she finally took the job, she didn't actually arrive or start for another three months.) In television, however, you may learn you have to start a job in a couple of days. If you live in Alexandria, Louisiana, can you move your life to L.A. to start a job that quickly? If not, no worries—agencies have a thousand other qualified candidates they can hire.

"Even shows [where] the writers rooms are outside of Los Angeles, which are not very many—we happened to have two last year . . . because the executive producers were based in New York—writers get hired from Los Angeles and move," says Horne. "So if you are just starting in this business and not living in Los Angeles, you're not seriously working to be a writer for television."

• **Professional TV writing credits**—Writers are more represent-able if they already have TV writing credits. They could be veteran TV writers, or they could be younger writers with a freelancer or two under their belt. The WGA requires TV shows to give at least two freelance episodes per season to writers not on the show's staff, and showrunners often give these opportunities to their assistants or low-level friends.

Having said that, "professional TV writing experience cuts both ways in terms of importance," says Kim. Most younger writers are searching for their first agent, but when it comes to more seasoned writers, agent sometimes wonder "why doesn't this writer have good representation? Was he fired? Is he unstaffable?

• **Other professional TV experience**—If you've never actually *written* for TV before, *non-writing* TV credits can also helpful. Perhaps you've been working as a script supervisor or first assistant director, allowing you to learn the processes of TV and form friendships with writers and producers. Maybe you've worked as a lighting designer or development executive. Having an industry job suggests a writer "has a working knowledge of how [the industry] works," says Meisinger. "Theoretically, although not necessarily, because they've been in and around writers who are actually on staff, their material should be more advanced."

I landed my current agent when I was a development executive at the Littlefield Company, transitioning to producing a reality show. IFC's *Out There* was created by *South Park* animation director Ryan Quincy. *90210* writer Scott Weinger began as a sitcom actor on *Full House* and *The Family Man*. While these credits may not be as valuable as actual writing experience, they at least give you a stamp of validation: you're a professional.

• **Professional accomplishments in a related field**—If you don't have professional TV credits, perhaps you have impressive credits in another medium. Maybe you'e published a best-selling novel. Or written a hit Off-Broadway play. In 2010, on the strength of her award-winning film *Humpday*, indie filmmaker Lynn Shelton landed her first TV directing job—on *Mad Men's* episode, "Hands and Knees." Before becoming an Emmy-nominated producer on *The Good Wife*, lawyer-turned-writer Craig Turk wrote speeches for politicians, including for Senator John McCain's 2000 presidential campaign.[1] And in August, 2012, FOX bought a television version of *Couple Time*, a web series written and produced by CAA-repped sketch performers Allyn Rachel and Patrick Carlyle.[2] Thus, other literary or entertainment accomplishments tell buyers, and agents, you have the talent, drive, and vision to produce marketable material.

• **Interesting life experience**—Agents love repping people who have fascinating life stories. Did you grow up on a kibbutz in Israel? Have you spent time in prison? When you were eighteen, did you elope with a cult leader and live on a free-love commune?

"Writers who have great life experience have better stories to tell," says NBC's Horne. Indeed, life experiences are the raw materials writers use to create or shape stories and, perhaps more importantly, gives those stories authenticity, genuine human truth. Plus, as a writer, much of what you're selling is your unique worldview and inner library of personal stories, so showrunners and agents alike look for people who can share these.

"You get some kid out of college–and I throw myself into this same category–when I came straight out of college, I was just mashing up other stuff," says *World War Z* and *Lost* writer Drew Goddard. "You haven't lived anything, so you're just funneling stuff you've watched and read of other people's experience through you. And quite frankly, there's a ton of people who can do that. It wasn't until I got life experience under my belt that I started to find my own voice [and get] jobs."

You don't have to be a former inmate or kibbutznik to have interesting life experience. *We all have amazing life stories–we just have to know how to mine and tell them.* Did you break ties with your parents because they didn't want you to marry your husband? Tell me what that felt like! Did you just get divorced and now find yourself back in the dating pool–at forty-three? Put me in your shoes! Are you a single father raising three kids? Your daily life is full of conflicts and adventures! "You can find your voice [even] if you've lived in a small town and got married young and had kids," says Goddard. If "you have something interesting to say about that life experience, you just have to find it and make sure you know it." Granted, if you haven't been an astronaut or a zoo veterinarian or a Syrian freedom fighter, you may have to work a bit harder to find the "color" in your life–but you're a writer! That's your job!

I know many writers, myself included, who keep journals and lists of fun stories they can tell in meetings with agents, execs, and showrunners. My list includes true stories like: "The time Matt and I conned the old lady with the lizard," "How I learned I'm racist," and "The time I busted a cocaine and crack ring." Your mission, as a storyteller, is to share these–not only on paper, but as a verbal entertainer.

Required Reading

Story Line: Finding Gold in Your Life Story, by Jen Grisanti–A magnificent guide to transforming your own experiences, thoughts, and feelings into gripping, relatable stories.

- **Well-positioned to get their own work**–As we discussed, agents love signing writers who are are in professional positions to get hired or promoted on their own. This could be a veteran writer already working on a TV show or a baby writer working as the assistant to a supportive executive producer. This doesn't make representatives lazy; it's just that breaking a baby is so hard, so time-consuming, so stressful, even hard-working managers or agents need all the help they can get. "This also helps because clients are in the know, and especially in this town, you're only as good as your information," says one manager. "If you can find out stuff before I can, that's very valuable."

- **Good in a room (personality/attitude)**–"Do I like you? Do I want to talk to you? Do I want to hang out with you? Are you 'good in a room?'" says Kim. "I look at it like, 'I would like to hang out with you for twelve hours in a writers room,' and I think a lot of people who would be hiring you would want to do that too."

TV writers spend "fourteen or fifteen hours a day, seven days a week" together, says Goddard. "There are very few people you don't want to strangle [after] fifteen hours in a room, and you have to try to not be one of those people."

Also, as a writer on staff, ninety percent of your ideas, pitches, and suggestions will get rejected or ignored, so you need to have thick skin. Thus, showrunners need to hire people who are "**good in a room**"–people with great attitudes who don't get easily discouraged.

Television is "more like being in a band than being a writer," Goddard continues. "If you're in a band, you have to worry what the other five members of your band are doing, or it's going to sound fucking terrible. You all have to be on the same page, and in order to do that properly, you have to be able to interact well with each other. The writers I've been in rooms with I see more than I see my own family. So it is a bond you need with one another."

Agents, therefore, as the people recommending you, want to know they're repping people who can fit this bill. Also, because getting writers work can be a long, hard slog—especially for babies—agents don't want to invest time in clients who are rude, unappreciative, or unpleasant to spend time with. "This is a business built on rejection," says New Wave manager Michael Pelmont, "and [reps] are on the forefront of that rejection. So [a client] has to be someone we really like, someone we really care about." He thinks a moment, then adds with a smile, "Or someone with a big quote."

I know it seems that aside from being a great writer, none of these other factors should matter, but sadly—whether you're a feature writer or a TV writer—they do. If "someone writes material that makes it stand out from the crowd, of course you want to meet with that person," says Jim Ehrich, a feature agent at Rothman Brecher Kim. But "the reality is: a lot of writing falls into that middle ground. It's like a bell curve . . . there are outstanding scripts that will blow you away, and there's a lot of stuff that's good, but doesn't stand out. [So] then you look to what makes someone unique. What gives them a voice? What makes them different from every other writer out there?"

So which combination of factors is the most important to agents and managers? Maybe a new writer has no professional experience, but she has hundreds of stories from her five years in Afghanistan. Is this writer staff-able? What about someone who's never been overseas, but has written four hilarious novellas about being a suburban husband? Or a recent college graduate who's written two great sitcom specs and is now working as an intern to a major showrunner?

In researching this book, I decided to ask representatives which qualities they valued most. I asked two different groups: scripted TV agents/managers and reality agents/managers. I then averaged their responses to get a general picture of the qualities TV lit representatives value. But before we look at their answers, rank them yourself—then compare your results to the professionals'.

Which of these factors *should* be most—and least—important to agents or managers looking for new clients in the following areas? Rank them from 1 (most important) to 9 (least important):

I Stand Corrected

"You don't mention a couple of things I think are very important," says Original Artists agent Matt Leipzig. "One is: *do you (the writer) generate ideas?* Another is: *Are you ambitious? Do you want to be successful?* Those things are important. It's hard to make somebody successful who doesn't want to be successful."

SCRIPTED TV

Quality	Rank (1–9)
Professional TV writing credits	____
Good in a room (personality/attitude)	____
Professional TV experience (non-writing)	____
Living in Los Angeles	____
Professional accomplishments in a related field	____
Interesting life experience	____
Professional connections	____
Great writing samples	____
Well-positioned to get their own work	____

REALITY TV

Quality	Rank (1–9)
Professional reality TV producing credits	____
Good in a room (personality/attitude)	____
Professional TV experience (non-producing)	____
Living in Los Angeles	____
Professional accomplishments in a related field	____
Interesting life experience	____

YOU AND YOUR AGENT

Professional connections _____
Great reality producing samples (demo reels, etc.) _____
Well-positioned to get their own work _____

Nice job. Now, here's how professional agents and managers ranked them:

SCRIPTED TV: THE RESULTS

1. Great writing samples
2. Good in a room (personality/attitude)
3. Professional TV writing credits
4. Well-positioned to get their own work
5. Interesting life experience
6. Professional accomplishments in a related field
7. Professional connections
8. Living in Los Angeles
9. Professional TV experience (non-writing)

Did I Lie to You?

Wait a second—"Living in L.A." is ranked nearly last! But you said . . .!

"You're right—I said aspiring television writers *had to live in Los Angeles* . . . and then those damn agents (and managers) went and ranked it 8 out of 9. *In my own book!* Look, I can take my lumps like the next guy; I stand corrected—maybe living in L.A. *isn't* that important. Except for one thing: the agents ranked "living in L.A." almost at the bottom—this is true. But coming in at #3 is "professional writing credits," followed immediately by "well-positioned to get their own work." And while "professional connections" ranked at an unimpressive #7, it's still ahead of "living in Los Angeles." So maybe you don't have to live in Los Angeles, *as long as you have professional TV writing credits and are well-positioned to get your own job!* Which usually means you're already working on staff or as some kind of prominent assistant (writers assistant, showrunner's assistant, etc.). And I don't know how you get those things *if you're not living in Los Angeles.*

REALITY TV: THE RESULTS

1. Professional reality TV producing credits
2. Good in a room (personality/attitude)
3. Professional connections
4. Living in Los Angeles
5. Well-positioned to get their own work
6. Interesting life experience
7. Great reality producing samples (demo reels, etc.)
8. Professional accomplishments in a related field
9. Professional TV experience (non-producing)

What Feature Agents and Managers Look For In New Clients

The world of feature screenwriting is just as competitive as television. While movie executives aren't filling positions on staffs like TV execs and producers, there are thousands of aspiring scribes clamoring to make the next big sale. One feature agent estimated he received 4,000 unsolicited queries per year. Wannabes are fueled by stories like that of Brad Inglesby, who, in 2008, was living with his parents in Pennsylvania, working at his dad's furniture company, when Relativity purchased his spec screenplay *The Low Dweller* (later renamed *Out of the Furnace*) for $650,000 against $1.1 million.[3] Inglesby has since gone on to become one of Hollywood's top screenwriters. In 2012, he sold *The All-Nighter* to Warner Brothers, *The Signal* to Indian Paintbrush, and was hired to rewrite Gareth Evans' award-winning Indonesian martial arts film, *The Raid: Redemption*, for Screen Gems.

Yet while stories like Inglesby's are inspirational, they're anomalies. The vast majority of writers don't sell million-dollar screenplays while living hundreds of miles from Hollywood. Most screenwriters get their start by slaving away in Los Angeles and selling their first screenplay for something closer to WGA minimum—about $125,000 on the high end (on the low end, about $35,000). Sure, $125,000 is nothing to sneeze at for a writer, but for a feature agent commissioning ten percent, it's less than $13,000 (or, if you sold a low-budget, non-original script, about $3,500). Again, like with baby television writers, this hardly sustains an agent's business.

So do feature agents look for the same factors as TV agents? Yes, although not necessarily in the same order of importance. "Staffing and development on the TV side is very much about getting into the club," says Verve agent Zach Carlisle. "There are a lot of fantastic writers out there, but getting into that first room or getting that first piece of development is hard without the relationship. On the feature side, if you have a great script you can gain a lot of heat quickly. One executive reads, two executives read, they start to pass it around, it makes its way to a studio [or] studio president; [suddenly] everyone wants to sit down with this person."

Let's repeat the same ranking exercise we did a moment ago, this time thinking about MP lit agents and screenwriters—which of these factors should be most—and least—important to an MP lit agent or manager looking for new feature-writing clients? Rank them from 1 (most important) to 9 (least important).

FEATURE SCREENWRITING

Quality	Rank (1–9)
Professional screenwriting credits	____
Good in a room (personality/attitude)	____
Professional film experience (non-writing)	____
Living in Los Angeles	____
Professional accomplishments in a related field	____
Interesting life experience	____
Professional connections	____
Great screenwriting samples	____
Well-positioned to get their own work	____

Done? Good. Now compare your responses to how the representatives ranked them:

FEATURE SCREENWRITING: THE RESULTS

Quality

1. Great screenwriting samples
2. Good in a room (personality/attitude)
3. Interesting life experience
4. Professional screenwriting credits
5. Living in Los Angeles
6. Professional accomplishments in a related field
7. Professional connections
8. Well-positioned to get their own work
9. Professional film experience (non-writing)

How do your rankings (in all three genres) compare to the representatives'? What do the results tell you about agents and managers' priorities and values as they hunt for new clients? Does this surprise you? Or were you and the agents psychically connected? Of course, agents and managers don't actually use a quantifiable test like this to determine whether someone is worth representing. Much of it is instinct, gut reflexes, and personal connection. If an agent is blown away by a brilliant script from a first-time writer living in Houston, will he sign her? Maybe—if he truly believes he can sell the script. Will a manager sign a baby writer who's a bit raw, but works for a great showrunner and has tons of industry friends? Perhaps, if he thinks that writer can mature and has a viable opportunity to staff. The problem, unfortunately, if you don't have enough of these qualities working in your favor, is even getting representatives to *look* at you.

Other Clues That Tell You *May* Be Ready for Representation

- "When legitimately established industry professionals have read your material and agreed that this is a business for you, then you can talk about pursuing an agent or a manager. Until then, I would equate it to *American Idol* auditions. Everybody goes into *American Idol* thinking they're prepared to be the next biggest pop star—right up until they stop singing and Simon Cowell goes, 'I don't know who told you you're good at this, but it sounds like cats are dying. Please go home.' It's a tough business. It's not for everybody. Even though somebody may be a good writer, with the competitive nature of shrinking budgets and fewer opportunities, it's not enough to be a good writer. You have to be an amazing writer to break in."–Lindsay Howard, VP, Television, APA
- "Another element for me . . . was being in a room and seeing what it's like. Even just [being] in a writer's *office*, you get a much different perspective of what goes on and what kind of skills you need. One of the first times I was in a writers room, I realized that writing is really a small part–not a very small part, but it's only a part of a skill set you need to be a writer in the room. Just learning dynamics of being in the room and pitching ideas and all that is a whole other ballgame that you have to be ready for. So for me, it helped to spend time in that environment and get used to it"–Kelly Galuska, writer (*Emily Owens, M.D.*)

Other Ways to Grab Agents' Attention

So you don't have enough qualities to score yourself an agent. You have talent, and you have some (presumably) terrific scripts, but you don't live in L.A., or you have no Hollywood connections, or you've never had any writing published or produced. Does this mean you can't attract representation? Not necessarily. There are two other ways you can garner the attention of an agent or manager:

1. **Make something.** Write, publish, or produce something fantastic that forces people to sit up and take notice. Stage an original play at your local theater and work hard to get positive press and reviews. Shoot an indie film and submit it to festivals, or rent out your local theater and screen it for your community. Publish (or self-publish) a best-selling novel!

"It's easier to get an agent for a book than it is for a screenplay," says Brendan Deneen. And he should know–Deneen has worked for film producers Harvey Weinstein and Scott Rudin; plus, he's been an agent at Fine Print Literary Management and an editor at Thomas Dunne Books. He now runs Macmillan Films, the production arm of Macmillan Publishing. "I would highly recommend aspiring writers not giving up on screenwriting ... but if you have an inclination to write books, it's an easier way to break in. An editor is more likely to respond than a movie exec, to be honest. And me— I'm open to hearing pitches from non-agented writers. I reject most of it, but I think it's fun."

Don't want to write a book? Put together a sketch group and perform at local comedy clubs or community functions—then shoot your material and post it online! "If you're a young content creator and you're not creating something [online], taking advantage of the low barriers to entry, all the tools and technology available to you, you're completely missing the boat," says UTA agent Brent Weinstein. "So many unbelievably talented and successful artists working in film, television, and digital media today were discovered because they took the initiative to make something and put it online. When my film and television colleagues signed Lena Dunham, she had really only done shorts online. That lead to her directing and writing *Tiny Furniture*, which was a hit at South By Southwest, and going on to create *Girls* for HBO. The guys who created *Mail Order Comedy* were doing online sketch comedy. Based on those online shorts, they were discovered by people at this agency ... and had an idea for a TV show (*Workaholics*). So if you're a writer, and you have a vision, and you're not already working in film or television, you should just be making stuff. Absolutely! Especially in certain genres. If you're a big dramatic writer, if your daily bailiwick is *Downton Abby*, which is amazing television, it's probably harder to display that type of skill-set through YouTube shorts. But if you're a comedian, or if you're a sci-fi or action director, there's a lot you can do to demonstrate your skill-set online and get discovered."

Want to be a film director but lack the budget for a full-length feature? Make a music video! In 2012, Seattle filmmaker Jon Augustavo directed "Thrift Shop," a rap video for local musicians Macklemore and Ryan Lewis. At 15,000 views, the video caught the eye of Lenny Beckerman, head of film and TV at Hollywood management firm Hello and Company. Beckerman tracked Augustavo down and signed him to Hello and Company, which boasts a roster of feature directors, like Kat Coiro (*Life Happens*, *While We Were Here*) as well as top video directors working with artists such as My Chemical Romance, Madonna, Kelly Clarkson, The Dixie Chicks, Motley Crue, Prince, The Killers, and The Rolling Stones.

I'm not saying any of these things is easy. They're all extremely difficult and take months—even years—of hard work, dedication, and passion. But if breaking into Hollywood, or getting an agent, were easy, everyone would be doing it! I mean, was anything truly worth doing ever easy? No! And being a working writer is no exception. My point is simply this: if you can't get an agent using traditional channels, sure—you may be at a disadvantage—but you don't have to be down for the count. So use whatever resources you have at your disposal.

2. **Move.** If you already live in L.A. (or, to a lesser degree, New York City), ignore this one, but if you don't, I'll say it again: *Move.* If you're serious about pursuing a writing career in Hollywood, it's a career transition you're going to have to make.

What Type of Representation Is Best For You?

So, everything checks out and you're ready for representation! The first question to ask when hunting for representation is: *what type of representation best suits me?* There are obviously different kinds of representatives: agents, managers, lawyers. Big companies, tiny companies, mid-level companies. Older, established firms; younger, more hip and nimble firms. Which is right for you?!

To be fair, you may not know until you begin meeting with people, asking questions, getting the vibe of various agents, managers, and companies. But it helps to understand the many options and variables. There are three general areas writers consider when searching for representation:

1. What kind of representation do you need: agent or manager?
2. Which type of company is best suited to help you fulfill your needs and goals?
3. Who at that company is the right individual for you?

"I Can't Just *Move!*"

A lot of people hem and haw when I say this—"I can't just *move*, I have a job . . . I have a family . . . I have a [insert reasoning here]." But the truth is: it's not that you *can't* move, it's that you don't *want to move*. Jobs can be quit or transferred. Families can be uprooted. Maybe these things aren't optimal—no one likes to uproot a family or ditch an important job—but there's a difference between being "not optimal" and "impossible." Which is fine, as long as you accept the fact that you're making a choice to prioritize other things over your writing career.

I'm not saying this as a criticism, I'm saying this as a simple fact. You've decided that certain things—having a steady income, keeping your family where they are—are more important to you than pursuing your writing career. People tend to get very insulted and defensive when I say this, as if laying out the realities of becoming a writer is somehow attacking their desire or passion for writing. But every job has barriers to entry. If you desperately want to be a doctor, yet can't afford med school . . . *you will not be a doctor*. If you want to be a professional football player, but don't play for a college team or can't get to a city having tryouts . . . *you will never be a professional football player*.

TV and screenwriting have their own barriers to entry, and if you want to succeed, you need to face these barriers realistically and strategize how to surmount them. If you're not ready to move *now*, fine, but start planning how and when you *will* move. If you're not willing to do that, you may need to take a look at your life and devise a new strategy. Maybe you decide to write movies inexpensive enough to be shot in your hometown. Or instead of becoming a screenwriter, you write plays you can put up at your local theater. Or e-books you can publish online. Or a stand-up act you can take around your state. The point is, if you truly want to break in as a professional you need to look at this as a career, not a "dream" or fantasy, and accept the realities of the business.

Words of Wisdom

"If young writers spent as much time *writing* as they did worrying about an agent, or trying to meet producers, or trying to take general meetings, or trying to network in any of these scenarios, they would get all the things they wanted; because at the end of the day, all that matters is your material. You live or die by your material. In a weird way, it's comforting—because as much as we think there's a velvet rope of Hollywood that you can't get behind, Hollywood is often a meritocracy; it's just sometimes hard to find it. But if you work hard enough and long enough and keep generating material, it does work out eventually."—Drew Goddard, screenwriter/director (*Cloverfield*, *World War Z*, *The Cabin in the Woods*)

AGENT OR MANAGER?

"Baby writers just need *some* kind of representation," says TV producer-turned-lawyer Charles Holland. "That's the hardest work, when someone is a baby writer. No one knows who they are, so you have to introduce them to everybody. You have to beg people to read them. You have to follow up. You have to introduce them to the whole town." Either an agent or a manager—or both—can do this, as long as they're smart, well-connected, communicative, and—perhaps most importantly—passionate about you and your work.

Unfortunately, "it's harder to get an agent today than it's ever been," says WME TV agent Richard Weitz. "I take on fewer people than I ever have."

This has helped fuel the rise of managers, who are also "more open to the idea of signing someone new that has no credits," says one manager. "Agencies are so busy, have so many clients, and are more concerned with signing really big brands."

Managers are also more inclined to "take on writers who have an interesting voice, who have potential, and work with them to make their scripts great," says Robyn Meisinger of Madhouse Entertainment. "An agent just wouldn't get involved in that nascent stage."

Indeed, managers are usually much more hands-on in the development of young writers' material. "I sign a writer based not on the script he gave me," says manager Lenny Beckerman, "but on the *potential* of the script I feel he could create with me."

Do I Need Both an Agent *and* a Manager?

"A lot of people are willing to pay the twenty percent to have an agent *and* a manager," says Weitz, "and most people don't need both." On one hand, having both an agent and a manager means you have twice as many people introducing you to buyers, gathering information, submitting your scripts, talking up your name. You double your chances of landing a job or making a sale. On the other hand, having both an agent and a manager means you're paying twice as much commission—which, for a low-level writer, can be a hefty dent in a paycheck. If you're an Article 13 staff writer—making, say, $100,000/year before taxes—you're paying $20,000 in commission right off the bat. Assume you're also paying about twenty-eight percent to taxes, you're suddenly bringing home only *$52,000*! (Which, in a city where many people pay almost $20,000 per year in rent, isn't a lot.) (If you're paying a lawyer, you're paying another five percent, bringing your net to $47,000. And if you're part of a writing team, you split that 50:50, bringing your own personal income to less than $24,000! To put that in perspective, the 2013 federal poverty line for a family of four was $23, 283.[4])

So is having both an agent and a manager worth it? "I admit I cry . . . a little bit when I see the cut in my check," says TV writer Paula Yoo (*Eureka*, *The West Wing*), who's repped at CAA and The Shuman Company, "but in the bigger picture, it's a drop in the bucket. The rewards are far greater—you have twice as many possibilities for getting a job, because you have twice as many people working to get you out there."

As New Wave manager Michael Pelmont puts it: "I'd rather pay twenty percent on $1 million than ten percent on $200,000. If you're smart about who you hire, the synergy should outweigh the extra commission."

That means carefully putting together a team where each party is working hard and fulfilling different duties. "My manager is my day-to-day guy," says Yoo. "We have much more one-on-one. I talk to him about ideas, pitch stuff to him, send him very, very rough drafts, have lunch with him, talk to him about his opinions. He vets everything, so by the time my agency gets something, they're getting the best product possible. Agencies are so busy, there's so much competition . . . it's in your best interest to give your agent the best draft you can."

Having both an agent and a manager is especially beneficial in certain situations, like staffing season. Since big agencies package and rep most of TV's showrunners, they're more incentivized to staff clients on shows where they represent the executive producer. And since most EP's are all repped by only a handful of organizations, this can make it difficult for other agencies to get clients in for meetings. Managers, however, often have relationships where agents do not—so they're often able to score otherwise out-of-reach meetings.

YOU AND YOUR AGENT

Managers are also good at organizing a client's other representatives—whether they need organizing, motivating, or scolding. This is especially helpful for writers who aren't great with confrontation, conflict, or other management of human resources. Feel like your agent's being too complacent in getting you meetings? Let your manager talk to him. Is your lawyer taking too long to close your new deal? Have your manager light a fire under her. (We'll talk about this more in Chapter 13.)

"It's crucial to have as many people on your team as possible," says manager Geoff Silverman. "It costs the client nothing until they get hired; that's just the cost of doing business in this town."

Do I Need a Lawyer?

Most low-level deals are fairly simple and standard. A screenwriter selling her first script, for example, will have little leverage to negotiate, unless her screenplay has managed to ignite an intense bidding war. (Which can actually happen. In April, 2012, Sony Pictures outbid Paramount and MGM to buy *El Tigre*, a spec comedy from newbie writers Aaron Buchsbaum and Teddy Riley, for mid-six figures.[5]) Likewise, a low-level TV writer is usually offered a standard staff deal with little negotiating room.

"In the beginning of your career," says Charles Holland, "a lawyer is not necessarily important." As your career progresses, however, and your deals begin incorporating backend, producer fees, net profits, separated rights, etc., it behooves you to have a lawyer on your team.

"We live in a world of slippery diabolical contracts that can really screw you over," says *Terminator 3* screenwriter Tedi Sarafian. "You've got to have an ugly animal in your cage to let out, look at these contracts, and fight the good fight. Because, unless you have a law degree and you really know what you're doing, you cannot read these

---

Can't I Just Use My Agency's In-house Lawyers?

Agencies do have in-house legal teams, yet while they occasionally deal with clients' matters, their purpose, first and foremost, is to service the agency. More importantly, "agency people are agency people," says attorney Charles Holland. "They're not an independent voice that's going to look out for you, [especially] against the agency. Who's going to read your agency agreement? Who's going to be on your side and look at things when you are dealing with another person in the agency, or something you don't want to talk to the agency about?

Ask the Producer

Q: Do I even need representation at all? I'm pretty level-headed; I like to network—can't I just do everything myself and keep my ten or twenty percent?

A: You could, presumably, do it all yourself, but "the best agent-client relationships form a sort of Voltron to do the work of many men and women," says *Promised Land* co-producer Mike Sablone. "There's a skill set good agents have that you, as a writer, presumably are *not* going to have. You want someone that is going to be an advocate, someone that can have more reach and more relationships than you have as one individual. Someone to make sure you're not getting fucked by deals, someone who is going to be able to draw a hard line in the sand. As much as it would be great to do everything yourself, and take all the money for yourself, there are many things your representation is going to do to help you in the long run."

things. There are so many little things to protect you on, like down the road, [when you say,] 'Can I have my script back?' And they're like, 'No, because you signed that contract and . . . paragraph 9, Section 8 says 'Herein not withstanding–' and all this stuff. You have to tell [your lawyer], 'Here's the deal: I want to own merchandizing,' or, 'I want to be able to get the package in a turnaround.' Attorneys get five percent of [whatever you make], but it's something you need to pay."

WHICH COMPANY IS RIGHT FOR YOU?

There are several factors to consider when exploring various agencies or management companies:

1. Size of the company
2. Track record
3. Professional inroads and relationships
4. Other clients
5. Your individual agent's own personality

Let's look at how each of them affects your search, your decision, and your relationship with the firm.

Size Matters . . . Or Does It?

As we've discussed, some are giant international corporations, with tentacles reaching into every medium and industry imaginable. Others are smaller, more focused. Many are tiny one or two-man shops. So which is right for an emerging writer? A seasoned veteran? A mid-level producer struggling to make it to the next tier?

"There's no real formula for success when it comes to literary agents. I certainly wouldn't correlate the size or the furnishings in [someone's] office with how good of an agent they are going to be for you," says agent Scott Hoffman, a founding partner of Folio Literary Management, which sells books and novelists to Hollywood.

While this may be true, the Big Four agencies do—for better or worse—dominate much of Hollywood. In 2011 and 2012, over ninety percent of all scripted broadcast shows were packaged by one of those companies, which also collectively claimed over ninety percent of 2012's prime time Emmy winners. Plus, of the twenty-four screenwriters credited on 2012's ten highest grossing movies, over sixty-two percent were repped by CAA, UTA, or WME—and those same agencies repped nine of 2013's eleven Oscar-nominated screenwriters! For writers looking for representation, this suggests several things:

1. The Big Four has a monopoly on much of Hollywood's five-star talent (not all, but much).
2. Those same agencies are Hollywood's top product suppliers.
3. Because those agencies provide buyers with most of their content-creators, those companies have direct access to staffing opportunities.

These qualities can be huge plusses for writers and artists repped at those firms, but they can also be a curse. "When you're an emerging writer, you can get lost at a big agency" says Roy Ashton, who left CAA in 2011 to head the TV lit department at mid-level Gersh. "Their priority is to high level clients or retainer clients. When you're a staff writer bringing in a small commission, compared to a producer who has multiple shows on the air, you're just not a priority."

In addition, CAA and WME are partially owned by outside investors, meaning they have important shareholders to satisfy. Even Resolution, the agency started in 2013 by former ICM topper Jeff Berg, received a cash injection of approximately $200 million from Arizona's Najafi Companies. Does this mean these companies can't effectively service smaller clients?

Not necessarily, but "agents at those places . . . spend a gigantic amount of their time—I would argue *half* their time—servicing big retainer clients," says Ashton. "And by doing that, they're not paying attention to writer clients, the core business."

Big agencies also have many more agents than smaller agencies. A single department in one of the Big Four agencies may have approximately thirty agents around the world; the same department at a mid-size agency may have only seven or eight. While this often means the larger agency has slightly better coverage of the town, and more hands on deck, it also means they have many more clients. A big agency may have hundreds, even thousands, of literary clients. Can a low-level writer stand out at a company where she's one of a thousand names? Will she get enough support when she's competing for jobs against scores of other clients? Who knows. But these are the plusses and minuses of signing with the Big Four.

Words of Wisdom

"The misconception is: 'If I get the biggest agent at the biggest agency, every door will be opened for me and I will be instantly successful.' If your writing is phenomenal, and you're the best writer ever, and you have the best agent there is . . . [there's] still a good possibility that it's *not* going to happen. It's not just you and your agent making the movie; there are a thousand other people that are actually going to make that movie, that are going to put that play up. There are a thousand people that have to weigh in, a thousand people's tastes and thoughts, both artistically and commercially, that butt up against you."—Mike Sablone, co-producer, *Promised Land*

Mid-level agencies, meanwhile (Paradigm, Gersh, APA, Resolution, Innovative), have fewer agents and fewer clients, allowing them to give clients more attention. "People who are more entrepreneurial might want to be at a smaller agency," says Ashton, "because they know they'll be a priority. They want to get their careers moving a little faster and have more activity . . . more access to the resources at that agency."

Mid-levels also attract talented mid and upper-level writers who may have been neglected at a larger firm. "People who have been at CAA or WME come to us because they haven't worked in a couple years," says one mid-level agent. At a mid-level agency, these writers are able to get the attention they need without being overlooked for bigger, more profitable clients.

Having said all this, mid-levels often have fewer high-level clients than bigger agencies. Of the ninety-three Prime Time Emmys handed out in 2012 (in all categories), mid-level agencies claimed only *nine*. Of those, only three were writing or producing awards, and they all went to APA clients: *The Daily Show*'s Hallie Haglund won for Outstanding Writing For A Variety Show, *Regular Show* writer Jack Thomas won for Outstanding Short-Format Animated Program, and *The Amazing Race* co-executive Giselle Parets won for Outstanding Reality Competition.[6] Likewise, the only mid-level agency to have an Oscar-nominated writer in 2013 was Gersh, whose Lucy Alibar co-wrote *Beasts of the Southern Wild*.[7] (And she signed with Gersh *after* her movie blew away audiences at the 2012 Sundance Festival.)

Thus, mid-level agencies must sometimes work harder to get their clients sales and jobs. They also, however, have something big agencies don't: agility. While big agencies often refrain from packaging writers or projects with producers or clients from rival companies, mid-level agencies—and even boutiques—have the ability to form and use relationships across the board.

"We represent a guy named Karl Gajdusek, who was a feature writer when he came in," says agent Amy Retzinger of Verve, a quickly rising agency that straddles the line between mid-level agency and boutique. He "pitched us an idea for a feature that sounded an awful lot like *Crimson Tide*. I [said], 'Have you thought about doing this for TV,' and he said, 'Yeah.' We said, 'Who are the producers you most admire?' and he said, 'Shawn Ryan and John Wells.' We don't represent either of them–Shawn Ryan is at WME and John Wells is at CAA, [but] we went to both and both wanted to do it. Ultimately, we decided to pair up with Shawn Ryan and put a show on the air called *Last Resort* at ABC. Truthfully, because Shawn Ryan is a WME client, you know damn well that if Karl had been at CAA, he never would have touched Shawn Ryan with a ten-foot pole. They only want to put their clients in business with pods they represent so they can get a whole package instead of splitting. But we're of the belief that a hundred percent of nothing is nothing, so if you're limited to putting your clients with people you represent, you might not make it the best . . . project it can be. So for our client, it was an advantage that we were willing to play with anybody, willing to get into business with any kind of agency. And if you're Shawn Ryan, you're pleased the project came to you."

Ask the Producer

Q: The industry seems to perceive certain agencies as being stronger than others, of having better writers. This may or may not be true–but how much of being a "good agency" is just perception?

A: "It *is* perception . . . but that makes a difference," says producer Doug McKay, a former VP at Phoenix Pictures (*Zodiac*, *License to Wed*). "Evaluating a script is a subjective thing; people–for good or ill–tend to take more seriously projects that are submitted from one of the major agencies, as opposed to agencies they've never heard of. It colors someone's subjective read if they feel like the script has come from a big agency or well known agent. And frankly, because the major places are powerful entities, a writer is more likely to find some synchronicity in terms of finding a director or actor for their project if the people that could get it made are also represented by that same agency."

Boutique agencies (Rothman Brecher Kim, Kaplan-Stahler, Vision Art, Alpern Group, etc.) have even fewer agents, and therefore fewer clients. While this occasionally makes it harder for them to cover the town and root out job opportunities, boutiques specialize in giving much more personalized attention to both clients and buyers. "We're not a clearinghouse," says Dennis Kim, a partner at Rothman Brecher Kim. "During staffing season, we do not go out there and back the truck up and dump everything on. If I'm talking to a showrunner and they're looking for a high-level female that does sci-fi and I don't have that person, or they're not available, I'll tell them. But I'll [say], 'If you want a *guy* that could do that–upper level–I have that. But I'm not going to send him to you [if] you don't need him.' Over time, writers . . . or showrunner-level people get it, and when I call, they answer because they know they aren't going to get twenty-five scripts from each level–they're going to get three to five."

Thus, boutiques are incredibly selective about who they represent. "I always read things to make sure I love it," Kim says. "It can't just be someone who happens to be on a show right now, so you're going to [represent them] because of their credits. I need to be passionate about the writing. [So] if I hear fifty no's [from buyers], it doesn't matter. We'll go and find the place and I'll staff you . . . because I believe in you 100 percent and I'm not going to bail on you [just because] ninety-five percent of people are passing."

Unfortunately, one of the biggest challenges for boutique agents is convincing potential clients—especially those just starting out—that they can compete with the big dogs. "If you don't have a working knowledge of the business, you've heard of CAA, you've heard of WME, you've watched *Entourage*," says Retzinger. So "as an agent at a smaller agency I have a bit more of an uphill battle to prove to this client exactly what I bring to the table." It's easy for naive young upstarts to get seduced by the flash and dazzle of bigger agencies, especially those repping movie stars like Tom Cruise and Mila Kunis.

"Perception-wise, I get it; if I were in their shoes I'd be like, 'I've got to check out [the big agency]," says Kim. "And some will succeed and some will not. [But] a lot come back to say, 'I made a mistake.'"

Track Record

Whether you're learning toward a Big Four agency or a small boutique, it's important to sign with an agency that has a proven track record. While the Big Four agencies have obvious track records, many smaller agencies are just as reputable. Rothman Brecher Kim, for instance, has only seven agents, but they represent stellar clients, including *Grimm* executive producer Naren Shankar, *Suits* creator Aaron Korsh, and *30 Rock* supervising producers Josh Siegal and Dylan Morgan, who—with the help of Rothman Brecher Kim—landed a two-year development deal at Sony Pictures TV in 2012. Researching an agency's track record can help illuminate the agency's standing and success in the industry. While you may not want to be at CAA or UTA, you also don't want to be at an agency that's never sold a project or only represents low-level writers. "[Buyers] know there's an element of quality control that comes from established agencies that they're not likely to get with agents they haven't heard of before," says Hoffman.

You also want to be wary of a new, untested agency that could evaporate tomorrow. "Agenting is like any other business," Hoffman explains. "Agencies fail all the time, because they're under capitalized, don't have enough working capital. There are agencies that pop in and out of business and leave their clients in a lurch, even ones that have been in business a long time. The last thing you want is to sign with an unstable agency that closes shop overnight, leaving you waiting for outstanding paychecks or with unclosed deals in limbo. While this can certainly happen with reputable companies (like in 2002, when CAA founder Michael Ovitz sold his latest venture, Artists Management Group, after founding it only three years earlier), it's more likely to happen with start-ups and first-timers.

Professional Inroads and Relationships

Film and television are, more than anything, relationship businesses, so whether you go with a long-standing agency like ICM, which began in 1975, or an upstart like Resolution, which opened its doors in 2013, you want to make sure your representatives have a multitude of deep, meaningful relationships throughout the industry. "Find somebody who has credibility, respect, and is well liked," says Kristina Speakman, Director of Current Series at Disney Channel. "Some people think you have to be [either] well liked *or* well respected, [but] they don't have to be separated. A good agent is both."

One way agents earn executives' respect and trust is by peddling only writers appropriate for certain projects. As a client, we often want our agent putting us up for *everything*; I remember once, years ago, calling my agent and at the time asking her to put me up for a Canadian sci-fi show I'd seen on cable. Was I right for this particular show? *Not even close.* But it seemed like an easy show to write for, and I figured Canadian shows were eager to hire American writers—why not?!

A good agent "is going to be honest," says Speakman. A good agent says, "'I know you're calling about [Alex], but he's really not right for that project. Alex is better suited for X, Y, and Z.' That's a guy you want in your corner."

Younger agents, of course, may not have tons of deep, trusting relationships, yet this is where they can benefit from working at companies with more seasoned veterans. "If you're an agent working at an established agency, you have the benefits of those shared relationships with people who have been there for a long time," says Hoffman, whose Folio Lit has fifteen agents. "We've got a bunch of younger agents here who are actively building their lists. So folks like me, my partners, and some of the more senior agents can make sure their submissions go to the top of [buyer's] piles. I can always say [to an editor or executive], 'Agent X from Folio has this amazing young adult novel.' Chances are I've had lunch with that editor a bunch of times, we've had drinks together, we've gone to each other's parties."

But what about a newbie with *no* relationships? How much harder is it for a fledgling agent or manager to make things happen for his clients? Can't someone just starting out make those introductions and relationships as he goes? Not usually, says TV writer Alison Brown, who worked as a showrunner's assistant before becoming a writer herself on shows like *Dog With a Blog* and *$#*! My Dad Says*. "I don't think their calls will be answered by executives [or] producers who run shows. I've worked on the desk of the people they call, and if my boss did not know who that person was, if it was some random schmo, he would not take the call. But if he knew who they worked for, it was a different story."

If you're thinking of signing with an agent and are unsure of the strength of his or her relationships, call around. Ask industry friends—producers, execs, other writers. Google the agent or agency; does the name pop up in relation to deals and sales? This can give you an idea of how well-connected the agent may be.

Other Clients

It's sometimes helpful, when searching for representation, to look at an agent or manager's other clients. Even if they don't work in your same medium or genre, are they artists you admire and respect? Does the agency seem to help people achieve a certain level of career success? Google the name of the agent or agency you're interested in. I like to combine search terms, like "[name of agency]" and "Deadline," or "Variety," so it brings up any mentions in the trades. You can also add terms like "spec script" or "showrunner." These help bring up deals or sales the agency has been part of. You can tell a lot by looking at these deals. For instance, when I Google "UTA" and "showrunner," I get numerous articles about UTA's showrunner clients: Ira Ungerleider, Darlene Hunt, Ken Sanzel, etc. When I Google boutique agency "Kaplan Stahler," I get articles about *Angel* co-creator David Greenwalt running NBC's *Kidnapped*, Jeremy Anderson and Patrick Moss partnering with producer Debra Martin Chase to sell the CW a modern-day adaptation of *Great Expectations*, former reality agent Alec Shankman launching Kaplan Stahler's digital department, and *Nurse Jackie* story editor Alison McDonald landing a deal at ABC to develop her short film, *She Got Problems*, as a TV pilot.

What these results tell me is that Kaplan Stahler may not represent as many showrunners as UTA, but they're forward, creative thinkers who find innovative ways to help clients succeed. (Kaplan Stahler is, in fact, one of the most successful and well-respected boutiques in town.)

Your Individual Agent's Own Personality

"The most important thing with your agent is your individual relationship," says Paradigm-repped TV producer Anupam Nigam (*Defiance*, *Psych*). "You want someone who understands your writing, somebody who understands what kind of shows you want to go up for, someone whose passionate about your writing." This, indeed, is probably the most important factor in selecting an agent or manager. After all, this person is going to be your business partner for, hopefully, a very long time. They'll not only own ten percent of your business, they'll be privy to and intimately involved with some of the most intimate parts of your life. The decisions you make together may affect—and will be affected by—when you buy a new house or car, have children, get married or divorced.

Thus, lot of finding the right agent is simply listening to your gut. When you first meet with this person, do you click? Do you have fun talking about mutual likes or dislikes? Can you make the same kinds of jokes? Do you riff off each other? Does this feel like someone you could talk to about your insecurities as an artist? Someone you'd trust reading imperfect, embryonic thoughts and pages of your most precious work? "I might be the best manager with the best clients, the most experience, the best relationships, and the best track record," says veteran manager Jeff Thal of Ensemble Entertainment, "but the guy I'm sitting across the desk from might think I'm not his type—he doesn't get me. He's not as comfortable as he is with somebody else, somebody who speaks his language in a way I don't. In most cases, that carries the day more than anything else."

You can also check in with industry friends; ask the opinions of execs, writers, and producers. When meeting with an agent, you can even ask to call a couple of clients—see how they feel about the agent. Do they always feel listened to and heard? Does he give constructive feedback? Does he share their visions for their careers?

Having said this, some writers want an agent whose personality matches their own; others prefer an agent whose personality is the total opposite. "You could say, 'I'm a nice guy, [so] I want somebody really tough to represent me, a bulldog, otherwise, I [know I'll just] take whatever deal comes,'" says showrunner Richard Gurman. Other

---

Insider's Tip

"These guys at CAA or WME great, but if there's a guy at [a smaller agency like] Paradigm that you feel could really bust his hump for you, then you're probably better suited there, as a baby writer, than at the big place. If you like the big guys because they have a lot of packaging opportunities, [and] they're there ready to sign you, sign with them—but bring a manager to the party, because you'll need to figure out how to navigate the waters of those bigger places."—Lenny Beckerman, manager, Hello and Company

---

Ask the Producer

Q: I know everyone says 'It's not about the agency, it's about the agent—go with the individual you like the best.' But certain agencies *are* more powerful and respected than others. So be honest—does a writer's agency affect your opinion even before you read that writer's work?

A: "[A writer's agency] certainly gives me some information about where [that writer] might be in his career. The general perception of someone at a big agency is they have talent, they have experience or potential, they have been involved in projects that have gone somewhere. There are many exceptions to that rule, but . . . the general perception is it's a symbol of status to be represented by one of those big agencies. The perception [of people repped at other agencies] is still that these are professional screenwriters. The question that pops into everyone's head is: 'Why are they not represented by one of the big agencies?' I don't think someone writes them off because they're not represented there, but its something to take note of.

"When I get material from any agency I've heard of, I take it very seriously. Many agents at those places are people whose opinions I trust. There are many writers who—given their druthers—would be represented by one of the larger places, so it does come into play. The question is: 'Have they been there before and are no longer there?' 'Are they working their way up to being represented by one of the bigger agencies?' At the end of the day, a piece of writing can only be evaluated by its own inherent quality, but the trappings of where a writer is represented colors many people's reads."—Doug McKay, producer and Phoenix Pictures executive (*What To Expect When You're Expecting, Black Swan*)

writers, those who are naturally aggressive or defensive, may want representation that's a bit softer. "It just depends on your personality."

However you'd like your representation to balance or complement your own personality, trust your instincts. Evaluate your agent on your personal connection; don't be swayed by the sexiness (or lack thereof) of the name or repuation of the firm. This is far less important than your relationship with one particular representative.

What Do *Buyers* Want from an Agent?

Just as writers seek out agents they like, someone who "gets" them, so do buyers. Executives and producers want to feel just as comfortable in their agent dealings as clients do, which is why they return time and again to buy projects, or writers, from agents they like and stop doing business with those they don't. "There's a fine line between under-selling and over-selling, [and] there's nothing worse than being oversold in that cheesy, salesman image we all have," says Brendan Deneen, who worked for Harvey Weinstein and Scott Rudin before founding Macmillan Films. "Those people exist. Cheesy, super-Hollywood—it's a turn-off. But if you have a good eye for clients, if you're passionate about your material without being overly aggressive, if you have a proven *track record* . . . these are the things that are attractive to buyers. You [want] somebody you can go out for lunch with, or a drink, and not only talk about business. Somebody you can talk to about your family, your interests, what movie you saw. You want to have fun with them. So agents who are real people, who have good eyes for talent, who are aggressive without being pushy, those are people I like to do business with. And those are successful agents."

WHO IS THE RIGHT POINT AGENT FOR YOU?

While many agencies use a team approach, you'll still have one point agent who's your main contact. This is the most important person on your team. Thus, people always ask: *How can I get the biggest, most powerful agent at the firm as my point person?* To which I always ask: *why do you want the biggest, most powerful agent at the firm?*

Personally, I want whomever's going to work hardest for *me*, and that's not always going to be the biggest, most powerful agent at the firm. Many times, it's young agents eager to prove their mettle who work the hardest, especially for lower-level clients who don't yet command the attention of a big-wig. The question you *should* be asking is: *how do I know which agent will work hardest for me?*

Strangely, this question may have different answers for features and television. In features, when young agents get promoted or hired, they're often placed on teams where their first order of business is to service clients of other agents. Maybe a senior agent has an incorrigible director he's sick of dealing with. Perhaps he reps a screenwriter who's grown cold and no longer lands top-level assignments. The senior agent will pawn these clients off on the junior. "The perception is that when you're a new agent, you're looking for clients," says manager Lenny Beckerman, head of film and television at Hello and Company, which shares clients with agencies like WME and Paradigm. "The irony is: it's the complete opposite. The new agent who gets promoted all of a sudden inherits a hundred clients, or forty clients, or fifty clients, because they just get jumped onto a team to service existing clients of the agency. The misperception is that a new agent needs clients. He doesn't."

Rather, it's often *senior* MP lit agents who are looking for hot new voices, young writers about to pop. In features, after all, a new writer can burst onto the scene with a killer spec screenplay that sells for hundreds of thousands of dollars, like in October, 2011, when Warner Brothers made a million-dollar deal for first-time writer Graham

Moore's *The Imitation Game*.[8] Suddenly, the CAA-repped Moore was the hottest writer in town, and less than two months after his first sale, Warner Brothers hired him to adapt Erik Larson's 2003 non-fiction bestseller *The Devil In the White City*.[9] So while upper-level agents still need to make sure their top clients are happy, they also let junior agents do much of the servicing, freeing them up to find and sign the next big thing.

"In television, it's totally different," says Beckerman. "A senior agent is concerned about showrunners, or supervising producers who are going to be showrunners." In TV, remember, it's much harder to "burst onto the scene." Showrunners become show-runners only after years of experience and working their way up the ladder. They also stand to generate much more revenue for an agency, thanks to packaging fees, so showrunners usually remain the sole province of upper-level agents. "There's no way, as a baby writer, you'll be represented by the top person," says Brown. "If you are, then you've done something [extraordinary]—[you made] a short that won an Oscar."

This means that while young TV agents may occasionally service older agents' clients, they're also eager to prove themselves. This is how young TV agents get promoted—by finding the next Carlton Cuse or Shonda Rhimes. "Partners are going to service the breadwinners," says agent-cum-manager Jeff Holland, a partner at The Cartel. "The junior agents or managers are going to hustle. They're going to get you all over town. Partners are going to spend ninety percent of their time working for ten percent of their clients. The ten percent that brings in ninety percent of their revenue. Their focus is going to be on appeasing Aaron Sorkin, Judd Apatow, and John Wells, not necessarily [a rising low-level writer]." Occasionally, however, young writers do explode onto the TV scene, like in August, 2013, when first-timer Mickey Fisher sold his sci-fi spec pilot, *Extant*, to CBS for a 13-episode on-air commitment.

"If I'm a writer who has an incredible amount of buzz," says lawyer Charles Holland, "I want the highest person I can get to take advantage of that buzz before it dissipates. If I'm a writer who needs to *establish* buzz, I want the person who will set themselves on fire for me. It's passion above everything else."

Unlike Fisher, of course, most TV writers do not start out with buzz, so they need that passionate young agent to knock down doors. "I often suggest to [new writers] that the best fit is to work with a newer agent at an experienced agency," says Hoffman. "Those people generally have more time to work on development . . . and they benefit from the relationships that older and more established people at the agency already have. So that fit generally works for folks who are just starting out in the business."

Approaching and Attracting Representation

Sometimes I talk to young writers looking for representation, and they say, "I had a great meeting with an agent at [insert name of agency]! They loved my script and we totally hit it off—they're just not taking on new clients right now."

This is bullshit.

"We're *always* open to finding new clients," says Pelmont. "The truth is: most of our clients, at any given time, are working. [But] if we're doing our job right, we're always hearing about stuff. There's nothing worse than hearing about opportunities and not having any clients available to put in those opportunities."

So what do agents and managers mean when they say "they're not taking on new clients?" "They don't like you," says Meisinger. "They don't believe in you. It's like a date—'I'm not that into you!'"

Having said that, hunting for new clients is not necessarily something agents and managers actively set out to do. It's a problem that usually takes care of itself. Young agents who get hired or promoted at larger agencies inherit senior agents' client lists. Veteran agents that get poached by other companies, or set out to start their own firms, have long-time relationships they take with them.

Nonetheless, one boutique agent estimated she received 2,500 submissions a year from writers hoping for representation. And a Big Four agent estimated his company received nearly 400 unsolicited queries *per day*–approximately 140,000 per year! Unfortunately, most of these writers will get rejected. In fact, most of these scripts or queries will go completely unread. Not because they're not good, but because agents with limited time and energy tend to only sign clients that come through particular channels. Want to get an agent? Understand those channels and use them.

Ask the Agent

Q: I know TV staffing season usually begins in April, so this February and March I started contacting agents, looking for representation. I heard back from only one person, and she told me she wasn't looking for new clients at that time. How could she not be looking?! Staffing season was only two months away; shouldn't she be *starving* for new clients?!

A: "By March, I'm already committed and invested in my current roster, making calls to shows, [so] it's hard to focus on somebody newer. [A good time to find representation is] summer/fall, after agents realize who worked and who didn't. They [realize] they've made a couple choices signing [writers] who didn't work out; their material isn't connecting or their samples are soft, so you part ways. Sometimes it's [also] good right before the holidays. Around Christmas it quiets down a lot; agents have time to catch up on their reading, and the barrage of pilots hasn't come in yet."–Jen Good, The Alpern Group

---

Channel 1: Referrals

Almost every agent and manager I spoke to for this book said *referrals* were, undoubtedly, their number-one way to find new clients. Now, this obviously doesn't mean agents *accept* all referrals; but referrals are moved to the top of their reading pile. This is for a couple of reasons:

1. Referrals suggest the writer has been vetted by someone the agent trusts: a friend, colleague, client, whomever;

2. If an agent receives a referral from a valued friend/colleague/client/whomever, he often feels an obligation to read the material fairly quickly. The agent may not *sign* the writer, but there's a strong chance he'll *read* the writer.

Also, certain referrals carry more weight than others, so it helps to strategize who refers you. Here's a ranking of the "weightiest," most meaningful referrals, based on another totally unscientific sampling of agents:

1. **Referrals from clients.** If a respected client appreciates a writer's work, that usually signals the agent that he'll appreciate it as well. Plus, representatives are eager to keep their clients happy, so, says one manager, "if a writer reads your work and says, 'Hey, you've got a good voice–let me talk to my agent for you,' that's the best approach."

2. **Referrals from producers or executives.** Because relationships with buyers are important for agents and managers to maintain, recommendations from producers or execs get read quickly; also, they suggest the writer is someone who has fans with purchasing power.

3. **Referrals from agents or managers.** Agents and managers refer clients to each other all the time. After spending weeks or months helping a client hone material, a manager may refer her to a great agent he thinks will enjoy her work. Similarly, agents introduce clients to managers when they feel the client's work may benefit from an extra set of eyes.

Channel 2: Get Your Own Job

You're scoffing, I can hear you. You're saying, "Uh, if I could get my own job, *why would I need an agent?!*" The unfortunate truth, however, is that breaking a baby is such hard work–especially in television–many agents *won't* sign a writer until they land their first job, or are on the verge of landing their first job. Get that first offer on your own, and I promise: any agent in town will be happy to negotiate it for you. And for what it's worth–getting your first job on your own isn't unheard of. Many TV writers score their first break by working as a writers assistant and getting promoted onto the staff. Others get freelance assignments from their showrunner bosses and friends. Put yourself in this position, finding an agent will become the easiest thing in the world.

Channel 3: Studio Writing Programs

As we discussed in Chapter 6, many of the major studios have writing programs designed to identify undiscovered talent and diverse voices, then staff those writers on the studio's TV shows. (Most studio writing programs focus solely on television writers.) "I know there are lot of [talented writers] out there," says Chris Mack, Vice President of the Warner Bros. Television Workshop. "The purpose of our writing program is to create a 'farm team' of talent . . . we can nurture and develop within the system, so when they're ready to create their own television shows, they know how to do it the Warner Bros. way."

Most programs take place over several weeks preceding staffing season. Over the course of the program, students write anywhere from one to three new television scripts and participate in educational exercises and activities. Mack's Warner Bros. program, for example, recreates an actual writers room to help writers rework their scripts and acclimate them to the world of collaborative writing. NBC's Writers On the Verge brings in performers from Upright Citizens Brigade to teach improvization skills needed for thinking on your feet. Writers On the Verge also has rounds of "speed dating" with various Universal TV execs to help writers learn the importance of making a great first impression. "I describe Writers on the Verge as a beauty school, a finishing school, for writers who are just that–on the verge," says NBC VP Karen Horne, who designed and runs the program. "It's not [a program] where I'm looking to teach structure, it's one where writers may have written a few good scripts, but it's to help them understand story and how to make their script good all the time."

Writers who complete the program are then shopped directly to shows and series. As an added incentive to showrunners, workshop writers who get staffed are often paid out of a separate budget maintained by the studio, so showrunners get a "free" writer who doesn't deplete their writing budget! Because program participants have such a leg up when it comes to staffing, and because their work has been vetted and developed by industry professionals, they're also highly attractive to agents looking for new clients. "It's because [their approval] is coming directly from a buyer," says Generate manager Kara Welker. You're "being vetted by those who want to buy, so if you're approved through their eyes, or through their process, it means a trained executive has seen your material and decided you belong in Hollywood."

Applying to Studio Writing Programs

Getting accepted into a studio writing program is highly competitive. In 2012, the Warner Bros. program, one of the most well-regarded in the industry, received 1,750 applicants from all over the country. They accepted nine. Different programs have different requirements. Some, like CBS and FOX, focus primarily on "diverse" writers. Others, like NBC's Writers on the Verge and Warner Bros., simply want the best writers possible, regardless of age, gender, or ethnicity. Every program, however, requires candidates to submit at least one or two writing samples, usually a sample spec of an airing show and/or a piece of original material. You can learn more about each program, and its application requirements, via the websites below:

- **CBS Writers Mentoring Program, Writers Fellowship, and Daytime Writers Initiative, and Directing Initiatives:** http://diversity.cbscorporation.com/page.php?id=23
- **Disney/ABC Television Writing Program, Directing Program, and NHMC Latino Television Writers Program:** http://writersworkshop.warnerbros.com/
- **Fox Writers Intensive:** www.fox.com/audiencestrategy/foxwritersintensive/
- **NBC Writers On the Verge:** www.nbcunicareers.com/earlycareerprograms/writersontheverge.shtml
- **Nickelodeon Writing Program:** www.nickwriting.com/home/
- **Warner Bros. Writers Workshop:** http://writersworkshop.warnerbros.com/

Channel 4: Festivals and Contests

First, a clarification: When I say "festivals and contests," I am not talking about every podunk screenwriting contest out there, and there are plenty. I am not talking about random "pitch festivals" or writing conferences. Yes—agents occasionally go to these. No—they do not actually find and sign clients there. I know conferences love to advertise that so-and-so was discovered at the conference and signed by an agent, but frankly: *I never believe it.* Usually, it's not a bona fide agent or agency, or the client wasn't officially "signed", or the agent just liked one particular project, and maybe offered to "help" in some vague way, but isn't actually providing service or representation. Most respectable agents do not fish for clients at conferences. In fact, if an agent approached me at a conference about representation I'd seriously question that agent's credentials. Why would an agent sign a complete nobody at a conference when he could instead sign somebody who already has the support of buyers or professionals? (This isn't to say conferences have no value, but we'll discuss this later in Chapter 15.)

Second, when I talk about festivals, I'm talking about the handful of high-profile festivals and contests frequented by the industry. Produce a film that gets accepted into Sundance, Cannes, South By Southwest, or Toronto, and you have a chance of meeting an interested agent. After *My Awkward Sexual Adventure* premiered at the 2012 Toronto Film Festival, Gersh signed its writer/star, Jonas Chernick, as well as director, Sean Garrity.[10] A few months later, at the 2013 Sundance Festival, CAA nabbed Francesca Gregorian, writer/director of *Emanuel and the Truth About Fishes*.[11]

Likewise, Hollywood pays little attention to contests, but there are a handful that attract the eyeballs of agents, managers, and buyers, like the Academy of Motion Picture Arts and Sciences' Nicholl Fellowships. In 2011, Nicholl finalists Chris Shafer and Paul Vicknair saw their winning script, *A Many Splintered Thing*, optioned by Wonderland Sound & Vision (*Supernatural*, *Chuck*), producer McG's production company at Warner Brothers. That same year, former Nicholl finalist Christina Hammonds Reed landed a job with Emmy-nominated producer Donald Rosenfeld (*The Tree of Life*) adapting Kevin Henkes' YA novel, *Olive's Ocean*.[12]

Best of the Fests

Want to submit your work to the few film festivals Hollywood actually cares about? Check out the textbox on page 152.

Agents and managers also monitor The Black List—which isn't a contest, per se—it's a list of Hollywood's ten best unproduced screenplays, according to top Hollywood executives and producers. Black List finalists have included household names like Aaron Sorkin (for *The Social Network*) and Quentin Tarantino (for *Django Unchained*), but they've also included fresher faces, like Rajiv Joseph and Scott Rothman, whose *Draft Day* topped the 2012 list and was optioned by Montecito Pictures and Paramount.[13] (It's worth noting that Joseph and Rothman weren't bright-eyed babies. Joseph was already a Pulitzer-nominated playwright writing on *Nurse Jackie*, and Rothman had sold screenplays to New Line and Warner Brothers.)

Similarly, Hollywood also takes note of The Sundance Lab, which admits a select number of applicants to a five-day intensive screenwriting workshop. The lab takes place in January, in conjunction with the Sundance Film Festival. Alumni include Darren Aronofsky, Wes Anderson, Anna Deveare Smith, Jose Rivera, Edward Burns, and Stephen Tolkin.

Hollywood's Top Screenwriting Contests (and things that are kinda of like contests)

- **Academy Nicholl Fellowship in Screenwriting:** www.oscars.org/awards/nicholl/
- **The Black List:** http://blcklst.com
- **Humanitas New Voices Program:** www.humanitasprize.org/ScriptDevelopment_NewVoices.html
- **Sundance Lab:** www.sundance.org/programs/screenwriters-lab/

THE WORST WAY TO FIND AN AGENT

Cold Calls and Unsolicited Submissions

"Every morning, I wake up, and there are about fifteen [unsolicited submissions in my email]," says Meisinger. "I don't know what happens in the middle of the night, but it's like—'Query!' They're all so generic, and they all come in such clumps that I read none of them. Sometimes, I'll open one and just look at a logline. And I'm like, 'Really? Why would you *ever*?!'"

No aspiring writer—especially those living outside Los Angeles—likes to hear it, but "the worst way to try to get an agent is by sending a query letter or unsolicited submission," says Hoffman. "Trying to find an agent by sending out blank query letters is similar to trying to find a job by shooting out blind resumes. It happens, but it should probably be the last thing you do rather than the first."

Young writers are always outraged by this, as if wading through stacks of thousands of random scripts is a perfectly efficient way to find your next multi-million dollar investment. After all, GM and Ford get most of their car designs by having random amateurs and hopefuls send in blueprints, so why not—oh, wait, they don't? Then why should Hollywood work any differently? The good news: no assistant or agent ever remembers—or notices—the name of the writer on the unsolicited script they just chucked in the trash. So submitting unsolicited scripts probably can't hurt you beyond wasting your time, energy, and office supplies.

Regardless of where a script comes from, agents have different ways of organizing incoming submissions. Some still prefer reading hard copies, so they prioritize scripts in various stacks: Tonight's Read, Weekend Read, Slush Pile, etc. Others prefer digital scripts, organizing and prioritizing with applications like Dropbox. Most agents try to get through their important submissions within two weeks. If this seems like a

Pinch some Pennies

I know at least 28.4 percent of you will ignore this advice and still send your scripts out to agents, but at least save yourself the time, energy, and money of enclosing a self-addressed stamped envelope (SASE). Most unsolicited submissions go into the trash *unopened*, so there's little point wasting *double* postage.

long time, remember: agents and managers aren't *only* reading scripts from wannabe clients. They're constantly getting in new drafts of projects from current clients, open assignments looking for rewriters, etc. So scripts from talented writers seeking representation usually take a backseat to current business matters.

When a manager or agent starts to read a script from a potential client, "I'm thinking, 'Can I sell it? Am I'm engaged? How's the writing?'" says Luber Roklin manager Bryan Brucks. "Having read thousands of scripts over fifteen years, I can usually tell on page two or three whether I want to represent that person or not."

If the manager or agent responds to the script, he contacts the writer to schedule an in-person meeting. Knowing a writer can write is essential, but reps also need to know if potential clients have enthusiasm, positive energy, and "the ability to communicate, express themselves, pitch, tell a story, engage in conversation, be memorable, be a dynamic person, and be someone you want to work really really hard for!" says Luber Roklin manager Bryan Brucks. "You have to see whether they're someone who can walk into a meeting with an executive at the end of his day, who's had fifteen meetings and the last thing he wants to do is be in that room—and the writer must go in and make that exec love him!"

The Meeting

Every agency and management company has a slightly different culture and style. Some present themselves as sleek, take-no-shit, corporate power-players. Others are hip, cutting edge, maybe a bit alternative. Still others feel casual, eschewing fancy offices with expensive artwork for more bare-bones, no frills operations. Some agencies are housed in gleaming skyscrapers. Others prefer a Bohemian back-alley warehouse. Whatever the vibe—meeting at an agency is an exciting, and often intimidating, experience.

What Should I Include in My Cover Letter to a Potential Agent or Manager?

First of all, why are you even asking this question?! Have you not been paying attention to everything you just read?! If you're sending a submission to an agent or manager you don't already know, or haven't been referred to, "it doesn't matter too much" says one TV agent. "I'm just going to ignore it anyway."

Assuming you *have* been referred, here are some quick pointers to writing an irresistible cover letter or email:

- Keep it short—no more than four to five sentences.
- Begin by referencing the common friend or colleague who referred you.
- Use proper grammar and syntax. "I don't want an email in all lower-case," says APA TV agent Alan Moore.
- Don't attach your script unless you have permission, or have been told to do so by the person referring you. Instead, ask the manager/agent if he'd like to read it.
- If you're attaching your resume (which you also shouldn't do without permission) it should be no more than one page.
- Refer to people by their first name; most professionals in Hollywood don't want to be called "Mr. Gordon" or "Ms. Davis."
- Don't begin with "Dear," which is too formal. Don't begin with "Hey," which is too informal. Try something like "Hi, Miles . . ."
- After mentioning your common friend/colleague, lead with any important info that may spark a manager's attention—if you recently sold something, landed a job, or won a prestigious honor, drop it in here.

Here's a sample of a nice cover email:

> Hi, Josh
>
> Eliot Clavin, an old friend from *Cyborg Love*, referred me to you—he may have told you I'd be emailing—so I wanted to drop you a quick note to say hello and introduce myself.
>
> I'm a recent Nicholl Fellowship Finalist, as well as a writers assistant on *Hate the Taste*, and knowing I'd been taking representation meetings, Eliot thought you and I might hit it off. (He also said you're a fan of Rocky's Pizza—which, I'm convinced, is mankind's greatest culinary creation.)
>
> Anyway, if you're interested, I'd love to send you a copy of *The Same Old Ground*, my screenplay that placed as a Nicholl Finalist. I know you're super-swamped, so if you don't have time, I totally get it.
>
> In the mean time, I hope you're well, and if you're ever up for a slice of Rocky's, lemme know! Talk soon.
>
> Teven Whitman

When you first arrive, you'll check in at the front desk. The receptionist, usually a super-cute twentysomething, will ask who you're meeting with. (FYI—they'll probably ask in a sightly suspicious tone, as if they're fully prepared to hear you say, "Oh, I don't have an appointment—I just wanted to see if someone could get my script to Martin Scorsese." It's not personal—they all act like this.) You'll say, "I'm here to see so-and-so," and they'll say, "Have a seat; I'll let her know." Eventually, the agent's assistant comes down to retrieve you—or, if an agent really wants to make a good impression, she'll come down herself.

If you're meeting at a smaller agency, or at an agency where only one person plans to represent you, there may be only one or two agents in the meeting. If you're meeting somewhere that uses a team approach, several agents—the entire team—will likely attend.

Preparing for an Agent Meeting

Finding the right agent or manager is like dating. You're hoping to find someone who's not only a creative and (in a way) spiritual partner, but someone who shares a vision for your work and career. If you see yourself as a genre writer, writing sci-fi and slasher films, but a manager sees you as a dark comedy writer, it's probably not a relationship that can survive the long haul. You're each going to want you to be producing different types of material and pursuing different types of jobs.

Here are tips from some of the industry's busiest writers, agents, managers, and execs on how to prepare for a "date" in Hollywood's meat market of representation:

- **Research the agency online and in the trades.** Know who their big clients are, what recent movies they've sold, what shows they've packaged. Who are their top agents? Do they have a successful talent department that could provide packaging opportunities? A book department that could provide interesting source material? Have they had any recent mergers? Have they recently hired or fired any prominent agents?
- **Be knowledgable and up-to-speed about what's going on in the industry and how the business works.** Agents and managers want to know they're not signing someone who will bombard them with questions like, "'Why do we do this? What does this mean?' It's like explaining the business to your parents who aren't in the industry. You have to go through what a general is, why you take a script into a studio, 'what do you mean I'm writing it on spec?' or 'why am I writing the producer's idea for free?' When you have to deal with that stuff it just becomes more work. Our time is finite, and instead of spending time on someone else, I'm answering questions that could have been Googled."–Literary manager
- **Research the individual agents you'll be meeting with, including junior agents and coordinators.** Was the department head previously at another agency? Why did he leave? Do any of the senior agents have backgrounds as executives or producers? Have any of the junior agents closed any news-worthy deals recently?
- **Clean yourself up, but not too much.** "One of the perks of being a writer is you get to dress like a twelve-year-old on a daily basis. But when it comes to meeting with an agent, try to spruce it up a bit. A good rule of thumb is don't look any dressier than a J Crew salesperson, unless you're going to an awards show."–Scott Weinger, co-producer (*90210*, *Privileged*, *What I Like About You*)
- **"Be 100 percent prepared to talk about who you are and what you're looking for in an agent.** Know what you want to do in the future. Have a firm understanding of where you want to be five or ten years down the road. Tell them exactly the trajectory you want for your career. I would even say, 'I want to be staffed on [this show]' so they know your sensibility right off the bat."–Alison Brown, TV writer (*Dog With a Blog*, *Worst Week*, *$#*! My Dad Says*)
- **Come in with ideas to write!** "It's amazing to me—writers come in and: *blank stare*. 'What do you mean, you have no ideas? You're a writer! What exactly is it you're doing all day, if you're not generating ideas?!' Be able to speak about what you want, what you want to say! The reason writers get blocked, the reason they have chunks of time where they're not generating material, is because cause they're not really thinking. Read! Read articles, read books, read magazines, read whatever, but get those wheels turning and things happen!"–Robyn Meisinger, manager/partner, Madhouse Entertainment
- **Don't bring gifts.** "It's generally weird to give gifts to agents who are not your agents. If you're trying to get an agent, they're going to look askance at anybody who sends them something—even if it's just of negligible value."–Scott Hoffman, partner, Folio Literary Management

How to Spot an Agent in the Wild

Archetypal agents "are usually wearing an extremely fashionable suit that's well tailored. They're usually fit—a body fat content of about five percent. Not all but many—the *real* sharks, who are very good agents, they're predators at that level—are lean and mean. There's [also] this level of grooming where they could be a European businessman *or* a Hollywood agent. And [they] possess and express an easy comfort with everybody; it's more personality than clothing. Agents are incredibly Alpha, *really* confident. They think fast, they talk fast, they grasp concepts fast and move on. It's like talking to your doctor, where you have to write down what you want to say before you walk in the door because he's only going to give you two minutes of his interest. That's [agents'] business agenda at work—they have a certain amount of personal coin they expend on you, because you're worth a certain amount on a business level. It sounds callous, but that's what the animal is. I don't think it's totally wrong—they are fascinating predators on that level."—Todd Holland, director/executive producer (*Go On, Malcolm in the Middle, The Larry Sanders Show*)

Who's in the Room with You?

When you're meeting with an agency, who they bring to the meeting says as much about how they'll service you as the words coming out of their mouths. Depending on the potential client, some agencies may send whole departments of ten or fifteen people—upper-levels, mid-levels, low-levels. Others may send only two high-level agents, equity partners in the company. And still others may send one upper-level agent and two or three junior agents. So when you're in that meeting, look around—the agents sitting around that conference table are often a good indication of who you'll be working most closely with.

For example, maybe you're meeting with a department head and two junior agents. This is a pretty good indication you'll be serviced mostly by junior agents. Sure, the department head is there, but that's only to look impressive and convince you to join the agency. Unless you're a top-tier client, you're not going to be working closely with an upper-level agent on a regular basis and if you were, if that was the agency's plan, why bother sending two lowly, unimpressive juniors? "I'd rather [meet with] three mid- to top-level agents than the top guy and a couple juniors," says one film producer, "because the top guy is not there for me, so now I'm with two juniors."

And what if you sit down with the entire department—does that mean you'll be serviced by all fifteen people? No way—no client receives (or even needs) that kind of treatment. This is designed to look impressive, to show off the agency's manpower and make you feel like you're getting the royal treatment.

"No matter who's in the meeting, always know who your day-to-day people will be," says reality showrunner Joke Fincioen (*Caged*). "Who's going to return your calls? Who's going to meetings with you? A department head may boost an ego, but better to connect with who is going to do the actual work." So again—look around: who's the lowest-level agent in the room? *This* is probably who will be doing most of your heavy lifting, although he or she may be supervised by a mid-level agent.

Now, if you're meeting with only the top two or three guys—CEO's or partners or department heads—you can be fairly certain these are the power-hitters who will be servicing you. But these types of meetings happen only for high-end clients. After all, if an agency is trying to impress and sign Martin Scorsese or Tony Gilroy or Angelina Jolie, they're not going to put them in a room with a bunch of middling and fledgling agents.

"[For my meeting the] agents came down themselves," says Brown, recalling a meeting at UTA, "and I remember wishing I had been a little more dressed up—because they were all dressed nicely. We went into the higher-up agent's office, and she had a spread of dried fruit and nuts, like a little Dean & DeLuca setup. I sat on the couch, next to my manager, and they sat in front of me in chairs and brought us drinks. I didn't do a lot of the talking, and I was surprised at that. They were comparing themselves to other agencies, saying they had the outreach, a lot of higher-up writers, a lot of female writers. [They were] trying to make it seem like a place where I would fit, where I would feel at home—and that they knew how to accommodate me and get me jobs that would be best suited for me. As a writer who wants an agent, you're nervous about getting them and wanting them to like you, [but] *they* were really selling themselves to *me*. Which was a shock."

Valuable Questions to Ask in an Agent Meeting

- How do you work with your clients? What's your process for developing ideas, pitches, and scripts?
- How do you differentiate from other agencies or management companies?
- How do you like to communicate with clients? Do you prefer phone? Email? Do you like to have scheduled weekly calls—or just check in whenever? How often do you talk to most of your clients?
- Do you use a team approach when covering the town? What studios, producers, and companies do you cover?
- How many of your clients are staffed on shows that are run or were created by other clients?
- What are some of your favorite shows that you've packaged?

Not-So-Valuable Questions to Ask in an Agent Meeting

- **Could I see your client list?** ("Unless you're a starfucker," says one agent, "it shouldn't matter. We're going to service you like anyone else and in the marketplace you're competing with everyone else on our list and every other agency's list anyway, so it doesn't matter." Also, a quick Google search should show you many of an agency's clients, so if you have to ask, it just shows you haven't done your homework.)

- **How many clients do you have?** (This is a question that seems important, says a high-level agent, but probably isn't. "If we're doing our job, you shouldn't feel like there are a thousand other people. I usually answer that question by telling people how many clients we actually have *available* at any given time, which is really small. We could have 10 million clients, but if 9,999,999 are working, who cares if we have 10 million clients?")

- **How many baby writers do you have?** I mean, baby writers take up massive amounts of time, so I don't want to be one of sixteen time-sucking baby writers. (Again: not that important. "Most agents don't want to represent baby writers" says one representative. "It's harder to get them work, and the money we make off babies is lower. So if we're even meeting with you, it's because we believe in you.")

- **Which studios, networks, or production companies do you do the most business with?** (Any legit agency should be doing business with *all* the major studios, networks, and production companies—and if you're unsure about the agency's legitimacy, you've got other issues to tackle. Also, this is information you can probably glean through a quick Google search, researching where the agency has recently sold shows or staffed big clients.)

The agents will also, undoubtedly, talk about your script and your writing process. What compels you to write the things you write? What's your writing schedule? Who are your biggest influences and inspirations? What are your favorite TV shows and movies? While flattery and attention are nice, a good agent will also lay out specifics for how they see your career developing—and how they'll help it along. "If [an agent] has a plan and a point of view for the writer and the material they've written, they're going to feel it," says WME TV agent Richard Weitz. And a plan does *not* include, "'We're reaching out to everybody. We throw it against the wall and hope it works.'" A plan should be calculated, tailored to the writer and his or her material. "'Your material sparks to *these* kinds of shows. Here are the people at studios and networks, and some of the writers we want to get it to, [writers and shows] we feel your writing directly relates to in order to move you forward.' [You want to] get them to know everybody in anticipation of staffing season, because that's basically what you're trying to do—staff them and break them in."

Insider's Tip

"Form a picture in your mind of where you are [today] and where you want to be, how you'd dream the world to be. Then question [agents] about what they think about that world and how they would get you there". —Charles Holland, entertainment lawyer/ TV writer

It's also good to have questions of your own to ask. After all, you are potentially embarking on a lifelong relationship, a partnership that will help your career sink or sail. Asking questions not only gets you information, it shows you're engaged, thinking practically, and informed about the industry.

Most meetings don't end with agents offering you a contract to sign right then and there—and you shouldn't be chomping at the bit to partner up right then, anyway. You want to take your time, make a smart decision. Usually, agents end the meeting by saying, "Well, thanks so much for coming in. It was great meeting you, and we'd love to have you here, if you'd like to be here." You can then take some time to think about your decision. You may have other representatives to meet. You may simply want to digest the meeting, think things over.

Ask for Client Referrals

Another helpful way of evaluating an agent or agency is by talking to other clients. Don't be afraid to ask for a couple of names to call or email. "Anybody worth their salt as an agent should feel confident giving out their clients' names," says Verve partner Amy Retzinger. "[Besides,] as a young writer, why not have an excuse to call up a bunch of writers who are on staff, or more senior than [you]? Maybe this person says 'Hey, keep me posted! I'm running a show at CBS, and if we ever need somebody, I'll call you!'"

Calling other clients is a great way to get important answers you may not get from agents themselves. How good is the agent about returning phone calls? What are the best ways to communicate with the agent? Does he or she give helpful creative notes?

"We signed somebody recently and gave them a list of ten clients," says manager Jeff Holland of The Cartel. We didn't think he would follow up with all ten, but he literally emailed and called every one of them and had a laundry list of questions. I thought that was a bit extreme, but he did his due diligence and we ended up signing [him]."

How Agents Decide if They Want You as a Client

Often, agents know before they even meet with you whether or not they intend to sign you; they won't waste their time with a meeting if they're not 99.9 percent sure they want you as a client. The meeting is just to make sure you're likable and not a psychopath. Many agents, however, especially at larger companies, must have their department heads, and sometimes the entire department, give their approval before taking on a new client.

How Much Do Age, Gender, and Ethnicity Matter?

If the world were perfect, age, gender, and ethnicity would have nothing to do with a writer's ability to get an agent. Unfortunately, the world is not fair and because age, gender, and ethnicity often *do* affect whether or not a writer gets hired, they also affect whether or not a writer can get an agent. They don't, however, always affect hiring decisions in the way you might think.

Age

"Everybody wants the young talented individual," says TV-writer-cum-entertainment-lawyer Charles Holland. "If you have somebody who's gray-haired and they're a beginner, they're going to have a hard time finding representation. If somebody's in their twenties, and they have good material, they're well-situated. Part of the reason agents are that way is that a lot of executives have that bias."

Having said this, every TV showrunner I know would much rather hire someone older, with deep reserves of life experiences and memories, than some young wunderkind fresh out of school. (In fact, according to a WGA study, the largest share of TV jobs in 2009 were held by writers ages forty-one to fifty, who claimed thirty-seven percent of available TV jobs.[14]) "Coming out of college, unless they're a brilliant writer and have lived an amazing life, [writers] just don't have the maturity," says Chris Mack, Vice President of the Warner Bros. Television Workshop. "When I was [a writer] on *ER*–I look about fifteen years younger than I really am, and I was thirty at the time–this guy asked me, 'How old are you?' I said, 'I'm thirty-one.' He walks away, and I go, 'Hey, you can't just ask that question and not tell me why you asked that!' and he says, 'I thought you were like twenty-one. And it's my opinion that a twenty-one-year-old hasn't lived long enough to tell America was life is all about.' That always kind of stuck with me and if you do read writers that are older, life brings [a depth] to the work."

Unfortunately, this doesn't necessarily make it easier for older writers to find an agent, even in television. Every agent wants to find the next Max Landis, the *Chronicle* writer who sold eight projects by the time he was twenty-seven. Just "like playing sports or looking at a draft pick," says Verve agent Zach Carlisle, you're "looking at potential, and if you see a piece of material you get really excited about–[but] maybe it's a little raw–and you read a second piece and it's better, if [the writer is] older, you think, 'Maybe they've reached their peak, maybe there's no more potential.' If they're younger, in their twenties or early thirties and it's their first or second piece of material, you feel like there is still more [mountain] to climb."

Race and Gender

The bad news: people of color and women are grossly unrepresented among the ranks of professional film and TV writers. In 2009, only *five percent* of working movie writers were minorities, and they earned only seventy-three percent of what their white male counterparts made. (The median income for white male writers was $76,517; minorities' median income was $55,653.) In television, minorities claimed ten percent of jobs and made seventy-eight percent of what white male writers earned.[15]

The good news: Hollywood is working to correct this. As we mentioned earlier, many TV studios have diversity programs in place, giving minorities a leg up when it comes to staffing. (Often, remember, diversity staff writers are "free." In other words, if a TV show hires a minority staff writer, the writer's salary is paid from a special studio fund, *not* from the show's regular writers budget. Thus, shows are motivated to hire minorities.) As a result, TV agents love finding talented minority writers, or "diversity writers," because they're often much easier to staff.

The WGA also has a handful of programs–such as the Feature Access Program, the Writer Access Program For Mid-Level Diverse Television Writers, and the Writers Training Program (for writers who aren't yet members of the WGA)–designed to boost numbers of working women and minority writers by getting their work to producers, executives, and agents. You can explore them yourself at the WGA's Diversity Department: www.wga.org/content/default.aspx?id=1042

"At my agency, I can take on whoever I choose," says N.S. Bienstock alternative agent Ra Kumar, "but I often seek the thoughts of other people I work with. We usually work as a team and have team qualities, [so] I want to make sure that if [my colleagues] are going to be working with someone, they like them and are interested in them."

As we discussed earlier, many considerations factor into an agency's decision to take on a client. Sure, that client must be talented and "good in a room," but what else does she have going for her? Is she a writers assistant about to be promoted? Did she just have a hot film at South By Southwest? Was she recently accepted into the Disney/ABC Television Writing Program? Has she spent years working as a respected sci-fi visual effects designer and has now written her own effects-heavy sci-fi film?

If an agency is really interested in a particular writer, and that writer is taking other agency meetings or uncertain about where he or she wants to sign, agencies may turn up the heat in their wooing efforts. Many may simply check in with the writer via phone or email. Some ply the writer with Lakers tickets and dinners at fancy restaurants. Others "use the other representatives in [the writer's] life," says Carlisle, "whether it's a manager or an attorney . . . to convey the passion that you felt."

"I know of some managers that say, 'If you don't cancel every meeting, I'm no longer interested in representing you,'" says manager Bryan Brucks of Luber Roklin. Personally, "I want to represent people I feel like I get along with, so if someone needs Lakers tickets for me to sign them, I don't want to work with them."

How to Decide which Agency Is Right for You

As you think about the agents you've met, weigh all the considerations we talked about earlier in the chapter. Do you care about being at a massive, muscular agency or would you rather be somewhere smaller, more familial, more nimble? Do you want an agent whose personality matches yours or balances your weaknesses? What if the most passionate agent works at the smallest, newest agency—does he still have the connections and relationships needed to propel your career? Do you feel like this agent understands your vision for your career and will make the appropriate decisions to help you realize it?

Aside from researching online and in the trades, another way to evaluate an agent is to ask the opinions and advice of industry friends: execs, writers, producers, other agents or managers, even assistants. Some good questions to ask people in the know:

- Do you enjoy interacting with this particular manager or agent?
- What kind of taste does this agent or manager have?
- Do you, or other buyers, trust this manager's opinions and suggestions? Is he an aggressive hard-seller or a casual soft-seller?
- Is this agent someone who gets things done?
- What's your perception of the company this agent/manager works for and the other clients they represent?
- How will your impression of this manager, or his other clients, color your impression of me?
- If you didn't know me personally, what would your general impression of me be based solely upon this particular agent or manager being my representative?
- How much personal attention do you think I'll get from this agent/manager? How does the amount of personal time they give me reflect on their stature in the industry, or their ability to get things done?
- Can this manager get his phone calls returned?

Also, "I would look at the culture of the agency," says Folio Lit agent Michelle Brower, who specializes in selling authors and literary properties to Hollywood. "Are they forward thinking? Are they adaptable?"

"It's a mistake to let
somebody represent you
because they're your uncle,
or your husband, or your wife.
It's also a mistake to have
somebody represent you
[because] you like their name,
they're at a [certain] firm, or
they're doing it as a favor.
You don't want someone
doing it as a favor."–Charles
Holland, entertainment
attorney

Do they have fingers in many different areas and businesses—and is this important to you? If you decide you want to write a novel or pitch a web series, or develop a reality show, will this agency be able to adequately service you? As the industry changes—with new distribution platforms and online channels appearing every day—is the agency positioned to maximize these developments?

Ultimately, "the number one thing is to find the person that believes in you and will do whatever it takes," says CAA-repped reality producer Biagio Messina (*Commercial Kings*). "If that person happens to be at a bigger agency—that's better. If that person is at a mid-level or boutique agency, then go to that mid-level or boutique agency. The power of one agent outweighs the power of the whole agency, but that doesn't mean that the big agency can't get you more, if your person who's fighting for you is at the big agencies."

As for Brown, "I met with two other agencies [besides UTA]," she says. "[One] made me feel like they probably weren't going to give me any individual attention. [At the other], I felt like I could call the guy up and he would be on the phone with me in a second; he would be easy to talk to, I could tell him anything, he'd always be available—but I felt like their reach wasn't [quite as strong]. I felt like UTA was perfectly in the middle. They were big, but would also be able to call me; they might not answer the phone [every time] I call, but they'd call me back. It was a perfect middle ground." Brown signed with UTA, and the very next staffing season, they placed her on Disney Channel's new series, *Dog With a Blog*.

Negotiating 101: The Ice Cream Rule

You've met with all the agents. You've heard all the sales pitches. You've weighed the pros and cons of each agency and gotten opinions from executives and producers. Finally, you've decided which agent you want to work with. Do you call him back and tell him the exciting news? *No–not yet*. Because first—you get ice cream.

"The Ice Cream Rule is a negotiating tactic," says Gerry Sadowski, a research analyst for Fox, Paramount, and Playboy TV. "Choosing which agent to go with, which deal to take, which contract to go after, each of those is a pretty big decision, and its easy to get caught up in that. The point [of the Ice Cream Rule] is to distance yourself . . . to take the heat off. When you're in the middle of a situation, it can be tough to see what's going on, to assess the path you should take for yourself. So when you've gathered [all] the information, when you're ready to make the decision, you put everything aside, walk away [and] get some ice cream—because ice cream is delicious. And you give yourself an opportunity to cool down, [to] come back and take a look at the opportunities in front of you and make your decision more responsibly, at arms length."

AGENCY PAPERS

You've just told your new agents the exciting news—you've decided to sign with them! Hugs all around! You both hope this will be a long, fruitful partnership. So . . . *now what?* Your agent may or may not ask you to sign **agency papers**, a contract governing the relationship between clients and their representation. Agency papers must follow rules and guidelines established by the WGA's **Artists Manager Basic Agreement (AMBA)** of 1976, also known as the WGA's **franchise agreement**. Each major union has its own franchise agreement officiating agent/client relationships and contracts (although as of September, 2013, SAG's franchise agreement has been expired since the early 2000s[16]).

The truth is: many agents don't bother asking clients to sign agency papers; they simply seal the deal with a verbal agreement and a handshake. It's important to know, however, that even without signing an actual contract, you are still bound by the rules of the agency's standard agreements. So if you're not sure what those are–*ask*. (And remember, even if you never see an actual contract, the agency must stay within the bounds of the WGA's franchise agreement.) The basic terms of most agency papers are:

• **Commission**–Most talent and literary agents charge ten percent, the maximum allowed by union franchise agreements. Agents and managers are allowed to commission *any* income you generate while being represented by them–even if you got the job yourself. Also, if you leave the firm–either by your own volition or because you're fired by your representation–your agency continues commissioning any income generated by work you did while under its banner. In other words, if you land a gig on *Nashville* while being represented at CAA, but you then fire CAA to be represented at Kaplan Stahler, CAA gets to keep commissioning your *Nashville* income. If Kaplan Stahler negotiates a raise, CAA continues commissioning the original amount; Kaplan Stahler commissions *only* the raise. (To learn more, see p. 302.)

Ask the Representative

Q: If I have more than one agency pursuing me, could I negotiate a lower commission–say, eight percent instead of ten percent?

A: Absolutely not. Not only will no legit agent or manager lower her commission, especially for a low or mid-level writer, but "if you're a baby writer, and you try to bring your percentage down, you're not really incentivizing your agent," says agent-turned-manager Lenny Beckerman. "Ten percent is not a lot of money in this market. [An agent] needs a lot of clients working until that ten percent buys something decent to live in. So I would not go with that. I would go with the idea of 'Who do you feel is going to be the best agent for you?'"

• **Term**–Agency contracts can tie a client to the firm for no more than two years at a time; this number, however, is negotiable and rarely binding. A client may also fire his agency if he fails to work or earn more than $10,000 in any ninety-day period. Of course, if a client is truly unhappy and wants to leave his agency, most agents won't obligate him to stay; usually, the agency doesn't want to rep the client any more than the client wants to be repped, and the two sides are more than happy to part ways.

• **Areas of representation**–Most agencies want to represent clients in all media: film, television, publishing, stage, digital, etc. But perhaps you already have a successful career, as well as representation, as a novelist–so you only want your new agency to handle your film and television work. You may be able to negotiate out of this. Jodie Foster, for example, is repped at ICM as an actor, but at UTA as a director.[17]

First Things First

"Every new client is a new project," says manager Kara Welker, a founding partner at Generate. "With every person who walks in the door there's a new list of tasks, things to accomplish. Usually, prior to signing that person, the goals are made clear, and hopefully you have said, 'I can do this.'"

Exactly what's on each client's "list of tasks" depends on the client's level and whether he works in TV or film. Let's say a manager signs a TV writer who has worked

Check Authorization–This grants employers permission to send your paychecks directly to your agency.

Bank Authorization–A statement allowing your agency to deposit checks into a bank on your account.

Danger! Agency Red Flags to Be Wary of

- An agency is not Guild-signatory, or has not agreed with the WGA's AMBA. To find out if a particular agency is Guild-signatory, consult the WGA's list of signatory agencies: www.wga.org/agency/agencylist.aspx
- An agency is not licensed or fails to meet its home state's legal operating requirements. You can research your state's agency requirements via the Association of Talent Agents, the trade organization representing talent agencies: www.agent association.com/frontdoor/agency_licensing_detail.cfm?id=571
- No agency should charge to read your material or consider you for representation.
- Agents and managers should never commission **residuals**, payments the writer receives when a movie or TV episode he wrote reruns on TV or On-Demand.
- Some agents may try charging you for photocopies, paper, postage, etc. *No.* Do not allow this. This isn't necessarily the sign of an untrustworthy agent, but don't allow it. Simply cross those parts out of the contract.
- An agency wants to commission more than ten percent; this is not allowed according to most franchise agreements, including the WGA's.
- Do not pay an agency any fees, such as registration fees, upfront! In fact, according to 2009's Krekorian Talent Scam Prevention Act, it is illegal in California to charge money in exchange for the hope of getting someone a job.[18]
- Agencies are not allowed to own or invest in client service businesses such as acting or writing coaches, head-shot photographers, writing or performing schools, printing operations, etc. Agents may also not refer clients to any such businesses in which they have even an indirect financial stake.[19]

It's Not You, It's Me: How to Let an Agent Down Gently

The good news: you've found an agent! The not-so-good news: you need to tell any other suitors that, unfortunately, you're marrying someone else (for now). It's important in these situations to be polite and considerate. After all, this person believed in you, they wanted you, they spent time and energy on you. That deserves respect and courtesy. Also, you never know when or how your paths might cross again. Agents switch agencies all the time. In January, 2013, former UTA agent Rob Kim joined forces with APA.[20] A month later, ICM lit agent Robert Lazar jumped ship for Resolution Agency, as did former CAA talent agent Isabella Brewster.[21, 22] Other agents leave representation to become execs or producers. In 2012, when *Two and a Half Men* co-creator Chuck Lorre inked a four-year TV and film development deal with Warner Brothers, he hired Bob Broder, the ICM agent who had negotiated Lorre's deal, to run his production company, Life's Too Short.[23] And Paradigm senior agent Ken Stovitz began as an agent at CAA, left to be an executive at Will Smith's Sony-based Overbrook Entertainment, then exited Overbook for Paradigm–bringing with him, as clients, Jada Pinkett Smith and Jaden Smith.[24]

Thus, today's rejected agent could be part of your agency's team tomorrow–or an executive you're hoping will buy your pitch! Therefore, when you call to break the bad news, keep it short, sweet, and polite: "You were great. Unfortunately, I'm going to go in a different direction, but thank you so much for everything."

Do I Want to Be "Hip-pocketed?"

Occasionally, agents "**hip-pocket**" a writer. This is like "pseudo-representation." Perhaps the agent isn't 100 percent certain she can sell this particular writer, so she wants a "trial period" to see how things go. Maybe the agent couldn't get the rest of her department to sanction signing this writer, so she's "hip-pocketing" the writer on her own. Or an assistant or coordinator has found a young writer she loves, and while the assistant is not a full agent, she offers to send out the writer's material. These are all forms of "hip-pocketing." (The agent's keeping the client in her "hip pocket," representing him on the side.)

"Hip pocketing frequently happens with lower-level writers," says The Cartel's Jeff Holland. "The time it takes to employ or get a baby writer working–it takes a lot more time than an upper-level position, and the revenue stream is so much lower, [so] you don't have a lot of time to spend on these baby clients." Thus, some agents would rather hip-pocket a writer than commit all their time and resources. There's no official agreement in these situations, but the relationship works similarly to a regular agent/client relationship, including ten percent commissions.

"It's certainly not a terrible thing if you have a friend, or someone wants to help you out, that can send out your stuff," says Verve coordinator Melissa Solomon, but "that should [not] be your goal."

Having said that, "we were hip-pocketed at [one of the Big Four agencies]," says reality producer Joke Fincioen (*Beauty and the Geek*, *Caged*), now repped at CAA, and "it was great in the sense that we could say, 'Yeah, we're with [this huge agency],' but we had to do all the work, all the hustling. The one time I needed [the agents] to make a phone call to legitimize a meeting with a big producer, they didn't want to make the call, so we said 'Screw you,' [and] walked away. I'd rather be at a boutique agency, with a junior agent who has been an agent for a year and fucking bleeds for us, than be hip-pocketed by somebody big."

Thinking Like an Agent

Q: I'm an unrepresented writer looking for an agent or manager. In Chapter 9, we talked about how agents "go wide" with a script in hopes of generating competition. Could I do the same thing? Could a writer looking for representation blast his script out to fifty agents or managers and say, "I'm sending this to you and forty-nine other people. It's a great script–so read fast, and if you're interested: let me know asap"? Would that work?

A: "I doubt it," says one big-time manager. "In this town, it's harder to get an agent for a screenwriter than it is to sell a script. There are more screenwriters–by ten, twenty, thirty times–than agents. So when you're an agent at an agency–big agency, small agency, medium agency–there's only a certain amount of writers you could represent, and only a certain amount of things you could read on a weekend. Especially agents who have families and obligations. How many scripts could you really read, as a person, and still have a life of some sort? [So] if somebody puts a gun to my head and says, 'Hey, you have to read this weekend or I'm not signing with you,' I'm not reading it that weekend. My feeling is: if he wants to sign with me, he must know something about me. He's researched me, how I've been with writers, how I treat them, what sales I had, what projects I've got going, and he thinks our relationship is going to be special enough that he'll give me the time to read. Just like I make a producer feel special by giving him a first look on a project, a writer should make me feel special by giving me a first look."

in the business a while. "If they are exceptionally good in a room, good at pitching, and have good samples ... [the] strategy might be more geared toward coming up with a pitch," says Thruline manager Chris Henze, who reps both TV and feature writers. "If somebody has exceptional spec material that hasn't been sent out, we'd talk about taking out the spec material. If it's somebody on the staff of a show, and the show's about to end, we're obviously going to be talking about staffing. What are their best samples? What do they want to do next? What kind of show should we be targeting to satisfy the next level of your career? Then we wait for them to become available and send samples for staffing."

If the new client is a low-level or baby writer, "I would probably encourage [them to write new] samples, whether it's a spec episode of a show or an original," Henze says. "I'd probably gravitate towards what attracted me to signing the person in the first place. So if they had a blog that was so impressive I had to represent them, I'd find a way to print parts of that blog, then have them back that up with some original material, whether it be an idea or a story or a spec script or even a sample of another show."

With feature writers, the representative's first step usually depends on whether or not the client has a new piece of material. This could be a new spec script, a short film, even an indie feature that's gotten into festivals. The agent or manager then sets about strategizing how to best expose this piece to buyers. Should they try the Shotgun Approach, sending it out wide, in hopes not only of selling it, but also introducing the writer to as many new executives and producers as possible? Or is the piece best served by slipping it to a handful of special producers?

If the writer doesn't have new material, a manager or agent may try to set them up on a "quick half-dozen generals," says manager Michael Goldberg of New Wave Entertainment, who reps sci-fi writer Damian Kindler (*Sanctuary*) and comedy writer Keith Heisler (*American Dad*).[25,26] "I like to use general meetings as a testing ground.

I try to make sure my writers have two or three ideas, so when they take rounds of generals, they're not just meeting an executive, putting a face to a name, they're testing to see if their idea is viable in the marketplace. It's a great way to get executives excited, workshop ideas, [and] check the competitive landscape to see what else is out there."

Good agents and managers will also talk with their client to figure out what they should write next. If they're a previously hot writer who's cooled off, or a young writer who has had success in the indie world, maybe they need to write something commercial to take their career to a new level. If they're a successful drama writer who wants to switch to comedy, they need to write something comedic. "I can't just tell people you're funny," says Henze. "Even if you go into a general and you're funny, people are going to read your dramas and not going to hire you because they want to read something you've written and laugh."

13   Working with Your Representation

"Having a relationship with your agent is like being in a marriage," says ICM agent Melissa Orton. "You have to be able to communicate with each other and say what one another needs. Communication needs to happen on both sides." While this sounds obvious, it's not uncommon for one or both sides of the partnership to—at some point—feel frustrated with the other. A writer friend called me a few days ago, fuming because his manager of three months hadn't gotten him a job on a TV show. Another friend, a manager, fired a long-time client (and close friend) because the client kept scolding her for not sending out his four-year-old *Family Guy* spec. Another friend, a successful feature writer, recently emailed me with a subject saying "Are all agents worthless?"

Most of these frustrations stem from poor communication. Sometimes writers and their handlers are communicating the wrong types of information to each other. Other times, one side or the other has unrealistic expectations about the relationship. Maybe there are certain obstacles making effective communication difficult. Or perhaps clients and their representatives just don't see eye to eye. Whatever the problem may be, the first step to improving agent/client communication is understanding where or how it may be failing.

Seven Things a Client Needs to Communicate to Their Representation

1. **Career goals**—Not every writer has the same career goals. Some want to become TV showrunners, creating and producing their own shows. Others are perfectly happy working on other people's shows, free from the stress and headaches of being a boss. Many want to write features and even direct. Any of these is a perfectly viable goal, but the road to becoming a sitcom showrunner is different than the road to writing and directing tentpole action flicks, and agents, unfortunately, aren't mind readers. If you want your representation's help in plotting a path to your goal, you need to articulate what that goal is—and the more specific the better. I always tell people, "the more laser-focused you can be, the more specific in your goals, the further you'll go faster." Saying "I want to write television" is not enough. "I want to write comedy" is only slightly better. Best: "I want to write single-camera family comedies a la *Modern Family* and *Trophy Wife*."

2. **Contacts and relationships**—Agents need to know who you have connections to. Are you neighbors with a Disney animation executive? Do you sit on your daughter's PTA board with the showrunner of a hot new AMC series? Did you attend a wedding this weekend and meet the director of the new *G.I. Joe* spinoff? Agents use every angle they can when trying to get you work, and all these bits of information help them navigate and grow your career.

3. **What you want to write on spec**—If agents don't know what you plan to write, they can't advise you on how marketable they think the idea will be, or whether or not it will help you realize your career goals. Perhaps more importantly, they can't strategize how to sell it for $3 million dollars! "It's fine to write your one-

million dollar indie piece," says *Conan the Barbarian* writer Sean Hood, "but be in communication with your agent about what you want to do with that. 'I want to direct it myself,' or 'I want to work with an indie director.' If you want to write a blockbuster script, talk to your agent about what is already out there. It's the agent's job to know what the market is looking for, what's already sold, what they're hearing from producers that they like."

4. **Specific jobs you may want**–Your agent or manager will not put you up for every single job. He can't. First of all, not every job is appropriate for you. Second, your agent has other clients he has to service, so sometimes he must evaluate who has the best shot of actually *getting* the job. Other times, you may hear of an opportunity your agent doesn't yet know about. In any of these cases, your agent can't help you get the job if he doesn't know you want it.

    So aside from talking to your agent about long-term career goals and hopes, you also need to keep him in the loop about your *short-term* goals and hopes. Read the pilots each spring and tell him which are your favorites. Inform him when you hear of a new job opening. I recently learned that some of my favorite sketch performers were doing a web series–which my agent rarely covers–so I asked her to find out if they needed any writers. (Sadly, they didn't.) The point is: don't be afraid to tell your agents what specific jobs you want, and to task them with going after them.

5. **Your priorities in a negotiation**–Sure, "sometimes money is important," says *Cloverfield* writer Drew Goddard. But sometimes writers are attracted to projects for other reasons as well. "Sometimes working with a specific director is important. Sometimes you have a passion for a project. Agents love hearing all of those things. They're not just about getting you the most money. They're about finding you the best fit–and it falls on your shoulders to communicate that to them."

6. **Status of projects you're working on**–Whether you're writing on a TV staff or speccing your own screenplay, your agent needs to know how things are going. Can he expect your new script in a month, or is it taking longer than expected? Is your TV-writing job going wonderfully, or are you worried they won't pick up your twenty-week option? "Your agent can only protect you if they know what's going on," says Hood. "So when producers start to ask for free rewrites and things they're not paying you for . . . if you don't let your agent in on it, they cannot be your advocate. So it's important to keep them abreast of what's going on–good or bad–on whatever work you happen to be doing."

7. **Things going on in your personal life**–You don't need to be an open book, but certain details of your personal life affect your career. If, for example, you're taking a part-time job that could lessen your ability to write or take meetings, your agent needs to know. If you have certain past experiences an agent can use to help get you work–such as being in prison, serving in the military, spending time in a cult–your agent needs to know. Maybe you've just had a baby, or survived a divorce, or lost your father to leukemia–these can actually be selling points! Perhaps it's pilot season, and ABC has a comedy about new parents, or CBS has a drama about teenagers navigating their parents' divorce! Maybe Relativity is looking for a closer to polish a script about a man dealing with leukemia–and your experiences with your dad make you the perfect candidate!

Seven Things Representatives Need to Communicate to their Clients

1. **What they need from the client**–Clients should always be writing new material, but managers and agents need to guide clients to write the "right" piece, the piece that will most help your representation get you work. For instance, if you've already specced *CSI* and *Law & Order: SVU*, your agent may need something lighter, more character-driven. Maybe your manager needs a demo reel of your

reality producing work. Perhaps your feature agent wants you to write something more commercial than your last script. Whatever it is, it's an agent's job to find you work and to let you know what resources he needs to do so.

2. **State of the marketplace**—"Your agent has to give you some idea about what the marketplace is like out there," says Hood. No one wants to spend six months working on a female buddy comedy if the market is already saturated with female buddy comedies. Likewise, if producers or studios are interested in futuristic action films, you may have a futuristic action script you could quickly revise—or a pitch you could whip into shape! Hollywood is a marketplace, and in order to fully participate as sellers, clients need to know what that marketplace is hungry for.

3. **Their own evaluations and analyses of ideas**—Managers and agents "need to communicate what they're responding to and not responding to in your material," says Verve agent Zach Carlisle. Is your first act not working? Do certain characters seem false or contrived? Is the B-story too cliched? Whether it's a screenplay, a sizzle reel, or the pitch for a new drama series, good reps do everything they can to prepare clients' material for the marketplace.

4. **What's going on with opportunities in play**—Neurotic clients hate being in the dark about what's going on with scripts or job opportunities. Has your manager sent out your new script? What about that staff job you went in for—is it filled? Representatives "always need to be updating someone when they have information," says Carlisle. "Don't wait for more information to come in—make sure the client knows what [is going on]. Also, make sure the client knows how the market responds to a piece of material. If people pass, give as much information as you can. 'This is why someone didn't respond: X, Y Z,' so they can better themselves and their career."

5. **Information to help prep for pitches or generals**—A writer going into a meeting with a producer or exec has a better chance of making a great impression if he's armed with helpful personal or professional information—and a good agent provides this. What shows or projects does the executive have in development? Do you and the exec have any mutual friends or colleagues? Are there personal touchstones that might make good talking points—stories about kids, schools, etc.?

6. **How agency changes may affect a client**—Sometimes agencies, or agents themselves, undergo changes that affect clients. Maybe a mid-level agency poaches a Big Four agent to come be a department head. Maybe an agent on your team is fired. Perhaps the company is merging with another firm or your point person is leaving to be a manager. It's essential for agents to keep clients in the loop about company changes—and how these changes may affect clients directly.

7. **Where the client stands in the industry**—For clients to be able to plan and build a career, they need to have an accurate picture of their place in the industry. What are a writer's chances of actually getting to run his own show? How does getting fired from a particular job affect a writer's reputation? How does *accepting* a particular job affect a client's reputation? It's essential for agents to give clients honest, straightforward perspective on where they stand professionally, how the industry perceives them, and how this fits into the larger context of their career.

None of this should be a newsflash to clients *or* agents; most know they need to be communicating. This doesn't mean, unfortunately, that writers and agents always do a great job of communicating. They often don't, which leads to many of the frustrations between clients and representation. But why don't agents and clients always communicate well? Ideally, they both *know* they're supposed to communicate, *right*? And ideally, they're in a co-dependent relationship: the writer needs the agent to get good jobs and deals, the agent needs the writer to book those jobs and make money. So they share the same goal. Why, then, do agents and clients so often *fail* to communicate clearly?

BARRIERS TO EFFECTIVE AGENT/CLIENT COMMUNICATION

Most people know that—in any type of relationship—communication is essential, yet despite everyone knowing this, communicating never seems to get easier. Parents misunderstand children. Husbands and wives keep secrets. Brothers and sisters throw punches instead of talking. Just like in a marriage or a family, agent/client relationships have no shortages of communication breakdowns. And when they occur, they're usually due to one of these eight common "communication barriers":

Barrier 1: Fear—"I Don't Want to Lose My Agent!"

Many writers place a massive premium on having representation. They think, "If I lose my agent, or can't get an agent, I have no career. I am nothing." They also believe having representation validates them. "Real writers have representation," they think. "If I don't have representation, I'm not a real writer. I have no value." Thus, writers are often terrified of doing or saying anything that could jeopardize their representation—or their chances of getting representation. They don't want to tell their agent, "That's not the kind of project I want to peruse", or "I get frustrated and nervous when I don't know what's going on with my script", or "I'm concerned I haven't had any meetings in six months"—because they fear upsetting—and losing—their agent. But are these concerns valid?

"The short answer would be *yes*," says one veteran manager, "because how do you sustain yourself in the business? How do you keep going? But the long answer is *no*—because more than anything else, it's all who you know. As long as you know the right people, you can get your material seen, and that's really key. Agents and managers are gatekeepers for the Hollywood community, but if you have someone at a studio or network, or your friend's a showrunner, or someone in a hiring position, you don't need to be repped. And guess what happens when you get [hired] on a show? You get repped right away."

My agent and I have a fantastic relationship; she works her ass for me. But that doesn't mean I don't pound the pavement to get jobs on my own. Sometimes I learn about a job from a contact, then have my agent use "official" channels to put me up for it. Other times, I get a job through someone I've previously worked with, but my agent gets me more money or a safer contract. The point is: agents are wonderful, but they're not the only way to survive Hollywood; in fact, even *with* a great agent, you'll need to keep pounding the pavement on your own. "There are many writers I know that don't have agents [and] are extremely talented," says *Mom* writer Kelly Galuska. "It's so much about timing and so many other elements."

Once you recognize and embrace this, you'll also recognize and embrace that there's life beyond your agent—helping to evaporate the fear of being without representation.

Barrier 2: We Forget to Think About the Long-term

You have a thorn in your side and you're anxious to hash it out with your manager or agent. Maybe you're angry at how she handled a particular negotiation. Perhaps you're disappointed in her response to your latest screenplay. Whatever it is, before you raise the issue, ask yourself: *is this a short-term problem or a long-term problem?*

"When negotiating with your agent, it is important to keep in mind that 'we either both win or both lose,'" says Donny Ebenstein, a negotiation and conflict resolution expert with two decades of experience. "Great agents make their money not by getting extra percentage points out of a client, or by getting someone to give them more stuff in negotiation. Their [long-term] success depends on having happy clients."

Thus, when you place a problem in the context of your long-term relationship, it often changes your perspective on the problem. You may be unhappy right now, but is this a problem that can—or should—affect your long-term relationship?

"Focusing on the long term brings out people's best behavior," says Ebenstein. Imagine, for example, you're driving to work and someone cuts you off on the freeway. Your yell and flip that person off. You're never going to see him again—who cares? But if you suddenly realize it's your neighbor, you *don't* flip him off, because you know you're going to have to see this person the next day. And the day after that. And after that. "Good behavior is like a tree, and the fruits get picked over time. They may not all get picked on the first day, but over time, if you culture and nurture it, you can keep picking the fruits."

Meet the Expert

Donny Ebenstein isn't someone you'd normally expect to find in a book about Hollywood. As a negotiation and conflict resolution expert, Ebenstein has helped build up mediation in Costa Rica's legal system, taught conflict resolution to teachers in a previously violence-ridden area of Colombia, and he's the author of *I Hear You: Repair Communication Breakdowns, Negotiate Successfull, and Build Consensus . . . In Three Simple Steps.* As Ebenstein can tell you, the art and skills of negotiating and communicating are the same whether you're negotiating a sitcom deal or helping the Israel Defense Forces coordinate security with the Palestinian Authority Police. So I thought it might be helpful to bring in an expert from outside the industry, someone who approaches negotiations—and relationships with negotiators—from a more "objective," free of detailed knowledge about if-comes, shopping agreements, or open assignments.

Barrier 3: Agents and Clients Have Different Goals

"Whenever you have a principal (client) and an agent, ideally, the agent's incentives should be lined up perfectly with the principal's," says Ebenstein. "In other words, what you want to achieve in your deal should perfectly match what the agent wants to achieve in your deal. But it's hard to get that right all the time. Everyone's an individual and we have different things we care about."

In other words, a writer/client may care about certain things—the amount of money she's paid, the length of a particular job—and she *assumes* the agent has the same cares, goals, or priorities . . . when in reality, the agent has his own agenda.

There's a joke that illustrates this nicely: A young man graduates law school, and his father, a prominent lawyer, gives him a job at the family firm. On the son's first day, his dad hands him a file and says, "Here you go, kid—I've been working on this case for twenty years." The young man comes back the next day, hands his dad the file, and says, "Hey, Pop—I solved the case!" And his dad says, "You idiot! That's the case that put you and your brothers through law school!"

So while we want certain things from a situation, our agent may want others—and whether we think the agent's goals are right or wrong, being cognizant of this gap can help us navigate certain conflicts. "We all try to be aware that there's this tension," says Ebenstein, "but we also have to be realistic; we don't have angels as our agents, we have human beings. Just because you said, 'This is what I hope happens,' doesn't mean that's what the agent hopes happens. And just because you say to your agent, 'This is my number one priority here,' doesn't mean the agent will agree that it should be your number priority, and it doesn't mean the agent will push for it as the number one priority."

This is one reason it's helpful, in the salad days of your relationship, to have an open conversation with your agent or manager about hopes, concerns, and expectations for the partnership. "In a lot of relationships, people enter with a whole set of preconceived notions [and] expectations," says psychotherapist Chuck Moshontz. "Great! Except the other person has a different map, and they're proceeding on *that* basis. So just put those maps out and compare them side by side. Ask 'What are you capable of doing for me? What do you need from me to make that job easier? What can I expect from you?' Get the lay of the land and the ground rules."

Even as the relationship evolves and you and your agent start to click, get in a groove, you may find you sometimes have occasionally different agendas. You may want to partner with a particular producer or piece of talent, and your agent may want you to partner with someone else. Perhaps you want to write a low-budget indie film you could possibly direct—while your agent wants you to take a rewrite job. "One of the ways to navigate that tension is to be transparent about it; make it a topic," suggests Ebenstein. "Say 'Listen, agent, I know you're pushing me to accept a particular assignment or offer, because you want to get work on the board. I know you care about my career, but it also helps you to get paid. I'm pushing back because I have different ideas about my career. Maybe they're not realistic, and I know you don't make any money if I don't accept work. I want it to work for both of us, and I don't want to waste your time, but I'm the client, and I need it to work for me, so let's find a way to navigate or balance that.'"

Barrier 4: Different Perspectives on the Same Situation

Even when agents and clients' goals are perfectly aligned, they can still have different approaches to a problem or scenario. Let's say Sarah, a mid-level writer, is up for a writing job on *Cruel Summer*, a hit drama series. The studio's initial offer came in lower than expected, but Sarah is unfazed; both she and her agent, Tony, are excited about the opportunity. So Tony dives into the negotiation, eager to seal the deal and land Sarah the job. But the deal falls through. Sarah, not surprisingly, is *pissed*. She blames Tony—he was too aggressive! Sure, the money was low, but so what?! Sarah would've taken the job! Now she has nothing! How could Tony screw this up?!

It usually helps to adjust your thinking, to try and see the situation from the other person's perspective; not necessarily to agree with it, but to help you understand it and see the whole picture. "If you felt your agent went in there and was too aggressive and screwed things up," says Ebenstein, "your story might be 'I tried to warn the agent and he did it anyway! Now I'm frustrated, and it damaged my reputation and relationship.' But the agent's story might sound like: 'My job is to protect my client. My client is sometimes naive and sells herself short; she doesn't establish or defend her worth in the marketplace, or she gets herself deals that are not worth taking. So I tried to be gentle, but if I wasn't gentle enough, it's not a reflection on me—it's a reflection on the lousy deal terms! Not only should my client not be frustrated, she should be thanking me! In six months, she'd have come crying back to me.'

"Those are two different narratives. Neither is more right, but it's not about being right, it's about seeing both sides. It's possible your agent didn't understand you weren't doing this for the money but rather for the creative opportunity, or she failed to realize you were doing this because of a personal relationship. But to make the conversation go better, you need to see multiple stories and points of view."

Barrier 5: Not All Clients Are Created Equal

While every writer hopes he's his agent's most important client, that's unfortunately not true for everyone. "The truth is, almost everybody prioritizes based on who's making the most money," says manager Jeff Thal of Ensemble Entertainment, whose clients include writer John Jarrell (*Romeo Must Die*) and director Ron Underwood (*City Slickers, Heroes, Once Upon a Time*). This can be a tough pill to swallow, especially for clients who aren't actively working. But agents, like writers, have mortgages to pay and families to feed.

Having said that, agents and managers don't *always* focus on their biggest breadwinners. "Sometimes your biggest clients don't need you because they're working on a series, it's a hit, they're successful," says Thal. "Months can go by where they don't need me for anything other than to stay in touch and think about the future. [Then] some new guy comes in with a great new spec pilot or feature I love, and I might spend a lot more time on him than I am on my big clients. My energy tends to go where the need is. If I have something new I believe in, I'm going to put a lot of time into it—even if it's a client who has no track record."

So the key to staying near the top of your agent's priority list, especially if you're not yet a multi-million dollar screenwriter is to *always be pumping out new material*. "Ultimately, the most successful clients," says Gersh partner Roy Ashton, "are clients who are constantly coming up with things on their own: working to find material, find stories, coming up with ideas, watching television, watching movies, figuring out how to construct a TV show they can go out and sell."

Similarly, what turns off many agents and managers "is the writer who hasn't generated any new material, and all he wants you to do is sell his old material," says Madhouse Entertainment's Robyn Meisinger. "Buh-bye. Move forward. Focus on the future."

Barrier 6: Agents and Managers Just Like Some Clients Better than Others

"What a lot of people don't realize," says New Wave manager Michael Pelmont, "is a big part of getting the most from your [agent or] manager is having that relationship, that friendship. I work hard for all my clients, [but] I'd be lying . . . if I said there weren't some clients I'm really *friends* with." Not every client necessarily wants (or needs) to be "friends" with his representation—and that's okay—but let's be honest: *friends like doing things for friends*. When my friend A.J., an elementary school teacher, needs a favor, I'm happy to help. The same goes for work matters. If an agent or manager must choose between spending an hour going over a script with a grumpy, defensive writer versus an easy-going, hilarious buddy—who do you think he's going to pick? "If someone seems like an asshole I'm probably not going to sign that person," says Pelmont. "Or if I sign him, I'm probably going to work a little harder for the guy I'm close with, [the guy] I have a good, healthy relationship with. That's human nature."

Barrier 7: Agents Can Be Intimidating

Negotiating with Nolan

"You may be playing catch with Nolan Ryan," says negotiation expert Donny Ebenstein, "but you can say, 'Nolan, everyone knows you have a great fast ball, but you're playing catch with *me*—so keep that in mind.'" In other words, feel free to ask your agent to slow down, explain things again, walk you through his thought process. And don't be afraid to spell out your own passion, concerns, worries, or fears.

It's true. After all, agents' whole purpose in life is to negotiate and manipulate to get what they want. And while that's great when they're on on the front lines, fighting for our livelihood, it can be intimidating when we're up against it ourselves, trying to articulate an idea we believe in or express a concern or disappointment. Especially because writers tend to be neurotic, non-confrontational, and conflict-adverse.

So how do we keep from getting talked out of things we want—such as being able to write certain scripts or pursue certain projects—if our agent thinks we should do something else? If we acquiesce, do we look like a sucker? If we express certain fears or concerns, will our agents see us as weak and wimpy?

"A great agent is somebody who is listening at all times to what a client wants," says Tanya Cohen of Verve, "and sometimes making hard decisions to turn down potential paying jobs in order to have integrity to an artist's vision."

It often helps to know agents are often just as nervous about appearing vulnerable or ineffectual in front of clients as we are in front of agents. "I had a client [call] the other day [and catch] me at a bad moment," says one veteran lit agent. "He called because he thought of an ending for this feature he's been writing. But we're on the phone, and he could tell I was bummed, so he says, 'What's wrong?' And he just kept poking until I was like, 'Fine, I got fucking fired [by a client] today, okay?! It was a client I had signed [six months ago] and I staffed her on [a drama show].' I [knew] I shouldn't be telling my client that someone fired me. You want to be represented by someone everybody knows, everybody likes, everybody respects, [and] a lot of being an agent is about perception. Is he gonna lose faith in me because someone's leaving me to go to [a rival agency]? To be that vulnerable to a client . . . it confuses me whether or not it hurts me."

I like this story becomes it reminds me that agents have neuroses and insecurities, too. They don't want clients to be unhappy or displeased any more than clients want agents to be unhappy or displeased.

Barrier 8: Different Communication Styles

Different people like to communicate in different ways. Some prefer phone conversations; others prefer email. Some write long wordy notes; others pound out abbreviated text messages. Some chat briefly several times a day; others go weeks without speaking a word. "It's up to [the agent and client] to determine the best way for them to maintain a level of communication with which they're both happy," says Folio Lit agent Scott Hoffman. "Ask the agent what the agent's communication style is, and the frequency with which the agent would prefer to communicate with the author."

There may be growing pains as new clients and agents become accustomed to each other's communication styles. There's nothing wrong with this; in fact, it's helpful to talk about these things out in the open. For example, my agent once told me it drives her crazy when I text her during the day. "If I'm in an important meeting and my phone goes off, I think it's an emergency," she said. "Then I look, and it's you asking about a pilot. And by the way—I do most of my communicating over email. So if you text something to my phone, I don't see it when I'm responding to emails later, and it doesn't get done."

Some agents or clients even like to schedule regular calls or meetings. "I have set calls with clients at least once a week," says N.S. Bienstock alternative agent Ra Kumar, "even if it's only for ten minutes to make sure we're on target. I'm kept honest and they're kept honest."

In the early stages of an agent/client relationship, the writer and her representation may speak more frequently. There are many introductions to be made, meetings to be taken, scripts to be submitted, new specs to be completed. New clients may also need more guidance from their representation. Which project does a baby writer's new agent think she should be pursuing? Who are the most important execs or producers for her to meet?

As the relationship settles into a stable working routine, communication may die down. If you're busy working on your new horror screenplay, or in the middle of production on a Nickelodeon series, there's no reason to talk to your agent every other day. Communication picks up when things get busy again. If your agent or lawyer is in the midst of negotiating your spec sale, or going out with your new reality pitch, you may talk several times a day. Then, once you're off writing or the show is in production, communication once again tapers away.

The important thing to remember is: even if you and your agent don't need to communicate *right now*, the lines of communication must be kept *open*. It's fine not to talk to—or hear from—your agent for weeks at a time, as long as neither side feels ignored and both feel comfortable reaching out when they need to. This means both parties must be willing to A) ask for what they need, and B) listen to their partner's needs. It's also important to understand that communication ebbs and flows. "There are times I'll go months without talking to my clients," says Hoffman, "if they're knee-deep in writing I don't need to be involved in."

APPROACHING YOUR REPRESENTATION ABOUT CONFLICTS

"We need to talk."–Perhaps the worst four words in the English language. Whether it's with your spouse, your parents, your fiance, your boyfriend, your kids, your employee, your agent, or your manager, no one likes to hear–or say–them. Maybe you feel your agent hasn't been selling your new screenplay as hard as he should. Perhaps you think your manager hasn't sent your spec pilot to the right kinds of production companies. Whatever your beef, as the captain of your career, you need to be willing to take the wheel of your agent/client relationship and put your issues on the table. Unfortunately, writers are great at creating and navigating conflict on the page, but in real life? Forget it. We're nervous, skittish, socially awkward, introverted, even reclusive. Let me write a script about someone in an uncomfortable situation–bam, done. But I'm at a total loss if I have to navigate that same uncomfortable situation myself.

So how should you approach your agent or manager when you're unhappy? Schedule an appointment at their office? Is it easier just to have your manager talk over the issue with your agent, so you can stay out of the fray?

Who Should You Talk To?

Agents and managers are different–and sometimes one more is more equipped to respond to certain problems than others. "The 'personal manager' is called personal for a reason," says Thal. "Managers are supposed to have fewer clients and give you more time and attention, so it would seem natural that you would have a closer, deeper, more open relationship with your manager." Thus, managers not only help writers develop and shape material, they also field frustrations and emotional issues. Their job, in fact, is to manage your entire professional life, including relationships with other representatives.

"A lot of times when my clients have problems with their agents, they tell me," says Brillstein Entertainment Partners manager Alex Murray, "and if I feel it's kind a 911 issue, I'll alert the agent and try and fix it. Address it head on. [Sometimes] I encourage the agent to call the client directly, have lunch or dinner, engage them a bit more. A lot of times, it just comes out of insecurity and a little distance, and once they hang out a bit, and see the agent is passionate, it fixes a lot of things."

How Should I Have This Difficult Conversation?

Rule One of conflict navigation: *don't do it in an email*! As anyone who's ever tried to send an inappropriate or sarcastic joke over email knows–emails are easily misread and misunderstood. Some things (like humor) don't always translate; others, like anger, are often amplified or distorted. "It depends on the situation, and how upset the client is, but I believe in personal connection, face-to-face interaction, dealing with things head-on," says Cohen. "Grab lunch, grab coffee, come into the office for a meeting. If you can't meet in person, do it over the phone."

When beginning the actual conversation, even though tempers may be running hot, address the situation with questions rather than attacks and accusations. "Curiosity is the first part, rather than condemnations or assumptions or blame," says Moshontz. "Ask, 'What is going on here? Why did this come down the way it did?' And don't answer it yourself–because you don't know! 'I find myself feeling that–you blew this, you screwed me, you're incompetent. I don't want to believe [that], so I want to understand from you what happened here.'"

It also helps to assume some level of responsibility or cooperation. Your goal, remember, is not to fire your representative or put him on the defensive. Your goal is to *improve your relationship*. So rather than saying, "You haven't gotten me a single pilot meeting this year; what's going on?!" try "I've noticed I haven't had any staffing meetings for a while. What should I be doing differently?"

"Take it on yourself and let the person start to talk," says Thal. "You might learn a lot more from that than being aggressive and pointing the finger. The other person may say, 'I have been a bit distracted lately for this or that reason,' or 'I haven't felt that your last two scripts were as good as the ones [you wrote] two or three years ago; we haven't been getting as good a response,' or 'I'm glad you brought this up because it's frustrating for me too. I'd love to still work with you, but we need to do something different.'"

Deal with It

Q: I know I should have open communication with my agent, and I shouldn't have panic attacks over being without representation. Still, whenever I'm worried or frustrated with my agent, I get nervous—and I tend not to express those things because I'm afraid of upsetting him. How can I get over this fear to foster effective communication with my representation?

A: "This is [actually] two questions in one," says Donny Ebenstein, who has taught negotiation and conflict resolution on five continents. "It's important to break the question into parts because it goes to the heart of what makes people more effective in negotiation, and communication in general. [The first] part of the question is: 'What do I do with my feelings? How do I manage them?' Fear, apprehension, nervousness. People need to grapple with their own internal reactions and experiences."

Step one in managing your emotions is to simply "identify, acknowledge, define, explore what you're experiencing," Ebenstein says. "The simple matter of talking it through with someone you trust, or thinking about it on your own, can be very helpful. That someone could be your agent, or someone else before you talk to your agent. 'What is my fear? What do I not want to have happen?' Make friends with that fear. Defining it is a big part of mastering it." After all, *your fear may be warranted.* Your agent or manager *may* leave if you say the wrong thing. But you can't deal with this fact—emotionally or practically—unless you acknowledge it.

It's also important to remember that *you can leave, too.* While the agent/client relationship is often compared to a marriage, this is one area where it's *not* like a marriage—neither of you is locked in for better or worse. *You can leave whenever you want.* Once you've acknowledged this, you can ask yourself: "Do I want to be partnered with someone who leaves me just because I express myself?" If you're with someone—whether in a marriage or a business arrangement—who leaves just because you voice your opinion or concerns, it's probably not a healthy relationship.

Now, the second part of the question: "how do you communicate?" says Ebenstein. "That's external: not what's in your head, what comes out of your mouth."

Often, the best answer is to be honest and lay your fears on the table. "State your needs, not as a demand but as a question," says psychotherapist Chuck Moshontz. "Start by saying, 'I'm worried. I'm angry . . . I'm nervous about having this conversation . . . but I don't know whether I should be or not, so I wanted to check it out with you.' Often, we—as human beings—look at ourselves as 'that thing over there' and 'a thing over here,' lobbing information back and forth, and we're not sure how it's landing. The truth is the other person is a partner in this conversation. [So] rather than two armed camps, fighting it out, opposing each other, it's two people sitting together, looking at the issue, trying to resolve whatever it is . . . together as a collaboration. How can we have this conversation—about what may be a difficult subject—*together*?"

Moshontz suggests rather than making "a declaration of 'God damn it—get me a job!'" which *may* alienate your representation, try saying, "'I'm nervous having this conversation', [or] 'I need a job real soon because my money is running out, how can we handle this?'"

By approaching conflicts this way, you create a comfortable space where both parties feel like part of a mutual partnership. This allows you and your manager or agent to work together, instead of at odds, to explore the problem and find solutions. "In order to get along in this world," says Moshontz, "we have to accept that others' realities have as much validity as [our own]. 'I am the center of the universe. I take that to be absolutely true. But I also take it to be absolutely true that so are you. And so is everybody else.' Having that perspective engenders respect for the other person's point of view. You don't have to agree with it—but you can recognize that it's right for them. And that [point of view] might be a deal breaker! You might say, 'I'm not down with that way of perceiving the world, so on that basis, I think it's best we part company.' Or you may say, 'Okay, that's not my experience, but in this instance, I trust yours.'"

WRITERS' MOST COMMON COMPLAINTS ABOUT AGENTS

"My Agent Never Calls Me Back!"

This complaint has become a Hollywood cliche, but that doesn't make it any less frustrating. And when it happens, it can be maddening. However—and I'm not excusing bad communication—it also helps to have some perspective.

"There are a lot of people who don't return every phone call," says Thal, "even if you're friends with them." He's right. I have close friends who take days to return calls—and I'm the same way. My brother and I sometimes play month-long games of phone tag, with days or weeks between voice mails. When it's our agent, however, someone we've entrusted with our livelihoods, we tend to set the bar higher than we do with other people. This isn't entirely fair—to us *or* the agent.

"The bar is inherently set higher in a relationship where one person is dependent upon another," says psychotherapist Moshontz. "It's not a psychological mechanism, it's the truth! It's even written into law. For example, in psychotherapist/patient relationships, there is a standard that is recognized: therapists have a certain obligation to care for clients in certain ways because there is a dependency—one person is dependent on the other, and the other person correspondingly has power over that person. So it's hard not to take it personally when you're the little birdie with your mouth open, waiting for the worm that only the mama bird can provide, and the mama bird flies off and doesn't come back for a week! The bar *is* set high!"

The first step in dealing with this is realizing that unreturned phone calls are rarely about *you*. Managers "deal with the same thing," Thal says, "whether it's agents or network executives or studio executives or producers. A lot of people are very busy, stressed, and under a lot of pressure. And some people just have bad phone manners."

Wait, what's that? *Managers* can't get all their calls returned?! Well, what's this tell us? That's right—*it's not about you*. "One of the great things we do to screw ourselves up is to take things personally," Moshontz explains. "People have all kinds of complicated reasons for not returning phone calls—logistical, psychological, whatever. So until you know otherwise, a good metacognition is to not take it personally, to recognize this may not be about you."

Having said that—if dropped calls have become a pattern, it may be worth having a conversation. Again, approach the situation with curiosity and concern rather than anger and accusations. "What I would say to your agent—your 'partner,' if you will," says Moshontz, is "'You know, this has happened three times in the last three months—I've called you and didn't get a call back for a week. I just want to better understand what goes on when that happens—because its hard for me not to take it like you don't care about me, you're not really working for me. Can you help me understand, from your point of view, why you don't return those phone calls?'" This allows your agent to answer without feeling defensive. He may say, "I'm sorry, my wife is pregnant, it's been a crazy month," or he may say, "Look, I'm not great at returning phone calls—can you build that into your expectations?" Or, "I haven't told anyone this, but I've been having some serious health issues." Or, "I have more important things to do than talk to you all day—I'll get to your calls when I get to them, you needy baby!"

Based on your agent's response, you can then decide whether the problem is fixable . . . or whether it's time to hunt for new representation.

All in the Timing

"What time of day your agent calls you back tells you where you rate in their life. My agent never calls me back before 7:00 at night, which makes me think he doesn't care about me at all. If they call you back the same day it means one thing; if they call you back before 11:00 a.m. it means they love you."—Veteran screenwriter

Is there truth in this? Maybe a little . . . I'm sure when Steven Spielberg calls CAA, his agent, Richard Lovett, picks up or calls back immediately. But most people aren't Steven Spielberg. That doesn't mean you won't be someday—even soon—but you're not yet. (However, if you *are* Steven Spielberg, and you're reading this book—I'm a huge fan! Call me!)

However, there's a more practical reason why agents return phone calls when they do. Remember, agents must make and return countless daily calls to execs, directors, managers, and producers, and those people aren't always easy to reach. "You have to plan phone calls to those people around the times when they are likely not in meetings, which usually start at the top of every hour," says APA agent Lindsay Howard. "So if they're not starting meetings until ten or eleven in the morning, you have between nine and ten to get people on the phone. Then it's cyclical toward the end of the hour before another one starts."

Of course, execs and producers aren't the only ones who are busy. Agents are also in meetings much of the day, so they often make calls while in the car or racing from one meeting to the next. Entire days can be spent playing phone tag. Thus, "a lot of people just routinely return all their calls at the end of the day," says literary manager Jeff Thal, "especially client calls." This isn't a comment on the importance of those clients. But since most executives and producers have specific office hours, agents have limited windows in which to reach them. Artists like writers and directors tend to have more flexible schedules, so agents push those calls to the end of the day. It's easier, for instance, to reach a writer at 7:30 p.m. than a Lionsgate exec. So, unless you have an extremely urgent matter, don't be insulted by your agent's end-of-day phone call.

Faster than the Phone

For clients who want quick responses, "we also have this thing called email," adds Ensemble Entertainment manager Jeff Thal. "Some people are much more reachable via email. It's more efficient, and they're quicker about returning emails than phone calls. Often, if I don't get somebody on the phone right away, I send an email—depending how urgent it is, five minutes later, or five days later—and say, 'Hey, I called you to check in on this, what's going on?' Eventually, they get back to you, so you have to be a bit patient."

Words of Wisdom

"The worst time to email your agent is between 12:30 and 2:30 in the afternoon. When I'm in the car on the way to lunch, I can't adequately respond. When I check it on my way back to the office after lunch, I forget to respond until later in the afternoon. It's terrible but it's true. *So please don't email your agent during those two hours.*"—Lindsay Howard, vice president, APA

"I Have a Fantastic Idea I'm Excited About . . . and My Agent Doesn't Want Me to Write It!"

Writers "are often so passionate about their own work they lose perspective on it," says Folio Lit partner Scott Hoffman. "Ironically, that's one of the ways in which agents can be most valuable to artists—particularly writers. We're able to be more dispassionate, to see the true worth of [a project]."

An agent or manager's job is to help nurture, guide, and facilitate a client's career. And while you may want to write a tear-jerking screenplay about your great-grandfather's gout, if that screenplay isn't commercial enough to sell, or "noisy" enough to get you attention and meetings, you've not only failed to advance your career, your representatives have failed to adequately advise you. This doesn't mean, of course, you must always take your agent's advice or write what he dictates. It does mean, however, that you should let him do what you're paying him to do: advise you on the best way to achieve your career goals. If, after chewing on his advice, you still want to write about Great-Grandpa's gout, go for it. Your final product may be so wonderful it changes your agent's mind . . . or it may be something that forces the agent to say,

"I'm sorry—I don't think I can sell this. Perhaps we should part ways." This is the risk you must be willing to take.

"The role of the agent to explain to the client, then let him make his own decision," says Hoffman. "And because I work with that client on a commission basis, whether I want to be involved in that project, or whether I want to be involved with a client whose commercial goals might differ from my own, is [an issue] that often winds up being a source of conflict between agents and clients."

"I Turned in My Script and My Reps Gave Me a Ton of Terrible Notes: It's like they don't understand the script—or me—at all! Can't they just shut up and *sell*?!"

"When I give a writer notes," says one manager, "it's always with the caveat that *they're* the writer and I'm just trying to help. I don't give people my own personal take, I try and respond the way I think the marketplace is going to respond, the way I think buyers are going to respond. Sometimes it's informed by having already submitted the material to a certain number of people to get feedback; sometimes it's just having done this for thirty years—there are a lot things I can anticipate people are going to say."

Does this mean you need to rush off and slavishly take your agent or manager's notes? Not necessarily. In fact, there are several ways you may choose to respond:

1. **Simply say, "Hm . . . that's interesting. Let me think on that for a while."** Whether they're from my agent, another writer, or an executive, I often find if I let notes sit and simmer for a while, I start to get my head around them. Other times, I find if I chew on a note for a few hours or days, I realize with even more certainty why it's not a great note and how to articulate this. Either way, it's frequently helpful *not* to respond in the moment. Chances are you'll have a more cemented opinion on the note later.

2. **Come up with a better fix.** Often, when agents or managers give a note, "I'm hoping [the writer] comes up with a better idea than what I threw out there," says Thal. "I'm not ever married to my own ideas. I'm trying to help them see weaknesses and give possible solutions."

Sometimes, writers need to see "the note behind the note." For example, maybe your agent has read your searing kitchen-sink drama and says "I think your main character needs a sidekick. What if we gave him a wisecracking clown?" Well, a wisecracking clown may be totally wrong, but "the note behind the note" may be that the main character needs a friend to talk to. Right now, the script is bogged down with voice-overs and internal monologues—by giving your protagonist a friend, a sidekick, he can verbalize internal thoughts in a more dramatic or comedic way.

3. **Articulate why the script works the way it does.** Sometimes, a well-articulated explanation goes a long ways in quelling an agent's issues. I am not endorsing fighting every note or bullheadedly defending your script. Quite the opposite. Your agent's note is very likely touching on a genuine flaw . . . but by explaining, "B has to work this way so that C can work this way," or "Moment X sets up Moment Y, which happens later," you illuminate your intent for the agent. Then he can either say, "Oh, I get it—now it makes sense," or he can say, "Well, if that's your intent, maybe the real problem is in the previous scene." Then, hopefully, he points out a flaw you *do* agree you should fix.

4. **Do nothing.** Everyone gives bad notes sometimes, but ignoring a note altogether is often the least productive response. Sure, it's momentarily easier, but in the long term, it improves neither the script nor your relationship with your agent. "I'm disappointed if [writers] don't address the notes in any form," says Thal. "I wonder why they're being complacent, because I'm usually pretty sure about the notes I give." Ignoring notes also sends your reps a message about how you'll deal with notes from showrunners, studios execs, or other employers. A big part of success in Hollywood hinges on how you respond to feedback; if you can't accept constructive criticism from your agents and managers, people supposedly on your team, it makes them less comfortable sending you into professional situations where you'll be expected to deal with notes from other people.

"Why Didn't My Agent Put Me up for this Job?!" or "How Come My Agent Didn't Know about this Job?!"

Sometimes, writers find out about an open writing assignment or staff job they think they're perfect for, and the agent didn't submit them. Usually, representatives just tell clients, "I didn't think the job was right for you." But the truth is, "you have a list you have to service," says one agent, and "you can't put everybody up for [the same thing], so you pick the people you want to put up for certain jobs." Usually, agents select candidates based on who has the most appropriate writing samples. Other times, they select clients who have a little more "heat," figuring they have the best chance of actually landing the job. Often, agents don't realize you might have *wanted* the job; perhaps you're typically a procedural writer, and your agent had no idea you wanted to be considered for SyFy's new time-travel series. In these cases, you and your representation may need to re-discuss your career goals—and the kinds of stepping-stones needed to accomplish them. Your agent or manager may not fully understand your vision for your career. Or *you* may not fully understand the types of jobs you should be pursuing to keep you on track.

Lastly, it's also possible that the concerns dredged up by this experience—by not getting submitted for a job you wanted—are founded: your agent has lost interest in you. Or has other clients he's more interested in. If "I've got ten story editors who write fantastic action [scripts, and] I can send two of them" in for a job, says one agent, "maybe I shouldn't be representing the other eight."

"Why Are You Still Negotiating?! Just Close the Damn Deal— I Need to Get Paid!"

Occasionally, negotiations drag on longer than expected, which can be nerve-racking for a client anxious about closing a deal and landing a job. There are several reasons, good and bad, that can extend negotiations:

- **There are important outstanding deal points.** If your quote for a spec purchase is $350,000, and a studio only wants to pay you $200,000, you probably don't want your agent to rush and close the deal. Not only will you accept a much lower price tag for this project, but accepting a lame offer resets your quote at a much lower value.
- **There are "unimportant" deal points still outstanding.** A writer recently told me she had accepted work on a TV show, only to have her negotiations drag on for several weeks past the date when she was supposed to start. When her lawyer finally closed the deal, he sent the client a note saying, "Congrats—we're closed! And we got that improved workman's comp clause we wanted." The client was furious. "*Workman's comp?!* I spend my entire day in a conference room with five other people—I don't need better workman's comp! I need to get *paid!*"

  This "is a point lawyers are sometimes guilty of," says entertainment attorney Charles Holland. "While we are trained to think in terms of legal concepts, sometimes we don't think in terms of practical effects—like somebody hasn't been paid. And creatives have almost always gone a period of time without being paid, so when they get something, they need to be paid! That's a practical thought lawyers are not always cognizant of because they get paid regularly."

  Having said this, a deal point that seems insignificant today may not be insignificant tomorrow. In other words, we value different things at different times. Let's say, for example, you're buying a new MP3 player online. You find the MP3 player you want on Amazon for $100. But you find the exact same MP3 player on another site, CheapDeals.com, for $85.00! "This is great," you think. "It's the same exact thing for $15.00 less!" However, when the MP3 player shows up four days later, it's damaged; the plastic case is cracked and the volume doesn't work. You email CheapDeals.com. You don't hear back. Three days later, you email them again.

They send you a link where you need to download a return form. You click on the link, but it doesn't work. You email them again. No response. Right about now, you're thinking, "This would be so much easier if I'd just bought this from Amazon!" Last week, price was your most important factor; a week later, however, *service* has become most important.

The same holds true for deals in Hollywood. Today, you may only care about getting a certain paycheck, but in two months, when you slip on a wet floor and break your leg, that workman's comp clause may prove pretty important. Thus, before you get anxious about seemingly unimportant deal points, talk to your representation about why these points are—or aren't—important to you. You may realize your lawyer is fighting for something extremely valuable. Or perhaps your lawyer realizes he's wasting time negotiating something meaningless to you.

- **Your agent/manager/lawyer just wants to win.** "There are certain types of people who love to negotiate," says conflict resolution expert Ebenstein, "but part of what they love is the contest, the game. They want to win." In some cases, this is fine; after all, we hire agents because they're not afraid to jump in the ring and fight to the death.

   On the other hand, we don't need negotiations to deteriorate into a pissing match. "If you (the client) feel like it's dragging, that's [usually] the sign of a pissing match," says Carlisle. However, "it's on you, as the client, to make sure your agent is giving you information about what's going on and then reacting to it. If you feel like, 'Hey, we're in a good place,' tell your agent to close. They'll argue with you, [but you can] listen to their argument and decide whether you want that or not. When you say 'close the fucking deal,' it's our job to close the deal."

"My Agent Should've Gotten Me More Money!"

Money is important—and most writers want to continue climbing the pay scale with each gig. So it's not unusual to hear writers complain that their agents didn't get them enough cash—which may or may not be true. What is *also* true, however, is that there are many important things to look at in a negotiation—and just because you may not be able to hit the dollar amount you want doesn't mean you can't find other equal or greater value in other ways.

In every negotiation, there's a tension between two concepts: "dividing" value (also called "claiming" value) and "creating" value. "'Dividing' value," explains Ebenstein, "is deciding who gets what slice of the pie. 'Creating' value is making the pie bigger, so there's more to go around." Most people are accustomed to think only in terms of dividing value. In other words: "I know there's only limited pie to go around, but I want to make sure I get the biggest possible piece of that pie. I want to divide it so I get the best value I can."

In normal business transactions, this is very straightforward. If you want an apple, you go to a grocery store, and the store says, "We have a limited number of apples. Therefore, we can give you an apple for one dollar." It's less straightforward, however, when you're selling not goods, but *services*. It's easy to say an apple costs one dollar. But how much does it cost to write a screenplay? Or write on the staff of a medical drama? This is harder to quantify. People have different creative processes; they contribute different things. Are great jokes worth as much as great stories? Is someone with flawless story logic as necessary as someone who punches up dialogue? You might think your services are worth $20,000 per episode; a studio may think your services are worth only $15,000 per episode.

It's easy, in these situations, to get bent out of shape—partly because we're so used to thinking only in terms of "dividing" or "claiming" value, grabbing our "fair share" of the finite pie. Thinking about "creating value," however, works a bit differently—especially when it comes to services.

Imagine you run a company that needs a certain computer software to process its books. The software costs $1,000 per year, so each year, you pay one twelfth ($83.33) every month. But this year, you get smart. You say to the software company, "I know I usually spread my $1,000 out over the course of a year. But what if this year, I pay everything up front in one lump sum? You get all your cash up front, and in exchange, I get a discount." This seems like a win-win; sellers love getting their complete payment up front, and you get a discount. You've just "expanded the pie"–*creating more value* for both parties!

"Everyone gets fixated on 'How much should I ask for?' or 'How much will I they offer me?'" says Ebenstein. "And they don't think about how to make that pie *bigger* so that both sides can get more." Once you've expanded the pie, *then* you can negotiate how to divide the pie. In our software scenario, for example, you may want a thirty percent discount, but the software company wants to give a ten percent discount. You now have to negotiate *this* issue, but at least you've already *created* more value for both parties.

Thinking in terms of a writer's deal–perhaps your quote is $20,000/episode ($440,000 for twenty-two episodes), but the studio wants to pay only $15,000/episode ($330,000 for twenty-two episodes). So you say, "I have an idea, studio. I'll do it for $15,000/episode but I also want a blind script deal for $100,000. If you were to pay me my quote *and* buy a script from me, it would cost you almost $440,000 (for 22 episodes, plus a developmental quote of $100,000). Doing it this way, you get my services, plus a new pilot–all for less than $450,000!" Thus, you've created value– for yourself *and* the buyer!

"Everyone thinks negotiations are zero-sum, but that's not always the case," explains Ebenstein. Development deals, of course, aren't the only way to expand the pie. If you can't get the actual dollar amount you want, maybe you can get guaranteed scripts or an episode to direct. "It's important for your agent to think about how to make the pie bigger."

"I Didn't Get a Credit on the Movie I Wrote–and It's My Agent's Fault!"

Actually–it's *not* your agents fault. It's the Writers Guild's fault. Credits aren't decided by movie studios or TV networks–they can't be negotiated by agents or managers– they are decided by the WGA, plain and simple. When a company–a movie studio, TV network, or production company–has a final shooting draft of a script, it submits to the WGA a "Notice of Tentative Writing Credits," detailing all the writers who shall receive onscreen credit (based on whose contributions have most impacted the final script). The company also sends this Notice, along with a copy of the final shooting script, to every writer who has worked on the project. If there has been only one or two writers, and they're properly credited, there's nothing to be done. Sometimes, however, a script has gone through multiple drafts and writers–but not everyone has been selected to receive onscreen credit. In these cases, an aggrieved writer can protest the credits.

Occasionally, the writers may collectively decide on their own who should receive and/or share on-screen credit. (To do this, the writers' decision must be unanimous.) Other times, writers ask for an **abritration**, a complicated process orchestrated by the WGA to determine which writers rightfully deserve credit. This includes collecting statements, testimonies, and drafts from writers involved with the project. One person who's not involved with the arbitration: your agent.

"I'm Scared if I Bug My Agent Too Much, She'll Get Annoyed and Lose Interest in Me"

"If a client is writing a spec and is just calling to say, 'Hey, I got five pages done today,' I definitely don't need to hear it," says Jim Ehrich, a feature agent at Rothman Brecher Kim. "That is a waste of time for a representative, to have that kind of status update call. Frankly, it takes away from time I could be doing something else for them, in terms of looking for a job." So what issues *are* okay to discuss with your representation?

To Learn More . . .

About the WGA's screen credit determination process download the WGA's Screen Credits Manual at http://www.wga.org/subpage_writersresources.aspx?id=167

- **Professional relationship issues** (with execs or producers, or even your own agents and managers)–Absolutely!
- **Personal relationship issues** (with significant others, family members, etc.)–Only if you and your representation are close personal friends. "The best agents are *always*–with artists–part therapist," says Hoffman. "A lot of what we do is make sure the emotional sides of our clients' lives are being reflected well in the work they're doing. But there can come a time when it gets to be too much for an agent to reasonably handle. It's a fine line everybody has to walk–what is appropriate to share with their agent, and what's better kept with their friends and their family and their therapist."
- **Creative and writing issues** (plot or outlining problems, joke pitches, etc.)–Of course! Althouth managers are usually better equipped to deal with these issues than agents, it's still best to use them only when you have genuine creative issues to discuss. "I like to know what [clients] are writing and if they're blocked," says one manager. "I don't need to know what they had for lunch."
- **Financial issues**–As the people charged with finding you employment, most managers and agents have a keen grasp of your financial situation. Thus, "calling me telling me you need a job probably isn't the best use of your time. We're on it," says another seasoned representative. "If it's like, 'Hey, I'm broke, I'm broke,' that infiltrates. You can scare off people with 'I'm desperate' vibes. And that's what's hard about our business. You kind of have to have that poker face–'everything's great and we're excited!' You have to present that, because–this sounds like a Tony Robbins thing–people want to be around successful people. I want to know you're going to kick ass."

REPRESENTATIVES' MOST COMMON COMPLAINTS ABOUT CLIENTS

"You're Not Producing Enough New Material."

Writers often complain agents aren't pushing their material hard enough. But the truth is: agents can only push material they believe is sell-able, and they evaluate what's "sell-able" based on their experiences in the marketplace. Can they be wrong? *Absolutely*. Can a script they think is uncommercial suddenly find the right home and get sold? *Without a doubt*. And when this happens, managers and agents are thrilled. But most of the time, their instincts are correct. So when writers are upset their representatives aren't pushing their material hard enough, the problem is rarely the agent's lack of selling; the problem is usually *the agent's lack of sellable material*. Maybe the writer's most recent script isn't commercial enough. Or worse–maybe the writer's most recent script isn't that recent–maybe it's two years old, or more, and the agent has sent it to everyone who would be appropriate.

Whatever the reason, the solution is simple: *write more material*. This is, after all, your job–*you're a writer*. Your job is to write, to constantly churn out new product. "I met a writer one time who said she writes two hours in the morning," says manager Robyn Meisinger, "and that's it. And not even two hours of writing–two hours of 'thinking!' We will not do well together. You treat this like a job. You are serious. You are focused. You are committed."

Feel free to ask your representation how much new material they expect–and what kinds of material they need. Sometimes an agent will tell you she needs something original, a pilot or a feature, every six months to a year. Other times, she may need a TV spec. When you finish that piece, talk to your agent about what to write next and start again!

"If a writer comes in here and says, 'I want to [write] a pilot a year'–No! That's nothing!" says Meisinger. "Thirty pages a year?! You should be able to do that in a month! If you're treating this like a job, a serious career, you should be writing at least three scripts a year. *At least*.

"What's This New Script? I Didn't Know You Were Writing This!"

One of agents' biggest pet peeves is when clients go off and write in isolation without first telling agents what they want to write. An agent's job is to help discern what's commercial and what's not, and what project will best represent you at this stage of your career. If you write something your agent or manager can't sell, you've just wasted months of your life.

Strangely, most clients *know* they're supposed to keep their agents abreast of what they're writing. So why do many still go off and write in a void without consulting their agents first? "Fear," says Moshontz, "of being told 'That's a stupid idea.' Of being told 'Don't do that thing that's lighting you up right now.' Exposing your enthusiasm, your creativity, your longing, your great idea . . . that's the essence of shame—to reveal a longing, a vulnerability, and have somebody say, 'That ain't right.' It's like the kid who brings home a great piece of artwork they drew in school—'Mommy, look at this!' But Mommy is busy, and the kid is deflated. Nobody wants that deflated feeling of being crushed."

Personally, I'd rather feel momentarily bummed when my agent ixnays a two-paragraph idea than totally crushed when she ixnays a 110-page screenplay it took six months to perfect. Thus, if you consult your representation first, they can not only weigh in on the project's commercial value, they can give creative notes or feedback that will save you time in the development or writing process. Maybe your agent loves the idea, but she thinks it should involve a murder instead of a bank robbery, or brothers instead of sisters, or it should be set in the Spanish Riviera instead of the French Alps. You may not agree with your agent's notes or she might give you the perfect insight to help you write a killer script! Either way, if you don't talk to her before writing, you run the risk of writing something that can't be used at all. And hey—you're paying your agents ten percent; you might as make them work for it!

Also, just because your agent isn't fired up about your idea doesn't mean you can't explain your passion and reasons and change her mind. It also doesn't mean you can't hear her objections and say, "Thank you, but I'm super excited about this. I'm going to write it anyway."

"Hopefully," says Moshontz, "there's enough flexibility in the relationship that the agent can say, 'Okay—as long as you know I may not be able to use it or sell it or like it.'" Often, when a writer has a particular story burning inside him, he produces a stellar piece of writing. Maybe it was something he just couldn't pitch well. Or perhaps he had to find the story as he wrote it. Or maybe the agent was right all along—it's *not* a commercial piece of work, but it's something that makes a tremendous writing sample.

I'm not advocating ignoring your agent's advice; I'm simply advocating *communicating* with your agent, listening openly to her advice, then making an informed decision.

Ask the Agent

Q: "I'm working on a show and I just don't feel like I'm the right match for it. I pitch different kinds of jokes, tell different kinds of stories. I'm trying to adapt to the show's sensibility, but it's a losing battle. Should I tell my agent? I'm afraid she'll see me as a failure and will lose faith in me. What should I do?"

A: "Be honest. Her *not* knowing almost gives her a handicap on how to serve you best. Maybe [single-camera comedy] just isn't your thing. I hear things like this and think 'Oh, she doesn't need to be on this show, she needs to be on *this* show.' I have a client who has literally been fired off two shows, and I'm about to put him on [a hit comedy], because I believe in him. He's kooky and weird and funny and bizarre, but when he was on [another hit comedy], he came to me and said, 'It's not working.' His manager would get upset: 'You should go in there and do everything they tell you to do.' And the writer was like, 'But they're telling fart jokes— I don't think that's funny.'" And I see what he's saying! So even though it was a hit show, it wasn't the right show for *him*.

> "If you have a close enough relationship with your agent, articulate the issue you're having, rather than just saying, 'It's just not going well.' Sometimes it takes a while to figure out what a client's nitch is. It's good for the agent to know that so she can prepare for the next thing. If she gets a call from [the showrunner] out of the blue, a week before your contract's up, and she thinks you're going to get renewed, [she] can't prepare for the next job. That's the most important part—for her to get one step ahead. Even for her to call [the network] and say, 'It doesn't seem to be working over there,' so she can do damage control on your name in that [network] camp. It's all how you spin it. By telling your agent, she can go out to the marketplace and say, 'It just wasn't the right show for her; she's not a single-cam writer.'"—Big Four TV lit agent

"I Don't Have Any Updates to Report–Stop Bugging Me!"

One thing managers and agents "find annoying is when clients are constantly calling or emailing, saying, 'What's going on? What are you doing?'" says Thal. "That implies a lack of trust or confidence. It's understandable that clients want to know what's going on in their careers and what kind of activity is happening. But when you have a relationship with somebody, a long-term relationship, at some point you hope they trust you're doing your best for them." Unfortunately, writers tend to be an insecure bunch, and simply saying "trust your agent or manager" doesn't make the insecurity go away. Even when a writer *forces* himself not to call, the feelings are still there, nagging and poking. So what can a poor writer do?

"If you're calling your manager or agent saying, 'What's going on? Anything happening?' that's not good," says manager Alex Murray of Brillstein Entertainment Partners. "You should be calling with something real, some feedback on a meeting you had, 'What about this [project],' 'What about that [opportunity].' Those are better calls than just calling to check in."

Personally, I always find I get anxious when I feel like my professional life is stagnating, losing forward momentum. This is when I most want to call my agent—"maybe *she'll* have some exciting news!" But when agents have exciting news, know what they do? *They call*. No agent or manager gets a piece of promising news, something that could lead to actual money, and *doesn't* tell the client. What would be the point of that?!

Thus, I often find the best way to feel like I'm reviving forward momentum is to actually *do something* that can push me forward. Namely—*write*! Start a new screenplay. Rewrite your pilot. Polish that reality idea you've been developing. Not only will this

---

If It Ain't Broke, Don't Ask Your Agent to Fix it

In 2009, America's average unemployment rate was 9.28 percent.[1] But not among TV and screenwriters. In Hollywood, *48.4 percent of the WGA was unemployed*—a 2.6 percent jump from 2007. Nevertheless, "I had a [writer] on [a hit drama] who said to me, 'I'm over it—I don't want to be on this show anymore,'" says one lit agent. "I was like, 'You're on [a hit drama]—you're lucky! You're on a successful show! It's on its eighth season!' But [as an agent,] you have to take care of her, so I got her a meeting on [a FOX pilot]. You want to make sure it's perceived you're still working for the client—even though for financial purposes, and career purposes, you want her to return to the successful show. [And as a writer,] you shouldn't rattle the cage to be on a show that may not work, because there are so few shows that work." (The FOX pilot ended up not going to series and the writer stayed on her original show.)

take your mind off your anxiety, it will result in something you (and your representation) can actually use. And if it's good, which it will be, you agent will be so fired up about it, you won't be able to get him to *stop* calling you!

"I Would've Asked for That–But the Client Didn't Tell Me He Wanted It!"

When negotiating a deal, it's important to think about all the things that may be important to you–besides money–and communicate these to your agent. If you don't, your agent will likely push to get you the largest possible paycheck–which is great … unless it comes at the expense of other points you may value. "Fixating on money and failing to reflect on different things you want satisfied in a deal is a classic mistake," says Ebenstein. "The antidote is to say, 'Of course money is important, I should research a range and shoot for the highest end of that range,' but there are also other things that matter."

For example, would you like to write your screenplay from your cabin in Vermont–making you unavailable for in-person meetings? Do you need to leave your TV staff job early on Monday nights to teach a college class? Do you want to try to direct an episode of your series this season? These things are important–and your agent needs to know! "Help your agent be a good representative by discussing other factors beyond money," says Ebenstein. "The agent isn't you and may not have a good handle on non-monetary drivers. Maybe you're like, 'Yeah, it's a lousy deal, but I want to be able to do this if it gets me more into the world of radio.' An agent may try to talk you out of it, or even feel adverse, because 'If you get less money, I get less money.' But this is where you need to be explicit about other things that matter to you–and why they matter. If your agent isn't motivated to help you get those other things, you might want to remind them that although they'll make less money in the short term, over the long term, agents that get clients what they want–even when it's not as financially beneficial to the agent–have happier and more loyal clients."

14 Parting Ways with Your Representation

FYI: Everything in the following story is true, except the names of those involved.

Life was good for Meg Einaudi. After years of producing reality shows for highly successful pods and networks, she had finally launched her own company, Panama Pictures. Business was booming. The company had a show airing on a major cable outlet, pilots in contention at several other networks, plus several promising projects in development. And then the phone rang. "Things have changed," said the voice on the other end of the line, "but it's all for the good; it's all for the better."

It was Joaquin Turner, Meg's TV agent at SMA (Strong Mid-Level Agency) who had represented her since the dawn of her career. Joaquin had taken Meg from being a virtual unknown, editing shows in the bedroom of her tiny Hollywood apartment, to a top-level showrunner, selling and producing series for broadcast and cable networks alike. He had also, he now informed her, just been fired.

Meg was in shock, but Joaquin assured her this was for the best; he and the agency hadn't been seeing eye-to-eye lately anyway.

"What are you going to do?" Meg asked.

"I've got some irons in the fire," Joaquin said. "Let's meet this week to discuss."

Meg hung up and called her development exec, Sadie Hyung, into her office. "I said, 'Oh my God—you won't believe the phone call I just got,'" Meg recalls, "and we were both like 'Holy shit, what just happened?!'"

Within the hour, the phone rang again, this time: Lyman Fry, Joaquin's former boss, and the head of SMA's reality department. "I know this is a huge upheaval," he said, "but we don't want you to leave the agency." Meg was hesitant; Joaquin, not Lyman, had been her guy—not only her point agent and primary contact at the company, but one of her closest friends. In the years she'd been at the agency, Meg had barely even spoken to Lyman. "Just hear us out," Lyman continued. "Give us a chance to make our pitch." Meg agreed, and they scheduled a meeting for a few days later.

For Meg, the timing of Joaquin's firing could not have been worse. Panama Pictures was about to shoot a new pilot, they had several shows in development, and they *needed* an agent to pitch their projects, set up meetings, and negotiate contracts. They were in a bind, and they needed to act fast. "At that point, we called the network executives we do business with and said, 'What do you think?'" Meg says. "Every single one of them said: 'use this as an opportunity to shop around.'" But one executive in particular said something else. "You guys are doing well," he said, "but you're not going to get much bigger unless you sign with a bigger agency. You have to start getting in rooms with more successful producers, more high-level execs. The only one way to do that is to take the leap. You have to leave SMA."

Meg was unsure. While she wasn't committed to staying at SMA, or even following Joaquin to wherever he landed, she'd always enjoyed the personal attention of a mid-level agency (and for, a brief time before that, a boutique). "With our agent, I always felt like I was one of his most important clients," says Sadie. "I knew if I went to one of the bigger agencies, my relationship with my agent would be less personal and more business."

After thinking it over, she figured taking meetings couldn't hurt. So with their lawyer's help, Meg and Sadie called friends and contacts at three of the Big Four agencies. "Within six days," they met with three of Hollywood's largest agencies, as well as SMA, their current home. To their surprise, all four meetings were completely different.

SMA "talked more about the past than the future," says Meg. They kept saying "'Look, we have a past together', to which I was like, 'Yeah, [but] I want to hear what we're going to do together in the future.'" The Big Four agencies, meanwhile, rolled out the red carpet. The first "pulled out the big guns," bringing their top agents into the meeting. The second "was pure vibrato-like bluster—'We know you want us . . . you're awesome, you know we're awesome, let's be awesome together!' I can't say it didn't feel good."

But at the third Big Four agency—Huge Powerful Agency (HPA)—the fanfare came to a screeching halt. "They did not say 'We want to sign you,'" says Meg. "They said, 'Why don't you come back and show us some of your pitches to see if we'd be a good fit?' I was like, 'Ach, I'm not being courted?! Fuck!' Then I [realized], 'You know what? This is smart. This is about a long-term relationship, not a great first date.'"

So Meg and Sadie scheduled a second meeting to present HPA with some ideas. The agents were impressed, but "We want to be completely, brutally honest," they said. "Just because we're HPA doesn't mean we're going to rep you across the board. Right now, we're interested in making you a very successful reality TV company. Do you want that?" Meg and Sadie nodded.

They left the meeting a few moments later and headed to a nearby cafe to hash things out. They immediately dismissed the first two Big Four Agencies; while they'd appreciated the enthusiasm, "it felt very much like *Jerry Maguire*-type stuff, where it's like 'Oh, I'm just a pawn in an agency war.'" They had also learned that Joaquin had taken a job at highly respected boutique agency on the east coast. "As a friend, I was super-excited for him," says Meg, but "I just didn't feel comfortable having an agent in [another state]."

This left only two contenders: SMA (their current agency) and HPA. It was not an easy decision. At SMA, they had a history, a short-hand, long-standing relationship; they were also a big fish in a medium-sized pond. At HPA, they worried they'd be lucky to be a minnow in a Great Lake. Sure, Panama had had some successes, but at a Big Four Agency, they'd be fighting for attention against the likes of *The Amazing Race* showrunner Bertram van Munster and *The X Factor* creator Simon Cowell.

The decision came down "to who we felt we could build a relationship with," says Sadie. "We weren't looking for a new best friend, but we were looking for someone we wouldn't mind talking to. [Someone] we wouldn't dread calling up." When Meg and Sadie left the cafe, they had made up their minds. They rushed back to the office to make the call.

"Hey, Meg! How's it going?!" asked Lyman Fry.

"Good," said Meg, but "I wanted you to hear this from me: I'm going to go with somebody else. I feel like I need to make a change, but . . . I want to thank you for everything you've done. You represent a lot of people we do business with, so I'm sure we'll continue our relationship that way."

Meg hung up the phone, looked at Sadie, and said, "Holy shit—we're about to sign with HPA!" And they did.

Since then, Meg and her Panama Pictures have been introduced to newer and bigger networks, and at networks where they already had acquaintances, "we've moved passed the 'meetings phase' and into the 'working together phase.'" They've also met with higher levels of talent and producers, and have even been "invited to participate in a few select development agreements with networks, through which we sold a series," Meg says. "I'm not sure these opportunities would have been brought to us at SMA."

BREAKING UP IS HARD TO DO

There are various reasons a client and an agency part ways. Sometimes clients fire agents for blowing an important deal. Other times, agents fire clients for failing to produce new work. I've seen writers panic over something in their personal life–a new baby, a divorce–and take it out on their representation. I've also seen agents who *don't* fire clients–even when they should–and instead let the client wither away, unemployed, wondering why no one's calling him back. And occasionally, as Meg Einaudi discovered, clients get put into uncomfortable positions thanks to internal agency politics.

Regardless of the details, a client and his representation ultimately part ways in one of two ways: either the client leaves voluntarily, firing his agency, or the client leaves involuntarily, in which case the agency fires him.

When Agents Fire Clients

No writer or producer likes to be fired, but "if you haven't been able to book a client a job or sell something for them in a couple years, you have to ask, 'What's not working here?'" says manager Dave Brown of Artists International. Firing someone isn't fun for either party; it's often as much of a disappointment for the agent as it is for the client. There are several reasons why agents fire clients:

1. **The client's not generating enough income**–Some agencies periodically run numbers on each client, and those not generating revenue get the axe. Of course, low- and mid-level writers aren't expected to earn as much as upper-levels, so agents compare income levels to expectation, and clients who aren't earning– *whack*. Having said this, the calculation isn't usually as cut-and-dry as a pure numbers game. "There are clients you keep even if they don't make a lot of money," says Verve partner Amy Retzinger. Some clients, for instance, may not generate a huge payday, but their work wins awards, earning respect for the agent and allowing the agency to have a presence at prestigious festivals and awards ceremonies. Other clients "write something so specific you're only putting them up for [certain kinds of] shows–a doctor-turned-writer who only wants to be on a medical show. That person's not going to take the same amount of time as a baby writer who wants to be put up for every show. It's a case-by-case basis, [but] if I'm putting in more work than I'm getting in reward, whether it's financial [or] personal," that person gets fired.
2. **The client is too difficult to work with**–Some clients repeatedly blow off meetings or auditions. Some consistently ignore their representatives' advice or script notes. Others may not be difficult in interactions with their representation, but their work behavior is so incorrigible it makes the manager or agent's job more difficult. I've seen writers fail to show up to work, act churlish to bosses or co-workers, sleep through meetings with actors and directors, fail to deliver promised scripts or assignments to their employers. While this behavior may not involve the agent directly, it means the agent has to keep starting over finding the writer work, and he or she has to constantly convince employers the writer has changed. "You have to do a cost/benefit analysis and figure out: is it worth it to put up with this headache and misery?" says Brown. "If you can't wrangle a client after a while, there's never going to be a good working relationship. You have to hug, shake hands, and go your separate ways."
3. **The client hasn't written anything new**–"My colleagues and I have high expectations of our clients," says Generate manager Kara Welker, who suggests writers should deliver at least three half-hour scripts to their agent each year– especially if they aren't actively working on paid assigments. "And if you aren't creating original material, you need to be responding to assignments we put out . . . like late night or daytime talk [shows that are] hiring. You need to be very responsive and hit your deadlines on those things. That's the minimum you need to be doing."
4. **The client and agent disagree about the direction of the client's career**– Sometimes clients and their representation have opposing visions of what material

the client should be producing, what goals she should be aiming for. Maybe a writer's agent wants her to be writing blockbuster sci-fi films, but the client wants to do low-budget thrillers. More often, however, the client and her representation have differing perspectives on where the client stands, career-wise, *right now*. "I had a client I signed at a festival—a hot, young, up-and-coming comedian at the very beginning of a comedy career," says one representative. "Within a year, I realized their ego was out of line with the reality of where they were in the grand sceme of comedy. We had the same goals with very different timelines, [but] they thought they should be up for jobs [going to] far more qualified comedians. I was like, 'Patience. You have to do the work, do the stepping-stones. You can't just go from A to Z. You have to build some groundwork. You don't go from being a 'New Face' at [a comedy festival] to being on *The Tonight Show*. You go from being a 'New Face' to having a bit on Comedy Central.' If the client and agent can't find common ground on where the client is and what she should be doing, one of them—usually the agent—says sayonara."

While I hope you're never in any of these situations, it's also important to recognize that *not* getting fired can be just as harmful. Obviously, no writer wants to get fired, but a client receives no benefit by staying at an agency that's not enthusiastic about representing him. "We almost never fire anybody," says one agent, "which is a mistake, because there's this sense of, 'What if that person makes five cents tomorrow?' Well, if it costs a dollar in your agent's time and energy to make five cents, then it doesn't make sense, but there's that attitude. Operating from fear."

Writers in this boat never get the full service and attention they need, and many never realize they need to fire their representation. Thus, both the client and their representation remain stuck in limbo, neither working effectively for the other, both careers floundering. Getting fired may hurt in the moment, but it may also spur you to do whatever needs to be done to reignite your career: writing new material, getting a new job, or finding a better agent, an agent who truly values you.

How Agents Prepare to Fire a Client

Usually, when an agent or manager is contemplating firing a client, they first have an open and honest conversation. "You can deliver things honestly while still being caring and loving," says Welker. "Usually, I would just say, 'Here are the things that are working and here are the things that are not. I would love to hear from you what's working [for you] and what's not. Maybe we can find a middle ground, because we need to get you working—and if that doesn't happen, we need to agree to part ways. But let's work towards making things better.'"

Of course, the writer-representative relationship "is a two-way street," says Artist International manager Dave Brown. "You [can always] say to your representative, 'What can I be doing? What samples do I need in my arsenal so I can be considered for premium cable shows as well as procedural network shows? You want to be able to work together on the same page."

If dialogue doesn't work, the manager or agent may decide to cut bait, especially if the client is openly upset with the agent. "You don't want an unhappy client out there in the marketplace talking about what a poor job their agent or agency's doing," says Retzinger. "You want to put an end to it sooner [than] later. You don't want to let that hang out there."

When an agent decides to fire a client, he first talks to his colleagues, the other agents on the client's team. The client, after all, may have great value to another department. If it's a TV agent that wants to fire the writer, maybe the film agents are less inclined to let her go and the solution is to assign the client a different TV agent. If the client is a money-earner, the agent may also need to get permission from his boss. "I remember when I wanted to fire [Tanner, a big television director]," says one agent.

"He had been [my boss's] long-term client, [but] I was in his life for about a decade. I wanted to fire him because he was a pain in the ass. And he was making money . . . more money than clients I kept, but it was just not worth it to me. He would get hired on a show, direct an episode, then he wouldn't get asked back. So I'd have to start over—whereas if I had put in the same amount of work with a guy who gets asked back time after time, then I [could] let [this director] go and just reap the reward. So I [told my boss] and he couldn't understand. He was like, 'What? But the guy makes money!' 'Yeah, but the opportunity cost does not make sense; I should be putting that effort into somebody else.' Long story short: you have to get permission from the other people on the team."

There's little else to be done in the way of preparations or protections. Agents, in a way, are more protected after a break-up than managers, because agents are licensed by the state and beholden to Guild franchise agreements, which contain certain rules. For example, after a break-up, clients must continue to pay commission to their former agents on any jobs procured during the client's time with that particular company. This is legally binding—even if the client never signed official agency papers. Because managers, however, aren't regulated and don't sign franchise agreements, they're much more exposed, which is why you sometimes see unfortunate situations where clients hire managers to help guide their career, then—when they fire the manager later—they refuse to pay owed commissions on the basis that the managers never should have been procuring them work (see page 17).

Your Commission Stays with the Agent

When clients part ways with their representation—regardless of who breaks up with whom—the original representation continues commissioning any work the client got while represented at the firm. So if Rhonda, an agent at Paradigm, books her client, Marco, a writing gig on CBS's *Elemenatary*, Paradigm commissions that job–ten percent of every paycheck. If Rhonda leaves Paradigm six months later to go to BAA (Big Ass Agency), taking Marco with her, Paradigm *still* commissions Marco – ten percent of every paycheck. Paradigm, in fact, gets to commission Marco as long as he works at *Elementary*. However, if Rhonda and/or BAA negotiate Marco a raise on *Elementary*, does Paradigm get to keep commissioning? *Yes* . . . but only the amount of Marco's paycheck that *they negotiated*. The raise itself is commissioned by BAA. In other words, if Marco had been making $6,000 per week, and BAA got him bumped to $7,000 per week, Paradigm would continue taking $600 out of Marco's weekly paycheck (ten percent of the original $6,000), while BAA would commission his additional $1,000 per week (a $100 weekly commission).

Even with no signed agency papers (which most agencies never use), the standard terms of agency agreements are binding, and management companies or agencies are often more than willing to sue to collect any owed commissions. In 2012, lit manager Stephen Crawford ditched Luber Roklin Entertainment to go to Industry Entertainment, taking with him *Nancy Drew* writer Tiffany Paulsen and *Eight Below* writer David DiGilio; the following year, Luber Roklin sued Crawford for allegedly telling his clients to stop paying their Luber Roklin commissions.[1] Similarly, in May 2013, UTA sued former client and *Scrubs* star, Donald Faison—who left the agency for APA—for more than $73,000 in supposedly unpaid commissions.[2] (As I'm writing this, both cases are still pending.)

How Agents Fire Clients

Firings usually happen over the phone. "On one hand, you think [doing it on the phone] is such a cop out," says Retzinger, but "nobody really wants to be dumped in person." Here's the way the conversation usually goes:

INT. RAUL'S HOUSE:

Raul has just answered the phone; it's his agent, Sabrina.

SABRINA: So . . . I'm sure this is not a surprise to you, but we've been having a little trouble making things happen for you.

RAUL: Uh-huh . . .

SABRINA: I've been thinking about it a lot, and I know it's not for lack of trying on my part, and I like you too much to keep muddling on this way. I think it's time for you to think about taking a different agent.

Raul digests this. A long, heavy silence. Finally. . .

RAUL: So what do I do now?

SABRINA: Talk to Logan, your manager. He's terrific. Have him make some calls and say you're leaving BTA (Big Talent Agency) and taking some meetings. Tell people it just wasn't a fit.

(Or, if you don't *have a manager, the agent may say . . .)*

SABRINA: You've got friends out there. Talk to them, get meetings with their agents.

RAUL: Are there things I could've done better?

SABRINA: You just didn't write enough, Raul. I need new material every year. More than that! You can't just let five years go by twiddling your thumbs. (Then . . .) Listen, I think you're talented, Raul. Let me know what I can do to help you; the door is open here.

Usually, this phone call is not a complete ambush. After all, agents rarely fire successful working writers, so there's probably been frustration and unhappiness on both sides. Other times, agents may first contact the client's manager, saying, "We don't want to represent this guy anymore. Why don't you talk it over with him, we'll lay low, and you can tell other agencies, 'We're looking for a change, some new blood on the team. We've been with Big Talent for a while, and we've run our course. It's time to move on.'" Even if the agent doesn't offer this up, feel free to ask her to do this. Most will, especially if you've had a friendly relationship.

Can You Recover from Getting Fired by Your Agent?

"It's absolutely something you can recover from," says SyFy's *Defiance* producer Anupam Nigam. "I've been in the business ten years now, and I'm on my second agent. If you've done a good job, if you've been on shows where you've worked with writers who are repped by different agents, the first thing I would do is call writers I trust, writers I consider friends, and ask about their agents. Would they mind showing my material to their agents? If you impress people—not just other writers, [even] network and studio executives—if you have a good rapport with them, it's not hard to call them and say, 'You know my writing; what agents do you think are a good match for me?' Hopefully, you'll find an agent that's a better fit."

Another great way to bounce back, both professionally and emotionally, is to "get off your butt and write something great," says screenwriter Tedi Sarafian (*Terminator 3, The Creature From the Black Lagoon*). This gives you "something people are going to want. Now you have a pulse. [Having] that next script; the next thing to talk about; that is the most important thing in the world."

Meeting with New Agents

After getting fired, the question on many writers' mind is: *"Will this mar me? Am I now 'tainted,' branded as the 'fired writer?' Will other agents view me as undesirable?"* Not necessarily. The first rule when meeting new representation is: *do not badmouth your old agents.* Most people in this town know each other, do business together, and are friends. So no matter how angry you are at your old reps, and no matter how justified that anger may be—*don't do it.*

"I have been in this position," says writer David Weinstein (*The Closer*, *Stevie TV*). "I have been young and stupid and said unfortunate things. You may get away with it, but let others talk shit about the people you know. It will . . . *never* do good for you to run your mouth about an agent's [or] manager's shortcomings, especially because [the new people] are just looking at you like you are full of sour grapes."

Often, when meeting with new agents, the topic won't even come up. If it does, don't be dishonest, but take the high road with an answer like, "It just wasn't working. They're great people—we just stopped clicking." If your old agency has agreed to let you say you left, you can say something like, "I just wanted a smaller home, somewhere I could be more of a big fish in a little pond." Sometimes, unfortunately, the new agent may already know what happened; it's a small town, after all—people talk. In this case, just be upfront and honest. "Let's address the elephant in the room," you might say. "Here's what happened, here's how I'm fixing the problem, and I'd love to be in business with you." This allows the new agent to be honest in return. He may say, "Trust me—you should be *glad* you got fired from that place. They just work on volume, so if you're not a top earner, you're not getting serviced anyway." Or he may say, "Well, in order to represent you, I need a new sample. Something I can use to reinvent you and reintroduce you to the town."

One red flag agents *do* watch for: clients who have been represented by too many different agencies. "If a person's been represented by four or five agencies, obviously they're jumping ship every so often because they're unhappy," says feature agent Jim Ehrich of Rothman Brecher Kim. "Do you really want to put your time and energy into someone that has that tendency just to leave and jump ship?"

Occasionally, a potential new agent or manager may even call your old representation to get the story. "I've made that call before and people have certainly called me about it," says manager Aaron Kaplan of Kaplan/Perrone Entertainment, but "I'm not going to shit-talk someone just because they were signed with us. It's probably the opposite—I'd speak well of them. Sometimes relationships [just] run their course. The only way I would say [something negative] to someone is to give them a real warning if [the client was] problematic in terms of paying commission. If [the client] said, 'I'm going to pay you ten percent,' but then didn't pay, I would make sure other people trying to sign him knew that as a risk. If it was a situation where creatively we weren't on the same page, or personally we didn't get along, [I wouldn't say anything bad]."

Your Agent Might Be an Asshole if . . .

Josie was working as an assistant to a big showrunner, whose pilot—after two years in development—had finally gotten a green light. "I, of course, wanted to be staffed on that show," Josie says, "and my boss said, 'I'm going to give you a script, then staff you if we get the back nine.' But I'd been with him through two development seasons with the same show, I knew the show inside and out; I wanted to be staffed from the beginning! My agent knew my history with [this boss], and I felt like he should've been calling him and advocating on my behalf. [But instead, my agent called and] asked *me* to talk up one of his *other* clients! I was shocked . . . that's *not* how the relationship should go. I made a point of saying, 'Have you talked about *me*?' And [the agent] was like, 'Well, [your boss] said he'd give you a script [and] staff you at the back nine, so we're not going to do anything.' And he did nothing! So I let him go."

WHEN CLIENTS FIRE AGENTS

"Sometimes a break is the best thing," says Weinstein. "I leave when I feel [my career is] not moving forward *or* we have some huge philosophical [difference] on what should be next for my career. At one point early on, I fired someone who had been a great agent because I was simply going through some kind of entitled feeling and I thought I could do better. She was actually one of the best agents I ever had, and the truth is—that was a huge mistake."

Indeed, writers have many reasons for axing their representation—some good, some not so good. The most common reasons for firing agents or managers are:

1. **Clients are unhappy with their service**—In the last chapter, we discussed reasons why clients get frustrated with representation: unreturned phone calls, bad creative notes, lack of job opportunities, insufficient income, etc. Exacerbate these enough, compound them, and clients reach a breaking point. Once a writer feels like an agent is actually *costing* him money, rather than helping to *earn* money, the relationship probably has a short fuse.

2. **Agent and client have different career goals**—Many agents and clients split up because they no longer "see eye to eye on the path of the writer," says screenwriter Francisco Castro (*Urban Games*, *Without a Trace*). Perhaps a writer wants to start directing and producing his own work, while his agent wants him to take high-profile studio assignments. Another writer may see herself as an indie writer/director, while her manager sees her more as a pure writer. Someone else wants to be a showrunner, but the agent thinks they need to keep focusing on staffing. In any of these cases, not only will the client and agent have totally different ideas of the kinds of opportunities to be pursuing, but they'll probably view the writer's work very differently. "I had an agent . . . who was just lukewarm [on everything I wrote, so] I was like, 'Oh, [they think] it sucks," says Sarafian. "Then I had this massive TV producer say, 'I love it' and their people are saying, 'I love it,' and all of a sudden the agent was like, 'Yeah, it's great!' When that happens, you wonder if you're with the right guy."

3. **Clients get enamored with larger, sexier agencies**—Many writers, when they start moving up the ladder of success, decide they need a more powerful agency. Sometimes a larger company comes to woo, or **poach,** them; other times the writer seeks out the agency himself. Thus, many writers ditch the smaller agent who helped them launch their career and sign with the massive juggernaut. "When you're at a mid-size agency, and you're not representing 400 clients, and the clients you've procured work for are working in rooms of people repped at other agencies, it's easy for a bigger agency to swoop in and say, 'Well, if *they* did that for you, imagine what *we* could do!'" says one mid-level agent. "That's something we're up against consistently. And when we're dumped for that reason, it's as hurtful as your boyfriend or girlfriend coming to you and saying, 'You're just not good enough for me.' Because it doesn't matter what you've done at that point—it's a weird business where you can get fired for doing something right. That, for me, is the hardest pill to swallow. I would love to get fired for doing something *wrong* one day." As another mid-level agent puts it: "We don't ever get fired for being bad agents. We get fired for [the name on our door], which is so fucking frustrating."

So is there truth to the notion that bigger agencies can more effectively take your career to "the next level," literary stardom? "There is no denying big agencies have a bigger arsenal of weapons which you can draw upon," says Thruline manager Chris Henze, who reps clients like *Psych* creator Steve Franks and actress Allison Janney (*Mom*, *The Help*). "They have a big directors list, they are probably handling producer pods, and if it's about exposing you to those people . . . you have to think about whether or not that's going to benefit you. It very well could. However, that's a very general situation. There are some incredible small agencies, and there are incredible agents at small agencies that give you [the same] attention a manager might. [They] are smart and will strategize. [They] are bulldogs and will find ways to get your material in front of the right people, even if they aren't representing them.

"[Also,] sometimes when you're at a big agency, you almost get exclusively exposed to people they represent, because they don't always play *outside* their agency as well as they play *inside* their agency. So if you want your material to be seen by a specific set of directors, and one of those directors is [represented by a rival] agency, you may be on your own. Or you may need your manager to expose it to them. Or it may get exposed by your agent, [but] with a little less enthusiasm. So . . . [being at a big agency] works well for some clients, [and] it works well for some at smaller places."

4. **The agent is leaving the agency**—Often, agents themselves get wooed away by rival companies. When this happens, most writers have a choice: they can stay at the original agency, or they can follow the agent to his new employer. We'll discuss this scenario, and its various options, in a moment.

How Writers Prepare to Fire an Agent or Agency

How to approach whether or not to fire or leave your agency depends on the reasons you're leaving. A writer following his point agent to a new company, for instance, needs to research and ponder different factors than a writer upset that his phone calls aren't returned. As we discussed in the last chapter, if you're unhappy with your agent's service, the first step is simply to discuss it. And while you may be able to have your manager handle certain issues for you, if you're seriously considering firing someone, you should have that talk openly and honestly. "I personally believe people should own up to things," says APA TV agent Alan Moore. "Be clear what the problem is, see what their reaction is, and if they're willing to fix it. [Maybe] you can move on and it's all good . . . or maybe it's just time to part ways. It's like dating; you're not going to leave [someone] because of one little thing, [but] you might say, 'Hey, let's talk about it.'"

If you've already started sniffing around other agencies, you may want to tread lightly. Sometimes a rival agent may be trying to poach you; other times, you may have sought out that other agent yourself, but how you handle this with your current representation depends on your relationship. "If you have a good relationship with your current representation, it may be worth having a frank conversation," says psychotherapist and relationship expert Chuck Moshontz. "Say, 'Look, if another agency did contact me, I would rather not go, if I can get [here] some of the things I [would] get with a bigger agency. What if we talked about: can I get this and this and this here . . . [things] I can get there, that I'm not getting here now?' If it's worth it to you to give your agent the chance, why not find out about it? [On the other hand,] if you've been looking to jump ship for a long time, why bother?"

Some agents get territorial, defensive, angry—so it may not be worth discussing until you're certain you're leaving. Others may feel comfortable saying, "You should absolutely go meet around. See what else is out there. If I'm not the right person for you, you shouldn't be here." Gauge your own relationship to anticipate how your agent may react.

What *Not* to Say

As you're meeting with possible new agents, know that many "don't like having potential clients come in and just rip their old agents," says feature agent Jim Ehrich of Rothman Brecher Kim. "It sounds like sour grapes. I like to hear a little more objectively what has and hasn't worked for that particular client in a particular place. If they're a hot feature person but the TV department's not paying attention—okay, I can understand that. There are just certain telltale things you hear in a conversation that would give you pause as an agent."

No Poaching Allowed

One red flag to watch out for: if a *manager* tries to poach you, or steal you from your current management company, *beware!* Reputable managers live by an unwritten code: *they don't poach clients.* Why? Since managers also produce, they often work with clients from many different management companies. Thus, it's not unusual for a manager at 3 Arts to call a manager at BenderSpink about one of her clients. But if managers are going to let clients work on other managers' projects, they need to know that client's not in danger of being stolen. So managers follow a special rule and refrain from wooing or poaching each other's clients.

"I get calls from non-clients all the time," says New Wave manager Michael Pelmont, or "another client I represent on a show will say, 'Hey, my friend who works on the show with me really wants to come in and meet with you—he's just not happy with the job his manager's doing.' And I say, 'I appreciate that, but until he dismisses that manager, I cannot talk to him. If he wants to fire that manager and take on a new manager, then by all means, but I will not meet with him while he's still engaged with another manager.'"

This obviously puts writers in a scary position, as most don't want to ditch their representation unless they know they have a new home. But even scarier is signing with a manager who may have an unscrupulous reputation. "There are managers who don't operate that way" and *do* poach, says Pelmont, "but I would be leery of them."

When things get especially tricky or confusing is when one of your agents—maybe your point agent—leaves for a competing agency, and you must make a decision: do you follow the agent to his new company, or stay with your current firm? As we discussed in Chapter 3, when agents are poached by other companies, it's frequently a top-secret operation until the ink is dry. But once the agent informs his old agency he's leaving, he must also inform his clients. "You say, 'I've decided to leave because it's the best thing for my business and my clients' business, and I'd like you to come with me,'" says Roy Ashton, who left CAA for Gersh in 2011. "You say why you're making the decision, why it's better not only for you—because the client doesn't want it to be about you, the agent, they want it to be about them, which is the way they *should* think. Hopefully, you have a relationship and a trust, a bond. You believe in each other and make that leap together."

However, just as the agent is frantically calling his clients—so are his co-workers at the old agency, hoping to keep the client for themselves. "Sometimes there's a really clear division of whose clients are [whose]," says APA's VP of Television Lindsay Howard, so "ideally, it's clear who they're [taking] and who they're not. And I think there should be some honor in that. You just accept there are certain people you'll lose and certain people you'll keep."

Unfortunately, many clients get caught in the middle. And this is where things get ugly. "It's a war," says one agent. "You have to mobilize, get your troops together, and figure out your plan of attack. You call those clients you want to retain and go, 'Look, so-and-so is a fantastic agent. They're going to go off and do something different. You signed here for a reason . . . there's a service and a personal touch you responded to in this company, and that continues to be our mission, our drive, our goal for you.'"

That, of course, is the "nice" version. In many cases, co-workers who were previously close friends lash out, backstabbing and trashing each other. One producer friend, Maia, told me that when her point agent, Joseph, left his agency for a bigger company, she went in to meet with the other agents who, led by the head of the department, proceeded to rip Joseph to shreds behind his back. "Not cool," Maia thought. "These guys were Joseph's friends—he stood up in their weddings!" Turned off, Maia ditched the agency and took her business elsewhere.

In these situations, clients must make an often difficult decision. Sure, it would be easier if people could be repped by two places, but most agencies insist clients are repped entirely by them. Occasionally, high-profile clients are allowed to split their representation. Jodie Foster, as we learned earlier, is repped at UTA as a director, and at ICM as an actor. Similarly, when long-time CAA agent Adam Kanter ditched CAA for Resolution, *The Bourne Identity* director/producer Doug Liman moved his film business with Kanter but left his TV business (which includes shows like *Suits* and *Covert Affairs*) at CAA. Most clients, however, aren't allowed this kind of leeway; agencies want to rep people across the board or not at all. (In fact, WME and CAA reportedly refused to sign Foster as a director if they couldn't represent her in all areas.[3])

When deciding whether to follow your agent or stay with the old company, it's important to meet with both agencies, just as if you were meeting with representation for the first time. At the old agency, you may learn interesting things about why your agent left or you weren't being fully serviced. The agents may say, "You never heard from some of us because your agent didn't wanted us calling you. He wanted to be your only contact." Or, "I used to put you up for jobs, but I don't know if your point agent passed along the information." You'll also want to find out: now that your point agent is gone, who will be your new point? Do you click with him? Does he "get" you? How will the team function differently without your old agent?

At the new agency, research the people and the company just as if you were meeting with representation for the first time. Ask "questions about their personal tastes," says Verve agent Tanya Cohen, "and some of the clients they've worked with, success they've had. Ask about their background, where they've come from, their passions. See if there's a connection, a meeting of philosophies, ambitions, if everything aligns. And get a general sense of why they're different, what makes them better than [your old agency]."

It may even help to "make a list of all the things you appreciate, have grown used to, with the agency you're with now, and all the things you will be better served by with the new agency," suggests Chuck Moshontz. "Have a conversation with the new agency: 'Can I get this, this, this, and this which I used to get from my old agent? Can I get this, this, this, and this [which] I'm expecting to get from you—that I *couldn't* get from my old agent?' Then you know in advance, and [you don't] come into it with all kinds of assumptions about what life will be like."

Also find out: will your old agent remain your point agent at the new agency? Who else will be on your team? How does this agency function differently than your last agency? Why are you better off at the new place, which already has many clients and relationships to service? Why will you be better served here than at your old agency, where you're already known? Most importantly, "look at the agents more than the agency," says Kaplan/Perrone manager Aaron Kaplan. "If you look at any of the big agencies, or any of the small one-man shops, it's all about who is going to be the one actually representing you."

Does the New Agency Want You?

Most of the time, agencies poach agents because they're interested in that agent's client list. When Resolution hired away ICM talent agent David Unger, what they really wanted was his roster, which included performers like John Hurt, Mickey Rourke, Courtney Love, and Ray Winstone.[4] This doesn't mean, however, that a newly poached agent is allowed to bring along every client. It's "a dollars and sense issue," says Jim Ehrich, a feature agent at Rothman Brecher Kim. "If the agency thinks they're going to make a lot of money with that [client] down the road, they say 'come on in.' If they think the person is going to be a waste of the incoming agent's time, someone that's not going to make a lot of money, they say 'don't bring them.'"

Other times, agents may use "the-new-agency-won't-let-me-bring-you" as an easy excuse to trim their client list of talent they no longer care about.

Pulling the Trigger

Getting fired by a client "feels like when you're in a relationship, and all of a sudden you feel somebody pulling away, and then they dump you," says one veteran lit agent. "You start to feel it coming. Sometimes there's no explanation for it. Sometimes the [client] has just decided they need to do something different, and it stinks."

It's never easy getting dumped, even in a business relationship. It's also never easy being the dumper. But sometimes you've tried everything to make a relationship work—talking things over, communicating differently—and it's not improving. As much as it hurts, you've made the decision: *it's time to part ways*.

Your goal now is to make the break as clean as possible—for both you and your old agent. "The cruelest way to end it is in a dishonest way . . . or to avoid it." says Moshontz. "As human beings, we are wired to seek pleasure and avoid pain. And it's painful to be in situations where what you're saying is causing somebody to crumble in front of you—or however you fear they're going to take it. But the truth is: it's going to be painful however it gets done. [So] how do you want to feel afterwards? Do you want to feel like you handled it with integrity? Or do you want to feel like you ducked out of something and slunk around the corner?"

The first rule of firing your agent: *do it in person or on the phone*. Do not do it in an email or a letter. Second, be honest and straightforward. "If you're firing somebody who's done a terrible job," says APA agent Lindsay Howard, try saying something like, "'I've given it a lot of thought. This isn't working out for me. I've decided to try something different, and I hope our paths cross again in the future.' That's an appropriate way of dealing with a flawed client relationship."

Also, note how quick that statement was. It doesn't leave room for conversation, discussion, or arguing. It's brief and to the point. Rip the band-aid off and say goodbye. Things get trickier, of course, if you're leaving not because your agent has failed, but because you want to try greener pastures. "When you [finally] have that phone call or do it in person," says Generate manager Kara Welker, "it is respectful and not belabored—[don't give] a laundry list of issues. Say you 'need to make some changes' and you 'would like to move on. I've made up my mind and this is what I'm doing.' A lot of managers, and certain agents, will put up a fight—[so] when that agent or manager argues back, 'No, no no no, you're not doing this,' you have to be prepared. Be certain in your gut this is what you want *before* you have the conversation. You need to be able to put your foot down and say, 'I'm sorry, I've made up my mind. This is what I'm doing.'"

Moshontz suggests having "a bottom line—and sometimes that bottom line needs to be repeated several times. 'Yes, I understand, and we're coming to an end here. I'm leaving. Yes, it would have been better if it had come at a better time than this—and now is the time.'"

"I lead with 'yes' almost all the time in my responses to others," says Moshontz. "Not as a way of buttering them up, but philosophically, standing from a place of 'Yes, I hear what you say,' 'Yes, I want to better understand.' And then the second part of the clause begins not with 'but,' but with '*and*.' 'Yes, I know what you're feeling is real and valid for you. It makes sense for you. *And* I see it a bit differently. *And* I've got my perspective on that. Acknowledge the other person is right. 'There is a difference, we're not the same.' [Make] the difference clear."

Agents respond to getting fired in different ways. Some say, "I'm disappointed to learn about your decision. There are reasons why I think this may not be the right move for you. Is your mind made up or can we discuss it?" Other agents get angry and hurl insults, or simply shut down the relationship with a cold, curt "Good luck," and that's the end of it. Smart and classy agents usually say something like, "I wish you the best, and I'm here if you need anything"; they know clients often come back after discovering a new agency is no better than the old agency. "A lot of times they fire you because of stuff that's out of your control," says one agent. "You just roll with the punches and move on to the next client. Sometimes they realize they made a mistake, and sometimes they don't."

What Agents Do After They've Been Fired

"The first thing anyone does when they get fired—if it's a client you really like and believe in—is you step back and just go *'Fuck!'*" says one seasoned agent, "because it *sucks*." The *second* thing a representative does is compose a **protection letter**, a document detailing all unfinished projects on which the agent or manager has worked on the client's behalf. This could be a TV show on which a writer is currently staffed or an unsold project the agency has been out pitching. Either way, your old representatives will try to continue commissioning them, including any unfinished projects they may have given notes or feedback on. Realistically, it's hard for agents or managers to lay claim to anything that hasn't been sold or has a deal put in place, but they'll try, and the client can refute or discuss anything he disagrees with. This is also why "if a writer knows they are going to get rid of an agent, they won't be showing them any of their new material," says Ehrich. "They'll use it to procure their next agent."

Ultimately, even the most dedicated, impassioned agent must pull himself together and move on. "Would I like to curl up in a ball, go home, and cry to my family or my fiancé? Absolutely," says another lit agent. But "I once asked [an agent friend] who's been doing this for many years, 'How do you survive this? It's such an emotional roller coaster.' And he said, 'I don't get too high with the highs, and I don't get too low with the lows.' That's something I try to bring into my business. It's hard, because you get emotionally invested with the people you're working with. But, when all is said and done, entertainment is a business. And sometimes business associates and business employees change."

Perhaps nothing illustrates this better than a (supposedly) true anecdote an agent recently told me, about legendary ICM talent agent Ed Limato getting fired by a major star at the height of his career (according to unsubstantiated rumor: Bill Cosby). Supposedly, Limato hung up the phone, turned to his assistant, and said, "All right—who else called?"

15   Networking in Hollywood

My mom always says, "It's not what you know, it's who you know." And as much as I hate to admit she's right about anything . . . she is. Networking is essential in Hollywood. You'll most likely not only get your first (and second) agent through your own contacts, you'll also get most of your jobs and sales through your own relationships - even once you have an agent! Yet before we dive into networking, let's do an exercise, a little mental Zumba. First, get a piece of paper and a pencil. Actually, I'll make this easier— I'll *give* you a piece of paper (unless you're reading this as an e-book, in which case— get your own paper). You're on your own for the pencil. Got a pencil? Good. We're going to make a list of five people you know and might want to network with. Not just any people, a specific five. I'll walk you through:

A)   The highest-level industry person you know personally (a VP at a studio, a high-powered agent, Ang Lee, Ang Lee's assistant, etc.):

_____

B)   The lowest-level industry person you know personally (an intern, an assistant, a part-time script reader, etc.):

_____

C)   A personal relationship with someone who's *not* in the entertainment industry, but knows someone who is (your dogwalker who knows Kate Winslet, your neighbor who worked for Mark Burnett, etc.):

_____

D)   The most recent industry person you've met (a receptionist you bumped into thirty seconds ago, a producer you had a date with last week, a lawyer you met yesterday at church, etc.):

_____

E)   Someone in Hollywood you don't know, but want to (a specific agent, the head of NBC, Jamie Foxx, etc.): _____

Now, rank those names below in order of the *most* valuable person to know (#1) down to the *least* valuable person to know (#5).

Next, beside each name write how or why you'd like to network with that person. How can this person help you? What do you hope to gain from them?

	Ranked Names	*How To Network With This Person*
1.	_____	_____
2.	_____	_____
3.	_____	_____
4.	_____	_____
5.	_____	_____

Finally, put your paper aside. We'll come back to it later.

Why We Network

"Networking gets a bad rap," says script coordinator Sam Miller (*The Exes*, *Malibu Country*), and he's right. Networking often conjures up images of slimy Sammy Glicks glad-handing their way through swanky clubs and studio backlots. The truth, however, is that networking can not only be an incredibly fun and productive career-building tool, it's also essential.

Wait a second, you don't know Sammy Glick?

Read *What Makes Sammy Run*, by Budd Schulberg. If it makes your stomach churn, congratulations—you're human. If it doesn't—you'll probably have a very long career in Hollywood.

We've seen, time and time again in this book, how showrunners like to hire people they know, or film execs turn to producers they've worked with, or video game developers want writers they know and trust. We've also seen how important it is to managers and agents to have clients with large networks of personal and professional relationships, how much easier this makes their job. Yet a lot of people assume networking is only for people who don't have enough genuine *talent* to succeed—"If she were a genuinely *good writer*, why would she need to network? Her work would stand on it's own!" Nothing, however, could be further from the truth. Writers still have to be immensely talented to get and keep jobs. But in an industry where the clamor of aspirants trying to break in is truly deafening, networking opens channels that allow our work to rise above the hubbub into the hands of readers and employers. Whether or not those readers and employers respond to our material is a different question—but networking opens those avenues. In fact, I often say we network for four primary reasons:

1. **To find people with similar tastes, preferences, and sensibilities**—This is especially important in an industry based on the creating, buying, and selling of art or entertainment, which are totally subjective. *Hostel* writer Eli Roth and *Saturday Night Live* writer Seth Meyers are both immensely talented, but if you're hiring the staff of an edgy new TV comedy, one is more appropriate than the other. Whether you're a film producer looking for someone to direct your indie sex comedy or a studio executive hiring a designer for a gritty family drama, you need someone who understands and appreciates the genre.
2. **It takes so much time, work, and energy to push any project forward, you need to work with people you like, and respect, and who share a vision.** This is true whether you're stuck in a TV writers room for fifteen hours a day or scraping together financing for your independent short film. Nothing in Hollywood is quick or easy, and if you're going to partner with people, you need a team of hard-working people who understand your worldviews—and whom you trust and respect.
3. **To meet business colleagues, partners, and peers**—Whatever business you're in, it's usually nice to be part of your business "community." Being in a community gives us friends, neighbors, and partners with whom we share helpful information, discuss community-related news, release worries and stresses. Doctors ask other doctors for second opinions. Plumbers refer clients to other plumbers. Teachers swap tips with other teachers.
4) **And this may be the most important reason of all—*Networking is not about what you can get, it's about what you can give.*** Obviously, the ultimate point of networking is to push ourselves forward and build our careers. But in order to do this, you have to make a *mental shift*. You have to stop looking for people who can help *you*—stop asking what benefits a particular relationship can bring you—and start looking for how *you* can help or benefit *other people*. When you talk to a video game executive looking to switch into animation, dig up job opportunities you can send her way. Run into a TV director casting a pilot? Email him actor suggestions. Know an intern hunting for her first full-time gig? Connect her to your neighbor, a Paramount HR exec.

Helping people allows you to be seen as generous and competent—someone who gets stuff done. Which means next time that intern or TV director or video game executive needs to hire or consult someone trustworthy, they'll turn to someone they see as reliable. Helping people also builds social and political capital. Help someone get a job or put together a project today—they'll be eager to repay the favor tomorrow.

Doing this successfully, however, requires keeping two things in the front of your head:

1. **Networking is a marathon, not a sprint.** Yes, you're doing things "selflessly" to build your own career, but do not expect short-term results. Many relationships take years or decades to bear any visible fruit. "I met . . . this producer . . . five years ago," says *Urban Games* screenwriter Francisco Castro. "He was always asking me, 'What's your next script?' and trying to figure out how it could be sold. [Then] he actually got assigned this project and needed a rewrite, [so] I was the first person he called, because he knew I could write fast. This is based on a five-year relationship of talking now and then, sending each other email updates, that kind of thing."

2. **Everything you give away, you give away *for free*.** In other words, no attaching conditions to your favors; no offering to help people only if they help you in return. Many of the favors you do may *never* get returned—at least, not in any practical fashion—but again: you're not doing favors to get quick or obvious returns. You're doing favors to build your image as a competent, generous person who *gets things done*.

What Do You Have to Offer?

The first step in helping people is knowing what available resources you have to offer. I often hear young people and aspirants say, "How am I supposed to help people? I have nothing to give, no way of helping!"

First of all, if you don't think you have anything helpful to offer, I'll tell you what you *do* have: *the wrong attitude*. And a total lack of the kind of creativity and resourcefulness needed to make it in Hollywood. In other words, if you said "I don't have anything to offer," pack up and go home, you failed the litmus test. Even if you just stepped off the bus yesterday, with nothing but the clothes on your back and the passion in your veins, you have something to offer. It might be:

• **A great work ethic**—Every employer in the entertainment business, whether it's a film director in Hollywood or a TV station manager in Mississippi, is looking for enthusiastic, tireless workers—especially if those workers are willing to work for free. So you wanna get your foot in the door? Offer to intern or volunteer for someone who needs your help. This could be at a local production company, a major film studio, or for a college student working on their thesis short. If you're in Los Angeles, a quick search on Google or Craigslist turns up numerous opportunities. (I checked Craigslist just now and found seventeen postings just today—and it's a Sunday! There were people searching for editors, stylists, assistants, writers, camera operators, you name it.) And while you may work for free for a while, you're actually being compensated in something almost as valuable as money—*relationships*. You're meeting gaffers, actors, directors, post producers, costumers, make-up artists—many of whom will go on to bigger and better things, and (if you impress them with your attitude and work ethic) take you with them. Besides, everyone you meet knows hundreds of other people, so while the set dresser you met last week may not have a job for you immediately, he may *know* someone to whom he's happy to recommend you!

• **Specialized skills**—If you're trained or educated in a particular area, put these skills to use! Maybe you've mastered the Alexa Plus 4:3 and could help a young director shoot a music video. Maybe you've got copyediting skills and could edit a writer's screenplay or treatment. Perhaps you just graduated with a Masters in Nineteenth-Century Russian History and could help the costume designer on an indie production of Tolstoy's *The Power of Darkness*. Or maybe you just make a great spaghetti sauce and could cater someone's weekend shoot. Whatever skills you have in your arsenal, figure out how to make them useful to people you'd like to know.

- **Connections to other people**—Another fantastic way to prove yourself an indispensable colleague is to connect people you know to *other* people you know. Perhaps a producer is looking for a composer—and your neighbor writes his own chamber music. By putting them in touch, you help not just one person, but *two!* Ka-ching—money in the Good Will Bank. You don't even need to match people for professional entertainment reasons. Maybe you know a talent manager looking for a good masseuse, or a dog-walker, or a babysitter—hook her up! She'll remember you as a reliable, trustworthy contact. (And by the way—introducing people to each other is seventy-five percent of a good agent or manager's job. Getting clients general meetings doesn't put immediate cash into a representative's pocket, but agents and managers know that by helping people start a relationship today, they're paving the way for income down the road.)

- **Inside information**—Information is currency. Every night, every weekend, every afternoon, assistants all over Hollywood get together for lunches, drinks, and networking parties. And one of the ways they build trust and rapport with each other is by trading inside information. Because they work so closely with their bosses, including listening in on phone calls, assistants are often the first to know which shows are getting picked up, which movies are getting green-lit, who's getting hired or fired. And by trading this information with other colleagues, they form closer, tighter relationships. Of course, you usually have to have a job in order to have access to the information, but once you're there, the ability to find or trade information makes you invaluable.

- **Money**—There's nothing wrong with "buying" your way into Hollywood. I'm not talking about paying people off or buying publicity. But Hollywood is an industry made up of producers and filmmakers scrambling to make projects, and one of the resources every project needs is *cash*. So if you have money, or access to money, use it! Financial consultant Ryan Kavanaugh had little Hollywood experience when he founded Relativity Media in 2004; what he *did* have, however, was connections to powerful venture capitalists, and he was able to match them with producers in need of financing. Similarly, David Ellison, son of multi-billionaire Larry Ellison, had struggled for years to break into Hollywood as an actor, then finally became a producer when he offered Paramount $350 million to co-finance *True Grit*, *Mission Impossible: Ghost Protocol*, and a new Tom Clancy film.[1] Obviously, not everyone has Ellison money—or connections to wealthy venture capitalists—but that's okay; there are plenty of producers patching together budgets of a few hundred or a few thousand dollars. If you have have some cash burning holes in your pockets, finding a worthy project—*or producing your own worthy project!*—is a great way to begin learning the business and meeting other players.

- **An available job**—Everybody needs a job. I'm guessing that's one of the reasons you're reading this book—you're trying to figure out how to best use representation to navigate Hollywood and find work. Well, then, you know how grateful people are to get jobs, so if you can be the person who helps someone land their next gig—you have forever won a special place in their heart. I run an internship program for students at my alma mater, Vanderbilt University, and I'm always struck by how eternally grateful people are when you help them find a position they want (even an unpaid internship). Many of my former interns have gone on to become executives, filmmakers, and agents—and I keep in touch with most of them. I no longer consider them students; they're now friends and colleagues, but it always feels nice, even years down the road, when they tell me how appreciative they are. I am also sure that one of these days—probably in the not-so-distant future—I'll be hitting them up for a job myself.

As you're reading this, I'm sure your brain has landed on hundreds of other things you have to offer, and how you can use those things to help other people. So the next question is:

Who Should You Be Networking With?

The first answer is: *everyone and anyone*. That's also the least helpful answer.

Aspirants often think they should network with people as high up on the food chain as possible. The decision-makers. After all, if you can form a great relationship with the president of Warner Brothers, or John Wells' VP of Development, or Ben Affleck—*you're in, right?!* You've got the ear of someone with real power, someone who can green-light your movie or produce your pilot!

Uh . . . *no*. Unless you become that person's absolute best friend. And most likely, they already have a best friend. The truth is: *you should be networking as low on the totem pole as possible*. Or at least at the same level where you are yourself. This is for several reasons.

First of all, higher-ups are busy with their own high-level projects and issues. The president of Warner Brothers isn't interested in next the next hot screenwriter; he's busy dealing with high-level writers, producers, and directors. Low-level people, however—assistants, coordinators, junior executives, etc.—are not only much more accessible, they're the gateway to their bosses. Assistants "have a lot of power . . . in terms of what information they pass on, or how they pass it on, to their boss," says digital producer Shilpi Roy, who began her career as the assistant to a VP at a production company. "When the assistant likes you, you are guaranteed to get a call back from the boss, you are guaranteed to get notes back on your script, and these things will happen in a timely manner."

When I took my first job as an assistant at the Littlefield Company, my boss Jennifer required me to go to lunch with assistants at all the networks and studios; she knew that if I had a rapport with the assistants, *her* calls would be returned much more quickly.

Perhaps more importantly, while higher-level execs and agents may have other priorities than reading through stacks of spec scripts, lower-level employees are *dying* to find the next hot screenwriter. "Those are the people that are hustling, trying to be recognized for their hard work," says Melissa Solomon, lit coordinator at the Verve Agency. "They're the ones out there trying to find information and material, so those would be your most feasible points of access. Eventually, you will meet those higher-ups and those decision-makers, [but] it's always going to be the C.E.'s and development execs and coordinators pushing the material up for them to notice."

Indeed, finding great new scripts and writers—and delivering them to their bosses—is how young execs and agents get promoted. They also swap info with each other; so if an assistant at WME reads an amazing sci-fi script, and two weeks later learns her friend, a low-level film exec at Imagine, is looking for a talented sci-fi writer, she passes it along. Also, "one of the reasons it's important to meet the next young up-and-coming class of soon-to-be-VP's," says Solomon, is "these are the people you're going to grow up in the industry with. We're out there, we're hungry, and we'll be running agencies and studios one day." In other words, people tend to rise through the ranks together. The assistant you're befriending today could be a showrunner or studio president in a matter of years, and—as we've learned—people like to hire their friends.

Three Main Ways of Networking

There's never a wrong time or way to make a new contact. You could meet your future producing partner in line at the supermarket. You could find an actor for your short

Bottoms Up!

A close friend of mine, a successful reality producer, is the daughter of a Belgian beer importer. When she was just starting out, meeting with execs, producers, and agents, she used to give a six-pack of Belgian beer to the assistant at each office. Miraculously, when she would call the exec/agent/producer later to pitch a new idea or follow-up, the assistant *always* made sure her call got put through or returned immediately.

Talk the Talk

Production Assistant–
An entry level position
responsible for low-level
tasks and errands, usually on
the set (or in the production
office) of a movie, TV show,
or commercial. Duties include
making copies, answering
phones, handing out walkie-
talkies, setting up lunch,
running errands for
producers, etc.

Talk the Talk

Logger–In reality television,
a low-level employee who
watches all the raw footage
from field shoots, logging
(and often transcribing)
important moments and
lines.

Talk the Talk

Runner–An entry-level
employee who spends most
of his or her time running
errands: picking up groceries,
delivering scripts, buying
office supplies, etc.

while playing at the dog park. I met Alpern Group agent Jen Good, who's featured throughout this book, because I used to be her barista at a Coffee Bean fifteen years ago! We stayed in touch, and have worked together and been friends ever since.

In Hollywood, however, there seem to be three tried and true methods of networking:

1. **Get a Job!**–Getting a job in the industry is, without a doubt, the absolute most effective way to network. In fact, it's so much better than the other two ways, which we'll get to in a moment, I'm tempted to say it's the *only* way to truly network. I won't say that, but the bottom line is: if you want to be taken seriously as a professional in the entertainment industry, *become a professional in the entertainment industry.*

This doesn't mean you have to score your dream job tomorrow. It just means you have to put yourself in a professional position where you're learning the business, gathering and trading information, and meeting other professionals. Most likely, this will be some kind of assistant position: **a production assistant (P.A.)**, an executive assistant, even a receptionist, **logger**, or **runner**.

These jobs are not glamorous. You'll often work sixteen hours a day, for little more than minimum wage, fetching coffee, collating scripts, picking up lunches. Your network of professional contacts, however, will grow exponentially on an hourly basis. Every day, you'll be meeting new people in person, talking to new people on the phone, scheduling and sitting in on meetings with your boss. You will interact and form relationships with writers, producers, executives, agents, and countless other professionals (not to mention assistants). You will meet more people faster than you ever thought possible, and every interaction is an opportunity to impress and prove your own competence and reliability.

"It's weird," says *World War Z* writer Drew Goddard, "but people don't think you're going to be a good writer if you give them [your] scripts [to read]. People think you're going to be a good writer if you get their coffee order right. If you can make their life easier, they're so much more likely to help you. Most P.A.s don't quite get that."

Entry-level and assistant jobs also allow you to meet other assistants, which–as we discussed–can be even more valuable than meeting higher-ups. "When I started in the mailroom at [an agency]," says Brian Berk, now a writers P.A. at ABC Studios, "I was working with a bunch of people in a small room. We had no choice but to interact with each other. I became good friends with some of those people not because I was consciously trying to network with them, but because they're fun people to hang out with. My best friend from my agency days, who I met in the mailroom, is now an agent. He's a great person to know in the industry, but more importantly, he's a great beer pong partner. Those types of relationships are usually better than the ones you get when you go to organized networking mixers and events."

Ask the Agent

Q: What's the best entry-level job in Hollywood, the best place to get my foot in the door and begin learning the ropes?

A: An agency mailroom–even if you have no desire to be an actual agent. "The agency is the hub of what's going on in the [entire] business," says Verve coordinator Melissa Solomon. "It's the agent's job to know what's going on in town, so they're talking to studios, producers, financiers, writers, directors, everybody. [Working at an agency] will allow you the most access to information, the most access to people you're going to talk to, or at least hear on the phone as an assistant. It's [listening to] your boss's phone calls where you learn the most things . . . it gives you a good idea of what other people do without having to work for them. It will allow you to better educate yourself and decide what path you want to go down." We'll talk more about agency mailrooms in the next chapter.

Good Reasons *Not* to Get an Industry Job

There are none. Whenever I suggest people get a job in the industry, I inevitably run into resistance. "I can't can't afford to take an entry-level job!" "I don't live in Los Angeles and have no professional entertainment opportunities near me!" "I want to be seen as a writer, not an assistant!" All of these, and any rebuttals people may have, are only one thing: *excuses.* Let me take a quick moment to dispel some of them for you:

*   **"I can't afford to take an entry level job"**—Correction: *you don't want to live an entry-level job lifestyle.* I get it. Entry-level jobs don't pay well, and for people who have reached a certain lifestyle or level of income, it's painful to take a step back. Makes perfect sense. But be honest with yourself: it's not that you "can't afford to take an entry level job," it's that you're prioritizing your lifestyle above a writing career. I am not criticizing that, I'm just pointing it out. You would rather live a certain lifestyle (not necessarily a lavish lifestyle, just not an "entry-level job" lifestyle) than pull out all the stops to have a writing career. By owning it, you can move on to figuring out the best way to getting around it.

    I sometimes hear an even lamer version of this excuse: "I've come too far in my career to start at the bottom. I'm a VP/lawyer/doctor/accountant/whatever, I can't go back to fetching coffee or making copies." Translation: "While my current job has nothing to do with writing, I think I've come far enough in this career that someone should just hand me a career in a different field." Obviously, a ridiculous sentiment. If a successful screenwriter suddenly decided to become a doctor, should she be able to skip med school because she's attained a high level of success in a totally different industry? Of course not. Every career path has barriers to entry; you don't get a free pass simply because you've proven yourself in a *totally unrelated field!* If you don't want to start at the bottom, that's fine—just admit to yourself that a writing career is not as high on your priority list as you might have thought. Do you want to be a writer? Yes. Do you want it badly enough to make certain sacrifices? No. There's nothing wrong with that; just don't fool yourself, or people you're asking for help, into believing this is a highly important goal. It's a hobby—and we approach hobbies differently than we approach careers.
*   **"I don't live in Los Angeles and have no professional entertainment opportunities near me."**—So move to Los Angeles. If this isn't an immediate possibility, start working to *make* it a possibility. In the mean time, get a job in whatever professional opportunities *are* near you. Work at a movie theater and start learning everything you can about theatrical exhibition and distribution from the owner or manager. Volunteer with the administrators of a regional or community theater. Take an entry-level job at your nearest TV station. Join the crew at a local production company; today, most small cities have production companies specializing in commercials, wedding videos, industrial videos, etc. These jobs may not be Hollywood, but they'll all give you an introduction to valuable skill sets and knowledge bases.
*   **"I want to be seen as a writer, not an assistant."**—Most of the time, the person saying this is working as some kind of waiter or barista. The good news is: they're right—by working as a waiter or barista, no one sees them as a lowly assistant. The bad news is: everyone sees them as a waiter or barista. Being worried about how you're viewed is a ridiculous concern (frankly, I'm guessing it's more of a self-deceptive excuse to avoid being an assistant). Whether you're an assistant or a barista, you're only going to get your first writing job by being a great *writer.* Being a barista, however, won't give you the relationships you need to get your work read. It will not help you ingratiate yourself to those who can hire you. You will just be a barista who can possibly write—although no one may ever know this. As an industry assistant, forming friendships and impressing employers, you become an indispensable *colleague* who can write.

2. **Networking Organizations and Events**—Hollywood is full of organizations and associations designed to help people network and build careers. Some host mixers at posh bars and nightclubs, others present educational lectures and panels. Some are strictly for working professionals, others target wannabes trying to break in. With a little research (and I'll do some of it for you right here), you'll find a vast array of networking opportunities for every style and career level. You'll find:

- **Professional organizations**—Hollywood has some fantastic organizations for working professionals. One of the best is the Junior Hollywood Radio and Television Society (JHRTS), an offshoot of the Hollywood Radio and Television Society (HRTS), which hosts panels and programs for high-level TV and media execs. JHRTS is geared toward junior execs, agents, coordinators, and assistants, and does a wonderful job putting on mixers and educational panels. Here are some top-notch organizations for professionals of all levels:

  Academy of Motion Picture Arts and Sciences—www.oscars.org
  Academy of Television Arts and Sciences—www.emmys.tv
  HRTS—www.hrts.org
  International Animated Film Society—www.asifa-hollywood.org
  JHRTS—www.hrts.org/JHRTSMain.aspx
  National Association of Latin Independent Producers—www.nalip.org
  National Association for Multi-Ethnicity In Communications—www.namic.com
  Next Gen Femmes—www.nextgenfemmes.com
  Organization of Black Screenwriters—www.obswriter.com
  Producers Guild—www.producersguild.org
  Women in Film—wwww.if.org

- **Classes and workshops** are a great way to improve and sharpen your skills while meeting other professionals and aspirants. Be warned: not all classes are worth the money, and Hollywood is filled with unqualified teachers, useless seminars, and bogus schools or workshops. Here, however, are some with reputations for providing quality training opportunities:

  The Groundlings—www.groundlings.com
  Improv Olympic—ioimprov.com/west
  The Second City—www.secondcity.com
  UCLA Extension—www.uclaextension.edu
  UCLA's School of Theater, Film, and Television: The Professional Program—www.filmprograms.ucla.edu
  Upright Citizens Brigade—www.ucbtheatre.com

- **Festivals and conferences**—Legitimate film festivals and conferences are one of the best places to hobnob with up-and-coming filmmakers and established professionals alike. There are also plenty of conferences and "pitch festivals" catering to aspirants, and while there's value to these, they're a different beast than festivals like Sundance, or conferences like RealScreen, that attract actual industry professionals. Many of these "amateur-oriented conferences" charge a few hundred dollars for two or three days worth of workshops, panels, and seminars, combined with a "pitch event," where attendees pitch their ideas to studio execs, agents, producers, etc.

Here's my take on these events (and I say this as someone who has spoken and taught at many): if you're attending in hopes of actually selling your project, *don't bother*. This is not how projects are bought and sold, any more than Ford selects new car designs by hosting a conference and letting amateur designers submit their blueprints. I know, I know—every one of these conferences claims "fifty people sold scripts last year," or "so-and-so made a $150,000 sale." But I would highly question the legitimacy of those statements. I'm not saying they're outright lies—I'm just saying they may be highly "spun" for the sake of promotion. Not to mention, most of the professionals attending these events are *not* actual producers, execs, or agents—they're assistants, coordinators, even interns, sent by their bosses to represent the company.

Having said this, if you're simply going to learn, to take classes and gather information, or to network with like-minded people, these conferences can be fun and valuable. The pitching activities can also be great "trial runs" for a real pitch. In other words, don't view the pitching portion as an opportunity to *sell*; view it as an opportunity to practice *presenting your idea*. Can you articulate your idea quickly and succinctly? Do you skip certain key points? Ramble? Are the jokes landing? Could you use a visual aid? (FYI—most of these events give pitchers a time limit, usually anywhere from two to five minutes—another construct that creates a totally unrealistic and inhospitable environment for actually *selling* something.)

I discussed some of the biggest film festivals (and markets) on page 152, but here are some other important events that attract industry professionals:

MIPCOM—www.mipcom.com
Montreal's Just For Laughs Comedy Festival—www.hahaha.com
NATPE—www.natpe.org/natpe/
New York TV Festival—www.nytvf.com/
RealScreen—http://realscreen.com

- **Alumni associations**—"Reach out to alumni from your college or any Greek organization you were involved in," says Lex Ardeljan-Braden, story editor at Radical Pictures (*Oblivion, Hercules*). "I found alumni are very helpful and remember what it's like trying to figure out what you're doing with your life." Check with your school—many even have special alumni organizations designed specifically for people working in entertainment, such as Harvardwood and the Northwestern University Entertainment Alliance.

- **Other great ways to meet people**—In nearly every major city, especially Los Angeles, countless organizations provide opportunities to network with entertainment amateurs and professionals alike. You can find networking functions at libraries and arts organizations, such as Center Theater Group's Fringe @ CTG, which supports theater and new plays in L.A.; civic and charity organizations such as Leveraging Up and Streetlights, both of which promote diversity in the entertainment community; churches and religious organizations, like the Jewish Federation's Entertainment Group; even sports leagues like Planet Social Sports or L.A.'s Prime Time Softball League, a summer league exclusively for professional TV creatives and crew members. (In the 2012 season championship, *Parenthood* beat *The Biggest Loser*, 18–17.)

And if you can't find an organization you like—start your own! One of the best ways to connect with other writers, and to get feedback on your work, is to start a writer's group: five to eight writers who gather regularly to read each other's work, offer constructive criticism, and trade helpful information and support.

3. **Connections/friends/relationships of people you already know**—In a world where everyone is less than six degrees away from everyone else, you may already be closer to Hollywood's insiders than you're aware. Does this mean you should email blast everyone you know, asking to be introduced to all their industry friends? Absolutely not. Relationships are valuable, and you want to treat yours—and other people's—with TLC and respect. It *does* mean, however, that every contact is valuable, as you never know who's connected to whom.

"When I went home [to New Jersey] for the holidays this past December," says Berk, "I went back to my old gym and got a guest pass. I had to sit down with the manager of the gym for a few minutes, and we started chatting. When he found out I worked in the entertainment industry in L.A., he told me that he had a writer friend who used to write for *Scrubs*, and he'd put me in touch. I didn't go to my old gym expecting to network, I went expecting to pump my guns and get my sweat on. To my surprise, I was able to do all of the above."

Networking Tips and Tools

Networking isn't easy for everyone—especially writers. After all, if writers were social geniuses, we wouldn't make a living holing ourselves up in tiny rooms and living out our fantasies on paper. But networking is an art that can be studied, learned, and practiced. Here are some great tools and techniques to help even the most nervous networker become a pro:

Take people to lunch or drinks—"When reaching out to an industry professional," says writer Benjamin Oren (*Cult*, *Crank Yankers*), "offering to take them for lunch, coffee or a drink goes a long way." Indeed, not only does a lunch/coffee/drinks invitation "go a long way"—it's probably the best networking tool in the book!

There's "nothing better than face-to-face interaction with someone," says Hunter Kinsella, Manager of Brand and Digital at Trium Entertainment (*MasterChef*, *The Biggest Loser*). "When they are debating whether to help the person they talk to over the phone or someone they have met, nine times out of ten, they will help the person they've met."

Of course, taking someone to lunch means *you pay*—but this is money well-spent. You're not simply buying people free lunches, you're investing in relationships that are going to pay off over time, leading to jobs, sales, and lucrative partnerships. Besides, you don't need to go somewhere expensive. Every city is filled with cool, relaxed sandwich shops, coffee houses, and bars—and the truth is, you just want a quiet place where you can sit and chat.

Going to lunch, coffee, or drinks is especially a great way to get to know assistants and coordinators, who work long hard hours and rarely get treated to anything nice. Buy an assistant a sandwich or a beer, you've already paved most of the road to a long-term friendship.

Also, remember: when you take a new contact to lunch/drinks/coffee, you are not taking them with the goal of asking for a job, giving them your script, or meeting their boss. You are not trying to *get* anything; you are only trying to *give*, or form a relationship. I usually invite people to lunch by saying "I'd love to hear about what you do," or "I'd love to talk more and hear your story," or "You've done such an amazing job building up your development slate, I'd love to pick your brain about how you get started." Granted, none of these seem like they're giving something tangible—but they are. First of all, everybody loves to talk about themelves, especially to a willing listener, and low-level people rarely have anyone seek them out to listen to their counsel. More importantly, you're not asking people for anything that takes effort on their part—a job, script notes, etc. You simply want to *learn* from them, and most people are flattered and honored to pass on their knowledge and insight.

Sure, you hope you end up in a relationship, but first you have to "get to know people not just for what they do. Get to know the *person*," says Stacy Greenberg, manager of development at Ron Howard's Imagine Television (*24*, *Arrested Development*). "People have a ton of 'work contacts,' but what sets you apart is if they consider you a 'work friend.' I hate even calling it networking because I think of it more as getting to know someone. When someone is too blunt about getting straight to business outside of work at networking events, it feels impersonal and cheesy."

Words of Wisdom

Drinks are a great way to "get [people's] cell phone [numbers]," says Trium Entertainment executive Hunter Kinsella. It's true; people usually swap numbers before meeting, just in case someone has to cancel last-minute. "I know that sounds creepy, but a cell phone is something someone will take to their next job; their work email will go away. Now you always have a point of contact with this person."

Lunch Hour

Unlike everywhere else in America, lunch in the entertainment industry is 1:00–2:00. Not 12:00. Not 12:30. *1:00.* Be aware of this as you schedule your lunches.

YOU AND YOUR AGENT

Set Networking Goals

"Make the commitment to yourself to meet with one new person a week," says Hunter Kinsella, an executive at Trim Entertainment (*The Biggest Loser, Masterchef*). Productive networking becomes much more do-able if we set specific goals like this. For example, I try to schedule at least four lunches, breakfasts, or drink meetings a week. At least one of these is with someone new, and the other three are with colleagues and contacts I already know. Both are important—one builds your Rolodex, the other strengthens pre-existing relationships. As a result, I often have lunches scheduled three or four weeks out. *This is not unusual.* As you set your lunches, you'll find that most agents, execs, producers, and assistants are booked several weeks into the future. Don't be alarmed or upset by this—it doesn't mean they're not eager to see you, it's just the way an industry rooted in relationships works. Plus, many lunch and drink meetings get rescheduled multiple times, so they get kicked further and further down the road. If your meeting gets rescheduled, this is not a comment on you, it's simply the function of the industry.

Another good networking goal: set aside a special period of time each day to answer emails, return phone calls, follow up after meetings, send your invitations to lunch or drinks. (I recommend thirty to sixty minutes each day.) Designating this time not only ensures your networking will get done, but it's good time management; emails and phone calls can become enormous time sucks, so it helps to put time limits on them. (Writing this chapter right now is taking forty-three times longer than it should because I keep checking email and Facebook.)

Research! Research! Research!

"Know who you're talking to before you sit down with them," says Kinsella. If you're meeting with an executive at AMC, even for a casual lunch, know what shows she covers. If you're having a drink with a screenwriter, watch or read some of his screenwriting work. See what you can learn on his Facebook page. Follow him on Twitter. Don't become a stalker, but be as knowledgeable as you need to be to have an informed conversation. Also, brush up on what's going on in the world today—especially the industry. Have there been any big movie sales? New development deals? Companies going under or coming together? Know what movies scored at the box office last weekend, and if possible see them. Watch last night's biggest TV shows and know what's going on with any "watercooler" series. Listen to the top singles on iTunes and Billboard. Read a couple of books on the *New York Times* bestseller list. Take a peek at the hottest viral videos. Play the latest blockbuster video game; know what makes the gameplay unique. If it's pilot season, read as many pilot scripts as you can—even beyond those covered by the person you're meeting; people love chatting about which pilots they liked or disliked, so have an opinion.

"Keep up with info online: Deadline, *Variety*, IMDB, blogs, movies, books," says Scott Bender, an assistant and intern coordinator at Mandeville Films. "I can't tell you how many times it's been beneficial to know little obscure facts about directors, producers, actors, because when that name comes up in conversation, you now have something to add. It's like my theory on current events, you don't have to read the whole article, just know the title and use some common sense to figure out the rest."

Have a Story

Whether at a business conference or on a first date, two people meeting for the first time eventually get around to asking, "So tell me about yourself—where you from?" There are two ways to answer this: with the boring minutae of your biography or with a quick, fun anecdote that illuminates who you are as a unique individual. The boring version: "Where you from?" "I grew up in Byron, Minnesota, till I was twelve, then my dad got transfered to Sioux City, so we moved there till I left for college in Colorado. I majored

Wanna Avoid the Siren Call of the Internet?

A great, inexpensive piece of software is Freedom, which disables your computer's Internet abilities for whatever period of time you designate. It's *great* if you're easily distracted by email, Twitter, etc. (I just turned mine on.) You can download it for about $10.00 at http://macfreedom.com.

Tracking Boards

One way to stay informed is by joining **tracking boards**, private online forums where industry professionals trade exclusive information and scripts. Most boards are founded and managed by agents, execs, managers, or assistants who admit only people they know and trust. "Trackula," for example, is a tracking board managed by Kailey Marsh, a manager at Station 3, who also founded "The Blood List," an annual ranking of the thirteen best unproduced horror screenplays.[2]

While boards tend to be invite-only, there *are* some tracking services available as paid memberships or subscriptions. Some of the most well-known are:

- Studio System— www.studiosystem.com
- Variety Insight— www.varietyinsight.com
- TrackingB— www.trackingb.com

in philosophy, then moved to L.A. to become a writer." UGH–SHOOT ME. Better: "Where you from?" "Byron, Minnesota–and we were the only Jews for a hundred miles. Everyone thought we were Mexican, which was awesome, because the guy who ran the Quickie Mart always gave me free tacos. When I got to Los Angeles, I figured I'd fit right in. Now there are so many Jews, I'm not only *not* considered a minority, but every TV show I know wants to hire Mexican diversity writers."

The second answer may be light on facts, but who cares? It has attitude and invites a response, opening the door for conversation. I actually keep a running list of stories I tell well, and before going in to a pitch or general, I review the stories, picking a couple that seem like they'll fit the tone of the meeting. There's "How I Learned I'm Racist," "The Time I Busted a Cocaine and Crack Ring," "The Penis Story," etc. I have certain stories I know are strong ice breakers, others that are great "closers", and some I use just to revive a sagging conversation.

The point is: you are a professional storyteller. Stories are your currency, your skill set, so use them to help you. There's no better way to prove to potential employers you're a brilliant storyteller than by keeping them entertained with stories!

Follow Up

"Generally, if I'm meeting someone, and it's casual, I'll send them an email afterwards," says Solomon. "'Hey, it was really great to sit down with you. Thank you for taking the time.' Always assume the other person is busier than you are, and you kind of make them feel that way."

When writing a thank-you email, I always like to mention something personal or unique from the meeting–a funny joke that happened, a beloved movie the person referenced, etc. If we bonded over our mutual love of rock music, I may send a couple of my current favorite MP3's, or recommend one of my favorite rock books, like Chuck Klosterman's amazing *Fargo Rock City.* If the other person mentioned they're working on a project about something specific–say, talking animals taking over the world– I may send them some Internet links to recent articles I'd read about animal intelligence or evolution. Basically, your job after the meeting is to maintain and strengthen the personal connection you created *during* the meeting. Sending a helpful recommendation not only says you were paying attention during the meeting, it also invites them to email you back, keeping open your lines of communication.

Do Free Little Favors

A great way to keep in touch with people is to check in periodically with small, kind favors. This could be as simple as inviting someone to lunch, or it could be something more specific and personal. Years ago, when I was an assistant at the Littlefield Company, one of the other assistants and I became friends with a young manager. We learned he *loved* Krispy Kreme donuts, so every year on his birthday we'd send a dozen Krispy Kremes to his office. He loved it, and while the annual Krispy Kremes eventually faded from our to-do list, we remain friends to this day.

Special events, like birthdays and holidays, also present great opportunities to touch base in friendly ways. Send birthday cards or emails. I usually spot someone's birthday on Facebook, then send a personal email–nothing is *less personal* then getting a generic "happy birthday" message among 500 other Facebook posts. Also, every Christmas, I create a mix CD of my favorite new songs of the year. I have them professionally made with cover art, liner notes, etc.–then mail them out to everyone I've worked with. The list grows and grows each year; I now make about 700 CD's. Is this effective? Do people care? Last year, *Psych* creator Steve Franks asked if I'd be interested in writing a *Psych* tie-in book, a fake how-to-be-a-detective handbook "written" by the show's fictional detective, Shawn Spencer. On my first day in the *Psych* offices, Steve introduced me to everyone by saying, "Chad and I have known each other for about fifteen years, and every Christmas he sends out this amazing CD of the year's best songs!" A) That made my week. B) It made every CD I had ever made totally worth it–not only because I like making the CD's, but because I have no doubt those CD's helped Steve and I stay connected, eventually leading to my writing *Psych's Guide To Crimefighting For the Totally Unqualified.*

Another great "excuse" to check in with kind words is when someone has some positive press. Maybe you see a friend or contact in the trades for getting a show picked up, or selling a project, or maybe you just saw their movie and enjoyed it. Everyone appreciates a simple "Hey–saw *Burn To Dust* this weekend–loved it! Kudos on a fantastic job, man–can't wait for the next one!" Even more valuable is emailing people when they've hit a down turn. If someone's show has been canceled, or their movie bombs, or they've just been fired–these are times when kind words can be even more helpful. A quick "Hey, Jake–heard the news about *Swan Dive* this morning, and just wanted to say: that show was fantastic, and whatever stupid decisions the network has decided to make, you should know: you have at least one massively disappointed fan out here. Lemme know if there's anything you need; talk to you soon."

Keep a Database of Contacts

"Keep track of who you meet [and] what your impressions of that person were," says writer/director James Seale (*Scorcher, Juncture*). Write down who you meet with, what you talked about, and special facts about them, whether it's "a ten minute conversation at a festival schmoozer, or someone whose name you got from a mutual acquaintance." Some people use their computer or phone's address book, scribbling important tidbits in the "notes" section. Other people use database software. Whatever system works for you is fine. Personally, I like a spreadsheet that allows me to sort info according to different criteria, and print quickly if I want to review the list with my agent. It looks like this (Table 15.1).

Finally Asking Someone to Help You

"You don't ask for sex on a first date," says *The Exes* script coordinator Sam Miller, "and you don't ask for a (script) read when you first meet." While it's tempting to ask a new contact to take a look at your screenplay or help you get a job, or introduce you to their boss, networking is about the long game. It's about building the relationship, nurturing it to a point where the other person doesn't feel pressured or inconvenienced to help a good friend.

For whatever reason, amateur writers often think it's a quick, easy favor asking someone to read their script. *It's not.* Reading a full-length screenplay can take at least a couple of hours, and reading it thoroughly, thinking about it, making notes, takes much longer. Even reading a one-page story description or beat sheet takes time. Sure, it may require only two minutes to speed read, but to really process and evaluate it properly may take ten or fifteen minutes. Or more. While this doesn't seem like a huge imposition, you're asking an incredibly busy individual who gets *numerous* requests

TABLE 15.1 Contact Database

Name	Company	When/How We Met	Notes/Personal Info	Action
Bradley, Jay	Thumbnail Entertainment	3/18/13–General meeting	Mentioned I had a spec pilot about all-girl rock band	Send pilot wk of 6/30 (on vacation till then)
Morrison, Sabrina	CAA	7/22/13–Marissa's birthday party	Has two daughters, discussed pre-schools	Email to set lunch (discuss pre-school options)
Grant, Tony	Pokerface Productions	5/13/12–JHRTS networking mixer	Loves snowmobiling; sent "Simple Pleasure" script–passed	Email to set drinks ("it's been way too long")

like this every day. Would you ask a doctor you've just met for a free physical? Would you ask a mechanic you don't know for a free oil change? Probably not. So why do people expect free favors from agents, execs, or producers they barely know? One answer, of course, is: it's in those people's job descriptions to find new scripts and writers! Yes, this is true. And if you give a new contact the greatest screenplay they've ever read, it will make their day. But if it's *not* the greatest screenplay they've ever read, it may very well be the end of your relationship. So if you're going to ask someone with whom you don't yet have a solid relationship to read your material, or give notes, or

---

Seven Trade Secrets from Master Networkers

- "I've never met a professional writer who carries business cards. Sure, cards are really cheap to get made and you might have a hilarious picture or witty remark that you think will make an impression, but what the card really says is 'I'm new here, and I'm kind of desperate.'"—Gabe Uhr, writer (*Cartoon Network Hall of Game Awards*, *Rock and Roll Roast of Dee Snider*)
- "Go to as many mixers as possible and order soda water with lime—it's cheap, it looks like you're drinking (thus a fun person), but you'll stay sober and avoid making a fool of yourself in front of strangers. If you're a socially awkward writer (like many are) you are allowed one drink."—Jason Coffey, showrunner's assistant (*Beauty and the Beast*)
- Do not "[brag] about *anything*. We are all at the bottom of the totem pole making $10/hour. You are not better than anyone. At the same time, don't complain too much. There is a middle ground of hope, humor, acceptance, and loss of dignity and pride that comes with a four-year degree being spent on years climbing upwards to this magical land of Hollywood tiers."—Scott Bender, assistant and intern coordinator, Mandeville Films (*The Fighter*, *Monk*)
- "When I interned at *Conan*, I got my job done in a timely fashion and made time to make relationships with people who worked there. Remember things [people] tell you—ask how the editor's weekend away was, or if the head writer's dog is recovering from surgery. When staff members asked about me, I used that small window to tell them about myself and what I want to do. They may not need to hire anyone now, but one day they may, and they might remember you and the day you said you were interested in producing. My last week at *Conan* I handmade 'thank you' cards for the staff. I'm not saying everyone should do this—I personally love any excuse to go to Michael's and buy glitter—but do something personal to give thanks that represents you well.'—Lauren Vally, production assistant, TV Guide Network
- "Don't blow someone off just because they're lower on the totem pole than you are. The kid in the mailroom that you just screamed at for accidentally binding two scripts together might become an agent sooner than you will. Or maybe he/she will end up at a studio or production company, and you'll have to go through him/her to set up a meeting, send a submission, etc. Hollywood is a small town. Make as many friends—and as few enemies—as possible."—Bryan Berk, writers P.A., ABC Studios
- "Hang out at places [industry professionals] hang out at. Walk out the front gates of a studio and find the nearest bar. Those spots can be relatively packed."—Gerry Sadowski, entertainment research analyst, Paramount, Fox, Playboy TV
- "Social networking has created enormous resources to meet up with other writers. But be careful—you can waste a lot of time with wannabe groups and get togethers. Make sure the people you are networking with have had a least some professional success in the business. Otherwise it won't really help you."—James Seale, writer/director (*Black Sash*, *Throttle*)

YOU AND YOUR AGENT

pass along your script, you'd better be ready to stake your relationship on it. Personally, I'm more conservative; I'd rather preserve the relationship and grow it until it becomes a genuine friendship, at which point, I have a much more responsive, helpful reader.

How, then, do you know when the time is right to "pop the question," to ask an important favor? One good indicator is "when the tables turn and someone asks you for a favor [first]," says *Promised Land* co-producer Mike Sablone. Once you've been asked a favor, the door is open to ask a return favor. Of course this may not happen, and most of the time "you just know when you know," says Verve's Melissa Solomon. It may take a week, a month, or several years before you feel ready to ask a particular individual for their help. Whenever it happens, you just have to feel "you have a connection. It's easy going, free-flowing—maybe you're texting the person, you guys are hanging out, it's cool."

Also, when you finally feel the time is right, never ask someone to read your material in hopes they'll pass it on to their boss or consider buying it. If you ask someone to read your material, ask them for their notes or opinions. Try something like—"Hey, I know you're super busy, but I'm in the middle of working on a new screenplay, and if you're not too swamped, I'd love to get your thoughts on it." Posititioning it like this is much less of an imposition because: A) You've removed pressure form your reader by letting them know you're hoping for expertise and guidance, not a sale. B) You've let the reader know the screenplay is a work in progress, suggesting you're less precious about the words and ideas in the script. If they dislike something, there's still time to fix it; in fact, you're *hoping* they point out the script's flaws. C) You've given the reader an out, an opportunity to say, "I am really busy—I just don't think I can do it right now." If your friend loves the script, they'll automatically pass it to their boss or ask if it's available to be bought or developed. Finding a great script, after all, is how people make their name and move ahead in Hollywood. So even if you've just asked for "notes," an astute assistant, coordinator, or junior exec always reads with one eye open for opportunities.

Do Wannabe Writers Really Need to Live in L.A.?

Q: These tips and suggestions all seem great . . . *for someone living in Los Angeles.* But what about those of us living out of state. Are we screwed? Is it really necessary for aspiring writers to live in Los Angeles?

A: Next to "Roth vs. Hagar," the "do-I-have-to-live-in-L.A." debate is the most divisive question in the history of entertainment. So I'm going to answer it for you now, once and for all. *YES.* If you want to be a professional TV or film writer (especially TV) you have to live in Los Angeles—at least when you're starting out. (And to answer the more important question: *it doesn't matter, as long as Eddie's on guitar.*)

Now, let me clarify: you can be a talented writer *anywhere.* You could be the world's most talented screenwriter ever and live in Omaha, Nebraska—but there's a difference between having talent and having a *career.* And in order to have a career, you need to be meeting and networking with other professionals—gathering information, learning how things work, finding and making opportunities, having a presence—which you can not do in Omaha. (I know, I know, I always hear from writers who live in other states and love telling me they used Facebook or Twitter to connect with Seth MacFarlane or Judd Apatow or a Paramount executive or an ICM agent or whatever. So they *can* network, see?! They *do* have relationships! Yeah, well—I have yet to meet anyone who lived in another state, connected with Apatow or MacFarlane or Paramount or whomever via social networking, and then *sold them a movie.* Do not mistake the fickle connectivity of the Internet with an actual relationship. We all meet hundreds of people online every year; ninety-nine percent of us don't get married that way.)

"I left L.A. a couple years ago [and] lived in Milwaukee for a year," says screenwriter Francisco Castro. "When I left, I still had projects on the burners, so I'd get calls. And I realized, 'I'm in Milwaukee now, [so] I can't take a meeting. I can do it on the phone or Skype!' But there is a whole different thing taking a meeting face-to-face. Yeah, you could jump on a plane, but that costs money, and you have to wait to get on that plane." Eventually, as Castro watched his projects and opportunities evaporate, he moved back to Los Angeles, where he just finished a new script, *Urban Games*, currently in production.

"Living here does give you something," says Original Artists agent Matt Leipzig. "There is a certain understanding of the system, the language, the personality, certain cliches like 'high-concept' or 'accessible' or 'sympathetic'—these nouns and adjectives that make writers bristle. If you live here, you talk to people, you meet with people, you spend time discussing your ideas and their ideas. Even if just osmotically, you get a better idea of how the system works. There's frequently a conceptual disconnect if a client never spent time here and hasn't immersed themselves in the system."

Having said all this, I'm not one to discount the other side. Dennis Kim, a partner at the esteemed Rothman Brecher Kim Agency, has clients in Canada, New Jersey, New York, Florida, and Portland. "Living in Los Angeles doesn't matter too much except for [television] staffing," Kim says. "For me, signing someone, I'm not thinking about it. But once we're in business, [we] have to be in constant communication, [and] I need you to commit [to spending some time here]. It doesn't have to be a month. Commit to five business days. Tell me what they are, give me a lead time. You're not going sightseeing, you're going to do three meetings a day, maybe more." Kim even likes to use out-of-towners' unavailability to create a bit of mystique with execs and producers. "Everyone knows [the writer's here for] a limited time. That almost gives him a little step up in stature, like "Oooh! This guy's coming in from [out of town]!" Kim says. Still, "you have to make sure that you're calling [producers and execs] even a week in advance saying, 'Remember: Client X is coming in for a limited time!'"

Also, one important caveat: Kim's out-of-town clients include a comic book writer, a novelist, and a radio/music producer. In other words, these clients may not be based in Southern California, but they've already achieved a certain level of literary or entertainment success. They have both cache *and* connections, and most of them are prepared—should they sell a project—to move to Los Angeles.

As an agent signing an out-of-town client, "you better make damn sure he's going to quit his life to get something going here," Kim continues. "That's where the pressure is. [The client has] got to dive in and say, 'I'm done with that. I'm going to commit.'"

One Last Bit of Exercise

I want you to return to the exercise we did at the top of the chapter. Find the list of five people you'd like to network with. Now, thinking about everything we just discussed, I want you to repeat the exercise here. Using your original list of names, re-rank them in order of the *most* valuable person to know (#1) to the *least* valuable person (#5). Then, in the space beside each name, write how you'd like to network with that person.

Ranked Names   *How To Network With This Person*

1. _____   _____

2. _____   _____

3. _____   _____

4. _____   _____

5. _____   _____

Compare your new answers to the answers you wrote at the beginning of the chapter. Have you re-evaluated who is the most important person to network with? Do you have different ideas about how to network with these people? If so, congratulations— you're already a much stronger, more prepared networker. Now go out there and meet someone!

16 The Best Place to Begin Your Hollywood Career

Gerry Sadowski was not a "suit guy." In his early-thirties, with a Bachelors Degree from Purdue, a Masters in mechanical engineering from UCLA, and a brand new MBA from USC, Sadowski was most comfortable in a Foo Fighters t-shirt, black leather jacket, and baseball cap. But on this particular morning, as he stepped off the elevator to begin his first day of work at The Endeavor Talent Agency, Gerry Sadowski was wearing a suit. "It can get pretty hot running around in a suit all day," Sadowski says, but agents "want everybody to be tip-top and put on a proper appearance, so it turns into a bit of an upfront expense to get a good rotation of suits."

Sadowski smoothed out his suitcoat, approached the front desk, and told the twenty-something receptionist he was here to start his first day. Smiling, the receptionist offered to lead him to Human Resources. They started down the sterile white hallway, one side lined with the glass walls of agents' offices, the other lined with cubicles containing headset-wearing assistants. Snippets of conversations swirled through the air like confetti at a New Years parade. "Peter Roth on line one," "three-picture deal," "says it's urgent," "forty-date tour." To an outsider, it might feel like a telemarketing operation had set up shop in a "fancy dentist's office." But to Sadowski, it felt "like you were in the heart of what really happens in Hollywood. Every creative part of production or entertainment [runs] through an agency in some way, shape, or form. The talent, the scripts, the directors—everybody's either represented or getting funneled through an agency. And it's all right in front of you."

Boasting clients like Christian Bale, Guillermo Del Toro, Amy Poehler, and Charlie Sheen, Endeavor was one of the most powerful and respected agencies in the world. Sadowski—even with three degrees from prestigious universities, and several years' experience as the top salesman for a Japanese robotics company—had needed a referral just to get in the door. Fortunately, he had a friend in the TV department who got him his first interview. From there, he met with H.R. executives as well as agents in television and MP lit. "The goal was to [see] if you have the fire to do what they do," Sadowski recalls. " I remember the TV literary agent asking me what shows I watched and then immediately 'Why did I like them?' [He wanted] to see if I had an eye for television, if I could identify what makes good TV. [Another asked], 'Do you have good taste? [And] how would you define good taste?'"

After four grueling rounds of interviews, writing sample coverage, and providing references, Sadowki's phone had rung. It was one of Endeavor's H.R. execs: "We'd like to extend an invitation for you to join the company." He had made it. "They say [getting a job at a Big Four Agency] is more competitive than getting into an Ivy League university," Sadowski says, "so it's very exciting."

The receptionist ushered Sadowski into the H.R. suite, where he was introduced to the other newcomers starting that day. After a brief orientation, the H.R. exec offered to show him to his office. Sadowski followed his guide past the windows of heavy-hitters like Patrick Whitesell, the agent who had discovered Matt Damon and Ben Affleck, and Ari Emanuel, the inspiration for *Entourage's* Ari Gold. Sadowski beamed; he was about to become one of them. "Here you go," said the H.R. exec. Sadowski turned to find himself standing before his new "office": a wall of tiny cubbies, carts loaded with packages, the constant whir of copy machines and printers, and a swarm of fresh-faced Millenials, sorting mail and collating scripts. "Welcome to the mailroom."

Sadowski smiled. He was in Hollywood.

Where Everyone Starts

There are numerous jobs you could find to break into Hollywood, but whether you land at a network, a production company, a second-year TV show, or a big movie studio, one thing is for certain. "Be prepared to start at the bottom," says writer Gabe Uhr (*The People's Choice Awards*). "I was an experienced industrial producer in the suburbs outside Washington, DC, and when I got to L.A., that experience translated to being a set production assistant."

You could have graduated top of your class from Stanford Law School, or founded your own million-dollar company in Madison, Wisconsin, or run an award-winning regional theater in Tennessee—when you get to Hollywood, you will start at the bottom. "This is one of the [few] businesses where, more than anything, it's about what you can do *right now*," says Michael Conway, Chief Administrative Officer at UTA. "I don't care if you went to Harvard. I want to know how fast you can dial ten digits on a telephone pad and get so-and-so on the phone for me. This business is not for people who tread water and wait around for someone to discover [them] and realize how brilliant [they] are. You have to go out and make things happen. Starting at the bottom, you appreciate it."

This usually means finding a job as some kind of assistant. **Production assistants (P.A.s)** are usually on the set or in the production office of a TV show or movie, doing basic grunt work: running errands, stocking supplies, filling the fridge, taking lunch or coffee orders. **Executive assistants** work at networks, studios, or production companies, managing the office of a particular exec: answering phones, updating calendars, organizing charts, tracking projects. **Producers assistants** work with showrunners like Blake McCormick (*Cougar Town*), or non-writing producers like Donald De Line (*Pain and Gain, The Green Lantern*). **Writers assistants**, while not yet official writers, are part of a TV show's writing staff; they sit in the writers room, typing every joke, story idea, and plot twist the writers pitch. They are essentially a court stenographer, creating a daily log of what happens in the room.

Writers Assistants

Being a writers assistant is often considered the best springboard to an actual staff writing job, as many showrunners fill their low-level positions by simply promoting their writers assistants. "I did [it] for a season and it was like going to comedy college," says *Men At Work* supervising producer Jessica Kaminsky. "I watched first-hand how a show got better each day of production. And lots of practical tips like how not to be precious about a joke—meaning if it doesn't get a laugh, it's out of there. I also learned how to act—and even more importantly, how *not* to act—in a room. But mainly, sitting in a writers room was incredibly motivating. If the weird guy who doesn't speak and looks like a serial killer can be in a room, well, then so can I."

Unfortunately, getting even an assistant job is incredibly competitive. When trying to become a writers assistant, for instance, "you're competing with every writers assistant [and] every person trying to break in as a writer or a writers assistant," says manager Jeff Holland of The Cartel. They're "just as competitive as staff writer positions. There might be even fewer writers' assistant gigs!"

Also, many high-powered execs and producers want assistants who come already loaded with experience and contacts. When an executive yells out, "Get me Paul Lee on the phone," he doesn't want his assistant to ask "Who's Paul Lee?" or to even need to look up the number. He wants you to *know*. (Paul Lee is, at the time I'm writing this, president of ABC.)

Thus, most professionals consistently recommend one job, above all others, as the single best way to break into Hollywood and learn the ropes: *Work at an agency.*

Even if you have no desire to become an actual agent, working at an agency is one of the best launching pads to any career in Hollywood: writer, executive, manager, producer, director. Agencies give you a "road map—knowing who's who, who to call, relationships [and] players . . . how to get things done," says Andy Bourne, who began as an agent's assistant at APA before becoming Sr. Vice President of Development at Closed On Mondays Productions, an NBC-based pod. "It's harder [to learn those things at a production company or studio]. The agencies are such a hub of information and commerce that so many things flow though your desk in any given day. The volume there creates a situation where you can learn exponentially. [Also,] at a production company, you're usually aligned with a studio and a network, so you'll be at ABC Studios, which means you'll be doing ninety percent of your business at ABC network. What ends up happening is: there are four other places in town, [but] you're not really going to have exposure to NBC, FOX, CBS and the CW because you end up in this ABC silo. Your education becomes narrow and focused."

Indeed, working at an agency is often considered "grad school" for Hollywood. You learn how to roll calls. What restaurants are appropriate for business lunches. How to write coverage. How to navigate sticky negotiations. Who gets invited to a big meeting and who doesn't. Which writers can sell something and which can't. You gain more knowledge, and meet more people, faster than you ever thought possible. And while you could learn all these things at other assistant jobs—at a network, studio, or production company—an agency's sheer *volume* of business trains you faster, harder, and better than most other jobs.

In fact, many network and studio executives won't even hire an assistant who hasn't had agency experience. "I'm a big believer in that," says 20th Century Fox Sr. VP of Development Dana Honor, who began her career as an assistant at CAA. "Working in an agency gives you a bigger global perspective of what the business is and what production companies do versus studios versus networks. You understand the nature of the business a bit more than your own small production company or your own small division in another company. It's a great experience to just learn all the different functioning parts of the business."

Thus, not only do many people begin their careers at an agency, they begin their careers at one special part of the agency in particular—*the mailroom.*

What is the Mailroom?

The mailroom is the nerve center of the entire agency. Every package, every script, every contract, every headshot is somehow shuttled through the mailroom. "It's like working at the post office, but you're delivering mail to the agency staff," says TV writer Kelly Galuska, who began as an assistant at ICM. "It's a social experience, too, because you're in there with all these people your age, they all want to do the same thing, and you're all down in the basement where the mail and packages come in. But you're also going upstairs four times a day delivering stuff . . . so you can watch all [the action] happen."

The mailroom is also home base for much of the agency's low-level support staff: **runners**, who deliver packages or pick up supplies outside the agency; **floaters**, substitute assistants who fill in when regular assistants are out of the office; and **cart-pushers**, the "mailmen" who sort and deliver mail to the agents.

"You come in, you're getting someone's coffee, you're answering someone's phone, you're doing grunt work," says Conway. "You're doing a lot of work beneath your set of skills, [but] it's a safe place to get grounded in a corporate culture. You learn the names and faces of people who work here, who are clients, what projects we're working on, who does what, how this organization works. You need to know that before you get on a desk and try working for an agent. It's also a big tradition. Everyone here has done it this way, everyone expects everyone else to go through the same process. It's like boot camp."

Indeed, working in the mailroom is a Hollywood tradition that has launched the careers of hundreds of agents and managers, as well as *The Normal Heart* playwright Larry Kramer, former *Cosmopolitan* editor-in-chief Helen Gurley Brown, and *Rocky* and *Goodfellas* producer Irwin Winkler. Walk into any agency mailroom in Hollywood, and you'll find thirty-five-year-old Princeton MBAs working alongside twenty-two-year-old UCLA graduates working alongside former lawyers and businessman. I know one Big Four agent who ran his own multi-million-dollar manufacturing company until, in his forties, he decided to switch gears and become an agent; he started in the mailroom. It doesn't matter how smart and talented you may be, or if you graduated summa cum laude from your film school, or if your father is president of Warner Brothers—working in an agency mailroom, you will learn more, meet more people, and understand the business faster than you've ever learned anything. "I had an MBA in entertainment from USC," says Sadowski. "I studied and studied, went over [everything], knew the business—the math and the finance—backwards and forwards, but *nothing* was like the mailroom."

Required Reading

Want a first-person glimpse into the mailroom without actually having to go? Read *The Mailroom: Hollywood History From the Bottom Up*, by David Rensin.

How to Find a Job at an Agency

The "first step," says *The Exes* script coordinator Sam Miller, is to "move to Hollywood. Few people can get you a job [while you're] outside of Hollywood." Unlike almost every other industry on Earth, where you can apply for a job, accept it, and then move to the city, most agencies in Hollywood won't even *consider* you until you're actually living in Los Angeles—especially for low-level positions like assistants and mailroom workers. This is for several reasons:

1. There's a huge flake-out rate, and employers hate hiring someone—or even interviewing them—only to have them bail on the opportunity. If someone doesn't live here yet, the the chance they'll flake is even greater.
2. As an assistant or mailroom worker, a big part of the job is running errands, knowing where to make special restaurant reservations, picking up supplies, etc. If you don't know the city, your ability to do those things is hampered. Agencies want to know they're hiring someone who can navigate the city, both geographically and culturally, and if someone doesn't even live here yet, there's a good chance he can't do that.
3. Low-level employees have an incredibly high turnover rate, so when employers are looking to hire someone, it's usually because someone has left or is leaving and the boss wants someone to start *tomorrow* (or within a few days). And while you may be the world's smartest, fastest, most savvy assistant, if you live in Little Rock or Portland or Chatanooga, you can't start tomorrow. There's such high demand for these jobs—and most of the jobs don't require incredibly specialized skill sets—it's much easier just to hire someone in L.A.

Unfortunately, once you're here, job-hunting doesn't get much easier. Most of the big agencies don't post employment information on their websites. They do, however, list their contact info, and you can email or send your resume to the agencies' H.R. departments. My advice: before sending your resume cold, call each H.R. department and get the name of the appropriate person. You're always stronger submitting personalized material. You can also sometimes find agency job listings on sites such as entertainmentcareers.net or showbizjobs.com—but many of those listings prove to be outdated or fruitless. What, then, is the secret?

"You have to know somebody," says Sadowski. "I got in because I knew agents at William Morris and Endeavor. That's the trick; the agency, the Hollywood side of things, is all about networking and knowing people. I can't think of how I would have been able to get in if I hadn't known someone."

"Having said that, agencies *do* look at resumes that just randomly come [in]," says Conway. "But, if someone says, 'I have a friend, blah blah blah'—we look at *all* of [those]. It's because we want to maintain those relationships—our relationships with people who we are referring candidates to. We want that pipeline. And if someone can come to me and say, 'I've got this great person who was an intern for us and they knocked it out of the ballpark . . . will you please take a look at this?' *Yes*, I'm going to take a look at it."

Of course, it's not always easy making connections—especially if you don't have a job. And while a few pages ago you read a brilliant chapter on networking, networking is a long-term game—and you need a job or an opportunity *right now*. So what do you do?

"The best way to break into the biz is through internships and temping," says DreamWorks Animation SKG executive Scott Seiffert. "Go after internships like a dog goes after a bone. They get you in the door and help you learn how things are really run." As an intern, you'll not only get to observe the business in action, you'll also make real connections, and many internships lead to full-fledged jobs. Producer Jim Whitaker (*The Odd Life of Timothy Green*) started his career as an intern at Ron Howard and Bryan Grazer's Imagine, then worked his way up to President of Motion Picture Production before landing a first-look deal at Disney![1] *Assassin's Creed* writer Corey May sold his first film pitch, an adaptation of Kenneth Grahame's children's novel *The Wind in the Willows*, to Disney after interning there as a USC grad student.[2]

The Yin and Yang of Internships

The good news about internships: you'll get up-close-and-personal experience, and the connections you make will, hopefully, lead to an eventual job. The bad news: most internships are unpaid—and possibly illegal. According to 1947's landmark Supreme Court ruling, Walling v. Portland Terminal Co., every worker at a company *must* receive minimum wage unless a worker is working solely for his or her training and educational purposes, not the betterment of the company. I.e., *interns*. When it comes to internships, employers are not required to comply with federal laws regarding compensation, discrimination, benefits, etc.—they are required only to appropriately train and teach the individual. In order to qualify, the intern/employer relationship must meet six qualifications laid out by the federal government to ensure the experience is purely educational; the intern, for example, must do no work that would be otherwise done by actual employees, and the company can get no legitimate benefit from the intern's presence.[3]

Thus, many employers require interns to get college credit, "proving" the intern is there to train and learn, not "work." If you're a college student, this usually poses no problem; most colleges and universities have easy-to-navigate paths for doing internships and receiving credit. If you're not a student, however, it can be a bit trickier. One suggestion: enroll at a local community college. Many community colleges, such as Santa Monica College, are relatively inexpensive (less than a few hundred dollars) and offer one-credit internship programs for exactly this purpose. So yes, you'll be "paying" to work, but if it's an experience that educates you in the business, introduces you to contacts, prepares you for a real job, and (hopefully) leads to genuine employment, it may be an investment worth making.

As we discussed in the last chapter, knowing when to ask contacts and relationships for favors is a delicate process. You don't want to ask too soon, so gauging the strength of the relationship is imperative. "Job-hunting is like trying to get laid," says ABC Studios writers P.A. Brian Berk. "You start off talking, then comes the hand holding, then you ask if she wants to come back to your place for (insert random excuse here). The next thing you know, it's 7:00 a.m. and you're digging through her purse trying to find her ID so you can figure out what her name is before she wakes up. Notice that *at no point* did either of you ever come right out and ask: 'Do you want to have sex with me?' Well, job-hunting works the same way. "When talking to your contacts, *never* come right out and ask for a job. Talk to them, check in on how they're doing, see what they've been up to. Ask things like, 'How did you start in the industry?' or 'What

If You Don't Live in L.A.

Get an industry job wherever you are! As I mentioned in the last chapter, most cities have at least some entertainment or related businesses: movie theaters, agencies, local TV stations, commercial production companies, regional theaters, etc. You can also check with your state's film commission, which may know of regional film festivals and conferences, visiting movie or TV shoots, or other local jobs and companies.

Job-Hunting Resources for Finding Agency Jobs

"The most helpful job-hunting resources you're going to find are your friends and your reputation," says one assistant. "In a tough job market, I've had friends be unemployed for literally [only] one day just because they had so many people recommending them for openings." Of course, if you're a misanthropic pariah, you may not have the friends you need to get you hired. In which case, you may need some other job-hunting resources:

Agency Contact Information
APA–www.apa-agency.com
CAA–www.caa.com
Gersh–www.gershagency.com
ICM–www.icmtalent.com
Kaplan Stahler–kaplanstahler.com
Paradigm–www.paradigmagency.com
Rothman Brecher Kim–9250 Wilshire Blvd Penthouse Beverly Hills, CA 90212; (310) 247–9898
UTA–www.unitedtalent.com
WME–www.wma.com

Industry Job-Hunting Websites
4 Entertainment Jobs–www.4entertainmentjobs.com
Cynopsis–Cynopsis.com
EntertainmentCareers.net–www.entertainmentcareers.net
EntertainmentJobs.com–www.entertainmentjobs.com
The Grapevine–www.grapevinejobs.com
Greenlight Jobs–www.greenlightjobs.com
Mandy–www.mandy.com
Media Match–www.media-match.com
Showbizjobs.com–www.showbizjobs.com
Staff Me Up–staffmeup.com

Temp Agencies Serving the Industry
The Comar Agency–www.comaragency.com
Executive Temps–executive-temps.com
The Friedman Agency–www.friedmanpersonnel.com

Other Helpful Resources
Association of Talent Agents' Classifieds–
    www.agentassociation.com/frontdoor/classifieds.cfm
CraigsList–Craigslist.org
Streetlights–www.streetlights.org
Temp Diaries' Job List–www.tempdiaries.com/p/job-list.html
UTA Joblist–UTA keeps a constantly updated list of exclusive industry jobs; unfortunately, it's rarely available online. If you want it, you need to know someone.
Workplace Hollywood–www.workplacehollywood.org

advice do you have for someone who's just starting out, like myself?' They know you're looking for a job, and often they'll come back and tell you to send them your resume because they know someone who's hiring, or they'll keep an eye out for entry-level jobs they come across."

When someone *does* ask what kind of job you want, *be specific*. Many young people say, "I'll do anything and everything—I just want to get my foot in the door," thinking they're more hire-able by sounding eager, ambitious, and open. Nothing could be further from the truth—*this answer actually makes you less hire-able*. Why? Because if I run a visual effects company specializing in low-budget movies, I do not want the kid who's interested in "anything and everything"; I want the kid who's rabidly passionate about visual effects, or post-production, or low-budget filmmaking! I want the kid who is so laser-focused on what she wants, I understand immediately how my job or internship will benefit her, and why she'll work tirelessly to impress me.

Having said that, "apply to *everything* and take every interview you can get," says Radical Pictures story editor Lex Ardeljan-Braden, whose first Hollywood job was at Paradigm. Look online at studios' corporate websites, use specialized job-hunting services, check Craigslist and the trades. Most listings will lead to dead-ends, but at least you're exploring every avenue. And if you do get an interview, says Ardeljan-Braden, even "though you might not be interested in the position, it could lead to something more up your alley. At the very least, it's in your best interest to get as much interview experience as possible."

What Your Resume Should Look Like

Short, simple, easy to read. The purpose of a resume is *not* to convince the agency to hire you; it's to convince someone you're worth interviewing. Most likely, whoever reads your resume is going to spend ten seconds glancing at it to discern whether you're even minimally qualified for the job. Your mission to make that decision as easy as possible—which means keeping your resume clean, crisp, and pleasing to the eye. I am constantly shocked at how many disorganized, unappealing resumes I see—narrow margins, tiny fonts, as much information as possible squeezed onto the page, as if the reader will actually want to peruse every detail of the applicant's last ten years.

One-Pagers Only!

Keep your resume to *one page*. No one likes reading pages upon pages, and there's no reason you can't fit all your relevant job info onto a single page. Also, if you're emailing your resume, a one-page PDF will show up in the body of the email. Anything over one page will not, which means your recipient has to open the PDF. This may not seem like a huge deal, but when you're trying to please a super-busy employer you want to make their job as easy as possible.

What Your Cover Letter Should Look Like

Like your resume, keep this short and sweet. One to three short paragraphs are usually enough to do the trick. The purpose of a cover letter or email is not to give the agency your life's story, but to quickly introduce yourself, explain how you learned about the position, and give a sense of your passion, enthusiasm, and personality. In other words, it's about quickly conveying information that can *not* be found on your resume. Agents and HR reps don't want to spend an hour—or even thirty seconds—poring over a cover letter; they simply want to see if you sound intelligent, professional, articulate, and enjoyable. Most assistants are hired based on whether or not they click with their interviewer—almost nothing can trump a strong personal connection—so the real goal is simply to get to the interview stage. Thus, the mission of your resume and cover letter is to quickly broadcast, "I'm someone worth meeting."

Sample Resume

What *Not* to Put on Your Resume

- Your high school (no one cares)
- Your college GPA (despite what your college career center told you, no one cares)
- Your "objective" (any employer knows your objective–*to fill the specific job opening they have*)
- Things you've written (unless they were sold, published, or won awards)

What Else *Not* to Put on Your Resume

"I don't ever want an actor working for me, because then I feel like I'm being used. If I see someone is taking stand-up classes at a local comedy club or something, I can tell they're trying to get the job for connections rather than experience."–Talent/literary manager

---

WOLFGANG TEMPLEMAN
1978 Ludovico Street
Los Angeles, CA 90025
323-555-0812
wtempleman@waxahatchee.com

ENTERTAINMENT EXPERIENCE

- **PRODUCTION ASSISTANT, "SWAN DIVE"**   Nov 2013 – Current
  Phosphorescent Pictures
  Assisted production coordinator in basic office management: monitoring/stocking supplies, answering phones, tracking daily script changes, organizing script deliveries, overseeing radio distribution, etc.

- **INTERN, "BEATS WORKIN"**   Jan 2013 – Nov 2013
  Nijmegen Productions
  Assisted producers in all aspects of daily local interest show: researched stories, liaised with guests and talent, scouted locations, inventoried equipment, monitored and ordered supplies/equipment, etc.

- **INTERN**   Aug 2012 – Dec 2012
  Mammoth Enterprises
  Assisted and participated in all aspects of industrial video and live event production company: managed event schedule, researched and booked vendors, compiled pitch presentations, etc.

- **ARTISTIC DIRECTOR**   Feb 2010 – Oct 2012
  Cherokee Ranch Players
  Founded and ran semi-professional children's theater company; wrote, directed, and produced three productions per year; hired actors, designers, etc.; oversaw all aspects of production and promotion.

OTHER EMPLOYMENT EXPERIENCE

- **ASSISTANT MANAGER**   Summers, 2009 – 2013
  Gazzarri's Cafe
  Began as part-time server, eventually becoming assistant manager; overseeing schedule management, employee training, weekly P&L reports, local advertising campaigns, customer service, etc.

- **GROUNDSKEEPER**   2009 - 2010
  Alden Falls High School
  Mowed lawns, tended gardens and landscaping, oversaw fertilizer distribution, monitored/ordered supplies, maintained riding mowers and other garden machinery, etc.

EDUCATION

- B.A. – Franzen College, 2014
- – American Theater Institute, Tennessee Williams Theater Center, Fall 2012

AWARDS & HONORS

- Ain't Talkin' 'bout Love – original stage play – WINNER: Eugene O'Neill Young Playwrights Award
- "Me Wise Magic" – original short story – Published: Emerging Voices 2012

Words of Wisdom

"I don't want to know where [you] went to first grade and [your] entire life on two pages in a cover letter. I want to know why you're applying for this position specifically. Why you?"

How to Ace an Agency Job Interview

Job interviews in the entertainment world are a bit different than interviews in other industries. Sure, you may talk about past job experiences and qualifications, but you'll also talk about your favorite movies or TV shows, recent books you've read, even great bands you're listening to. And while this sounds like insignificant fluff, interviewers aren't just making small talk, they're looking to see if you have, and can articulate, a point of view. In other words, they don't ultimately care about *what* you like; they want to know *why* you like what you like.

"If you have to sit and kind of 'Ummmm, ohhhhh,' and struggle to talk about what films you like, you're basically killing yourself," says Conway. "If I say 'What do you watch on television? What is your favorite show?' and you don't have a favorite show . . . why are you in the room with me? If you sit here and say 'I want to represent actors,' and you can't name five actors you would like to represent, or who you're really impressed by . . . why are you in the room?"

You and your interviewer could have totally different tastes, as long as you can articulate the reasons behind your likes and dislikes. You could enjoy listening to Train, the worst band in the history of music, and it's fine—*as long as you can articulate why you like Train.* (Which no one can, so that answer's pretty much a lose-lose.)

Great organizational skills are also a must, since assistants are not only managing their boss's calendar, they're managing the calendars of all the agent's clients—which could be upwards of fifty or sixty people.

Finally, agents look for someone with "a great attitude, a degree of humor, [and the] ability to roll with the punches," says Matt Leipzig, a feature agent at Original Artists. "Somebody who is intuitive . . . somebody whose personality will add to the office."

"You are the face of your boss's business," adds Galuska. "Everything is going through you before it gets to him. So you want to be good on the phone, you want people to like you on the phone, and if [your boss] needs you to get information out of somebody, you want to be able to get it because you're friends with people and [they] like you."

Also, remember—getting a job at an agency, especially a big agency, rarely requires acing an interview; it usually requires acing *several* interviews. "You always interview with H.R. first," says Galuska. "They can tell right away if you'll be able to survive what kind of environment they have. H.R. knows all the agents and they know the personalities that fit with these agents, so if you seem like a confident person who's going to work hard, they'll push you to the next round."

Questions to Ask in an Interview

"The core of what you want in an assistant is someone who helps make your life better, [someone] who helps you function more productively," says agent Matt Leipzig of Original Artists. Thus, many agents evaluate assistant candidates by the questions they ask. Going into a job interview, prepare some strong questions that illustrate how you will approach this job, how you hope to make your agent/boss's life easier. Good questions may include:

- How can I help you be better at what you do?
- What's the most important thing you want from your assistant?
- How do you start your day? What's the first thing you like done every morning?
- What do you make sure you have done every night before you go home?
- How much of this job is clerical and how interested are you in my being involved, at the appropriate time, in reading scripts, writing coverage, sitting in on meetings?
- What else can I do to make myself indispensable?

Questions *Not* to Ask

- Where can I go from this position?
- How quickly do you promote?
- What are my hours?
- When is my lunch break . . . and how much time do I get?
- How much vacation time am I allowed?

YOU AND YOUR AGENT

The second round of interviews usually involves meeting with agents themselves, or sometimes agents' assistants. It's customary in Hollywood for assistants who get a new job to find their own replacement before leaving. Assistants "know what their boss wants, what their boss needs, what kind of person will work with their boss, so their boss trusts them to hire someone that will fit," says Galuska. "I remember when I left, feeling this tremendous amount of guilt because I was leaving and I knew how everything worked. No one I could find would know as much as I knew right away, because I had the key to [my boss's] business. So, if you like your boss, you want someone who will be good for them."

Thus, if you're interviewing to assist a specific agent, you may very well interview first with that agent's assistant. If the assistant likes you, he or she will pass you on to the boss, and possibly, from there, to other agents at the company. This can often be, as Sadowski learned, a three or four round process.

Ask the Agent

Q: I want to be a writer, but I know starting at an agency is a great way to get my foot in the door. If I'm applying for a job as an agent or manager's assistant, should I tell them my goal is to be a writer? Or should I lie and say I want to be an agent or manager?

A: "That's a little tricky," says Thruline manager Chris Henze. "Telling someone you want to be a writer can sometimes not be great for you getting the job. If you're going in to be somebody's assistant, they most likely just need a really great assistant. [So] it's not in your best interest to go in and say, 'I want to be a writer on a TV show, that's my goal, that's what I'm here working for,' because you're essentially saying, 'I don't have that much interest in what you do, but I want you to entrust your business to me on a daily basis.'"

Having said that, "I don't want [people] to lie," says agent Matt Leipzig of Original Artists. "I just want them to have a sense of passion and investment in what they're doing, not just marking their time. I want to feel like they want to do the job really well, that they're enthusiastic about it."

I suggest explaining how and why you feel working as this particular agent's assistant will propel you toward your ultimate goal. Something like, "You represent my four favorite screenwriters, which not only means you *like* the same things I do–it means you know how to *sell* the types of things I want to sell. And if I'm going to learn to navigate this industry, I want to learn from the best. You won't find anyone to work harder for you than I will–because you won't find anyone who wants to learn as much from you."

Sometimes, however, bosses aren't keen on hiring someone with outside aspirations. Or rather, they're concerned an assistant's outside aspirations could interfere with their job. If you sense this is the case with your prospective boss, I still wouldn't lie, but try something like this: "I'd love to write at some point; it's something I do on the side. But right now I'm just interested in learning the business of the business. It could only help me as a writer, if that's what I decide to do down the line, to understand how people are represented and deals are done. So right now, I really just want to work hard and learn how you and your business work."

How to Get Promoted Out of the Mailroom

Congratulations–you got the job! Sure, your $250,000 college education is being used to sort mail, make copies, and pick up lattes, but you're sorting mail, making copies, and picking up lattes in Hollywood! The agency mailroom is where Expedia and

Insider Secrets to Crushing an Agency Job Interview

- "Before going into your interview, research the person who is interviewing you as well as the company. Know who they rep in all areas. Also, be sure you're familiar with both general and entertainment news. [Scour] Deadline, *The Los Angeles Times*, and *The New York Times* the day of your interview to have a couple of talking points."–Lex Ardeljan-Braden, story editor, Radical Pictures (*Oblivion, Hercules: The Thracian Wars*)

- "1. If you are early you are on time, if you are on time you are late, and if you are late don't bother showing up. There are hundreds of people who want that job, don't blow it by being late. 2. Have multiple copies of your resume on hand. 3. Make sure you know your resume well. If you wrote it three months ago and they ask you about something on it, be sure you can elaborate and talk about it. 4. Remember the interviewer's name. Say it once while you are shaking their hand and meeting them. Bring it up once in the conversation and say it again when you leave."–Lauren Vally, production assistant, TV Guide Network

- "Be calm and not overly confident. Do so much research on the job, company, show, interviewer, etc . . . then keep it in your back pocket. I made the mistake once of touting to my interviewer that we went to the same college–that, combined with nerves and enthusiasm, made me look like a stalker. I didn't get the gig. Once I decided to chill out and actively listen, I understood what the needs of the jobs were, then positioned myself as the best person to meet them."–Jason Coffey, showrunner's assistant (*Beauty and the Beast, Desperate Housewives*)

- "Two things any interviewer wants to hear: 'I love what you do' and 'I'm willing to do anything.' They might ask you what your favorite show or movie is. Have a prepared answer, then ask them the same question. Show you're more interested in them than anyone else they've interviewed."–Sam Miller, script coordinator (*The Exes*)

- "Don't shit on any people, movies, or shows because you don't know who's listening. The hair person could be married to a producer. And no matter the ratings, box office, or critical reception, any show on TV, or any movie released, is a success by the mere fact that it has survived long enough to make it to the screen. Most projects die long before then."–Gabe Uhr, writer (*People's Choice Awards*)

- "Even though you've had some internship experience, don't act like you know everything. 'Cause you don't. Instead, come in humble and hungry. Ready to do whatever it takes to learn what you need to get to the next level. People notice that."–Hunter Kinsella, manager, Trium Entertainment (*MasterChef*)

IAC/InterActiveCorp. Chairman Barry Diller started,[4] so you must be doing something right. Besides, this is just square one; it won't take long for you to make it to square two.

"I see Hollywood as a big game of Frogger," says *The Exes* script coordinator Sam Miller. "You start on a lily pad. You jump to another one closer to the other side. Sometimes something comes up and you have to jump back. But eventually, if you string enough lily pads together, you get to the other side." Most agency mailroom workers make their first jump to a new lily pad by "floating," working as a temporary assistant for agents whose assistants are out of the office. This is how you learn the ropes of the job as well as the idiosyncrasies of each individual agent; it's also how you prove you're ready to be bumped up onto a full-time desk. Thus, getting good floater assignments can be incredibly competitive among mailroom workers, and often comes down to one thing–*relationships*.

"Make friends with the assistants," says Sadowski. "They'll give your preferential treatment, especially if you're a good floater, because they don't want any problems with their agent."

Assistants are also great educational resources because "they're not that far removed from floating," Sadowski continues. Ask assistants about their jobs: how they organize their bosses' offices, which calls or meetings are important, any practical do's or don'ts. "Assistants are well connected, they're on all the calls, they know the people . . . they have information, and a lot of them are open to talking. [Eventually,] an assistant gets bumped up, an assistant leaves, [or] a new agent comes over and doesn't have an assistant. At that point, H.R. has some idea of who the better floaters are, so they pick from the ones they consider the most competent . . . and that's how you end up at an assistants desk."

Most assistant appointments aren't immediately permanent; there's usually a trial period, so if things don't work out, the agent can send the assistant back to the mailroom and pick another.

What It's Like "Being on a Desk"

"One of the main reasons I wanted to work at an agency," says Galuska, who first assisted a talent agent at ICM, "is because I'd heard how tough a skin you need, and I was like, 'Okay, I'm going to see if I have one. And if I don't, I'm going to get one, because everything after that will be easier,' and that proved to be true."

As an agent's assistant, your job is to "[run] this agent's life," Galuska says. It's not unusual for assistants to take in their bosses' dry-cleaning or shop for a spouse's birthday present. Most importantly, however, "it's a lot of management . . . sending your boss to places he needs to be, making sure he's on calls [or] at meetings he needs to be at. Then, as silly and *Entourage*-y as it sounds—rolling phone calls, listening to calls your boss is having, remembering information without being told, taking care of whatever was asked to be taken care of. You've got a headset—you look like a telemarketer—and you're doing five other things at the same time."

And remember, "you're managing not only your boss's schedule, but the schedule of every person he has on his client list. If you're representing actors, you're managing all their audition schedules—making sure [they have] every piece of information they need to get to their auditions at the right place, at the right time, with the right people—and you're the one to blame if that doesn't happen! [Plus,] your boss is pitching clients from the whole agency, so he's talking to casting directors and saying, 'What kind of person are you looking for?' As an assistant, I get all those people's head shots, all their resumes, all their information, I compile a letter and send all that out to casting agents on my boss's behalf."

Most agents' assistants arrive at the office between 7:30 and 8:00 a.m., well before their bosses. This way, they can look at the schedule, see where their agent needs to begin his day (many agents start with a breakfast meeting), and download any important information. Then, as the agent travels to his first meeting, the assistant **rolls calls** from the office. "It's just phone calls all day," says Galuska, and "replying to emails, sending out submissions . . . over and over. Once your boss leaves, you catch up on everything you didn't have time to do during the day: submissions, sending out audition information, whatever it is. It just piles up."

During the year's busiest times—like pilot season or staffing season—agency assistants often leave the office at 9:00 or 10:00 p.m. But is this the end of their day? Unfortunately not. Most assistants are expected to build their network by going to dinner or drinks with other assistants. Then, when they arrive home, they have scripts to read and cover for their bosses.

As you get more comfortable in your assistant role, you'll probably begin looking for opportunities to show you can do more than just answer phones and schedule meetings. "Prove you can make a difference in the bottom line, and you're engaged and passionate about it," says Thruline's Henze. "Listen to phone conversations and find a way to support the business. Step in and say, 'Hey, I read this article . . . I just want to expose it to everybody to see if I'm crazy, but this seems like a good TV show.'

Misunderstood

At a big agency, the word "'assistant' is a bit of a misnomer," says UTA's Michael Conway. "When you say 'assistant,' most people think of someone who's doing a lot of secretarial work. Yes, you have to be a great secretary, that's a given. But at the same time, you also have to start thinking like a junior-level agent. How do you get a client paid? How are deals negotiated? You're on every single phone call an agent makes. You listen to every single negotiation that goes down. You're taking notes, understanding it, figuring it out. 'This is an incredibly nutrient-rich environment,' as [UTA CEO] Jeremy Zimmer likes to say, and your job is to absorb as much as you can. Read everything you can get your hands on–[anything] that's on a Black List, that's got someone attached, that's got financing behind it, and you have to have a point of view. You have to be able to walk into a room and talk intelligently about whether or not you like this and why. You can't walk into a room and say 'Oh, I thought it was kind of cool.' That gives no one anything."

How to Survive as an Agent's Assistant

- Always arrive early. "Everyone in California is late all the time, but you cannot be late even once, and you cannot complain that others are late always or that nothing ever starts on time. There are no excuses for being late ever."–Gabe Uhr, writer (*Cartoon Network Hall of Game Awards*)
- "DON'T LIE!! If you mess up, try to fix it, but don't lie. Good employees make mistakes, good employees don't lie."–Stacy Greenberg, manager, Imagine TV (*Arrested Development, 24*)
- "If you had a connection (friend, family) help you get your job, do not over-extend [that] connection in the workplace–or if you are interviewing for a job, do not bring up your relationship with this person more than once, unless the interviewer asks. At work, do not bring that person up in conversation every time you speak to your boss/co-workers. That person may have gotten you in the door, but only you can prove you are worthy of staying."–Lauren Vally, production assistant, TV Guide Network
- "Don't brag about student films, or what famous person you met because it's your mom's cousin's ex-boyfriends roommate. No one cares and you look like a stalker."–Rachel Burger, assistant, Kaplan/Perrone Entertainment
- "Cry in the bathroom, not in the office. Just take everything with a smile and know you are working towards the greater good. Never let it affect you to the point you become upset–we are not performing surgery, we are providing entertainment, so don't let it ruin you. Just put one foot in front of the other, and if you keep at it, someone will hopefully notice. Otherwise, there is always Vegas."–Scott Bender, assistant and intern coordinator, Mandeville Films (*The Fighter, 21 & Over*)
- "Setup Google news alerts for your job. That way, whenever your [boss or company] gets a review or mention somewhere, you get an email. You'll be the first in your office to know when some news broke and it makes you look great to your boss."–Sam Miller, script coordinator, (*The Exes*)
- "IMDB Pro and StudioSystem are your best friends. They'll provide the 'who works where' and 'who made what' information that will help put together all the pieces of what your boss is talking about."–Lex Ardeljan-Braden, story editor, Radical Pictures (*Oblivion*)
- "The most important person you'll work with, other than your boss, is your boss's boss's assistant. That's the person who knows everything that's going on and has friends all over town. They can help you more than anyone else in the office."–Sam Miller, script coordinator (*Malibu Country, The Exes*)

> - "If you're not sure what [scripts or packages] should be sent out, double check. Better to ask your boss a second time than send out the wrong version of something and make your boss look stupid. Nothing worse than making your boss look stupid."–Hunter Kinsella, manager, Trium Entertainment (*The Biggest Loser*)

Or, 'I noticed you've been talking to one of your clients about writing a western, and I saw this article I thought was interesting about the history of westerns."

This, after all, is how assistants get promoted–by proving they can think like an agent or executive and contribute to the health and growth of the company. "This is a true apprenticeship," says Conway, "not necessarily a warm and fuzzy environment; people aren't gonna pat you on the back and tell you how great you are. That's your job. You come in, you're expected to be great. We're all type-A personalities, we're all overachievers, we're all ambitious, we're motivated, we're scrappy, we're resourceful and entrepreneurial. That's who we are. Some days you hit it out of the ball park, some days you don't. If you don't that's okay. You dust yourself off, you get back in the game, and no one's gonna think anything less of you."

For an aspiring writer (or director, producer, actor, designer), working for an agent is not only a terrific education on the business itself, it's an invaluable chance to see–up close and personal–how agents go about representing their clients. You'll hear, first-hand, how agents pitch different clients over the phone. You'll see what keeps a client in her agent's good graces. Perhaps most importantly, you'll learn exactly how high the bar is set in terms of staffing writers or selling their work.

"An agent I worked for had so many [clients] he couldn't do anything for because they didn't have a lot of experience or they weren't at the same level of talent as other people," says one assistant-turned-writer. "[When I started looking for representation],

---

A Production Assistant's Journey, by Brian Berk (writers P.A., ABC Studios)

Technically I'm unemployed right now. But that's part of the nature of doing freelance P.A. work. Since moving to L.A. from the east coast, I've had three Hollywood assistant jobs, all of which have been pretty different experiences, so I'll break it down:

1st job: Assistant to producers at a feature production company
This job, which actually started as an unpaid internship, really broke me into the industry. I learned the 'lingo' (i.e. what things like 'LW' or 'Left Word' mean), learned some of the major players in the feature world, and, most importantly, got exposed to reading and covering a lot (A LOT) of scripts. The people here were the ones who got me the interview at my next job.

2nd job: [Agency assistant]
The vast majority of what I know about Hollywood, I learned here. Names I read on Deadline weren't just names anymore, they're people I remembered [my boss] talking to. I knew the companies they worked for, if they were comedy or drama people, and I could sometimes even remember their assistant's name. I also saw firsthand how writers get staffed on TV shows, how writers get pilots on the air, how negotiations work and deals get done.

Aside from what I learned at the desk, another huge perk of working at an agency is networking. I met a ton of people at [the agency], from clients to agents to other assistants. Some of those assistants are agents already, some will be soon, some will move to another side of the industry and become studio execs or producers, etc. They're all good people to know. This job also kept me busier than any other job I've had, especially during staffing season. You have to be able to multitask, be able to get lots and lots of things done without forgetting anything (ALWAYS WRITE STUFF DOWN), and you'll often go home feeling fried. It's not an easy job, but for what you gain from it, it's definitely worth it (even if you don't necessarily want to be an agent).

3rd job: Writers' P.A.

Landing a job as a writers' P.A. put me on a more direct path to what I want to do—write for TV. Definitely not as demanding as my previous jobs, but I love being in the writers room and spending time with people who write for a living. If the writers, and the showrunners in particular, like you as a writers' P.A. or writers assistant, then there's a good chance you'll be able to move up the ladder to staff writer, story editor, etc. if you're lucky enough to get on a show that stays on the air for a while.

Agency Training Programs

Many agencies have special training programs specifically designed to prepare young people to become agents. Admission is highly competitive. UTA, for example, received approximately 3,000 applications in the first six months of 2013 alone. Some programs, like Paradigm's, are open to outside applicants; other programs, like ICM's, require wannabes to spend a year working at the agency before applying.[5] Candidates go through a rigorous vetting process that includes written essays and multiple interviews. Only 126 of UTA's 3,000 applications advanced to the interview stage, and of those, a mere twenty-seven trainees were hired. That's an acceptance rate of less than .89 percent! Harvard's 2013 admission rate? 5.8 percent.

Different programs work differently, but once admitted, most trainees begin in the mailroom, even if they've already been working as an agent's assistant. There they learn the basics of their agency's operations and the business overall, as well as attend seminars, meetings, lectures, and workshops. ICM, for example, has trainees mock up their own network TV schedules and go through simulated contract negotiations.[6] UTA trainees head to a classroom every afternoon between 3:00 and 5:00 for "UTA U," where they attend classes taught by agents and executives from throughout the industry. After four weeks, trainees are given an exam; if they don't score ninety percent, they're given one week to study and improve. If they still don't pass the second time, they're given the boot.

Eventually, qualified trainees are eligible to land on a desk. Some float first; others immediately land with a specific agent. Ultimately, most trainees spend twelve to eighteen months on one desk before being transferred to a different department; the goal is to give trainees as broad an experience as possible. Although there's no guarantee, it usually takes about three years for trainees to progress from the mailroom to becoming a fully-fledged junior agent.

"There's an enormous amount of dedication you have to throw at this," says Michael Conway, who runs UTA's program. "You have to be incredibly passionate about film and television and actors, writers, directors, and pop culture and music and books and history and politics and sports and everything in between. Whatever your client is passionate about you need to understand something about it. Some people come in and after two years, [they] become a commodity in this business. If you've worked at an agency for two, three years, everyone in town wants you to come work for them . . . you're going to be poached."

Here's info on training programs at top-rated agencies. Not every agency makes training program info public, so if you're interested in an agency not listed here, contact them directly (you'll find contact info for many agencies in Appendix 2).

UTA—www.unitedtalent.com/#training
ICM—careersla@icmtalent.com
Paradigm—www.paradigmagency.com/about/agenttrainee
Innovative Artists—www.innovativeartists.com/training-program.html

First Day of Class

Some agency training programs admit participants only once a year; others begin a new "class" every two or three months.

I was hyper-aware of that. When agents were reading [my] work and started responding, getting in touch, [I was] like, 'Okay, this person knows when someone's ready to be staffed, and he's coming after me. I'm doing *something* right.'"

Moving On: How *Not* to Stay an Assistant Forever

Whether you want to be a writer, director, producer, executive, or agent, one thing's for sure: *you don't intend to stay an assistant forever*. Having said this, most bosses will expect you to give them at least a year, and leaving your current position—or using it to get your next gig—can be a delicate process. Hopefully, your relationship with your boss is open, warm, and friendly enough that you can be honest about your goals and enlist his or her help. "You have to be careful," says Henze, "because you don't want that to imply you are now going to [do] your job in a half-assed fashion. [However,] it's not going to be entirely surprising to any boss to hear 'Gosh, now that I've been here for [six months or a year], I've got to be honest . . . I'm starting to gravitate toward production.'"

Best case scenario: your boss offers to make some calls for you, put in a good word, and proactively help you take the next step. A strong agent obviously has numerous connections with producers, executives, writers, showrunners, managers, even other agents—and few things carry more weight with a potential employer than the praise of someone's current boss.

On the other hand, "if you've got [a boss] who's tightly wound and really concerned about his business, you have to be careful about what you say," Henze cautions. "Generally, you want to be honest. [Nobody] likes 'I'll be sneaky and pretend I want to be here, but I'm secretly putting myself out there.' That never ends well. There has to be a level of trust. It's probably important to say up front: 'I'm [trying to figure] this out. I'd love your input and understanding, but please know I'm really good at my job, and it's a priority for me. This doesn't mean I'm not going to continue to be great at this and give 100 percent. It just means I'm gravitating toward another division of the industry.'"

When you're finally ready to ask for your boss's help, know *precisely what you want to do*. Don't ask him to call showrunners looking for writers P.A.'s, executives needing assistants, *and* agencies wanting coordinators. These are three very different jobs, and while you may be eager to leave your assistant days in the dust, failure to be laser-focused suggests you don't know what you want or what your skill set is.

It's also important to use your boss, as well as other colleagues, wisely. Hollywood is a small industry, and as we've discussed, paths undoubtedly cross and re-cross over and over again. I know agent's assistants who have gone on to become executives, hiring or staffing their former boss's clients. I know writers who began as assistants to showrunners, then later sold a show and hired their old boss. I know people who started working for producers, then became agents, and now represent those same producers! Hollywood is, if nothing else, *all about relationships*, so it's imperative to keep yours intact.

BIRTH OF AN AGENT

"Melissa Solomon, do you have what it takes?" This was not the question Verve coordinator Melissa Solomon expected to be answering this early on a Monday. She had just flown back to L.A. from a ten-year college reunion in New Orleans, and she was still recovering from the weekend. Her plane had been delayed, so she had greeted with relief a company-wide email saying all employees would begin the day with a mandatory tour of Verve's new offices, which were still under construction.

Yet now, as founding partner Bryan Besser led the company through the new space, talking about color themes and design elements, Solomon was suddenly being singled out. "Yes," she answered, unsure what would happen next.

Besser ushered everyone into a hallway, where Solomon was presented with four doors. On each door was a riddle. Solomon stepped up to the first one: *When you're an agent, you have to be out wining and dining. Never leave home without this.*

"Uh . . . like American Express?" Solomon asked.

She opened the door. Gift-wrapped on a table inside was, indeed, an American Express—the Verve company card. Solomon grinned; she knew exactly what was happening. She plowed through the other three riddles, opening each door to find a new phone, a wireless headset, and a black power suit.

And then she realized—*there was a fifth door.* Hesitantly, she opened it. "Congratulations!" said the man inside. It was Jon Hoeber, screenwriter of *Whiteout*, *Red*, and *Battleship*. And now—her client. After beginning her career as a lawyer, then starting over and spending years as an assistant, and eventually a coordinator, Melissa Solomon had finally become an agent.

What This Means for You

It means there's a new agent out there, hungry to find the next big writer, director, or producer. Hungry to find the person reading this book. And tomorrow there will be another. And another. And another. And with every new agent comes a wealth of new opportunities.

It also means you've reached the end of this book. Or rather, the beginning. Perhaps of your career. Perhaps of a relationship with a new agent or manager. Or maybe it's the *re*-beginning, a chance to restart or repair a relationship that's been damaged. Ultimately, I hope this book has helped you see your relationship with your representation, or your future representation, differently. Perhaps it's helped you understand why your agent is able to (or *not*) make certain things happen. Maybe it's given you insight into how, as a client, to improve your own communications. Or made you realize you're not ready for representation at all.

Most importantly, I hope you close this book knowing what your representation *can't* do. They can, after all, do a lot. They can open doors, make introductions, offer feedback, negotiate deals, hold your hand and play therapist. Some can navigate Hollywood at the highest levels, constructing new kinds of deals and partnerships that create whole new revenue streams and forms of entertainment. But the one thing no agent can do—no matter how strong or powerful he may be—is make you *a great writer*. Only you can do that—and this is where you hold all the strength and power of your career. Create something brilliant—the next *Parks and Recreation* or *Argo* or *Dancing With the Stars*—and you can have your pick of agents. You can call all the shots.

So why are you still reading? Put this book down and go do the most crucial thing you can do to help your career:

Go write something. Write something brilliant. Something personal. Something that will make audiences sit up and take notice of you. And hopefully, somewhere in that audience, will be Hollywood's next hot-shot representative.

(That's it. Book's over. You can stop reading.)

(Seriously. I'm not kidding this time. I just wrote 344 pages—I have nothing left to say.)

Part VI
Appendices

Appendix One: **Glossary**

AAA–A term referring to big-budget video games developed and released by any of the major publishers such as Electronic Arts, Microsoft, Sony, etc.

Above-the-Line–Filmmakers, artists, or professionals that must be factored into a budget before production begins; this usually includes only writers, directors, producers, and actors.

Accounting–The agency department responsible not only for auditing, bookkeeping, and monitoring internal finances, but also for tracking and processing clients' checks.

Adjusted gross profits (or adjusted gross receipts)–Profits generated by a particular property, minus certain expenses such as a reduced distribution fee, interest, and/or overhead. Sometimes known as *modified adjusted gross profits.*

Agency–A company designed to represent artists or craftsmen in the entertainment marketplace, helping them procure work, negotiate contracts, and stay legally and professionally protected. Agencies, unlike management companies, must usually abide by their home state's licensing and bonding requirements.

Agency papers–A contract outlining the terms of a relationship between an agency and client.

Agency training program–A program designed to train aspirants and assistants to become professional agents in the entertainment industry.

Agent–Someone who represents professional artists and tradesmen, attempting to procure clients work, negotiate deals, introduce them to buyers, and protect them legally and professionally.

Alliance of Motion Picture and Television Producers (AMPTP)–The trade organization responsible for representing nearly 400 movies studios, production companies, and TV networks in negotiations for collective bargaining agreements with agencies, writers, directors, editors, and actors.

Alternative TV–While the term "alternative television" is often used interchangeably with "reality TV," "alternative TV" may also include sketch comedy shows, talk shows, stand-up specials, game shows, competition shows, etc.

Arbitration–The Writers Guild's process for determining which screenwriters deserve credit on a particular piece of work.

Article 13–In the Writers Guild's Schedule of Minimums, Article 13 refers to entry-level TV writers. These writers, unlike Article 14 writers, are considered "pure writers"; they are paid weekly (not episodically), and are not paid for additional "producing duties" such as editing, casting, etc.

Article 14–According to the Writer's Guild's Schedule of Minimums, Article 14 writers include any non-entry-level writer (story editor or above) on the writing staff of a TV show. These writers have "producing duties" in addition to writing responsibilities, so they're paid script fees for their writing work, and episodic fees for non-writing duties such as set design meetings, casting, editing, etc.

Artists Manager Basic Agreement (AMBA)–A contractual agreement negotiated between the Writers Guild of America and Hollywood's talent agencies, governing the relationships between writers and agencies. Also known as a *franchise agreement*.

Assistant—An individual charged with managing the office and supporting the business of an agent, manager, executive, producer, or other entertainment professional. Assistants' duties often blur the line between the professional (answering phones, rolling calls, maintaining calendars) and the personal (shopping for gifts, picking up dry-cleaning, dog walking, etc.).

Association of Talent Agents (ATA)—Non-profit trade organization representing talent and literary agencies, notably in negotiations with artists' unions such as the Writers Guild, Directors Guild, etc.

Attach—To formally commit an artist or element to being involved with a project. An actor may attach to a screenplay, committing himself to star; a director may attach to a TV pitch, committing herself to direct the pilot and oversee the direction on the series; etc.

Attachment—An individual or element who attaches himself or herself to a project.

Auspices—Elements, such as producers or actors, attached to a project.

Baby writer—A writer who has not yet sold a project or been professionally staffed on a TV show.

Backend—Money generated once a project has been distributed in the marketplace; this usually involves income through ticket sales, syndication, etc.

Backend compensation—Money paid to writers, artists, or professionals once a TV show, movie, or video game begins generating backend revenue or profits.

Bank authorization—A signed document stating that an agency or management company may deposit checks into their account on the client's behalf.

Beat—A single piece of story information.

Beat out—To outline a story, or construct it according to the simplest units of story information.

Beat sheet—A simple step-by-step outline or document detailing a story according to beats.

Below-the-Line—Term referring to filmmaking professionals who are *not* factored into a budget before production begins; this usually involves anyone not responsible for steering the creative direction of the pilot: lighting designers, accountants, costumers, electricians, etc.

Big Four—Term referring to Hollywood's four biggest agencies—CAA, WME, ICM, UTA—which control the lion's share of Hollywood's above-the-line talent.

Blind script deal—A deal in which a writer is contracted to write an as-yet-undetermined script.

Block—A thematically related chunk of TV scheduling. In the fall of 2013, CBS scheduled a "comedy block" from 8 pm–10 pm on Monday nights: *How I Met Your Mother*, *We Are Men*, *2 Broke Girls*, *Mom*.

Board of directors—A group of appointed members who oversee an agency or company's operations.

Booking sheet—A document detailing the commission, or other types of income, generated by an agent's client on a particular job. A new booking sheet is filled out each time a client lands a gig or makes a sale.

Boutique—A small literary agency that usually has only a handful of agents and focuses on only one area of representation, such as literary, talent, or modeling.

Box office bonus—Financial bonuses, usually paid to a screenwriter, actor, producer, or director, based on a movie achieving certain benchmarks in box office revenue.

Branded entertainment—Advertiser-generated content designed to look and feel like traditional entertainment, while subtly promoting a product or service. The online series "The 4 to 9'ers," for example, written and directed by TV director/producer James Widdoes (*Two and a Half Men*, *The King of Queens*), was funded and produced by Subway.[1]

Break a baby—To get a baby writer his or her first job or sale, the first break.

Break-even number—The benchmark number, often identified in agents' contracts, at which the agent's income exceeds his or her overhead and expenses; in other words, the number at which the agent is now generating pure profit for the company.

Broadcast network—A television distributor which delivers content (shows, sports, news, etc.) to television sets via radio waves.

Business manager—A representative charged with handling a client's financial life: bills, insurance, wealth management, etc.

Business affairs—The department of an agency, studio, network, or production company that handles legal concerns in regards to contracts and negotiations.

Busted (pilot)—A television pilot that has been shot, but is not selected to move forward as an on-air series; a rejected television pilot.

Cable network—A television distributor delivering content (shows, sports, news, etc.) via wires, or *cables*, connected directly to cable boxes attached to consumers' television sets.

Capping—The practice of limiting how much commission an agent can earn from a particular client.

Call sheet —A list of incoming and outgoing phone calls, usually maintained by an assistant for an agent, executive, or producer. (Also known as a *phone sheet*.)

Cart-pusher—A mailroom worker who pushes the mail carts up and down the halls, delivering or picking up incoming/outgoing mail to and from individual offices.

Certificate Of Authorship (C.O.A.)—A legal document, signed by a writer, stating any work written is owned by the employer.

Channel—The homepage of a content creator, where all that creator's work can be accessed online. Most channels live on YouTube, although other video-sharing websites may offer channels as well. (In television, "channel" also refers to either a particular television station, like Des Moines, Iowa's KCCI, or the band of radio waves over which a particular station is broadcast. KCCI, for example, broadcasts on Channel 8, the band between 180 and 186 megahertz.)

Check authorization—A signed document granting an employer permission to send a writer, producer, or other employee's checks directly to that person's agency.

Closer—A high-level writer hired to do the final pass, often a joke or dialogue punch, on a script.

Commencement—The act of officially beginning work on a script or project, usually signified by the paying of "commencement fees."

Commission—A percentage of income paid to a representative or employee. Agents, managers, and lawyers, for example, often charge clients commission ranging from two percent to twenty-five percent of the client's income (depending on the medium or industry).

Consulting producer—A high-level TV writer who has a different contractual obligation than the rest of the writing staff; a consulting producer may come in three days a week, or work on the show for only a short time, or have limited duties and responsibilities.

Contained movie—A movie set entirely in one place (such as *Cube*, *Saw*, *Rope*, etc.) and, as a result, can be done for a specific price point.

Content Management System—Software allowing online content to be published or revised from a single, central interface.

Contingent compensation—Monies paid to a screenwriter only if his or her movie gets made.

Coordinator—A low-level position at an agency, network, studio, or production company (usually a transitory position between assistant and agent/executive) responsible for supporting an entire department. A television lit coordinator, for example, may track, monitor, and organize information regarding competitive TV development, daily ratings reports, writers' credits, etc.

Coverage–1. At an agency, the process of gathering development information from a specific territory. One agent, for example, may be responsible for "covering" Sony, Disney, and Paramount, then reporting his findings back to his agency colleagues. 2. A report, usually written by an assistant or professional "script reader," evaluating the plot and commercial prospects of a literary property. Also see *script coverage*.

Covering agent–A low-level agent whose duties include coverage, or checking in on the development activities of various territories, then reporting back to his or her department. (Also known as *junior agent* or *servicing agent*.)

Credit(s)–1. A writer, producer, or other employee's title on a project (e.g., "executive producer," "production coordinator," "story editor," etc.) 2. An entertainment professional's resume. ("I have a job opening on my show. Send over your credits and I'll try and get you hired.")

Current executive–An executive at a television network, studio, or production company responsible for overseeing shows already on the air.

Cutscene–A video game scene over which a player has no direct control. Cutscenes are usually narrative scenes appearing at the beginning or end of a particular level or mission.

Deal memo–A legally binding document outlining the primary points of a contract; deal memos are often used as precursors to "longforms," or complete and detailed contracts.

Deficit financing–The process of funding a TV show or project by paying more than you will immediately earn back, hoping to turn a profit on the project's backend. Most scripted TV shows are deficit financed by one of the major studios: Sony, ABC Studios, CBS Studios, Universal Television, 20th Century Fox, or Warner Brothers.

Demo reel–A clip reel showcasing highlights of a particular director or performer's work.

Department head–An agent responsible for overseeing the direction and operations of a particular department (motion picture lit, TV talent, personal appearances, etc.).

Development deal–An arrangement, usually with a studio or production company, in which a writer, producer, performer, or director is contracted to create or develop a particular property.

Development executive–A TV or film executive charged with overseeing the creation and maturation of original content and projects.

Development report–A chart or report tracking the status of internal or competitive projects.

Development season–The annual period (usually July–October) when broadcast television networks, studios, production companies, and writers buy, sell, and develop new content.

Development studio–Companies responsible for conceiving, designing, and actually making video games–which are then marketed and distributed by publishers.

Digital media–Non-traditional methods, platforms, and mediums used for producing and distributing creative content or entertainment, including the Internet, mobile phones and devices, social networking, video games, etc.

Directors Guild of America (DGA)–Hollywood's labor union representing film and TV directors, assistant directors, stage managers, unit production managers, etc.

Discretionary fund–A pool of money used by a production company to finance its own projects outside of any deal with its home studio.

Distributor–An entity responsible for delivering product from producers to consumers. In television, distributors are broadcast or cable networks. In film, distributors usually deliver movies from producers or studios to exhibitors or home video and online retailers.

Diversity writer–A TV writer of minority descent.

Docusoap–A narrative reality show following the serialized stories of a cast of characters; although docusoaps are "non-scripted," they're designed to resemble traditional scripted programs.

Dumb money–Film funding coming from investors with no creative or practical voice in the production process.

DVD bonus–A financial bonus paid to a writer, director, actor, or producer when a movie achieves certain benchmarks in DVD sales or revenue.

Episodic fee–Per episode money paid to TV writers for duties above and beyond traditional writing tasks, such as set design meetings, casting, sound mixing, etc.

Equity partner–A high-level agent/partner who has invested capital in the company.

Exclusivity–A contractual clause determining whether a writer or artist is bound to a single project or can work on other projects.

Exhibitor–A company such as a movie theater that screen films for audiences.

Feature–Full-length motion picture.

Film festival–An event dedicated to the screening of films, usually in celebration of films related by genre, theme, budget, geography, etc. While most festivals use a submission and acceptance process, some also incorporate a competition element, awarding prizes to various movies. A few, such as Sundance and Cannes, are important shopping grounds for agents and distributors looking for films or filmmakers.

Film market–A conference or expo at which sellers (filmmakers, producers, agents, etc.) and buyers (distributors, foreign sales agents, etc.) converge to peddle and acquire film projects. Unlike festivals, which often accept a limited number of submissions, markets are open to almost anyone who wishes to pay the entrance fee.

Financier–An organization or individual that provides funding for film projects.

First-dollar gross–A film's overall gross receipts *before* the subtraction of expenditures and other deductions.

First-dollar gross participant–A high-level actor, writer, director, or producer whose backend compensation is based on a film's first-dollar gross, not net profits.

First-look–A contractual arrangement in which a film or television studio provides a producer with financing and/or practical resources in exchange for the right of first refusal on any material the producer generates.

First party developer–A video game developer who makes both video games and video game consoles. Microsoft, for example, makes consoles like the XBox One, as well as games like *World of Tanks* and *Max: The Curse of Brotherhood*.

First position–A project that contractually must take top priority or precedence over other projects.

Floater–An agency mailroom employee who serves as a temporary assistant, filling in as needed when agents' assistants are unavailable.

Foreign sales agent–Agents who specialize in selling the distribution rights of films to foreign distributors.

Format-driven (aka "format-based")–A reality show whose stories stem from a format designed to spark conflict; this could include competition-elimination shows, like *American Idol* and *Survivor*, or game shows, like *Wheel of Fortune* and *Jeopardy*.

Franchise agreement–See **Artists Manager Basic Agreement (AMBA)**.

Freelance script– An episode of a TV show to be written by a writer who's not part of the regular staff.

Full-service–An agency that provides services to all types of artists and clients–above-the-line, below-the-line, talent, lit, music, digital media, music, etc.–and has the ability to service areas or a career that may straddle many disciplines.

General content platform–Video-sharing sites that invest in developing or producing original content. Although general content platforms usually have terrific reach, most don't have the deep pockets of more premium platforms.

General meeting–A casual meet-and-greet between an artist and an executive, producer, or agent.

Getting agented–Getting manipulated or sold by an agent.

Going wide–To submit a screenplay or project to many buyers at the same time.

Guaranteed compensation–The purchase price of a screenplay, or what the writer must be paid whether the script gets greenlighted for production or not.

Guaranteed scripts–The number of scripts per year a television writer is contractually promised to write and get paid for.

Guild-signatory–An agency, production company, studio, or project that has agreed to abide by rules negotiated by Hollywood's labor unions or Guilds.

Hip pocket–To work unofficially with an agent or client; in other words, an individual agent agrees to represent someone on the side, without a formal agreement or the consent of the agency.

If-come deal–A TV development deal in which a studio or production company agrees to pay a writer or producer for a project only if it sells to a network.

Incoming call client–In agency parlance, a client who is so in-demand she no longer needs to be submitted for jobs; buyers and employers simply seek her out.

Independent financing–Funding for a film that doesn't come from the traditional Hollywood studios.

IP (Intellectual Property)–Ideas, artworks, or other often unquantifiable works created by artists and producers.

Joke packet–A compilation of jokes, monologues, or sketches used to help writers get jobs on TV talk shows, sketch shows, prank shows, etc. Also see *sketch packet*.

Junior agent–A low-level agent whose duties involve covering territories and servicing clients of more veteran agents. Also see *servicing agent* and *covering agent*.

Last writer bonus–Money paid to the rewriter of a screenplay if he is the last writer to be hired before the project gets greenlighted.

Leave-behind–A treatment or document left behind after a pitch meeting.

Legal affairs–The agency, network, or studio department that deals with legal concepts and minutiae; occasionally, legal affairs and business affairs are the same department.

License–To sell off specific rights of a project (distribution, exhibition, merchandising, etc.) for a limited time.

License fee–Money paid to acquire specific rights to a project. A broadcast network, for example, will pay a TV studio a license fee for the rights to air the first run of a TV show; the studio, however, retains ownership and can relicense any subsequent airings or reruns.

Literary–Relating to literary disciplines such as writing or directing.

Loan-out–The act of loaning a contracted employee to another company. Often, when writers or other artists incorporate, they form a production company which then "loans them out" to other TV shows, projects, or companies.

Lock–A guarantee of employment. If a writer or employee is locked to a particular project, they can not be fired.

Major–One of the six large, deep-pocketed movie studios: Paramount, 20th Century Fox, Disney, Sony, Universal, or Warner Brothers.

Mailroom–The "post office" of an agency, the mailroom processes all incoming and outgoing packages, makes script or CD/DVD copies, etc. Although most studios and networks have their own mailrooms, "the mailroom" generally refers to agency mailrooms, where countless entertainment professionals get their start.

Man month rate–The monthly rate of hiring one person or a team of people.

Manager–1. A talent or literary representative neither licensed by the state nor bound to union franchise agreements. 2. A low-level executive at a network, studio, or production company.

Market area–A geographic region where the population all has access to the same TV stations, radio stations, newspapers, etc. Also known as *Designated Market Area (DMA) or Television Market Area*.

Media conglomerate–A collection of media or entertainment-related businesses and corporations all operating under the umbrella of one large corporation.

Mid-level–1. Large agencies that don't have the high employee counts or massive client rosters of the Big Four, but still operate in many disciplines and businesses. Mid-level agencies are generally considered: APA, Gersh, Innovative, Paradigm, and Resolution. 2. Article 14 writers above story editor, but not yet upper-level (executive story editors, co-producers, and producers).

Mid-season–Usually January through March or April, a period midway through the traditional television season when networks launch new shows they refrained from launching during the fall premiere season.

Milestone–Benchmarks determining when video game writers or developers' work will be evaluated, and when they will be paid.

Mini-major–Up-and-coming film studios that are slightly smaller than traditional majors. The mini-majors are generally considered to be: CBS Films, FilmDistrict, Lionsgate, MGM, Relativity, and The Weinstein Company.

Minimum Basic Agreement (MBA)–Document defining the relationship between screenwriters and Hollywood's buyers/employers, as negotiated by the WGA and studios, networks, or producers represented by the Alliance of Motion Picture and Television Producers. The MBA covers such topics as reuse of written materials, health and pension funds, compensation, etc. (Other unions, such as the DGA and SAG-AFTRA, also have MBAs, but they're simply called "Basic Agreements.")

Modified adjusted gross profits–Profits generated by a property, minus certain expenditures such as a reduced distribution fee, interest, and/or overhead. Sometimes known as *adjusted gross profits*.

Multichannel network (MCN)–Organizations or companies that aggregate thematically related channels and content creators. See also *vertical brand*.

Music Agents–Licensed representatives representing musicians and performers; music agents may book concerts or tours, negotiate record deals, etc.

National Conference of Personal Managers (NCOPM)–A trade organization representing talent and literary managers.

Negative cost–The cost of producing and shooting a film, or making an actual negative.

Net profits–A TV show or movie's backend profits, or box office receipts, minus certain fees and expenses.

Network–A distributor of television content. (So named because broadcast networks, the original TV distributors, were literal networks of local stations.)

Network Needs Document–A document compiled and distributed by an agency, usually internally and to clients, detailing the creative or programming needs of a particular television network.

NewFront–Digital media's version of the upfront presentations, in which companies unveil new programming slates and schedules to press and advertisers.

Non-equity partner–A high-level agent who has been promoted to partner but has no capital invested in the company.

Off-network (also, "off-net")–Usually refers to the cable networks; "off-network" syndication, for example, involves syndicating TV shows to cable networks instead of local broadcast stations.

On the bubble–Shows with an uncertain future; they could be canceled, they could be renewed.

One-liner–A one sentence encapsulation of a movie or TV show's most basic story.

Open writing assignment–A job opportunity in which a writer is hired to develop, write, or adapt a script or treatment based on someone else's IP.

Option–Contractual arrangement by which a buyer acquires rights to a property or project for a limited amount of time. When the time expires, the rights revert to the original owner or creator.

Option date–The date on which an option on a particular project or property expires and the rights revert back to the original owner or artist.

Optional steps–Additional rewrites on a project requested of a writer by a studio or buyer; these are different from guaranteed steps, rewrites to which the writer is contractually obligated.

Original material–Literary material based wholly on the writer's own IP, as opposed to an adaptation, open writing assignment, or TV sample spec.

Online entertainment–Web series, shorts, and other video content designed specifically for the Internet; also, agency departments that deal with online content.

Output deal–A contractual arrangement in which a distributor pre-pays for distribution rights to a specific number of projects produced by a production company.

Overall deal–A development deal in which a TV studio pays a showrunner, writer, producer, or production company a specific amount of money in exchange for exclusive rights to that entity's development for a specific amount of time.

P & A–Prints and Advertising, one of the most expensive costs in distributing and marketing a film.

Package–*Noun:* 1. A film or television project that has been bundled with creative attachments or auspices such as a showrunner, producers, or actors. 2. In television, the fee paid to an agency for compiling a package. 3. *Verb:* to put together, or bundle, elements into a package.

Packaging agent–A senior TV agent who focuses on packaging projects with high-level clients rather than covering territories or servicing low-level clients.

Packaging fee–The fee paid to an agency by a network, studio, or production company for delivering a TV package.

Paper team–*Verb:* to pair together two individual TV writers so as to pay them lower fees. *Noun:* a team of writers that has been artificially paired by a network, studio, or production company in order to pay them lower fees.

Partner–An upper-level agent who either helped found the company, bought into it at a later date, or has been promoted to a high-level, decision-making position.

Pass–To reject a script, project, or submission

Penalty–A fee imposed on a TV network for not greenlighting a script to pilot.

Personal appearances agents–Agents who book lectures, performances, and live appearances for comics, authors, or other public personalities.

Personality-driven (aka "personality-based")–A reality show whose appeal stems from the charisma of its host or cast rather than a format designed to incite conflict; shows such as *The Ellen DeGeneres Show* and *Here Comes Honey Boo Boo* are personality-driven shows.

Phone sheet–A constantly updated record of an agent, executive, or producer's incoming and outgoing phone calls or messages. Also known as a *call sheet.*

Pilot–A sample episode of a TV show, or online project, used to help a distributor determine whether or not to green-light the project to series.

Pilot season–The annual period (usually January–May) when broadcast TV networks green-light a select number of scripts to pilot. Studios then produce those pilots, and networks decide which pilots will become series.

Poach–To steal a client or agent from a rival agency.

Pod / P.O.D.–A Production Overall Deal, an overall deal for an organized production company (as opposed to an individual writer or showrunner).

Point agent–The head agent on a client's team of representatives.

Points–The 100 backend percentage points of a movie, TV show, or other property.

Position–The contractual level of priority where a project must rank. (First position projects take top priority, second position projects take second priority, etc.)

Post-production–The stage of production following principal photography, in which various pieces of a film or TV show are edited together and enhanced with visual effects, sound effects, etc.

Preemptive deal–An early offer to acquire a film or property before other buyers have a chance to bid.

Pre-production–The stage of production preceding principal photography; pre-production usually consists of set designing, location scouting, casting, script revisions, etc.

Premium digital content platform–Online distributors with the resources to acquire and develop expensive, high-quality content. Netflix, for example, invested approximately $100 million in its high-profile series *House of Cards.*[2]

Principal photography–The period in which a TV show or movie is actually filmed.

Producer–One who shepherds the practical, creative, or financial development and completion of a film, TV show, or other property. In television, many producers are writers as well.

Producer deal–A contractual arrangement in which a studio or financier offers a producer financial or practical support in exchange for exclusive or semi-exclusive rights to the producer's development. Also see *studio deal* or *production deal.*

Producer fee–Monies paid to a producer, usually by a studio or financier, for rendering producing duties on a particular project.

Product integration–The weaving of an advertiser's product or service into the narrative or cosmetic fabric of a show or movie so it feels organic to the piece.

Production–The act of making an actual film, TV show, or other filmic property.

Production bonus–Extra money paid to a writer if his or her script gets greenlighted to production. See also contingent compensation.

Production company–A company or organization that develops, produces, and occasionally finances film or TV projects.

Production deal–A contractual arrangement in which a studio or financier offers a producer or production company financial or practical support in exchange for rights (either exclusive or semi-exclusive) to material the producer develops. Production deals can include both overalls and first-looks. See also studio deal.

Progress-to-production–Production deals requiring the studio to meet specific benchmarks in order to retain rights to a particular project. For example, the studio may have until a particular date to begin casting or hire a director, ensuring the project continues moving forward.

Public relations–Management of a company or individual's public persona via interviews, media appearances, etc.

Publicist–Representative hired to supervise an artist or company's public relations.

Publisher–Large companies responsible for producing, distributing, and marketing video games.

Punch up–To improve individual jokes or lines of dialogue within a script.

Put deal–A studio deal requiring a production company's home studio to make a certain number of the company's projects. *Argo* producer Graham King, for example, had a four-movie put deal at Sony before moving his company, GK Films, to Warner Brothers in 2012.[3]

Put pilot–A pilot script or pitch which has received a production commitment from a network even before being written.

Quality Assurance (QA)–The process, or the department responsible for the process, of testing various stages of a video game to make sure they work appropriately.

Quote–An artist's price tag, based on his or her last job, for rendering particular services.

Reality TV–Usually, any television content that does not use a traditional script or can't be classified as news or sports. At some networks or studios, this includes docu-series (such as Style's *Tia and Tamera* and the CW's *Breaking Pointe*), competition/elimination shows (like CBS's *The American Baking Competition* or NBC's *The Winner Is . . .*), and even game shows or talk shows.

Representation–Acting, negotiating, or speaking on behalf of someone else; professional representatives often help clients find employment, negotiate contracts, develop or produce material, meet inaccessible people, access exclusive information, and protect themselves legally.

Retainer–A fee paid to keep representatives "on call," even when their services aren't being utilized.

Revenue share–A video game deal in which a development studio and publisher split the profits from a particular game.

Rip reel–A video compilation of movie and TV clips, used by directors to land open assignments.

Rolling calls–The process of "rolling" through a series of phone calls by having an assistant stay on the line and patch his/her boss into various calls remotely.

Royalty–1. In television, money paid to a show's creator each time a new episode airs. 2. In video games, the term *royalty* is used interchangeably with *revenue share* or *backend*.

SAG-AFTRA (Screen Actors Guild–American Federation of Television and Radio Artists)–Hollywood's labor union representing film and TV performers, hosts, and broadcasters. It was formed in 2012 through the merger of previously separate unions, SAG and AFTRA.

Scale–The minimum payment contractually allowed by a labor union, according to Basic Agreements negotiated with film or TV networks, studios, and production companies.

Scale deal–A deal in which film exhibitors and distributors split a movie's box office gross. The amount of the split is determined by the success of the movie.

Schedule of Minimums–A document defining minimum payments for various screenwriting duties as negotiated by the WGA and the studios, networks, and production companies represented by the Alliance of Motion Picture and Television Producers.

Script commitment–A commitment by a TV studio or network to pay a writer to develop and write a particular project, even if that project fails to get picked up and produced as a pilot or series.

Script coverage–A report detailing the plot of a script, treatment, or other literary property, and critiquing its commercial prospects. Script coverage is usually written by an assistant or professional "script reader."

Script fee–The amount of money a writer is paid to write a particular script.

Servicing agent–A low-level agent whose duties include servicing the agency's existing clients (as opposed to signing new clients), as well as "covering" various territories. (Also known as *covering agent* or *servicing agent*.)

Set–A round of notes or revisions to be delivered by a screenwriter, as requested by a film studio. Most screenwriting contracts specify a specific number of guaranteed and/or optional sets.

Senior agent–An upper-level TV agent who services high-level clients and packages projects rather than handling low-level clients or covering territories.

Series commitment–A TV pitch or pilot script which a network has guaranteed to order to an on-air series, occasionally even before the pilot has been written or produced.

Set-up bonus–Money paid to a screenwriter when an independent producer who has acquired the rights to a screenplay succeeds in setting it up with a financier or studio.

Shared production bonus–Money shared between a script's original writer and a rewriter when the script is greenlighted for production (as opposed to a sole production bonus).

Shopping agreement–A short document defining the relationship between a writer or producer and a creative attachment (actor, director, etc.).

Shopping an offer–The act of taking a studio or production company's offer to purchase a project and using it to persuade rival companies to make a better offer.

Shotgun approach–To submit a screenplay or project simultaneously to as many buyers as possible in hopes of creating competition.

Showrunner–The head writer and producer of a TV show. Often (but not always) the show's creator, the showrunner is in charge of everything from the writers room to casting to set design to post-production.

Showrunner meeting–A meeting with a showrunner for possible employment on a TV show.

Sizzle reel–A short video "trailer" used to help sell a reality show.

Sketch packet–A compilation of sketches, bits, or jokes used to help a TV writer get a job on talk shows, sketch shows, prank shows, etc. Also see *joke packet*.

Slate–A docket of projects in various stages of development or production.

Sole production bonus–A bonus a studio pays to a screenwriter when the writer's screenplay is greenlighted, and he or she is the only writer on the project (as opposed to a shared production bonus).

Spec Day–The designated day for 'going wide' with a script.

Spec grid–A document used by agents to track their screenplay submissions to various companies.

Spec pilot–A TV pilot written without first being set up at or commissioned by a network.

Spec script (or "spec")–Any "speculative" script or a script which has been written without first being commissioned by a network, studio, or production company. In TV, most "specs" refer to sample specs, scripts of airing TV shows written as calling cards for staffing.

Specialty arm–The branch of a movie studio dedicated to developing, producing, or distributing non-mainstream movies. This could include genre pictures, low-budget movies, experimental or indie films, etc.

Staff–*Noun:* The team of writers responsibile for developing and writing stories and episodes for a TV series. *Verb:* to get hired on a writing staff.

Staff writer–The entry level position on a TV writing staff.

Staffing book–A book compiled by an agency to be used as a staffing aid, containing credits or resumes of every TV literary client at the company.

Staffing meeting–1. For agents, staffing meetings take place between major agencies and the various scripted departments at TV networks and studios (current comedy, current drama, drama development, comedy development). They allow each agency to walk executives through their entire roster of TV lit clients, in preparation for TV staffing season. 2. For writers, staffing meetings with network, studio, or production company executives usually concern staffing opportunities on particular shows. These are usually the gateway to showrunner meetings, the final step before getting hired onto a writing staff.

Staffing season–In broadcast television, the annual period (April–early June) when new and returning TV shows hire their writing staffs.

Station group–A company that owns and manages multiple local TV stations.

Strike price–A penalty paid by a studio if it fails to green-light a screenwriter's script into production.

Strip–*Verb:* To air a TV show on a daily basis. *Noun:* a TV show that airs on a daily basis.

Studio–In television, a company responsible for financing, developing, producing, and owning television content. In film, studios cover the same functions–and also distribute. (In TV, distribution is usually done by the networks.)

Studio deal–A contractual arrangement in which a studio or financier offers a producer or piece of talent financial and/or practical support in exchange for rights to material the producer develops. Production deals can include both overalls, first-looks, and talent holding deal. See also *production deal* and *producer deal*.

Studio writing program–Studio-sponsored training programs designed to prepare aspiring TV or film writers for a professional career; most programs then funnel writers onto the studio's own TV shows or projects.

Summer booking season–The annual period from November through April when music agents book much of the upcoming summer's concerts and tours.

Summer concert season–The busiest, and most lucrative, period for music acts and agents. Music departments are often one of the largest revenue drivers of big agencies.

Surety bond–A bond guaranteeing that one party, the principal, must pay damages to a second party, the obligee, if the principal fails to live up to certain promises, obligations, or responsibilities. Some states, such as California, require talent agents to post a surety bond before taking on clients.

Sweeps–A quarterly process in which the Nielsen Company, America's main analyst of TV viewership, takes highly accurate audience measurements.

Syndication–The process of selling, or re-selling, a television show directly to local stations or cable outlets. Many syndicated shows are reruns of programs that have already aired on broadcast networks. Others, like *Steve Harvey*, are sold into *first-run syndication*, meaning they have no broadcast run; they're simply sold right to local stations.

Talent–Relating to performance or performers, such as actors, hosts, or musicians. Actors and on-air personalities, for example, are often referred to as "pieces of talent," while their representatives are "talent agents" or "talent managers."

Talent Agencies Act–California's 1978 law requiring agents to be licensed and bonded before engaging in business.

Talent holding deal–A contractual arrangement in which a film or TV studio offers an actor, host, or other piece of talent a financial sum in exchange for exclusive use of that performer's talents. In other words, an actor under a talent holding deal is only allowed to act in that studio's shows, pilots, or projects.

Targeted producer approach–A script submission strategy in which an agent or manager submits a screenplay to a handful of producers, one person at a time, hoping to make each producer feel wanted and special.

Term–The length of a time a contract or deal stays in effect.

Term writer–TV writers who are hired for a specific amount of time, rather than the entire run of a series or a set number of episodes.

Territory–1. A particular movie studio and all its related specialty arms and production companies. 2. A geographic region covered by a film distributor. For example, Martin Scorsese's movie *Silence* was distributed by IM Global's Apsara in Asian territories like Malaysia, Indonesia, Philippines, and India, and by Paradiso in Benelux (Belgium, the Netherlands, and Luxembourg).[4]

Theatrical distribution–Distributing a movie to traditional movie theaters and exhibitors.

Third party developer–A development studio that makes video games for other companies' consoles, or whose games can be played on any console.

Title–A writer, producer, or other employee's position, or credit, on a project (i.e., "supervising producer," "set designer," "production assistant," etc.). See also **credit(s)**.

Tracking board–An online forum, usually invite-only, where executives, producers, agents, and assistants swap information, scripts, and job opportunities.

Transactional attorney–An attorney specializing in deals, contracts, and business documents.

Treatment–A short document detailing the story, characters, and/or world of a movie or TV show.

Turnaround–The state in which a screenplay has been developed by a studio that then passes on the project, making it available to other buyers. If another studio or financier acquires the project, it must repay the first buyer's development costs.

Unsolicited submission–A script, treatment, or project sent to an agent, manager, or buyer without being requested first.

Upfront buying season–The annual window, usually in May, June and July, when cable and broadcast networks pre-sell much of their next season's advertising inventory.

Upfront presentation–A giant gala, kicking off the upfront buying season, in which a network promotes its upcoming schedule to advertisers, local stations, and media.

Upfronts–A term often used in reference to spring's broadcast and cable upfront presentations. Advertisers and ad salespeople, however, use it in reference to the upfront buying season.

Vanity deal–A studio deal offered to someone for political reasons. It could be offered to an executive as part of a severance package or an actor the studio wants to cast in movies.

Vertical brand (or "vertical")–An online organization of thematically related channels and content creators. See also *multichannel network*.

VOD–Video On Demand.

Writers Guild of America (WGA)–Hollywood's labor union representing film and TV writers. The Guild is actually composed of two separate but affiliated unions, the WGA, West and the WGA, East.

WGA minimum–The minimum amount of money a union writer may receive for rendering services, such as writing a television episode or rewriting a screenplay. See *scale*.

Writers assistant–An assistant charged with supporting the writing staff of a TV show. Writers assistants are responsible for recording and transcribing every joke, story, character idea, or bit of dialogue discussed in the writers room. They also oversee each outline, treatment, and script getting from the writing staff to the production staff; they facilitate notes sessions with networks and studios; and track and monitor script changes. While a demanding job, and quite different from other Hollywood assistant jobs, being a writers assistant is often a great springboard to getting promoted to staff writer.

Writers room–1. The room where a TV show's writing staff convenes to write episodes of the show. 2. Another name for the writing staff itself.

Writing staff–The team of writers responsible for brainstorming, outlining, writing, and rewriting every episode of a TV show.

Appendix Two: **Agency Contact Info and Resources**

AGENCIES

The agencies listed on the following pages are by no means the only agencies in Hollywood. In fact, I list these agencies not as recommendations, but because they're WGA-signatory companies I've worked with, in some capacity or other, over the years. This doesn't necessarily guarantee they're good, or a fit for every writer. I'm publishing this list simply as a resource to help as you research companies, job prospects, or the general landscape of Hollywood. (Also, most of these agencies will *not* accept unsolicited submissions, so sending your stuff will most likely result in nothing more than a wasted stamp.)[1]

Agency For The Performing Arts
405 S. Beverly Dr.
Beverly Hills, CA 90212
P: 310–888–4200
www.apa-agency.com

The Alpern Group
15645 Royal Oak Rd.
Encino, CA 91436
P: 818–528–1111
www.alperngroup.com

Beth Bohn Management, Inc.
Ste. #508
2658 Griffith Park Blvd.
Los Angeles, CA 90039
P: 323–664–2658
www.bethbohn.com

Brant Rose Agency
Ste. #1584 B
6671 Sunset Blvd.
Los Angeles, CA 90028
P: 323–460–6464

Creative Artists Agency
2000 Ave. Of The Stars
Los Angeles, CA 90067
P: 424–288–2000
www.caa.com

David Shapira & Associates
193 N Robertson Blvd.
Beverly Hills, CA 90211
P: 310–967–0480

Don Buchwald & Associates
Ste. #2200
6500 Wilshire Blvd.
Los Angeles, CA 90048
P: 323–655–7400
www.buchwald.com

Gage Group, Inc.
Ste. #505
14724 Ventura Blvd.
Sherman Oaks, CA 91403
T: 818–905–3800

Gersh Agency, Inc.
6th Floor
9465 Wilshire Blvd.
Beverly Hills, CA 90212
P: 310–274–6611
www.gershagency.com

ICM Partners
10250 Constellation Blvd.
Los Angeles, CA 90067
310–550–4000
www.icmtalent.com

IFA Talent Agency
Ste. #490
8730 Sunset Blvd.
Los Angeles, CA 90069
P: 310–659–5522

Innovative Artists
1505 Tenth St.
Santa Monica, CA 90401
P: 310–656–0400
www.innovativeartists.com

Irv Schechter Company
Ste. #300
9460 Wilshire Blvd.
Beverly Hills, CA 90212
P: 310–278–8070

JKA Talent & Literary Agency
12725 Ventura Blvd.
Studio City, CA 91604
P: 818–980–2093
www.jkatalentagency.com

Kaplan Stahler Agency
Ste. #923
8383 Wilshire Blvd.
Beverly Hills, CA 90211
P: 323–653–4483
kaplanstahler.com

Metropolitan Talent Agency
7020 La Presa Drive
Los Angeles, CA 90068
P: 323-857-4500

N.S. Bienstock, Inc.
(NOTE: Bienstock is not WGA-
signatory, as it does not have a
traditional literary department. It
does, however, represent reality
producers, and most of reality TV
is not unionized.)
Ste. #333
250 West 57th Street
New York, NY 10107
P: 212-765-3040
F: 212-757-6411
E: nsb@nsbtalent.com
www.nsbienstock.com

Original Artists
9465 Wilshire Blvd., Ste. 870
Beverly Hills, CA 90212
P: 310-275-6765
www.original-artists.com

Paradigm
North Bldg.
360 N Crescent Dr.
Beverly Hills, CA 90210
P: 310-288-8000
www.paradigmagency.com

Preferred Artists
Ste. #1421
16633 Ventura Blvd.
Encino, CA 91436
P: 818-990-0305

**Rebel Entertainment Partners,
Inc.**
Ste. #456
5700 Wilshire Blvd.
Los Angeles, CA 90036
P: 323-935-1700
www.reptalent.com

Resolution
Floor 23
1801 Century Park East
Los Angeles, CA 90067-2325
P: 424-274-4200

Rothman Brecher Kim Agency
Penthouse
9250 Wilshire Blvd.
Beverly Hills, CA 90212
P: 310-247-9898

Stars, The Agency
4th Floor
23 Grant Ave.
San Francisco, CA 94108
P: 415-421-6272
www.starsagency.com

The Susan Smith Company
1344 N Wetherly Dr.
Los Angeles, CA 90069
P: 310-276-4224

United Talent Agency, Inc.
UTA Plaza
9336 Civic Center Drive
Beverly Hills, CA 90210
P: 310-273-6700
www.unitedtalent.com

**Verve Talent & Literary Agency
LLC**
Ste. #500
6330 San Vicente Blvd.
Los Angeles, CA 90048-5455
P: 310-558-2424
www.vervetla.com

WME Entertainment
3rd Floor
9601 Wilshire Blvd.
Beverly Hills, CA 90210
P: 310-248-2000
www.wma.com

MANAGERS

Hollywood now teems with far more management companies than agencies; this list
doesn't even attempt to be comprehensive. Rather, I've tried to include most of the
industry's heaviest hitters, as well as some reputable smaller firms and boutiques. Again,
this list isn't intended to help you find representation (most of these places won't accept
unsolicited submissions), but simply to help you research different kinds of
representatives, job opportunities, and the industry itself.

3 Arts
4th Floor, Ste. 400
9460 Wilshire Blvd.
Beverly Hills, CA 90212
T: 310-888-3200

Anonymous Content
3532 Hayden Ave.
Culver City, CA 90232
T: 310-558-3667
F: 310-558-2724
www.anonymouscontent.com

Benderspink
Suite #E
5870 West Jefferson Blvd.
Los Angeles, CA 90016
T: 323-904-1800
www.benderspink.com

Big Frame
8965 Lindblade Street
Culver City, CA 90232
www.bigfra.me

**Brillstein Entertainment
Partners**
Ste. #350
9150 Wilshire Blvd.
Beverly Hills, CA. 90212
T: 310-275-6135
www.bepmedia.com

The Cartel
Ste. #B
8252 1/2 Santa Monica Blvd.
West Hollywood, CA 90046
T: 323-654-3333
cartelent.com

Circle of Confusion
8931 Ellis Avenue
Los Angeles, CA 90034
T: 310-253-7777
www.circleofconfusion.com

Generate/Alloy–LA
Ste. #200
1545 26th Street
Santa Monica, CA 90404

Generate/Alloy–NYC
151 W 26th Street
New York, New York 10001
T: 212-244-4307
www.alloydigital.com/studio

Hello and Company
1641 N. Ivar Avenue
Hollywood, CA 90028
T: 323-465-9494
helloandcompany.com

Hollywood Studios International
Ste. #600
9107 Wilshire Blvd.
Beverly Hills, CA 90210
T: 310-358-9007
www.hsifilms.com

Industry Entertainment
955 Carrillo Dr.
Los Angeles, CA 90048
T: 323-954-9000

Kaplan/Perrone Entertainment
Suite #513
280 S. Beverly Dr.
Beverly Hills, CA 90212
kaplanperrone.com

Levity Entertainment
Ste. #1111
6701 Center Drive West
Los Angeles, CA 90045
T: 310.417.4800
E: info@leg-corp.com
www.leg-corp.com

Luber Roklin Entertainment
8530 Wilshire Blvd.
Beverly Hills, CA 90211
T: 310-289-1088

Madhouse Entertainment
Ste. #110
10390 Santa Monica Blvd.
Los Angeles, California 90025
T: 310-587-2200
F: 323-782-0491
www.madhouseent.net

Management 360
9111 Wilshire Boulevard
Beverly Hills, CA 90210
T: 310-272-7000
management360.com

Mosaic Media Group
10th Floor
9200 Sunset Blvd.
Los Angeles, CA, 90069
T: 310-786-4900

New Wave Entertainment–L.A.
2660 West Olive Avenue
Burbank, CA 91505
T: 818-295-5000

New Wave Entertainment– N.Y.C.
10th Floor
35 West 36th Street
New York, NY 10018
www.nwe.com

Rain Management Group
1631 21st Street
Santa Monica, CA 90404
T: 310-954-9520
F: 310-496-2769
www.rainmanagementgroup.com

ROAR
8th Floor
9701 Wilshire Blvd.
Beverly Hills, CA 90212
T: 310-424-7800
www.roar.la

The Shuman Company
Fourth Floor
3815 Hughes Ave.
Culver City, CA 90232
T: 310-841-4344
F: 310-204-3578

Silver Lining Entertainment
7th Floor
421 South Beverly Drive
Beverly Hills, CA 90212
T: 323-370-1500
F: 323-370-1555

OTHER RESOURCES

These organizations aren't representatives themselves, but they work with agents and managers in some regard, and often offer helpful resources.

Association of Talent Agents
Ste. #930
9255 Sunset Blvd.
Los Angeles, CA 90069
T: 310-274-0628
F: 310-274-5063
www.agentassociation.com

National Association of Talent Represenatatives
150 West 25 Street #1200
New York, NY 10001
NATRmail@gmail.com
www.natragents.com

National Conference of Personal Managers
T: 1-866-91-NCOPM
www.ncopm.com/

Writers Guild of America, West–Agency Department
7000 W 3rd St.
Los Angeles, CA 90048
T: 323-782-4502
www.wga.org/agency/agency list.aspx

Websites, Blogs, Twitter Feeds, and Podcasts

TRADES AND INDUSTRY NEWS SOURCES

Looking for inside news about the world of entertainment? These sources will keep you up-to-date on what's going on in TV, film, video games, and music. Some are exclusively online, others still produce print publications, but they all offer slightly different perspectives on their corner of the industry. Read them all regularly, and you'll be the most well-informed person in Hollywood.

Actor's Access–www.actorsaccess.com (This isn't really a trade or news source, but even if you're not an actor, this subscription-only resource from Breakdown Services will keep you abreast of what's shooting.)

Advertising Age–adage.com

AdWeek–www.adweek.com

Backstage–www.backstage.com

Below the Line–www.btlnews.com

Billboard–www.billboard.com/biz

Box Office Mojo–Box office results and calculations–www.boxofficemojo.com

Broadcasting & Cable–www.broadcastingcable.com

Cynopsis–www.cynopsis.com

Deadline Hollywood Daily–www.deadline.com/hollywood

Facts on Pacts–www.variety.com/charts/facts-on-pacts/ (Variety's chart tracking studio production deals in the film world)

Gamasutra–Gamasutra.com

Games Industry International–Gamesindustry.biz

Hollywood Reporter–www.hollywoodreporter.com

Joystiq–Joystiq.com

Multichannel News–www.multichannel.com

Kotaku–Kotaku.com

Polygon–Polygon.com

TV Media Insights–www.tvmediainsights.com

Scoggins Report–specscout.com

Studio System News–www.studiosystemnews.com

TVBytheNumbers–www.tvbythenumbers.com

TVWeek–www.tvweek.com

Variety–www.variety.com

Vulture–www.vulture.com

The Wrap–www.thewrap.com

BLOGS AND WEBSITES

Wanna get helpful business or writing advice straight from Hollywood's hottest writers? Here are some of the best blogs and websites offering tips, insights, and helpful services.

The Aspiring TV & Screenwriting Blog–Honest info from articulate aspiring writers working in the industry–http://aspiringtvwriter.blogspot.com/

The Bitter Script Reader—Guidance and perspectives from a veteran script reader—http://thebitterscriptreader.blogspot.com

Black List—An annual survey of Hollywood's best unproduced screenplays, according to industry professionals. Also, a screenplay recommendation and evaluation service—blcklst.com

. . . By Ken Levine: The World As Seen By a TV Comedy Writer—A blog by TV writer/producer Ken Levine (*Cheers, Frazier, M*A*S*H*)—http://kenlevine.blogspot.com/

Complications Ensue: The Crafty TV and Screenwriting Blog—A blog by screenwriter/author Alex Epstein (*Crafty Screenwriting: Writing Movies That Get Made*)—http://complicationsensue.blogspot.com

Directors Notes: The What, Why, and How of Independent Filmmaking—www.directorsnotes.com

Earl Pomerantz: Just Thinking—http://earlpomerantz.blogspot.com/- A blog by TV writer/producer Earl Pomerantz (*The Mary Tyler Moore Show, The Cosby Show, Family Man*)

Famous Mark Verheidens of Filmland—A blog by TV writer/producer Mark Verheiden (*Hemlock Grove, Falling Skies, Battlestar Galactica*)—http://verheiden.blogspot.com/

The Futon Critic—TV news and development tracking—www.thefutoncritic.com

Gavin Polone—A blog by outspoken (and usually right) manager/producer Gavin Palone (*Curb Your Enthusiasm, Twisted, Conan O'Brien Can't Stop*)—http://nymag.com/author/gavin%20polone/

Go Into the Story—A blog by screenwriter/teacher Scott Myers (*K-9, Alaska, Trojan War*)—http://gointothestory.blcklst.com

Good in a Room—Pitching advice and interviews with writers from *Good in a Room* author Stephanie Palmer—www.goodinaroom.com

Jane Espenson on Huffington Post—A blog by TV writer/producer Jane Espenson (*Once Upon a Time, Husbands, Buffy the Vampire Slayer*)—www.huffingtonpost.com/jane-espenson

John August—A blog by screenwriter/producer John August (*Corpse Bride, Frankenweenie, Charlie and the Chocolate Factory*)—Johnaugust.com

Joke and Biagio: Producing in Hollywood—A blog by reality TV writer/producers Joke Fincioen and Biagio Messina (*Beauty and the Geek, Caged, Commercial Kings*)—www.jokeandbiagio.com

Kung Fu Monkey—A blog by film and TV writer John Rogers (*Leverage, Catwoman, Transformers*)—http://kfmonkey.blogspot.com/

On Writing Online—The online magazine of the Writers Guild of America, East—http://onwritingonline.org/

Running With My Eyes Closed: Life at the Intersection of Television and Digital—A blog by TV writer/producer Jill Golick (*Ruby Skye, P.I., Metropia*)—www.jillgolick.com

Screenwriting.io: Answering Basic Questions About Screenwriting—A Q & A Web site supervised by screenwriter John August—http://screenwriting.io

Script Magazine—The online version of formerly print magazine *Script*—www.scriptmag.com

ScriptChat—Weekly live online chats with film and TV writers—http://scriptchat.blogspot.com/

ScriptShadow—Frequented by Hollywood assistants, a review site evaluating both professional and amateur scripts—scriptshadow.net

TVLine—Michael Ausiello's Web site of TV news and opinions—http://tvline.com/

FUN AND HELPFUL TWITTER FEEDS

Many TV and film writers use Twitter to connect with fans, try new jokes, voice political opinions, or even just open a window into their creative processes. So if you're looking to get up-close-and-personal with great screenwriters, here are Twitter links and handles for some of my favorites.

Aaron Korsh—TV writer/producer (*Suits*, *Notes From the Underbelly*, *The Deep End*)—https://twitter.com/akorsh9

Agent Trainee—An anonymous agent trainee tweets about life in Hollywood—https://twitter.com/AgentTrainee

Andrew Marlowe—TV writer/producer and screenwriter (*Air Force One*, *Hollow Man*, *Nick Fury*, *Castle*)—https://twitter.com/andrewwmarlowe

Benedek Myers—Screenwriting news—https://twitter.com/screenwritingMC

Bitch Pack—Promoting female screenwriters and screenwriting—https://twitter.com/biatchpack

Bitter Script Reader—Snarky insights from a Hollywood script reader—https://twitter.com/BittrScrptReadr

Bill Lawrence—TV writer/producer (*Cougar Town*, *Scrubs*, *Spin City*)—https://twitter.com/vodka

Bill Prady—TV writer/producer (*The Big Bang Theory*)—https://twitter.com/billprady

Box Office Mojo—Daily box office results and analysis—https://twitter.com/boxofficemojo

Damon Lindelof—TV and film writer/producer (*Lost*, *Prometheus*, *Star Trek Into Darkness*)—https://twitter.com/damonlindelof

Dan Harmon—TV writer/producer (*The Sarah Silverman Project*, *Community*)—https://twitter.com/danharmon

DumbInternSaysWhat??—An anonymous writer quotes idiotic interns around his office—https://twitter.com/DumbInternSays

Elan Gale—TV producer (*The Bachelor*, *The Bachelorette*, *Bachelor Pad*)—https://twitter.com/theyearofelan

Emily Kapnek—TV writer/producer (*Parks and Recreation*, *Hung*, *Suburgatory*)—https://twitter.com/emilykapnek

Hart Hanson—TV writer/producer (*Bones*, *The Finder*)—https://twitter.com/harthanson

International Screenwriters Association—News, classes, and resources for screenwriters—https://twitter.com/networkisa

Jeff Eastin—TV writer/producer (*Graceland*, *White Collar*)—https://twitter.com/jeffeastin

Jeff Lieber—TV writer/producer (*Lost*, *Necessary Roughness*, *Pan Am*)—provides rules for showrunners— https://twitter.com/JeffLieber

Jim Michaels—TV producer (*Everybody Hates Chris*, *Supernatural*, *Odyssey 5*)—https://twitter.com/thejimmichaels

Julie Plec—TV writer/producer (*The Originals*, *Kyle XY*, *The Vampire Diaries*)—https://twitter.com/julieplec

Kurt Sutter—TV writer/producer (*Sons of Anarchy*, *The Shield*)—https://twitter.com/suturing

Lorene Scafaria—Screenwriter (*Nick and Norah's Infinite Playlist*, *Seeking a Friend For the End of the World*)—https://twitter.com/LoreneScafaria

Louis C.K.—Because he's the greatest comic on the planet—https://twitter.com/louisck

Michael Rauch—TV writer/producer (*Royal Pains*, *Love Monkey*, *Life is Wild*)—https://twitter.com/michael_rauch

Michael Schur—TV writer/producer (*Brooklyn Nine-Nine*, *The Office*, and the greatest TV comedy ever: *Parks and Recreation*) – https://twitter.com/kentremendous

Mystery Executive—a working entertainment exec doles out snarky behind-the-scenes observations about the business of Hollywood—https://twitter.com/mysteryexec

Rick Dunkle—TV writer/producer (*Criminal Minds*)—https://twitter.com/rickdunkle

Robert Dillon—Screenwriting news, interviews, advice, links—https://twitter.com/rdlln

Scott Myers—Screenwriter (*Alaska*, *K-9*, *Trojan War*), Black List blogger—https://twitter.com/gointothestory

ScriptChat–Weekly live online chats with film and TV writers–https://twitter.com/scriptchat

Shawn Ryan–TV writer/producer (*The Shield*, *Last Resort*, *The Unit*)–https://twitter.com/ShawnRyanTV

Shonda Rhimes–TV writer/producer (*Grey's Anatomy*, *Private Practice*, *Scandal)*–https://twitter.com/shondarhimes

Steve DeKnight–TV writer/producer (*Spartacus: War of the Damned*, *Dollhouse*, *Smallville*)–https://twitter.com/stevendeknight

Steve Levitan–TV writer/producer (*Modern Family*, *Back To You*, *Just Shoot Me*)–https://twitter.com/stevelevitan

Warren Leight–TV writer/producer (*Law & Order: SVU*, *In Treatment*)–https://twitter.com/warrenleighttv

PODCASTS

Podcasts are portable, free, and have an intimacy you don't get with television. Here are some of the best exploring writers, writing, and the business of Hollywood.

The Business–KCRW's weekly radio show going behind the scenes of the film and TV business–www.kcrw.com/etc/programs/tb

Directors Notes: The What, Why, and How of Independent Filmmaking–www.directorsnotes.com/

Film School with Mike Kaspar–KUCI 88.9 FM's series of interviews with indie filmmakers–www.kuci.org/filmschool

Martini Shot–KCRW's weekly look at Hollywood . . . as seen through the eyes of veteran comedy writer Rob Long–www.kcrw.com/etc/programs/ma

Meet the Filmmaker–Apple's series of interviews with writers, directors, actors, and filmmakers–http://podgallery.org/meet-the-filmmaker/

The Nerdist Writers Panel–A weekly panel of writers from film, comics, television, and music–www.nerdist.com/podcast/nerdist-writers-panel

On the Page: Screenwriting–Screenwriting teacher Pilar Alessandra interviews writers, directors, authors, performers, and storytellers–www.onthepage.tv/2012/?page_id=141

Producing Unscripted–How to produce and break into reality television, from producers Joke Fincioen and Biagio Messina (*Scream Queens*, *Dying To Do Letterman*)–http://producingunscripted.com

The Q&A with Jeff Goldsmith–Intimate interviews with top-tier writers and directors–www.theqandapodcast.com/

Scriptnotes–Screenwriters Craig Mazin and John August discuss all aspects of screenwriting: the creative, the social, the practical, the legal–http://johnaugust.com/podcast

Storywise–Former TV exec and script consultant Jen Grisanti interviews today's top screenwriters and authors–http://jengrisanticonsultancy.com/category/podcasts/

This Week In Comedy–Writer/comedian Ed Crasnick hosts a series of interviews with America's top comics and comedy creators–www.edcrasnick.com/podcast.php

TV Media Insights–TV guru Marc Berman's daily podcast of TV ratings, news, and trivia–www.tvmediainsights.com/topics/podcast/

TV Writer Podcast–Gray Jones' semi-monthly series of interviews with TV's hottest writers, producers, and showrunners–www.tvwriterpodcast.com/

WTF–Comedian Marc Maron interviews filmmakers, writers, artists, comics, and musicians–www.wtfpod.com/podcast

Appendix Four: **Periodicals, Books, and Scripts**

PERIODICALS

There aren't many quality print publications left anymore, but here's a handful of good ones published exclusively for Hollywood insiders.

Emmy–Official magazine of the Academy of Television Arts & Sciences–
www.emmys.tv/emmy-magazine
DGA Monthly–Official magazine of the Directors Guild of America–hww.dga.org/
News/DGAMonthly.aspx
Produced By–Official magazine of the Producers Guild of America–www.producers
guild.org/?page=produced_by
Written By–Official magazine of the Writers Guild of America, West–www.wga.org/
writtenby/writtenby.aspx

BOOKS

As writers, it's important to always be writing. But it's just as important (if not more) to always be *reading*. And if you're looking to read about the entertainment business– or how to break in–here are some fantastic works to give you an inside glimpse.

The Agency: William Morris and the Hidden History of Show Business, by Frank
Rose
Artistic Differences, by Charlie Hauck
The Big Picture: Money and Power in Hollywood, by Jay Epstein
Clearance & Copyright: Everything You Need to Know for Film and Television,
by Michael C. Donaldson
Contracts for the Film & Television Industry, by Mark Litwak
**Dealmaking in the Film & Television Industry: From Negotiations to Final
Contracts**, by Mark Litwak
Desperate Networks, by Bill Carter
Getting It Done: The Ultimate Production Assistant Guide, by Joshua Friedman
**Good in a Room: How To Sell Yourself (and Your Ideas) and Win Over Any
Audience**, by Stephanie Palmer
Guide To Literary Agents, edited by Chuck Sambuchino

Hollywood 101: The Film Industry, by Frederick Levy

The Hollywood Assistants Handbook: 86 Rules for Aspiring Power Players, by Peter Norwalk and Hillary Stamm

Hollywood Dealmaking: Negotiating Talent Agreements for Film, TV and New Media, by Dina Appleton and Daniel Yankelevits

Hollywood Economist: The Hidden Financial Reality Behind the Movies, by Edward Jay Epstein

Hollywood Game Plan: How to Land a Job in Film, TV, and Digital Entertainment, by Carole M. Kirschner

L.A. Fadeaway: A Novel, by Jordan Okun

The Late Shift: Letterman, Leno, and the Network Battle for the Night, by Bill Carter

The Mailroom: Hollywood History From the Bottom Up, by David Rensin

The Men Who Would Be King: An Almost Epic Tale of Moguls, Movies, and a Company Called DreamWorks, by Nicole LaPorte

The Pocket Lawyer for Filmmakers: A Legal Toolkit for Independent Producers, by Thomas A. Crowell

The Production Assistant's Pocket Handbook, Caleb Clark

Reel Power, by Mark Litwak

Small Screen, Big Picture: A Writer's Guide to the TV Business, by Chad Gervich

This Business of Television, by Howard J. Blumenthal, Oliver R. Goodenough, and Howard Blumenthal

Top of the Rock: Inside the Rise and Fall of Must See TV, by Warren Littlefield and T.R. Pearson

The War For Late Night: When Leno Went Early and Television Went Crazy, by Bill Carter

Where Did I Go Right: You're No One in Hollywood Unless Someone Wants You Dead, by Bernie Brillstein and David Rensin

When Hollywood Had a King: The Reign of Lew Wasserman, Who Leveraged Talent into Power and Influence, by Connie Bruck

The Writer Got Screwed (but didn't have to): Guide to the Legal and Business Practices of Writing for the Entertainment Industry, by Brooke A. Wharton

SCRIPTS

Books and magazines are great, but if you wanna be a screenwriter, you also have to read scripts. Lots of 'em. Screenplays, TV shows, whatever you can get your hands on. And not transcribed scripts—actual scripts, the way the writers wrote them.

If you work in the industry, or have industry friends and contacts, you can usually get scripts from agents, managers, or executives. You can also hole yourself up in the Writers Guild's library (7000 W 3rd St, Los Angeles, CA 90048), which contains scripts for nearly every movie and TV show ever produced! (Non-WGA members welcome!) If neither of these is a possibility, try local bookstores, which occasionally sell published screenplays. These days, however, the best resource is often the Internet, where several sites offer downloadable scripts—sometimes for sale, sometimes for free:

Scripts On the Net–www.roteirodecinema.com.br/scripts/titles.htm
Drew's Script-O-Rama–www.script-o-rama.com
Simply Scripts–www.simplyscripts.com
TV Writing–https://sites.google.com/site/tvwriting/
Internet Movie Script Database–www.imsdb.com

Acknowledgments

Just as agents work in teams to cover the town and represent their clients, this book could not have been written without the teamwork and support of over 200 people. I'm just the guy who gathered the information; it's everyone else who contributed their time, energy, knowledge, and experiences that brought it to life. None of this would have happened without them.

First, three people whose hard work and infinite patience were invaluable in pushing this rock up the hill. Peter Linsley and Dennis McGonagle—I can only imagine how many times you guys cursed my name, but someday, bards will sing of your patience and generosity. Elinor Actipis—this all started with you; I can't thank you enough for your belief in it, and while we didn't actually get to do much together, I hope we can find something else soon.

Also, Melissa Sandford, Matthew Scotti, Kattie Washington, and the rest of the team at Focal Press: I hope this book makes tons of money and you all get raises.

Lindsay Howard, you are the best agent in Hollywood and an even better friend. *A message to all other writers: if you're looking for an agent who will stand by you even when you want to work on a passion project that is probably totally uncommercial (and she's told you as much) ... if you're looking for an agent who believes in you even when you fall on your face and are convinced you have no right to be in this business ... if you're looking for an agent who understands your voice and knows what you should be writing even better than you do ...* I have bad news: she's already taken—look somewhere else.

To APA, which has been hugely supportive of this project in every way: you have all been warm and amazing partners over the years—and I look forward to many more.

To the best group of assistants ever assembled. First: Erin Hotchkiss and Mandee Kulaga, thanks for always being there. Second: Lindsay Baird, Conor Fallen Bailey, Daniel Vincent Discenza, Hannah Fasick, Eric Fram, Juliana Ruth Gensheimer, Tim Hamilton, Soulan Jiang, Camilla Ruth Kaplan, Matthew Keeney, Daniel Larios, Kim Li, Larissa Marie May, Rebecca Slater, Leah Steuer, Harris Tartell. To everyone reading this: if you're ever writing a book and need tireless helpers to transcribe interviews, implement revisions, copy edit or format, these guys are the best, hands down.

Again, thank you to all the news sources, outlets, and websites whose wonderful research and reporting made this job do-able. *Variety*, Deadline Hollywood, *The Hollywood Reporter*, *The Los Angeles Times*, *The New York Times*, The Wrap, Vulture, *The New York Post*, *TV Week*, Yahoo, *The Chicago Tribune*.

Of course, the real authors of this book are all the amazing people who trusted me enough to give me their knowledge and insight. I hope people reading this book know what a rare gift they've been given. Thank you, thank you, and thank you: Hal Ackerman, Chris Alexander, William M. Akers, Lex Ardeljan-Braden, Jordana Arkin, Roy Ashton, Lenny Beckerman, Joel Begleiter, Scott Bender, Brian Berk, Beth Blickers, Andy Bourne, David Boxerbaum, Michelle Brower, Alison Brown, Dave Brown, Bryan Brucks, Rachel Burger, Zach Carlisle, Francisco Castro, Diablo Cody, Jason Coffey, Tanya Cohen, Michael Conway, Christine Crowe, Gil Cunha, Duppy Demetrius, Brendan Deneen, Donny Ebenstein, Jim Ehrich, Jonathan Eirich, Joke Fincioen, BJ Ford, Kelly

Galuska, Alexis Garcia, Jeremy Garelick, Diana Glazer, Mike Goldberg, Drew Goddard, Jennifer Good, Jim Gosnell, Stacy Greenberg, Richard Gurman, Richard Hare, Marchele Hardin, Garry Hart, Chris Henze, Scott Hoffman, Charles Holland, Jeff Holland, Todd Holland, Dana Honor, Sean Hood, Karen Horne, Rich Hull, Ali Iali, Alex Johnson, Jessica Kaminsky, Marc Kamler, Aaron D. Kaplan, Kristyn Keene, Dennis Kim, Kirby Kim, Hunter Kinsella, Chris Knight, Aaron Kogan, Amanda Kogan, Adam Kolbrenner, Ra Kumar, Heather Lazare, Matt Leipzig, Josh Levenbrown, Todd Lieberman, Debbie Liebling, Warren Littlefield, Will Lowery, Jennifer Lurey, Chris Mack, Patty Mann, Doug McKay, Kate McKean, Robyn Meisinger, Shelly Mellot, Biagio Messina, Julie Miesionczek, Sam Miller, Joe Minton, Gregg Mitchell, Alan Moore, Chuck Moshontz, Rick Muirragui, Alex Murray, Julie Nathanson, Kent Nichols, Anupam Nigam, Daniel Noble, Erin Oremland, Ben Oren, Melissa Oren, Lindsay Orman, Melissa Orton, Amy Retzinger, Shilpi Roy, John Peaslee, Michael Pelmont, Sarah Penna, Michael Plonsker, Jillian Profetta, Ashley Sackerman, Gerry Sadowski, Tedi Sarafian, Matthew Saul, Ryan Saul, David Sanchez, Eric Schaar, Tony Segall, Scott Seiffert, John Seitzer, Matt Shakman, Geoff Silverman, Greg Snodgrass, Melissa Solomon, Kristina Speakman, Charlie Stickney, Don Tannenbaum, Jeff Thal, Stacy Traub, Gabe Uhr, Jennifer Vally, Lauren Vally, Shelagh Wagener, Dean Ward, Lesley Webster, Scott Weinger, Brent Weinstein, Dan Weinstein, David Weinstein, Richard Weitz, Kara Welker, Patrick Whitesell, Paula Yoo, Mason Ziluca.

An equally enormous note of gratitude to all the other agents, managers, producers, writers, and executives who allowed me to interview them off the record, giving me brutally honest information and wisdom. Every major agency in Hollywood is represented in this book, whether they're credited or not.

Paper or Plastik—half this book was written at your tables. And while I know that drives you crazy (and I owe you $6,749.63 in tips), the truth is: there are few places in L.A. buzzing with as much infectious creative energy as you guys. To anyone reading this in L.A.—if you *haven't* been to Paper or Plastik (5772 W Pico Blvd.), *go*. Part-cafe, part-dance studio, part-experimental theater space, it's the La Rotonde of Los Angeles.

Mom and Dad—thanks for reading and copy editing. Not just this, but everything for the last forty years. Also, now I can do those thank-you notes.

Kelly, Max, and Miles—I can come home now. Thanks for waiting for me. I love you.

Notes

Author's Note

1 Tatiana Siegel, "Next Gen 2012: Hollywood's Fastest-Rising Stars - Jason Cunningham," *The Hollywood Reporter*, November 7, 2012, www.hollywoodreporter.com/lists/jason-cunningham-387035

2 Variety Staff, "Fast-Rising Tenpercenters," *Variety*, October 27, 2012, http://variety.com/2012/scene/people-news/fast-rising-ten percenters-2-1118061180

3 Tatiana Siegel, "Next Gen 2012: Hollywood's Fastest-Rising Stars–Michael Kives," *The Hollywood Reporter*, November 7, 2012, www.hollywoodreporter.com/lists/michael-kives-387054

1 No Vocation Without Representation

1 Phil Rosenthal "'ER' final episode: Networks unlikely to deliver such a drama again." *Chicago Tribune*, March 29, 2009, accessed May 22, 2013, http://articles.chicagotribune.com/2009-03-29/business/0903280052_1_medical-drama-warren-littlefield-nbc-and-warner-bros

2 Lesley Goldberg, "CW, 'Veronica Mars' Creator Rob Thomas Adapting Peter Morgan's U.K. Mini 'Metropolis'." *The Hollywood Reporter*, October 16, 2012, accessed May 22, 2013, www.hollywoodreporter.com/live-feed/cw-veronica-mars-rob-thomas-metropolis-peter-morgan-379326

3 Nellie Andreeva, "Writer Thompson Evans & Producer Warren Littlefield Sell Dramas To Fox And NBC," *Deadline Hollywood*, November 7, 2012, accessed April 9, 2013, http://tv.yahoo.com/news/writer-thompson-evans-producer-warren-littlefield-sell-dramas-180827317.html

4 "Travel Agents," Questex Travel Group, accessed April 7, 2013, www.travelmediakit.com/travel-agents

5 Nellie Andreeva, "Billy Crystal-Starring Comedy From Matt Nix & Larry Charles Lands At FX With Pilot Order," *Deadline Hollywood*, May 22, 2013, accessed May 28, 2013, www.deadline.com/2013/05/billy-crystal-starring-comedy-from-matt-nix-larry-charles-lands-at-fx-with-pilot-order

6 Eriq Gardner, "James Cameron Sued For Stealing 'Avatar' (Again)," *The Hollywood Reporter*, January 25, 2012, accessed May 22, 2013, www.hollywoodreporter.com/thr-esq/james-cameron-sued-stealing-avatar-284803

7 Eriq Gardner, "CBS' 'The Talk' Sued by Author Claiming She Pitched Similar Motherhood Show," *The Hollywood Reporter*, October 22, 2012, accessed May 22, 2013, www.hollywood reporter.com/thr-esq/cbs-talk-sued-381666

2 Types of Representation

1 Lacey Rose and Lesley Goldberg, "CBS Orders Stephen King's 'Under the Dome' Straight to Series for Summer 2013," *The Hollywood Reporter*, November 29, 2012, www.hollywood reporter.com/live-feed/stephen-king-under-dome-cbs-summer-395495

2 "Talent Agency Licensing," ATA: Association of Talent Agents, last modified February 6, 2013; accessed April 17, 2013, www.agentassociation.com/frontdoor/agency_licensing_detail.cfm?id=742

3 Matthew Belloni, "What is CAA's Role in AXS?" *The Hollywood Reporter*, January 24, 2012, www.hollywoodreporter.com/news/what-is-caas-role-axs-284775

4 David K Li, "$einfeld rakes in $2.7 billion," *New York Post*, June 7, 2010, www.nypost.com/p/entertainment/tv/einfeld_rakes_in_bil_RFu9jOStArywzQ8I5rSvAJ

5 Eriq Gardner, "Personal Managers Group Sues To Stop Enforcement of the Talent Agencies Act," *The Hollywood Reporter*, November 13, 2012, accessed April 9, 2013, www.hollywood reporter.com/thr-esq/personal-managers-group-sues-stop-389786

6 "Hollywood Managers: Calif. Talent Agencies Act Unconstitutional," CBS News, November 13, 2012, accessed April 8, 2013, http://losangeles.cbslocal.com/2012/11/13/hollywood-managers-calif-talent-agencies-act-unconstitutional

7 Eriq Gardner, "California Judge Shoots Down Challenge To Talent Agencies Act," *The Hollywood Reporter*, March 6, 2013, accessed April 9, 2013, www.hollywoodreporter.com/thr-esq/california-judge-dismisses-talent-managers-426263

8 "WhoRepresents?.com Newsletter," September 19, 2011, accessed April 8, 2013, http://archive.aweber.com/whoreps/EPLaY/h/WhoRepresents_com_Newsletter.htm

9 "Management 360 Ups Darin Friedman, Eryn Brown To Partner Level," *Deadline Hollywood*, June 22, 2011, accessed April 8, 2013, www.deadline.com/2011/06/management-360-ups-darin-friedman-eryn-brown-to-partner-level

10 Josef Adalian, "'Sex' Scribe Puts Pilots on Two Nets," *Variety*, November 7, 1999, accessed April 8, 2013, http://variety.com/article/VR1117756420

11 Alison Hart, "APA Stealing Gumer Away," Glam, January 29, 2009, accessed April 8, 2013, http://ca.glam.com/apa_stealing_gumer_away

12 Claire Hoffman, "From Boutique Agency To ICM Brass," *The Los Angeles Times*, July 29, 2006, accessed April 8, 2013, http://articles.latimes.com/2006/jul/29/business/fi-silbermann29

13 Christopher Lisotta, "Gersh Agency Acquiring Boutique Talent Firm Dytman & Associates," *TV Week*, August 2006, accessed April 9, 2013, www.tvweek.com/news/2006/08/gersh_agency_acquiring_boutiqu.php

14 Robert Simonson, "Gersh Acquires Joyce Ketay Agency" Playbill, January 10, 2006, accessed April 9, 2013, www.playbill.com/news/article/97245-Gersh-Acquires-Joyce-Ketay-Agency

15 Hilary Lewis, "Whose Agent Just Got Fired?," Business Insider, October 13, 2008, accessed April 9, 2013, www.business insider.com/2008/10/whose-agent-just-got-fired-

16 Michael Cieply, "Agents Replaying a Hollywood Drama," *The New York Times*, July 27, 2008, accessed May 22, 2013, www.nytimes.com/2008/07/27/business/media/27agent.html?page wanted=all

17 Nikki Finke, "William Morris: It's a Takeover, Not a Merger," *LA Weekly*, May 27, 2009, accessed May 22, 2013, www.laweekly.com/2009-05-28/news/william-morris-it-39-s-a-takeover-not-a-merger

18 Michael Cieply, "A Merger of Agencies Shakes Up Hollywood," *The New York Times*, April, 27, 2009, accessed May 22, 2013, www.nytimes.com/2009/04/28/business/media/28talent.html?pagewanted=all

19 Danielle Bernin, "David Lonner leaving William Morris Agency," *Jewish Journal*, April 28, 2009, accessed April 9, 2013, www.jewishjournal.com/hollywoodjew/item/david_lonner_leaving_william_morris_agency_20090428

20 Kim Masters, "Why Studios Don't Pay To Make Movies Anymore (Analysis)," *The Hollywood Reporter*, December 13, 2012, accessed May 22, 2013, www.hollywoodreporter.com/news/disney-fox-paramount-sony-fox-400727

21 Ben Fritz, "Sony Pictures Cutting Back on Production," *The Los Angeles Times*, October 30, 2012, accessed May 22, 2013, http://articles.latimes.com/2012/oct/30/entertainment/la-et-ct-sony-pictures-cutbacks-20121030

22 "2012 Worldwide Grosses," Box Office Mojo, accessed April 10, 2013, accessed May 22, 2013, www.boxofficemojo.com/yearly/chart/?view2=worldwide&yr=2012

23 Nikki Finke, "Pay Cuts And Layoffs At Major Agencies," *Deadline Hollywood*, January 9, 2008, accessed April 9, 2013, www.deadline.com/2008/01/agents

24 Rebecca Winters Keegan, "Financial Crisis Puts Squeeze on Hollywood," *Time*, September 18, 2008, www.time.com/time/business/article/0,8599,1842122,00.html

25 Margaret Heidenry, "When the Spec Script was king," *Vanity Fair*, March 2013, www.vanityfair.com/hollywood/2013/03/will-spec-script-screenwriters-rise-again

26 Dorothy Pomerantz, "2011 Was a Bad Year at the Box Office. Expect 2012 To Be Worse" *Forbes*, January 3, 2012 www.forbes.com/sites/dorothypomerantz/2012/01/03/2011-was-a-bad-year-at-the-box-office-expect-2012-to-be-worse

27 Nikki Finke, "Lionsgate-Summit Laying Off 12% Of Staff: Film And Home Entertainment Hit Hardest," *Deadline Hollywood*, March 9, 2012, accessed April 9, 2013, www.deadline.com/2012/03/lionsgate-summit-laying-off-12-of-workforce

28 Paul Bond, "Jeffrey Katzenberg on DreamWorks Animation's 'Very, Very Difficult' Layoffs," *Hollywood Reporter*, February 26, 2013, accessed May 22, 2013, www.hollywoodreporter.com/news/jeffrey-katzenberg-dreamworks-animations-very-424699

29 Nikki Finke, "Metropolitan Agency Not Closing Doors," *Deadline Hollywood*, March 18, 2008, accessed April 9, 2013, www.deadline.com/2008/03/did-writers-strike-put-agency-out-of-biz

3 Anatomy of an Agency

1 Julia Boorstin, "Hollywood's Most Powerful Agency Loses Big Client," CNBC, June 11, 2007, accessed April 9, 2013, www.cnbc.com/id/19171154/Hollywood039s_Most_Powerful_Agency_Loses_Big_Client

2 "ICM's Andrew Francis Joins UTA Licensing," *Deadline Hollywood*, November 2, 2012, accessed April 9, 2013, www.deadline.com/2012/11/andrew-francis-joins-utas-licensing-team/#more-365132

3 "Hasbro and Discovery Communications Announce Joint Venture to Create Television Network Dedicated to High-Quality Children's and Family Entertainment and Educational Content," Discovery News, April 30, 2009, accessed April 9, 2013 http://corporate.discovery.com/discovery-news/hasbro-and-discovery-communications-announce-joint

4 Kim Masters, "DreamWorks Secures Additional Funding from Reliance," *The Hollywood Reporter*, April 10, 2012, www.hollywoodreporter.com/news/dreamworks-secures-additional-funding-reliance-310123

5 Mike Fleming Jr., "CAA Finalizes Joint Venture Deal With Indian Talent Agency KWAN," *Deadline Hollywood*, October 18, 2012, accessed April 9, 2013, www.deadline.com/2012/10/caa-closes-joint-venture-deal-with-indian-talent-agency-kwan

6 Leena Rao, "Kleiner Perkins Heads To LA; Partners With USC And United Talent Agency For New Startup Accelerator," *Techcrunch*, March 26, 2013, accessed April 9, 2013, http://techcrunch.com/2013/03/26/kleiner-perkins-heads-to-la-partners-with-usc-and-united-talent-agency-for-new-startup-accelerator

7 Claire Hoffman, "Gersh Talent Agency to Acquire Sports Firm," *Los Angeles Times*, March 23, 2006, http://articles.latimes.com/2006/mar/23/business/fi-gersh23

8 Jeff Sneider, "APA buys additional digs," *Variety*, July 12, 2011, www.variety.com/article/VR1118039736?refCatId=29

9 Daniel Miller, "'Big Bang' Star Jim Parsons Signs With CAA," *The Hollywood Reporter*, June 6, 2012, www.hollywoodreporter.com/risky-business/big-bang-star-jim-parsons-334268

10 Nikki Finke, "Gersh Loses Two Actors, Signs Two Actors," *Deadline Hollywood*, January 29, 2009, accessed April 9, 2013, www.deadline.com/2009/01/gersh-loses-two-actors-signs-two-actors

11 Nikki Finke, "Gersh Loses Two Actors, Signs Two Actors," *Deadline Hollywood*, January 29, 2009, accessed April 9, 2013, www.deadline.com/2009/01/gersh-loses-two-actors-signs-two-actors

12 Jeff Sneider, "APA buys additional digs," *Variety*, July 12, 2011, http://articles.latimes.com/2006/mar/23/business/fi-gersh23

13 Liz Mullen, "Gersh Agency exits football, keeps baseball and MMA," Sports Business Daily, February 18, 2008, accessed April 9, 2013, www.sportsbusinessdaily.com/Journal/Issues/2008/02/20080218/This-Weeks-News/Gersh-Agency-Exits-Football-Keeps-Baseball-And-MMA.aspx

14 Mike Fleming, "Carano wins starring role in major action film, Mixed Martial Arts, accessed April 9, 2013, www.mixedmartialarts.com/news/186140/Carano-wins-starring-role-in-major-action-film

15 Philiana Ng, "'Supernatural': Misha Collins to Return as Series Regular in Season 9," *The Hollywood Reporter*, February 25, 2013, www.hollywoodreporter.com/live-feed/supernatural-misha-collins-season-9-424318

16 "MGM taps Schut 'Macabre' scribe," IMDb, August 9, 2004, accessed April 9, 2013, www.imdb.com/name/nm1134230/news?year=2004

17 Lesley Goldberg, "Amy Poehler-Produced 'Broad City' Lands Series Order at Comedy Central," *The Hollywood Reporter*, March 13, 2012, www.hollywoodreporter.com/live-feed/amy-poehler-broad-city-comedy-central-428256

18 Nikki Finke, "Rick Yorn Exits The Firm; Julie To Follow," *Deadline Hollywood*, October 19, 2008, accessed April 9, 2013, www.deadline.com/2008/10/rick-yorn-leaves-the-firm-julie-to-follow

19 Claude Brodesser-akner, "What Talent-Agency Merger Could Mean for Brands," Adage, April 28, 2009, accessed April 9, 2013, http://adage.com/article/madisonvine-news/entertainment-marketing-endeavor-william-morris-merger/136304

20 Mark Lacter, "Agency deal is done," La Biz Observed, April 27, 2009, accessed April 9, 2013, www.laobserved.com/biz/2009/04/agency_deal_is_done.php

21 Darren Heitner, "Model Rule 1.5–Fees," Sports Agent Blog, December 11, 2007, accessed April 9, 2013, www.sportsagentblog.com/2007/12/11/model-rule-15-fees

22 Mike Sielski, "Out of Sight but Not Yet Out of Mind Will a Lost Season Damage Tebow's Marketing Appeal?," *Wall Street Journal*, December 28, 2012, http://online.wsj.com/article/SB10001424127887324669104578207730413497410.html

23 Nellie Andreeva, "The CW Greenlights Mystery Drama Pilot," *Deadline Hollywood*, January 4, 2012, accessed April 9, 2013, www.deadline.com/2012/01/the-cw-greenlights-mystery-drama-pilot/

24 Matthew Belloni, "'MILLIONAIRE' AFTERMATH: CELADOR LEAVES DOOR OPEN TO SUE AGENTS," Thr, Esq., July 8, 2010, accessed April 9, 2013, http://reporter.blogs.com/thresq/2010/07/millionaire-aftermath-agency-angst-dogs-celador.html

25 Meg James, "Warner to Let TV Stations Offer Sitcom Reruns Online," *Los Angeles Times*, May 8, 2006, http://articles.latimes.com/2006/may/08/business/fi-warner8

26 Leslie Ryan, "Packaging Prime Time," *TV Week*, July 2003, accessed April 9, 2013, www.tvweek.com/news/2003/07/packaging_prime_time.php

27 Mike Fleming Jr, "QED Pays $1 Million For David Ayer WWII Spec Script 'Fury'," *Deadline Hollywood*, February 13, 2013, accessed April 9, 2013, www.deadline.com/2013/02/qed-pays-1-million-for-david-ayer-wwii-spec-script-fury/

28 Alex Ben Block, "'Friends' Picked Up By Tribune Through at Least 2017," *The Hollywood Reporter*, June 27, 2011, www.hollywoodreporter.com/news/friends-picked-up-by-tribune-205895

29 Nellie Andreeva, "Regis Philbin Not Retiring From Showbiz; Plots Next Career Move; Fires Talent Agent," *Deadline Hollywood*, January 19, 2011, accessed April 9, 2013, www.deadline.com/tag/regis-philbin-career

30 Nikki Finke, "CAA Signs Kelly Ripa And Mark Consuelos," *Deadline Hollywood*, April 12, 2011, accessed April 9, 2013, www.deadline.com/2011/04/caa-signs-kelly-ripa-and-mark-consuelos/

31 Borys Kit, "Universal Picking Up Charlize Theron Sci-Fi Project 'Agent 13'," *The Hollywood Reporter*, April 20, 2012, www.hollywoodreporter.com/heat-vision/charlize-theron-agent-13-universal-314702

32 Tim Kenneally, "'Rock of Ages' Broadway Producer Sues Over Movie Version," *The Wrap*, July 6, 2011, accessed April 9, 2013, www.thewrap.com/movies/article/rock-ages-broadway-producer-sues-over-movie-version-28865

33 Nellie Andreeva, "WME Signs Production Co. BermanBraun," *Deadline Hollywood*, April 19, 2011, accessed April 9, 2013, www.deadline.com/2011/08/wme-signs-production-co-berman-braun/

34 Zorianna Kit, "Mandate picks up Aziz Ansari project," *The Hollywood Reporter*, May 10, 2010, www.hollywoodreporter.com/news/mandate-picks-aziz-ansari-project-23432

35 AJ Marechal, "Reality shop Collins Avenue inks with WME," *Variety*, October, 4, 2012, http://variety.com/2012/tv/news/reality-shop-collins-avenue-inks-with-wme-1118060294

36 Nellie Andreeva, "UPDATE: Kelsey Grammer Heads To UTA," *Deadline Hollywood*, March 6, 2013, accessed April 10, 2013, www.deadline.com/2013/03/kelsey-grammer-leaves-wme-likely-headed-to-uta

37 Matthew Belloni, "Barbra Streisand Signs With UTA," *The Hollywood Reporter*, March 6, 2013, www.hollywoodreporter.com/risky-business/barbra-streisand-signs-uta-426295

38 Steve McLellan, "USPS Mails McCann Erickson AOR Creative Win," *MediaPostNews*, April 2, 2013, accessed April 10, 2013, www.mediapost.com/publications/article/197159/usps-mails-mccann-erickson-aor-creative-win.html#axzz2Pa5JcBXF

39 Stuart Elliot, "Talent Agency Adds Brand Strategy Unit," *The New York Times*, June 3, 2012, www.nytimes.com/2012/06/04/business/media/united-talent-agency-adds-brand-strategy-unit.html?_r=0

40 Todd Longwell, "APA: Percentery's synergies," *Variety*, November 19, 2012, http://variety.com/2012/more/news/apa-percentery-s-synergies-1118062384

41 Bill Gorman, "'Big Bang Theory' Has The Most Remembered Product Placement Among Dramas/Sitcoms; 'American Idol' Had Most Placement Overall," TV By The Numbers, December 20, 2011, accessed April 10, 2013, http://tvbythenumbers.zap2it.com/2011/12/20/big-bang-theory-has-the-most-remembered-product-placement-among-dramassitcoms-american-idol-had-most-placement-overall/114288

42 Nicole Pedersen, "Paramount and Mattel to Reanimate MAX STEEL as a Feature Film," Collider, July 13, 2009, accessed April 10, 2013, http://collider.com/paramount-and-mattel-to-reanimate-max-steel-as-a-feature-film

43 Chris Schrader, "Legendary Pictures Developing an Edgy 'Hot Wheels' Movie," Screenrant, 2012, accessed April 10, 2013, http://screenrant.com/hot-wheels-movie-fast-and-furious-five-schrad-120021

44 "WME Signs The Knot and Miss Universe Organization," Licensing Book Online, June 16, 2011, accessed April 10, 2013, http://licensingbook.com/wme-signs-the-knot-and-miss-universe

45 Becky Ebenkamp, "Coke Reduces CAA's Role In Its Hollywood Script," *AdWeek*, January 16, 2006, accessed April 10, 2013, www.adweek.com/news/advertising/coke-reduces-caas-role-its-hollywood-script-83554

46 Mike Fleming Jr, "CAA Now Involved In Schmattah Business," *Deadline Hollywood*, February 4, 2010, accessed April 10, 2013, www.deadline.com/2010/02/caa-now-involved-in-schmattah-business

47 Jefferson Graham, "Creative Artists Agency gets into celebrity tech start-ups," USA Today, April 18, 2012, http://usatoday30.usatoday.com/tech/columnist/talkingtech/story/2012-04-18/caa-startup-incubator-moonshark/54394716/1

48 Joe Flint, "Investment bank EMC becomes a force in sports and entertainment," *Los Angeles Times*, March 20, 2012, http://articles.latimes.com/2012/mar/20/business/la-fi-ct-caa-evolution-media-20120320

49 Georg Szalai, "'South Park' Creators Trey Parker, Matt Stone to Launch Own Studio," *The Hollywood Reporter*, January 14, 2013, www.hollywoodreporter.com/news/south-park-creators-launch-studio-412113

50 Rosemary Mercedes, "Broadcasting Media Partners Completes Acquisition of Univision," Univision Communications, Inc. March 29, 2007, accessed April 17, 2013, http://corporate.univision.com/2007/press/broadcasting-media-partners-completes-acquisition-of-univision/#.UW8YKILQH-5

51 Brent Lang and Sharon Waxman, "TPG Capital Buys 35% Interest in CAA," The Wrap, October 1, 2010, accessed April 17, 2013, www.thewrap.com/movies/article/tpg-buys-35-interest-caa-21379?page=0,2

52 Daniel Miller, "Alec Gores Buys Showbiz Law Firm's Beverly Hills Building for $24 Million," *The Hollywood Reporter*, February 22, 2012, www.hollywoodreporter.com/news/alec-gores-beverly-hills-building-wilshire-293859

53 Dawn C. Chmielewski, "Creative Artists Agency sells 35% stake to TPG," *Los Angeles Times*, October 1, 2010, http://articles.latimes.com/2010/oct/01/business/la-fi-ct-caa-20101002

54 Roger Vincent, "William Morris gets a deal in a down market," *Los Angeles Times*, September 29, 2008, http://articles.latimes.com/2008/sep/29/business/fi-morris29

4 The Life of an Agent

1 Bernard Weinraub, "Phil Gersh, a Leading Agent In Hollywood, Is Dead at 92," *The New York Times*, May 12, 2004, www.nytimes.com/2004/05/12/us/phil-gersh-a-leading-agent-in-hollywood-is-dead-at-92.html

2 Gavin Polone, "Polone: So How Much Do Hollywood Players Make?," Vulture, March 14, 2012, accessed April 10, 2013, www.vulture.com/2012/03/hollywood-salaries-studio-president-agent-lawyer.html

3 Kim Masters, Daniel Miller, "ICM Executives to Buy Out Majority Owner Rizvi Traverse," *The Hollywood Reporter*, December 9, 2011, www.hollywoodreporter.com/news/icm-rizvi-traverse-jeff-berg-chris-silbermann-272038

4 Seonjin Cha, "Psy's 'Gangnam Style' Hits 1 Billion Views on YouTube," Bloomberg, December 21, 2012, www.bloomberg.com/news/2012-12-22/psy-s-gangnam-style-hits-1-billion-views-on-youtube.html

5 Jungyoun Park, "Korean talent agency cuts IPO size after key star's drug scandal," Reuters, October 19, 2011, accessed April 10, 2013, www.reuters.com/article/2011/10/19/ygentertainment-ipo-idUSL3E7LJ0IM20111019

6 "The Secrets of Hollywood Agency Mailrooms," *The Hollywood Reporter*, November 3, 2011, www.hollywoodreporter.com/news/hollywood-mailroom-secrets-CAA-ICM-UTA-WME-257222?page=2

7 Gavin Polone, "Polone: So How Much Do Hollywood Players Make?," Vulture, March 14, 2012, accessed April 10, 2013, www.vulture.com/2012/03/hollywood-salaries-studio-president-agent-lawyer.html

8 Michael Cieply, Peter Lattman, "C.A.A. Sells 35% Stake to TPG," *New York Times Dealbook*, October 1, 2010, accessed April 10, 2013, http://dealbook.nytimes.com/2010/10/01/tpg-to-buy-a-35-stake-in-c-a-a

9 Brooks Barnes, "A-Listers, Meet Your Online Megaphone," *The New York Times*, November 10, 2012, www.nytimes.com/2012/11/11/business/oliver-luckett-of-theaudience-building-online-fan-bases.html?pagewanted=all

10 Peter Lauria, "Talent agency CAA mulls Silicon Valley office," Reuters, August 24, 2011, www.reuters.com/article/2011/08/24/us-creativeartists-idUSTRE77N6CR20110824

11 Gavin Polone, "Polone: So How Much Do Hollywood Players Make?," Vulture, March 14, 2012, accessed April 10, 2013, www.vulture.com/2012/03/hollywood-salaries-studio-president-agent-lawyer.html

12 "The Secrets of Hollywood Agency Mailrooms," *The Hollywood Reporter*, November 3, 2011, www.hollywoodreporter.com/news/hollywood-mailroom-secrets-CAA-ICM-UTA-WME-257222?page=4

13 Nikki Finke, "Paradigm Hiring Abrams Youth Department," *Deadline Hollywood*, July 26, 2011, accessed April 10, 2013, www.deadline.com/2011/07/paradigm-hiring-abrams-youth-department

14 Nikki Finke and Nellie Andreeva, "AGENCY MUSICAL CHAIRS: Buchwald's Youth Department Moves To Abrams Artists," *Deadline Hollywood*, July 29, 2011, accessed April 10, 2013, www.deadline.com/2011/07/agency-musical-chairs-buchwalds-youth-department-moves-to-abrams-artists

15 Mike Fleming Jr, "WME Signs Anna Faris, Jackie Earle Haley," *Deadline Hollywood*, June 13, 2012, accessed April 10, 2013, www.deadline.com/2012/06/wme-signs-anna-faris-jackie-earle-haley/#more-285798

16 Todd Longwell, "APA: Percentery's synergies," *Variety*, November 19, 2012, http://variety.com/2012/more/news/apa-percentery-s-synergies-1118062384

17 Dominic Patten, "CAA Taken To Court By Dan Aloni For $5M; Agent Says Owed Bonuses & Vacation Pay," *Deadline Hollywood*, November 5, 2012, accessed April 10, 2013, www.deadline.com/2012/11/caa-taken-to-court-by-dan-aloni-for-5m-agent-says-owed-bonus-vacation-pay

18 Nikki Finke, "CAA Retreating … with Tom Cruise," *Deadline Hollywood*, April 14, 2010, accessed April 10, 2013, www.deadline.com/2010/04/caa-retreating-with-tom-cruise

19 Kim Masters, "CAA Retreat: Insiders Hear Presentations by Lorne Michaels, Steve Burke, Selena Gomez," *The Hollywood Reporter*, April 23, 2012, www.hollywoodreporter.com/risky-business/caa-selena-gomez-steve-burke-lorne-michaels-315099

5 A Quick Overview of the TV Business

1 Writers Guild of America, West, Inc., "Annual Financial Report," June 29, 2012, accessed on April 8, 2013, www.wga.org/uploadedFiles/who_we_are/annual_reports/annualreport12.pdf

2 "Disney's Earnings Dip But Still Top Analyst Forecasts," MoneyNews, February 5, 2013, accessed on April 8, 2013, www.moneynews.com/Companies/Disney-earns-analyst-forecast/2013/02/05/id/489046

3 "Home," CBS Corporation, last modified April 11, 2013, www.cbscorporation.com/index.php

4 "Music site Last.fm bought by CBS," BBC News, May 30, 2007, http://news.bbc.co.uk/2/hi/technology/6701863.stm

5 Annlee Ellington, "CBS wins sweeps, NBC beaten by Univision," *Phoenix Business Journal*, February 28, 2013, www.bizjournals.com/phoenix/morning_call/2013/03/cbs-wins-sweeps-nbc-beaten-by-univision.html

6 "'Por Ella Soy Eva' Finale Reaches 8.8 Million Viewers and Makes Univision No. 1 Network among Adults 18–49 and Adults 18–34," Univision Communications, Inc., last updated March 11, 2013, http://corporate.univision.com/2013/press/por-ella-soy-eva-finale-reaches-8-8-million-viewers-and-makes-univision-no-1-network-among-adults-18-49-and-adults-18-34/?utm_source=rss&utm_medium=rss&utm_campaign=por-ella-soy-eva-finale-reaches-8-8-million-viewers-and-makes-univision-no-1-network-among-adults-18-49-and-adults-18-34#axzz2NMDTlnoG

7 "'Walking Dead' Propels AMC Networks," *Wall Street Journal*, February 26, 2013, http://online.wsj.com/article/SB10001424127887323884304578328013837954522.html

8 Bill Gorman, "2010–11 Season Broadcast Primetime Show Viewership Averages," TV by the Numbers, June 1, 2011, http://tvbythenumbers.zap2it.com/2011/06/01/2010-11-season-broadcast-primetime-show-viewership-averages/94407

9 Brian Steinberg, "Cartier's Three-Minute Gem Extends Demand for Longer Spots," Ad Age, March 7, 2012, http://adage.com/article/tuning-in/cartier-s-3-minute-ad-gem-extends-demand-longer-spots/233154

10 Brian Steinberg, "'American Idol,' NFL Duke it out for Priciest TV Spot," Ad Age, October 24, 2011, http://adage.com/article/media/chart-american-idol-nfl-duke-priciest-tv-spot/230547

11 "The Amazing Race: Spring 2011–12 Ratings," TV Series Finale, May 8, 2012, http://tvseriesfinale.com/tv-show/the-amazing-race-spring-2011-2012-ratings-22173

12 "Family Guy: Ratings for the 2011–12 TV Season," TV Series Finale, May 23, 2012, http://tvseriesfinale.com/tv-show/family-guy-ratings-2011-2012

13 Brian Steinberg, "'American Idol Duke it out for Priciest TV Spot," Ad Age, http://adage.com/article/media/chart-american-idol-nfl-duke-priciest-tv-spot/230547

14 Anthony Crupi, "In Their Prime: Broadcast Spot Costs Soar," June 22, 2011, www.adweek.com/news/television/their-prime-broadcast-spot-costs-soar-132805

15 Brian Steinberg, "Cartier's Three-Minute Gem Extends Demand for Longer Spots," Ad age, March 7, 2012, http://adage.com/article/tuning-in/cartier-s-3-minute-ad-gem-extends-demand-longer-spots/233154

16 Peter Lauria, "Exclusive: Low ratings could end cable deal for Gore's Current TV," *Chicago Tribune*, April 4, 2012, http://articles.chicagotribune.com/2012-04-04/business/sns-rt-us-currenttv-timewarnercablebre83404p-20120404_1_keith-olbermann-time-warner-cable-low-ratings/2

17 Liana B. Baker, "Discovery Channel upstaged by murderers, stalkers," Reuters, April 12, 2012, http://blogs.reuters.com/mediafile/2012/04/12/discovery-channel-upstaged-by-murderers-stalkers

18 Christopher Palmeri, "Disney Junior's McStuffins Battles Dora for Pre-Schoolers," Bloomberg, March 23, 2012, http://mobile.bloomberg.com/news/2012-03-22/disney-junior-s-mcstuffins-battles-dora-for-pre-schoolers?BB_NAVI_DISABLE=BIZ

19 Derek Thompson, "3 Very Simple Reasons Why You Can't Get HBO Go, Exclusively," *The Atlantic*, June 6, 2012, www.theatlantic.com/business/archive/2012/06/3-very-simple-reasons-why-you-cant-get-hbo-go-exclusively/258209

20 Anthony Crupi, "Cable Unit Props Up Ailing NBC," Adweek, November 2, 2011, www.adweek.com/news/television/cable-unit-props-ailing-nbc-136266

21 Anthony Crupi, "Cable Unit Props Up Ailing NBC," Adweek, November 2, 2011, www.adweek.com/news/television/cable-unit-props-ailing-nbc-136266

22 James Warren, "'Cosby Show' Syndication: 'Arrogant' Hardball," *Chicago Tribune*, May 4, 1988, http://articles.chicagotribune.com/1988-05-04/features/8803140143_1_stations-per-episode-bill-cosby

23 "Sheen's lucky seven," *New York Post*, November 17, 2010, www.nypost.com/p/entertainment/tv/sheen_lucky_seven_Sp9AofvilFML5PtSZNzdLK

24 Greg Braxton, "'Seinfeld' Syndication Fees Likely to Surge," *Los Angeles Times*, January 28, 1998, http://articles.latimes.com/1998/jan/28/entertainment/ca-12753

25 David K. Li, "$einfeld rakes in $2.7 bil," June 7, 2010, www.nypost.com/p/entertainment/tv/einfeld_rakes_in_bil_RFu9jOStArywzQ8l5rSvAJ

26 Nikki Finke and Nellie Andreeva, "BIG SYNDIE DEALS: 'Glee to Oxygen; 'Modern Family' To USA," *Deadline Hollywood*, June 29, 2010, www.deadline.com/2010/06/big-syndication-deals-for-20th-tv-oxygen-gets-glee-usa-buys-modern-family

27 Nellie Andreeva, "'The Good Wife' Off-Network Rights Sell to Amazon, Hulu, Hallmark Channel, Broadcast Syndication for

Nearly $2M An Episode," *Deadline Hollywood*, March 13, 2013, www.deadline.com/2013/03/the-good-wife-off-network-rights-sell-to-amazon-hulu-hallmark-channel-broadcast-syndication

28 James Warren, "'Cosby Show' Syndication: 'Arrogant' Hardball," *Chicago Tribune*, May 4, 1988, http://articles.chicagotribune.com/1988-05-04/features/8803140143_1_stations-per-episode-bill-cosby

29 L.J. Davis, "Hollywood's Most Secret Agent," *New York Times*, July 9, 1989, www.nytimes.com/1989/07/09/magazine/hollywoods-most-secret-agent.html?pagewanted=all&src=pm

30 Marisa Guthrie, "'Two and a Half Men' Shutdown Could Cost CBS, Warner Bros. Millions," Backstage, January 31, 2011, www.backstage.com/news/two-and-a-half-men-shutdown-could-cost-cbs-warner-bros-millions

31 Nellie Andreeva, "Greg Berlanti Back at Warner Bros. Television with Mega Deal," *Deadline Hollywood*, March 1, 2011, www.deadline.com/2011/03/greg-berlanti-back-at-warner-bros-television-with-mega-deal

32 Nellie Andreeva, "'Bones' Producer Carla Kettner Inks Overall Deal with Sony, Joins 'Mob Doctor' as EP," *Deadline Hollywood*, June 13, 2012, www.deadline.com/2012/06/bones-producer-carla-kettner-inks-overall-deal-with-sony-joins-mob-doctor-as-ep

33 Nellie Andreeva, "'Up All Night' Creator Emily Spivey Inks Overall Deal With 20th Century Fox TV," *Deadline Hollywood*, February 21, 2013, www.deadline.com/2013/02/up-all-night-creatoremily-spivey-inks-overall-deal-with-20th-century-fox-tv

34 Ben Grossman, "Perpetual Development," Broadcasting and Cable, July 9, 2006, www.broadcastingcable.com/article/101246-Perpetual_Development.php

35 Michael O'Connell, "NBC Orders Medical Drama Pilot from '90210' Writers," *The Hollywood Reporter*, October 8, 2012, www.hollywoodreporter.com/live-feed/nbc-orders-medical-drama-pilot-gabe-sachs-jeff-judah-377078

36 Daniel Kreps, "Trent Reznor Developing 'Year Zero' Mini-Series For HBO," Rolling Stone, September 28, 2010, www.rollingstone.com/music/news/trent-reznor-developing-year-zero-mini-series-for-hbo-20100928

37 Ronald Grover, "NBC All Action, No Talk As Network Tries To Rebound," Bloomberg, September 9, 2010, accessed April 8, 2013, www.bloomberg.com/news/2010-09-10/nbc-all-action-no-talk-as-last-place-network-tries-to-rebound.html

38 "Upfronts 2012: CBS makes bold moves, TBS touts 'Cougar Town,'" *Los Angeles Times*, May 16, 2012, http://latimesblogs.latimes.com/showtracker/2012/05/upfront-2012-cbs-tbs-cougar-town.html

39 "Garden Staked: CBS Cancels Made in Jersey," TV Line, October 10, 2012, http://tvline.com/2012/10/10/made-in-jersey-cancelled

40 Michael O'Connell, "NBC Cancels 'Do No Harm,'" *The Hollywood Reporter*, February 8, 2013, www.hollywoodreporter.com/live-feed/nbc-cancels-do-no-harm-417513

6 Staffing Season–How Agents Help Clients Get Hired

1 Nellie Andreeva, "How Agencies Did At This Year's Upfronts: New Scripted Series Package Scorecard," *Deadline Hollywood*, May 20, 2012, www.deadline.com/2012/05/how-agencies-did-at-this-years-upfronts-new-scripted-series-package-scorecard

2 Lesley Goldberg, "'Game of Thrones': By The Numbers," *The Hollywood Reporter*, April 14, 2011, www.hollywoodreporter.com/news/game-thrones-by-numbers-178659

3 www.wga.org/uploadedFiles/writers_resources/ep_append.pdf

7 Development Season–Selling Your Own TV Show

1 Nellie Andreeva, "Comedy Central Gives Cast-Contingent Pilot Order to 'Bad Advice From My Brother," *Deadline Hollywood*, February 28, 2013, www.deadline.com/2013/02/comedy-central-gives-cast-contingent-pilot-order-to-%E2%80%98bad-advice-from-my-brother%E2%80%99

2 Michael O'Connell, "Ricky Martin Inks TV Holding Deal With NBCUniversal," *The Hollywood Reporter*, July 7, 2012, www.hollywoodreporter.com/live-feed/ricky-martin-tv-show-glee-evita-nbcuniversal-355835

3 Lesley Goldberg, "CBS Adapting Cameron Diaz Starrer 'Bad Teacher' With Hilary Winston," *The Hollywood Reporter*, October 5, 2012, www.hollywoodreporter.com/live-feed/bad-teacher-hilary-winston-cbs-376821

4 Nellie Andreeva, "'Battlestar Galactica's Ron Moore to Adapt 'A Knight's Tale' As Drama Project for ABC," *Deadline Hollywood*, September, 21, 2012, www.deadline.com/2012/09/a-knights-tale-battlestar-galacticas-ron-moore-adapting-movie-as-series-for-abc

5 Nellie Andreeva, "Liz Brixius Signs Deal with Universal TV," *Deadline Hollywood*, April 24, 2012, www.deadline.com/2012/04/liz-brixius-signs-deal-with-universal-tv

6 Nellie Andreeva, "Comedy Writer-Producer Tucker Cawley Signs Deal With Universal Television," *Deadline Hollywood*, www.deadline.com/2012/05/comedy-writer-producer-tucker-cawley-signs-deal-with-universal-television

7 Nellie Andreeva, "Gina Fattore Sells Drama To NBC With Dawn Parouse, Inks Overall Deal With Universal TV," *Deadline Hollywood*, September 10, 2012, www.deadline.com/2012/09/gina-fattore-sells-drama-to-nbc-with-dawn-parouse-inks-overall-deal-with-universal-tv

8 Nellie Andreeva, "Jason Katims Inks New Deal With Universal TV, Hires Michelle Lee As Development Exec," *Deadline Hollywood*, June 29, 2012, www.deadline.com/2012/06/jason-katims-makes-new-deal-with-universal-tv

9 Nellie Andreeva, "DJ Nash Inks Overall Deal With Universal TV, Joins 'Up All Night' As Exec Producer," Yahoo! TV, May 30, 2012, http://tv.yahoo.com/news/dj-nash-inks-overall-deal-universal-tv-joins-211223757.html

10 Nellie Andreeva, "'Parenthood' Co-Executive Producer Sarah Watson Inks Overall Deal With Universal TV," *Deadline Hollywood*, March 26, 2012, www.deadline.com/2012/03/parenthood-co-executive-producer-sarah-watson-inks-overall-deal-with-universal-tv

11 Nellie Andreeva, "Writer Harris Wittels Inks Overall Deal With Universal TV, Will Continue On 'Parks & Rec,'" *Deadline Hollywood*, June 12, 2012, www.deadline.com/2012/06/writer-harris-wittels-inks-overall-deal-with-universal-tv-will-continue-on-parks-rec

12 Nellie Andreeva, "PILOT SEASON: Spec Market Heats Up With Josh Schwartz's 'Misfits' & Christ Carter's 'Unique,'" *Deadline Hollywood*, January 8, 2012, www.deadline.com/2012/01/pilot-season-spec-market-heats-up-with-josh-schwartzs-misfits-and-chris-carters-unique

13 Nellie Andreeva, "Glen Mazzara Signs Overall Deal With Fox TV Studios," Yahoo! TV, March 14, 2013, http://tv.yahoo.com/news/glen-mazzara-signs-overall-deal-fox-tv-studios-173022083.html

14 Nellie Andreeva, "'Mad Men' Writer-Producers Andre & Maria Jacquemetton Ink Deal With Warner Bros TV," *Deadline Hollywood*, March 1, 2013, www.deadline.com/2013/03/mad-men-writerproducers-andre-maria-jacquemetton-ink-deal-with-warner-bros-tv/#more-444014

15 Lesley Goldberg, "Baz Luhrmann Inks Two-Year Development Pact With Sony Pictures Television," *The Hollywood Reporter*, September 24, 2012, www.hollywoodreporter.com/live-feed/baz-luhrmann-sony-pictures-television-deal-373684

16 Josef Adalian, "Mouse Nibbles WMA," *Variety*, December 19, 2001, http://variety.com/2001/more/news/mouse-nibbles-wma-1117857591

17 Matthew Belloni, "'Millionaire' Aftermath: Celador Leave Door Open To Sue Agents," *The Hollywood Reporter*, July 8, 2010, http://reporter.blogs.com/thresq/2010/07/millionaire-aftermath-agency-angst-dogs-celador.html

18 Matthew Belloni, "Lawsuit Claims CAA Cheated TV Creators Out of Millions in Profits," *The Hollywood Reporter*, July 11, 2011, www.hollywoodreporter.com/thr-esq/lawsuit-claims-caa-cheated-tv-209735

19 Ted Johnson, "Creatives sue CAA over packaging," *Variety*, July 12, 2011, http://variety.com/2011/tv/news/creatives-sue-caa-over-packaging-1118039738

20 Matt Belloni, "'Millionaire' aftermath: Celador leaves door open to sue agents," *The Hollywood Reporter*, December 21, 2010, www.hollywoodreporter.com/blogs/thr-esq/millionaire-aftermath-celador-leaves-door-64056

21 Edvard Pettersson and Tori Richards, "Disney Loses 'Who Wants To Be A Millionaire' Trial," Bloomberg, July 7, 2010, accessed April 17, 2013, www.bloomberg.com/news/2010-07-07/disney-loses-who-wants-to-be-a-millionaire-suit-must-pay-269-4-million.html

22 Ben Fritz, "Disney loses appeal in $269-million 'Millionaire' case," *The Los Angeles Times*, December 4, 2012, http://articles.latimes.com/2012/dec/04/entertainment/la-et-ct-disney-millionnaire-appeal-20121203

23 Leslie Ryan, "In Depth: Packaging Prime Time," *TV Week*, accessed April 16, 2013, www.tvweek.com/news/2003/07/packaging_prime_time.php

24 "The Bachelor (U.S. TV series)," Wikipedia, last modified April 3, 2013, http://en.wikipedia.org/wiki/The_Bachelor_%28U.S._TV_series%29#International_versions.

25 "Dutch Watch," Nederlands Film Festival, last accessed April 16, 2013, www.filmfestival.nl/profs_en/news/news/dutch-watch

26 Bill Carter, Desperate Networks (New York: Doubleday, 2006), 204-207.

27 David Bauder, "ABC's 'Housewives' starts strong," The Boston Globe, October 6, 2004, www.boston.com/news/globe/living/articles/2004/10/06/abcs_housewives_starts_strong

28 Robert Bianco, "A good season, with reason," *USA Today*, April 27, 2005, http://usatoday30.usatoday.com/life/television/news/2005-04-26-tv-lookback_x.htm

29 Dorothy Pomerantz, "TV's Biggest Moneymakers," *Forbes*, April 10, 2012, www.forbes.com/sites/dorothypomerantz/2012/04/10/tvs-biggest-moneymakers-2/?partner=comcast.

30 Nellie Andreeva, "'Desperate Housewives' Stars Finalizing New Deals, Paving Way to Season 8 Pickup," *Deadline Hollywood*, April 11, 2011, www.deadline.com/2011/04/desperate-housewives-stars-finalizing-new-deals-paving-way-to-season-8-pickup

31 Lesley Goldberg and Lacey Rose, "ABC Orders Big Thunder Mountain Drama, Gothic Monster Soap, Ryan Reynolds Entry to Pilot," *The Hollywood Reporter*, January 29, 2013, www.hollywoodreporter.com/live-feed/abc-orders-big-thunder-mountain-416634

32 Nellie Andreeva, "CBS' 'Rules Of Engagement' Renewed For Seventh Season With 13-Episode Order," *Deadline Hollywood*, May 21, 2012, www.deadline.com/2012/05/cbs-rules-of-engagement-renewed-for-seventh-season-with-13-episode-order

8 A Quick Overview of the Feature Business

1 Michael Cieply, "Many More Indie Films Are Released, but Not Very Widely, Study Finds," *New York Times*, April 9, 2012, http://mediadecoder.blogs.nytimes.com/2012/04/09/many-more-indie-films-are-released-but-not-very-widely-study-finds

2 Ray Subers, "Paramount Wins 2011 Studio Battle," *Box Office Mojo*, January 11, 2012, accessed April 28, 2013, http://boxofficemojo.com/news/?id=3345

3 "Sony Classics Buys Rights To 'At Any Price,'" *Deadline Hollywood*, Last modified August 3, 2012, www.deadline.com/2012/08/sony-pictures-classics-acquires-rights-to-at-any-price

4 "Sony Pictures Classics Acquires Zac Efron, Dennis Quaid Film 'At Any Price,'" The Wrap, August 3, 2012, accessed April 28, 2013, www.thewrap.com/deal-central/column-post/sony-pictures-classics-acquires-zac-efron-dennis-quaid-film-any-price-50751

5 "Post-'Office,' Steve Carell Ponders Doomsday With Keira Knightley," *Deadline Hollywood*, March 31, 2011, www.deadline.com/2011/03/post-office-steve-carell-ponders-doomsday-with-kiera-knightley

6 Peter Bart, "Fox Searchlight defies tentpole tyranny," *Variety*, April 30, 2012, www.variety.com/article/VR1118053211

7 Pamela McClintock, "Paramount's Insurge refines its gameplan," *Variety*, October 23, 2010, www.variety.com/article/VR1118026147?refCatId=16

8 "Studio Market Share," Box Office Mojo, accessed April 21, 2013, http://boxofficemojo.com/studio/?view=company&view2=yearly&yr=2012&p=.htm

9 Mike Fleming Jr., "Universal Acquires 'Family Therapy' Pitch For Jason Bateman's Aggregate Films," *Deadline Hollywood*, March 19, 2013, www.deadline.com/2013/03/universal-acquires-family-therapy-pitch-for-jason-batemans-aggregate-films

10 Dominic Patten, "Gold Circle Buys 'Eden' Spec Script by Olatunde Osunsanmi," *Deadline Hollywood*,March 26, 2013, accessed April 21, 2013, www.deadline.com/2013/03/gold-circle-buys-eden-spec-script-by-olatunde-osunsanmi

11 Glen Chapman, "Leonardo DiCaprio Attached to Dennis Lehane Adaptation Live By Night," Den of Geek, Last Modified April 16, 2012, accessed April 28, 2013, www.denofgeek.us/movies/19049/leonardo-dicaprio-attached-to-dennis-lehane-adaptation-live-by-night

12 Mike Fleming Jr., "Nick Hornby To Adapt Cheryl Strayed Memoir 'Wild' For Reese Witherspoon And River Road," *Deadline Hollywood*, November 29, 2012, www.deadline.com/2012/11/nick-hornby-to-adapt-cheryl-strayed-memoir-wild-for-reese-witherspoon-and-river-road

13 Mike Fleming Jr., "Lionsgate Lands Movie Rights to Zombie Vidgame 'Dead Island,'" *Deadline Hollywood*, September 27, 2011, www.deadline.com/2011/09/dead-island-movie-rights-land-at-lionsgate

14 Daniel Miller, "Sacha Baron Cohen Signs First-Look Deal With Paramount," *The Hollywood Reporter*, February 29, 2012, www.hollywoodreporter.com/risky-business/sacha-baron-cohen-dictator-paramount-296024

15 McNary, Dave. "Dream Works Signs Carla Hacken to First Look Deal." *Variety*, April 15, 2013. http://variety.com/2013/film/news/dreamworks-signs-carl-hacken-to-first-look-deal-1200371050

16 Claudia Eller, "Disney to Sign Deal with Rudin," *Los Angeles Times*, April 19, 2005, http://articles.latimes.com/2005/apr/19/business/fi-rudin19

17 Ben Fritz, "Producer Scott Rudin signs first-look deal with Sony Pictures," *Los Angeles Times*, June 30, 2011, http://latimesblogs.latimes.com/entertainmentnewsbuzz/2011/06/producer-scott-rudin-signs-first-look-deal-with-sony-pictures.html

18 Mike Fleming Jr., "Relativity Makes Two-Year Production Deal With Channing Tatum," *Deadline Hollywood*, December 3, 2010, www.deadline.com/2010/12/relativity-makes-two-year-production-deal-with-channing-tatum

19 Pamela McClintock, "Danny Boyle signs 3-year deal," *Variety*, June 11, 2009, www.variety.com/article/VR1118004862?refCatId=13

20 Greg Kilday, "Universal Extends Its Pact With Working Title Films Through 2015," *The Hollywood Reporter*, April 27, 2012, www.hollywoodreporter.com/news/universal-extends-pact-working-title-films-les-miserables-317579

21 Greg Kilday, "Universal and Imagine Extend Production Pact Through 2016," *The Hollywood Reporter*, January 10, 2012, www.hollywoodreporter.com/news/universal-imagine-deal-280283

22 Mike Fleming Jr., "Warner Bros Re-Ups Todd Phillips' First Look Deal As He Sets Four Films to Helm," *Deadline Hollywood*, February 6, 2012, www.deadline.com/2012/02/warner-bros-re-ups-todd-phillips-first-look-deal-and-sets-his-next-four-films

23 "Warner Bros. Ending Deal with Producer Joel Silver." *The Hollywood Reporter*, April 27, 2012, http://tv.yahoo.com/news/warner-bros-ending-deal-producer-joel-silver-195203612.html

24 Tatiana Siegel, "'Fifty Shades of Grey' Movie Producers Considering Surprising Screenwriters (Exclusive)," *The Hollywood Reporter*, August 7, 2012, www.hollywoodreporter.com/news/fifty-shades-grey-producers-screenwriters-359080

25 Greg Kilday, "Universal and Imagine Extend Production Pact Through 2016," *The Hollywood Reporter*, January 10, 2012, www.hollywoodreporter.com/news/universal-imagine-deal-280283

26 Jeff Sneider and Justin Kroll, "Producers jockey for 'Fifty Shades of Grey,'" *Variety*, June 14, 2012, www.variety.com/article/VR1118055531

27 Tatiana Siegel, "'Fifty Shades of Grey' Movie Producers Considering Surprising Screenwriters (Exclusive)," *The Hollywood Reporter*, August 7, 2012, www.hollywoodreporter.com/news/fifty-shades-grey-producers-screenwriters-359080

28 Marc Graser, "Heavy hitters pick up slack as studios evolve," *Variety*, February 24, 2012, http://variety.com/2012/film/news/heavy-hitters-pick-up-slack-as-studios-evolve-1118050682

29 Rachel Abrams, "TWC closes $75 mil UBS pact," *Variety*, June 20, 2012, www.variety.com/article/VR1118055808

30 Christopher Helman, "Meet Tim Headington, Billionaire Oil Tycoon Behind Oscar Winners 'Hugo' and 'Rango,'" *Forbes*, February 27, 2012, www.forbes.com/sites/christopherhelman/2012/02/27/meet-tim-headington-billionaire-oil-tycoon-behind-oscar-winners-hugo-and-rango

31 Michael Fleming, "Sanders set for film, theater," *Variety*, March 20, 2007, www.variety.com/article/VR1117961505?refCatId=1238

32 Deborah Sontag, "FILM; A Couple Go For a Morning Dive. . .," *The New York Times*, August 1, 2004, www.nytimes.com/2004/08/01/movies/film-a-couple-go-for-a-morning-dive.html?pagewanted=all&src=pm

33 Rachel Abrams, "Slate debate: Investors now get to pic & choose," *Variety*, February 24, 2012, http://variety.com/2012/film/news/slate-debate-investors-now-get-to-pic-choose-1118050685

34 Marc Graser and Rachel Abrams, "Thinking outside the studio lot," *Variety*, February 24, 2012, http://variety.com/2012/film/news/thinking-outside-the-studio-lot-1118050683

35 Patti Payne, "Behind the Scenes with Patti Payne," *Puget Sound Business Journal*, November 4, 2011, www.bizjournals.com/seattle/print-edition/2011/11/04/margin-call-and-its-seattle-back.html?page=all

36 "Michael Benaroya: Film Financier to Watch," The Wrap, April 2, 2012, accessed April 28, 2013, www.thewrap.com/movies/article/michael-benaroya-financier-36719

37 "Venture Capital Firm Sues Rizvi Traverse, Claims It Was Taken On Indie Pic 'Tekken,'" *Deadline Hollywood*, August 25, 2011, www.deadline.com/2011/08/venture-capital-firm-sues-rizvi-traverse-claims-it-was-taken-on-indie-pic-tekken

38 John Hopewell, "Studiocanal picks up 'RoboCop': Film group to distribute in U.K., France and Germany," *Chicago Tribune*, July 11, 2012, http://articles.chicagotribune.com/2012-07-11/entertainment/sns-201207111238reedbusivarietynvr1118056441-20120711_1_studiocanal-robocop-film-group

39 "Ryan Kavanaugh: The Fall and Rise." *Malibu Magazine*, 2013, http://malibumag.com/new/article/ryan_kavanaugh_the_fall_and_rise#.UXOcEILQH-4

40 "Red Granite Partners on International as Production Starts in Braddock, Pennsylvania," Zamm, April 5, 2012, accessed April 28, 2013, www.zamm.com/articles/news/casting-heats-up-on-relativity-medias-currently-titled-out-of-the-furnace

41 "'Veronica Mars' Movie Kickstarter Closes Out At $5.7M," *Deadline Hollywood*, April 14, 2013, www.deadline.com/2013/04/veronica-mars-kickstarter-5-7-million

42 Alan Duke, "Church gets more drama than it bargained for in film," *CNN*, April 13, 2013, http://religion.blogs.cnn.com/2013/04/13/church-gets-more-drama-than-it-bargained-for-in-film/?hpt=hp_c1

43 Bill Lodge, "Feds charge two in film tax credit case," *The Advocate*, April 7, 2013, http://theadvocate.com/home/5631211-125/feds-charge-two-in-film

44 Todd Longwell, "APA: Percentery's synergies," *Variety*, November 19, 2012, http://variety.com/2012/more/news/apa-percenterys-synergies-1118062384

45 Pamela McClintock, "Paramount No. 1 in 2011 Global Market Share With $5.17 Billion," *The Hollywood Reporter*, January 2, 2012, www.hollywoodreporter.com/news/paramount-transformers-kung-fu-panda-277322

46 Etan Vlessing, "Lionsgate Posts Loss, Despite 'Hunger Games' Fattening Revenue Line," *The Hollywood Reporter*, May 30, 2012, www.hollywoodreporter.com/news/lionsgate-hunger-games-posts-loss-331000

47 "Murdoch Spreads Risk, Nets $400 Million From 'Avatar' (Update2)," Bloomberg, Last modified March 15, 2010, www.bloomberg.com/apps/news?pid=newsarchive&sid=aZWgwaFj6lqM

48 Mike Fleming Jr., "Sundance: 'Austenland' To Sony WorldWide Acquisitions For North Of $4 Million; Sony Pictures Classics To Release In U.S.," *Deadline Hollywood*, January 21, 2013, www.deadline.com/2013/01/sundance-austenland-to-sony-worldwide-acquisitions-for-north-of-3-million/#more-409541

49 "AFM: Phase 4 Acquires Virginia Madsen- Starring Drama 'Long Time Gone,'" *Deadline Hollywood*, November 6, 2012, www.deadline.com/2012/11/phase-4-acquires-drama-long-time-gone

50 "Going Bionic: Distributing Independent Films Internationally—(Almost) Criminal Contract Clauses, Part 1," *Film Threat*, January 8, 2013, www.filmthreat.com/features/59799

51 Gene Goodsell, "Film & TV Packaging," Entertainment Agent Blog, November 12, 2009, accessed April 28, 2013, http://entertainmentagentblog.com/2009/11/12/film-tv-packaging

52 Mike Fleming Jr., "'Saw'-Maker Twisted Pictures Carves Worldwide Output Deal with Wild Bunch," *Deadline Hollywood*, January 10, 2012, www.deadline.com/2012/01/saw-maker-twisted-pictures-carves-worldwide-output-deal-with-wild-bunch

53 Nikki Finke, "'The Avengers' Now Biggest Opener! Shocking $200M Record Domestic Weekend: Expecting $642M Global From First 12 Days," *Deadline Hollywood*, May 6, 2012, www.deadline.com/2012/05/avengers-now-260-5m-overseas-could-reach-585m-worldwide-through-sunday-with-u-s-canada-russia-china-openings

54 "Specialty Box Office: Holdovers 'Amour', 'Quartet' Flourish In Expansions," *Deadline Hollywood*, January 20, 2013, www.deadline.com/2013/01/indie-films-holdovers-amour-quartet-silver-linings-playbook-strong-in-expansions

55 "Specialty B.O. Preview: 'The Playroom', 'Lore'; Plus 'Amour', 'Quartet' Expand," *Deadline Hollywood*, February 8, 2013, www.deadline.com/2013/02/indie-films-coming-out-the-playroom-lore-plus-quartet-amour-expand/#more-424966

56 "Top 10 U.S. & Canadian Circuits," NATOonline, Last modified June 24, 2010, accessed April 28, 2013, www.natoonline.org/statisticscircuits.htm

57 Erin Duffy, "Opera screenings open new venue and revenue for Mercer movie theaters," *The Times of Trenton*/nj.com, December 25, 2011, www.nj.com/mercer/index.ssf/2011/12/opera_screenings_open_new_venu.html

58 Richard Verrier, "Movie theaters turn to live event screenings to fill seats," *Los Angeles Times*, April 10, 2010, http://articles.latimes.com/2010/apr/20/news/la-ct-theater20-20100420

9 Original Material—Specs and Pitches

1 Noah Isackson, "Pitch Man," *Chicago Magazine*, May 2006, www.chicagomag.com/Chicago-Magazine/May-2006/Pitch-Man

2 "Forget the Oscars. Films need foreign viewers, not American prizes," *The Economist*, February 17, 2011, www.economist.com/node/18178291

3 Nellie Andreeva, "The Gotham Group Signs First-Look Deal With ABC Studios," *Deadline Hollywood*, July 27, 2012, www.deadline.com/2012/07/the-gotham-group-signs-first-look-deal-with-abc-studios

4 "Jetset Studios Launches New Production Division Repped by Benderspink," PRWEB, July 27, 2011, accessed April 28, 2013, www.prweb.com/releases/jetset-studios/benderspink/prweb8665280.htm

5 Nellie Andreeva, "Benderspink Re-Ups First-Look Deal With CBS TV Studios," *Deadline Hollywood*, March 8, 2013, www.deadline.com/2013/03/benderspink-re-ups-first-look-deal-with-cbs-tv-studios

6 Meg James and Dawn C. Chmielewski, "Hollywood awaits how Peter Chernin will fare with new venture," *Los Angeles Times*, July 26, 2011, http://articles.latimes.com/2011/jul/26/business/la-fi-ct-chernin-20110726

7   Mike Fleming Jr., "Paramount Selects Football Comedy 'Draft Day' Spec With Ivan Reitman Attached," *Deadline Hollywood*, June 20, 2012, www.deadline.com/2012/06/paramount-selects-football-comedy-draft-day-spec-with-ivan-reitman-attached

8   Mike Fleming Jr., "Summit Buys 'Spinback' Spec; Scott Speer To Helm Mystery Set In Electronic Dance Music World," *Deadline Hollywood*, February 11, 2013, www.deadline.com/2013/02/summit-buys-spinback-spec-scott-speer-to-helm-mystery-set-in-electronic-dance-music-world

9   Jeva Lange, "Actress Carey Mulligan on Daisy in 'Great Gatsby': 'She's like a Kardashian,'" *Daily News*, April 17, 2013, www.nydailynews.com/blogs/pageviews/2013/04/actress-carey-mulligan-on-daisy-in-%E2%80%98great-gatsby%E2%80%99-%E2%80%98she%E2%80%99s-like-a-kardashian%E2%80%99

10 "Revolution turns to sci-fi," *Variety*, November 11, 2004, www.variety.com/article/VR1117913428/?refCatId=10

11 "Next," Box Office Mojo, Last modified April 27, 2013, accessed April 28, 2013, www.boxofficemojo.com/movies/?id=next.htm

12 Dan Ackman, "Hollywood's Star Power Failure," *Forbes*, June 19, 2003, www.forbes.com/2003/06/18/cx_da_0619stars.html

13 Kristen Acuna, "The Biggest Box-Office Bombs Of 2012," Business Insider, December 26, 2012, accessed April 28, 2013, www.businessinsider.com/box-office-bombs-of-2012-2012-12?op=1

14 Eduardo Porter and Geraldine Fabrikant, "A Big Star May Not a Profitable Movie Make," *The New York Times*, August 28, 2006, www.nytimes.com/2006/08/28/business/media/28cast.html?pagewanted=all&_r=1&

15 Eduardo Porter and Geraldine Fabrikant, "A Big Star May Not a Profitable Movie Make," *The New York Times*, August 28, 2006, www.nytimes.com/2006/08/28/business/media/28cast.html?pagewanted=all&_r=1&.

16 "The 15 Most Profitable Movies of All Time," CNBC.com, Last modified 2013, www.cnbc.com/id/39083257/page/5

17 Dorothy Pomerantz, "The Biggest Box Office Flops Of 2012," *Forbes*, November 14, 2012, www.forbes.com/sites/dorothypomerantz/2012/11/14/2012s-biggest-movie-turkeys

18 Nancy Tartaglione, "Millennium Films, West Coast Film Partners Enter $100M Co-Finance Pact," Deadline London, May 19, 2012, www.deadline.com/2012/05/millennium-films-west-coast-film-partners-enter-100m-co-finance-pact

19 Fred Schruers and Joshua L. Weinstein, "10 Producers Who Will Change Hollywood In 2012," Business Insider, April 3, 2012, http://mobile.businessinsider.com/producers-who-will-change-hollywood-2012-4/8-super-crispy-entertainment-jonathan-schwartz-and-andrea-sperling-8

20 Sharon Waxman, "A Small Film Nearly Left for Dead Has Its Day in the Sundance Rays," *The New York Times*, January 23, 2006, www.nytimes.com/2006/01/23/movies/MoviesFeatures/23sund.html?_r=0

21 Paul Sullivan, "Lights. Camera. Invest! Putting Filmmaking in the Portfolio," *The New York Times*, April 27, 2012, www.nytimes.com/2012/04/28/your-money/filmmaking-as-an-alternative-investment.html?pagewanted=all&_r=0

22 Reynders, McVeigh Capital Management, LLC, accessed April 28, 2013, www.reyndersmcveigh.com/team.php

23 Paul Sullivan, "Lights. Camera. Invest! Putting Filmmaking in the Portfolio," *The New York Times*, April 27, 2012, www.nytimes.com/2012/04/28/your-money/filmmaking-as-an-alternative-investment.html?pagewanted=all&_r=0

24 Mike Fleming Jr., "Not So Fast, Avi Lerner! 'Chainsaw' Rights Holder Slices Sequel Plans," *Deadline Hollywood*, January 9, 2013, www.deadline.com/2013/01/not-so-fast-avi-lerner-chainsaw-rights-holder-slices-sequel-plans

25 "Universal Wins Bidding War for 'Snow White and the Huntsman,'" The Wrap, Published September 29, 2010, www.thewrap.com/movies/column-post/universal-wins-bidding-war-snow-white-and-huntsman-21311

26 Pamela McClintock, "'Abraham Lincoln' logs film right sale," *Variety*, October 4, 2010, www.variety.com/article/VR1118025081/?categoryid=13&cs=1&ref=vertfilm

27 Mike Fleming Jr., "Warner Bros Buys Hot Spec, Matt Damon Circles As Star And Director," *Deadline Hollywood*, May 6, 2011, www.deadline.com/2011/05/warner-bros-buys-hot-spec-matt-damon-circles-as-star-and-director

28 Karyn Scherer, "The Hollywood shell game," *The New Zealand Herald*, December 13, 2010, www.nzherald.co.nz/business/news/article.cfm?c_id=3&objectid=10693123

29 "'The Option, The Sale, The Rewrite & The Meeting' or 'We Don't Need No Stinkin' Meeting Option,'" Writers Guild of America, West, www.wga.org/subpage_writersresources.aspx?id=191

30 "April 24, 2013," 2013 episode of *The Daily Show with Jon Stewart*. (Comedy Central, Mad Cow Productions, Comedy Partners, Hello Doggie, Mobile Video Productions Inc.)

31 Borys Kit, "'Rampage' Writer Hired To Work On 'Ben 10' Film," *The Hollywood Reporter*, February 20, 2013, www.hollywoodreporter.com/heat-vision/rampage-writer-hired-work-ben-422896

32 www.deadline.com/2013/04/kimberly-peirce-to-helm-the-brand-alessandro-camon-scripted-drama-on-aryan-brotherhoods-violent-prison-reign

10 Writers-for-Hire–Open Assignments and Rewrites

1   "'The Option, The Sale, The Rewrite & The Meeting' or 'We Don't Need No Stinkin' Meeting Option,'" Writers Guild of America, West, accessed April 28, 2013, www.wga.org/subpage_writersresources.aspx?id=191

2   Mike Fleming Jr. "Jack Ryan Getting David Koepp Rewrite." *Deadline Hollywood*, April 28, 2011. www.deadline.com/2011/04/jack-ryan-getting-david-koepp-rewrite

3   Mike Fleming Jr. "Sony Pictures Acquires Publishing Phenomenon 'The Rosie Project.'" *Deadline Hollywood*, April 25, 2013. www.deadline.com/2013/04/sony-pictures-acquires-publishing-phenomenon-the-rosie-project

4   Tatiana Siegel. "Top scribes reap pic rewrite riches." *Variety*, April 24, 2010. http://variety.com/2010/film/news/top-scribes-reap-pic-rewrite-riches-1118018205

5   Kim Masters. "Why Studios Don't Pay to Make Movies Anymore (Analysis)." *The Hollywood Reporter*, December 13, 2012. www.hollywoodreporter.com/news/disney-fox-paramount-sony-fox-400727

6   Ryan Nakashima. "Hollywood And Big Budget Movies: Is The Love Affair Over?" The Huffington Post, September 17, 2011, accessed April 28, 2013, www.huffingtonpost.com/2011/09/17/hollywood-big-budget-movies_n_967559.html

7   Lacey Rose. "Hollywood's Most Expensive Movies." *Forbes*, December 18, 2006. www.forbes.com/2006/12/18/movies-budget-expensive-tech-media-cx_lr_1214moviebudget.html

8   Kristen Acuna, "Movie Ticket Sales Are Down 100 Million From A Decade Ago [Chart]," Business Insider, September 4, 2012, www.businessinsider.com/see-how-movie-ticket-sales-have-drastically-declined-over-the-past-decade-2012-9

11 Navigating a New World

1   Liz Shannon Miller, "What happens if your web series doesn't hit it big?" Gigacom.com, August 14, 2011, accessed May 28, 2013, http://gigaom.com/2011/08/14/what-happens-when-youre-not-the-guild-one-creator-speak

2   Lesley Goldberg, "Amy Poehler-Produced 'Broad City' Lands Series Order at Comedy Central," *The Hollywood Reporter*, March 13, 2013, www.hollywoodreporter.com/live-feed/amy-poehler-broad-city-comedy-central-428256

3   Tiffany Lee, "'Nashville' casts 13 and 6-year-old YouTube viral singing stars Lennon and Maisy Stella," Yahoo.com, October 9, 2012, accessed May 28, 2013, http://tv.yahoo.com/blogs/fall-tv/nashville-casts-13-6-old-youtube-viral-singing-204411890.html

4   Lesley Goldberg, "YourTube Breakout Ray Williams Johnson Sells Comedy to FX," *The Hollywood Reporter*, May 17, 2013, www.hollywoodreporter.com/live-feed/youtube-breakout-ray-william-johnson-524675

5   Daniel Miller, "THR's 2012 Digital Power 50," *The Hollywood Reporter*, January 11, 2012, www.hollywoodreporter.com/lists/digital-domains-280391

6   Brian Stelter, "NPR Wants to Click With Those Who Tweet," *The New York Times*, March 12, 2013, www.nytimes.com/2013/03/13/arts/nprs-generation-listen-seeks-audiences-in-their-20s.html?_r=0

7   John Gaudiosi, "New Reports Forecast Global Video Game Industry Will Reach $82 Billion By 2017," *Forbes*, July 18, 2012, www.forbes.com/sites/johngaudiosi/2012/07/18/new-reports-forecasts-global-video-game-industry-will-reach-82-billion-by-2017

8   "Top Ten Highest Grossing Video Games Ever," Digital Battle.com, February 21, 2012, accessed May 26, 2013, http://digitalbattle.com/2012/02/21/top-10-highest-grossing-video-games-ever/

9   Brian Altano, "The Billionaire Movie Club: The 15 Highest Grossing Films of All Time," *IGN*, March 6, 2013, www.ign.com/articles/2013/03/06/the-billionaire-movie-club-the-15-highest-grossing-films-of-all-time

10 Tom Magrino, "EA Contracts UTA," *GameSpot*, July 23, 2008, www.gamespot.com/news/ea-contracts-uta-6194934

11 Wayne St. Amand, "Crimson Hexagon, Leading Social Intelligence Company, Signs with United Talent Agency and Adds Agency to Client Roster," *Crimson Hexagon*, July 11, 2011, www.crimsonhexagon.com/crimson-hexagon-leading-social-intelligence-company-signs-with-united-talent-agency-and-adds-agency-to-client-roster

12 Daniel Miller, "THR's 2012 Digital Power 50," *The Hollywood Reporter*, January 11, 2012, www.hollywoodreporter.com/lists/digital-domains-280391

13 Lucas Shaw, "Youtube Stars Align With Their CAA for the Digital Set," *The Wrap*, April 30, 2012, www.thewrap.com/media/article/youtube-stars-align-their-caa-digital-set-37371

14 Jake Coyle, "Ben Stiller Spoofs 'The Bachelor' With 'Burning Love' Web Series," *The Huffington Post*, June 13, 2012, www.huffingtonpost.com/2012/06/13/ben-stiller-spoofs-the-bachelor-burning-love_n_1594580.html

15 Mike Shields, "BRB! I'm Watching Awesomeness," *Adweek*, June 25, 2012, www.adweek.com/news/technology/brb-im-watching-awesomeness-141364

16 Sam Gutelle, "Dreamworks Animation Acquires Awesomeness TV for $33 Million," *Tubefilter*, May 5, 2013, www.tubefilter.com/2013/05/01/dreamworks-animation-awesomeness-tv/

17 Andy Forssell, "Summeritme...and the Viewing is Easy," *Hulu*, May 20, 2012, http://blog.hulu.com/2012/05/20/summertime%E2%80%A6and-the-viewing-is-easy/

18 Rich Mbariket, "CES 2012: 'Electric City' Budget In Excess of $2 Million! Most Expensive Web Series of All Time?" *Web Series Network*, January 11, 2012, http://webseriesnetwork.com/profiles/blogs/ces-2012-electric-city-budget-in-excess-of-2-million-most-expensi

19 Amrita Khalid, "Why Isn't *Cybergeddon*, the Most Expensive Web Series of All Time, Going Viral?" *Slate*, October 8, 2012, www.slate.com/blogs/future_tense/2012/10/08/cybergeddon_can_anthony_e_zuiker_s_yahoo_web_series_succeed_.html

20 "Anthony E. Zuiker's Digital Blockbuster Cybergeddon Set to Premiere Globally on Tuesday, September 25, Exclusively on Yahoo!" Yahoo! News Center, last modified September 6, 2012, http://pressroom.yahoo.net/pr/ycorp/anthony-e-zuikers-digital-blockbuster-238253.aspx

21 Jill Goldsmith, "CAA Showcases Digital Productions," *Variety*, April 26, 2012, http://variety.com/2012/digital/news/caa-showcases-digital-productions-1118053196

22 Michael O'Connell, "Amazon Passes on 'Zombieland' Pilot," *The Hollywood Reporter*, May 17, 2013, www.hollywoodreporter.com/live-feed/amazon-passes-zombieland-pilot-524640

23 "Made-for-Internet Movie Debuts on YouTube," *The Independent*, March 14, 2011, www.independent.co.uk/arts-entertainment/films/madeforinternet-movie-debuts-on-youtube-2241507.html

24 Paloma M. Vazquez, "'Being Henry': An Interactive Film by Range Rover," *PSFK*, May 4, 2011, www.psfk.com/2011/05/being-henry-an-interactive-film-by-land-rover.html

25 "Ad Sales at 2013 Digital Newfronts Could Surpass $1 Billion," *SmartBrief*, April 8, 2013, www.smartbrief.com/04/08/13/ad-sales-2013-digital-newfronts-could-surpass-1-billion#.UYPoaoLQH-5

26 Michael Learmonth, "Digital Newfronts Poised to Rake in $1 Billion in Ad Deals," *Advertising Age*, April 8, 2013, http://adage.com/article/digital/digital-newfronts-rake-1-billion-ad-deals/240751

27 Brian Stelter, "Subscribers Help Propel Netflix Gain," *The New York Times*, April 22, 2013, www.nytimes.com/2013/04/23/business/media/netflix-reports-strong-revenue-on-strength-of-subscribers.html?_r=0

28 Rebecca Sun, "Youtube Star iJustine Signs With UTA (Exclusive)," *The Hollywood Reporter*, April 16, 2013, www.hollywoodreporter.com/news/youtube-star-ijustine-signs-uta-440418

29 Geoffrey A. Fowler, "Now Playing on a Computer Near You: A Fruit With an Obnoxious Streak," *The Wall Street Journal*, April 26, 2010, http://online.wsj.com/article/SB10001424052748703404004575198410669579950.html?mod=WSJEUROPE_hpp_sections_tech

30 Nellie Andreeva, "Hit YouTube Series 'The Annoying Orange' to Become Animated TV Show," *Deadline.com*, April 13, 2011, www.deadline.com/2011/04/hit-youtube-series-the-annoying-orange-to-become-animated-tv-show

31 Lesley Goldberg, "Cartoon Network Adds More 'Regular Show,' 'Annoywing Orange,' 'Gumball,'" *The Hollywood Reporter*, January 7, 2013, www.hollywoodreporter.com/live-feed/cartoon-network-annoying-orange-regular-show-gumball-409211

32 Wendy Getzler, "Viral Brand The Annoying Orange Gets Toy Deal," *Kidscreen*, October 5, 2011, http://kidscreen.com/2011/10/05/viral-brand-the-annoying-orange-gets-toy-deal

33 "AOL's Investment in Original Programming Takes Center Stage at Digital Content Newfront With Launch of New 2013 Video Slate," AOL.com, April 30, 2013, http://corp.aol.com/2013/04/30/aol-s-investment-in-original-programming-takes-center-stage-at-d

34 Dana Kerr, "Yahoo rolls out six original shows and new TV partnerships," cnet.com, April 29, 2013, http://news.cnet.com/8301-1023_3-57582013-93/yahoo-rolls-out-six-original-shows-and-new-tv-partnerships

35 http://adage.com/article/madisonvine-digital-entertainment/branded-entertainment-brands-flock-web-series/145276

36 www.tubefilter.com/2012/12/13/video-game-high-school-freddiew-freddie-wong-budget-costs

37 www.pastemagazine.com/blogs/lists/2012/12/the-10-best-web-series.html

38 Gabriel Beltrone, "Perrier Invites You to a 'Secret Place' Where Sparkling Water Makes People Get Crazy," *Adweek*, April 2, 2013, www.adweek.com/adfreak/perrier-invites-you-secret-place-where-sparkling-water-makes-people-get-crazy-148352

39 Chris Lee and John Horn, "A Bawdy CAA Party at Sundance Shocks Guests, Including Clients," *Los Angeles Times*, January 24, 2013, http://articles.latimes.com/2013/jan/24/entertainment/la-et-mn-sundance-caa-20130125

40 Robert Seidman, "USA Network Secures Primetime Interactive Emmy Nomination for 'PSYCH: HashTag Killer," *TVbytheNumbers*, July 19, 2012, http://tvbythenumbers.zap2it.com/2012/07/19/usa-network-secures-primetime-interactive-emmy-nomination-for-psych-hashtag-killer/142143

41 Enid Burns, "Mobile Ad Spend is Starting to Look Like Serious Money," *E-Commerce Times*, April 18, 2013, www.ecommercetimes.com/story/77818.html

42 Anthony Ha, "Internet Ad Revenue Reaches $31B in 2011, Mobile Up 149 Percent (IAB Report)," *TechCrunch*, April 18, 2012, http://techcrunch.com/2012/04/18/iab-revenue-report-2011/

43 Kate Arthur, "9 TV Shows That Make Everyone Think Cable's Doing Better Than It Really Is," *BuzzFeed*, April 3, 2013, www.buzzfeed.com/katearthur/walking-dead-duck-dynasty-ratings

44 Lucas Shaw, "YouTube Star Freddie Wong Launches A Summer Blockbuster—Without a Film Studio," *The Wrap*, August 23, 2012, www.thewrap.com/media/article/freddie-wong-launches-summer-blockbuster-without-studio-or-youtube-53041?page=0,0

45 Mike Shields, "The Collective Scores With Video Game High," *Adweek*, July 19, 2012, www.adweek.com/news/technology/collective-scores-video-game-high-142004

46 Catherine Laughlin, "Florence Native Becomes a Social Media Superstar," *PhillyBurbs*, May 20, 2013, www.phillyburbs.com/news/local/burlington_county_times_news/florence-native-becomes-a-social-media-superstar/article_9cb52ff2-bdc4-55b9-9e6c-c45d5a7a01ce.html

47 Susan Young, "Youth Impact Report 2012: Channeling Talent," *Variety*, September 13, 2012, http://variety.com/2012/tv/news/lucas-cruikshank-moving-beyond-fred-figglehorn-1118058833

48 Denis Faye, "One Singular Sensation," *Written By*, February/March, 2011, 20.

49 Marc Graser, "Disney Plans New 'Star Wars' Games Through Electronic Arts," *Variety*, May 6, 2013, http://variety.com/2013/digital/news/electronic-arts-to-make-new-star-wars-games-1200466418

50 "Products," Land Ho! www.landho.co.jp/en/works/game/index.html

51 "Sony Pictures Consumer Products and Ubisoft Collaborate to Develop a New Video Game Based on Sony Pictures Animation's the Smurfs 2 Feature Film," *Gamasutra* and *GamesPress*, April 10, 2013, www.gamasutra.com/view/pressreleases/190220/SONY_PICTURES_CONSUMER_PRODUCTS_AND_UBISOFT reg_COLLABORATETO_DEVELOP_A_NEW_VIDEO_GAME_BASED_ON_SONY_PICTURESANIMATIONrsquoS_THE_SMURFStrade_2_FEATURE_FILM.php

52 Kev Geoghegan, "Will L.A. Noire Change the Game for Actors?" *BBC News*, May 27, 2011, www.bbc.co.uk/news/entertainment-arts-13507355

53 Ana Douglas, "Here are the 10 Highest Grossing Video Games Ever*," *Business Insider*, June 13, 2012, www.businessinsider.com/here-are-the-top-10-highest-grossing-video-games-of-all-time-2012-6?op=1

54 Dave McNary, "Boss Media Rousts 'Wake Cycle,'" *Variety*, October 18, 2011, http://variety.com/2011/film/news/boss-media-rousts-wake-cycle-1118044698

55 Marc Graser, "Scribe Guides Blockbuster Game," *Daily Variety*, October 16, 2012. www.accessmylibrary.com/article-1G1-306971948/scribe-guides-blockbuster-game.html

56 "Top Game Design Programs," The Princeton Review, www.princetonreview.com/game-design.aspx

12 Finding Representation

1 Stephen Battaglio, "Meet John McCain's (Boston) Legal Eagle," *TV Guide*, February 28, 2008, www.tvguide.com/biz/Meet-John-McCains-8595.aspx

2 Nellie Andreeva, "Fox Buys Comedy Based On 'Couple Time' Web Series With Ellen Degeneres Producing," *Deadline Hollywood*, August 15, 2012, www.deadline.com/2012/08/fox-buys-comedy-based-on-couple-time-web-series-with-ellen-degenres-producing

3 Mike Fleming, Jr., "'Crazy Heart's' Scott Cooper Takes On 'The Low Dweller' For Relativity Media," *Deadline Hollywood*, April 11, 2011, accessed May 26, 2013, www.deadline.com/2011/04/crazy-hearts-scott-cooper-takes-on-the-low-dweller-for-relativity-media

4 Erin McClam, "There may be millions more poor people in the U.S. than you think," NBC News, May 3, 2013, accessed May 23, 2013, http://inplainsight.nbcnews.com/_news/2013/05/03/17671753-there-may-be-millions-more-poor-people-in-the-us-than-you-think?lite

5 The Deadline Team, "Sony Buys Action-Comedy Spec 'El Tigre,'" *Deadline Hollywood*, April 26, 2012, accessed May 23, 2013, www.deadline.com/2012/04/sony-buys-action-comedy-spec-el-tigre

6 Nikki Finke, "Top Agency Count: Primetime Emmys 2012," *Deadline Hollywood*, September 28, 2013, accessed May 26, 2013, www.deadline.com/2012/09/top-agency-count-primetime-emmys-2012

7 "The 2012–2013 Awards Season Breakdown – Updated," Who?Represents.com, last modified January 10, 2013, accessed May 26, 2013, www.whorepresents.com/news/2012-2013-awards-season-breakdown-updated

8 Nikki Finke, "Warner Brothers Buy Script About Math Genius Alan Turing For Leonardo DiCaprio," *Deadline Hollywood*, October 11, 2011 www.deadline.com/2011/10/warner-bros-buys-spec-script-about-math-genius-biopic-because-leonardo-di-caprio-chasing-lead-role

9 Mike Fleming, Jr., "Warner Brothers Sets Black List Top Scribe Graham Moore For 'Devil in the White City'; Leonardo DiCaprio To Play Serial Killer," *Deadline Hollywood*, December 16, 2011, www.deadline.com/2011/12/warner-bros-sets-black-list-top-scribe-graham-moore-for-devil-in-the-white-city-leonardo-dicaprio-to-play-serial-killer

10 Mike Fleming, Jr., "Gersh Signs Toronto Helmer Trio," *Deadline Hollywood*, October 15, 2012, www.deadline.com/2012/10/gersh-signs-toronto-helmer-trio

11 The Deadline Team, "Tribeca Film & Well Go Acquire 'Emanuel and the Truth About Fishes," *Deadline Hollywood*, May 13, 2013, www.deadline.com/tag/emanuel-and-the-truth-about-fishes

12 Mike Fleming, Jr., "Elle Fanning To Star in Feature Adaptation of Kevin Henkes Novel 'Olive's Ocean,'" *Deadline Hollywood*, August 15, 2012, www.deadline.com/2012/08/elle-fanning-to-star-in-feature-adaptation-of-kevin-henkes-novel-olives-ocean

13 Nicole Sperling, "2012 Black List: The Top Ten Unproduced Scripts In Hollywood," *The Los Angeles Times*, December 17, 2012, http://articles.latimes.com/2012/dec/17/entertainment/la-et-mn-2012-black-list-the-top-ten-scripts-20121217

14 "Recession and Regression: The 2011 Hollywood Writers Report," Writers Guild of America, West, May 18, 2011, accessed April 30, 2013, www.wga.org/uploadedFiles/who_we_are/hwr11execsum.pdf

15 "Recession and Regression: The 2011 Hollywood Writers Report," Writers Guild of America, West, May 18, 2011, accessed April 30, 2013, www.wga.org/uploadedFiles/who_we_are/hwr11execsum.pdf

16 Jonathan Handel, "SAG and AFTRA Unveil Merger Documents (Analysis)," *The Hollywood Reporter*, January 31, 2012, www.hollywoodreporter.com/news/sag-aftra-merger-documents-286128

17 Nikki Finke, "TOLDJA! Director Jodie Foster Signs With UTA," *Deadline Hollywood*, March 13, 2012, www.deadline.com/2012/03/jodie-foster-uta-agency-representation-directing-movies/

18 Daniel Holloway, Ivan Lopez-Muniz, "Roses, O'Brien Case Prove Kerkorian Talent Scam Prevention Act Has Teeth," *The Hollywood Reporter*, August 11, 2011, www.hollywoodreporter.com/news/roses-obrien-cases-prove-krekorian-222355

19 "California Labor Code Section 1700.40," last modified February 22, 2013, accessed May 26, 2013, http://law.onecle.com/california/labor/1700.40.html

20 Nellie Andreeva, "Rob Kim Leaves Untitled Entertainment, Joins APA As VP," *Deadline Hollywood*, January 29, 2013, www.deadline.com/2013/01/rob-kim-leaves-untitled-entertainment-joins-apa-as-vp/

21 Borys Kit, "David Unger and Robert Lazar Leaving ICM," *The Hollywood Reporter*, February 20, 2013, www.hollywoodreporter.com/news/david-unger-robert-lazar-leaving-422651

22 Nikki Finke, "Ex-CAA Agent Isabella Brewster to Resolution," *Deadline Hollywood*, February 20, 2013, www.deadline.com/2013/02/ex-caa-agent-isabella-brewster-to-resolution

23 Joe Flint, "ICM's Bob Broder exits firm to work with TV producer Chuck Lorre," *The Los Angeles Times*, September 10, 2012, http://articles.latimes.com/2012/sep/10/entertainment/la-et-ct-icm-agent-bob-broder-leaves-firm-to-work-with-tv-producer-chuck-lorre-20120910

24 Daniel Miller, "Ken Stovitz returns to the agency fold with Paradigm," *The Los Angeles Times*, February 27, 2013, http://articles.latimes.com/2013/feb/27/entertainment/la-et-overbrook-entertainment-executive-ken-stovitz-joins-talent-agency-paradigm-20130227

25 Studio System News, "Rep Moves: WME, Fortitude, Resolution," May 23, 2013, access May 28, 2013, www.studiosystemnews.com/rep-moves-wme-fortitude-resolution

26 Studio System News, "Rep Moves: APA, CAA, ICM, Resolution, Circle of Confusion, New Wave Ent.," March 7, 2013, access May 28, 2013, www.studiosystemnews.com/rep-moves-apa-caa-icm-resolution-circle-of-confusion-new-wave-ent/

13 Working with Your Representation

1   "Labor Force Statistics From the Current Population Survey," Bureau of Labor Statistics, last modified April 19, 2013, accessed April 19, 2013, http://data.bls.gov/timeseries/LNS14000000

14 Parting Ways with Your Representation

1   Matthew Belloni, "Luber Roklin Sues Manager Over Commissions From Ex-Clients," *The Hollywood Reporter*, February 6, 2013, accessed May 22, 2013, www.hollywoodreporter.com/thr-esq/luber-roklin-sues-manager-commissions-418995
2   Matthew Beloni, "UTA Sues Another Ex-Client For Commission," *The Hollywood Reporter*, May 9, 2013, accessed May 22, 2013, www.hollywoodreporter.com/thr-esq/uta-sues-client-commissions-520268
3   Nikki Finke, "TOLDJA! Director Jodie Foster Signs With UTA," *Deadline Hollywood*, March 13, 2012, accessed May 21, 2013, www.deadline.com/2012/03/jodie-foster-uta-agency-representation-directing-movies
4   Nikki Finke, "2ND UPDATE: David Unger Leaves ICM Partners For Resolution; Also Robert Lazar," *Deadline Hollywood*, February 20, 2013, accessed May 21, 2013, www.deadline.com/2013/02/talent-agent-david-unger-leaves-icm-resolution-bound

15 Networking in Hollywood

1   Nikki Finke, "The Son Also Rises: David Ellison Funding 1/2 Of Paramount's 'Mission Impossible 4', 'True Grit', and Jack Ryan," August 16, 2010, accessed May 23, 2013, www.deadline.com/2010/08/the-son-also-rises-david-ellison-funding-12-of-paramounts-mission-impossible-4-true-grit-jack-ryan
2   Jeff Sneider, "'Maggie tops 2011 Blood List," *Variety*, October 31, 2011, accessed May 23, 2013, http://variety.com/2011/film/news/maggie-tops-2011-blood-list-1118045326

16 The Best Place to Begin Your Hollywood Career

1   Borys Kit, "Ex-Imagine Exec Lands Disney Prod'n Deal," *The Hollywood Reporter*, April 7, 2010, accessed May 24, 2013, www.hollywoodreporter.com/news/ex-imagine-exec-lands-disney-22396

2   David Bloom, Cathy Dunkley, "'Wind' Blows Well For Tyros," *Variety*, February 6, 2002, accessed May 24, 2013 http://variety.com/2002/film/news/wind-blows-well-for-tyros-1117860378
3   Peter I. Minton, "6 Legal Requirements For Unpaid Internship Programs," Forbes.com, April 19, 2013, accessed May 24, 2013, www.forbes.com/sites/theyec/2013/04/19/6-legal-requirements-for-unpaid-internship-programs
4   "Top Execs Who Started At the Bottom," CNBC.com, accessed May 25, 2013, www.cnbc.com/id/43896634/page/8
5   Cynthia Littleton, "ICM invests in next gen," *Variety*, June 6, 2011, accessed May 24, 2013, http://variety.com/2011/tv/news/icm-invests-in-next-gen-1118038049
6   Cynthia Littleton, "ICM invests in next gen," *Variety*, June 6, 2011, accessed May 24, 2013, http://variety.com/2011/tv/news/icm-invests-in-next-gen-1118038049

Appendix 1

1   David Castillo, "Subway Shows Us How To Do Branded Entertainment," Product Placement News, May 22, 2013, accessed June 9, 2013, http://productplacement.biz/201305225181/branded-entertainment/subway-shows-us-how-to-do-branded-entertainment.html
2   Kim Masters, "David Fincher Battles Over Budget on Netflix's 'House of Cards,'" *The Hollywood Reporter*, March 7, 2012, accessed June 15, 2013, www.hollywoodreporter.com/news/netflix-house-cards-david-fincher-media-rights-capitol-297444
3   Mike Fleming Jr., "Graham King Makes First Look Warner Bro Deal For GK and Brings 'Jersey Boys' Musical With Him," *Deadline Hollywood*, September 13, 2012, accessed June 12, 2013, www.deadline.com/2012/09/graham-king-makes-first-look-warner-bros-deal-for-gk-and-brings-jersey-boys-musical-with-him
4   Mike Fleming Jr., "Cannes: Martin Scorsese's 'Silence' Sells in Key World Territories," *Deadline Hollywood*, May 30, 2013, accessed June 15, 2013, www.deadline.com/2013/05/cannes-martin-scorseses-silence-sells-key-world-territories

Appendix 2

1   "Guild Signatory Agents and Agency," WGA.org, accessed June 12, 2013, www.wga.org/agency/agencylist.aspx

Index

Note: **bold** page numbers indicate tables and figures.

190–191; agent's new clients, desirable qualities in 246–248; agent's reading of 162–163; commerciality of 159–161; contracts for see movie contracts; development of 161–164; festivals/contests 262–263; "going out" with see "going out" with screenplays/screenwriters; manager's roles with 161, 162; online/printed information for 160, 363–368; open assignments see open assignments/rewrites; pitching 164; purchase prices 186; subjects for 158–160; turnaround and 191; upfront/backend payments for 34, 348

script commitment 125–126, 356
script coverage 45, 356
script fees 98–99
senior agents 45, 46, 47, 192, 197, 199, 203, 256, 258–259, 266, 274, 354, 356
servicing agents 45, 356
shopping the offer 183–185, 357
shotgun approach 164, 165–173, 276–277, 357; agent's/manager's commissions/fees 170–171; cover letters for 168–169; passes 169–170, 172–173; preemptive deals and 167–168; spec grids for **169**; targeting strategies 165–167; timing of 167
show chart 88
showrunner meetings 71–72, 80, 90–96; for comedy shows 93–94; follow-up tips/referral calls 96; number of 92; pilot screenings at 93; short notice of 92–93; showrunner's priorities in 91–92; success in, seven tips for 95
showrunners 6, 59, 68–69, 244, 357; and agents 73, 90–91
sizzle reels 18, 119, 357
sketch/joke packets 75, 352, 357
Sony 8, 25, 38, 48, 63, 145
spec scripts/pilots 66, 67, 73, 79, 357
specialty arms 48, 146, 147, 151, 165–166, 203, 357
sports agents 11, 22, 34, 381
staffing books 76–77
staffing meetings 80, 89–90
staffing season see hiring TV writers
staff writers 97, 99, 101–102, 103, 291
stand-up comedy 6, 10
studio deals 5, 116, 122, 147, 159, 174, 176, 200, 201, 264, 357
studio/network charts 88–89, **89**
studios, movie see movie studios

studio writing programs 79, 261–262, 358
Sundance Film Festival 51, **52**, 151, 152, 155, 156, 254, 262, 318, 351
surety bonds 13, **23**, 358
sweeps 61, 358

Talent Agencies Act (TAA, 1978) 13, 17–18, 358
talent agents/agencies 7, 12, 14, **15**, 31, 42, 48, 176, 177–178, 358; brands and 38–39; and business managers, compared 22; contact information/resources 362
talent holding deals 121–122, 358
television advertising 26, 39, 61–62
television agents 59, 71–107; and baby writers 239–241; new clients, desirable qualities in 241–246
television audiences 26, 61
television commercials 12, 61, 63, 317
television contracts 97–103; agent-client communication in 102; cable vs. broadcast 99; COA and 103, 349; exclusivity in 100–101; fee minimums/pay scales 97–99, 100; first/second positions 101, 129, 351; five deal points in 97; lawyers and 103; longform 103; option dates 104, 354; problems with 102–103; raises/promotions in 100; staff writers 101–102; title/credit in 99–100, 293, 350
television executives/executive producers 6, 8, 11, 18–19, 78, 81–82; and "agenting" of writers 82–83, 351; current/development 70; in general meetings 84–87; hierarchy/job titles 75; writer's charts **82**
television industry 3–4, 59–70; annual schedule 66–69, **68**, 106, **106**, **140**; development season 66–67, 108–140; hierarchy/job titles 69–70; income generated by 59; and movie industry, compared 59–60, 145, 150; online/printed resources for 363–368; overall/first-look deals 65, 66; pilot season 66, 67–68, 354; reality shows see reality TV; staffing season see hiring TV writers; station groups/market areas 63; sweeps periods 61, 358; syndications 63–64, 358; types of company in 60–66; upfront presentations 67, 68, 359;

see also broadcast networks; cable TV/cable networks; television studios
television packages see packages/packaging fees
television production companies 3, 11, 38, 60, 64–65
television studios 60, 62–64, 357; networks and 62–63, 67; ownership of 62; and production companies 64–65; revenue streams of 63–64
television writers 67, 68–69; agent's priorities for 79–80; annual schedule of **68**; aspiring/baby see baby writers; cancelled shows and 106–107; diversity 76, 270–271; freelance 105, 351; head see showrunners; hiring see hiring TV writers; mid-/upper-level 77, 78, 79, 80, 87; pay scales for 100; payment to 104–105, 274, 348, 349; pitches/quotes see pitching for television; "punch up"/"beat out" roles of 69, 348, 355; and the "room" 69–70, 359; staff 97, 98, 101–102; teams of 91, 118
term writers 97, 358
theatrical distribution 143, 358
Time-Warner 60, 62, 65, 145
tracking boards 48, 122, 321, 358
transactional attorneys 20, 358
turnaround 180, 191, 358
TV lit agents 14; in hiring process see hiring TV writers; revenue stream of see packaging fees
Twitter 75

Univision 40, 60, 61
upfront presentations 67, 68, 111
UTA (United Talent Agency) 3–4, 23, 26, 28, 29, 38, 133, 184, 211, 256, 332, 342

vanity deals 148, 359
vertical brands see MCNs
Viacom 145

video games 31, 147, 211, 224–236; academic 235; conventions/industry news sources 236, 363; development 226–228, 229; development studios 225, 234, 235; future of 236; industry structure 225–226; negotiating deals for 228–229; original ideas/adaptations 227; QA testing 229, 235; revenue shares/royalties for 229; writers see video game writers